Numbers

'Is God's promised redemption really unstoppable, even if the people of God disintegrates spiritually? This wonderful little devotional from Chris Wright will really make the book of Numbers come alive for you. And, as you will discover, the answer is a resounding "Yes"!'
Marcus Honeysett, Executive Director, Living Leadership

Ruth

'Ideal for anyone wanting to work God's Word into their busy routines, these bite-sized banquets from the book of Ruth reveal our loving Father weaving the loose and messy ends of our everyday lives into his beautiful, eternal purposes in Christ.'
Derek Burnside, Principal, Capernwray Bible School, England

Ezekiel

'In these simple but profound devotional thoughts on the message of Ezekiel, Liam Goligher inspires, challenges and comforts us in equal measure. He reminds us that God is closer than we think, and hope is deeper than we could imagine.'
Malcolm Duncan, Lead Pastor, Dundonald Elim Church, Northern Ireland

Habakkuk

'Jonathan Lamb has done an excellent job of making Habakkuk accessible and exciting. The message that God is in control and is enough, even in the most difficult circumstances, rings out loud and clear for the reader today.'
Clare Heath-Whyte, author of a number of books including First Wives' Club *and* Old Wives' Tales

John 14 – 17

'These devotional guides are excellent tools.'
John Risbridger, Minister and Team Leader, Above Bar Church, Southampton, and Chair of Evangelical Alliance Council

Romans 5 – 8

'John Stott explains these challenging chapters with great clarity . . . He enables us to get our heads around core truths for the Christian journey and leads us into praise and thankfulness to the Jesus of the gospel.'
Hugh Palmer, Rector, All Souls, Langham Place, London

Colossians
'Here is a book that is sound and solid, but also beautifully simple – an exceedingly rare combination. It is Steve Brady at his best interpreting Paul the apostle at his best.'
R. T. Kendall, speaker and former Pastor of Westminster Chapel, London

1 Thessalonians
'This devotional series is biblically rich, theologically deep and full of wisdom. I recommend it highly!'
Becky Manley Pippert, speaker, author of Out of the Saltshaker and into the World *and creator of the Live/Grow/Know course and series of books*

2 Timothy
'This helpful series will facilitate a prayerful, intelligent, systematic reading of the Bible, so that God's voice is clearly heard.'
David Cook, speaker and former Principal, Sydney Missionary and Bible College, Australia

Hebrews
'Insightful, pastoral, warm and encouraging. Charles Price has a gift for mining the gold and making it glitter.'
Martin Salter, Associate Pastor, Grace Community Church, Bedford

James
'I was truly encouraged as I used this devotional each day.'
Peter Maiden, International Director Emeritus, Operation Mobilisation, and Minister-at-Large, Keswick Ministries

Revelation 1 – 3
'What rich food indeed is served up with these terrific short devotionals from the letters to the seven churches. Paul Mallard does three things so very well: he opens up the text faithfully, he connects to people warmly and, above all, he lifts up Jesus in all his magnificence. Readers are in for a real treat – and, if taken to heart, this book will do you the power of good. Warmly commended!'
Ray Evans, Lead Pastor, Grace Community Church, Bedford, and Church Leadership Consultant, Fellowship of Independent Evangelical Churches UK

Food for the Journey

Food for the Journey

365-DAY DEVOTIONAL

Edited by Elizabeth McQuoid

INTER-VARSITY PRESS
36 Causton Street, London SW1P 4ST, England
Email: ivp@ivpbooks.com
Website: www.ivpbooks.com

First published as single volumes under name of Bible book 2016, 2017 and 2018.

First published as Omnibus edition, containing all twelve volumes, 2019

British Library Cataloguing-in-Publication Data
A catalogue record for this book is available from the British Library.

ISBN: 978–1–78359–730–7
eBook ISBN: 978–1–78359–731–4

Typeset in Great Britain by CRB Associates, Potterhanworth, Lincolnshire
Printed in Great Britain by TJ International Ltd, Padstow, Cornwall

Inter-Varsity Press publishes Christian books that are true to the Bible and that communicate the gospel, develop discipleship and strengthen the church for its mission in the world.

IVP originated within the Inter-Varsity Fellowship, now the Universities and Colleges Christian Fellowship, a student movement connecting Christian Unions in universities and colleges throughout Great Britain, and a member movement of the International Fellowship of Evangelical Students. Website: www.uccf.org.uk. That historic association is maintained, and all senior IVP staff and committee members subscribe to the UCCF Basis of Faith.

Contents

Application and commentary for each day by Elizabeth McQuoid

Preface

What do you do when you need refreshment? Book a holiday, go for a hike in the hills, sit in front of the TV . . . ? We refresh our bodies in various ways. But God says that true refreshment, the type that nourishes your soul and sustains you on life's journey, is only found in him. And so the psalmist says:

> The law of the LORD is perfect,
>   refreshing the soul.
> The statutes of the LORD are trustworthy,
>   making wise the simple.
> The precepts of the LORD are right,
>   giving joy to the heart.
> The commands of the LORD are radiant,
>   giving light to the eyes.
> (Psalm 19:7–8)

This *Food for the Journey* compilation is a feast for your soul, providing this much-needed sustenance. It is a year's worth of devotionals designed to deepen your relationship with God and to equip you to live for him wherever life's journey takes you.

We invite you to savour the rich variety of Bible books and Bible teachers included in this volume. Twelve Bible books, covering a whole raft of topics, have been brought together in one special compilation edition. You'll find the books are not arranged according to their order in the Bible, but around a unifying theme, and each theme is introduced by a psalm. Psalm 1 introduces the books of Numbers, Hebrews and 1 Thessalonians, which call us to live today in the light of the future. Ezekiel, John 14 – 17 and Romans 5 – 8, introduced by Psalm 51, confront us with the dreadful nature of sin, its consequences and the saving activity of God through Jesus' death and resurrection, and the ministry of the Spirit. Psalm 13 introduces Habakkuk, James and 2 Timothy, which all engage, in different ways, with the question of suffering. The connecting theme of the final section – the books of Ruth, Colossians and Revelation 1 – 3 – introduced by Psalm 2, is the person of Jesus Christ.

The pages of this devotional are deliberately undated for a guilt-free experience! If you have to miss a day for any reason, just pick up the next day where you left off.

The twelve devotionals were originally sermons delivered at the Keswick Convention in the English Lake District. Where necessary, the language has been updated but, on the whole, they are the messages you would have heard had you been listening in the tent on Skiddaw Street. Each day of the devotional ends with a fresh section of application designed to help you apply God's Word to your own life and situation. Whether you are a Convention regular or have never been to Keswick, this *Food for the Journey* volume is a unique opportunity to study the Scriptures with a Bible teacher by your side.

Our prayer is that these devotionals will become your daily feast, a nourishing opportunity to meet with God through his Word. Read, meditate, apply and pray through the Scriptures given for each day and allow God's truths to take root and transform your life.

If these devotionals whet your appetite for more, you can visit our website <www.keswickministries.org> to find the full range of books, study guides, CDs, DVDs and MP3s available. Why not order an audio recording of the sermon series to accompany your daily devotional?

Let the word of Christ dwell in you richly.
(Colossians 3:16, ESV)

Food for the Journey

Day 1

Read Psalm 1
Key verses Psalm 1:1–3

· ·

¹ *Blessed is the one*
who does not walk in step with the wicked
or stand in the way that sinners take
or sit in the company of mockers,
² *but whose delight is in the law of the* LORD,
and who meditates on his law day and night.
³ *That person is like a tree planted by streams of water,*
which yields its fruit in season
and whose leaf does not wither –
whatever they do prospers.

When you're going on a journey, some items demand to be put first on the packing list and/or to be put out first. When the journey is a long one, food is at the top of the list. Without sustenance, energy levels will drop and the journey will become a struggle, not a joy, and may even fail.

Psalm 1 is, spiritually speaking, first on the list. It is placed at the beginning of the Psalter – and of this collection of *Food for the Journey* – for a reason. It sets the tone for all that follows, to shape our attitudes, thoughts and values.

Of course, the psalmist knows that the world is complex, ambiguous, fraught. But here, with the God-given eye of faith, is the insistence – as Jesus himself taught – that there are two ways and two destinies. There is no middle ground. There is no neutrality. There are righteous and wicked, innocent and guilty, those who listen to God's Word and those who don't, those who live God's way and those who don't.

The first way (verses 1–3) is the way of blessing or happiness (verse 1). It is the way of prospering, of flourishing (verse 3). It is the way that

God 'watches over' (literally 'knows'; verse 6). The way is defined negatively in verse 1. It means *not* doing certain things or – more specifically – not lingering approvingly and listening to the wrong kinds of voices. Look at how the people are described ('wicked', 'sinners', 'mockers'). Look at the progression of the verbs highlighting the dangers of getting ever more involved ('walk', 'stand', 'sit').

This way is marked by a different desire – delighting in God's instruction (or 'law' or 'Word'). And it has different habits or thought processes – meditating on God's instruction day and night. To speak of 'day and night' is another way of saying 'all the time'. It suggests learning and reciting – how else with no lights could an Israelite meditate on it at night?

Every day we face a choice. What will we pack for our journey? Who will we listen to? Who will we spend time with? What will we value? Will we delight in the Word of God? Will we meditate on it day and night?

Ultimately, it's a matter of trust. The early Christians were called people of 'the Way' (Acts 19:9). Will we walk Jesus' way?

Introduction
Numbers

Christopher Wright

Is God faithful?

The children of Israel were first-hand witnesses of God's amazing faithfulness. He had led them out of slavery in Egypt and opened up the Red Sea for them to cross. By Numbers chapter 10, the Israelites were about to leave Mount Sinai, and God was with them: 'By day the pillar of cloud did not fail to guide them on their path, nor the pillar of fire by night to shine on the way they were to take. You gave your good Spirit to instruct them' (Nehemiah 9:19–20).

The future looked bright. Yet, despite all the evidence of God's faithfulness, the rest of the book of Numbers is a catalogue of grumbling, in-fighting and rebellion by God's ungrateful people. Instead of embracing freedom, they longed for the food they had eaten in slavery and wanted to return to Egypt (chapter 11). There was division at the very heart of the nation's leadership, and factions emerged, jockeying for status and ambition, with complete disregard for humility or holiness (chapters 12 and 16). Fear and unbelief stoked rebellion among the people, and they refused to enter Canaan (chapters 13 – 14).

Such rebellion was not without its consequences. God took the people at their word and a whole generation died in the wilderness, never setting foot in the Promised Land. However, despite these repeated failures, God remained faithful. He even used the pagan seer, Balaam, to affirm his determination to bring Israel to the land of promise, highlighting in glorious technicolour that his blessing on Israel rested not on her faithfulness but on his sovereign will (chapters 22 – 24).

Like the Israelites, God's people still fail him and test his patience. But nothing – not our sin, not the circumstances of our lives, nor the anti-Christian agenda growing in the West – will thwart God's redemptive plan. Though we face danger, suffering and even death, we can be sure of God's ultimate protection and eternal blessings.

These selected readings from the book of Numbers testify to God's faithfulness and invite us to trust him for today and all our tomorrows.

Day 2

Read Numbers 10:11–13, 29–36
Key verses: Numbers 10:29–31

••

²⁹ Now Moses said to Hobab son of Reuel the Midianite, Moses' father-in-law, 'We are setting out for the place about which the Lᴏʀᴅ said, "I will give it to you." Come with us and we will treat you well, for the Lᴏʀᴅ has promised good things to Israel.' ³⁰ He answered, 'No, I will not go . . .' ³¹ But Moses said, 'Please do not leave us. You know where we should camp in the wilderness, and you can be our eyes.'

What a difference a year makes!

It has been almost exactly a year since the Israelites left Egypt and arrived at Mount Sinai. And in that time they have experienced the miracles over Egypt as they left, the Passover, the great crossing at the Red Sea and the making of the covenant at Mount Sinai. There was the terrible time when they rebelled against God and were almost destroyed, but received God's forgiveness. Then they spent some months building the tabernacle. But now it is time to move on: 'The Lᴏʀᴅ our God said to us . . . , "You have stayed long enough at this mountain"' (Deuteronomy 1:6).

In Numbers 10:29, Moses turns to the family of Jethro (also known as Reuel), who first welcomed him to Sinai. Jethro is now his father-in-law (see Exodus 18). Moses speaks to Hobab, Jethro's son, his brother-in-law, and invites him to accompany him on his journey. Hobab initially declines, but it seems that he eventually agrees because he turns up in Judges chapters 1 and 4. We also read about the Canaanite people of this particular community, later called the Kenites, subsequently being among the Israelites.

So, who is really leading the people at this point? God? Yes: we are told in verse 33 that the Ark of the Covenant, representing the very presence of God, is going before them as they move, and the cloud of God's presence is seen by day and the pillar of fire by night. God is in charge. What about Moses? He was appointed by God, and in verse 35 we see that he has the authority to say when they are going to leave and where they will stop and camp. So what about Hobab? In verse 31, Moses says to him, 'You will be our eyes. You know where the water is, you know where the oasis is; you have the local expertise.'

Moses has God's authority, God's presence and God's guidance, yet he asks for Hobab's eyes. He is confident in God but doesn't despise human expertise and wisdom.

God has given each of us a work to do for him. Perhaps, like the Israelites, he is calling you to begin a new venture. Spend time in God's presence; seek his guidance. But remember, God has strategically placed mature believers in your life so you can learn from their wisdom and experience. Be humble, be ready to learn from others, recognize that 'You are Christ's body – that's who you are! . . . Only as you accept your part of that body does your "part" mean anything' (1 Corinthians 12:27, MSG).

Day 3

Read Numbers 11:1–9
Key verses: Numbers 11:4–6

. . . .

> [4]*The rabble with them began to crave other food, and again the Israelites started wailing and said, 'If only we had meat to eat!* [5]*We remember the fish we ate in Egypt at no cost – also the cucumbers, melons, leeks, onions and garlic.* [6]*But now we have lost our appetite; we never see anything but this manna!'*

The future is bright.

God's people are on the move. They are led by God, with the presence of God's Spirit, led by Moses and a man with brilliant expertise, Hobab, and with the wonderful promises of good things that God has put ahead of them. Moses mentions twice to Hobab the good things that God has promised to Israel (10:29, 32).

So Numbers 11:1 is a bit of a shock. 'The people complained about their hardships.' The Hebrew word 'hardships' conveys the idea of evil. I'm sure the narrator is quite deliberately contrasting the double use of 'good' in what Moses says to Hobab with this immediate use of 'evil' in the language and the attitude of the people. They are grumbling, rebellious and disobedient. The scene in verses 1–3 – the people grumbling, God's anger and judgment, followed by Moses' intervention and the containment of the problem – is replayed throughout the book.

You would be surprised at what the people complain about. What do you think the Israelites would remember the most about the years of slavery in Egypt? Just one year before this event they were an oppressed, exploited minority, being beaten and put to slave labour in Egyptian agriculture and construction projects, doing all the dirty work that the Egyptians didn't want to do. What do they remember? The hard labour, the humiliation, the genocidal murder of the little boys? No. They remember the fish. It was very tasty, and it was free. Talk about a selective memory! They reckon that a healthy diet in slavery is better than a normal diet in freedom. They have been having a miracle a day – manna – but it isn't good enough and they find it boring. How perverse!

We are not so different from the Israelites. When our circumstances are difficult, we are quick to question whether God loves us and is for us. We conveniently ignore all the miracles of grace that God performs each day – simply because life has not turned out how we had hoped or imagined. We quickly forget God's faithfulness to us in the past, the times when we have seen his goodness, the answered prayers and the guidance we have received. Today, open your eyes to see God's mercies and remember his acts of kindness to you. Literally, count your blessings; write them down in a list. Praise God for who he is and all he has done.

I will remember the deeds of the LORD;
    yes, I will remember your miracles of long ago.
I will consider all your works
    and meditate on all your mighty deeds.
(Psalm 77:11–12)

Day 4

Read Numbers 11:4–15
Key verses: Numbers 11:12–14

. . . .

[12] Did I conceive all these people? Did I give them birth? Why do you tell me to carry them in my arms, as a nurse carries an infant, to the land you promised on oath to their ancestors? [13] Where can I get meat for all these people? They keep wailing to me, 'Give us meat to eat!' [14] I cannot carry all these people by myself; the burden is too heavy for me.

'I'm a failure; get me out of here!'

Moses is a gifted leader. He has had all the training, expertise and experience of forty years of government service under Pharaoh, but this massive community protest causes him to doubt his own leadership.

In verse 10, we read, 'The LORD became exceedingly angry, and Moses was troubled.' That's actually a little weak, as the original text says that the people's complaints are evil in the eyes of Moses. The narrator is yet again contrasting the good things that were supposed to be happening at the end of chapter 10 with the evil that is happening now. Moses and God are quite rightly angry. Moses has told Hobab that things are going to be good, but now he sees that things have become terribly bad.

It's ironic that, in verse 11, Moses accuses God of doing evil to him. The word used in verse 10 is used again here: 'God, why did you do evil to me?' Moses suggests that God should be taking his responsibility as a parent a little more seriously, rather than dumping all the chores on to the nanny. He says, 'Lord, I can't take it any more.' This outburst is almost a complete collapse of his self-confidence as a leader. We can look at this positively and say that, at the very least, Moses is not presented here as a James Bond figure. In films, it's amazing how quickly the hero comes up with a solution and always knows exactly what to do. Nor is Moses a management guru, expertly sitting down to diagnose the problem, coming up with creative ideas that will lead to solutions that everyone agrees to and then moving forward. Moses simply collapses. He is face down before the Lord in desperate inadequacy, desperate dependence. There's an absence of self-sufficiency. But I think there's something more serious here. This crisis is causing Moses to doubt not only his own leadership, but God himself.

Feelings of inadequacy and facing criticism are commonplace in Christian ministry. Sadly, opposition does not just come from unbelievers. We also face 'friendly fire' from fellow Christians. Such scenarios can cause us to doubt God, when the exact opposite course of action is needed. When you are wounded, cling to Christ more closely, look to him for strength and guidance, trust his Word and his promises. Use this time of weakness to deepen your relationship with Christ. Look to him alone for validation and approval.

> Look to the LORD and his strength;
>   seek his face always.
> (Psalm 105:4)

Day 5

Read Numbers 11:16–25
Key verses: Numbers 11:16–17

....

> [16] The LORD said to Moses: 'Bring me seventy of Israel's elders
> who are known to you as leaders and officials among the people.
> Make them come to the tent of meeting, that they may stand
> there with you. [17] I will come down and speak with you there,
> and I will take some of the power of the Spirit that is on you and
> put it on them. They will share the burden of the people with
> you so that you will not have to carry it alone.'

For the first time we hear that Moses is a man of God's Spirit: 'the
Spirit that is on you'. What does that mean?

It certainly doesn't mean that Moses has instant solutions to every
problem, nor does it give him some super status. Remember that the
man whom God describes here in verse 17 as having 'the Spirit' is
the man who in verses 11–15 isn't able to cope. We might say,
paradoxically, that the fact that Moses knows he has the Spirit of
God reinforces a lack of self-sufficiency. Moses knows that only God
can solve the problem, and yet he still feels alone, impotent and
inadequate. So God says, 'I'll tell you what I'll do: I'll spread the
Spirit around. I'll put the Spirit on seventy more people so they can
help you carry the load.'

Back in Exodus 18, the administrative load has already been shared
and delegated, on the advice of Jethro, so this event is probably
talking more about the sharing of spiritual leadership, of widening
the circle of those to whom God has given gifts, those who are able
to administer pastoral wisdom. In verses 24–25, the elders come
together before the watching people. They're not appointed by
some election; they're summoned by God's representative, and God

authenticates them by letting them prophesy. This probably means that they speak some kind of word from God.

Moses is perfectly willing to accept the gifts of the Spirit to and in other people, and that is a sign of his spiritual maturity. Moses teaches us that the Spirit is for sharing. Even though God raises up remarkable individuals within his community of people, of all ages, he still intends it to be a shared leadership, exercised alongside the gifts of others. The New Testament clearly endorses this: the Spirit of God distributes his gifts not just for the one man at the top, but to be shared.

God has shared his Spirit with the other believers in your home group, those with whom you serve on rotas, the people you get on with in church – and those you don't! What a sobering thought. Remember Barnabas – even though all the activity in the church outside Jerusalem was very different from his own Jewish up-bringing, when he 'saw what the grace of God had done, he was glad' (Acts 11:23). Today, thank God when you see his Spirit working in someone else's life. Find practical ways to encourage that person to continue using their gift for God.

Day 6

Read Numbers 11:24–30
Key verse: Numbers 11:29

···

²⁹But Moses replied, 'Are you jealous for my sake? I wish that all the Lᴏʀᴅ's people were prophets and that the Lᴏʀᴅ would put his Spirit on them!'

How do you cope when the unexpected happens?

In the camp, there is an outburst of unscripted, unsupervised charismatic activity. Two men, Eldad and Medad, registered elders, remained in the camp rather than going out to the tent. Yet the Spirit also rests on them and they begin to prophesy. Joshua, son of Nun, Moses' assistant, is outraged and says, 'Moses, my lord, stop them!' (verse 28). Perhaps he is concerned this is a breach of good order, perhaps he thinks it is bad manners, perhaps he is afraid of a loss of control, or perhaps he thinks it is an implied insult to Moses. Often when people are in some position of senior leadership, you find a bunch of acolytes who draw their own authority and status from being servants of the servant of God. Anything that threatens the leader's authority also threatens theirs. Quite possibly, Joshua sees the threat to Moses' authority and wonders how it's going to affect him.

In verse 29, we have Moses' reply: 'Are you jealous for my sake?', as if to say, 'It's not a problem to me, so why is it a problem for you?' Moses has no desire for office, status or prestige. If God wants to share his gifts around, it's no problem for Moses. In fact, he says that he wishes all of God's people would be prophets. Perhaps he thinks that if they were all prophets, he wouldn't have to be the one sorting out everyone else's problems! Perhaps it is simply that Moses has a deep security in his relationship with God. He has no need to prove anything, and that in itself is a mark of great spiritual maturity.

Our reactions in church and the Christian world, especially when things are unexpected and not quite what we want, can be like Joshua's: 'Stop them; we can't have that going on.' Or our reaction can be like that of Moses. We can be led by the Spirit of God and renounce the attributes that the world usually links to strong leadership: self-sufficiency, status, ambition and control.

Check your heart – are you jealous, are you motivated by status and prestige, do you like to be in control? Like Moses, seek security, not in your position or title, but solely in your relationship with God. You are 'in Christ'. You may lose your job, or have to relinquish ministry responsibilities, or your family circumstances may change. You may feel that everything that gave you your identity has been stripped away. But grasp the truth that you are totally complete, accepted, righteous, alive and secure in Christ. Ask the Holy Spirit to help you renounce worldly leadership traits in favour of pursuing spiritual maturity.

> Do not tie your joy, your sense of well-being, to power in ministry. Your ministry can be taken from you. Tie your joy to the fact you are known and loved by God; tie it to your salvation; tie it to the sublime truth that your name is written in heaven.
> (Don Carson, *A Call to Spiritual Reformation*, IVP, 2011, p. 141)

Day 7

Read Numbers 11:18–23, 31–35
Key verses: Numbers 11:33–34

. . . .

> ³³ *But while the meat was still between their teeth and before it could be consumed, the anger of the LORD burned against the people, and he struck them with a severe plague.* ³⁴ *Therefore the place was named Kibroth Hattaavah, because there they buried the people who had craved other food.*

Sometimes physical symptoms mask more serious health issues. In a similar way, God perceives that there is more to the people's whining than simply boredom with manna. He sees his people turning away from the whole project of salvation. The Israelites were crying out in the slavery crisis in Exodus and now they are saying, 'We were better off in Egypt.' They have the living God among them, but have rejected him. 'So,' says God, 'you want meat, I'll give you meat until you're sick of it' (verses 18–20).

The writer tells us in verse 31 that 'a wind went out from the LORD'. In Hebrew that's the word *ruah*, which is exactly the word that is translated as 'Spirit'. The wind or Spirit of God solves the meat crisis by bringing so much quail in on the wind that the people are able to net it and everyone has buckets full. But it leads to serious illness, as we read in verse 33. It sounds as though, before the actual supply of birds is finished, it goes bad. The plague that is described is quite possibly food poisoning. Perhaps they don't let the meat dry out properly or they don't salt it properly. The result is more graves in the wilderness. The place, in English, is called, 'Graves of craving'. The people craved meat and it leads to their punishment, judgment and suffering.

In the same way, we need to be careful about what lies beneath when there is a culture of complaint and protest in any Christian community. In church, complaints about simple things like food, rotas and the use of money can actually hide a deeper discontent and a deeper failure, especially the failure to understand the deeper plan and purpose of God for us as a church. Sometimes our behaviour can be very thoughtless and faithless, and our memories can be very short. In spite of all the good things that God has built into the past, and all the good things that he has for the future, we effectively put God's purposes in rewind.

It is frightening to think that we can be so consumed by grumbling and dissent that we fail to comprehend God's plan for us. But this danger is real for both the church and individuals. God is working in your difficult circumstances, your grief and your suffering, whether you can see it or not. Don't get so wrapped up in your complaints that you miss God's comfort, what he is trying to teach you and how he wants to use you. Today, instead of complaining, will you trust that God, who has worked in your past, is now working in your present?

Day 8

Read Numbers 12:1–9
Key verses: Numbers 12:1–2

. . . .

> [1]*Miriam and Aaron began to talk against Moses because of his Cushite wife, for he had married a Cushite.* [2]*'Has the LORD spoken only through Moses?' they asked. 'Hasn't he also spoken through us?' And the LORD heard this.*

'Who does he think he is?' This is the essence of Aaron and Miriam's complaint against Moses.

At first glance, the conflict seems to revolve around sibling rivalry. Moses is the younger brother, and you can imagine Aaron and Miriam's jealousy that he is still getting the limelight after all these years.

There also seems to be an ethnic issue. Verse 1 mentions twice that Moses' wife, most likely his second wife, is a Cushite. Cush was an important, powerful kingdom just south of biblical Egypt, in what we could now call southern Egypt or part of northern Sudan. His wife would have been a black African. We are not exactly sure why Aaron and Miriam object to this marriage, but ethnic prejudice and racial hatred seem to play a part.

However, verse 2 exposes the real source of the conflict. Even though Aaron and Miriam have been appointed by God to their roles (Micah 6:4) – Aaron is a high priest, the head of the whole priesthood in Israel, and Miriam is a prophet (Exodus 15:20) – they are jealous of Moses' position. Moses is the one through whom God is revealing his will, law and word, and Aaron and Miriam question his unique relationship with God and his uniqueness in relation to them.

In terms of biblical history and salvation, at this stage of the biblical revelation, Moses certainly does occupy a unique position. It is not because he claims or wants it, but because God has chosen him and put him there. It is a familiar tactic among the discontented and disaffected, and it insinuates an arrogance about Moses that the narrator is going to tell us is not there. It accuses him of a monopoly that he does not want; it implies that Moses is hogging all the gifts and status, when in fact that is the opposite of what he wants (Numbers 11). And so Aaron and Miriam protest. They both have God-given gifts and responsibilities of their own. But this is a case of spiritual jealousy, discontent and an attack on a brother. It may look like a family feud, but there is a profoundly spiritual issue attached.

In John 21, Jesus reinstated Peter after his denial. When Jesus spoke to him about his ministry and how he would die, Peter's first reaction was to look at John, Jesus' beloved disciple, and ask, 'Lord, what about him?' Jesus replied, 'What is that to you? You must follow me' (verses 21–22). Don't waste time looking around at other people's gifts and how God is using them: what is that to you? Just make sure you are following God and serving him where he has placed you. We won't have to give an account of how anyone else has used their gifts, only how we have used ours (2 Corinthians 5:10).

Day 9

Read Numbers 12:1–9

Key verses: Numbers 12:2–3

· ·

²'Has the LORD spoken only through Moses?' they asked. 'Hasn't he also spoken through us?' And the LORD heard this.
³(Now Moses was a very humble man, more humble than anyone else on the face of the earth.)

How do you deal with conflict or attacks on your character?

Notice the contrast between the way that Aaron and Miriam are behaving and the way that Moses conducts himself. We read that Miriam and Aaron begin to talk against Moses. We want to ask where and to whom. To each other? To other people? To other family members? And they ask whom? Themselves? Anyone who will listen? The rest of the Levites? There's a campaign going on – a subtle, subversive undermining of Moses. But what does Moses say in response? Nothing. And it seems that the narrator gets embarrassed by this silence. The narrator says that the Lord hears what they are saying, but Moses says nothing, and the reason is that Moses is the most humble man on earth. Moses is not a character who gets into a dogfight of attack, defence and counter-attack. There is a dignified silence.

One of the things I've learnt in my limited experience of Christian leadership is that self-defence is rarely, if ever, the right response to being attacked, accused or misinterpreted. The more you try to defend yourself, the more you dig yourself into a hole and make the accusations sound as if they are true. Moses' example reminds us that spiritual authority and personal humility are not incompatible, but integral to each other; the one is part of the other. Humility is the very essence of a Christian leader among God's people.

Humility is not just for Christian leaders but for all disciples of Christ. Today, reflect on Jesus' humility and what it means for you, in your particular situation, to cultivate his mindset.

> In your relationships with one another, have the same mindset
>   as Christ Jesus:
> who, being in very nature God,
>   did not consider equality with God something to be used
>   to his own advantage;
> rather, he made himself nothing
>   by taking the very nature of a servant,
>   being made in human likeness.
> And being found in appearance as a man,
>   he humbled himself
>   by becoming obedient to death –
>   even death on a cross!
> (Philippians 2:5–8)

Can you serve your boss and others at work, helping them to succeed and be happy, even when they are promoted and you are overlooked? Can you work to make others look good without envy filling your heart? Can you minister to the needs of those whom God exalts and men honour when you yourself are neglected? Can you pray for the ministry of others to prosper when it would cast yours in the shadows?
(Donald Whitney, *Spiritual Disciplines for the Christian Life*, NavPress, 1991, p. 122)

Day 10

Read Numbers 12:1–9
Key verse: Numbers 12:7

. . . .

> [7] . . . *my servant Moses;*
> *he is faithful in all my house.*

We all know those words of Jesus that we hope to hear ourselves: 'Well done, good and faithful servant.' Most of us expect to die before we hear them. What happens here is that Moses hears them at this precise point of accusation.

God deals with the quarrel by directly confronting the participants and calling them together into his presence. He summons them to the Tent of Meeting and comes down in a pillar of cloud (verses 4–5). We already know that Moses is humble. But now God tells Aaron and Miriam that his servant Moses is faithful (verse 7). Addressing Moses as 'my servant' is in itself a term of high honour combined with humble status. This title of 'my servant' is given to very few people in the Old Testament. God says it about Caleb, for example, in Numbers 14:24; it's said about David quite regularly, but it's a rare term of honour, spoken about someone who is going to do the will and purpose of God.

The fact that Moses is God's servant means that he has access to the whole of God's estate. God is saying, 'All of my affairs are entrusted into his hands.' God is saying that he exercises trust in Moses. He trusts him to confront Pharaoh and to stand firm in all the pressures of the plagues. He trusts Moses to lead this people; he trusts Moses to reveal his law and his name, as Yahweh the God of Israel. And God says, 'My servant Moses has not been a disappointment to me. He has been faithful in every department of my house.' It doesn't mean that Moses doesn't make any mistakes, but God is saying that he is a trustworthy house manager.

Can God trust you? Will you remain faithful to him when your prayers seem to go unanswered? Will you keep serving when you can't see the results? Will you work zealously when only God sees your effort? Will you obey him in the small, daily, apparently insignificant moments of life rather than looking to make grand gestures?

Faithfulness isn't very glamorous. We prefer to applaud success. Today, determine to leave the outcomes with God and concentrate on getting ready for his return by faithfully obeying his Word and doing whatever work he has entrusted to you (Matthew 24:36–37; 25:21).

> It gave me great joy when some believers came and testified about your faithfulness to the truth, telling how you continue to walk in it. I have no greater joy than to hear that my children are walking in the truth.
> (3 John 1:3–4)

> Be a loyal servant of Christ so that one day you will hear him say, 'Well done, good and faithful servant!'
> (Matthew 25:21)

Day 11

Read Numbers 12:1–9

Key verse: Numbers 12:8

....

⁸*With him I speak face to face,*
clearly and not in riddles;
he sees the form of the LORD.
Why then were you not afraid
to speak against my servant Moses?

We talk of having 'mountaintop' encounters with God: times when our experience and appreciation of him is magnified. Perhaps the concept comes from Moses' breathtaking encounters with God, many of which happened on mountains.

God certainly distinguishes between ordinary everyday prophets, to whom he gives messages and dreams, and Moses. With Moses, it's different, as God says, 'With him I speak face to face.' The words in verse 8 convey the idea of speaking mouth to mouth. God says that 'Moses speaks what I say'. There is a direct correlation between the word of Moses and the word of God. God's law and truth and self-revelation at this point in biblical history are coming through this man of God. That is part of the reason for the scriptural authority of Moses. Not only is Moses God's servant, but he is also God's friend. Moses has a unique intimacy with God.

Listen to Exodus 33:11–13:

> The LORD would speak to Moses face to face, as one speaks to a friend . . .
>
> Moses said to the LORD, 'You have been telling me, "Lead these people," but you have not let me know whom you will send with me. You have said, "I know you by name and you have found favour with me." If you are pleased with me, teach me your ways so I may know you.'

Moses wants to know God as a friend, and God honours that request. So in Numbers 12:8, God says that Moses 'sees the form of the LORD'. It doesn't mean that Moses sees God as he is, but that Moses clearly sees some visible expression of the presence of God. Exodus 24, the story of the making of the covenant, tells of some people who see God. They have a one-off, visual experience of the presence of God. The rest of the people, we are told in Deuteronomy 4:12, 15, see 'no form'; there is only a voice on the day that the Lord speaks through the fire. Moses has a unique experience of the presence of God, so much so that when he goes out of the presence of God, his face is shining in such a way that the people are afraid of him.

God affirms his approval of his chosen leader Moses, not because of his great power, resourcefulness or managerial skills, but because he is a humble man, a faithful servant, a unique communicator and a true friend of God.

Is it obvious when you have spent time with Jesus? When Moses meets with God, his face shines. Your face may not shine, but you may be more patient in difficult situations, quicker to forgive, joyful rather than critical, kind rather than bitter. Time with God – studying and praying through his Word (and then obeying it) – is the only way that we become more like Christ. Make these times a priority. Then, like a candle in a cracked clay jar (2 Corinthians 4:7), the life of Christ will shine out through you and draw others to the Saviour.

Day 12

Read Numbers 12:1–9
Key verses: Numbers 12:7–8

. . . .

> [7] . . . my servant Moses;
> he is faithful in all my house.
> [8] With him I speak face to face,
> clearly and not in riddles;
> he sees the form of the LORD.

Can you imagine being there when Jesus leads Cleopas and his friend in a Bible study? Luke 24:27 says, 'And beginning with Moses and all the Prophets, he explained to them what was said in all the Scriptures concerning himself.' Perhaps Jesus mentions Numbers 12, as he is clearly anticipated in this chapter. Notice how Moses is a portrait of the Lord Jesus Christ:

- *Humble*. Moses is a humble man; so is Jesus. That's how he's assessed in Isaiah 53:2–3: 'He had no beauty or majesty to attract us to him, nothing in his appearance that we should desire him. He was despised and rejected by mankind, a man of suffering, and familiar with pain.' Jesus says that 'whoever wants to be first must be slave of all. For even the Son of Man did not come to be served, but to serve, and to give his life as a ransom for many' (Mark 10:44–45).

- *Faithful*. Just as Moses is faithful, so is Jesus. The writer of the book of Hebrews picks up on this language of Moses and applies it to Jesus in Hebrews 3:6: 'Christ is faithful as the Son over God's house.' In the preceding verse, he says, '"Moses was faithful as a servant in all God's house," bearing witness to what would be spoken by God in the future.' Jesus knows that he comes from the Father and is going to the Father. He is secure in his own Sonship, and so he is able to take the status of a servant and act humbly.

- *The unique revelation of God.* Moses sees the form of God, whereas Jesus is in the form of God; he is a member of the Godhead. As Paul puts it in Philippians 2:6, Jesus is 'in very nature God'. Hebrews 1:1–2 explains that 'God spoke to our ancestors through the prophets at many times and in various ways, but in these last days he has spoken to us by his Son'.

God's words about Moses, although historically true about him, are prophetically true about Jesus, who also bears the mark of God's approval.

Moses' life points to Christ, and so should ours. Instead of blending in with the world, our lifestyles should be so distinct and winsome that people start asking, 'Why?' Think: does how you spend your time and money differ greatly from your non-Christian neighbours? The way you treat work colleagues, what you post on Facebook, the activities in which you encourage your children to be involved: do these point people towards Christ?

If I make you light-bearers, you don't think I'm going to hide you under a bucket, do you? I'm putting you on a light stand. Now that I've put you there on a hilltop, on a light stand – shine! Keep open house; be generous with your lives. By opening up to others, you'll prompt people to open up with God, this generous Father in heaven.
(Matthew 5:14–16, MSG)

Day 13

Read Numbers 12:10–16

Key verses: Numbers 12:10–11, 13

. . . .

> [10]*When the cloud lifted from above the tent, Miriam's skin was leprous – it became as white as snow. Aaron turned towards her and saw that she had a defiling skin disease, [11]and he said to Moses, 'Please, my lord, I ask you not to hold against us the sin we have so foolishly committed . . .'*
>
> [13]*So Moses cried out to the Lord, 'Please, God, heal her!'*

We often get angry when our plans are derailed, the computer crashes, or even just waiting in a queue! In stark contrast, God's anger is holy and righteous, and Aaron and Miriam feel the full force of it.

God leaves the Tent of Meeting and, when the cloud lifts, Miriam is afflicted with a skin disease. This is not leprosy in its modern form, but probably some form of flaking skin disorder, with the skin described as falling off like snow. Aaron is horrified; in that culture, the shame on his sister is also a shame on him.

The irony is that Aaron has complained that Moses is usurping the full right to pray and speak to God, but now Aaron doesn't feel it is right to go straight into the presence of God, high priest though he is, so he turns to Moses. And here, for the first time, Moses speaks. This is the only time he speaks in this chapter, and when he does, it is to pray for his sister: 'Please, God, heal her!' (verse 13). This is a mark of the likeness of Christ, who tells us that we should love those who persecute us (Matthew 5:44), and who says, 'Father, forgive them, for they do not know what they are doing' (Luke 23:34). Moses asks God to heal his sister, and God does so, after a period of time – a week of disgrace, in which the lesson will be learnt by Miriam and the whole community.

Raymond Brown in his commentary puts it like this: 'Moses learnt the importance of silence and let the LORD do the talking . . . Aaron learnt the value of prayer' – though he was a high priest, he had to learn the power of the prayer of others (his own brother). 'Miriam learnt the generosity of grace', because eventually she was pardoned, cleansed, healed and restored, and 'the people learnt the seriousness of sin', although we have to say that they didn't learn it very well (Raymond Brown, *Numbers*, The Bible Speaks Today, IVP, 2002, p. 111).

What about us? What do we learn? It depends on whom you identify with in the story. Is the Holy Spirit convicting you that you are behaving like Miriam and Aaron: critical, undermining and jealous, guilty of discontent? If so, let's repent of our ways. Is the Holy Spirit impressing on you the humility of Moses, his integrity in leadership, his reliance on God in difficult days? Is the Holy Spirit urging you to trust God, let him vindicate you and, in due course, exalt you? For God's glory, make it your ambition to be his humble servant.

Day 14

Read Numbers 13:1–33
Key verses: Numbers 13:30–33

• •

^{30} *Then Caleb . . . said, 'We should go up and take possession of the land, for we can certainly do it.'*

^{31} *But the men who had gone up with him said, 'We can't attack those people; they are stronger than we are.'* ^{32} *And they spread among the Israelites a bad report about the land they had explored. They said, 'The land we explored devours those living in it. All the people we saw there are of great size* ^{33} *. . . We seemed like grasshoppers in our own eyes, and we looked the same to them.'*

They don't know it yet, but the Israelites are on the brink of arguably the most awful catastrophe in their history up to this point. They arrive at the very southern edges of the land of promise, the oasis that is there at Kadesh, and they decide to send spies into the land. The spies' initial report is very positive. They tell Moses, 'We went into the land to which you sent us, and it does flow with milk and honey!' (verse 27). They even bring back a big bunch of grapes to prove how fruitful the land is.

But then something happens. In verse 28, the spies' report very suddenly shifts into a grossly exaggerated negative account. Caleb silences the people and urges, 'We should go up and take possession of the land, for we can certainly do it.'

The other ten spies say, 'Sorry, but we can't.' The ten spies then spread negativity and an inferiority complex among the people: 'We can't attack those people . . . We seemed like grasshoppers in our own eyes' (verses 31, 33). Their account breeds fear among the Israelites, which Moses records in Deuteronomy 1:28–29:

Our brothers have made our hearts melt in fear. They say, 'The people are stronger and taller than we are; the cities are large, with walls up to the sky. We even saw the Anakites there.'

Then I said to you, 'Do not be terrified; do not be afraid of them.'

As Raymond Brown puts it, the spies 'magnified the problem and then minimised the resources that they had', and their report leads to the people's rebellion (*Numbers*, The Bible Speaks Today, IVP, 2002, pp. 118–119). 'That night all the members of the community raised their voices and wept aloud. All the Israelites grumbled against Moses and Aaron, and the whole assembly said to them, "If only we had died in Egypt! Or in this wilderness!" ' (Numbers 14:1–2).

It is easy to look at the huge problems in our world, the rising opposition to Christianity and the massive task of evangelism, and to feel so fearful and inadequate that we don't actually do anything. But remember that you serve in God's name, with his power and resources. He promises to equip you for all that he calls you to do. Just as he multiplied the five loaves and two fish, he can multiply your efforts and use them for his glory. Today, take heart from God's word to Joshua:

Have I not commanded you? Be strong and courageous. Do not be afraid; do not be discouraged, for the LORD your God will be with you wherever you go.

(Joshua 1:9)

Day 15

Read Numbers 14:1–12

Key verse: Numbers 14:11

· ·

> [11] *The* LORD *said to Moses, 'How long will these people treat me with contempt? How long will they refuse to believe in me, in spite of all the signs I have performed among them?'*

Listening to a sermon is often a good way to understand a Bible passage. Sometimes the Bible helps us by providing a sermon on its own text, and that's what we get in Deuteronomy 1. In chapters 1 – 3, Moses remembers what happened in the book of Numbers, and preaches to the next generation of Israelites on the basis of this.

Moses' sermon explains what happened in Numbers 13 – 14:

> But you were unwilling to go up; you rebelled against the command of the LORD your God. You grumbled in your tents and said, 'The LORD hates us; so he brought us out of Egypt to deliver us into the hands of the Amorites to destroy us.'
> (Deuteronomy 1:26–27)

There is this grumbling rebellion against God and a rejection of God's plans, the whole purpose of the redemption. The Israelites have been brought out of Egypt and they want to go back. Even worse than that, they attribute false motives to God. They say, 'He only brought us out of slavery because he wanted to kill us here.' They also say, 'The LORD *hates* us' (Deuteronomy 1:27, italics added). That's incredible. What they have just experienced is the biggest demonstration of the love and faithfulness of God in the entire Bible, apart from the cross: the story of the exodus. It's the Old Testament story of God's redemption, faithfulness, love and power. God has poured his love on these people and they turn around and say, 'Do you know what? God hates us.'

They say, 'We'd rather be dead. We'd rather go back to slavery' (Numbers 14:1–3). What is God's response? He says in verse 11, 'How long will these people treat me with contempt? How long will they refuse to believe in me?' It's very strong language. It's the kind of language that is used about David's adultery with Bathsheba (2 Samuel 12:14).

This rebellion in the wilderness is not just a rejection of Moses or the leadership; it is a rejection of God himself. The Israelites have a choice to make: they can either please God, and have God be pleased with them, through their courage, obedience and faith; or they can oppose and stand against God, and be afraid of those whom God has already defeated (Numbers 14:8–9).

There is a story of a father trying to get his young son to sit down. The father kept asking the boy to sit, but the boy determinedly refused. At last the boy sat down, but he looked his father in the eye and said, 'In my heart I'm standing up!' We may not have rebelled against God as spectacularly as the Israelites, but often our hearts are just as defiant. In the Holy Spirit's power, stop disobedience taking root. Be grateful instead of grumbling; be intentional about remembering God's faithfulness to you. Daily acknowledge and submit to his sovereign will.

Day 16

Read Numbers 14:1–12
Key verses: Numbers 14:10–11

....

¹⁰But the whole assembly talked about stoning them. Then the glory of the Lord appeared at the tent of meeting to all the Israelites. ¹¹The Lord said to Moses, 'How long will these people treat me with contempt? How long will they refuse to believe in me, in spite of all the signs I have performed among them?'

You saw how the Lord your God carried you . . . until you reached this place. In spite of this, you did not trust in the Lord your God, who went ahead of you on your journey, in fire by night and in a cloud by day. (Deuteronomy 1:31–33)

Unbelief is the root cause of the massive rebellion in Numbers 14.

In the same way, unbelief vexes Jesus throughout his ministry. Remember when he is unable to do any good work because of the unbelief among the people? 'You of little faith,' he once says to his disciples (Matthew 8:26). Of course, unbelief can afflict us at any point, even as mature Christian believers, when we're confronted with a future that seems uncertain or when God calls us into some new path of obedience. It is one thing to sing and celebrate all that God has done in the past, but it is quite another to be sure that he'll provide in the future. Unbelief can weave into our hearts and lead to disobedience.

This episode at Kadesh is so serious that it echoes on through the Bible. In Psalm 106:24–27 we read:

Then they despised the pleasant land;
    they did not believe his promise.
They grumbled in their tents
    and did not obey the Lord.

So he swore to them with uplifted hand
    that he would make them fall in the wilderness,
make their descendants fall among the nations
    and scatter them throughout the lands.

In the New Testament, Paul mentions this rebellion in 1 Corinthians 10, and so does the writer of Hebrews, in chapter 3:16–19:

Who were they who heard and rebelled? Were they not all those Moses led out of Egypt? And with whom was he angry for forty years? Was it not with those who sinned, whose bodies perished in the wilderness? And to whom did God swear that they would never enter his rest if not to those who disobeyed? So we see that they were not able to enter, because of their unbelief.

Unbelief slithers into our hearts and spreads its poison. Has it stopped you talking about Jesus to colleagues in the office or praying fervently? Has it prompted you to prize financial security or to overly protect your children from any hardship and disappointment? Has it stopped you recognizing God's daily blessings? Has unbelief in who God is, what his Word says and what his promises mean for you led you into some disobedience? Today, repent of your unbelief; ask for God's help to take him at his word and trust him with your life. Cry out to God like the father in Mark 9:24: 'I do believe; help me overcome my unbelief!' If it would be helpful, pray with a mature Christian about your struggles.

Day 17

Read Numbers 14:10–25

Key verse: Numbers 14:19

∙∙∙

[19] In accordance with your great love, forgive the sin of these people, just as you have pardoned them from the time they left Egypt until now.

How do we intercede for people? What should we pray?

God is ready to wipe the Israelites out, but Moses steps into the breach between the people and the wrath of God. He intercedes for them and appeals to God to hold back his anger and bear their sin. He appeals to:

- *God's reputation* (verses 13–16). News of the Exodus means God is already making a name for himself around the region (Exodus 15:14–15). So, Moses argues, 'If you kill the Israelites, what will people think? They will think either that you are incompetent or that you are malicious. They will think you brought the Israelites out of Egypt and planned a future for them but your plan collapsed, or you brought them out to raise their hopes and then dash them. Is this what you want people to say about you?' Moses is concerned about the name and reputation of God.

- *God's character* (verses 17–19). After that awful incident of the Golden Calf, Moses asked to see God's glory. God hid Moses in the cleft of the rock and declared his name, Yahweh: 'The LORD, the LORD, the compassionate and gracious God, slow to anger, abounding in love and faithfulness, maintaining love to thousands, and forgiving wickedness, rebellion and sin. Yet he does not leave the guilty unpunished' (Exodus 34:6–7). Now Moses says, 'Remember these words, remember your own name?' Then he pleads in Numbers 14:17, 'Now may the Lord's strength be displayed, just as you have declared.' Essentially, Moses is saying,

'I understand your anger. But you have an even greater strength because you are Yahweh. You are the God who has the power to forgive, to carry iniquity and to go on being faithful. That's what makes you the God that you are. That's your real strength. If you want to be really strong, then carry them and forgive them.'

- *God's promise* (verse 16). Moses mentions the land that God promised to Abraham (Exodus 32:12–13). His boldness is astonishing. It's almost as if he is saying, 'How can you contemplate destroying all these people? If you can't keep your promise to Abraham, how can I know you'll keep your promises to me? Is that the kind of God you are?'

- *God's covenant* (verse 19). Moses boldly reminds God of the covenant he made with the Israelites at Mount Sinai (Deuteronomy 9:26). God can't abandon his own people; the ones he brought out of Egypt.

What does Moses teach us about praying? He prays about the things that matter most to God. In Psalm 138:2, David affirms, 'You have exalted above all things your name and your word' (ESV). Moses appeals to the very things that are God's priorities, and pleads with him to act to the glory of his name, to act consistently with his own character and in accordance with his promise. Use this as a framework as you pray for others today.

Day 18

Read Numbers 14:20–38

Key verses: Numbers 14:32–34

• •

³²But you – your bodies will fall in this wilderness. ³³Your children will be shepherds here for forty years, suffering for your unfaithfulness, until the last of your bodies lies in the wilderness. ³⁴For forty years – one year for each of the forty days you explored the land – you will suffer for your sins and know what it is like to have me against you.

God's forgiveness does not mean we escape the consequences of our actions. He responds to Moses' appeal with a declaration of forgiveness (verse 20); the people will not be wiped out instantly. However, this does not mean there will be no punishment. God will continue his plan and purpose through the next generation, but this generation of adults have had their last chance. Their rebellion against God has left him with no alternative but to punish them.

In verses 21–24 we read God's general statement of what is going to happen. Notice the contrast here between what this generation of Israelites has seen and what they will now never see. They have seen all the miracles of God, the exodus and Sinai, but they will never see the Promised Land because of their contempt for God and their persistent rebellion. God says that this has happened ten times. This could be rhetorical, but rabbis and Jewish scholars have in fact come up with ten instances in Exodus and Numbers of grumbling, murmuring and rebellion: at the Red Sea (Exodus 14), Marah (Exodus 15), the Desert of Sinai (three times in Exodus 16), Rephidim (Exodus 17), Sinai (Exodus 32), Taberah (Numbers 11:1–3), Kibroth (Numbers 11:4–34) and here at Kadesh (Numbers 13 – 14).

In verses 26–35, God goes a little further, filling in the specific details of the punishment. The point of the contrast here is not between what the Israelites have *seen* and will now never see, but between what the Israelites have *said* and how God takes them at their word. Earlier in the chapter they said, 'We wish we'd died in Egypt or here. We'd rather be dead than go on.' God says, 'Very well, have it your way' (verse 28). They also said that their children would be captured as plunder (verse 3) but God says, 'No, they won't. They will be shepherds here in the wilderness until all the parents die off, and then they will go in and enjoy the land that you can't have' (verse 33). This is a sobering tale of a people unrepentantly resistant to God's plan for them, who constantly reject his grace, provision, purposes and love.

For the Israelites, the punishment for sin is death. Likewise, our sin warrants death, but thank God that Jesus died in our place; he became our substitute. He appeased God's wrath and he paid the penalty our sin deserved so that we don't have to (Romans 6:23). We now enjoy a relationship with God where God himself, the Holy Spirit, helps us live to please him. Praise God for this glorious gospel of grace.

Day 19

Read Numbers 14:26–45
Key verses: Numbers 14:42–43

....

*⁴²Do not go up, because the L*ORD *is not with you. You will be defeated by your enemies, ⁴³for the Amalekites and the Canaanites will face you there. Because you have turned away from the L*ORD*, he will not be with you and you will fall by the sword.*

Is there a future for God's people?

After God announces his punishment, the people respond with great mourning and a futile effort at belated obedience. They try to enter Canaan but they are beaten back, because the Lord isn't with them. That generation is finished, but God hasn't finished with his plans or the salvation, ultimately, of the world through them. The next thirty-eight years that they are to spend in the wilderness will not be wasted time. In fact, there are two ways in which we can look at this narrative of Kadesh and the following story of the later generation in the wilderness. We can look at it through the eyes of Psalm 95:10–11, where God declares his anger. We can also look at how Moses speaks to the Israelites in Deuteronomy 8:2–3 about the same event:

> Remember how the L*ORD* your God led you all the way in the wilderness . . . to humble and test you in order to know . . . whether or not you would keep his commands. He humbled you, causing you to hunger and then feeding you with manna, . . . to teach you that man does not live on bread alone but on every word that comes from the mouth of the L*ORD*.

God gives them bread to teach them that there are things more important than bread: the word and promise of God. 'Know then in your heart that as a man disciplines his son, so the L*ORD* your God disciplines you' (Deuteronomy 8:5). At one level, the years in the desert are a huge waste of time, the result of sin and rebellion, yet God turns it into a learning experience, an act of parental discipline, and an opportunity for grace and obedience.

It's interesting that in 1 Corinthians 10:11, Paul says that these things are written as *warnings* for us. But in Romans 15:4, he says that these things are written to *teach* us, 'so that through the endurance taught in the Scriptures and the encouragement they provide we might have hope'. Where is the encouragement in this passage? It is that God turns the wilderness into a time of fresh opportunity to love, trust and obey him.

You may feel like you are living in the wilderness because of some past act of rebellion, disobedience to God or folly. Your life feels blighted; you feel you've missed plan A and you're now in plan B. Don't fall for that nonsense! God is patient. You may be in a time of discipline, as the Israelites were in the wilderness, but it's not your final destination or where he wants you to stay. Redeem the time, and return to God in love and obedience. When you do, he will respond with grace and blessing.

Day 20

Read Numbers 16:1–15
Key verses: Numbers 16:1–3

. . . .

> ¹*Korah . . . and certain Reubenites – Dathan and Abiram, sons of Eliab, and On son of Peleth – became insolent* ². . . *With them were 250 Israelite men . . .* ³*They came as a group to oppose Moses and Aaron and said to them, 'You have gone too far! The whole community is holy, every one of them, and the LORD is with them.'*

It only takes a few complaints to trigger widespread rebellion. Here, two groups are involved in this challenge against Moses, but it starts out as independent grumbles involving three or four individuals: Korah of the Levites, and Dathan and Abiram of the Reubenites.

Korah and the Levites were discontented over their status (verse 3). They appeal to very plausible scriptural truth, that the whole community of God's people is holy. This is true: Israel as a whole was intended to be God's holy people (Exodus 19:6). The narrator intends a flashback to Numbers 15:37–41, where God commanded the Israelites to sew tassels on to the hems of their garments so that, even on their clothing, everyone in the community would be reminded of their holiness. So, asks Korah, 'Why are Aaron and the priests regarded as more holy than anyone else? What's so special about them?' This is jealousy expressing itself as an issue of equality.

The second theological theme that they appeal to is that the Lord is among all the people (verse 3). This is again true. The tabernacle itself is a symbol of the presence of God in the midst of the whole people (Exodus 29:45). Korah argues, 'God dwells among all of us, so what gives Aaron and the priests special right of access into the presence of God?' Again, it's a demand of equality, based on spiritual truth. But they're ignoring the particular calling and symbolic function that God has laid on Aaron and the priests in the tribe of Levi.

What are they really after? In verses 9–11, Moses exposes their real motives: they are dissatisfied with the roles that God has given them. The Levites have a tribal responsibility to carry and look after the tabernacle. But within the tribe of Levi, Aaron and his family have a specific priestly responsibility. It is they alone that God has commissioned to come to the altar to do the manipulation of the blood for the sacrifices: to speak the words of atonement and blessing, to enter once a year into the holy presence of God, along with many other duties. The Levites (through Korah) are discontented with what God has given them and jealous of what God has given to others (Aaron and sons); they have ambitions for a higher level of authority, and all the perks that go with it.

Do you desire the status, prestige or label of 'leader', in whatever ministry context you serve, more than actually being a godly servant-leader? Don't give selfish ambition room to grow. Instead, make much of Christ. Pray that you would be a leader like King David, who:

shepherded [the Israelites] with integrity of heart;
with skilful hands he led them.
(Psalm 78:72)

Day 21

Read Numbers 16:1–15
Key verse: Numbers 16:3

....

³ *They came as a group to oppose Moses and Aaron and said to them, 'You have gone too far! The whole community is holy, every one of them, and the* LORD *is with them. Why then do you set yourselves above the* LORD*'s assembly?'*

Resisting authority, of any sort, is quite common today, but it's not a new phenomenon. It is at the heart of Dathan and Abiram's objection to Moses. It's probable that the second half of verse 3 is Dathan and Abiram's complaint: 'Why then do you set yourselves above the LORD's assembly?' In other words, 'Who gave you the right to be in charge?' There is a tension between the equality of all God's people and the God-appointed role and necessity that there should be leaders. It's a tension that God's people have never seemed to get quite right.

But there is much more than a theological conflict. Moses summons these people in to try to sort this out, but they refuse to meet him (verses 12, 14). In verses 13–14, there are perverse and defiant accusations against Moses: 'Isn't it enough that you have brought us up out of a land flowing with milk and honey to kill us in the wilderness? And now you also want to lord it over us!' They attribute to Moses the same evil intention that they attributed to God: 'You brought us out to kill us in the desert. That's what you want, isn't it, Moses? You want us all dead. You want to lord it over us.'

Why are these people not going into a land of milk and honey? It isn't because Moses doesn't lead them there; it is the people who refuse. They hold God's leaders in contempt and they refuse to accept the leadership that God has appointed. Here we see the perversity of the people who attribute their own failure to the leadership of the people.

This account is not a licence for self-appointed tyrannical leaders to demand unquestioning submission. Neither is it a prohibition against ever questioning our leaders. Certainly we need to be careful about putting ourselves in opposition against those who are in leadership over God's people. Any challenges need to presented with gentleness and respect, 'speaking the truth in love' (Ephesians 4:15). How do you treat your church leaders? Is there anything you could do to show your support and appreciation of them?

> Remember your leaders, who spoke the word of God to you. Consider the outcome of their way of life and imitate their faith . . . Have confidence in your leaders and submit to their authority, because they keep watch over you as those who must give an account. Do this so that their work will be a joy, not a burden, for that would be of no benefit to you.
> (Hebrews 13:7, 17)

If you are a church leader, meditate on Paul's charge to the Ephesian elders:

> Keep watch over yourselves and all the flock of which the Holy Spirit has made you overseers. Be shepherds of the church of God, which he bought with his own blood.
> (Acts 20:28)

Day 22

Read Numbers 16:1–15
Key verse: Numbers 16:15

¹⁵ *Then Moses became very angry and said to the* Lord, *'Do not accept their offering. I have not taken so much as a donkey from them, nor have I wronged any of them.'*

Being a leader among God's people is often like being blotting paper. Blotting paper used to mop up spilt ink in the days when people used fountain pens. Sometimes that's what leaders have to do: absorb the mess and clean it up. But on this occasion, Moses becomes very angry. We're told in Numbers 12:3 that Moses is a very humble man. So what sparks this reaction?

I think it is the last phrase of verse 13 where they accuse him of 'want[ing] to lord it over us'. The first time that Moses heard these words was forty years earlier in Egypt, when he tried to help his own people by killing an Egyptian (Exodus 2:14). That led to forty years in the wilderness for Moses. Now these people have been so rebellious that Moses is going to have to spend another forty years in the wilderness with them. And the tune still hasn't changed. They are still accusing him of wanting to 'lord it over' them. Moses knows deep in his heart that he would rather be anywhere else than in this position of leadership, so this is an unjust accusation against him. And he becomes very angry, and protests to God against the accusation, which he feels is so unforgivably unfair. He says, 'I have not taken so much as a donkey from them' – a typical Jewish way of declaring your own innocence. He's saying, 'Lord, I've done nothing to deserve this kind of accusation. Don't forgive them; don't accept their offering.'

This is the same man who, in Exodus 32:32, asked God to blot his name out of the Book of Life rather than destroy anyone, the same man who pleaded with God to forgive the people for the rebellion (Numbers 14:13–19). But Moses is a man of flesh and blood, and he explodes with anger.

Think of Abraham, David, Peter, Paul – any leader from the Bible – and you will find an individual who failed, usually more than once. Every believer is familiar with failure, with times when we have too easily given into sin rather than lived up to our holy calling as God's children. But with God, failure isn't final. Repentance offers us a fresh opportunity to live for him in love and obedience. Today, will you ask for and accept God's forgiveness? Will you rely on the Holy Spirit to learn from past failure and move forward in his strength?

> Most Bible characters met with failure and survived. Even when the failure was immense, those who found leadership again refused to lie in the dust and bemoan their tragedy. In fact, their failure and repentance led to a greater conception of God's grace. They came to know the God of the second chance, and sometimes the third and fourth.
> (Oswald Sanders, *Spiritual Leadership*, Moody Publishers, 1967, p. 134)

Day 23

Read Numbers 16:16–40

Key verses: Numbers 16:33, 35

....

³³ They [those associated with Korah] went down alive into the realm of the dead, with everything they owned; the earth closed over them, and they perished and were gone from the community . . . ³⁵ And fire came out from the LORD and consumed the 250 men who were offering the incense.

Like in the best of stories, the suspense builds as the narrator interweaves what happens to Korah and the Levite supporters with what happens with Dathan, Abiram and his Reubenite supporters. First, look at God's verdict on Korah and the Levites. They claim to be as holy as the priests, so Moses jumps to the defence of his brother Aaron and proposes a test (verses 16–19). He says, 'Bring your censers. Light your fires, burn the incense and let's see if God accepts you.' What happens? Verse 35: 'And fire came out from the LORD and consumed the 250 men who were offering the incense.' The verdict is clear, verse 40: 'This was to remind the Israelites that no one except a descendant of Aaron should come to burn incense before the LORD, or he would become like Korah and his followers.'

What happens to Dathan and Abiram? God tells Moses to warn the Israelites to separate themselves from these defiant rebels. Verses 28–30 are important to the way in which Moses describes the actual conflict: 'This is how you will know that the LORD has sent me to do all these things and that it was not my idea.' Moses passes the decision on to God, saying, 'Let God show the truth.' The truth is twofold: positively, that 'God sent me', and negatively, 'This is not my idea. This has all come from the will, purpose and plan of God.' Moses' authority and plan of action have all come from God and he wants the people to know who they are really opposing: they are showing contempt for God, not just for Moses.

Judgment is immediate and extraordinary (verses 31–34): 'the ground under them split apart and the earth opened its mouth and swallowed them and their households . . .together with their possessions'. Part of the horror of the story is that the God who created the earth for our blessing and enjoyment uses it for his awesome judgment. In both cases, God acts to defend what he has established: Aaron's unique priesthood and Moses' unique authority. Neither of them vindicates themselves; God makes his verdict unmistakable.

God's judgment is real and serious. Despite what it looks like in the world around us, sin will not go unpunished. Jesus paid the penalty for sin when he died on the cross, so that those who belong to him will meet him as Saviour rather than Judge (Hebrews 9:26–27). But those who reject Christ, who continue in unrepentant, defiant rebellion, will face the full force of God's wrath (Romans 2:5). Pray for unbelieving family members and friends to accept the gospel and turn to Christ while there is still time to repent.

Day 24

Read Numbers 16:20–45
Key verse: Numbers 16:22

....

²²But Moses and Aaron fell face down and cried out, 'O God, the God who gives breath to all living things, will you be angry with the entire assembly when only one man sins?'

We can pray sitting, standing or kneeling; we can pray anywhere and at any time. There is no posture that makes our prayers more accept-able to God. However, our posture does reveal something about our attitude to prayer and what we are praying about.

Three times in this one chapter, Moses falls on his face (verses 4, 22, 45). Twice in this chapter Moses specifically intercedes with God; he falls on his face to plead for mercy and seeks to provide atonement. On the two occasions, in verses 21 and 45, God speaks identical words: 'Get away from this assembly so that I can put an end to them at once.'

In verse 22, Moses acts in response to that when he appeals to the justice of God, just as Abraham did when he interceded for Sodom and Gomorrah (Genesis 18:16–33). Moses intercedes with God on the basis of his known character. He's the God of all people, the God of justice, and so Moses says, 'You must judge, but let your judgment be discriminating on those who are truly the offenders.' Moses prays that God will act appropriately and not punish the whole of his people for the offence of a few.

In verse 41 we read, 'The next day the whole Israelite community grumbled against Moses and Aaron. "You have killed the LORD's people," they said.' Neither aspect of this accusation is true. Moses and Aaron haven't killed anyone; it was God, who acted without human agency. And Korah, Dathan and Abiram, by their actions, have ceased to be part of the Lord's people. They set themselves up as enemies of God. The tragedy in the Old Testament is that the whole people of Israel would discover what it would mean to have God as their enemy and no longer to be treated as his people.

Notice that there is an awesome and fearless escalation of sin. It starts with Korah, then it becomes a gang of four (with Dathan, Abiram and On), and then all 250 of the leaders. A day later it becomes the whole of Israel. There is something frightfully infectious about sin.

What is your usual posture for praying? Today, try a different posture – kneeling, lying prostrate, or perhaps standing with your hands open in front of you. A new posture won't make your prayers any more acceptable to God, but it might help you stay focused and pray more deliberately. Spend time interceding for others, praying not just for their physical needs but also for their spiritual ones. Like Moses, cry out to God to be merciful and to act according to his own character.

> As for me, far be it from me that I should sin against the Lord by failing to pray for you.
> (1 Samuel 12:23)

Day 25

Read Numbers 16:42–50
Key verses: Numbers 16:46–47

....

46 Then Moses said to Aaron, 'Take your censer and put incense in it, along with burning coals from the altar, and hurry to the assembly to make atonement for them. Wrath has come out from the LORD; the plague has started.' 47 So Aaron did as Moses said, and ran into the midst of the assembly. The plague had already started among the people, but Aaron offered the incense and made atonement for them.

There is a false dichotomy that says that the Old Testament God is the God of wrath and the God of the New Testament is a God of mercy. The wrath and mercy of God are in both Testaments. This story gives us a glimpse of the meeting of that wrath and mercy.

In verse 45, God threatens total destruction, and in verse 46, Moses acts, no longer only in prayer. Moses sends Aaron, Israel's great high priest, the one whom God himself has appointed, to stand in the gap and to atone for his people. Aaron physically puts himself between the people of God and the wrath of God. The language of atonement is spoken of twice (verses 46–47). It's the same word that is used in the context of the sacrifices mentioned in Leviticus, when it speaks of both the cleansing away of sin and the averting of the wrath of God from the sinner. Aaron, here as elsewhere, is a symbolic portrait of the work of the Lord Jesus Christ.

The emphasis in the concluding verse is that only Aaron can function as the high priest, and that's confirmed in chapter 17 through the budding of Aaron's staff, proving that he is the one whom God has chosen to stand as his atoning agent. At this point in Israel's history, Aaron is the only one who can make atonement for all Israel, and we know from the Scriptures that Jesus is the only one appointed by

God who can make atonement for all the world and all humanity. He is the 'Lamb of God, who takes away the sin of the world' (John 1:29). Let's give thanks to God for his grace.

Aaron, the high priest, atones for the sins of the Israelites, but he points forward to our Great High Priest. Whereas Aaron and his descendants have to offer sacrifices for their own sin as well as the sins of the people and to keep repeating the ritual – because the blood of bulls and goats never effectively and finally deals with sin – Jesus is the once-and-for-all atoning sacrifice (Hebrews 7:23–28). His sacrifice on the cross cleanses us from sin and satisfies God's wrath.

> So then, since we have a great High Priest who has entered heaven, Jesus the Son of God, let us hold firmly to what we believe. This High Priest of ours understands our weaknesses, for he faced all of the same testings we do, yet he did not sin. So let us come boldly to the throne of our gracious God. There we will receive his mercy, and we will find grace to help us when we need it most.
> (Hebrews 4:14–16, NLT)

Day 26

Read Numbers 22:1–20

Key verses: Numbers 22:5–6

....

⁵ Balak said:

'A people has come out of Egypt; they cover the face of the land and have settled next to me. ⁶ Now come and put a curse on these people, because they are too powerful for me. Perhaps then I will be able to defeat them and drive them out of the land. For I know that whoever you bless is blessed, and whoever you curse is cursed.'

Fear is spreading. This moving horde of Israelites that came out of the wilderness have defeated the Amorites. Moab, the kingdom where the Israelites are camping at this point, is scared that it will suffer the same fate. Of course, only the Israelites know that God has told them not to attack Moab or to take any of its land (Deuteronomy 2:9). The king of Moab, Balak, is certain he cannot defeat the Israelites in battle, so he decides to turn to sorcery and sends for the best magician around: Balaam, the son of Beor. It takes about three weeks for the king's messengers to reach Balaam and three weeks to get back, and they do the journey twice, so it takes Balak more than three months to get hold of Balaam.

In verses 7–20, Balak's messengers arrive and bring their fee. It's late, so they stay the night. Balaam consults God, who gives him two clear instructions: 'Do not go with them', and, 'You must not put a curse on those people, because they are blessed' (verse 12). The next morning Balaam gives an answer to the embassy from Moab, but he only gives half of God's answer. He says, 'God has told me not to come' (verse 13). He doesn't tell them that God has told him not to curse them.

So the men go back to Balak and report the answer (verse 14). Balak doesn't know Balaam has been told not to curse them, and assumes it's just a question of a higher fee. So he sends a higher offer. Balaam gives a remarkable reply: 'Even if Balak gave me all the silver and gold in his palace, I could not do anything great or small to go beyond the command of the LORD my God' (verse 18). Is this pagan seer genuinely talking like this? Or is this a safety clause in the contract that he hopes he can waive later on?

In the night, God tells Balaam to go to Balak, 'but do only what I tell you' (verse 20).

Balaam is a pagan seer, and yet God uses him. God does not confine himself to using the godly and upright to fulfil his plans and purposes. He used Pharaoh to release the Israelites from Egypt (Exodus 12:31), the Babylonians to punish the Israelites (Habakkuk 1:5–6) and Cyrus the pagan king of Persia to free the Jews from Babylonian captivity (Isaiah 44:28). Even today, although unbelievers do not recognize it, God is achieving his purpose through them. Today we can trust in God's sovereignty, knowing that his will is being accomplished.

Day 27

Read Numbers 22:21–40
Key verse: Numbers 22:31

....

³¹ *Then the* LORD *opened Balaam's eyes, and he saw the angel of the* LORD *standing in the road with his sword drawn. So he bowed low and fell face down.*

What makes God angry?

In verse 22, Balaam is doing what God has told him to do and sets off for Moab, yet God is very angry. Why? The only explanation is that God perceives that Balaam's intention in going is wrong. Balaam makes his living by manipulating gods and spirits to do whatever purpose he gets paid for. So he's probably expecting that, when the time comes, he'll be able to do the same again and collect the biggest fee from the richest customer he has ever had: the king of Moab.

God sends his angel to confront Balaam, and the comedy with the donkey begins. Three times in the story the angel of God, with a drawn sword, stands in front of Balaam and the donkey. Balaam doesn't see the angel, but the donkey does, and three times the donkey tries to avoid taking action. In verses 28–30, God even opens the mouth of the donkey.

The narrator piles irony upon irony in this part of the story. Think of the number of contrasts happening here. The man on the donkey is called a seer, but he can't see what's in front of his eyes; the donkey sees what the seer can't. Balaam gets paid to be eloquent: this dumb animal gets beaten until he's the one who talks first. The donkey turns aside from the way his master wants him to go, as Balaam is intent on doing. Balaam gets angry with the donkey; God is angry with Balaam. Balaam says he would kill the donkey if only he had a sword in his hand instead of a stick; the angel, who does have a sword in his hand, says that it is only the donkey that saves Balaam's life. Balaam is trying to get the donkey to do what Balak is trying to get Balaam to do – what he wants. Balaam tries beating; Balak tries bribing. The results are equally ineffective. Balak, the king of Moab, is blind to the reality of the God that he's dealing with: so is Balaam until God opens his eyes. The donkey sees the angel of God and then God opens its mouth. Eventually Balaam, God's other ass in the story, is led to see the revelation of God and compelled to speak God's words.

Are your eyes open to what God is doing? Like Balaam the seer and the Pharisees in the New Testament, sometimes it is the very people who claim to have spiritual sight who are the most blind. We need God to open our eyes, not only for the first time at conversion, but daily so that we are alive to who he is, to what he says in his Word and to what he's doing in the world. Ask God to open your eyes and then, like Balaam, fall on your face in worship and do whatever he tells you to do.

Day 28

Read Numbers 23:1–12

Key verse: Numbers 23:8

....

> [8]*How can I curse*
>   *those whom God has not cursed?*
> *How can I denounce*
>   *those whom the* Lord *has not denounced?*

If we go out to eat at a high-class restaurant or buy an expensive gift, we expect to get our money's worth. Balak is definitely not getting what he paid for, because Balaam is unable to curse the Israelites. Why? Because these are the people whom God promised in his blessing with Abraham:

> I will bless those who bless you,
>   and whoever curses you I will curse.
> (Genesis 12:3)

Old Testament Israel was protected by this promise.

There is a further hint at this in Numbers 23:10, as Balaam says, 'Who can count the dust of Jacob or number even a fourth of Israel?' This reference to the dust of the people is clearly an echo of Genesis 13:16. God promised Abraham that his descendants would be as numerous as the sand on the shore, the dust on the earth and the stars in the sky. Here are a people who stand under the protection of God because of what God has promised to Abraham.

Israel in the Old Testament is unique. In verse 9, Balaam says, 'From the rocky peaks I see them, from the heights I view them. I see a people who live apart and do not consider themselves one of the nations.' This doesn't mean that the Israelites are hermits or that there's exclusiveness here. God is saying that he has done things to and for Israel that he has done for no other nation. This is affirmed in Deuteronomy and elsewhere.

Why are these people unique? Why is God doing this? We return to Abraham again; it is for the sake of the nations, and ultimately for the blessing of the nations. This is God's mission, which is why he makes these promises and provides this protection. Balaam is so impressed with this first oracle that he wishes he could share it: 'Let me die the death of the righteous, and may my final end be like theirs!' (verse 10). Tragically, he does not (Numbers 31:8).

As believers, we sin and fail God spectacularly (see Numbers 25 for Israel's failure). But, just like the Israelites, our sin does not exclude us from God's family; we're still his people, still in a covenant relationship with him. Our sin does not cancel out God's great blessings and promises. Even as a church, though we are a community of failed sinners, we are still a community of God's people who trust in his protection, vision and promise. Today, praise God that we live under his overarching protection, promises and blessings. Though we often waver in our commitment and obedience to him, he never wavers in his commitment to us. While we are often faithless, he is always faithful. He is the great Promise-keeper. We can trust who he is and everything he says.

Day 29

Read Numbers 23:13–26
Key verses: Numbers 23:21–22

. . . .

²¹ *No misfortune is seen in Jacob,*
  no misery observed in Israel.
*The L*ORD *their God is with them;*
  the shout of the King is among them.
²² *God brought them out of Egypt;*
  they have the strength of a wild ox.

Sometimes we lose sight of the awesome holiness and 'otherness' of God, and we treat him as if he were our puppet: someone we can control and manipulate. We twist his words and take them out of context until he says what we want him to say. Before the second oracle, Balak tries to manipulate this God, whoever he is, into a change of mind. He finds out, as we all do, that this is not possible: 'God is not human, that he should lie, not a human being, that he should change his mind' (verse 19). In verses 18–24, Balaam utters his oracle. Again there are no curses, only blessing: 'I have received a command to bless; he has blessed, and I cannot change it' (verse 20).

Verse 21 is a little puzzling in its first half: 'No misfortune is seen in Jacob, no misery observed in Israel.' Perhaps it means that, in spite of all the problems, Israel will survive. Or perhaps the NIV is right in the footnote translation that says, '[God] has not looked on Jacob's offences or on the wrongs found.' The sins are there, but God will ultimately cleanse and forgive them.

The real point of this second oracle comes in the second half of verse 21 and verse 22: God has brought these people up out of Egypt and now he's among them as the victorious king. Balaam says, 'There is no divination against Jacob, no evil omens against Israel. It

will now be said of Jacob and of Israel, "See what God has done!"'
(verse 23). The salvation, the redemption and all that God has done
for these people is God's work, and Balaam says, 'I can't stand
against them; it's the work of God.' God's people are secure: God is
their King (verse 21), their Redeemer (verse 22) and their Protector
(verse 23).

God is in the rescue business. The salvation and redemption of
the Israelites in the exodus was all God's work. And our salvation
and redemption, won by Christ on the cross, is all God's work too;
we can't take any credit (Colossians 1:13–14). Now God lives not
just *among* us as our victorious King, as he did with the Israelites,
but *in* us. Paul explains the great privilege we have:

> Christ in you, the hope of glory.
> (Colossians 1:27)

Today, thank God for his presence in your life – submit to him as
King, worship him for the price he paid to be your Redeemer, rest
secure knowing that he is your Protector. Pray that the Holy Spirit
would help you to say 'no' to sin and 'yes' to righteousness, so
that Christ would feel more and more at home in your heart.

Day 30

Read Numbers 23:27 – 24:14

Key verses: Numbers 24:5–7

．．．

> [5] *How beautiful are your tents, Jacob,*
>   *your dwelling-places, Israel!*
> [6] *Like valleys they spread out,*
>   *like gardens beside a river,*
> *like aloes planted by the LORD,*
>   *like cedars beside the waters.*
> [7] *Water will flow from their buckets;*
>   *their seed will have abundant water.*

God is not limited in those through whom he can speak. He has been speaking through Balaam all along, but the narrator of Numbers makes very clear that, in this third oracle, Balaam is speaking by the Spirit of the living God (verse 2). The last time we saw the Spirit of God was in chapter 11, when the Spirit was on Moses and the seventy elders. Here, the Spirit comes on a pagan seer.

At this point, Balaam appears to realize what he's up against:

> When Balaam saw that it pleased the LORD to bless Israel, he did not resort to divination as at other times, but turned his face towards the wilderness. When Balaam looked out and saw Israel encamped tribe by tribe, the Spirit of God came on him and he spoke his message. (Numbers 24:1–3)

The first oracle is about the past: the promise of God to Abraham. The second oracle is closer to the present because it refers to the exodus and the Sinai experience, and how God is in the midst of these people. This third oracle (and the fourth) looks much more into the future, and to the blessing and the peace that is going to come to this people. God's people will be secure because of his abundant provision for them. Verses 5–7 are a beautiful picture of that provision.

The word for 'beautiful' is the same word that we heard in Numbers 10:29 when Moses said to Hobab, 'the LORD has promised *good* things to Israel' (italics added). Even Balaam can see this good as he looks to the people. This is a picture of peace, prosperity and abundance, and at one level it's poetic: it points towards an ideal picture of Canaan to which Israel will go, and centuries later will lose because of its sin.

This picture of the land points us forward to the Lord Jesus Christ. In the New Testament, the land of Israel is no longer significant as territory; instead, it is taken up into what we now have in Christ. The writer to the Hebrews explains that we don't belong to an earthly city, but are citizens of God's country and part of his family (Hebrews 11:13–16). The Old Testament teaching on the land also points further into the future, to God dwelling with his people in the new heaven and the earth.

You are rich! You may look around at the material wealth of others and shake your head but, as believers in Christ, we enjoy abundant provision. 'In Christ' we know out-of-the-world peace that money can't buy; we experience our heavenly Father's mercy, grace and kindness daily; and we look forward to a breathtaking inheritance, for ever with the Lord in the new heaven and the new earth. Today, prove the sufficiency of Christ; rely on him alone to satisfy your deepest needs.

Day 31

Read Numbers 24:14–25
Key verse: Numbers 24:17

∙∙∙

> ¹⁷ *I see him, but not now;*
>   *I behold him, but not near.*
> *A star will come out of Jacob;*
>   *a sceptre will rise out of Israel.*
> *He will crush the foreheads of Moab,*
>   *the skulls of all the people of Sheth.*

How do you respond when your plans are frustrated? Balak is extremely angry and reprimands Balaam: 'I summoned you to curse my enemies, but you have blessed them these three times. Now leave at once and go home! I said I would reward you handsomely, but the LORD has kept you from being rewarded' (Numbers 24:10–11).

Balaam replies, 'I'm sorry. I said I wasn't going to be able to bring anything but blessings. Now I'm going to warn you about what you and the Moabites can expect in the future.'

The fourth oracle runs from verses 15 to 25 and is God's messianic promise. The key text is verse 17. In Old Testament history, as these oracles were recorded and eventually passed on, this would have been seen as referring to King David, who did subdue Moab and the other kingdoms. A sceptre, a king, arose in Israel who did exactly what Balaam had said. But as we look at this verse and the great sweep of biblical history, it also points forward to David's greater Son, to the one who will come as the Messiah King, to Jesus, who will bring with him the reign of God, not just over Israel, but ultimately over all the nations of the world.

These four oracles have taken us from the distant past to the distant future, from Abraham to the Messiah. In this inspired poetry of a soothsayer, God, through his Spirit, spreads before us his whole counsel. First, we have God's promise to Abraham and his blessing on Israel for the sake of the whole world. Second, Balaam speaks about God's redemption of his people, the exodus, which prefigures the cross, as the New Testament teaches us. Having redeemed his people, God remains present among them. Third, Balaam speaks about God's provision for his people, in both this world and the world to come. Fourth, he mentions God's messianic reign, the one who would come in the form of David but ultimately in the servant messianic kingship of Christ. What a declaration of the ultimate security of God's people!

You may be serving God in a tough situation, or perhaps you are fearful for your church, where the Christians are vulnerable and young in the faith. God's words of promise and protection are for you. They do not mean you will not suffer persecution, danger or death, but they do mean that the Lord knows those who are his, and he will protect you for eternity. Paul's words leave us in no doubt that we have a sure foundation for our faith, hope and future:

> For I am convinced that neither death nor life, neither angels nor demons, neither the present nor the future, nor any powers, neither height nor depth, nor anything else in all creation, will be able to separate us from the love of God that is in Christ Jesus our Lord. (Romans 8:38–39)

For further study

If you would like to do further study on Numbers, the following books may be useful:

- Raymond Brown, *The Message of Numbers*, The Bible Speaks Today (IVP, 2002).

- Dennis Cole, *Numbers* (New American Commentary) (Broadman & Holman, 2000).

- Iain Duguid, *Numbers*, Preaching the Word (Crossway, 2006).

- Roy Gane, *Leviticus, Numbers*, NIV Application Commentary (Zondervan, 2004).

- Gordon Wenham, *Numbers* (Tyndale Old Testament Commentary) (IVP, 2008).

If God has fed you through your study of the book of Numbers, why not buy the individual Food for the Journey on Numbers and give it to a friend (available from ivpbooks.com)?

Introduction
Hebrews

Charles Price

Fix your eyes on Jesus

Sometimes we don't see what is right in front of our eyes.

Somehow we miss the obvious, fundamental truths staring us in the face.

Many of the Jewish people in the first century certainly did.

When God called Abraham, he promised to make him into a great nation and bless the whole world through his 'seed', his descendant: Christ. Abraham's descendants, the Hebrew people, were God's chosen people. But this promise – not just to set them apart as a distinct people but to bless the world through them – was fulfilled in the coming of the Messiah. The whole of Old Testament history, from Abraham on, orientates around the fact that one day the Messiah would step into history. But when the Messiah actually came, no-one recognized him. 'He came to that which was his own, but his own did not receive him' (John 1:11).

This letter to the Hebrews, by an unknown author, was written to address some of the fundamental misunderstandings the Jewish people had about Jesus. The author was writing to correct their ignorance of who Christ was and to explain how he completes and fulfils Israel's history, law, ceremonial rituals and priesthood.

We too can have a misconstrued understanding of Jesus and his work. So the writer to the Hebrews helps us focus our attention on the supremacy of Christ in divine revelation and the sufficiency of Christ in Christian experience. Jesus is not just a contributor to divine revelation. He *is* the divine revelation; he is the ultimate and final expression of truth. Neither does he play a passive role in our Christian lives. He is not just an onlooker or a spectator; he is the central participant.

We must not relegate Jesus to being the patron of our systematic theology, whereby we do things in his name but have become detached from him. We can't view him merely as a teacher or an example to follow. As we explore sections of the book of Hebrews, we will find that Jesus' role is so much fuller and so much more active.

Will you 'fix your thoughts' and '[fix] your eyes on Jesus' (Hebrews 3:1; 12:2) and, along with the first readers, discover how glorious Christ really is?

Day 32

Read Hebrews 1:1–14
Key verses: Hebrews 1:1–2

....

¹In the past God spoke to our ancestors through the prophets at many times and in various ways, ²but in these last days he has spoken to us by his Son, whom he appointed heir of all things, and through whom also he made the universe.

God speaks.

The writer to the Hebrews takes this fact for granted. But it is a breath-taking truth. Contrary to all the other gods people have worshipped down through the ages, we have a God who speaks to us.

God has always spoken. The very first introduction we have to God in Genesis 1 is of a God who speaks. Ten times in Genesis 1 the Hebrew can be translated 'and God said': 'And God said, "Let there be light"' (verse 3); 'And God said, "Let there be a vault between the waters"' (verse 6). If God speaks, it follows that he has something to say that lies outside the realm of human knowledge.

Psalm 19 tells us about the natural revelation of God. Verses 1–4 say:

The heavens declare the glory of God;
   the skies proclaim the work of his hands.
Day after day they pour forth speech;
   night after night they reveal knowledge.
They have no speech, they use no words;
   no sound is heard from them.
Yet their voice goes out into all the earth,
   their words to the ends of the world.

The psalmist tells us that God speaks every night when the stars come out. Look across the vastness of the universe and see God speaking about his greatness and power. Every time a money spider runs across your desk, God is telling you about his attention to detail and his interest in the smallest things.

Over the next few days we will look at other, more specific ways God speaks to us. But, today, pause and appreciate God's general revelation.

Creation is God speaking to you.

Look around you. Whether you live in the inner city, the suburbs or the country, take time to appreciate God's creation. In the vastness of the sea, the snow-capped mountains, the star-filled sky, the intricacies of a spider's web, the colours of a flower petal and moss growing over stones, God speaks. What is he saying? How do these truths help you in the circumstances of your life today?

Use the following verses to praise God for how he reveals himself through creation:

Who shut up the sea behind doors
when it burst forth from the womb . . .
when I said, 'This far you may come and no farther;
here is where your proud waves halt'?
Have you ever given orders to the morning,
or shown the dawn its place?
(Job 38:8, 11–12)

For in [Christ] all things were created: things in heaven and on earth, visible and invisible, whether thrones or powers or rulers or authorities; all things have been created through him and for him. He is before all things, and in him all things hold together.
(Colossians 1:16–17)

Day 33

Read Hebrews 1:1–14; 3:1–6
Key verses: Hebrews 1:1–2, 4, 14; 3:2, 5

....

¹*In the past God spoke to our ancestors through the prophets at many times and in various ways,* ²*but in these last days he has spoken to us by his Son . . .* ⁴*So he became as much superior to the angels as the name he has inherited is superior to theirs . . .*

¹⁴*Are not all angels ministering spirits sent to serve those who will inherit salvation? . . .*

³:²*[Jesus] was faithful to the one who appointed him, just as . . .* ⁵*'Moses was faithful as a servant in all God's house,' bearing witness to what would be spoken by God in the future.*

In what other ways does God speak?

The writer to the Hebrews explains the four key means by which God has spoken in the past.

- **Prophets**. The role of a prophet was to listen to God and to speak his words (Jeremiah 23:22). Prophets communicated God's message through preaching, often prefacing their message with, 'Thus says the Lord'. They used poetry and song. Isaiah 5, for example, is the song of a vineyard. Prophets spoke through drama (Ezekiel once had to eat a scroll!) and personal experience. Hosea was told to marry a prostitute called Gomer. Her unfaithfulness mirrored Israel's unfaithfulness to God. Hosea's broken heart was a pale reflection of God's hurt.

- **Priests**. The priesthood is implied in Hebrews 1:3 and is developed more fully in chapters 5 – 10. The role of the priest was to offer sacrifices on behalf of the people. This ritual purification ceremony performed by the priests spoke of God's holiness, our sinfulness and the extreme lengths required to satisfy the just wrath of God against sin.

- *Angels*. The word 'angel' is often translated 'messenger'. Angels are waiting for God to give them instructions to carry messages. Seventeen times in the Old Testament and on seven occasions in the New Testament angels visited people, and each time the message they brought was binding (2:2–3).

- *Moses*. Exodus 33:11 says, 'The LORD would speak to Moses face to face, as one speaks to a friend.' Moses is given special mention here because of his unique place in the revelation God gave to the Hebrew people. God revealed his law to Moses, and it became the plumb line, the chief legal authority, in the history of Israel.

God speaks. Are you listening?

We wish we could hear God's audible voice. The problem may not be about God speaking, but our listening. God spoke in the past and still speaks today: 'So, as the Holy Spirit says: "*Today*, if you hear his voice . . ."' (Hebrews 3:7, italics added). The Bible is God's Word to us (2 Timothy 3:16; 2 Peter 1:21). Pray that you would be attentive to God's voice; be expectant that he has something to say to you. As you read Scripture, ask the Holy Spirit to reveal God to you and to help you obey all that he tells you to do. Keep this daily time with God a high priority.

Bible Matters by Tim Chester (IVP, 2017) is a helpful book on this subject if you would like to read further.

Day 34

Read Hebrews 1:1–14; 2:5–9; 3:1–6
Key verses: Hebrews 1:1–2

....

¹*In the past God spoke to our ancestors through the prophets at many times and in various ways, ²but in these last days he has spoken to us by his Son, whom he appointed heir of all things, and through whom also he made the universe.*

God saved the best till last.

Look at verses 1–2 again. Jesus is God's final Word, because in him is the fullness of God's revelation.

He was superior to the priests. They had to offer sacrifices continually for their own sin and the sins of the people (Hebrews 7:27). But Jesus is seated in heaven now because no more sacrifices are needed (Hebrews 1:3). His death was a one-off event, sufficient to pay the penalty for sin in full.

Hebrews 1:5–8 explains why Jesus is also superior to the angels. God never spoke to angels the way he spoke to his Son. When he became a man, Jesus was made lower than the angels, but now he is back in his rightful place, 'crowned with glory and honour' (2:9).

Jesus is superior to the prophets, priests, angels and Moses, not because he was a better preacher, had a better message or was more trustworthy. Their message was true and they were all bearing witness to the truth. But Jesus is supreme because he is himself the truth (John 14:6). He himself is the message and therefore has unmatched supremacy in God's revelation.

This letter to the Hebrews was written to a group of people so wrapped up in all the true things God had revealed through his agents in the past that they had missed the fulfilment to which it all pointed: Christ.

Don't make the same mistake. Don't study the Bible to acquire knowledge or rules for life (John 5:39–40). Look for Christ in the Scriptures. Meet him there.

Jesus is the truth, and his teaching was shamelessly centred on himself. Meditate on the following words of Jesus. Let them encourage and equip you for the day ahead.

I am the bread of life. Whoever comes to me will never go hungry, and whoever believes in me will never be thirsty.
(John 6:35)

I am the light of the world. Whoever follows me will never walk in darkness, but will have the light of life.
(John 8:12)

I am the gate; whoever enters through me will be saved . . . I have come that they may have life, and have it to the full.
(John 10:9–10)

I am the good shepherd. The good shepherd lays down his life for the sheep.
(John 10:11)

I am the resurrection and the life. The one who believes in me will live, even though they die.
(John 11:25)

I am the way and the truth and the life. No one comes to the Father except through me.
(John 14:6)

I am the vine; you are the branches. If you remain in me and I in you, you will bear much fruit; apart from me you can do nothing.
(John 15:5)

Day 35

Read Hebrews 1:1–3; 2:1–18
Key verse: Hebrews 1:3

· ·

³*The Son is the radiance of God's glory and the exact representation of his being, sustaining all things by his powerful word.*

'What is truth?' asked Pilate, the Roman governor (John 18:38).

That is a universal question that most people ask at some point. Is there such a thing as truth?

Today it is unpopular to talk about absolute truth. Truth is whatever works for you. Your opinions and assertions are just as valid as mine. But Jesus went beyond that to claiming to *be* the truth. He claimed to be the truth about:

- *God.* If you want to know what God is like, look at Jesus. Everything Jesus is, God is. Paul says in 2 Timothy 1:12, 'I know *whom* I have believed' (italics added). He does not say, 'I know *what* I have believed.' Knowing what you believe is important, but Christianity is about knowing someone, not something! We can learn facts about God, such as that he is omniscient (all-knowing), omnipotent (all-powerful), omnipresent (in all places), eternal and immutable (unchanging), but these truths won't establish a relationship and provoke us to love him. The more we know, love and trust Jesus, the more we will know, love and trust God. In fact, it is only when we know Christ that we know God.

- *Humanity.* Hebrews 1:3 is speaking not just about Jesus' deity but also his humanity. Human beings were created in God's image, to portray the truth about him (Genesis 1:27). That means that if you were to look at Adam, you would see the visible, physical portrayal of the invisible, spiritual God. Adam would be kind because God was kind. The way Adam treated Eve, the way they looked after the animals and tended the garden, showed what God was like. But together they sinned, and God's image was tarnished. Their life and behaviour no longer showed what God was like. Jesus came as the 'second man', the 'last Adam' (1 Corinthians 15:45). He is the radiance of God's glory, the truth about God that humanity was intended to express. We were created, and are now redeemed, to portray a physical and visible expression of the moral character of God, of which Jesus was the prototype.

Schools, the government, magazines and the media inform our thinking about what it means to be human. They shape our moral character by subtly, in a myriad of different ways, influencing our values, priorities and attitudes.

Select and read an account from one of the Gospels. What do you learn in the character of Jesus about the character of God? How is this to be your character too?

Today, Jesus is our life, and his character is to be expressed in every task, conversation and encounter. Ask the Holy Spirit to live the character of Christ in you. As King David prayed:

> Show me your ways, LORD,
>   teach me your paths.
> Guide me in your truth and teach me,
>   for you are God my Saviour,
>   and my hope is in you all day long.
> (Psalm 25:4–5)

Day 36

Read Hebrews 2:1–18
Key verses: Hebrews 2:10–11

∙∙

¹⁰In bringing many sons and daughters to glory, it was fitting that God, for whom and through whom everything exists, should make the pioneer of their salvation perfect through what he suffered. ¹¹Both the one who makes people holy and those who are made holy are of the same family. So Jesus is not ashamed to call them brothers and sisters.

We talk of 'going to glory' when we die, meaning we are going to heaven. But that's not how the Bible uses the term 'glory'. When the Bible speaks of glory, it refers to the character of God.

John says of Jesus, 'The Word became flesh and made his dwelling among us. We have seen his glory, the glory of the one and only Son, who came from the Father, full of grace and truth' (John 1:14). In Jesus we see what God is like: we see the character of God; we see the glory of God.

Sin is the extent to which we 'fall short of the glory of God' (Romans 3:23). Sin is not so much a measurement of how bad we are, but of how good we are not! We have come short. We don't show what God is like any more. We've become selfish and live for our own agendas. Now, in Jesus, we see the glory of God fully expressed – but more than that, we see one whose goal it is to bring 'many sons and daughters to glory'. Restoring what was lost in the fall, restoring God's glory to human experience, was the object of Jesus' work and ministry.

That's why Colossians 1:27 says, 'Christ in you, the hope of glory.' Jesus brings us back to glory, the glory we have sinned against and come short of. The Scriptures are true, but it is Christ who is the truth; Christ who by his indwelling presence in your life makes this journey real. It was foreshadowed in the time of the prophets, but now in Christ we see how he equips us to be what God intended human beings to be.

You are God's image-bearer.

Yes, sin has tarnished that image, but even now Jesus is restoring us to glory in a continuing process. 'We all, who with unveiled faces contemplate the Lord's glory, are being transformed into his image with ever-increasing glory, which comes from the Lord, who is the Spirit' (2 Corinthians 3:18). One day, when Jesus returns, we will fully and finally be like him (Philippians 1:6).

Until then, join God in his work.

'Contemplate the Lord's glory' by:

• keeping your focus on Jesus (Hebrews 12:2);
• adopting his attitudes (Philippians 2:5);
• studying and meditating on his Word (John 17:17);
• allowing God's Word to renew your mind and thoughts (Romans 12:2).

Take an honest look at your tarnished image of God. In what specific ways does Christ need to be more evident within you? Pray that the Holy Spirit would continue his process of transformation so that you might represent God well to all the people you meet today.

Day 37

Read Hebrews 3:7–19

Key verses: Hebrews 3:7–11

∙∙

> *⁷ So, as the Holy Spirit says:*
> *'Today, if you hear his voice,*
> *⁸ do not harden your hearts*
> *as you did in the rebellion,*
> *during the time of testing in the wilderness,*
> *⁹ where your ancestors tested and tried me,*
> *though for forty years they saw what I did.*
> *¹⁰ That is why I was angry with that generation;*
> *I said, "Their hearts are always going astray,*
> *and they have not known my ways."*
> *¹¹ So I declared on oath in my anger,*
> *"They shall never enter my rest." '*

A picture speaks a thousand words.

Here we have a graphic description of the exodus to press home the first of five stark warnings that occur in this epistle. Jewish Christians would know the story well. It was the most glorious event in Israel's history, when God intervened and delivered them from years of slavery. But it was also one of the most disastrous events in their history. They spent forty years in a wilderness, going nowhere and doing nothing.

The writer retells this story because it is full of typology and pictures that point to Christ and our Christian life. Egypt is portrayed as slavery to sin, as we read in the book of Jude. The Passover lamb is a picture of Christ (John 1:29). The exodus itself depicts deliverance from sin. In fact, at the transfiguration, Jesus' death is called his exodus (Luke 9:31). Crossing the Red Sea is a picture of baptism, of death to the old life and resurrection to the new (1 Corinthians 10:2).

Canaan is portrayed in Hebrews 4 as resting in Christ and enjoying the fullness of his presence in our lives.

The problem was that the first generation of Israelites who left Egypt never got to Canaan. The journey that should have taken only eleven days (Deuteronomy 1:2) took them forty years! The writer's point is that they were saved from slavery in Egypt but did not enter into the fullness of God's purposes for them, and instead got stuck going round in circles because they weren't listening to God.

The same can happen to us. We stop listening to God and, although we are saved, we make little or no progress in our Christian lives. Saved but stuck!

Are you saved but stuck?

'The preaching isn't inspiring.' 'I'm too busy to read my Bible.' 'My spouse doesn't encourage me.' We can come up with a host of excuses for why we're spiritually stuck in a rut. But sometimes we've got to face up to the fact that we are distant from God because we choose to be. It is our responsibility. Instead of listening to, obeying and trusting God, we ignore him.

As the Holy Spirit speaks to you today, respond to God's love, mercy and grace with obedience.

Pray with the psalmist:

> GOD, teach me lessons for living
>   so I can stay the course.
> Give me insight so I can do what you tell me –
>   my whole life one long, obedient response . . .
> Give me a bent for your words of wisdom,
>   and not for piling up loot.
> Divert my eyes from toys and trinkets,
>   invigorate me on the pilgrim way . . .
> See how hungry I am for your counsel;
>   preserve my life through your righteous ways!
> (Psalm 119:33–40, MSG)

Day 38

Read Hebrews 3:7–19

Key verses: Hebrews 3:16–19

. . . .

16 Who were they who heard and rebelled? Were they not all those Moses led out of Egypt? 17 And with whom was he angry for forty years? Was it not with those who sinned, whose bodies perished in the wilderness? 18 And to whom did God swear that they would never enter his rest if not to those who disobeyed? 19 So we see that they were not able to enter, because of their unbelief.

When the Israelites crossed the Red Sea, God didn't wipe his brow and say, 'Phew, they're out! That's it – mission accomplished!'

Leaving Egypt was not the goal. God rescued the Israelites from Egypt so that they could enter into Canaan and, from there, bless the world. God had made his purpose clear when he called Moses at the burning bush: 'I have come down to rescue them from the hand of the Egyptians and to bring them up out of that land into a good and spacious land, a land flowing with milk and honey' (Exodus 3:8).

God's plan that he revealed to Moses wasn't anything new. He was keeping his promise to Abraham and re-establishing the original purpose for which he had set Israel apart. Many times in the wilderness he reminded the Israelites of this purpose: 'I am the LORD your God, who brought you out of Egypt to give you the land of Canaan and to be your God' (Leviticus 25:38; also Deuteronomy 6:23).

Why did God save you? To ease your guilty conscience? So you might be forgiven? So you could go to heaven instead of hell? These are wonderful aspects of the gospel. But in the New Testament, in the preaching of Jesus and in the preaching of the apostles (and we have nineteen messages or fragments of messages in the book of Acts: eight by Peter, nine by Paul, one by Stephen and one by Philip), going to heaven is never once given as the reason for becoming a Christian. That is a consequence, but it's never the reason.

So what is the reason?

The reason is that we might be reconciled to God and live in fellowship and union with him. Paul summed up God's desire for us: 'that you may be filled to the measure of all the fullness of God' (Ephesians 3:19). The goal of the Christian life is not to get us out of hell and into heaven, but to get God out of heaven and into us.

When you became a Christian, God did not wipe his brow and say, 'Phew, that's it! He/she is saved!' He had much grander plans, much larger ambitions, for you. Don't be satisfied with a rescue ticket to heaven. Live the life God intended for you now in the power he provides. Press on to Christian maturity (see what this looks like in Ephesians 4) and be filled with all the fullness of God.

Pray Paul's prayer for yourself:

I pray that out of his glorious riches he may strengthen you with power through his Spirit in your inner being, so that Christ may dwell in your hearts through faith. And I pray that you, being rooted and established in love, may have power, together with all the Lord's holy people, to grasp how wide and long and high and deep is the love of Christ, and to know this love that surpasses knowledge – that you may be filled to the measure of all the fullness of God.
(Ephesians 3:16–19)

Day 39

Read Hebrews 3:7 – 4:2

Key verses: Hebrews 4:1–2

∙∙

[1] Therefore, since the promise of entering his rest still stands, let us be careful that none of you be found to have fallen short of it. [2] For we also have had the good news proclaimed to us, just as they did; but the message they heard was of no value to them, because they did not share the faith of those who obeyed.

Fish and chips. Salt and vinegar. A toddler's grubby hands and newly painted walls. Some combinations work together, but others . . . well, they just don't. In these verses we are presented with one combination that works and one that doesn't.

Throughout chapter 3, God has stated why the Israelites didn't get into Canaan. Verses 7–8 say:

> Today, if you hear his voice,
>   do not harden your hearts
> as you did in the rebellion.

And again, in verse 10:

> That is why I was angry with that generation;
>   I said, 'Their hearts are always going astray,
>   and they have not known my ways.'

Their hearts were hard, unbelieving and wayward. Hard hearts combined with faithlessness is a fatal combination (4:2). So even though the Israelites heard the good news, it didn't do them any good because they refused to combine it with faith.

God offers us a better, a winning, combination: the truth, the good news of the gospel, combined with faith.

Perhaps the good news was preached or explained to you. You may have accepted the truth and become a Christian. Your sins have been forgiven and you've received the gift of eternal life. But that was just the start. You need to keep on believing and trusting. You need to combine truth with continuing faith.

Truth in itself doesn't do us any good unless it is combined with faith. The Authorized Version talks of it being 'mixed with faith' (Hebrews 4:2, KJV). If you detach truth from faith, it is of no value.

The combination we need is truth coupled with faith.

We will look at what faith is tomorrow. But today, give yourself a spiritual health check and examine your heart. You might not describe yourself as 'hard-hearted' towards God, but perhaps your devotion is compromised by being coupled with a particular sin. It could be:

• refusing to forgive someone who has hurt you;
• jealousy towards someone in church;
• spending habits that are out of control;
• a pornography habit you can't break;
• sexual activity outside marriage.

What once bothered us doesn't bother us anymore. What once activated our conscience doesn't seem to anymore. What we knew was outside of God's boundaries, and therefore functionally outside of ours, lives inside our boundaries, and it doesn't matter to us anymore. It is a scary place to be. The hard heart is a stony heart. It is not malleable anymore. It's hard and resistant to change, no longer tender and responsive to the squeeze of the hands of the Spirit. There is evil in our hearts and in the acts of our hands, and we're okay with it. Could there be a more dangerous place for a believer to be?

(Paul David Tripp, *Dangerous Calling*, IVP, 2012, p. 72)

Day 40

Read Hebrews 3:12 – 4:2
Key verses: Hebrews 4:1–2

....

¹Therefore, since the promise of entering his rest still stands, let us be careful that none of you be found to have fallen short of it. ²For we also have had the good news proclaimed to us, just as they did; but the message they heard was of no value to them, because they did not share the faith of those who obeyed.

What is faith?

Is it a mystical force you conjure up if you close your eyes and really believe something strongly enough to make it happen?

Is it a leap in the dark when you've run out of facts?

No. Faith is not believing that black is white. Nor is it a substitute for facts. Indeed, faith needs facts; it needs an object. And it is the object in which you place your faith that determines the validity of it. You could have a lot of faith in thin ice, but you'd still sink!

When you sit on a chair, you exercise faith. What does that mean? It means you sit down, trusting the chair to take the strain. When you have faith in an aircraft it means you get on board, trusting the plane to fly through the air. So what is faith in God? It is acting in obedience and trusting God to work.

On their release from Egypt, the Hebrews had ample evidence of God's utter sufficiency in his work on their behalf. But as soon as they got to Kadesh Barnea, they forgot about daily dependence on him and looked only to themselves.

Twelve men were sent to explore the land God had promised them (Numbers 13:1–2). They saw the bountiful produce, but were over-awed by the powerful inhabitants. Ten of the spies, conscious of their own inadequacy and lack of experience in warfare, concluded, 'We can't attack those people; they are stronger than we are' (Numbers 13:31). Only Joshua and Caleb spoke up, reminding the Israelites that God was with them, working on their behalf (Numbers 14:6–9).

We too have seen God working on our behalf. We've experienced his forgiveness and his Holy Spirit within us. But, having been saved by faith, we try to live by human effort, detached from dependence on God.

One of the features of the Christian life is that our lives become explicable only in terms of God working in us and through us. Would your marriage be different if you weren't a Christian? Would your family life be different if you weren't living in the power of the risen Christ? Would your church be different if God were to withdraw?

Have you become detached from dependence on God? Have you become so aware of how large the obstacles are, or how great your inadequacy is, that you have stopped letting God be God? Think through all the ways that God has worked on your behalf in the past. Write these blessings down and thank God for them.

Remember, you are not putting your faith in something flimsy. You are putting your faith in the creator and sustainer of the universe, who wants to work in your situation. Will you have faith today?

Day 41

Read Hebrews 4:1–11

Key verses: Hebrews 4:9–11

••

> ⁹*There remains, then, a Sabbath-rest for the people of God;* ¹⁰*for anyone who enters God's rest also rests from their works, just as God did from his.* ¹¹*Let us, therefore, make every effort to enter that rest, so that no one will perish by following their example of disobedience.*

Is it helpful to bring up the past and dwell on previous mistakes?

Sometimes.

The writer is not retelling the exodus story to discourage his readers by saying, 'Look at what the Israelites did. You are in danger of doing the same thing.' Having given them the bad news of their unbelief and failure to live by faith in God, he wants to remind them that 'the promise of entering his rest still stands' (verse 1).

This word 'rest' is repeated often in these verses. What do we mean by 'rest'? More importantly, what does the Bible mean by 'rest'? The writer defines it in verses 9–10 as 'a Sabbath-rest'. In other words, he is saying that there is a human experience that corresponds with the divine experience of God's rest.

Why did God rest at the end of creation? God's energy is inexhaustible, so he didn't rest because he was tired. He rested because he had finished. Big difference. The Sabbath-rest is a picture of God's sufficiency. The Christian calendar caught up with this principle only after the resurrection of Jesus and the gift of the Holy Spirit, and now we rest on the first day of the week, symbolically portraying the truth that we rest in the sufficiency of his risen life.

Jesus still offers rest to those who come to him in dependence, relying on his sufficiency (Matthew 11:28–30).

Affirm with the psalmist:

> Yes, my soul, find rest in God;
>   my hope comes from him.
> Truly he is my rock and my salvation;
>   he is my fortress, I shall not be shaken.
> My salvation and my honour depend on God;
>   he is my mighty rock, my refuge.
> Trust in him at all times, you people;
>   pour out your hearts to him,
>   for God is our refuge.
> (Psalm 62:5–8)

Resting means daily depending on God. In the psalmist's words, it is trusting him 'at all times' (verse 8). This is a big statement – one we continually need to be intentional about putting into practice. Is there a relationship, situation or concern you need to entrust to God today? Will you demonstrate your dependence on God's sufficiency by trusting him with it?

Day 42

Read Hebrews 4:1–11

Key verse: Hebrews 4:11

....

¹¹*Let us, therefore, make every effort to enter that rest, so that no one will perish by following their example of disobedience.*

Did you notice what seems like a contradiction in chapter 4?

The writer tells us to depend on God, but then says, 'Let us, therefore, make every effort to enter that rest.' Having to make an effort to enter into a place of rest certainly sounds like a contradiction!

But think for a moment.

If I were to ask you, 'What makes your car work?' you would say, 'The engine.' The engine is the power that takes the car down the road. Without the engine, the car is good for nothing. Jesus Christ, by his indwelling Holy Spirit, is the power that enables us to live the Christian life. As he said, 'apart from me you can do nothing' (John 15:5).

But right now your car has an engine under the bonnet that is doing nothing. Why? Because it needs a driver to put it in gear and steer it down the road. What makes the car go? Is it the engine? Is it the driver? It is both!

What makes the Christian life work? Is it Christ? Is it me? It is both: we're workers together with God. Of course, Christ, like the engine, is the indispensable part: he works in us to will and to act according to his good purpose (Philippians 2:13). He works in us to motivate, direct and channel us. But you and I have to learn to become the driver, to exercise those disciplines that keep us in touch with God. The driver's job is to enable the power of the engine to make contact with the wheels so that the car is empowered to go down the road. Our responsibility is to enable God's indwelling power to make contact with our life as we bring him into every situation and circumstance.

Obedience to God and dependence on him cannot be separated. Obedience without dependence will lead to legalism. Dependence without obedience will lead to unhealthy mysticism. But obedience coupled with dependence on him for the resources we need will lead to dynamism.

'There remains,' says the writer, 'a Sabbath-rest for the people of God.' God is inviting you to live in the richness of everything that's intended for you. God calls this 'entering into rest'. There will be nothing you face in your life that is bigger than the resources you have in the Lord Jesus Christ.

But you will never prove it until you trust and obey.

Would you like to experience more of the power of God? The key is obedience and trust together. Throughout the history of Israel every act of God was precipitated by an act of obedience. Think about Joshua leading the people across the River Jordan. It was only as the priests placed their feet in the water, in obedient response to, and dependence on, God, that God parted the waves before them (Joshua 3). The principle still operates. What obedience does God require from you today? As the provocative title of John Ortberg's book states, 'If you want to walk on water, you've got to get out of the boat' (Zondervan, 2001).

Day 43

Read Hebrews 4:14 – 5:10
Key verses: Hebrews 5:1–4

....

¹Every high priest is selected from among the people and is appointed to represent the people in matters related to God, to offer gifts and sacrifices for sins. ²He is able to deal gently with those who are ignorant and are going astray, since he himself is subject to weakness. ³This is why he has to offer sacrifices for his own sins, as well as for the sins of the people. ⁴And no one takes this honour upon himself, but he receives it when called by God, just as Aaron was.

What image does the word 'priest' bring to mind? Flowing robes, confessional booths, salacious newspaper headlines?

'Priest' is not a popular word in the Protestant vocabulary, particularly in nonconformist circles. Indeed, the word never appears in the letters of Paul, Peter, James or Jude, nor in the writings of John. This is the only epistle in which the word 'priest' occurs, and it occurs twenty-eight times: in every chapter from 2 to 10, and then as the writer sums up at the end of chapter 13.

Hebrews 5:1 explains that a priest is an intermediary who stands between two parties and connects them with each other. The priest stood between God and humanity for the purpose of bringing them together and reconnecting them. And in the book of Hebrews the emphasis is on the priesthood of Christ. In fact, twenty-four of the twenty-eight references to priest have to do with the priesthood of Christ.

The Jews reading this letter would have been able to understand Jesus' priesthood because they were familiar with the Levitical priesthood – what the book of Hebrews calls the Aaronic priesthood. From the tribe of Levi, Moses' brother, Aaron, and his family line were chosen to be priests (Exodus 28:1). When Aaron died, his son, Eleazar, replaced him. And before the Israelites entered Canaan, the Lord set apart the whole tribe of Levi, of which Moses and Aaron were members, to serve as priests (Deuteronomy 10:6–9). The function of the priests was right at the very core of their worship. If the priests didn't turn up, worship shut down.

We, too, need a priest. We need someone to bridge the gap between us and a holy God, someone to represent us before God, someone to act as an intermediary.

Jesus is our great high priest. He connects us to God and pleads our case when we sin. He prayed for us in John 17 and is still interceding for us before God the Father.

> Therefore he is able to save completely those who come to God through him, because he always lives to intercede for them.
> (Hebrews 7:25)

> Who will bring any charge against those whom God has chosen? It is God who justifies. Who then is the one who condemns? No one. Christ Jesus who died – more than that, who was raised to life – is at the right hand of God and is also interceding for us.
> (Romans 8:33–34)

We confess our sins to Christ, our high priest, grateful that his death was sufficient to pay the price for our sins. His intercessory role as our priest connects us with the Father. Think of the sins you have already committed today – the secret sins and the persistent ones. Repent and take strength from knowing that Jesus is praying for you. He is bringing your name before the Father.

Day 44

Read Hebrews 7:1–28

Key verses: Hebrews 7:11, 16–17

• •

¹¹*If perfection could have been attained through the Levitical priesthood . . . why was there still need for another priest to come, one in the order of Melchizedek, not in the order of Aaron? . . . ¹⁶[Jesus] has become a priest not on the basis of a regulation as to his ancestry but on the basis of the power of an indestructible life. ¹⁷For it is declared:*

> *'You are a priest for ever,*
> *in the order of Melchizedek.'*

The writer to the Hebrews had a problem. The priests in the line of Aaron did not accurately or adequately foreshadow the priesthood of Christ.

Jesus was not a Levite and therefore was not qualified to serve as a priest (7:14). The Aaronic priests were subject to weakness (5:2) – they had to deal with their own sin before addressing the sins of the people (7:27); they could offer sacrifices for the forgiveness of sin, but not clear the conscience of the worshipper (9:9); and they had to repeat the sacrifice again and again – their work was never finished (10:11).

So the author rummages around in Old Testament history and finds an obscure man, Melchizedek, mentioned briefly in Genesis 14:18–20 and referred to in Psalm 110:4.

Melchizedek could represent Christ because of some key similarities:

• *He has no genealogy* (7:3). The Aaronic priesthood was based entirely on genealogy. You couldn't be a priest if you couldn't trace your ancestry back to Aaron (Ezra 2:62). But just as no mention is made of Melchizedek's genealogy, Jesus had no father and mother in his ultimate origin (John 1:1–2).

• *He lasts for ever* (7:3). 'Without beginning of days or end of life, resembling the Son of God, he remains a priest for ever.' Again, this is arguing from the silence of Scripture, which mentions nothing of Melchizedek's death.

• *He is king of righteousness, and being king of Salem means he is king of peace* (7:2). These themes of righteousness and kingship correspond to Christ, as the writer explains in 1:8:

> But about the Son he says,
>> 'Your throne, O God, will last for ever and ever;
>>> a sceptre of justice will be the sceptre of your kingdom.'

• *He elicits the same response* (7:4). When Abraham returned from a victorious battle, he gave Melchizedek 10% of everything he possessed. Whereas the Levitical priests collected a tenth from the people, Abraham had no obligation to pay Melchizedek: he gave it voluntarily. In the same way, our response to Jesus is voluntary. The Holy Spirit is involved in our coming to Christ, but we are not forced to come: the way is open to us to come voluntarily.

What a great high priest we have! He ministers in 'the power of an indestructible life', so is able to save completely and for all time. Worship him today.

> Before the throne of God above
> I have a strong, a perfect plea;
> A great High Priest, whose name is Love,
> Who ever lives and pleads for me.
> My name is graven on his hands,
> My name is written on his heart;
> I know that while in heaven he stands
> No tongue can bid me thence depart.
> (Charitie Lees Bancroft, 'Before the Throne of God Above', 1863)

Day 45

Read Hebrews 7:1–28

Key verses: Hebrews 7:26–28

• •

²⁶Such a high priest truly meets our need – one who is holy, blameless, pure, set apart from sinners, exalted above the heavens. ²⁷Unlike the other high priests, he does not need to offer sacrifices day after day, first for his own sins, and then for the sins of the people. He sacrificed for their sins once for all when he offered himself. ²⁸For the law appoints as high priests men in all their weakness; but the oath, which came after the law, appointed the Son, who has been made perfect for ever.

'It is finished.'

Jesus' cry from the cross signalled that no more blood need ever be shed for sin. The temple curtain, the barrier that separated the Most Holy Place from the people and which could be approached only by a priest with blood on the Day of Atonement, was torn, not as a human act from bottom to top, but as a divine act from top to bottom. From that moment, every priest in Israel was out of a job.

Jesus offered himself once and for all, and then he sat down (8:1).

The writer to the Hebrews states that this qualifies Jesus to be our priest and mediator. The grounds of our access to God and our accessibility to God are not based on our personal credentials, any more than they were based on the personal credentials of the Israelites. They could approach God only because of the credentials of the priest. And we have a priest who is totally adequate: who you are, what your history is, what your background is, what sins you are up to your neck in – all this is irrelevant to the sufficiency of Christ to serve as our priest. We can approach God through Christ our priest, because it's the priest who is acceptable to God; it's the priest who addresses God and reconciles us.

That's why it says in Hebrews 4:14–16:

> Since we have a great high priest who has ascended into heaven, Jesus the Son of God, let us hold firmly to the faith we profess. For we do not have a high priest who is unable to feel sympathy for our weaknesses, but we have one who has been tempted in every way, just as we are – yet he did not sin. Let us then approach God's throne of grace with confidence, so that we may receive mercy and find grace to help us in our time of need.

Jesus is your perfect high priest. So, today:

- hold firmly to the faith you profess (Hebrews 4:14);
- receive mercy and grace in your time of need (4:16);
- draw near to God (7:19);
- be assured of your salvation (7:25);
- serve God without guilt (9:14);
- look forward to your eternal inheritance (9:15);
- accept that you have been made holy (10:10).

Today, talk to your priest, the Lord Jesus Christ. Confess your sins and thank him for his strength and help as you bring your needs before him.

Day 46

Read Hebrews 8:1–13
Key verse: Hebrews 8:10

....

> ¹⁰ *This is the covenant I will establish with the people of Israel*
> *after that time, declares the Lord.*
> *I will put my laws in their minds*
> *and write them on their hearts.*
> *I will be their God,*
> *and they will be my people.*

What had gone wrong?

Hebrews 8:7–12 is a direct quotation from Jeremiah 31, containing a prophetic announcement and a definition of a new covenant God promised he would bring to the house of Israel. Clearly, there was something wrong with the first covenant or it wouldn't have needed to be replaced (verse 7).

The two covenants are concerned with the same law, so there was nothing wrong with the law itself. Indeed, the law is unchangeable because it is a revelation of the moral character of God, which is immutable, unchanging. For example, when the law says, 'You shall not commit adultery', it is because God is totally faithful and this is an expression of his character. That's why Jesus said, in the Sermon on the Mount, that 'until heaven and earth disappear, not the smallest letter, not the least stroke of a pen, will by any means disappear from the law until everything is accomplished' (Matthew 5:18). God doesn't change, doesn't wind down, doesn't grow up, and doesn't get better. So the law, which expresses his character, is as un-changeable as he is.

There was nothing wrong with the law itself; the failure was in the people's ability to keep it. Moses had come down the mountain with the law of God, and the people agreed to obey it. They repeated their declaration in the book of Deuteronomy, and they said it again in the book of Joshua and at various other intervals. But they couldn't keep their promise. Of course they couldn't!

The fundamental difference between the two covenants is that under the old covenant the onus was on the people. They had to keep the Ten Commandments. 'You shall have no other gods before me.' 'You shall not make for yourself an image.' 'You, you, you . . .' In contrast, under the new covenant, the onus is on God. God said, 'I will put my laws in their minds and write them on their hearts. I will be their God . . . I will forgive their wickedness.'

The first covenant was, 'You do it'; in the new covenant, God said, 'I will do it.'

Today, rest in the freedom and joy of knowing that your salvation and the security of your covenant relationship with God are not dependent on you. They are based solely on Christ's work on the cross and his resurrection life in you. So, if you are:

• aware of your failure and inability;
• frustrated with your own sense of inadequacy;
• discouraged by events within and around you;

. . . remember, it is Christ's relentless working in you that is the basis for your relationship with God and your fruitfulness. It is Christ's performance that counts, not yours.

Day 47

Read Hebrews 8:1–13; 10:8–18
Key verse: Hebrews 8:10

. . . .

¹⁰ *This is the covenant I will establish with the people of Israel*
    after that time, declares the Lord.
I will put my laws in their minds
    and write them on their hearts.
I will be their God,
    and they will be my people.

Have you ever house-trained a dog or a cat? You reward good behaviour and discipline bad behaviour. If you do it well, your pet may behave perfectly – but only as long as you are there! The animal's modified behaviour is on the basis of reward for the good and punishment for the bad; there is no moral consciousness involved.

All the law can ever do is house-train us. Written on tablets of stone, it was external. It could demand righteousness but never accomplish it. At best, it might house-train us by its offer of reward or punishment.

How do you know if you've been house-trained? Check how you live when nobody is looking. If you live one way when people are looking and another way when they're not, you haven't been sanctified – you've just been house-trained!

The new covenant changes all this. No longer is the law imposed from the outside; it is placed inside us by the indwelling power of the Holy Spirit. The same law, once written on stone, is now written on our hearts and minds. The new covenant doesn't revise the law; it simply relocates it.

And as well as having a new priest ministering for us, we have a new power operating in us: the indwelling presence of the Spirit of Jesus Christ.

The Holy Spirit implements this new covenant (Ezekiel 36:27; John 14:17). What were commands under the old covenant actually become promises under the new (Romans 8:3–4). So when the law says, 'You shall not steal', you don't. Why? Because you are more disciplined than you used to be? No. It's because the Spirit of God is in you; he gives you a hunger and a thirst for righteousness, and he works in you to will and to do his good pleasure. This righteousness doesn't work from the outside in, by our trying to keep the law and do better. It's a righteousness that is released from the inside out as the Spirit of God writes the law of God in our hearts. That's why righteousness in the New Testament is described as fruit (Philippians 1:11). Fruit is a consequence of life; and the fruit of righteousness flows out naturally because the Spirit of God is in us.

Thank God for every evidence of the Spirit's work in your life – every decision, action, thought and conversation that is God-directed and God-initiated. Thank the Holy Spirit that it is his business to write God's law in even larger letters on our hearts as an expression of his righteous character.

Daily rely on the Holy Spirit's resources.

- If you are facing sexual temptation, draw on the Spirit's help to do what the law commands: 'You shall not commit adultery' (Exodus 20:14).
- If you struggle with greed, draw on the Spirit's help to do what the law commands: 'You shall not covet' (Exodus 20:17).
- If you are struggling to get your priorities right, draw on the Spirit's help to do what the law commands: 'You shall have no other gods before me' (Exodus 20:3).

Day 48

Read Hebrews 8:10–12; 9:11 – 10:25

Key verses: Hebrews 8:10–11

. . . .

> ¹⁰*This is the covenant I will establish with the people of Israel*
> *after that time, declares the Lord.*
> *I will put my laws in their minds*
> *and write them on their hearts.*
> *I will be their God,*
> *and they will be my people.*
> ¹¹*No longer will they teach their neighbours,*
> *or say to one another, 'Know the Lord,'*
> *because they will all know me,*
> *from the least of them to the greatest.*

Teachers, business colleagues, church ministers, spouses, friends. We have a variety of people in our lives, but with whom do we have deep relationships? It is those individuals we *know*, not just *know about*.

God said the new covenant would produce a new relationship. People would no longer be taught about the Lord; instead, 'they will all know me' (Jeremiah 31:34). There would be a new intimacy. The law would be in their hearts.

In 2 Peter 1:3 it says, 'His divine power has given us everything we need for a godly life through our knowledge of him who called us by his own glory and goodness.'

And 2 Peter 3:18 says, 'Grow in the grace and knowledge of our Lord and Saviour Jesus Christ.'

That's why we spend time in our Bibles: not to get to know the Bible but to get to know Christ, who is revealed through the Scriptures. The living Word is revealed through the written Word.

The least of us to the greatest will know God. That's an interesting progression. Knowledge of God is not obtained. It's received; it's dependent on revelation. As Jesus said in Matthew 11:25–26, 'I praise you, Father, Lord of heaven and earth, because you have hidden these things from the wise and learned, and revealed them to little children. Yes, Father, for this is what you were pleased to do.' That's why we come in humility, as children, and say, 'Lord, reveal more of yourself.'

And out of this new relationship – knowing God, knowing *whom* we have believed – comes a new righteousness (2 Timothy 1:12). The more we know Christ, the more we become like him. It's a process: we're being transformed from one degree of glory to another, in his image.

Paul says, 'Of this gospel I was appointed a herald and an apostle and a teacher. That is why I am suffering as I am. Yet this is no cause for shame, because *I know whom I have believed*, and am convinced that he is able to guard what I have entrusted to him until that day' (2 Timothy 1:11–12, italics added).

Because Paul knows God, he can obey him, face suffering, share the gospel, trust him with his life and not be anxious about the impact of his ministry. Today, spend time in God's Word so you can know him better and become more like him. Look forward to the day you will know him fully: 'For now we see only a reflection as in a mirror; then we shall see face to face. Now I know in part; then I shall know fully, even as I am fully known' (1 Corinthians 13:12).

Day 49

Read Hebrews 8:10–12; 9:11–15; 10:1–25
Key verses: Hebrews 8:12; 9:13–14

....

¹²For I will forgive their wickedness
  and will remember their sins no more . . .
⁹:¹³The blood of goats and bulls and the ashes of a heifer sprinkled on those who are ceremonially unclean sanctify them so that they are outwardly clean. ¹⁴How much more, then, will the blood of Christ, who through the eternal Spirit offered himself unblemished to God, cleanse our consciences from acts that lead to death, so that we may serve the living God!

Remember the days when everyone had a cheque book?

The paper a cheque is written on is intrinsically worthless; it is valid only for as much cash as there is in the bank. However, if you've no cash in the bank, you can postdate a cheque to the end of the month when you will receive your salary. You write the postdated cheque and the debt is covered. But it's not removed.

The blood of bulls and goats was like a cheque: worthless in itself. It covered sin but did not remove it (Hebrews 10:11). But when Jesus, on the cross, cried, 'It is finished', he was saying, 'There's cash in the bank! The cheque is now valid!' And all the Old Testament believers cashed their cheques.

Now we're dealing with the real currency, not the postdated cheque. The real currency is not the blood of bulls and goats, but the precious blood of Christ. This currency doesn't just cover sin; it removes sin, to the extent that the Father says, 'I will remember their sins no more.' This doesn't mean that God is forgetful. It means he never recalls our sin; he never brings it up again. This promise has nothing to do with what we deserve, but everything to do with the quality of our priest.

Jesus is both the sacrifice and the priest. He didn't merely offer sacrifices; he *was* the sacrifice, and it's by his blood that we, with confidence, have access to God. The whole saving work of Christ is encompassed in this new covenant. Our sins are forgiven at the cross. Having been forgiven, we come to the empty tomb so that we might get to know the living Christ and the power of his resurrection. And from there we go to Pentecost, where God says,

'I will put my Spirit in you and move you to follow my decrees and be careful to keep my laws' (Ezekiel 36:27).

This is the new covenant. Are you living in the good of it?

If you've confessed your sin to God, don't keep dwelling on it and wallowing in guilt. Believe the Father's promise: 'I will remember your sins no more'. You are forgiven by the precious blood of Christ. Savour this truth and serve in the joy of it.

> When Satan tempts me to despair
> And tells me of the guilt within,
> Upward I look and see him there
> Who made an end of all my sin.
> Because the sinless Saviour died
> My sinful soul is counted free.
> For God the just is satisfied
> To look on him and pardon me.
> (Charitie Lees Bancroft, 'Before the Throne of God Above', 1863)

Day 50

Read Hebrews 10:32 – 11:40
Key verses: Hebrews 11:1–2, 6

....

¹Now faith is confidence in what we hope for and assurance about what we do not see. ²This is what the ancients were commended for . . .

⁶And without faith it is impossible to please God, because anyone who comes to him must believe that he exists and that he rewards those who earnestly seek him.

I will make you into a great nation . . .
and all peoples on earth
   will be blessed through you.
(Genesis 12:2–3)

This was God's promise to Abraham. From a human point of view, it was physically impossible. Abraham was seventy-five and his wife sixty-five. She was long past childbearing age but, even if she hadn't been, the Bible tells us she was barren. Nevertheless, Abraham trusted God's promise (Hebrews 11:11; Romans 4:3).

No doubt the couple expected the promised baby to arrive in nine months, but the promise of God rang in their ears for twenty-five years before Isaac arrived. God is never in a hurry. God said that the seed of Eve's womb would crush the head of the serpent (Genesis 3:15). When she gave birth, Eve said, 'I have brought forth a man', perhaps thinking that this was the promised seed to crush the head of the serpent (Genesis 4:1). They called him Cain, but he wasn't the promise at all: he became a murderer. Millennium after millennium went by before the cry of the baby was heard in Bethlehem. God takes his time (see also Isaiah 5:19).

Isaac was born and grew up. No doubt Abraham anticipated he would marry at the age of twenty, have a baby every year for the next twenty years and get this nation on the road! But Isaac didn't marry till he was forty. Abraham had to employ a servant to find him a wife and, of all the women he could have chosen, the woman he found was barren. It was twenty years before Rebekah eventually conceived and gave birth to twins Jacob and Esau.

Abraham recognized that God often works slowly. Jesus said in John 8:56, 'Your father Abraham rejoiced at the thought of seeing my day; he saw it and was glad.' Abraham acknowledged that God's purpose and plan was something bigger than his children or grandchildren and that he was to wait patiently for God to fulfil his promise.

When we walk by faith, we do not know what God is doing; we have to wait. And God takes his time. Like Abraham, we need to trust God.

Are you waiting for God to act? Waiting for him to bring your children to salvation, to vindicate you in a difficult work situation, to restore a broken relationship? Will you bring God pleasure by trusting him in these dark days (Hebrews 11:6)? Faith is being sure that God knows what he is doing. One day, God's purposes will be fulfilled. The writer urges us:

> You . . . joyfully accepted [your suffering] . . . because you knew that you yourselves had better and lasting possessions. So do not throw away your confidence; it will be richly rewarded.
>
> You need to persevere so that when you have done the will of God, you will receive what he has promised.
> (Hebrews 10:34–36)

Day 51

Read Hebrews 10:32 – 11:40

Key verses: Hebrews 11:24–29

²⁴ *By faith Moses, when he had grown up, refused to be known as the son of Pharaoh's daughter.* ²⁵ *He chose to be ill-treated along with the people of God rather than to enjoy the fleeting pleasures of sin.* ²⁶ *He regarded disgrace for the sake of Christ as of greater value than the treasures of Egypt, because he was looking ahead to his reward.* ²⁷ *By faith he left Egypt, not fearing the king's anger; he persevered because he saw him who is invisible.* ²⁸ *By faith he kept the Passover and the application of blood, so that the destroyer of the firstborn would not touch the firstborn of Israel.*

²⁹ *By faith the people passed through the Red Sea as on dry land; but when the Egyptians tried to do so, they were drowned.*

At last God was going to rescue his people!

In the encounter at the burning bush, God told the eighty-year-old Moses that he was going to save his people (Exodus 3:7–9). The proviso was, 'I'll do it through you. You have to step out in obedience and trust me.'

So Moses did. He faced Pharaoh and eventually, after God had sent the tenth plague, the Israelites were released and Moses led them out of Egypt. When they got to the Red Sea, the sea hemmed them in in front, the Egyptian army hemmed them in behind and they began to panic. They complained to Moses, who replied with the remarkable affirmation: 'Do not be afraid. Stand firm and you will see the deliverance the LORD will bring you today . . . The LORD will fight for you; you need only to be still' (Exodus 14:13–14).

This didn't mean they just stood on the banks and did nothing. God told Moses to keep the people moving and to hold out his staff over the sea all night. This must have been a strange sight, but Moses had learned that you must obey what God says and trust who God is. As God parted the waves, Moses demonstrated that faith sees beyond circumstances.

You may be wondering why God has allowed a particular set of circumstances to come into your life. You want to do God's will, you are trusting his purposes, you stepped out in faith, but things have gone wrong. You are not the first to have been there. But faith sees beyond circumstances. God is going to fulfil his purpose.

Take heart from Hebrews 11. These men and women of faith did not experience one success after another. From a human perspective, their lives were full of failure, conflict, difficulty and tragedy. And yet God was at work. Will you join this gallery of saints and, even when you can't see what God is doing, 'live by faith, not by sight' (2 Corinthians 5:7)? Although your circumstances may look bleak, keep trusting who God is and obeying all that he tells you to do.

Day 52

Read Hebrews 11:1–40
Key verses: Hebrews 11:31–34

....

> ³¹*By faith the prostitute Rahab, because she welcomed the spies, was not killed with those who were disobedient.*
>
> ³²*And what more shall I say? I do not have time to tell about Gideon, Barak, Samson and Jephthah . . . ³³who through faith . . . gained what was promised . . . ³⁴whose weakness was turned to strength; and who became powerful in battle and routed foreign armies.*

There are some surprising names in this Hebrews 11 list of people who lived by faith.

Rahab the prostitute is mentioned. Two spies sent to check out the land of Canaan hid in her house. She helped them escape and told them, 'I know that the LORD has given this land to you' (Joshua 2:9). She had heard about the Lord drying up the Red Sea and how the Israelites had destroyed Sihon and Og. She knew that their God was *the* God.

She spoke with certainty. She didn't know any theology. She didn't have a history of God's leading as the spies had. And yet this prostitute took God at his word.

Samson, too, messed up his life. He was one of the judges. He was born to be a Nazirite, which meant he was not supposed to drink wine, go near any dead body or cut his hair. But he broke all those vows. His big problem was his promiscuity; he fell easily in and out of love. He fell in love with Delilah and foolishly told her the secret of his strength. Eventually the Philistines captured him, gouged out his eyes and locked him up. In his cell, his hair, which had been cut off, grew again and God restored his strength. When he was brought into the temple he prayed, 'God, just one more time, give me strength.' He pushed against the pillars and brought the building down, killing himself and the others inside (Judges 16). The whole story of Samson is tragic but, despite his weakness and his failings, he trusted God and is listed in this catalogue of those who lived by faith.

In 2 Chronicles 16:9 it says, 'The eyes of the LORD run to and fro throughout the whole earth, to show Himself strong on behalf of those whose heart is loyal to Him' (NKJV). God is looking for those who will let him show himself strong on their behalf.

That's why Rahab and Samson make the list.

Your life may have fallen apart for all kinds of reasons. Your failings and flaws may be obvious for all to see. God is not looking for you to be the finished article. The Holy Spirit will work at producing fruit in you and making you more like Christ. But, in the meantime, you can trust God. Ask God to demonstrate his strength in and through your life. Today, pray, 'God, I take you at your word. I trust in you.'

Day 53

Read Hebrews 11:1–40

Key verses: Hebrews 11:35–40

....

35 *Women received back their dead, raised to life again. There were others who were tortured, refusing to be released so that they might gain an even better resurrection.* 36 *Some faced jeers and flogging, and even chains and imprisonment.* 37 *They were put to death by stoning; they were sawn in two; they were killed by the sword. They went about in sheepskins and goatskins, destitute, persecuted and ill-treated –* 38 *the world was not worthy of them. They wandered in deserts and mountains, living in caves and in holes in the ground.*

39 *These were all commended for their faith, yet none of them received what had been promised,* 40 *since God had planned something better for us so that only together with us would they be made perfect.*

Don't get the idea that if you have faith in God, you'll avoid all hardships in life; that you'll never get sick, never get down, never be depressed and never be hurt.

We might be forgiven for assuming from the earlier verses that faith in God means, ultimately, that we're never beaten, we're not overcome and we don't really get hurt – but that's not true. The writer to the Hebrews gives examples of people commended for their faith who died, were persecuted and suffered greatly.

Stephen is the first martyr recorded in the book of Acts. As he was being stoned to death, he looked up and saw Jesus, standing at the right hand of the Father (Acts 7:55–56). Normally Jesus is portrayed as sitting at the Father's right hand. Some have said he was standing to welcome the martyr home. Maybe. But although Stephen saw Jesus standing at the right hand of the Father, Jesus didn't intervene.

He saw Stephen's blood-soaked face and he didn't rescue him. God allowed the death of Stephen. Among other things, he was sowing seeds in Saul of Tarsus that day. That arch-enemy of the church would later become a Christian and a great champion of the gospel.

Like Stephen in the New Testament, these characters from the Old Testament in Hebrews 11 didn't escape conflict and tragedies, but they persevered through them by faith, trusting that God had a plan.

We, too, need to trust that there is a bigger picture than the limited aspects we can see.

Remember, if without faith it is impossible to please God, then the reverse is also true – with faith it is impossible *not* to please God. You can go to bed tonight and say, 'I may have had a rough day, a day I would not like to live through again, but I know I've lived today in dependence on him, trusting him to work out his purpose. Faith is being sure of what we hope for. It may not be in my hand now, but I know that God is going to bring about his work; he's going to accomplish his purpose.'

Will you trust God like this and join the list of those commended for their faith?

Day 54

Read Hebrews 11:32 – 12:1
Key verse: Hebrews 12:1

....

¹Therefore, since we are surrounded by such a great cloud of witnesses, let us throw off everything that hinders and the sin that so easily entangles. And let us run with perseverance the race marked out for us.

There are only two options in the Christian life: you either press on to maturity or you subject the Son of God to public disgrace (Hebrews 6:1–6).

Pressing on to maturity is the appeal not only in chapter 6, but also throughout the book, and it is here again in chapter 12.

How are we to mature? The writer tells us to look around at the 'cloud of witnesses' he has described in chapter 11. These individuals experienced God and they are witnesses to us of God's sufficiency in times of need. If you are facing a big problem, look again at Abraham and ask, 'How did he trust God?'; 'How did Moses trust God?'; 'How did these men and women of Hebrews 11 trust God?' Then you can ask the question, 'How am I to trust God in the light of their example?'

The writer is saying, 'You are not the first one on this journey. You are not the first one to face troubles and temptations. I've given you a catalogue of just some of the people from the past who knew God. They are witnesses to us that he is the same yesterday, today and for ever' (see Hebrews 13:8).

Don't look at the past with rose-tinted glasses. These characters from the chapter of faith experienced obstacles, temptations, frustrations and almost-constant battle. They are reminders to us that God does his best work in tough situations. Again and again he proves his sufficiency to us when we are at the end of our own resources.

Their God is our God.

Think about the Bible heroes who have inspired you and also the individuals who have been influential in your own spiritual journey. What have you learned about being faithful to God and about God's sufficiency from watching their lives? Thank God for these men and women, and realize that, like you, they have faced troubles and temptations. Reflect on how they dealt with these crises. How can you depend on the resources they relied upon?

Remember, their God is your God. So trust God's unchangeable character and his bountiful sufficiency. 'Anything God has ever done, He can do now. Anything God has ever done anywhere, He can do here. Anything God has ever done for anyone, He can do for you' (A. W. Tozer, quoted in *Leadership Weekly*, 9 October 2002). Just think: even today your life could be a witness testimony to God's sufficiency, spurring someone else on in the faith.

Day 55

Read Hebrews 11:23–28; 12:1
Key verse: Hebrews 12:1

· ·

¹Therefore, since we are surrounded by such a great cloud of witnesses, let us throw off everything that hinders and the sin that so easily entangles. And let us run with perseverance the race marked out for us.

Have you heard any sermons about 'throwing off' recently?

'Throwing off' the things that entangle us is not something we hear a lot about these days. We want to be positive and affirm the good without exposing the bad. Yes, the gospel is positive, but self-denial is as much a part of Christian experience as living in the fullness of God. Taking up the cross is as much a part of the Christian life as enjoying his resurrection life. Brokenness is God's agenda for us as a prelude to wholeness. Dying with Christ is necessary that we might live with him. Too often we want the benefits without the obligations.

Hebrews 12 talks about the things we need to throw off. Look at just one example from the life of Moses. He refused to be known as the son of Pharaoh's daughter (Hebrews 11:24–25). Having been adopted into the royal family of one of the greatest nations on earth, he had all the privileges of such a position laid at his feet, but he denied himself those privileges – not because they were in themselves wrong, but because they would interfere with God's purpose for him. That's why Hebrews makes this analogy of running the race. There is nothing wrong with big boots, but you don't wear them when you are running a race. There is nothing wrong with a heavy coat, but don't wear it if you want to reach the finish line. And there are things in life that are not intrinsically wrong, but aren't good when measured against bigger criteria: 'What enables me to further God's interest, God's purpose, God's agenda in my life?' Because that which hinders his purpose and agenda, that which impedes my growth in holiness, may not be wrong for somebody else, but it needs to come out of my life.

> We tend to rate our spiritual life according to what we see in the people around us. We use the lives of our friends to gauge how well we are doing spiritually. If we're going to the same number of services, have the same standard of living, use the same language, then we must be doing all right. But Hebrews says you are to run the race God marked out for *you* – not for someone else. Is there something morally neutral, or even good, that is hindering God's purpose or agenda for your life? An attachment to family ties when God is asking you to serve him overseas? A desire to be comfortable instead of giving sacrificially? It might be a small thing: God nudging you to do a Bible study when you meet with your friend, instead of just having a coffee and a chat. What is impeding your holiness?

Day 56

Read Hebrews 11:24–25; 12:14–17

Key verse: Hebrews 12:16

....

16 See that no one is sexually immoral, or is godless like Esau, who for a single meal sold his inheritance rights as the oldest son.

Sin is pleasurable.

That's why we have a problem with it. If sin wasn't enjoyable and attractive, we wouldn't be tempted by it. We face a continual struggle to live beyond satisfying our senses and succumbing to the popular motto, 'If it feels good, do it.'

You can imagine the pleasures of sin Moses could have enjoyed growing up in the royal palace. No doubt he could have clicked his fingers and got any girl or anything else he wanted. But he recognized that pleasure was fleeting, lasting only a season, and he was committed to serving God for life. So he denied himself the pleasures of sin, choosing instead to be ill-treated by the Egyptians alongside the Israelites.

We think of sex as the big 'lust of the flesh' to avoid, but, if you look carefully in the Bible, you may discover that food is. In the Garden of Eden, Eve ate the forbidden fruit. Esau, for a plate of food, lost his birthright. The Israelites wanted to return to captivity in Egypt because they missed the food! 'If only we had meat to eat! We remember the fish we ate in Egypt at no cost – also the cucumbers, melons, leeks, onions and garlic' (Numbers 11:4–5). The first temptation Satan gave Jesus was, 'If you are the Son of God, tell these stones to become bread' (Matthew 4:3).

Food and sex have many similarities. Both relate to physical appetites which, if not kept under control, can lead us into sin. Here the writer associates Esau's loss of his birthright for a plate of food with sexual immorality. Both are legitimate appetites we are tempted to fulfil illegitimately.

In our day, the anonymity, accessibility and affordability of Internet pornography make it highly addictive. This sin is rampant among Christians as well as non-Christians. Again, it is appealing illegitimately to a legitimate sexual appetite. But it will entangle and destroy you. (For further information and help, see *The Porn Problem* by Vaughan Roberts, The Good Book Company, 2018.)

Whatever your particular sin, whatever vulnerability you face, look back to the great cloud of witnesses. Their God is your God. He was sufficient for them, and he will be sufficient for you.

> Clothe yourselves with the Lord Jesus Christ, and do not think about how to gratify the desires of the flesh.
> (Romans 13:14)
>
> O Father, make known to us the glory of your Son! O Spirit, shine the light of the knowledge of the glory of Christ Jesus into our hearts! Blind us to all but him. Captivate us with his splendor, that we, like Moses, might say no to the passing pleasures of sin. Help us to rest in Christ alone as the treasure greater than all earthly rewards.
> (Sam Storms, *The Hope of Glory*, Crossway, 2008, p. 212)

Day 57

Read Hebrews 12:1–29
Key verses: Hebrews 12:1–2

. . . .

¹ Let us run with perseverance the race marked out for us, ² fixing our eyes on Jesus, the pioneer and perfecter of faith. For the joy that was set before him he endured the cross, scorning its shame, and sat down at the right hand of the throne of God.

What do you focus your attention and energies on?

In Hebrews 3:1, the writer urges us, 'Fix your thoughts on Jesus.' Here in 12:2, the charge is to fix our eyes on Jesus. The context is the catalogue in chapter 11 of people who lived by faith. Then the writer says that Jesus is the 'pioneer and perfecter of faith' – or, as the New King James Version puts it, 'the author and finisher of our faith'. The object in whom we place our faith is Christ. He is therefore both the beginner of our faith and, as he goes on being the object in whom we place our trust, the finisher of our faith.

If we are going to grow and mature in the Christian life, we don't move beyond Christ to something more! Every day we live in fresh dependence on him. It follows, therefore, that the more we fix our attention on him, the more we get to know him and the more we're going to trust him. The reason why we don't trust God is, very simply, because we don't know him well enough. The more we get to know him, the easier it becomes to trust him.

One of the most important things in the Christian life is getting to know God better, supremely by getting to know Christ. That's why we read the Bible: not to get to know the Bible, but to get to know Christ. The more confident we are of the object of our faith, the less conscious we are of the faith itself. If you had the option of making a long journey in either a brand-new BMW or a forty-year-old VW Beetle and you chose the Beetle, someone might commend you for having a lot of faith! If you chose the BMW, no-one would mention your faith – because the more confident we are in the object of our faith, the less conscious we are of the faith itself. The more we know God, the less conscious we are of any risk element and the fact that we live by faith.

Alec Motyer said of Epaphroditus, the gospel worker who delivered Paul's letter to the Philippians, 'He took a calculated risk, involving the expenditure of all he had, relying only on the trustworthiness of Jesus Christ. He staked all on Jesus, knowing that he could not fail' (*The Richness of Christ*, IVP, 1966). What is stopping you expending all that you have for Christ? Do you need to get to know him better? Do you need to get rid of distractions and fix your eyes on him more intently? Ask the Holy Spirit to help you be obedient to God and 'do whatever he tells you' (John 2:5).

Day 58

Read Hebrews 12:1–29

Key verses: Hebrews 12:1–3

••

¹Let us run with perseverance the race marked out for us, ²fixing our eyes on Jesus, the pioneer and perfecter of faith. For the joy that was set before him he endured the cross, scorning its shame, and sat down at the right hand of the throne of God. ³Consider him who endured such opposition from sinners, so that you will not grow weary and lose heart.

The Christian Gospel is that I am so flawed that Jesus had to die for me, yet I am so loved and valued that Jesus was glad to die for me. (Tim Keller, *The Reason for God: Belief in an Age of Scepticism*, Hodder and Stoughton, 2009, p. 179)

Christ went gladly and willingly to the cross for you. But don't ever get the idea that he went waltzing to the cross saying, 'Oh well, this is all par for the course.' In the Garden of Gethsemane he said, 'Father, if it is possible for this cup to be taken from me, if there's any other way that a man or woman, a boy or girl can be reconciled to a holy God; if there's any other way, please let that be the way; but if there is no other way, your will be done.' In such a spirit, he went to the cross and endured the agony.

We might speculate about the physical agony, but we can't even begin to understand the spiritual agony Jesus suffered. He cried out in anguish, 'My God, my God, why have you forsaken me?' (Matthew 27:46). The very atmosphere of hell descended on him in those hours of darkness. Why did he do it? The writer to the Hebrews says it was 'for the joy that was set before him'.

What was the joy set before him? The prophetic statement about the cross in Isaiah 53 helps us to understand. Verse 11 says, 'He shall see of the travail of his soul, and shall be satisfied' (KJV). You and I were the joy set before him. Jesus endured the cross for the joy of knowing that human beings might be redeemed and reconciled to God.

The cross demonstrates just how much Christ loves you.

Difficult circumstances often leave us questioning God's love. We say to ourselves, 'If God really loved me, surely he would take this cup of suffering away from me?' Hebrews 12:2 confronts us with the startling truth: God loves you with an unfailing, everlasting, Calvary love. Before you were even born, Jesus knew you. He endured the agony of the cross because his mind was fixed on you and on how you could be reconciled to God. Today you may endure suffering, but trust him in dark days, knowing you are known, loved and cared for. This truth can thrill your heart and spur you on to greater devotion.

I have loved you with an everlasting love;
    I have drawn you with unfailing kindness.
(Jeremiah 31:3)

Day 59

Read Hebrews 12:4–29
Key verses: Hebrews 12:5–7

· ·

⁵And have you completely forgotten this word of encouragement that addresses you as a father addresses his son? It says,
> *'My son, do not make light of the Lord's discipline,*
> *   and do not lose heart when he rebukes you,*
> *⁶because the Lord disciplines the one he loves,*
> *   and he chastens everyone he accepts as his son.'*
⁷ Endure hardship as discipline; God is treating you as his children. For what children are not disciplined by their father?

When life is tough, we are tempted to assume something is wrong with us. We may be embarrassed about our financial struggles, job uncertainty, physical suffering or strained relationships. We worry that our troubles might be a sign of our own failure, lack of faith or disobedience.

But hardship is not something to be embarrassed about. Suffering is a fact of life and one of the ways in which God teaches and moulds us. Like a loving parent, God disciplines us for good (verse 7). We don't look for suffering, but again and again it is God's agent for good in our lives. Through it we discover what real values are, and through it God may conform us to the image of Jesus. 'It is good for a man to bear the yoke while he is young' (Lamentations 3:27). Suffering is productive: it produces 'perseverance; perseverance, character; and character, hope' (Romans 5:3–4).

Philippians 1:29 reminds us that suffering for Christ is part of the package of Christianity: 'For it has been granted to you on behalf of Christ not only to believe in him, but also to suffer for him.' We don't suffer in spite of God's will because we live in a fallen environment; we suffer according to God's will: 'So then, those who suffer according to God's will should commit themselves to their faithful Creator and continue to do good' (1 Peter 4:19). In a mysterious way, suffering can be a prelude to glory, the foretaste of great blessing to come (Romans 8:17–18).

As we mature in Christ, we look at the situations and hardships of life that we come up against and allow them to be God's tool to mould us into richer, deeper people, as he intends.

> Don't be surprised when you suffer. Expect it! And don't despise the hardships that come your way. Instead, pray that God would help you see your circumstances as he does.
>
> Friends, when life gets really difficult, don't jump to the conclusion that God isn't on the job. Instead, be glad that you are in the very thick of what Christ experienced. This is a spiritual refining process, with glory just around the corner . . . So if you find life difficult because you're doing what God said, take it in stride. Trust him. He knows what he's doing, and he'll keep on doing it.
> (1 Peter 4:12–13, 19, MSG)

Day 60

Read Hebrews 12:4–29
Key verses: Hebrews 12:10–11

∙∙

[10] [Human fathers] disciplined us for a little while as they thought best; but God disciplines us for our good, in order that we may share in his holiness. [11] No discipline seems pleasant at the time, but painful. Later on, however, it produces a harvest of righteousness and peace for those who have been trained by it.

Hope is essential to life.

We orientate our life around future hopes, high expectations or longings. It may be something as trivial as a holiday, or it may be watching our children and perhaps grandchildren grow up. Looking forward in hope is one of the ingredients of a healthy life, materially and spiritually. It alters how we feel about the present.

This theme of looking forward runs throughout this whole letter. Go back to Hebrews 11:10 and Abraham 'was looking forward to the city with foundations, whose architect and builder is God'. Hebrews 11:16 says that the men and women listed were 'longing for a better country'. Moses, too, was looking ahead to his reward; that's why he chose the disgrace of the people of God. The goal that kept them looking forward and pressing on is explained in Hebrews 12:10: 'God disciplines us for our good, in order that we may share in his holiness.' Sharing the holiness of God is our ultimate hope, for it alone brings deep satisfaction to our souls.

Hope in the Bible is a confident expectation based not on wishful thinking, but on the revelation God has given us in his Word.

No matter what situation we are in, through faith we can look beyond our circumstances and say, 'There is a city, whose foundation and builder is God. There is a future for which I am being prepared. It is a journey from which it is impossible to fall away, for we have been eternally sealed in that journey by the Holy Spirit.'

The writer to the Hebrews describes our hope in Christ as 'an anchor for the soul, firm and secure' (Hebrews 6:19). Whatever troubles are swirling around you right now, let your hope in Christ and all that God has planned for you hold you fast. Draw peace and strength from knowing that your future is secure. God's glorious plan and purpose for you will be fulfilled.

> Therefore we do not lose heart. Though outwardly we are wasting away, yet inwardly we are being renewed day by day. For our light and momentary troubles are achieving for us an eternal glory that far outweighs them all. So we fix our eyes not on what is seen, but on what is unseen, since what is seen is temporary, but what is unseen is eternal.
> (2 Corinthians 4:16–18)

> May the God of hope fill you with all joy and peace as you trust in him, so that you may overflow with hope by the power of the Holy Spirit.
> (Romans 15:13)

Day 61

Read Hebrews 13:1–25

Key verses: Hebrews 13:20–21

....

[20] Now may the God of peace, who through the blood of the eternal covenant brought back from the dead our Lord Jesus, that great Shepherd of the sheep, [21] equip you with everything good for doing his will, and may he work in us what is pleasing to him, through Jesus Christ, to whom be glory for ever and ever. Amen.

Perhaps more than ever before, people are watching to see whether our lives express our beliefs. Many are sick of outward pretence and genuinely hunger for authenticity and integrity.

The author of Hebrews knew the value of practical Christian living and describes what spiritual maturity looks like. After all the teaching and warnings, the letter concludes with loving application. The issues that were prevalent in the church then – sex, money, power, suffering and worship – are still hot topics today. Yet, despite the cultural norms and pressure to conform in our own particular society, the writer urges us to live distinctive lives, explicable only by the work and presence of God within us.

Whether talking about being content and not loving money (verse 5), or about obeying our leaders (verse 7), he explains that the motivation for our behaviour is God living within us. Throughout the chapter, Jesus' supremacy – and his role as mediator of the new covenant and pioneer of faith who is always available to his people – is the focus.

The great promise is that the God who guided the Israelites in the days of the old covenant, who intercedes for us today and who will take us to 'the city that is to come' (verse 14), is unchanged and unchangeable. 'Jesus Christ is the same yesterday and today and for ever' (verse 8). He is completely trustworthy and, if our faith is firmly rooted in him, we can be sustained and guided through difficult times (verses 5–6).

Yes, we have to be diligent and persevere, but even as we do so, God is at work in us and through us. As this prayer of blessing in verses 20–21 highlights, spiritual growth is possible. We have the God who planned and brought about our salvation and who raised Jesus from the dead, and the living Lord Jesus who guides and keeps us, and who gave us the Holy Spirit to equip us and enable all that God has called us to be and to do.

What grace!

Perhaps God is asking you to step out into a whole new area of service. Perhaps he is challenging you about your spiritual growth. Whatever he is calling you to be or to do, press on with confidence. Obey wholeheartedly, knowing that God will keep his promise to equip and enable you.

> May God, who puts all things together,
>   makes all things whole,
> Who made a lasting mark through the sacrifice of Jesus,
>   the sacrifice of blood that sealed the eternal covenant,
> Who led Jesus, our Great Shepherd,
>   up and alive from the dead,
> Now put you together, provide you
>   with everything you need to please him,
> Make us into what gives him most pleasure,
>   by means of the sacrifice of Jesus, the Messiah.
> All glory to Jesus forever and always!
>   Oh, yes, yes, yes.
> (Hebrews 13:20–21, MSG)

For further study

If you would like to do further study on Hebrews, the following commentaries may be useful:

- Raymond Brown, *The Message of Hebrews*, The Bible Speaks Today (IVP, 2000).

- F. F. Bruce, *The Epistle to the Hebrews*, New International Commentary on the New Testament (Eerdmans, Revised edition, 2011).

- George H. Guthrie, *Hebrews*, NIV Application Commentary (Zondervan, 1998).

- Tom Wright, *Hebrews for Everyone* (SPCK, 2003).

If God has fed you through your study of the book of Hebrews, why not buy the individual Food for the Journey on Hebrews and give it to a friend (available from ivpbooks.com)?

Introduction
1 Thessalonians

Alec Motyer

'Keep on pressing on'

Do you need to hear these words today?

'Keep on pressing on' was the theme of the first letter Paul ever wrote. It was a message that the Thessalonians, and every believer since, has needed to hear.

Paul visited Thessalonica, a bustling commercial seaport, on his second mission trip, along with his companions Silas and Timothy. As was his custom, Paul preached in the synagogue, and a number of Jews, as well as many Gentiles and some prominent women, accepted the gospel. Unfortunately, the visit was cut short after only four or five weeks when Paul was hounded out of the city by Jewish opposition (Acts 17:1–9).

But, amazingly, by the time he left, there was a fledgling church.

Paul wrote to these new believers to fill in details and explain mis-understandings about the second coming, to urge them to live well in Christian community and to give further instructions about godly living, all the while encouraging them to press on in holiness regardless of outside opposition. His prayer for them was that they would become all that they ought to be in character and conduct.

Whatever age or stage of the Christian life you are at, whatever cir-cumstances you are facing, Paul's message to 'Keep on pressing on' is for you. Let the encouragements, challenges and truths from 1 Thessalonians spur you on in your spiritual journey, so that, like these New Testament believers, we would become all that we ought to be in character and conduct.

Day 62

Read 1 Thessalonians 1:1–10
Key verse: 1 Thessalonians 1:1

• •

¹Paul, Silas and Timothy,
To the church of the Thessalonians in God the Father and the Lord Jesus Christ:
Grace and peace to you.

Complete the phrase, 'I'm in . . .' What is the first word that comes into your mind? Perhaps your answer was, 'I'm in work', 'I'm in hospital', 'I'm in university', 'I'm in pain', or simply, 'I'm in a rush'!

Although each of us faces different scenarios, there is a banner that can be put over the life of every Christian: we are 'in God the Father and the Lord Jesus Christ'.

When we become Christians, God, like a careful gardener, gently takes us out of the habitat in which we were living, and he transplants us into himself. Our union with him means that we are planted into a system perfectly suited to the new nature we have been given, a system specially designed to cultivate our growth, development and fruitfulness.

Remember the image of the vine and the branches Jesus used in John 15? The branches are in a system that has been perfectly designed to maintain their health, growth and fruitfulness. We are also in a system that has been perfectly designed for our holiness, development and usefulness. We have been planted into God the Father and the Lord Jesus Christ. And all the life of God the Father and God the Son, bound together as one God, surrounds us as soon as we become Christians. His life is there for us to put our roots into and draw our nourishment from, so that we grow straight, true, clean and fruitful.

Did you notice that Paul gives Jesus his full title in this verse? Paul doesn't want us to miss the amazing nature and privilege of our union. We are united with the Lord, God himself. He comes to us not only as Lord but as Jesus, the one who understands us and can perfectly minister to our needs. And he comes as Christ, the one who was anointed to be the totally perfect Saviour of sinners.

Are you beginning to feel like a protected species? Are you beginning to realize how precious you are to God?

It is easy to look at life simply from an earthly perspective: we are 'in a family crisis', 'in a reshuffle at work', 'in remission' or sometimes just 'in a rush'. But consider the difference it makes to see your life from God's perspective: you are 'in God the Father and the Lord Jesus Christ'. The breathtaking miracle of your salvation means you are now united with God. You have his life to strengthen you, his Word to nourish you, his Spirit to guide you. Meditate on the image of the vine and the branches from John 15. Be a Psalm 1 believer: sink your roots deeply into Christ today (see Day 1).

Day 63

Read 1 Thessalonians 1:1–10
Key verse: 1 Thessalonians 1:1

∙∙

> ¹*Paul, Silas and Timothy,*
>   *To the church of the Thessalonians in God the Father and the Lord Jesus Christ:*
>   *Grace and peace to you.*

What do you think you most need, to grow as a Christian? Sometimes we imagine we would be able to make better strides as disciples if only God were more explicit with his guidance, quicker to answer our prayers and keener to change our circumstances. But God's means of growth is to nourish us with his grace and peace.

Grace is not something God gives; not something he hands out like medicine. There is no such thing as grace apart from God. Grace is God being gracious. It is the free, undeserved, unmerited movement of God sharing himself with his people as our Father and as our Lord Jesus Christ. Our salvation was an act of sheer grace (Ephesians 2:4–5). And now, through Jesus' death, God offers us the perfect setting to live and grow, in union with him. There we find God's fatherly love, saving mercy and eternal power surrounding us.

He also offers us peace. Of course, peace begins with a restored relationship with God. But peace also means 'peace and fulfilment in our own being'. When God ministers peace to us, he is ministering to us all those things that bring us to fulfilment and full maturity: peace with God; the peace of a truly fulfilled humanity; peace in society; peace in fellowship with our Christian brothers and sisters. God's peace, his *shalom*, is not simply the absence of war but also the wholeness, well-being, rest and contentment that we experience when we live in union with him.

What are the 'extras' you are looking for to speed up your Christian growth? Are you waiting for clearer guidance, better circumstances or even deeper spiritual experiences? Stop! God has given you everything you need to grow as a disciple: he has given you himself. Your union with God is a treasure store, and it contains all you will ever need for life and godliness. You first became aware of God's grace and peace when you were saved. But that was just the beginning! Experiencing God's grace and peace daily nourishes your faith and helps it grow. Give thanks today for all the evidence of God's grace in your life, and rest in his peace, knowing that your wholeness and well-being are not wrapped up in your achievements, but only and always in Christ.

Day 64

Read 1 Thessalonians 1:1–10
Key verses: 1 Thessalonians 1:2–3

....

²We always thank God for all of you and continually mention you in our prayers. ³We remember before our God and Father your work produced by faith, your labour prompted by love, and your endurance inspired by hope in our Lord Jesus Christ.

When people look at you, what do they make of your life? Is it obvious from your actions and behaviour that you are a Christian?

In Thessalonica, the young believers are already bearing fruit. They are only weeks old in the faith and yet the evidence of their new life is obvious. John the Baptist once said, 'Produce fruit in keeping with repentance' (Matthew 3:8). And Paul is echoing his point. If we are truly repentant, it will show; spiritual experience is a matter not of claim, but of evidence. And being fruitful isn't for the few, it isn't for some time in the future; it is something that happens from the moment we are saved. We demonstrate our new life in Christ by our faith in God, our love for others and our hope in Jesus' return.

Notice that Paul doesn't apologize to the Thessalonians that their faith requires hard work and endurance. He assumes it is quite normal that being a Christian is demanding. However, when we face struggles, we are often quick to wonder, 'What is God thinking about?' Well, he is thinking about the fact that he calls us to live by faith, to live in love and to exercise hope. He is calling us to be what we are. The troubles and toils of life, which demand faith, hard work and endurance, are not unnatural experiences. They are the conditions God chooses for our growth.

Circumstances may be difficult and you may feel very weary, but don't give up. Hold on to faith: faith in Christ saved you, so trust him with every difficulty you face today. Hold on to love: keep on loving your church family in practical, self-sacrificing ways. Hold on to hope: endure each day knowing that one day soon Jesus is coming back. Remember, struggles are good soil for growth, so don't waste them! Pray that your perseverance and fruitfulness will point someone to Jesus today.

Day 65

Read 1 Thessalonians 1:1–10
Key verses: 1 Thessalonians 1:4–5

....

> [4]*For we know, brothers and sisters loved by God, that he has chosen you,* [5]*because our gospel came to you not simply with words but also with power, with the Holy Spirit and deep conviction. You know how we lived among you for your sake.*

My friend was explaining to her adopted daughter how loved and precious she was. She said, 'Other mums and dads just have to accept whatever child they get, but we *chose* you.'

Out of God's great love he *chose* us. God looked at us and said, 'Yes, I want that one.' We may worry, 'What about my choice? Didn't I choose Jesus to be my Saviour?' Well, we need to remember that we were 'dead in [our] transgressions and sins' (Ephesians 2:1). We couldn't even exercise repentance and faith: we were spiritually dead, without a spark of life. 'But because of his great love for us, God, who is rich in mercy, made us alive with Christ' (Ephesians 2:4–5). God had to take the initiative. There is no way we can come to life in Christ until he first gives us life. And he gave us life simply because he loved us.

So what happened? How does salvation work out at ground level, where we are lying dead in our trespasses and sins? Verse 5 of 1 Thessalonians 1 explains, first, that the gospel was preached. Second, God's power was doing its life-giving, quickening work, creating in us the capacity to hear the good news. God's Holy Spirit power brings to us what by nature we could never have – a vision of Jesus, the gift of repentance and an ability to believe. Third, conviction was created. God's Word came with 'deep conviction', convincing us of its truth and saving power.

So God's election, his choice of us, works outward, from the inner reality of his love to the outward preaching of the gospel: the exercise of the power of the Word of God, the energy of the Holy Spirit, producing conviction and giving the ability to repent and believe.

In the Bible, election (God's choice of us) is presented not as a theological conundrum to solve, but as evidence of God's inexplicable love for us. Do you have any idea how loved you are? We know it in our heads, but sometimes the truth does not reach our hearts. Reassess your vision of God today – he is not distant and aloof from your suffering and anxiety; he is not a stern taskmaster waiting for you to make the grade. He is your heavenly Father, who gave you the precious gift of spiritual life simply because he loves you. He looked at you and said, 'I want you to be my son; I want you to be my daughter.' You are loved, you are valued, you are precious. Let the words roll around on your tongue and seep into the core of your being. Today, allow this truth to govern your emotions and shape your thoughts and actions.

Day 66

Read 1 Thessalonians 1:1–10

Key verses: 1 Thessalonians 1:6–8

. . . .

⁶You became imitators of us and of the Lord, for you welcomed the message in the midst of severe suffering with the joy given by the Holy Spirit. ⁷And so you became a model to all the believers in Macedonia and Achaia. ⁸The Lord's message rang out from you not only in Macedonia and Achaia – your faith in God has become known everywhere. Therefore we do not need to say anything about it.

Who are your role models? Who are the Christians you look to for inspiration and encouragement in the faith?

Here, Paul promotes the Thessalonian church as a model. He does so not because the believers are perfect, but because of the priority they place on the Word of God.

First, they receive God's Word. Understanding and accepting the Bible message was core to their salvation and also tied them straight away into a system of imitation. In receiving the Word of God, they aligned themselves with the apostles, the men of the Word, and with the Lord Jesus, that great Man of the Word.

Second, they persevered in the Word. Despite the persecution, the Thessalonians continued to accept God's truth, believe his promises and trust his Son. We may not face the same type of persecution, but our faith will be tested to see if we hold on to God's Word in difficult times. Notice that the Thessalonians' perseverance was not a grim determination. The Holy Spirit gave them the spiritual joy of knowing the truth. And every time we open our Bibles, determined to persevere in the Word, the Spirit is ready to impart his own joy.

Third, they shared the Word: 'The Lord's message rang out from you not only in Macedonia and Achaia – your faith in God has become known everywhere.'

It was their focus on the Bible that made this church a model for others. The Word of God called it into existence, converted its members, and gave focus to its life and substance to its message.

What about your church? What about you? Are you a Bible person? Are you persevering in the Word of God? Are you sharing it with others?

On a scale of one to ten, rate the importance of the Bible in your life. Think about the influence it has on your decision-making, how you raise your family, how you plan for the future and how you use your leisure time. Christians are called 'people of the Book', but is it really true? Is devotion to the Bible the distinguishing mark of your life? Don't wait any longer. Give the Bible back its rightful place: read it, study it, meditate on it. Allow it to transform you. Who knows, God could use your passion for his Word as a model for others.

Day 67

Read 1 Thessalonians 1:1–10
Key verses: 1 Thessalonians 1:9–10

....

⁹They themselves report what kind of reception you gave us. They tell how you turned to God from idols to serve the living and true God,¹⁰and to wait for his Son from heaven, whom he raised from the dead – Jesus, who rescues us from the coming wrath.

Many Christians struggle with doubt. 'How can I be sure I'm really saved?' 'How can I know my sins are forgiven?' These questions plague us, stripping us of joy and peace and hampering our service.

Of course, if it was down to us and our abilities and reliability, then certainly our salvation would be in doubt. But our salvation is entirely dependent on that single, blessed, central, all-sufficient person: our Lord Jesus Christ.

These verses remind us that Jesus' resurrection is the decisive proof that his work of salvation was effective. God raising Jesus from the dead was heaven's sign of confirmation that his work at Calvary was complete. Jesus' resurrection was the Father's 'Amen' to the Son's cry, 'It is finished.'

The consequences of Jesus' work on the cross continue. However, when Paul says that Jesus 'rescues us from the coming wrath' – present tense – he doesn't mean that the work of salvation is still going on. Salvation was achieved once and for all on the cross. Jesus is not forever rescuing; he simply rescues for ever. So when Paul looks forward to that Day of Judgment and of standing before God, he has no fear. He has been rescued from the coming wrath. The same is true for us.

Some of us remember the exact moment when we 'turned to God'. The rest of us know we did; we just can't pinpoint the exact date and time of our conversion. But, whenever it happened, the important thing to remember is that when we 'turned to God', we entered into the finished work of salvation, and into an eternal security in which we never need to fear God's wrath.

The devil is a grand master of doubt and lies – he's had years of practice! He whispers in your ear, 'If you were really saved, surely you wouldn't have done that?' and 'Could God really forgive that terrible sin?' Jesus' resurrection stands as a line in the sand, a marker for all eternity, that the devil has been defeated and your sin has been paid for. Because of Christ's sacrifice, you are clothed in his righteousness and can look forward to that final day when you are welcomed into heaven. Bring your doubts, the sins that plague you and the failures of the past, and leave them at the foot of the cross. 'It is finished.' Rejoice in so great a salvation!

Day 68

Read 1 Thessalonians 2:1–16

Key verses: 1 Thessalonians 2:1–4

· ·

¹You know, brothers and sisters, that our visit to you was not without results. ²We had previously suffered and been treated outrageously in Philippi, as you know, but with the help of our God we dared to tell you his gospel in the face of strong opposition. ³For the appeal we make does not spring from error or impure motives, nor are we trying to trick you. ⁴On the contrary, we speak as those approved by God to be entrusted with the gospel. We are not trying to please people but God, who tests our hearts.

Every generation of Christians has to ask, 'How can we best share the gospel?' As culture, technology and resources change, what does effective evangelism look like? How can we share the gospel in ways that bear fruit in positive, unmistakable, lasting conversions?

Paul reminds the Thessalonian believers that his first visit to them was a fruitful time for the gospel, as people immediately turned to God. Why was this visit so successful? What was the reason for so many conversions? Paul gives two reasons. His first reason (we'll look at the second tomorrow) was the truth factor. He faithfully shared the gospel, which is the truth about and from God.

Twice in these four verses, Paul mentions the gospel. In verse 2, he talks of 'his gospel', which literally means 'the gospel of God'. Paul uses many parallel expressions. For example, he speaks of 'the gospel of his Son' (Romans 1:9), by which he means that the Lord Jesus is the sum and substance of the gospel. He is the great subject of the gospel; he is its great content. Similarly, when elsewhere he speaks of 'the gospel of the grace of God' (Acts 20:24, ESV), he means that the gospel message is a ministry of imparting the grace of God.

But here, by 'the gospel of God', he means origin and ownership. The gospel originated from God himself, and he is the owner and master of it.

Effective evangelism means us sharing the mighty gospel of God.

Have you ever found yourself in a conversation where, un-expectedly, you have the opportunity to share the gospel? Often when we are caught off guard, we don't know quite what to say. The temptation is to sugar-coat the gospel, to avoid talking about sin or judgment and to focus instead on the wonderful purposes God has for believers. Prepare for those conversations. What are the core components of the gospel? Practise presenting the gospel faithfully and gently. Research gospel resources that you would feel comfortable giving to your friends and colleagues. And, most importantly, pray. Pray for opportunities to share the gospel and wisdom when those opportunities arise. If you don't already pray regularly for unbelievers to become Christians, choose five friends or family members and commit to praying for them daily.

Day 69

Read 1 Thessalonians 2:1–16
Key verses: 1 Thessalonians 2:1–4

....

> ¹*You know, brothers and sisters, that our visit to you was not without results. ²We had previously suffered and been treated outrageously in Philippi, as you know, but with the help of our God we dared to tell you his gospel in the face of strong opposition. ³For the appeal we make does not spring from error or impure motives, nor are we trying to trick you. ⁴On the contrary, we speak as those approved by God to be entrusted with the gospel. We are not trying to please people but God, who tests our hearts.*

Many of the people we rub shoulders with will never darken the door of a church. They will never listen to a sermon. However, they are still watching to see if our 'walk' matches our 'talk'.

Look again at verses 1–4, where Paul gives us the second reason why his evangelism to the Thessalonians was so effective. Paul brought the truth of the gospel to the Thessalonians with a holy and dedicated life, and a heart approved by God. Effective evangelism has never been about simply saying the right words or knowing the right facts. God entrusts the gospel to those whose lives he has tested and approved. What exactly is God looking for? Or, more precisely, whom is God looking for?

- *Those who consciously rely on God's strength*. The freedom and courage that Paul and his friends experienced as they shared the gospel was not human stoicism, nor was it making light of their suffering; it was a conscious reliance on 'the help of our God'.

- *Those who present the good news simply*. 'Tell you his gospel' in verse 2 literally means 'chatting' the gospel.

- *Those who are not concerned about themselves.* Paul faced 'strong opposition', which refers to the danger and threats in Philippi, and also to the hesitations within his own heart. However, he was prepared to accept the risks and live with the hesitation.

- *Those who have integrity.* Paul had integrity of mind, emotion and will. His conscience was clear because he told the truth about the gospel and he did not use deceitful methods.

- *Those who desire to please God.* If Paul had not been flogged in Philippi, he would not have known whether he was promoting the gospel for his own purposes or out of a desire solely to please God. His willingness to suffer revealed his true motives and that he was 'approved by God to be entrusted with the gospel'.

Do you share these defining traits? Could God entrust you with his gospel?

The gospel is never delivered in a vacuum; it comes wrapped up in our personalities. Our lives are adverts for the gospel. Take time to pray through these traits. Ask God to highlight the areas where you need to change and ask for his Holy Spirit's help. And do not despise your suffering – who knows whether the suffering that you have just passed through, or are passing through, or which will start today or tomorrow, may be God approving you to be entrusted with the gospel. Accept his discipline, hold on to him, love him with a pure heart, live out the gospel and pray intentionally for opportunities to share Christ with others.

Day 70

Read 1 Thessalonians 2:1–16
Key verses: 1 Thessalonians 2:5–9

. . . .

> [5]*You know we never used flattery, nor did we put on a mask to cover up greed – God is our witness.* [6]*We were not looking for praise from people, not from you or anyone else, even though as apostles of Christ we could have asserted our authority.* [7]*Instead, we were like young children among you.*
>
> *Just as a nursing mother cares for her children,* [8]*so we cared for you. Because we loved you so much, we were delighted to share with you not only the gospel of God but our lives as well.* [9]*Surely you remember, brothers and sisters, our toil and hardship; we worked night and day in order not to be a burden to anyone while we preached the gospel of God to you.*

Evangelism is not meant to be a guilt-inducing extra in our already busy lives. Each of us has work colleagues, family, a circle of friends – people we already have relationships with but who do not yet know Jesus. Paul urges us to invest our lives into these people, and he gives us an illustration of how to do it: a nursing mother.

Perhaps a better translation of the sentence in verses 7–8 would be, 'Just as a nurse-mother cherishes her very own children, so we cherished you.' A mother will certainly cherish her children. But a nurse is trained, and here she is looking after her own children. Paul says that if you are going to be evangelists, you have got to demonstrate these qualities of tenderness, love and care. Essentially, un-self-seeking devotion is vital.

What did this look like in practice? Well, in verses 5–6, Paul explains how he shunned self-advantage: he didn't try to cajole people with clever words; he didn't need to cover up any greed; he didn't expect to be praised or put on a pedestal. Instead, he pursued what was to the Thessalonians' advantage: he worked tirelessly so they wouldn't need to give him financial support, and so the gospel would be free to them. He sums it up: 'We loved you so much, we were delighted to share with you not only the gospel of God but our lives as well' (verse 8).

What a picture for us to copy!

Think about the five individuals you chose on Day 68. How could you be a nurse-mother to them? How could you demonstrate self-sacrificing love and care, and work for their advantage? Pray through your day and all the specific opportunities you have to 'share life' with these people. If your plans go awry today and people interrupt your schedule, see this as God giving you an extra opportunity to show self-sacrificing love! Meditate on the self-giving of Christ as your motivation today.

Day 71

Read 1 Thessalonians 2:1–16
Key verses: 1 Thessalonians 2:10–12

....

¹⁰You are witnesses, and so is God, of how holy, righteous and blameless we were among you who believed. ¹¹For you know that we dealt with each of you as a father deals with his own children, ¹²encouraging, comforting and urging you to live lives worthy of God, who calls you into his kingdom and glory.

As we chat about the gospel in our workplaces, colleges, homes and the ordinary routines of daily life, Paul gives us another picture. Whereas the illustration of the mother emphasized self-sacrificing devotion, the illustration of the father highlights holy living and encouraging teaching. Paul was like a mother and a father to the Thessalonians as he shared the gospel with them. He urges us to follow his example and to:

- *Be a role model.* Paul modelled holiness to the Thessalonians: 'You are witnesses . . . of how holy, righteous and blameless we were among you' (verse 10).

- *Guide in the right direction.* In verse 12, Paul both encourages and exhorts the Thessalonians. Like a father, he gave positive encouragement to guide them in the right direction and was there to comfort them when they failed. But all the time, undergirding the encouragement and comfort, his purpose was to share the truth with them.

- *Remind them of God.* Like a father, Paul reminded the Thessalonians 'to live lives worthy of God' (verse 12). He reminded them of the sufficiency of God and the obedience their great King deserved. He also urged them to persevere in their faith, reminding them of the future glory awaiting them.

You might not like the idea, but people are watching you. Your children, work colleagues, college friends, parents at the school gate, people in your home group or book group – they are all watching you. They are taking notice of whether your actions and conversations match your beliefs. They are looking to see whether your faith really is authentic and makes a difference to your life. Pray that you will model Christ well today. Pray that instead of consisting of gossip or trivia, your conversations will point people to the way of truth and encourage them to press on in the faith, looking forward to heaven.

Day 72

Read 1 Thessalonians 2:1–16
Key verses: 1 Thessalonians 2:13–14

· ·

13 And we also thank God continually because, when you received the word of God, which you heard from us, you accepted it not as a human word, but as it actually is, the word of God, which is indeed at work in you who believe. 14 For you, brothers and sisters, became imitators of God's churches in Judea, which are in Christ Jesus: you suffered from your own people the same things those churches suffered from the Jews.

Today, many of us have multiple copies of the Bible, in various translations and on numerous electronic devices. It is easy to become complacent about the fact that the Bible is actually divine truth. Although they were brought to us through human agents, the words we read are the very words of God in the fullest sense. So how should we respond to the Bible? How did the Thessalonians respond?

- *They 'received' it* (verse 13). The Thessalonians recognized it was authoritative.

- *They 'accepted' it* (verse 13). More than just recognizing the authority of the Word of God, they opened their minds and hearts to it and welcomed it as something lovely.

- *They believed it*. The Word was 'at work in you who believe' (verse 13). They believed the Bible's teaching and promises, and then, in faithful obedience, acted upon its commands.

- *They 'suffered'* (verse 14). Paul has already spoken about this in 1 Thessalonians 1:6. As before, it is not the form of the testing that matters, but its inevitability. Their reception of the Word was tested by the onset of persecution. The Word of God is always challenged.

Part of our true reception of the Word is not only to receive it as authoritative, to welcome it as lovely, to believe and obey it, but to persevere in its truth in the face of any odds.

Do you recognize yourself in Paul's description of the Thessalonians? Have you received God's Word? Have you accepted it, believed it and suffered for it? What is holding you back from fully trusting the divine Word of God? Is there a promise you need to hold on to, a command you need to obey, or a circumstance you need to persevere in? Meditate on these verses from Psalm 119. Pray that God would increase your love and devotion to his Word, so you could say with the psalmist:

> I meditate on your precepts
>   and consider your ways.
> I delight in your decrees;
>   I will not neglect your word.
> (verses 15–16)

> You are my portion, LORD;
>   I have promised to obey your words.
> (verse 57)

> How sweet are your words to my taste,
> sweeter than honey to my mouth!
> (verse 103)

> Your statutes are my heritage for ever;
> they are the joy of my heart.
> (verse 111)

> Your promises have been thoroughly tested,
> and your servant loves them.
> (verse 140)

Day 73

Read 1 Thessalonians 2:1–16
Key verses: 1 Thessalonians 2:14–16

· ·

> [14] *You suffered from your own people the same things those churches suffered from the Jews* [15] *who killed the Lord Jesus and the prophets and also drove us out. They displease God and are hostile to everyone* [16] *in their effort to keep us from speaking to the Gentiles so that they may be saved. In this way they always heap up their sins to the limit. The wrath of God has come upon them at last.*

The gospel is only 'good news' if you accept it.

These verses are about those who reject the Word of God. Paul explains that the Jews 'killed the Lord Jesus and the prophets and also drove us out'. Essentially, they had the Word of God in the loveliest, personal form of Jesus; they had the Word of God in the inspired form of scriptural prophecy; they had the Word of God in its up-to-date form of New Testament apostleship – and they rejected it out of hand. They also rejected the Word of God's evangelistic benefit for the world: 'They . . . are hostile to everyone in their effort to keep us from speaking to the Gentiles so that they may be saved.'

Paul is not being anti-Semitic. But he's saying that where there is refusal of Jesus, a rejection of the prophets, a driving out of the apostles and a barring of the evangelistic message – where there is that fourfold rejection of the Word of God, there cannot be anything else but the utmost judgment of God.

This is no polemic, but simply a basic statement of a dreadful but inescapable fact: when people reject the Word of God, they come under judgment in its full and final form.

The judgment of God is a sobering thought. Pray for an openness to the gospel in the various ministries your church is involved in: the Sunday school, toddler group, ministry among the older folk and the youth. Think of the times you will hear God's Word today: in the music playing on your headphones, the sermon you downloaded to listen to as you travel, the devotional time you have with your family, the Bible study you will join this evening. Pray that, in each of those instances, you will accept God's Word as his message to you, whether that is a rebuke, a challenge, an encouragement or a comfort. As Paul exhorts us in Colossians 3:16: 'Let the message of Christ dwell among you richly.'

Day 74

Read 1 Thessalonians 2:17 – 4:8

Key verses: 1 Thessalonians 2:17–20

. . . .

17 But, brothers and sisters, when we were orphaned by being separated from you for a short time (in person, not in thought), out of our intense longing we made every effort to see you. 18 For we wanted to come to you – certainly I, Paul, did, again and again – but Satan blocked our way. 19 For what is our hope, our joy, or the crown in which we will glory in the presence of our Lord Jesus when he comes? Is it not you? 20 Indeed, you are our glory and joy.

How would you describe your relationship with the other people in your church, home group, those you serve alongside on the rota?

Paul describes his separation from the Thessalonians using a very strong image, of 'orphaned' children. He has already described his relationship with them as like that of a nurse-mother and a caring, directing, loving father. He also frequently addresses these believers as 'brothers and sisters'. In fact, he uses the term 'brothers' more frequently in his letters to the Thessalonians than when he writes to any other church. He is a mother to them, he is a father to them, he is a brother among brothers, and now he is a child bereaved of its parents. How greatly Paul loved these Thessalonian Christians!

This is no formal or pretend relationship. Paul describes himself being snatched away, bereaved, for a short time, 'in person, not in thought'. His heart is engaged in this relationship. He longs for them with an 'intense longing'. Indeed, he says in verse 19 that the prospect of the coming of the Lord Jesus itself would be less a matter of hope, joy and glory if Paul thought they were not going to be ready.

How deeply, how affectionately, how from the heart Paul loves these Thessalonians.

We talk about church being a family. And most of the time we rub along like a family, albeit a rather dysfunctional one! But one sharp word, a minor disagreement, and we quickly forget about our family ties in favour of factions and cliques. Pray for your own church, that there will be unity, love and understanding among you. Pray that you will play your part by avoiding gossip, forgiving, encouraging and, where necessary, building bridges and seeking peace. Look for an opportunity to show love and care to someone from your church today.

Day 75

Read 1 Thessalonians 2:17 – 4:8
Key verses: 1 Thessalonians 2:17–20

• •

¹⁷ But, brothers and sisters, when we were orphaned by being separated from you for a short time (in person, not in thought), out of our intense longing we made every effort to see you. ¹⁸ For we wanted to come to you – certainly I, Paul, did, again and again – but Satan blocked our way. ¹⁹ For what is our hope, our joy, or the crown in which we will glory in the presence of our Lord Jesus when he comes? Is it not you? ²⁰ Indeed, you are our glory and joy.

Are you giving Satan too much or too little credit for what's going on in your life?

Today we are looking again at verses 17–20 because we need to get Satan's power into perspective. Satan is mentioned by name only nine times in Paul's letters. Compare that with the hundreds of times that Paul refers to Jesus. In the Bible, Satan does not operate as a free agent, but only within the sovereign purposes of God. The story of Job, for example, reminds us that Satan can only operate within the permission, direction and limitation of God (see also Revelation 20).

Isaiah describes the way God runs history as like a horse (Isaiah 63:13–14) and its rider. The horse has the energy to jump a fence, but will not get over it unless the rider directs him to it. In this picture, Satan is the horse and on his back is the great divine rider, directing all that sinful power and energy to perform holy purposes. Satan always has the Lord on his back!

So we need to get Satan's power into proportion. There is a super-natural power raging against us. There is ceaseless malevolence, the god of this world, who prevented Paul reaching Thessalonica. But isn't it marvellous that Paul couldn't get back? As a result, he and his companions had a much better and richer experience. They learnt that, apostle or no apostle, ministry or no ministry, God was looking after his church.

We can begin to see why the Lord directed Satan to put up the roadblock: so that Paul could learn, so that the Thessalonians could learn, so that we could learn that our spiritual welfare rests in the hands of God.

As you reflect on the frustrations, sadness and suffering that have marked your life, do not be dismayed or despondent. Satan is not some wild horse riding roughshod over your life, going where he wants, doing what he chooses. Yes, imagine Satan as a horse, but with God as the divine rider, permitting, limiting and determining every step. To the untrained eye, it might look as if Satan is winning a victory. But, as Paul and countless others would testify, God will use even Satan's actions to accomplish his purpose in your life. Cling to God's sovereignty and his good purposes today.

Day 76

Read 1 Thessalonians 2:17 – 4:8
Key verses: 1 Thessalonians 3:1–5

....

¹So when we could stand it no longer, we thought it best to be left by ourselves in Athens. ²We sent Timothy, who is our brother and co-worker in God's service in spreading the gospel of Christ, to strengthen and encourage you in your faith, ³so that no one would be unsettled by these trials. For you know quite well that we are destined for them. ⁴In fact, when we were with you, we kept telling you that we would be persecuted. And it turned out that way, as you well know. ⁵For this reason, when I could stand it no longer, I sent to find out about your faith. I was afraid that in some way the tempter had tempted you and that our labours might have been in vain.

Have you ever asked God, 'Why?' 'Why am I suffering like this?' 'Why is the person I love suffering like this?'

The 'trials' (verse 3) that we face may be persecution; they may be the ordinary troubles and difficulties of life, but Paul knows that they often 'unsettle' believers. With troubles come doubt and a shaking of faith, and the pressure of Satan to lever us away from firm and believing attachment to the Lord Jesus Christ.

Paul has explained that suffering is what 'we are destined for', but we, like the Thessalonians, don't want to believe it. James says, 'Consider it pure joy, my brothers and sisters, whenever you face trials of many kinds' (James 1:2). But we don't listen to him; we don't consider it joy. Peter says, 'Do not be surprised at the fiery ordeal that has come on you to test you' (1 Peter 4:12). We don't believe him either; we think it very strange indeed. And we go on with our 'Why? Why?' and our doubting of the goodness of God.

But Paul says not to let Satan tempt us when trials come. Grasp today, and hold from today, the fact that this is not strange, but an inevitability. It is part of our discipleship, it is what we were 'destined' for (verse 3; see also Acts 14:22).

When Paul wrote to the Philippians, he said, 'You know my imprisonment, contrary to what you might have expected, is becoming a real testimony to the gospel, because they know that I am in prison for Christ – I am on duty for the gospel' (Philippians 1:12–13, paraphrased). It is the same word 'destined' here. Suffering is where we are on duty for God; it is the appointed sphere of our discipleship. It is what we were 'destined' for. So the real question should not be 'Why?', but 'What?' 'What should I do in this situation to grow in my discipleship, to demonstrate my devotion to Christ?'

When I was going through a particular trial, a friend wisely said to me, 'You will never pass this way again. Make sure there is something in it for him.'

Read Psalm 23. Why does God sometimes lead us by green pastures and quiet waters? Why is our portion sometimes the dark valley? What comes between the two in Psalm 23? 'He guides me along the right paths for his name's sake' (verse 3). What is the right path? It is a path that makes proper sense to God. We think the only proper path is the one that makes sense to us, and when suffering comes, we say, 'It doesn't make sense.' Yes, it does. It makes sense to him. That's all that matters. Trust in the sovereign hand of God today, and remember, 'You will never pass this way again. Make sure there is something in it for him.'

Day 77

Read 1 Thessalonians 2:17 – 4:8
Key verses: 1 Thessalonians 3:6–10

· ·

⁶But Timothy has just now come to us from you and has brought good news about your faith and love. He has told us that you always have pleasant memories of us and that you long to see us, just as we also long to see you. ⁷Therefore, brothers and sisters, in all our distress and persecution we were encouraged about you because of your faith. ⁸For now we really live, since you are standing firm in the Lord. ⁹How can we thank God enough for you in return for all the joy we have in the presence of our God because of you? ¹⁰Night and day we pray most earnestly that we may see you again and supply what is lacking in your faith.

What do you think a 'successful' Christian life looks like? How would you describe a 'victorious' Christian life?

If we imagine that Christian victory means never again being tempted by Satan, we will quickly become disillusioned. Likewise, if we imagine that being a Christian means experiencing heaven on earth, no more trials or suffering, we will be sorely disappointed.

Paul doesn't say to the Thessalonians, 'What a mighty victory you have scored in driving Satan out and drastically changing your circumstances in answer to prayer.' That is not the essence of earthly victory. And yet they have scored a triumph. Paul describes it as news that was just as good as the gospel, a fresh injection of life for which he didn't know how to thank God enough.

So what is their victory? It is Christian stability: 'now we really live, since you are standing firm in the Lord' (verse 8). And it is also Christian virtue, as shown in verse 6: 'Timothy . . . has brought good news about your faith and love.' Paul has already mentioned their faith, love and stability in 1:3. For him, Christian victory is not in the drama, but in faith, love and stickability in the ordinary realities of life.

Despite your prayers, your circumstances may not change, and you may still feel Satan prowling round you like a hungry lion. Don't be discouraged. God never promised us heaven on earth; trials and suffering are part of his plan. Pray for yourself and your loved ones who are going through difficult times, that you will stand firm in the Lord, demonstrating faith and love. Some days, holding on to God is all we can do, but it is all we need to do! God is not looking for dramatic displays of devotion, but faithfulness in the everyday ordinariness of life. Meditate today on Paul's outrageous criteria for victorious Christian living: 'We remember before our God and Father your work produced by faith, your labour prompted by love, and your endurance inspired by hope in our Lord Jesus Christ' (1 Thessalonians 1:3).

Day 78

Read 1 Thessalonians 2:17 – 4:8
Key verses: 1 Thessalonians 3:11–13

....

[11] Now may our God and Father himself and our Lord Jesus clear the way for us to come to you. [12] May the Lord make your love increase and overflow for each other and for everyone else, just as ours does for you. [13] May he strengthen your hearts so that you will be blameless and holy in the presence of our God and Father when our Lord Jesus comes with all his holy ones.

How would you describe your prayer life? Our prayers are often a good indicator of the state of our relationship with God and a mirror to our own soul. Can you see how Paul's focus shifted during the course of his prayer? Do you need to follow his example?

In verse 10, Paul prays, 'Night and day we pray most earnestly that we may see you again and supply what is lacking in your faith.' Paul felt that the Thessalonians' spiritual welfare was largely dependent on him being there to minister to them. He was anxious that, without his care and guidance, Satan would be gaining ground. But then Timothy reported back that the Thessalonians were getting on fine in Paul's absence.

Paul then returns to prayer with a completely different attitude, leaving it entirely to God whether he ever gets back to see them or not. He prays, 'Now may our God and Father himself and our Lord Jesus clear the way for us to come to you' (verse 11) – but whether he gets there or not, what does it matter? Paul realizes that God is looking after his people. It is the Lord who will cause their love for one another to increase and their hearts to be strengthened. The welfare of the church rests in the hands of a sovereign and loving God.

This realization shifts the focus of Paul's prayer, from verse 10 to verses 11–12. It is as if he is saying, 'If the Lord brings me back, great! But if he doesn't, he is there and he will make you perfect in holiness, and he will make your faith and your love go on increasing and out-reaching. You are all right. You are in the hands of God, and I'm happy to leave you there.'

It is easy to develop a messiah complex, assuming that events or circumstances depend solely on our organization and active participation. But the lesson Paul learnt is one we need to grasp – God is in control, not us! It is not up to us to orchestrate our children's lives, our parents' lives or our spouse's life. Entrusting our loved ones into God's hands shouldn't be a last resort, but a first port of call. Name the loved ones who are on your mind. Picture them in the hands of God. Pray Psalm 121 for them.

> I lift up my eyes to the mountains –
>   where does my help come from?
> My help comes from the LORD,
>   the Maker of heaven and earth.
>
> He will not let your foot slip –
>   he who watches over you will not slumber;
> indeed, he who watches over Israel
>   will neither slumber nor sleep.
>
> The LORD watches over you –
>   the LORD is your shade at your right hand;
> the sun will not harm you by day,
>   nor the moon by night.
>
> The LORD will keep you from all harm –
>   he will watch over your life;
> the LORD will watch over your coming and going
>   both now and for evermore.

Day 79

Read 1 Thessalonians 2:17 – 4:8
Key verses: 1 Thessalonians 4:1–8

....

¹As for other matters, brothers and sisters, we instructed you how to live in order to please God, as in fact you are living. Now we ask you and urge you in the Lord Jesus to do this more and more. ²For you know what instructions we gave you by the authority of the Lord Jesus.

³It is God's will that you should be sanctified: that you should avoid sexual immorality; ⁴that each of you should learn to control your own body in a way that is holy and honourable, ⁵not in passionate lust like the pagans, who do not know God; ⁶and that in this matter no one should wrong or take advantage of a brother or sister. The Lord will punish all those who commit such sins, as we told you and warned you before. ⁷For God did not call us to be impure, but to live a holy life. ⁸Therefore, anyone who rejects this instruction does not reject a human being but God, the very God who gives you his Holy Spirit.

Are you growing in holiness? Just as physical growth signals health, so does spiritual growth.

Paul is urging the Thessalonians to press on in the matter of holiness. And his plea is as follows:

- *Keep obeying God.* Paul had given the Thessalonians instructions and they were to keep on obeying these commands from God. Obedience to God is how we pursue holiness.

- *Keep knowing God.* The Thessalonians were clearly struggling with sexual morality. Paul's answer to their temptation was to 'know God'. If we are plagued with lapses into sexual sin, then the key is to be an informed believer, continually striving to get to know God better.

- *Keep fearing God.* God will punish those who sin; he is the avenger. A healthy fear of God keeps us on the track of holiness.

- *Keep trusting God.* Verse 7 reminds us that God called us not to an impure life, but to holiness. Holiness is not an external objective, rather the reality to which we have been brought. God has called us into the context of holiness, and we have got to learn to become what we are. So we say to God, 'I am desperately unholy in all my inclinations; I desperately want to be holy. I believe that you have given me all that I need to be holy, therefore it is worth all the striving and struggling.'

- *Keep relying on the Holy Spirit.* God's Spirit within us is called the Holy Spirit because it is his task to administer holiness to us, as we walk with God. God forever keeps on giving us his Spirit, and we live a holy life when we enjoy, respect and draw upon that Spirit.

How would you rate your growth in holiness? Have you grown in holiness in the past week, past month or year? Think through Paul's recipe for holiness:

- Is there a particular area of your life where God is asking you to obey him?
- What measures are you taking to know God better? What are your devotional times like? How is your prayer life?
- Do you have an appropriate fear of God? Does fear of disobeying God keep you faithful?
- Is there something you need to trust God for?
- Are you relying on the Holy Spirit or are you trying to please God in your own strength?

You started the journey of faith well, so don't give up now. Keep pressing on! God has given you all the means to grow in holiness, so ask for his strength and help today.

Day 80

Read 1 Thessalonians 4:9–18
Key verses: 1 Thessalonians 4:9–10

∙∙

⁹ *Now about your love for one another we do not need to write to you, for you yourselves have been taught by God to love each other.* ¹⁰ *And in fact, you do love all of God's family throughout Macedonia. Yet we urge you, brothers and sisters, to do so more and more.*

Is your church worth joining? Have you created an atmosphere of Christian love which attracts outsiders as you share the gospel with them?

Paul believes that it is only from a strong base of love that the church can reach out to the world. He knows that the Thessalonians already love one another, but he urges them to do so more and more because brotherly love is such a foundational principle for the church.

He explains that they have been 'taught by God to love each other'. When the Thessalonians became Christians, God shared his mind with them, so Christian intuition began to govern their relation-ships. But more than that, Paul taught them from Scripture about loving one another. Our intuition to love must be confirmed, strengthened, directed and controlled by the teaching of the Word of God.

Love within the church is not a requirement that can be set to the side; it is for now. It is not a requirement that can be exhausted. It is something that must always be on the increase, an immediate and endless obligation for the people of God.

We are never too old, too far along in the faith or too busy to be reminded about the need for love. If there is no love in the church, then we have nothing to offer the world. It is costly to love – it takes time and energy, and it interferes with our personal plans – but it is non-negotiable. Meditate on Jesus' words in John 13:34–35.

> A new command I give you: love one another. As I have loved you, so you must love one another. By this everyone will know that you are my disciples, if you love one another.

Consider Christ's love for you. How does that define the type of love you should have for others in your church? What difference will loving like this make?

Day 81

Read 1 Thessalonians 4:9–18
Key verses: 1 Thessalonians 4:11–12

• •

[11]Make it your ambition to lead a quiet life: you should mind your own business and work with your hands, just as we told you, [12]so that your daily life may win the respect of outsiders and so that you will not be dependent on anybody.

Think about your own church and the occasions when there has been strife or division.

Paul suggests that brotherly love breaks down because of frenzied activity, undue interference in people's lives and trading on the goodwill of others. So he urges the Thessalonians to safeguard their love by the following:

• *Lead a quiet life.* Paul is talking about tranquillity of temperament rather than circumstances. Be a tranquil person; be amenable.

• *Mind your own business.* Look after your own needs.

• *Work with your hands.* Earn your own living.

If you live like this, first, it will impact your evangelism. The world will notice and respect a church where these qualities exist. Second, you will not 'be dependent on anybody' and 'you will not have any need'. This seems a strange phrase, but the background is Acts 2 – 4, when no-one had any needs because no-one considered their possessions their own, and distribution was made to anyone who had need.

So, if we are tranquil in temperament, if we mind our own business and earn our own living, the world will sit up and take notice, and we will be in a position to cultivate and cherish and support a loving fellowship.

What is your ambition? What is the passion or driving force in your life? Not many of us would say our primary ambition was to love our church family! But accept Paul's challenge. Make it your goal this week to love the people in your church. This may mean working on your temperament, not being nosy and interfering unnecessarily in people's lives, or working hard to support yourself rather than expecting others to bail you out.

With Paul's words in front of you, ask yourself, 'Am I increasing the love quota in my church or am I a drain? Is my behaviour likely to attract people to church or put them off?' Invite the Holy Spirit to convict, challenge and encourage you. Allow him to search your heart and reshape your ambitions.

Day 82

Read 1 Thessalonians 4:13–18
Key verses: 1 Thessalonians 4:13–14

. . . .

¹³Brothers and sisters, we do not want you to be uninformed about those who sleep in death, so that you do not grieve like the rest of mankind, who have no hope. ¹⁴For we believe that Jesus died and rose again, and so we believe that God will bring with Jesus those who have fallen asleep in him.

Death is one of the few certainties of life.

Paul, full of pastoral concern, wants the Thessalonians to be well informed. They are anxious that fellow believers who have died would miss the second coming. So Paul allays their fears and reminds them, and us, that we can face the sorrows of life and look forward to the glories of heaven because we know that:

- *Death has been transformed.* For us, death is the impenetrable and irreversible reality, but for Jesus it is the sleep from which he will shake us awake, just like he did with Jairus' daughter in Mark 5.

- *Grief has been transformed.* How is our grief different from that of those who do not know Christ? Surprisingly, perhaps, our grief is sharper. We feel grief more keenly because our emotions have been sharpened by the regenerating work of the Holy Spirit. Our grief is also different because it is in the context of eternal hope; while we grieve, we also have the glorious expectation of a joyful reunion.

- *Hope has been transformed.* The Christian hope is sure and certain because it is based on Jesus' finished work. When he died and rose again, we were associated with that death and resurrection, so that we both died and rose with him. So we have the sure hope that after our death there will be resurrection and transformation.

As Christians, we are not immune from sorrow. We will face the death of loved ones just like our non-Christian neighbours. And, like Jesus weeping at Lazarus' tomb, we will feel that grief keenly. But Jesus' death and resurrection mean that, more than anything else, our mourning is transformed. We grieve only for a short time, knowing that one day soon those who are asleep in Christ will rise to meet him in the air. If you are mourning today, allow these truths to penetrate your grief. If you are supporting those who grieve, encourage them with these words. With gentleness, lift their eyes to the horizon to watch expectantly for the imminent return of Christ – our sure and certain hope. Paul says:

> Listen, I tell you a mystery: we will not all sleep, but we will all be changed – in a flash, in the twinkling of an eye, at the last trumpet. For the trumpet will sound, the dead will be raised imperishable, and we will be changed.
> (1 Corinthians 15:51–52)

Day 83

Read 1 Thessalonians 4:13–18
Key verses: 1 Thessalonians 4:13–14

··

¹³Brothers and sisters, we do not want you to be uninformed about those who sleep in death, so that you do not grieve like the rest of mankind, who have no hope. ¹⁴For we believe that Jesus died and rose again, and so we believe that God will bring with Jesus those who have fallen asleep in him.

Woody Allen famously said, 'I'm not afraid of death; I just don't want to be there when it happens.'

While we may not fear death, many of us fear the process of dying. We are anxious about the pain, the loss of control and the dependence on others. But Paul's words speak comfort to our hearts.

Verse 14 literally refers to those who have fallen asleep not 'in' but 'through' Jesus. This means that our death is stage-managed by him, that the circumstances of our dying have been organized by his sovereign hand, and that the timing of our death has been decided in heaven. It is all through Jesus. Through him we go to be with him. And, going to be with him, we have a guarantee that those who have died before he comes will nonetheless share in his coming, because God will bring with him those who sleep through Jesus. If that should be his portion for us, we will not miss out on any of the glory of the second coming. We might even have a better view of it! We will come with him, having been with him.

Take comfort and strength from the promise that God is sovereign and that even your death will be stage-managed by him. In the meantime, learn submission, patience and dependence on God. Then, when the final act comes, you will be ready to play your part with humility and obedience.

Meditate on Dietrich Bonhoeffer's words:

> Death is only dreadful for those who live in dread and fear of it. Death is not wild and terrible, if only we can be still and hold fast to God's Word. Death is not bitter, if we have not become bitter ourselves. Death is grace, the greatest gift of grace that God gives to people who believe in him. Death is mild, death is sweet and gentle; it beckons to us with heavenly power, if only we realize that it is the gateway to our homeland, the tabernacle of joy, the ever-lasting kingdom of peace.
>
> How do we know that dying is so dreadful? Who knows whether, in our human fear and anguish, we are only shivering and shuddering at the most glorious, heavenly, blessed event in the world? Death is hell and night and cold, if it is not transformed by our faith. But that is just what is so marvelous, that we can transform death.
> (Eric Metaxas, *Bonhoeffer: Pastor, Martyr, Prophet, Spy*, Thomas Nelson, 2011, p. 531)

Day 84

Read 1 Thessalonians 4:13–18

Key verse: 1 Thessalonians 4:16

. . . .

16 For the Lord himself will come down from heaven, with a loud command, with the voice of the archangel and with the trumpet call of God, and the dead in Christ will rise first.

Have you ever wondered what the return of Christ will be like?

We do not know many details, but one is guaranteed: his second coming will be very different from his first. Christ's return will be heralded with a loud command, presumably from God the Father, for who else knows when Christ is going to return and who else has the authority to give this command? The archangel Michael, the leader of the angel armies, will announce Christ's victory (see Jude 9; Daniel 10:13, 21; 12:1; Revelation 12:7). And then the trumpet will sound. Why will there be a trumpet?

- It is the trumpet of Exodus 19:16, which signals 'God is here'.

- It is the trumpet of Joel 2:1, which signals that the great and awesome day of the Lord has at last come.

- It is the trumpet of jubilee in Leviticus 25:9, announcing the release of slaves and the remission of debts.

- It is the trumpet of Isaiah 27:12–13, which sounds so that the people of God scattered in Egypt and Assyria may be brought home to Zion.

- It is the trumpet of Matthew 24:31, where the angels of God gather the elect from the four corners of the earth.

The trumpet of God will gather his elect from past, present and future, and from north, south, east and west.

Are you looking forward to that day?

I remember as a child wanting Christ to return, but hoping that he would wait until after Christmas! Even as adults we can get so caught up in the good things of life – family, friendships, cele- brations, work, holidays – that Jesus' return is not a top priority. We talk about it, but we don't yearn for it.

Close your eyes and imagine the scene: Jesus Christ himself coming down to walk on earth, the skies shuddering as God the Father gives the command and the archangel announces his victory. The trumpet blasts, gathering all the family of God to their heavenly home. The glory and majesty of Christ will be unmistakable – every eye will see it.

Pray that as you go through today, Christ's return will shape your behaviour, attitudes and thoughts: 'You ought to live holy and godly lives as you look forward to the day of God and speed its coming' (2 Peter 3:11–12).

Day 85

Read 1 Thessalonians 4:13–18
Key verses: 1 Thessalonians 4:16–17

. . . .

> ¹⁶*For the Lord himself will come down from heaven, with a loud command, with the voice of the archangel and with the trumpet call of God, and the dead in Christ will rise first.* ¹⁷*After that, we who are still alive and are left will be caught up together with them in the clouds to meet the Lord in the air. And so we will be with the Lord for ever.*

What will happen to us at the second coming?

Paul explains that the bodies of those who have died will be raised to meet their souls, which once left them, and there will be a mighty reconstitution of a totally redeemed humanity. But what about us who remain? Paul says, 'We who are still alive and are left will be caught up together with them in the clouds to meet the Lord in the air.'

There is obviously symbolism here. In the Bible, clouds are the presence of God. After the exodus, God lived among the people in a cloudy, fiery pillar. The cloud said, 'God is here.' When Jesus, Peter, James and John stood on the Mount of Transfiguration, the cloud overshadowed them, and out of the cloud came the voice that said, 'This is my Son: God is here' (see Matthew 17:5). And we will be caught up in the clouds, into the very presence of God. The air is the usurped dominion of Satan, the prince of the power of the air (Ephesians 2:2). But we will enter into his usurped dominion because he will be gone for ever. Only Jesus reigns.

The symbolism is important – with Jesus we will be caught into the presence of God; we will enter into his eternal triumph. But there is also objectivity and reality: we will be caught up. The phrase literally means 'we will be snatched' from the earth. And if we are alive on that day, we will be lifted bodily into heaven and stand before Jesus in the fullness of redemption. We will meet him in the clouds in the air.

Therefore encourage one another with these words.
(1 Thessalonians 4:18)

Paul writes these verses not to satisfy our curiosity or to give us a timeline for future events. These verses are to spur us on, to encourage us in the faith. So tell yourself these words; speak them to your own heart.

If you are:

- struggling with health or family issues;
- facing unemployment;
- battling mental illness;
- grieving;
- celebrating success at work or in your family;
- living with financial hardship or poverty;
- caught up in the mundane routines of life.

Remember: 'We . . . will be caught up . . . in the clouds to meet the Lord in the air. And so we will be with the Lord for ever.'

Today, in your conversations with other believers, 'encourage [them] with these words'.

Day 86

Read 1 Thessalonians 5:1–11

Key verses: 1 Thessalonians 5:1–5

• •

> [1]*Now, brothers and sisters, about times and dates we do not need to write to you* [2]*for you know very well that the day of the Lord will come like a thief in the night.* [3]*While people are saying, 'Peace and safety', destruction will come on them suddenly, as labour pains on a pregnant woman, and they will not escape.*
>
> [4]*But you, brothers and sisters, are not in darkness so that this day should surprise you like a thief.* [5]*You are all children of the light and children of the day. We do not belong to the night or to the darkness.*

Many people mock the idea of God's judgment. They don't believe it will ever come; they think that God is too nice to mete out judgment, or that they are too good to deserve it.

For those who complacently believe that life will always go on as it has done, and that their past will never catch up with them, Christ's return spells disaster. Paul makes it clear that although we cannot put a date on Christ's return, like a thief it will come unexpectedly and, like labour pains, it will be inescapable.

However, believers do not need to fear Christ's return because:

• *We are not in darkness*. Darkness means ignorance, estrangement from God (Ephesians 4:18). We no longer live in darkness; we live in a new setting, a new environment. As Paul reminds us in Colossians 1:12–13, '[Give] joyful thanks to the Father, who has qualified you to share in the inheritance of his holy people in the kingdom of light. For he has rescued us from the dominion of darkness and brought us into the kingdom of the Son he loves.'

- *We are children of the light, children of the day.* As well as a new setting, we have been given a new nature, one with new powers of behaviour built in, but also the characteristic lifestyle that goes with daytime.

- *We are not of the night.* We owe it nothing; it cannot command our loyalty. We have been brought into a new setting, we have been given a new nature, and we have been called to a new commitment. We live already, in our essential Christian nature, in that day into which he will usher us at his second coming. The day is coming; but, in reality, that day has dawned because already we are living in the light, with a new nature, new powers of behaviour and a new allegiance to the Lord Jesus Christ. And when the day comes, all that we have now as potential, and all that we enjoy in part, will come into full bloom.

When we were young and going out anywhere, my dad would remind my brother, sister and me to behave well by saying, 'Now remember who you are and to whom you belong.' Today, remember who you are: you are a child of God, a son or daughter of the King of kings. You have a new nature; you have been brought into God's kingdom; you owe no loyalty to Satan. One day, who you are and to whom you belong will be obvious for everyone to see; your royal status will be unmistakable. In the meantime, live up to your high calling. In the Holy Spirit's power, live as a child of God and don't allow Satan a foothold in your life. You belong to a new kingdom, with a new nature, new values and a new purpose. Today, 'remember who you are and to whom you belong'.

Day 87

Read 1 Thessalonians 5:1–11

Key verses: 1 Thessalonians 5:6–11

· ·

> [6] *So then, let us not be like others, who are asleep, but let us be awake and sober.* [7] *For those who sleep, sleep at night, and those who get drunk, get drunk at night.* [8] *But since we belong to the day, let us be sober, putting on faith and love as a breastplate, and the hope of salvation as a helmet.* [9] *For God did not appoint us to suffer wrath but to receive salvation through our Lord Jesus Christ.* [10] *He died for us so that, whether we are awake or asleep, we may live together with him.* [11] *Therefore encourage one another and build each other up, just as in fact you are doing.*

What if, on the day Jesus returns, you are having a bad day, spiritually speaking? On Sunday, of course, you were full of enthusiasm, but on the day he returns you are having a spiritual day off. What will happen to you?

Of course, Paul urges us, who belong to the day, to live like people of the light – to be clear-headed and spiritually alert. He says we shouldn't be sleeping. Here, 'sleep' is not a reference to a believer's death (as in 1 Thessalonians 4:13), but to natural sleep and moral laxity (see Mark 13:36). We are no longer in darkness by circumstances or nature. We have a new position, a new loyalty – and now a new responsibility, to moral alertness.

This doesn't mean we must make dramatic preparations for Christ's return, but we do have to put our armour on! We are to put on faith and love as a breastplate and the hope of salvation as a helmet. This is the third time in this letter that Paul urges us to be people of faith, hope and love. This armour is the characteristic hallmark of believers.

It is what equips us to go on trusting God, come what may, and living in the obedience of faith.

We know all this. But what happens if we are having an 'off' day when Christ returns?

The good news is that our great confidence in relation to Jesus' return is not connected with anything that we do or are, but with what God in Christ has done for us. We have been appointed eternally for the personal and full possession of salvation, through Jesus' death. His death covers all our sins, including the sins of laxness that make us unfit for his return.

Stop seeing your quiet times, prayer life or church service as bargaining chips to get into God's good books. When Christ returns, you will be able to stand in his presence not because of your good deeds or spiritual exercises, but because of the robes of righteousness given to you by God.

Inevitably there will be spiritual 'off' days when you are not as alert or focused on God as you should be. But don't let these days knock you off course. Remember that you 'belong to the day', you are 'in Christ', and your relationship with God is eternally secure. There is nothing you can do to make God love you any more and nothing you can do to make him love you any less.

So don't wait to give God grand displays of devotion, but seek to obey him in the regular routines of life. Today, put your armour on and keep pressing on in faith, love and hope.

Day 88

Read 1 Thessalonians 5:12–22
Key verses: 1 Thessalonians 5:12–13

••

¹²Now we ask you, brothers and sisters, to acknowledge those who work hard among you, who care for you in the Lord and who admonish you. ¹³Hold them in the highest regard in love because of their work. Live in peace with each other.

Have misunderstandings and arguments with leaders ever caused dissension in your church? If you are a leader, have you ever been hurt by the words or actions of church members?

Interestingly, when Paul talks about living for the day of the Lord, and describes what living in faith, hope and love means in practice, the first item on his agenda is church leadership.

There is no such thing in the New Testament as a church without leaders, or a church with only one leader. We don't know many details about their role, except that there was a distinct emphasis on teaching and ministering the Word.

In this section, Paul gives us three commands: to acknowledge the leaders who work among us; to esteem them highly because of their work (not because of personal attachment); and to respond to their leadership by creating a peaceful community.

Paul is adamant that brotherly love in the church doesn't do away with leadership, and that having leaders should not create dissent. They are to work hard, to offer Christlike leadership and to 'admonish you'. The word 'admonish' conveys the idea of tender loving care with a little bit of grit – rebuke where necessary, offering direction when necessary, but doing so with tender loving care. That is leadership.

Authority is rarely respected these days. So perhaps it seems strange that the first evidence of our pressing on in faith, hope and love is how we treat our leaders. How well are you doing in this area?

- Do you bristle at the first sign of admonition?
- Are you anxious to make your leaders' lives easier by living in peace?
- In what practical ways do you esteem them?
- Do you support them because of personal attachment or because of the work they do?

If you are a leader, consider the following:

- Are you working hard for the good of the church?
- Are you prepared to admonish others, even when it makes you unpopular?
- Is there sufficient evidence of Christlike servant leadership?

Whether you are a leader or a church member, pray through what it means for you to 'Live in peace with each other'.

Day 89

Read 1 Thessalonians 5:12–22
Key verses: 1 Thessalonians 5:14–18

· ·

> [14] *And we urge you, brothers and sisters, warn those who are idle and disruptive, encourage the disheartened, help the weak, be patient with everyone.* [15] *Make sure that nobody pays back wrong for wrong, but always strive to do what is good for each other and for everyone else.*
>
> [16] *Rejoice always,* [17] *pray continually,* [18] *give thanks in all circumstances; for this is God's will for you in Christ Jesus.*

Mark Twain is credited with saying, 'It is not the things I don't understand in the Bible which trouble me, it is the things I do understand.'

These nine commands are quite troubling. There is no mistaking that they are non-negotiable – Paul starts the section by writing 'we urge you', and ends with 'this is God's will for you in Christ Jesus'. Also, there are seven references to an unqualified obligation: we are to be like this to everybody, all the time.

What are these traits that should mark our lives? Paul gives three groups of commands:

• *Minister to each other.* We are to warn those who do not contribute to the fellowship or who are disruptive. The word 'warn' is the same word used in 1 Thessalonians 5:12: tender loving care with a pinch of grit. While the leaders demonstrate this, they are not separate from the congregation, but rather they are an example of what a Christian is to be like. So it is not left only to the leaders to show tender loving care, but also to those who are alongside them. Where necessary, this will mean rebuke and redirection. We are also to encourage the disheartened – those who are depressed and don't have the energy to deal with life – and to help the weak.

- *Live out a Christlike character*. We have to be patient. If the word 'long-tempered' existed, it would fit perfectly here. We are not to retaliate. We are to be people of unparalleled goodness, always pursuing what is good for others.

- *Hold on to God in all circumstances*. Circumstances are often such that it is impossible to rejoice or give thanks. Notice that Paul doesn't say 'give thanks for everything', but 'give thanks in all circumstances'. No matter what the circumstances are, or what we are suffering, Jesus hasn't changed. Salvation, the Scriptures, heaven and the second coming haven't changed. This is a command, calling us to live spiritually: to live consciously in the light of spiritual truth, to fill our minds constantly with the work of salvation, to renew ourselves in the presence of the Holy Spirit, to rejoice in the Holy Scriptures, to thank God for Christian fellowship, to attend Communion, to look forward constantly to Jesus. When the going is rough, this is the last thing we feel like doing, but it is a great discipline.

And notice that right at the heart of this command to live spiritually is 'pray continually'. That is to say, face the whole of life – its infinite variety, all its seemingly impossible demands, our needs and necessities – in the place of prayer. Because when we are not able, God is supremely able.

Today, will you hold on to God and give him thanks? As you minister to and with people in your church, as you have opportunities to practise patience and goodness, as you deal with all sorts of trials and suffering, will you determine to give thanks to God? If it helps, take time to write down everything for which you are thankful. There may be little about your circumstances that is praiseworthy, but give God thanks for Jesus, your salvation, the Word of God in your hands and the promises it contains. Today, try to deliberately pause once every hour to give God thanks. Be intentional about looking for reasons to be grateful and praise God.

Day 90

Read 1 Thessalonians 5:12–22
Key verses: 1 Thessalonians 5:19–22

· ·

[19]Do not quench the Spirit. [20]Do not treat prophecies with contempt [21]but test them all; hold on to what is good, [22]reject every kind of evil.

When we read verses like 1 Thessalonians 5:14–18, which command us to 'give thanks in all circumstances', it is tempting to roll our eyes and mutter, 'Yes, but Paul didn't know what I have to deal with!'

But think about Paul's circumstances. He wasn't living in an ivory tower, wrapped in cotton wool. He had just been flogged in Philippi. He had the marks on his body. If we find it a tall order to minister to others, live out a Christlike character and hold on to God in all circumstances, doubtless Paul did too. So who is on our side and what do we have going for us? Paul reminds us that we have:

• *The Holy Spirit.* The Holy Spirit here is pictured as fire (see also Matthew 3:11–12; Acts 2:1–4). His job is to create for God a clean, pure and holy people. The Holy Spirit is the fire that creates that holiness.

• *The Bible.* In Paul's day, the churches only had the Old Testament, but even that wasn't in everyone's hands. So God used prophecy to bring the Word of God to the people of God. Mostly this was words of declaration, but sometimes it was prediction. For us, the Word of God is complete, so in a fundamental sense we don't need prophecy. But even if someone were to say, 'I have a word of God for you,' we would still test it by Scripture. We are to be Bible people, listening intently and applying God's Word to our lives.

- *Our moral commitment.* Whether a word of prophecy comes to you in church, a thought occurs to you in your quiet time, or you are wondering whether a certain course of action is right – whatever has to do with living the life of Christ on earth – test it. Be a discerning believer, exercise your God-given faculty of criticism, bring it back to the touchstone of Scripture, pray about it, ask the Holy Spirit to illuminate you about it. And once you have come to a conclusion as to what is right and what is wrong, then go for it!

Reread God's commands in verses 14–18, slowly and deliberately. Which ones do you struggle with most? Stop trying to be obedient in your own strength – that is doomed to failure! Today, ask the Holy Spirit to refine, purify and create holiness in you. Spend time reading the Scriptures and applying them to your own life. Be intentional as you go through the day, and test everything: your choices, your actions, your thoughts. Pray about them and see if they align with Scripture.

God did not intend you to go on this journey of faith alone. He has given these means of grace to equip you to move forward with conviction. Meditate on his promise: 'His divine power has given us everything we need for a godly life through our knowledge of him who called us by his own glory and goodness' (2 Peter 1:3).

Day 91

Read 1 Thessalonians 5:12–28
Key verses: 1 Thessalonians 5:23–28

··

²³ May God himself, the God of peace, sanctify you through and through. May your whole spirit, soul and body be kept blameless at the coming of our Lord Jesus Christ. ²⁴ The one who calls you is faithful, and he will do it.

²⁵ Brothers and sisters, pray for us. ²⁶ Greet all God's people with a holy kiss. ²⁷ I charge you before the Lord to have this letter read to all the brothers and sisters.

²⁸ The grace of our Lord Jesus Christ be with you.

Paul never ends his letters, 'with warm good wishes'. Even his signing-off packs a punch!

He reminds the Thessalonians to be:

• a praying church – 'Brothers and sisters, pray for us';

• a loving church – 'Greet all God's people with a holy kiss';

• a Bible-loving church – 'Have this letter read';

• a church founded, kept and nourished in grace – 'The grace of our Lord Jesus Christ be with you.'

How could the Thessalonians, how can we, live up to such exacting standards? Paul reminds us, above all, that we have God himself on our side. Often we feel that the task is beyond us, that we will never be ready for Jesus when he returns. But the Bible promises that God will sanctify you. He will preserve you, in an all-embracing, completed holiness that touches every part of your being and covers all that you are. This is what 'sanctify' and 'keep' mean here: he will preserve you in relation to himself – your spirit; he will preserve you in your personality – your soul; he will preserve you in holy living in your body. Our faithful and all-sufficient God will sanctify and keep you ready for Christ's return.

Even today, God will fulfil his promise to sanctify and keep you. His methods are unorthodox. He uses suffering and trials, devoted church service, the encouragement and example of other believers, and all the various strands of our lives to sanctify us.

Paul reminds us, 'He who began a good work in you will go on putting the finishing touches to it until the day of Christ' (Philippians 1:6, paraphrased). Be conscious as you go through your day that God is using circumstances, pain, conversations and choices to sanctify you. Keep your eyes open and look out for these finishing touches. Don't resist his work. Instead, see any challenges to your comfort and priorities, any trials, any admonition from church friends, as getting you ready, so that there will be no single blemish to spoil Jesus' return.

Join Paul, the Thessalonians and countless other believers today as you speed the return of Christ.

For further study

If you would like to do further study on 1 Thessalonians, the commentaries listed here may be useful:

- James H. Grant Jr and R. Kent Hughes, *1–2 Thessalonians: The Hope of Salvation*, Preaching the Word (Crossway, 2015).

- Gene L. Green, *The Letters to the Thessalonians*, The Pillar New Testament Commentary (IVP, 2009).

- Richard Mayhue, *1 & 2 Thessalonians: Triumphs and Trials of a Consecrated Church*, Focus on the Bible (Christian Focus, 1999).

- Leon Morris, *1 and 2 Thessalonians*, Tyndale New Testament Commentaries (IVP, 2009).

- John Stott, *The Message of Thessalonians: Preparing for the Coming King*, The Bible Speaks Today (IVP, 1991).

If God has fed you through your study of the book of 1 Thessalonians, why not buy the individual Food for the Journey on 1 Thessalonians and give it to a friend (available from ivpbooks.com)?

Day 92

Read Psalm 51
Key verses Psalm 51:1–3

· ·

For the director of music. A psalm of David. When the prophet Nathan came to him after David had committed adultery with Bathsheba.
¹ Have mercy on me, O God,
    according to your unfailing love;
according to your great compassion
    blot out my transgressions.
² Wash away all my iniquity
    and cleanse me from my sin.
³ For I know my transgressions,
    and my sin is always before me.

What ground have we covered so far on our journey? Our first three studies, on Numbers, Hebrews and 1 Thessalonians, all call us to live today in the light of the future. Numbers calls us to keep obeying God as we look forward to our inheritance in the Promised Land. Hebrews highlights the supremacy of Jesus and urges us to keep trusting him so we can enter the heavenly rest (Hebrews 4:9). And Paul reminds the Thessalonians – and us – to be confident of the gospel and to keep living it out until Christ returns (see 1 Thessalonians 5:23).

Our next three studies, on Ezekiel, John 14 – 17 and Romans 5 – 8, also have a certain unity. They face full on the dreadful nature of sin and its fearful consequences. The only way forward is through God's saving activity – ultimately in Jesus Christ, his life, death, resurrection and in the powerful ministry of the Spirit.

That brings us to Psalm 51. No psalm prepares us better for the themes that are coming. Although it speaks of one particular situation – of

David's response to the prophet Nathan when Nathan confronted him about his adultery and murder (see 2 Samuel 11 – 12), as a psalm in Israel's songbook it gives words for everyone to use.

Look at the words David uses for sin: 'transgressions', 'iniquity', 'sin'. 'Transgressions' speaks of breaking away from God; 'iniquity' denotes a distortion, something not agreeing with God's will; 'sin' indicates a failure or a miss. Note how there is no hiding from sin or blaming it on anyone else. There may be extenuating circumstances, but ultimately no-one else is responsible. God is completely right in his verdict (verse 4). And this has been our life story from the very beginning (verse 5).

Look what God needs to show: 'unfailing love', 'great compassion'. Look at what God needs to do: 'have mercy', 'blot out', 'wash away', 'cleanse'.

And David knows God also needs to 'renew a steadfast spirit within me' (verse 10; see also Ezekiel 36:26). God's life-giving breath is utterly vital for God-shaped living.

Come to the Lord with hands and heart open in prayer, and say or sing:

> Nothing in my hands I bring,
> Simply to the cross I cling;
> Naked, come to Thee for dress;
> Helpless look to Thee for grace;
> Foul, I to the fountain fly;
> Wash me, Saviour, or I die.
> (Rock of Ages, Augustus Toplady, 1776)

Thank him for his cleansing and forgiveness through Jesus Christ's death on the cross. Thank God for the gift of his Spirit to empower us to live for him.

Introduction
Ezekiel

Liam Goligher

A better vision

What has been your most memorable birthday?

Ezekiel ben Buzi will certainly never forget his thirtieth birthday.

He has been trained as a priest and brought up to believe that when he turns thirty his life's work would begin. He has spent years anticipating this moment when he would be ordained and eligible to serve in the temple. So you will forgive Ezekiel if he wakes up feeling discouraged on his birthday.

Instead of being in Jerusalem, he is a captive in Babylon. In 605 BC, King Nebuchadnezzar subdued Judah and took some hostages back to Babylon, including Daniel and his three friends. A few years later, Judah's King Jehoiakim rebelled. Nebuchadnezzar subdued Jerusalem and, along with the temple treasure, took some of the nobles, royal family and priests back with him to Babylon. Among the group was this trainee priest. The day Ezekiel turns thirty, he is five years into his captivity in Babylon.

To say that life hasn't turned out as Ezekiel was anticipating is probably an understatement. Instead of to the priesthood, God calls him to be a prophet. Instead of living in the holy city of Jerusalem, he is an exile in Babylon. Instead of serving in the temple, he is surrounded by a plethora of pagan gods.

But, on his thirtieth birthday, God gives Ezekiel a vision for the exiles.

Many of these displaced Jews are having a crisis of faith. Where is God in this horrifying situation? Has he been defeated by the Babylonian gods? If he is still in control, why doesn't he intervene? Ezekiel's timely vision confronts the Jews with the severity of their sinfulness and the necessity of divine judgment. It is hard to hear the news that they will not be going home any time soon. But Ezekiel's words offer comfort and hope, reminding them of God's sovereignty and the promise of future restoration.

Perhaps, like Ezekiel's, your life has not turned out as you had anticipated or hoped. Perhaps some tragedy has left you asking questions similar to those the Jews are asking: 'Where is God?' 'Why doesn't he intervene?' 'Does he really care?'

The book of Ezekiel spans forty-eight chapters. We only have space for an introductory look at selected passages. Together, they trace the main contours of Ezekiel's message. Realizing that we are as sinful and disobedient as the dislocated Israelites will not be easy reading. However, Ezekiel's vision also amazes us with God – his sovereignty and Holy Spirit power. The prophet's message encourages us to take heart and to keep striving for holiness, even through difficult days, because the reality God has in store for us is greater than even Ezekiel imagines. Ezekiel points us forward – not just to the restoration of temple, land and people – but to a far greater salvation: the final perfect temple and a holy city. He points us to Christ who opens up heaven for us.

Day 93

Read Ezekiel 1:1–28
Key verses: Ezekiel 1:25–28

· ·

25 Then there came a voice from above the vault over their heads as they stood with lowered wings. 26 Above the vault over their heads was what looked like a throne of lapis lazuli, and high above on the throne was a figure like that of a man. 27 I saw that from what appeared to be his waist up he looked like glowing metal, as if full of fire, and that from there down he looked like fire; and brilliant light surrounded him. 28 Like the appearance of a rainbow in the clouds on a rainy day, so was the radiance around him.

This was the appearance of the likeness of the glory of the LORD. *When I saw it, I fell face down, and I heard the voice of one speaking.*

Have you ever been speechless?

When Ezekiel has a vision of the glory of God – the visible manifestation of God's presence – he is lost for words.

He repeats phrases like 'what looked like' and 'the appearance of', straining at imagery to convey the splendour of God.

First, he sees the Lord, the divine warrior, riding in a storm, surrounded by fire and lightning (verse 4). Storms and lightning are often associated with theophanies, appearances of God, in the Bible.

Next he notices the cherubim (verses 5–14). They each have four faces: the face of a human being, the highest of God's creation; the face of a lion, the highest wild animal; the face of an ox, the highest domestic animal; and the face of an eagle, the highest bird. These cherubim embody the highest attributes of creation. They are the guardians of God's holiness, his heavenly bodyguard. They are the ones that keep Isaiah away in the temple, crying, 'Holy, holy, holy' (Isaiah 6:3).

The cherubim are also God's law-enforcers. They stand at the gate of the Garden of Eden with their swords drawn, barring the way back into God's presence for those who have rebelled (Genesis 3:24). Their presence is a sign that God is going to judge his people. But, as in Genesis 9, the rainbow signals that, in his wrath, God will remember mercy.

And at the centre of the vision, God, in human form, sits on the throne.

Ezekiel falls on his face before God.

There is no other adequate response.

As you look at what is happening around the world, in your church and in your personal life, perhaps you're asking the same question as the exiles: 'Where is God?' Like them, we desperately need a fresh vision of God. Reread Ezekiel's vision, be still in God's presence, and pray for a renewed appreciation of his glory. Physically and spiritually, bow low before him. Remember, God is still on the throne. Humbly acknowledge his sovereignty over world affairs and all the details of your life.

Day 94

Read Ezekiel 1:1–28
Key verses: Ezekiel 1:19–21

....

¹⁹*When the living creatures moved, the wheels beside them moved; and when the living creatures rose from the ground, the wheels also rose.* ²⁰*Wherever the spirit would go, they would go, and the wheels would rise along with them, because the spirit of the living creatures was in the wheels.* ²¹*When the creatures moved, they also moved; when the creatures stood still, they also stood still; and when the creatures rose from the ground, the wheels rose along with them, because the spirit of the living creatures was in the wheels.*

What does the vision mean?

The storm that races across the desert, the living creatures with their legs and their wings, the wheels within wheels spinning around – all of this describes a scene of motion, action and speed. The point is that the Lion of Judah is not caged, back in Jerusalem. He is restless and marching around with Ezekiel and all the other exiles in Babylon.

Ezekiel describes a massive war chariot, with one exception: normally a chariot can move only forward and backward. This chariot is multi-directional – it can move forward, backward, upward, downward and sideways. It can move in any direction it wants to, at the speed of light or faster. Verses 20–21 tell us why: because it is driven by the Spirit of God. 'Wherever the spirit would go, they would go.'

God wants to encourage and warn the Israelites that he is God over the whole earth and is with them wherever they go. He is sovereign just as much in Babylon as he is in Jerusalem. He is with them where they are, far from home.

The same Lord who led the exiles out of Egypt and stayed with them in Babylon is Lord of his church today. Jesus says to us, 'I am with you always' (Matthew 28:20). When you go to the office, when you sit by the bedside of a sick loved one, when you travel away from home – God is present with you.

Psalm 139:7 asks, 'Where can I go from your Spirit? Where can I flee from your presence?' The answer is, 'Nowhere!' As we go through the routines of life, deal with suffering and bereavement, go to hospital appointments and job interviews, and witness to friends, Jesus says to us, 'I am with you.' Meditate on Psalm 139 and the promise that, wherever you go today, God will be with you. Grasp the challenge and comfort of this truth. Listen to God's leading, rely on the strength of his Spirit, and look out for his purposes in all your activities and conversations.

Day 95

Read Ezekiel 2:1–10
Key verses: Ezekiel 2:3–5

. . . .

³He said: 'Son of man, I am sending you to the Israelites, to a rebellious nation that has rebelled against me; they and their ancestors have been in revolt against me to this very day. ⁴The people to whom I am sending you are obstinate and stubborn. Say to them, "This is what the Sovereign Lord says." ⁵And whether they listen or fail to listen – for they are a rebellious people – they will know that a prophet has been among them.'

Is the Bible a divine book?

Prophecies being fulfilled, salvation history unfolding and key themes weaving their way through the text all point to God's divine authorship.

Notice, for example, the connections between the books of Ezekiel and Revelation. Both begin with a theophany – an appearance of God in Christ. In Revelation, the Lord is walking among the churches; in Ezekiel, God is among his people wherever they are. The two books have a similar message and carry a warning from God.

When you glance through Ezekiel chapter 2, you'll find the word 'rebel' and 'rebellious' repeated; that's how God sees his people. No other people have had so much done for them nor so consistently rejected the Word and the will of God as these people have. Like a rebellious vassal state, they have sided with the enemy instead of their liege Lord (verse 3). They are a disobedient race, a hardened people, who refuse to recognize God's sovereignty.

Consequently, Ezekiel's call is not going to be an easy one. He is not being sent like a Wycliffe missionary into an area that has never heard the truth. That would be an easier job because at least the people would listen. The Israelites, though they have the Scriptures, though they know that Ezekiel is God's servant, will not listen to him.

As Chris Wright points out in his commentary,

> It is still tragically true that in some parts of the world . . . God's Word receives a better hearing among those who have never heard it than among those established churches who have grown hard and deaf in their resistance to the movements of God's Spirit.
> (*The Message of Ezekiel*, The Bible Speaks Today, IVP, 2001, p. 57)

Remember Jesus' words repeated through the early chapters of Revelation: 'Whoever has ears, let them hear what the Spirit says to the churches.'

What is God saying to you and your church? Not many of us set out to resist God, but, over time, if we are not listening to him in his Word, his voice will grow faint. Today, listen for God speaking to you and obey all that he tells you to do.

> Everyone who hears these words of mine and puts them into practice is like a wise man who built his house on the rock.
> (Matthew 7:24)

Day 96

Read Ezekiel 3:1–19
Key verses: Ezekiel 3:11, 17

....

> ¹¹*Go now to your people in exile and speak to them. Say to them, 'This is what the Sovereign* LORD *says,' whether they listen or fail to listen . . .* ¹⁷*Son of man, I have made you a watchman for the people of Israel; so hear the word I speak and give them warning from me.*

Do you feel called by God?

Some Christians have a very clear sense that God has called them to a particular career or ministry. Ezekiel is called by God, but his is a call we all share, regardless of our job title, age or stage of life.

God calls Ezekiel to take his Word seriously and to live a life of compliant obedience to that Word. Specifically, he is called to be:

• *A spokesman.* Like all prophets, Ezekiel can't decide his own message, audience or how his words will be received. He is to consume the Word of God (3:1), absorb the Word into the totality of his life, and then proclaim it.

   We too have been given a book that we are to inwardly digest. We have not been given a blank sheet on which we can write our own message, but a book with writing on every page, with no room for additions (2:9). And we are to proclaim its message. This will be a bittersweet experience, because although the Word tastes sweet as it thrills our hearts and satisfies our souls, it is an unpopular message many will reject.

• *A watchman.* Ezekiel's job is to remind the people that judgment is coming. God's wrath against all the ungodliness and unrighteousness of men and women will soon be revealed. Many other prophets in Ezekiel and Jeremiah's day fudge the issue of judgment

(Jeremiah 6:13–14). There is a temptation for us to do the same – to sugar-coat the gospel so we only talk about God's love. But we are called to be watchmen and women, urging people to flee from the coming wrath. We need to tell people the bad news as well as the good news. As the American pastor and author Tim Keller explains, 'We are more wicked than we ever dared believe, but more loved and accepted in Christ than we ever dared hope' ('More Wicked but More Loved', 4 February 2015, <dailykeller.com>).

We don't all have the gift of evangelism, but we are all spokespeople and watchmen. That means being ready and willing to share the gospel – the difficult truth as well as the good news – not just through the witness of our lives, but with words as well. Don't dwell on the rejection you may face: that is part of the job description. The prophets, apostles and even Jesus himself faced rejection. Instead, be motivated by the urgency of the task and the privilege of introducing people to Jesus.

Today, look out for opportunities to share your faith. Pray that your words would be full of truth, compassion and hope.

Day 97

Read Ezekiel 2:1–2; 3:8–15

Key verses: Ezekiel 2:2; 3:12, 14

. . . .

²As he spoke, the Spirit came into me and raised me to my feet, and I heard him speaking to me . . .
    *³:¹²Then the Spirit lifted me up, and I heard behind me a loud rumbling sound as the glory of the L*ORD *rose from the place where it was standing . . . ¹⁴The Spirit then lifted me up and took me away, and I went in bitterness and in the anger of my spirit, with the strong hand of the L*ORD *on me.*

Have you ever had a 'mountaintop' experience of God? Some special encounter with him, perhaps in your quiet time or during a worship service at church?

These times are precious, but they are not an end in themselves. I imagine Ezekiel might have preferred to lie there on the ground, awed by his majestic vision of God. But it isn't paralysis that God wants; it is reasonable service.

Ezekiel is not on his knees for very long before the Spirit comes and enables him to stand up. Notice how central the Spirit of God is to this vision. It is the Spirit who raises Ezekiel to his feet, strengthens him, makes him as tough as his opponents, deposits him among the exiles, puts him in the place of service and equips him for the task.

It is interesting that Ezekiel can't even stand up without the Spirit lifting him (2:1–2). Perhaps, like many Old Testament prophets, he is reluctant to step out in service. He needs God's equipping and enabling. Yet we seem to be able to stand up, preach, plan, counsel and minister without the Spirit! In practice, our theology is one of self-reliance, whereas God wants us to rely on him.

If God speaks to you from his Word, he is speaking to you so he might push you into service. And he equips you for the ministry to which he calls you. He gives his Spirit to strengthen and enable you.

Don't serve in your own strength; rely on his.

Stop. You can't do everything in your own strength – raising your children, serving in church, being faithful at work, looking after others. God's plan was never to save you by grace and then make you live by your own efforts. You have the ever-present, ever-ready, eternal God living within you – listen to him and lean on him. He is your guarantee of glory, assurance of salvation, comforter, counsellor, guide, sanctifier, advocate in prayer and giver of gifts for service. Invite the Holy Spirit to direct every action and to give wisdom for every conversation today. Walk through your days in tandem with him and see his fruit more and more on display in your life (Galatians 5:22–25).

Day 98

Read Ezekiel 2:1 – 3:10
Key verses: Ezekiel 3:1–4

....

> [1] *And he said to me, 'Son of man, eat what is before you, eat this scroll; then go and speak to the people of Israel.'* [2] *So I opened my mouth, and he gave me the scroll to eat.*
>
> [3] *Then he said to me, 'Son of man, eat this scroll I am giving you and fill your stomach with it.' So I ate it, and it tasted as sweet as honey in my mouth.*
>
> [4] *He then said to me: 'Son of man, go now to the people of Israel and speak my words to them.'*

Do you have a nickname – a name given by friends and family that highlights one of your particular character traits?

In chapters 2 and 3, God repeatedly calls Ezekiel 'son of man', emphasizing his humanity and mortality. God will accomplish his work among the exiles through a son of man – one who obeys his Word and is committed to suffering whatever God sends along his path in order to accomplish God's will.

Have you heard that name anywhere else in the Bible? I think this is one of the reasons why Jesus prefers the title 'Son of Man' in the Gospels. He is fulfilling Daniel's vision of the heavenly being, and also this image in Ezekiel of the 'son of man' who suffers, serves and speaks the Word of God. Ultimately, God is going to accomplish his purpose through Jesus, the Son of Man, who will come into the world.

Ezekiel's imagery and metaphors are used not just in the Gospels, but also in the book of Revelation. In chapter 1, John sees a similar vision: one like a son of man, dressed in a robe reaching down to his feet, with a golden sash around his chest, his head and hair white as snow and eyes like blazing fire. John is seeing the Lord Jesus on his throne.

Like the prophet Ezekiel, we are to bring God glory through faithful obedience. We are to listen to, and speak, God's words regardless of the obstacles, confident we are following in Jesus' footsteps. Draw strength from the one who has finished the work God gave him to do and is now seated on heaven's throne in sovereign power.

Jesus has gone before us, blazing a trail, the ultimate Son of Man who was obedient to his Father in every way. Imagine yourself following his footprints as you daily journey on this path of humility, self-denial and God-honouring service. Faithful Christians past and present are cheering you on. Jesus is waiting for you at the finish line. Keep your eyes focused on him and ask the Holy Spirit for renewed strength to run the particular race God has set for you.

> Do you see what this means – all these pioneers who blazed the way, all these veterans cheering us on? It means we'd better get on with it. Strip down, start running – and never quit! No extra spiritual fat, no parasitic sins. Keep your eyes on *Jesus*, who both began and finished this race we're in. Study how he did it. Because he never lost sight of where he was headed – that exhilarating finish in and with God – he could put up with anything along the way: Cross, shame, whatever. And now he's *there*, in the place of honor, right alongside God. When you find yourselves flagging in your faith, go over that story again, item by item, that long litany of hostility he plowed through. *That* will shoot adrenaline into your souls!
> (Hebrews 12:1–3, MSG)

Day 99

Read Ezekiel 8:1–18
Key verses: Ezekiel 8:9–12

. . . .

⁹*And he said to me, 'Go in and see the wicked and detestable things they are doing here.'* ¹⁰*. . . and I saw portrayed all over the walls all kinds of crawling things and unclean animals and all the idols of Israel.* ¹¹*In front of them stood seventy elders of Israel . . . Each had a censer in his hand, and a fragrant cloud of incense was rising.*

¹²*He said to me, 'Son of man, have you seen what the elders of Israel are doing in the darkness, each at the shrine of his own idol? They say, "The* LORD *does not see us; the* LORD *has forsaken the land."'*

It is uncomfortable to think God is angry with his people.

Ezekiel has been using symbols to show the people that, because of their sin, the wrath of God is coming; and they don't like it. One day the exiled elders of Judah visit Ezekiel, hoping he will have a new message: that Jerusalem will be safe and that God will rescue them. Being so far away from home, they find it tempting to pin all their hopes on the future of the city of Jerusalem.

Suddenly, as they are talking, Ezekiel is swept up into a vision. He is taken from Babylon on a virtual reality tour round the temple in Jerusalem so he can understand why God is so angry and why destruction is coming.

The first scene takes place outside the temple where the goddess Asherah is being worshipped, involving all kinds of sexual immorality. Then the tour moves progressively closer to the heart of the temple precincts. We see the elders, key people from the community, worshipping the Egyptian gods. In case the Egyptians win the power struggle with the Babylonians, these businessmen are looking after their interests and garnering Egyptian goodwill. The elders' assumption is that, as God has deserted them, they need other sources of help. The women also, in verses 14–15, are weeping for Tammuz, a Babylonian god of nature, at the north gate of the temple itself.

Like a betrayed lover, God is jealous. He is angry that his covenant people have become idolaters, worshipping false gods.

Are we idolaters?

If we sacrifice relationships to win the blessing of the god 'career', we are idolaters. If we squander the precious hours of our lives for the god of 'entertainment', we are idolaters. If we crave the self-affirmation we get from sex or power, we are idolaters. If our self-worth is measured by our net worth, we are idolaters.

And God is jealous.

Ask the Holy Spirit to reveal where, consciously or unconsciously, someone or something has taken God's place in your life. Has career, family, money or image become a false god? Reflect on God's faithfulness to you in the past and return to 'the love you had at first' by picking up the spiritual habits you practised when you were passionate about Christ: Bible study, prayer and wholehearted service (Revelation 2:4–5).

Day 100

Read Ezekiel 8:1–18
Key verses: Ezekiel 8:16–17

. . . .

[16]He then brought me into the inner court of the house of the LORD, and there at the entrance to the temple, between the portico and the altar, were about twenty-five men. With their backs towards the temple of the LORD and their faces towards the east, they were bowing down to the sun in the east.

[17]He said to me, 'Have you seen this, son of man? Is it a trivial matter for the people of Judah to do the detestable things they are doing here?'

You can't have your cake and eat it!

But that is exactly what the Israelites are trying to do.

From verse 16 onwards, Ezekiel is taken into the heart of the temple, the space reserved for the priests and Levites, immediately in front of the Most Holy Place. In that sacred spot where God is worshipped, the people are bowing with their bottoms up to the Most Holy Place and their heads down to the rising sun coming from the east.

The Israelites haven't stopped worshipping the God of Israel. They are just not sure they can get by with his help alone, so they are covering themselves, politically and spiritually. They are prepared to worship God as long as their worship is modified by the new realities of life in which the gods of Babylon are strong.

Notice that God does not make any comment when the Canaanites worship their Canaanite gods or the people of Babylon worship their Babylonian gods. But he is provoked to jealousy when his people, who believe that he is the God who has acted in the past, prostitute themselves to other idols. He is angered when his own people want a private faith but also want publicly to admit that anti-God ideas, accepted by society, have won the day.

The message of chapter 8 is that we must be intolerant of idolatry among ourselves. God will not be treated simply as one option among many.

Are you trying to have your cake and eat it? Sometimes we don't even realize it, but we allow our money, health, reputation, family, even our role in church, to be a security blanket – an extra layer of comfort, another source of value and esteem. Check your heart: are you idolizing these things? Our sovereign God does not need to be, and will not tolerate being, one option among many. Take time to meditate on Paul's charge:

> Don't let the world around you squeeze you into its own mould, but let God re-mould your minds from within, so that you may prove in practice that the plan of God for you is good, meets all his demands and moves towards the goal of true maturity.
> (Romans 12:2, PHILLIPS)

Day 101

Read Ezekiel 9:1–11
Key verses: Ezekiel 9:8–10

• •

> [8]*While they were killing and I was left alone, I fell face down, crying out, 'Alas, Sovereign LORD! Are you going to destroy the entire remnant of Israel in this outpouring of your wrath on Jerusalem?'*
>
> [9]*He answered me, 'The sin of the people of Israel and Judah is exceedingly great; the land is full of bloodshed and the city is full of injustice. They say, "The LORD has forsaken the land; the LORD does not see." * [10]*So I will not look on them with pity or spare them, but I will bring down on their own heads what they have done.'*

People say there can't be a God because a good God would put an end to the evil in the world.

God is patient, but he does not shut his eyes to human sin. He is not indifferent. Judgment cannot be held back for ever.

For centuries, various kings of Israel and Judah have come along and led the people into one idolatrous action after another. But, in chapter 9, Ezekiel has a vision of God's intervention. And judgment begins, not with the unbeliever, but with the believer (1 Peter 4:17).

Our body is a temple of the Holy Spirit, so we must honour God with it, not pamper it in self-indulgence or abuse it (1 Corinthians 6:19–20). What must God think of the believer who professes to believe in the sovereignty of God on Sunday, but every other day looks for worldly solutions to his or her problems? Or the one who swears allegiance to Christ on Sunday, but serves the bottom line the rest of the week?

Next, God visits judgment on the church, his covenant people; corporately, they too are his temple. What does he think of our half-hearted evangelism, our toying with New Age ideas, our tolerance of old heresies, our questioning of some of the basic truths of the Bible, our elevation of subjective truth over the objective truth of Scripture? What does he think about leaders who deny Jesus' resurrection or who, in an attempt to appear relevant, play down God's judgment and wrath?

God is not indifferent. He will not tolerate this for ever. Judgment is coming.

Almighty and most merciful Father, we have wandered and strayed from your ways like lost sheep. We have followed too much the devices and desires of our own hearts. We have offended against your holy laws. We have left undone those things that we ought to have done; and we have done those things that we ought not to have done; and there is no health in us. But you, O Lord, have mercy upon us sinners. Spare those who confess their faults. Restore those who are penitent, according to your promises declared to mankind in Christ Jesus our Lord. And grant, O most merciful Father, for his sake, that we may live a disciplined, righteous and godly life, to the glory of your holy name. Amen.
(Prayer of Penitence, *Common Worship: Daily Prayer*, Church House Publishing, 2005)

Day 102

Read Ezekiel 9:1–11
Key verses: Ezekiel 9:3–6

· ·

> ³ *Then the* Lord *called to the man clothed in linen who had the writing kit at his side* ⁴ *and said to him, 'Go throughout the city of Jerusalem and put a mark on the foreheads of those who grieve and lament over all the detestable things that are done in it.'*
>
> ⁵ *As I listened, he said to the others, 'Follow him through the city and kill, without showing pity or compassion.* ⁶ *Slaughter the old men, the young men and women, the mothers and children, but do not touch anyone who has the mark.'*

Can we escape God's final, inevitable judgment?

Only if we have the mark of God on us.

In Ezekiel's vision, the angel is commanded to go through the city putting a mark on the foreheads of those who grieve and lament over the detestable state of the nation. Those with the mark are saved from God's judgment.

Revelation 7:3 talks about the mark, the seal of God, on the foreheads of the servants of the Lord. These are people with a broken and contrite spirit who weep over the sin of their church and nation. They repudiate the standards of the people around them. Like Daniel, there is no spirit of criticism in them (see Daniel 9). They are not coming to God saying, 'Do something about those sinful people.' They are saying, 'Forgive me for my sin.'

Remember also that protective mark, the dab of blood from the Passover lamb, put on the doors of the Hebrew homes as the angel of death came to visit (Exodus 12:12–13). In the Bible's larger story-line, the mercy of God in the midst of judgment finds its ultimate expression in the person of Jesus Christ. His blood shed on the cross saves us from the coming wrath.

Turn to Jesus to find refuge from God's wrath. Only his blood shed on the cross can wash away your sin, remove your guilt and appease God's anger. Don't seek security in other people or things; don't try to save yourself through effort and good works; don't be so distracted by other people's sins that you don't repent of your own. Let Jesus' blood cleanse you and mark you out as a child of his grace. Today, thank God that you are headed for heaven, dressed in robes of righteousness, with his name written on you (Revelation 9:4; 14:1; 22:4).

Day 103

Read Ezekiel 10:1–22
Key verses: Ezekiel 10:4–5, 18

....

> ⁴ Then the glory of the LORD rose from above the cherubim and moved to the threshold of the temple. The cloud filled the temple, and the court was full of the radiance of the glory of the LORD. ⁵ The sound of the wings of the cherubim could be heard as far away as the outer court, like the voice of God Almighty when he speaks . . .
>
> ¹⁸ Then the glory of the LORD departed from over the threshold of the temple and stopped above the cherubim.

They never believed it would happen.

The Jews never believed that Judah and Jerusalem would be devastated because they didn't think God would abandon the temple. Jeremiah mocked the people for their false confidence. They kept repeating, 'The temple of the LORD', as if by simply saying this mantra they would be supernaturally protected from danger (Jeremiah 7:4).

But, shocking though it might be, the city falls. God is moving somewhere else (Ezekiel 9:3). The winged chariot begins to move (10:4–5); the glory of the Lord departs from the threshold of the temple (10:18); it leaves the city and rests above the mountain (11:22–24).

God has made his message clear. He is not God of a place but of people. He is passionately concerned for their spiritual life. He is prepared to sacrifice their reputation, comfort and success if he can bring them back to the place where they are purified, repentant and effective for him again. He is far more concerned about the holiness of his people than about their happiness. His goal is restored relationship with those in exile: 'They will be my people, and I will be their God' (11:20).

God has not changed. He still prioritizes holiness over happiness, and is passionately concerned about our spiritual growth. And as John Calvin comments, 'The scourges of God are more useful to us because when God indulges us we abuse his clemency and flatter ourselves and grow hardened in our sin' (quoted in Iain Duguid, *Ezekiel*, NIV Application Commentary, Zondervan, 1999, p. 115).

Christian people don't do well in good days. We grow fat, flabby and lazy. We need to hear preaching that challenges what we are pinning our hopes on, where our priorities lie, and all the other idolatries of our day.

Just as God purges a people, so he disciplines us as individuals. See this discipline of God for what it really is – not evidence that he has abandoned you, but proof of his love. Don't waste your suffering, but use this time of being laid low to grow in your faith. Draw close to God, acknowledge your dependence on him, trust him for all that is to come, thank him for his grace and mercy, and allow him to purify you.

> Consider it pure joy, my brothers and sisters, whenever you face trials of many kinds, because you know that the testing of your faith produces perseverance. Let perseverance finish its work so that you may be mature and complete, not lacking anything.
> (James 1:2–4)

Day 104

Read Ezekiel 11:1–25

Key verses: Ezekiel 11:22–23

· ·

²² Then the cherubim, with the wheels beside them, spread their wings, and the glory of the God of Israel was above them. ²³ The glory of the LORD went up from within the city and stopped above the mountain east of it.

Do you have a 'special' place – somewhere you keep returning to, somewhere that holds precious memories?

The Mount of Olives is a special location in the Bible, simply because of the number of times God visits it.

At the end of chapter 11, the glory departs from Jerusalem and hovers above the Mount of Olives, just east of the city. Remember, five hundred years later, the glory of God would be visiting the temple again – this time not as a cloud of fire, not with cherubim, but in a person: 'We have seen his glory, the glory of the one and only Son, who came from the Father, full of grace and truth' (John 1:14). The glory of God revisits the temple twice, and on both occasions he clears the temple. He is looking for righteousness, and finds unrighteousness; for holiness, and finds sinfulness; for true worship, and finds a den of thieves.

The glory comes and the glory leaves, pausing at the city gate to be stripped, scorned, ill-treated and crucified. The glory leaves and pauses again on the Mount of Olives, to give his last words to his church to go into all the world. His people are to spread the gospel throughout the whole world. People from every tribe and tongue and nation are to be gathered under his kingship.

On that mountain he promises to be with his people to the ends of the earth. That presence can be found wherever his people are, even when they find themselves exiled in a strange land. And to that Mount of Olives he will come again, in power and glory; when 'the kingdom of the world has become the kingdom of our Lord and of his Messiah, and he will reign for ever and ever', and every creature, the cherubim and the redeemed, will sing, 'Hallelujah! For our Lord God Almighty reigns' (Revelation 11:15; 19:6).

One day soon, perhaps today, Jesus will return to the Mount of Olives. His second coming will be very different from his first. He will come in power, majesty and glory; everyone will bow before him and confess him as Lord (Philippians 2:10–11). Until then, let Jesus' last words on the mountain shape your priorities, and encourage, reassure and spur you to action: 'Go and make disciples of all nations . . . I am with you always, to the very end of the age' (Matthew 28:19–20).

Day 105

Read Ezekiel 34:1–10
Key verses: Ezekiel 34:4–5, 10

. . . .

[4]You have not strengthened the weak or healed those who are ill or bound up the injured. You have not brought back the strays or searched for the lost. You have ruled them harshly and brutally. [5]So they were scattered because there was no shepherd, and when they were scattered they became food for all the wild animals . . . [10]I am against the shepherds and will hold them accountable for my flock. I will remove them from tending the flock.

The world is divided into three camps: those who make things happen, those who watch what's happening and those who have no idea what is happening!

The ones who make things happen are the leaders. Leaders can do a power of good, but those corrupted by power are a menace. God addresses Israel's corrupted leaders in chapter 34. He uses the title 'shepherd', a very familiar one in the ancient world, a metaphor for the king or god of a state or country. This title is always used to emphasize the responsibility of those in power to enforce social righteousness.

The Lord is angry with these former kings of Judah because they have failed to fulfil their role as shepherds. Of course, these shepherds do not own the flock; they are employed as stewards to look after the sheep, answerable to the Chief Shepherd. Notice that God repeatedly calls his people 'my sheep'.

Nevertheless, the monarchy of Israel is responsible for much of the nation's apostasy. They introduced idolatry, they arranged foreign alliances, trusting foreign powers to protect and provide for them instead of trusting God, and they enforced harsh rule which threatens the reputation of God, who is known as compassionate and merciful.

And because of the absence of a true shepherd, the people of God have been scattered. God holds the kings responsible for tearing the tribes of Israel apart – ten in the north, two in the south, and in constant warfare with each other.

Ezekiel warns that, because of the shepherds' sinful self-interest, judgment is coming on them. They now face a greater enemy than any they have ever fought: the Lord himself.

Many of us have leadership responsibilities – as a small-group leader, parent, manager or an employer. Do you see your leadership as a status symbol or a boost to your ego? Do you use people for your own convenience? Sometimes our motives are mixed, and the influence that comes with our role corrupts our hearts. Today, take a spiritual health check. Ask God to point out areas of sinful self-interest, circumstances where you are not trusting him fully, or times you have failed to represent him well to his people. Avoid God's judgment: repent and return to the Chief Shepherd.

Day 106

Read Ezekiel 34:11–24

Key verses: Ezekiel 34:12, 14

. . . .

> ¹²*As a shepherd looks after his scattered flock when he is with them, so will I look after my sheep. I will rescue them from all the places where they were scattered on a day of clouds and darkness . . . ¹⁴I will tend them in a good pasture, and the mountain heights of Israel will be their grazing land. There they will lie down in good grazing land, and there they will feed in a rich pasture on the mountains of Israel.*

What does a true leader look like?

God uses the term 'shepherd' to describe a true leader. We may see the image of a shepherd as a sentimental one. But often in the ancient world a shepherd was regarded as more of a cowboy: tender with his sheep; tough in the way he had to live.

God promises the people a coming shepherd who will be tough and tender, one who will gather the scattered nations. 'I will search for the lost and bring back the strays,' says the Lord (verse 16). We hear that again on the lips of Jesus, who says, 'The Son of Man came to seek and to save the lost' (Luke 19:10). Isaiah 40:11 gives us this description of the Lord our Shepherd: 'He gathers the lambs in his arms and carries them close to his heart; he gently leads those that have young.' In contrast to Israel's previous kings, the Lord can be trusted not to scatter the flock; to teach and not deceive; to feed and not fleece the flock.

This idea of the shepherd feeding and tending the flock is taken up in the New Testament and used of leadership within local churches. Paul describes the role of the Ephesian elders: 'Keep watch over . . . all the flock of which the Holy Spirit has made you overseers. Be shepherds of the church of God, which he bought with his own blood' (Acts 20:28). The rest of Acts 20 indicates that this means testifying to the gospel of God's grace, warning people day and night with tears and proclaiming the whole counsel of God. You feed people by telling them the Word of God, and sharing about a judgment that's coming and the love of God that can rescue them from it.

If you have a responsibility in your local church, whatever level it is, you are a shepherd of God's flock. Fulfil that calling willingly (1 Peter 5:2–3). Make sure you are doing it to serve people. You are there to care for, woo and win them. Love God's people. Love them to death; love them into the kingdom: that's the role of the shepherd.

How would you rate yourself as a leader? Don't be tempted to adopt the world's criteria to judge how you are getting on. The role of God's shepherd is to care for the spiritual, material and emotional needs of the flock. Today, be quick to demonstrate servant leadership, to value people as individuals and to outdo yourself in showing love (1 Peter 1:22; 4:8).

Day 107

Read Ezekiel 34:11–24
Key verses: Ezekiel 34:15–16

. . . .

15 I myself will tend my sheep and make them lie down, declares the Sovereign LORD. 16 I will search for the lost and bring back the strays. I will bind up the injured and strengthen the weak, but the sleek and the strong I will destroy. I will shepherd the flock with justice.

What is God's solution to a history of bad shepherds?

Ezekiel points further into the future and explains that God will change not the nature of the office, but the nature of the occupant. God will replace the bad shepherds with a good shepherd: someone like David, a king after God's own heart.

Who is this shepherd? Psalm 23:1 says, 'The LORD is my shepherd.' The New Testament unfolds this answer even further. Jesus says, 'I am the good shepherd' (John 10:11). Jesus actually bases what he says on this passage from Ezekiel, and it is a radical thing to say. His listeners are shaken, and they question whether he is demon-possessed or raving mad (John 10:19–20). They later pick up rocks to throw at him (John 10:31). What is it about this title that provokes such an extreme reaction?

Jesus knows exactly what he is saying when he calls himself the 'good shepherd'. He is saying that Herod, King of Judah, is not a true king. But more than that, he is calling himself by the title used for God himself.

Jesus is separating himself from all the other kings, messianic pretenders and freedom fighters who call themselves 'shepherds' and are trying to unite the people behind their goal of driving out the Romans. The violent methods of these revolutionaries mean that many following these shepherds will be killed. Jesus reminds the people that, in contrast to these leaders, he has their interests at heart, he loves them and he will lay down his life for them.

Jesus comes as the one shepherd who will unite the flock; there will be one flock and one shepherd (John 10:16). He is the good shepherd who will look for the one lost sheep (Luke 15:3–7). He is the discerning shepherd who, in the final judgment, will separate the sheep from the goats (Matthew 25:31–46, again using Ezekiel 34 language). And when it comes to his church, he is the Chief Shepherd to whom all the under-shepherds report (1 Peter 5:4). Jesus is the fulfilment of all God's promises to King David: the ultimate Shepherd-King.

Politicians, celebrities, even some church leaders, parade as shepherds, claiming to have your best interests at heart while using your allegiance to build their personal empire and reputation. But Jesus is the only one who loves you enough to lay down his life for you. He is your Shepherd-King who alone provides protection, refreshment, guidance, satisfaction, comfort and support. Meditate on the truths of Psalm 23. Listen for your Shepherd's voice and determine to follow wherever he leads.

Day 108

Read Ezekiel 34:25–31
Key verses: Ezekiel 34:25–26, 28

....

²⁵ *I will make a covenant of peace with them and rid the land of savage beasts so that they may live in the wilderness and sleep in the forests in safety.* ²⁶ *I will make them and the places surrounding my hill a blessing. I will send down showers in season; there will be showers of blessing . . .* ²⁸ *They will no longer be plundered by the nations, nor will wild animals devour them. They will live in safety, and no one will make them afraid.*

What difference will Jesus' coming make?

In place of the curses of the Sinai covenant that the Israelites have experienced under the judgment of God – wild animals, drought, famine, the sword – they are now going to experience safety, rain in its season, fruitfulness and peace; *shalom* will reign.

That Hebrew word *shalom* – peace – is much more than simply the cessation of warfare and the absence of strife. It conveys a comprehensive state of wholeness and well-being. It suggests a people who are free from fear and insecurity and at peace with themselves; a people who have a relationship with God – the hostility has been resolved and they are reconciled to him; and a people who are also reconciled to nature.

Many of us are afraid of storms, street crime, what other people think, failure, economic downturn, poverty, old age, sickness, bereavement, death. When Jesus comes into our world, he says, 'I've come to deal with those basic fundamental fears and insecurities that lie at the very core of your human nature. I've come to bring peace right into the heart of your life. I've come to bring a peace that the world cannot give or take away.' That's why Ezekiel promises that when the king comes, there will be no fear at any time, and no-one to make them afraid (verse 28). The good shepherd defines the measure of the *shalom*: 'I have come that they may have life, and have it to the full' (John 10:10).

The *shalom* of God is not an activity or an afternoon of undisturbed dozing; it is not boring – there is no need for you to look at your watch when you're enjoying this peace. It is a life where every minute satisfies, every second is worth savouring, each hour has new pleasures; a life where activity is fulfilling and every sensation brings pleasure.

Being reconciled to God means enjoying a restored relationship with him. This is real, everlasting, not-dependent-on-feelings peace. Don't let fears or anxieties rob you of this peace. Instead, bring your prayer requests to God. Invite him to minister his *shalom* to your heart and mind (Philippians 4:6–7).

> May the Lord of peace himself give you peace at all times and in
> every way.
> (2 Thessalonians 3:16)

Day 109

Read Ezekiel 34:25–31
Key verses: Ezekiel 34:29–30

....

29 I will provide for them a land renowned for its crops, and they will no longer be victims of famine in the land or bear the scorn of the nations. 30 Then they will know that I, the LORD their God, am with them and that they, the Israelites, are my people, declares the Sovereign LORD.

The Bible is full of promises.

Here, Ezekiel speaks of a renewed covenant, at the heart of which is this wonderful promise of God: the Lord is your God and you are his people. Instead of having a monarchy divided by sin, God's people will be united under one shepherd. Instead of an undistinguished succession of monarchs, there will be a single ruler after God's own heart.

Christians experience the blessings of this covenant in a different way from those who lived under the old covenant. One of the things we need to remember is that, in the Old Testament, many of the promises of God are put in terms that the people would understand. For example, the people of God have a particular relationship with the land in which they live. It is God's land, they are his tenants, and the fertility of that land is very often a spiritual thermometer, as Chris Wright puts it, of the relationship between Israel and their God (quoted by Iain Duguid in *Ezekiel*, NIV Application Commentary, Zondervan, 1999, p. 354). So the blessings of God are often described in terms of the fertility of the land.

But Israel fail miserably in their duties. Time and again they break the terms of their relationship with God. Ezekiel talks about Israel as a vine that is not producing the fruit that God is looking for. But when

Jesus, the new ruler, comes under the new covenant, he says, 'I am the true vine' (John 15:1).

The whole message of the New Testament is about the perfect obedience of Christ in our place. He makes peace by the blood of his cross, so even though we are covenant-breakers by nature, we can have every spiritual blessing in Christ. Through his death on the cross, those who were far away and those who were near are brought together into one new humanity, all by Christ in this new covenant.

Jesus keeps God's covenant on our behalf, so 'no matter how many promises God has made, they are "Yes" in Christ' (2 Corinthians 1:20). Thank God that he is the great promise-keeper. Worship Jesus for dying in your place. Ask the Holy Spirit to help you keep your part of this new covenant relationship today.

> May the God of peace, who through the blood of the eternal covenant brought back from the dead our Lord Jesus, that great Shepherd of the sheep, equip you with everything good for doing his will, and may he work in us what is pleasing to him, through Jesus Christ, to whom be glory for ever and ever. Amen.
> (Hebrews 13:20–21)

Day 110

Read Ezekiel 34:1–31

Key verse: Ezekiel 34:31

· ·

31 You are my sheep, the sheep of my pasture, and I am your God, declares the Sovereign LORD.

An engagement ring symbolizes a real relationship, but with the promise of more to come. Similarly, there is an 'already but not yet' aspect to the new covenant.

The peace we enjoy today is real but partial, because we still live in a fallen world. We experience trials of various kinds; we still know moments of panic, hours of boredom and days when we struggle with pain. Sometimes these are the results of our foolish choices; at other times, they are not. Sometimes obedience results in material blessing; sometimes it results in persecution, hardship and loss.

Yet even here, in the midst of sin, trials and temptation, we can experience inexpressible joy because of the nearness of the Shepherd. We see the blessings in part, though not in fullness. Creation around us still longs for the revelation of the new heaven and the new earth. These light and momentary troubles of ours are nothing in comparison with the glory that awaits us in Christ.

One day, when Christ returns, all of this will be gloriously and fully fulfilled as God gathers together his worldwide flock from many nations and brings them into his presence. There will be no more suffering, no more pain, and no more disharmony with God, my neighbour or even with the world around me (see Isaiah 11:6–9).

The Lamb of God, sacrificed in our place, has become our Shepherd-King. Make every effort to stay close to him. Feed on his Word, listen for his voice, accept his protection and put your trust in him. Keep serving, keep fighting sin, keep pursuing righteousness and keep your focus on glory, because the wait is almost over. One day soon, perhaps today, the engagement will culminate in the marriage supper of the Lamb.

> For the Lamb at the centre of the throne
>> will be their shepherd;
> 'he will lead them to springs of living water.'
>> 'And God will wipe away every tear from their eyes.'
> (Revelation 7:17)

> And when the Chief Shepherd appears, you will receive the crown of glory that will never fade away.
> (1 Peter 5:4)

Day 111

Read Ezekiel 36:16–32

Key verses: Ezekiel 36:18–21

....

18So I poured out my wrath on them because they had shed blood in the land and because they had defiled it with their idols. 19I dispersed them among the nations, and they were scattered through the countries; I judged them according to their conduct and their actions. 20And wherever they went among the nations they profaned my holy name, for it was said of them, 'These are the LORD's people, and yet they had to leave his land.' 21I had concern for my holy name, which the people of Israel profaned among the nations where they had gone.

The Bible talks about it, preachers teach about it, but what does it really mean to be holy? In the Old Testament, if something was dedicated for God's use, it was said to be holy. So, for example, certain foods and garments were holy because they were used exclusively in God's service (1 Samuel 21:4; Leviticus 16:4).

In the ancient world of Israel, people understand the concepts of holiness and ceremonial cleanness. Not only are certain things the people eat either clean or unclean, but there are also clean lands and unclean lands.

In this chapter, what God is saying to the Israelites is that even while they are living in the holy land, the clean land, they are desecrating it by their behaviour and idolatry. They are turning it into a place of death, making it a place unfit to live in. Instead of staying away from the thing that has been defiled, they have become defiled by it (verse 17). They are acting as if they belong to the unholy lands of the Gentiles (verse 19). And so God says, 'You want to live as if you're not God's chosen holy people? Then I'll send you out among the unholy, unchosen ones, to live the way you are really living!'

Not only are the people defiled and needing to be cleansed, but they are also disobedient and needing to be reconciled to God (verses 26–28). The story of Israel, from the moment of their rescue from Egypt to their settlement in the Promised Land, right up to Ezekiel's time, is one of constant disobedience to God. The whole story of their history is one of entrenched disobedience to God.

God's rebuke to the Israelites pierces our hearts sharply too. How often have we been guilty of not living as the holy people of God? Rather than living distinctive lives, we prefer to blend in with the culture and its values. It's understandable – it is hard to be different – but it is so far from the calling God has in mind for us. Ask God to show you specific areas where your lifestyle and choices reflect the culture around you, and ask for his help to be the salt and light God designed you to be.

Day 112

Read Ezekiel 36:24–36
Key verses: Ezekiel 36:25–27

. . . .

²⁵I will sprinkle clean water on you, and you will be clean; I will cleanse you from all your impurities and from all your idols. ²⁶I will give you a new heart and put a new spirit in you; I will remove from you your heart of stone and give you a heart of flesh. ²⁷And I will put my Spirit in you and move you to follow my decrees and be careful to keep my laws.

A heart transplant is a massive operation. And the Israelites need one.

In Hebrew, the heart is the place where we think, decide and will. The spirit is the life-breath, the driving force, which empowers our hearts. It is our aspirations, attitudes, disposition and motivation. The Israelites need their hearts and spirits to be transformed; they need to think and feel differently; and that's what God promises to do (verse 26).

God's intention is to produce heart obedience in his people. This is a creative act on God's part. The Spirit of God will indwell and recreate them in ways that will change and form their will and their ability to follow God's decrees and to keep God's laws. This was God's original intention when they came into the Promised Land (Leviticus 26:3).

The Israelites are not simply sick and in need of some kind of treatment. They are sinners in need of cleansing, rebels in need of reconciliation with their sovereign, dead and in need of life. They have made themselves totally unfit to inhabit God's land and to exist in God's presence. They are offensive to a holy God – and that is our predicament too (Ephesians 2:3).

It is not simply that we're not making the most of life, not fulfilling our potential as human beings or missing out on the spiritual dimension of our humanity. We are under God's wrath and judgment. What we need is radical new birth. Nothing less than this will do. Simply modifying the parameters of our lives, re-socializing ourselves so we behave better, will not cut it. Simply handing someone a list of rules and regulations will certainly not do it. We need to be born again, and that is precisely the good news that the gospel proclaims.

We don't really like talking about God's judgment or wrath. It is more palatable to present the gospel as a way of life that provides meaning and purpose. But don't miss the point. Don't sell the gospel short. The good news is that when we were facing God's wrath and could do nothing to save ourselves, God took the initiative to save us. Jesus' death on the cross paid the penalty for our sin. God's Spirit now dwells within us, gives us a heart transplant and makes obedience possible. That is truly good news worth rejoicing in and sharing with others.

> You see, at just the right time, when we were still powerless, Christ died for the ungodly. Very rarely will anyone die for a righteous person, though for a good person someone might possibly dare to die. But God demonstrates his own love for us in this: while we were still sinners, Christ died for us.
> (Romans 5:6–8)

Day 113

Read Ezekiel 37:1–13
Key verses: Ezekiel 37:1–3

....

> [1] *The hand of the* L*ORD* *was on me, and he brought me out by the Spirit of the* L*ORD* *and set me in the middle of a valley; it was full of bones.* [2] *He led me to and fro among them, and I saw a great many bones on the floor of the valley, bones that were very dry.* [3] *He asked me, 'Son of man, can these bones live?'*
> *I said, 'Sovereign* L*ORD*, *you alone know.'*

Ezekiel is transported to Death Valley.

Chapter 37 is a vivid picture of Israel's predicament from God's perspective. But it is also the human predicament. In many ways, this chapter is a dramatic illustration of what chapter 36 has been teaching.

The prophet is introduced to a scene of total death – the remains of a mighty army scattered in the valley where once he saw the glory of God. He walks to and fro among the bones. This is the ultimate picture of despair and hopelessness. That valley of dry bones is where all our plans for the future end up: those years at university, those years invested in our business, career or family. We are all headed to the place of death.

God asks, 'Can these bones live?'

Ezekiel doesn't answer God's question, but bats it right back and says, 'You alone know.'

In New Testament terms the question would be, 'What can be done for the men and women who are without hope and without God? The people we are trying to win for Christ – our friends and family members – are dead before God; they are in the valley of dry bones. What will God do to bring life to those bones?'

Ezekiel himself points us to the answer. No Jew, especially not a priest, would want to be among the dead, as that would bring ritual defilement. But God makes Ezekiel walk to and fro through the valley, rubbing his nose in it. And this is the story of Ezekiel's life: he is absolutely absorbed in the will and work of God in his generation. God calls him 'son of man', and he serves the work of God, getting utterly defiled, going in and out among these dead people.

This son of man, Ezekiel, is a picture of the Son of Man who comes into our world and exposes himself to all the defilement of our sin for our salvation.

> We don't like to think about the valley of death. But maybe we need to dwell on Ezekiel's image for a while to appreciate what we have been saved from (Ephesians 2:1), and the desperate plight our loved ones are still in. The task of evangelism and the need for the Holy Spirit to open blind eyes is urgent. What would our friends say to us if they ended up in hell and we hadn't even warned them? Pray for opportunities to share the good news of the gospel with someone today.

Day 114

Read Ezekiel 37:1–14
Key verses: Ezekiel 37:4–6

. . . .

> ⁴ Then he said to me, 'Prophesy to these bones and say to them, "Dry bones, hear the word of the LORD! ⁵ This is what the Sovereign LORD says to these bones: I will make breath enter you, and you will come to life. ⁶ I will attach tendons to you and make flesh come upon you and cover you with skin; I will put breath in you, and you will come to life. Then you will know that I am the LORD."'

Of all the ridiculous things that we find Ezekiel doing in this book, this has to be the most ridiculous.

God tells Ezekiel, 'Prophesy to these bones and say to them, "Dry bones, hear the word of the LORD!"' God is commanding his servant, 'Preach to the dead! Preach the promise of new life and breath and the knowledge of God.' And so Ezekiel preaches the words God has given him to speak. There's no magic rite, no secret incantation, no conjuring trick – it's just the plain, simple, straightforward speaking of God's truth. It is the proclamation that makes the difference.

The New Testament uses Ezekiel's picture, describing people as dead in their trespasses and sins (Ephesians 2:1). It is a graveyard out there! Getting people to believe our message is impossible. If new life is going to happen in our nation, it will be through preaching. God has promised he will bless the preaching of his Word.

And notice that it is the preaching of the Word of God and the action of the Spirit of God which together accomplish resurrection. The proclamation of the Word of God creates the context into which the Holy Spirit is happy to move in power to do his resurrection work in these people's lives. Jesus reminded Nicodemus of this key truth in John 3. He told him he needed to be born again by water and the Spirit: by the cleansing ministry of the Spirit through the Word that renews.

The real secret of spiritual life for our churches and our nation lies in the Word and the Spirit, by proclamation and prayer.

Meditate today on the power of God's Word and the Holy Spirit.

For the word of God is alive and active. Sharper than any double-edged sword, it penetrates even to dividing soul and spirit, joints and marrow; it judges the thoughts and attitudes of the heart. (Hebrews 4:12)

You were washed, you were sanctified, you were justified in the name of the Lord Jesus Christ and by the Spirit of our God. (1 Corinthians 6:11)

Pray that the truth of God's Word and the power of his Spirit would revive your soul, inspire your obedience and lead you into a deeper experience of God.

Day 115

Read Ezekiel 37:15–28
Key verses: Ezekiel 37:21–23

• •

21 This is what the Sovereign LORD says: I will take the Israelites out of the nations where they have gone. I will gather them from all around and bring them back into their own land. 22 I will make them one nation in the land, on the mountains of Israel. There will be one king over all of them and they will never again be two nations or be divided into two kingdoms. 23 They will no longer defile themselves with their idols and vile images or with any of their offences, for I will save them from all their sinful backsliding, and I will cleanse them. They will be my people, and I will be their God.

If we promise someone something – whether it is to babysit their children or to take them out for a meal – we usually have a good idea how and when we will fulfil that promise.

Through Ezekiel, God promises to renew the life of his people. But how and when does God fulfil that promise?

Like many Old Testament prophecies, this promise has been fulfilled at various levels. The first was when the exiled Jews returned to Jerusalem. They came back to their land, where they experienced spiritual renewal. They rebuilt the city and the temple; they reclaimed the land in response to the prayers of people like Daniel and the preaching ministry of people like Ezra. Yet it wasn't a long-lasting work.

The primary level at which this prophecy of renewal was fulfilled was at Pentecost, when the Spirit of God became an indwelling presence in the hearts of individual believers. The prophecy has also been fulfilled at various points in church history, when God has visited his people at periods we call 'revival'. The Spirit of God has stirred people to pray, and, flowing from the prayer and proclamation of the Word, whole communities have been transformed by the Word and the Spirit of God.

I believe the prophecy is yet to be fulfilled with respect to Israel. Their hearts are still hard to the gospel. But the apostle Paul suggests that a day is coming when the fullness of the Gentiles will have come in, and God's mercy will again be directed towards his ancient people (Romans 11:25–32).

Of course, this prophecy is going to be ultimately fulfilled when God brings us to the new heaven and the new earth. When Jesus returns, God will make us perfect both in body and in soul.

Personal renewal, those times of increased intimacy with God, happen at various times and in various ways in our Christian life. They always start with repentance. But that, as with every part of our salvation, begins with God, who saves and cleanses us. When the gospel message finds a home in our hearts, we do not view ourselves in a better light. Rather, we see ourselves as the chief of sinners. But we also grow in our understanding that, though we are far worse than we could ever have imagined, we are more loved than we ever dreamed possible.

Today, repent of your sins and pray for God's cleansing. Also rejoice that you are so greatly loved.

Day 116

Read Ezekiel 37:14–28
Key verses: Ezekiel 37:26–28

••

> ²⁶I will make a covenant of peace with them; it will be an everlasting covenant. I will establish them and increase their numbers, and I will put my sanctuary among them for ever. ²⁷My dwelling-place will be with them; I will be their God, and they will be my people. ²⁸Then the nations will know that I the LORD make Israel holy, when my sanctuary is among them for ever.

We guard our reputations fiercely. It's important to us that we are well thought of.

God is also keen to guard his reputation and restore the honour of his name. The whole emphasis in these verses is on people knowing that 'I the LORD have spoken, and I will do it' (Ezekiel 36:36; 37:14). Previously, God's name has been defiled among the nations, as people said, 'What kind of God is he? Look at these devastated people, dispossessed of their land. What kind of God is the God of Israel, that this should happen? He must be a weak God. Our gods, the gods of Babylon and Egypt, are stronger.'

But God says, 'I am going to do this work and the Gentile nations are going to see that I have done it' (Ezekiel 36:22–23). Chapter 37 ends with the emphasis that there is only one way to salvation. There is only one shepherd, one ruler, one flock.

All this is good news, not just for the people but also for the Lord himself. The crucifixion, resurrection and then exaltation of Jesus; the miracle of new birth in countless lives; the future conversion and ultimate resurrection of the dead: all this will, in the long run, vindicate his name among the nations. The act of salvation through Jesus Christ will, at the end of history, be the very thing that brings greatest glory to God, and that ought not to surprise us, for there is nothing higher than this.

For God to delight in his own perfections is entirely appropriate; to delight in anything less would be idolatry for him. The exaltation of God is the great end of salvation as well as creation.

Exalting God is not just the chief business of heaven; it should be our consuming passion now. How do we exalt God? Every time we choose to do his will rather than our own, every time we give him the praise he is due, every time we advance his cause, we are exalting God. Today, look for opportunities to exalt God. Honour him with your lips and your life.

Glorify the Lord with me:
let us exalt his name together.
(Psalm 34:3)

Day 117

Read Ezekiel 40:1–16

Key verses: Ezekiel 40:1–2

. . . .

> [1] *In the twenty-fifth year of our exile, at the beginning of the year, on the tenth of the month, in the fourteenth year after the fall of the city – on that very day the hand of the LORD was on me and he took me there.* [2] *In visions of God he took me to the land of Israel and set me on a very high mountain, on whose south side were some buildings that looked like a city.*

Have you ever been hill-walking? Sometimes it is not easy to see the path, and the climb is arduous. But when you reach the summit, the view is spectacular.

From chapter 40 onwards, Ezekiel takes us up a mountain and gives us a breathtaking view of an entirely new world, centred on the temple of God. Moses climbed up Mount Nebo and was allowed to see the Promised Land. In this vision, Ezekiel is also taken up a very high mountain and enabled to see the ultimate Promised Land: the new heaven and the new earth. Death Valley has now been raised above all the mountains of the world, and the temple of God is going to be established. Out of the resurrection life that God is going to breathe into people by his Word and Spirit, he is going to build a temple.

Notice the date in verse 1: 'In the twenty-fifth year of our exile, at the beginning of the year'. Ezekiel is mentioning this figure – twenty-five – because he is flagging up to those reading the book that they are halfway to the Year of Jubilee (see also Ezekiel 46:17). Every fifty years, on the tenth day of the seventh month, the people of Israel celebrate a Year of Jubilee. Slaves are released, the land is liberated from bondage, and debts are cancelled. The Year of Jubilee becomes a great picture of salvation, the final vindication of God.

Ezekiel is prophesying to a people faced with the absence of God. He gives these exiles, with their temple destroyed and their city devastated, a glorious vision of what it will be like when God is present in all his fullness, might and power. He thrills their hearts with a vision of heaven and reminds them that they are almost there. They are on their way to the Year of Jubilee, when they'll experience full salvation and the final vindication of God.

Take a trip up the mountain. Read God's description of heaven in Revelation 21 – 22. Soak up that spectacular view of God's new world and all he has planned for you. Today, if God seems silent, or if you face temptations, struggles and disappointments, hold on to that glorious vision. Hope in God and trust his promises.

Day 118

Read Ezekiel 43:1–12
Key verses: Ezekiel 43:1–5

••

¹Then the man brought me to the gate facing east, ²and I saw the glory of the God of Israel coming from the east. His voice was like the roar of rushing waters, and the land was radiant with his glory. ³The vision I saw was like the vision I had seen when he came to destroy the city and like the visions I had seen by the River Kebar, and I fell face down. ⁴The glory of the LORD entered the temple through the gate facing east. ⁵Then the Spirit lifted me up and brought me into the inner court, and the glory of the LORD filled the temple.

Ezekiel's vision is so graphic, we can almost hear God's glory surging back into the temple.

In chapter 11, Ezekiel saw a vision of the glory of the Lord departing from the Most Holy Place. Now, in chapter 43, the description of the temple culminates in the glory of God coming back through the eastern door to be present with his people (verse 4).

The God who marched before Israel through the desert now lives with them on his holy hill. Of course, the Israelites never believed God's presence was tied to any geographical spot (2 Chronicles 6:18). While the temple represents the presence of God, it never limits it, for God is in the midst of his people. Ezekiel's ministry teaches these exiles that the indestructible temple is the presence of God in glory among and with his people, wherever they find themselves (11:16).

Interestingly, Luke's Gospel begins in the temple with Jesus being brought in for dedication. Held in the hands of Simeon, he is described as 'the glory of your people Israel' (Luke 2:32), a title often used to refer to the temple. Where do we see the temple in the New

Testament? Where is the radiance of God's glory? John says, 'We have seen his glory, the glory of the one and only Son, who came from the Father, full of grace and truth' (John 1:14).

John makes the link clearer when he records Jesus turning over the tables of the temple traders. Jesus isn't simply making a statement against those who are ripping off the tourists coming to worship God. He halts the way the temple does its business; he suspends the process of offering sacrifices. And this leads to a discussion about who Jesus is. The people ask for a sign. 'Jesus answers them, "Destroy this temple, and I will raise it again in three days." They reply, "It has taken forty-six years to build this temple, and you are going to raise it in three days?" But the temple he had spoken of was his body' (John 2:19–21).

You cannot read Ezekiel's description of that perfectly holy temple without using your New Testament to tell you that God's final, perfect temple is Jesus.

God is not just among us and with us but he is *in* us – 'Christ in you, the hope of glory' (Colossians 1:27). Today, reflect on this awesome privilege and responsibility: 'Do you not know that your bodies are temples of the Holy Spirit, who is in you, whom you have received from God? You are not your own; you were bought at a price. Therefore honour God with your bodies' (1 Corinthians 6:19–20).

Day 119

Read Ezekiel 43:10–27
Key verses: Ezekiel 43:10–12

....

> ¹⁰ *Son of man, describe the temple to the people of Israel, that they may be ashamed of their sins. Let them consider its perfection,* ¹¹ *and if they are ashamed of all they have done, make known to them the design of the temple – its arrangement, its exits and entrances – its whole design and all its regulations and laws. Write these down before them so that they may be faithful to its design and follow all its regulations.*
> ¹² *This is the law of the temple: all the surrounding area on top of the mountain will be most holy. Such is the law of the temple.*

Imagine the temple as a gate (see Ezekiel 48:30–35).

Like a gate, the temple provides access to God's presence. Many times a day people come to the temple to offer sacrifices, acknowledging that they can only approach this holy God if their sins have been paid for.

At the same time, the temple is also a gate to keep people out of God's presence. Gentiles can't get into the temple compound, women can get in only so far, men a bit further, priests further still, but only the high priest is able to get into the Most Holy Place, and that just once a year. The temple emphasizes the barrier of sin that keeps people away from God.

So the temple is both a barrier and a means of access. It systematically excludes certain groups and keeps others at a distance, but at the same time offers a way for people to come to know God.

The climax of Ezekiel's temple description is this massive altar that dominates the sanctuary. It is bigger than the altar described in Leviticus. It is bigger than the altar the Jews actually constructed when they rebuilt the temple. This altar signifies God's grace and welcome, and takes a central place because it is only by sacrifice that this reconciliation and acceptance take place.

But even the blood of goats and bulls can't take away sin (Hebrews 10:4). What sacrifice makes us absolutely acceptable to God? There is only one sacrifice for all time: the sacrifice of our Lord Jesus. He is the real gate (John 10:7–10).

> Therefore, brothers and sisters, since we have confidence to enter the Most Holy Place by the blood of Jesus, by a new and living way opened for us through the curtain, that is, his body, and since we have a great priest over the house of God, let us draw near to God with a sincere heart and with the full assurance that faith brings, having our hearts sprinkled to cleanse us from a guilty conscience and having our bodies washed with pure water.
> (Hebrews 10:19–22)

It is right to feel shame when we see our sin in the light of God's perfection (Ezekiel 43:10). But Christ's sacrifice has completely dealt with your sin. God's wrath is satisfied – you are justified and forgiven. Jesus' death provides a pathway into God's presence, and your heavenly Father is waiting to welcome you with open arms. Today, meditate on Hebrews 10:19–22 and let God's Word nourish your soul.

Day 120

Read Ezekiel 44:10–31
Key verses: Ezekiel 44:13, 15–16, 23

....

¹³ They [the Levites who served idols] are not to come near to serve me as priests or come near any of my holy things or my most holy offerings; they must bear the shame of their detestable practices . . .

¹⁵ But the Levitical priests, who are descendants of Zadok and who guarded my sanctuary when the Israelites went astray from me, are to come near to minister before me; they are to stand before me to offer sacrifices of fat and blood, declares the Sovereign LORD. ¹⁶ They alone are to enter my sanctuary; they alone are to come near my table to minister before me and serve me as guards . . .

²³ They are to teach my people the difference between the holy and the common and show them how to distinguish between the unclean and the clean.

What is happening inside the temple?

Ezekiel describes a reformed priesthood offering worship. It is a God-centred community, a holy people in a holy place.

Under the old covenant, the people were separated from the priesthood. And we still tend to view holiness as something reserved for the 'spiritual elite' – missionaries and ministers. But God's desire has always been that his people serve him as priests (Exodus 19). Christ's death has made that possible. As Peter explains, 'You are a chosen people, a royal priesthood, a holy nation, God's special possession, that you may declare the praises of him who called you out of darkness into his wonderful light' (1 Peter 2:9). We are the God-centred community, a holy people in a holy place, that Ezekiel spoke of.

So 'as you come to him, the living Stone – rejected by humans but chosen by God and precious to him – you also, like living stones, are being built into a spiritual house to be a holy priesthood, offering spiritual sacrifices acceptable to God through Jesus Christ' (1 Peter 2:4–5).

When we give generously to God's work, that is a fragrant offering, an acceptable sacrifice, pleasing to God. When we sing and celebrate what God has done, we are offering him a sacrifice of praise. And more than that, our whole lives can be offered as a living sacrifice to God (Romans 12:1).

These New Testament images of sacrifice and priesthood are taken straight out of Ezekiel and remind those of us who are Christians, indwelt by the Holy Spirit, that we are called to holiness.

It doesn't matter what label you might give yourself – you could be a student, a parent, unemployed or retired – your primary role is that of a priest. God has placed you in a specific context, with a specific set of relationships and responsibilities, to be his priest there. What does that look like for you? What are the spiritual sacrifices you are offering to God? How is your holiness making an impact? Ask for God's help to be his priest. Today, serve sacrificially, make every effort to be holy, and devote yourself to God and his work.

Day 121

Read Ezekiel 47:1–12
Key verses: Ezekiel 47:1, 12

••

> [1] *The man brought me back to the entrance to the temple, and I saw water coming out from under the threshold of the temple towards the east (for the temple faced east). The water was coming down from under the south side of the temple, south of the altar . . .*
>
> *[The stream became a river.]* [12] *Fruit trees of all kinds will grow on both banks of the river. Their leaves will not wither, nor will their fruit fail. Every month they will bear fruit, because the water from the sanctuary flows to them. Their fruit will serve for food and their leaves for healing.*

Whether you are in the Amazon jungle or the Highlands of Scotland, wherever a river flows, there is life.

We notice that a river flows from the south side of the temple – interestingly, that's the place of sacrifice. Other prophets spoke of this. Joel prophesied of a day when a fountain would flow from the Lord's house (Joel 3:18). Zechariah said, 'On that day living water will flow out from Jerusalem' (Zechariah 14:8).

Jesus, the final temple, also uses the image of a river bringing life. Sitting by the well with the Samaritan woman, who is excluded from the temple, he offers her a way to worship God. Jesus tells her, 'Everyone who drinks this water will be thirsty again, but whoever drinks the water I give them will never thirst. Indeed, the water I give them will become in them a spring of water welling up to eternal life' (John 4:13–14).

Similarly, in John 7:37–38, 'Jesus stood and said in a loud voice, "Let anyone who is thirsty come to me and drink. Whoever believes in me, as Scripture has said, rivers of living water will flow from within them."'

The river motif runs throughout Scripture, right to Revelation. In Revelation 22, the Lamb is among his people, and God is there with them. We read of 'the river of the water of life, as clear as crystal, flowing from the throne of God and of the Lamb' (verse 1). Ezekiel says that where that river flows, everything will live. It brings life and healing to the nations.

Jesus still offers living water. He said, 'I have come that they may have life, and have it to the full' (John 10:10).

Does your spiritual life feel stagnant? Perhaps you have tried many ways to jump-start it. But there is really only one way: come to Christ. Return to him and drink deeply: spend time in his presence, praying and reading his Word. Let his living waters cleanse you from sin, revive your soul and satisfy the deepest longings of your heart. We look forward to the day when God will renew the whole of creation, but you can experience renewal today. You can be a Psalm 1 Christian – refreshed and fruitful – if you plant your roots deep in Christ and drink from his life-giving stream (see Day 1).

Day 122

Read Ezekiel 48:1–35
Key verses: Ezekiel 48:29, 35

. . . .

²⁹ *'This is the land you are to allot as an inheritance to the tribes of Israel, and these will be their portions,' declares the Sovereign LORD . . .*
³⁵ *'The distance all around will be 18,000 cubits.*
'And the name of the city from that time on will be:
THE LORD IS THERE.*'*

Are you spending your children's inheritance, or have your parents spent yours? Don't worry. Every child of God has a guaranteed inheritance!

In chapter 48, Ezekiel picks up the city metaphor again as he talks about the land that is the inheritance of God's people. Every tribe has a portion, an allotted space in this heaven Ezekiel is describing.

Remember the language Jesus uses in Matthew 5 when he quotes Psalm 37:11: 'the meek . . . will inherit the earth'. The word for 'earth' used here can be translated 'land'. Right now we don't have a land; we're still aliens and strangers. As the author of Hebrews explains, 'Here we do not have an enduring city, but we are looking for the city that is to come' (Hebrews 13:14). Ezekiel 48 is saying that in that city there will be a place for you.

Jesus likewise encourages his disciples:

My Father's house has many rooms; if that were not so, would I have told you that I am going there to prepare a place for you? And if I go and prepare a place for you, I will come back and take you to be with me that you also may be where I am.
(John 14:2–3)

The book of Revelation picks up much of its imagery from Ezekiel's heavenly vision. John presents us with a new Jerusalem. In this new city, the people of God are from both the old and the new covenants because the names of the apostles as well as the prophets are written on the foundations and walls of the city. All of God's people are there.

There is only one difference. John says, 'I did not see a temple in the city, because the Lord God Almighty and the Lamb are its temple' (Revelation 21:22). This is the definitive New Testament explanation of Ezekiel's vision. The Lord God Almighty and the Lamb are the city's temple. The entire city has become a holy place. There is no altar, because the Lamb, the one who made the sacrifice, is at the heart of the new Jerusalem. Everyone who is there has got in because of the sacrifice Jesus made on the cross.

Ezekiel's last words describe the city: 'THE LORD IS THERE.' And we hear the echo of John's words in Revelation 21:3: 'Look! God's dwelling-place is now among the people, and he will dwell with them. They will be his people, and God himself will be with them and be their God.'

Ezekiel's vision of heaven is our destiny. We are almost there.

What would make heaven heaven for you? An end to pain, seeing loved ones again, discovering the answers to all your questions? In truth, heaven will be heaven simply because God is there. Being with God and enjoying him for ever – this is your inheritance. While you wait, don't lose heart; don't let doubts or grief throw you off course. Stay faithful, keep pressing on: you are almost there!

For further study

If you would like to do further study on Ezekiel, the following books may be useful:

- Iain Duguid, *Ezekiel*, NIV Application Commentary (Zondervan, 1999).

- John Goldingay, *Lamentations and Ezekiel for Everyone* (SPCK, 2015).

- Derek Thomas, *God Strengthens: Ezekiel Simply Explained* (Evangelical Press, 2004).

- Christopher Wright, *The Message of Ezekiel*, The Bible Speaks Today (IVP, 2001).

If God has fed you through your study of the book of Ezekiel, why not buy the individual Food for the Journey on Ezekiel and give it to a friend (available from ivpbooks.com)?

Introduction
John 14 – 17

Simon Manchester

Troubled. Confused. Uncertain.

After three years with Jesus, there is still so much the disciples don't understand.

They are reeling from the news that someone in their inner circle will betray the Lord. Perhaps worse still is Jesus' prediction that their fiery and courageous friend Peter will deny him, and that Jesus' death is imminent. It is unthinkable.

On this night of nights, with the agony of Calvary approaching and his own heart heavy, what will Jesus say to them? What comfort can he possibly offer? What essential truths does he want the disciples to grasp?

Reclining at the meal table, Jesus answers questions, teaches and prays for his disciples. In this final tutorial, he wants to remind them of his love and his steadfast faithfulness, and that he is utterly trustworthy. Regardless of what is to come, he is in complete control, and the coming days will unfold according to his sovereign plan. He reassures them that his death will open up the way to heaven for them, and, until his return, his Holy Spirit will guide them into all truth. He anticipates the opposition they will face, but reveals how their union with him will keep them and make them fruitful. In these last moments together, Jesus is passionately interested in their holiness, unity and perseverance.

Today, disciples of Jesus still feel troubled, confused and uncertain. Perhaps we are asking different questions, but we still wrestle with doubts and concerns. Jesus longs to bring reassurance and, even now, he is praying for you. The apostle John invites you to listen in on this final tutorial and hear these essential truths. Let Jesus' words take root in your heart and mind; let them reshape the focus and priorities of your life and bring you comfort and hope.

Day 123

Read John 13:31 – 14:14

Key verses: John 13:31 – 14:3

. . . .

³¹ Jesus said, 'Now the Son of Man is glorified and God is glorified in him. ³² If God is glorified in him, God will glorify the Son in himself, and will glorify him at once.

³³ 'My children, I will be with you only a little longer. You will look for me, and just as I told the Jews, so I tell you now: where I am going, you cannot come.

³⁴ 'A new command I give you: love one another. As I have loved you, so you must love one another. ³⁵ By this everyone will know that you are my disciples, if you love one another.'

³⁶ Simon Peter asked him, 'Lord, where are you going?'

Jesus replied, 'Where I am going, you cannot follow now, but you will follow later.'

³⁷ Peter asked, 'Lord, why can't I follow you now? I will lay down my life for you.'

³⁸ Then Jesus answered, 'Will you really lay down your life for me? Very truly I tell you, before the cock crows, you will disown me three times!

^{14:1} 'Do not let your hearts be troubled. You believe in God; believe also in me. ² My Father's house has many rooms; if that were not so, would I have told you that I am going there to prepare a place for you? ³ And if I go and prepare a place for you, I will come back and take you to be with me that you also may be where I am.'

Worry is usually our default setting. We worry about our family, job, finances, singleness, reputation, the future, and a host of other big and small issues. We've heard Jesus' command, 'Do not let your hearts be troubled', but we don't know how we could possibly apply it. Is Jesus really asking us not to worry?

His words in John 14:1 sound like the start of a conversation, but we're actually joining it part way through. Jesus has just washed his disciples' feet, they have had their last meal together, and Judas has left. Jesus has told them that he is going to die and rise again three days later, but they will not be coming with him on this particular journey; they are going to stay and love one another.

The only thing Peter hears from this whole conversation is that Jesus is going to die. And he objects! Jesus says he can follow him later, but Peter says, 'No, I'll follow you now; in fact, I'll die for you. That's how capable I am.'

Jesus immediately replies, 'Do not let your hearts be troubled. You believe in God; believe also in me.'

Do you see what Jesus is doing? He is saying, 'Peter, you are not that brave, you are not going to be that successful, you're going to disown me, and you are not worth trusting in. Put your trust in something trustworthy, in someone who can deal with your fears. You trust in God; I am not inferior to God. Trust in me. I will take care of the future.' Notice how many times 'I' is repeated in verses 2–3, Jesus is saying, 'I go, I prepare, I'll come, I'll take – I, I, I. Trust me. I'll do this, not you, Peter.'

Jesus' answer to troubled hearts – then and now – is to trust him.

'Do not let your heart be troubled' – this is God's command to you today. The only real antidote to worry is trusting in Jesus. The problem is that many of us, like Peter, are DIY or do-it-yourself Christians. We like to depend on our own abilities. We want to do things ourselves and we can't quite accept that salvation is not something we have to contribute to. Maybe we need to say, 'It's going to be Jesus who will do the work: he will be the Saviour; he will carry me through. It's him I should be trusting, and there must be less focus on me and much more on him.' What do you need to trust Jesus with today?

Day 124

Read John 14:1–14

Key verses: John 14:2–3

....

> ² *My Father's house has many rooms; if that were not so, would I*
> *have told you that I am going there to prepare a place for you?*
> ³ *And if I go and prepare a place for you, I will come back and*
> *take you to be with me that you also may be where I am.*

How can we be sure of heaven?

Jesus promises us a future with him: that's what will make heaven,
heaven (verse 3). But how can we be certain?

In verse 2, Jesus says, 'I am going to prepare a place for you.' The NIV
says, 'I am going *there* to prepare a place for you' (italics added).
And so most people mistakenly think that Jesus is saying, 'I am going
to heaven to prepare a place for you.' They imagine him going up to
heaven with a hammer and chisel to prepare a room for us.

But Jesus is not saying that. He is saying, 'I am going *out* to prepare
a place for you. I am not going *up* to prepare a place for you. I am
going *out* – out of this room, *out* of this city, and when I am on the
cross, I am going to be *out* of fellowship with the Father. And because
I am going *out*, you can go *in*. Because I get the *exit*, you get the
entrance; because I get *banished*, you get *welcomed*.'

Mark 15 describes the scene. On the cross, Jesus cries out, 'My God,
my God, why have you forsaken me?' And suddenly the temple
curtain splits from top to bottom (verses 34, 38). Jesus was separated
from his Father's presence so we could be welcomed in.

If getting to heaven depended on us, then we really would have something to worry about. But take heart, there is nothing we can do to earn our place in heaven; no tradition to keep or ritual we can perform. Your future is totally secure because it has nothing to do with your achievements, obedience or goodness. Your entrance into heaven, your place at the heavenly banquet, is certain solely because of Jesus' death on the cross. Because he paid the punishment for your sin, because he appeased God's wrath, your relationship with God is restored, your home in heaven secure.

Meditate on how much your place in heaven cost Jesus. Worship him today for the price he was willing to pay. Delight in the truth that you are greatly loved by an awesome God! 'For God so loved the world that he gave his one and only Son, that whoever believes in him shall not perish but have eternal life' (John 3:16).

Day 125

Read John 14:1–14
Key verses: John 14:4–7

. . . .

> [4] *'You know the way to the place where I am going.'*
>
> [5] *Thomas said to him, 'Lord, we don't know where you are going, so how can we know the way?'*
>
> [6] *Jesus answered, 'I am the way and the truth and the life. No one comes to the Father except through me.* [7] *If you really know me, you will know my Father as well. From now on, you do know him and have seen him.'*

Sometimes we make Christianity sound too complicated. We talk in theological jargon, forgetting that, in essence, Christianity is all about a person – it is all about Christ.

Thomas has been following the conversation around the dinner table, and in sheer desperation he blurts out, 'We don't know where you are going, so how can we know the way?'

Jesus recognizes that explaining the crucifixion would be too difficult for the disciples to understand. So instead, he says, 'I want you to focus on me, the person. Let's not talk so much about atonement, reconciliation, redemption. Let's just concentrate on me.'

And then he says the famous words in verse 6: 'I am the way and the truth and the life.' Thomas is asking, 'Is there any way to God?' and Jesus answers, 'I am the way.'

This is the sixth time Jesus uses the phrase 'I am' in John's Gospel. 'I am' is a derivative of Yahweh, Jehovah, and therefore Jesus is using an explosive phrase when he describes himself again and again as 'I am'. He is declaring that he is the eternal God in the flesh. He also attaches highly significant metaphors. So when he says, 'I am the bread,' or 'I am the shepherd,' there are huge Old Testament implications.

During this last supper together, Jesus wants the disciples to know that they can trust him because he is the way to God: because he is the truth, he is reliable; and what flows from him is the life that is for ever, that is unbreakable. Jesus wants these men to understand that knowing and trusting him is just the same as knowing and trusting God the Father.

Jesus is the way to God, the truth about God and the life of God, because he *is* God. Today, Jesus says to you: 'I am sufficient. I am sovereign. I am the God who sees you. I am your provider. I am faithful. I am righteous. I am gracious. I am compassionate and merciful. I am eternal. I am your refuge. I am your healer. I am your restorer. I am your defender. I am your rock. I am your redeemer.'

Bring your circumstances and needs before him now, and imagine him responding by reminding you that he is 'I am . . .' Which of his character traits would he want to remind you of today?

Day 126

Read John 14:1–14
Key verse: John 14:6

....

> ⁶*Jesus answered, 'I am the way and the truth and the life. No one comes to the Father except through me.'*

'Tolerance' is a popular word these days. In our multifaith, multicultural society, 'tolerance' is seen as the only way to preserve unity.

But what is tolerance? When people speak of tolerance, they often mean, 'I will love you as long as we can both agree that whatever we say is all true.' But making our love for people conditional on agreeing that everything is true doesn't make sense – in the world or the church.

We must have a different understanding of the term 'tolerance', one that loves people regardless of disagreements on the issues. True tolerance says, 'I will love you whatever you say or do. I may completely disagree with what you are saying, but I will keep being patient and kind and I will stay with you.'

Although not primarily dealing with the question of whether there are many ways to God, this verse does stand in the face of plural religions. Jesus' statement, 'I am the way and the truth and the life. No one comes to the Father except through me', shatters the contemporary view of tolerance.

But Jesus can see more clearly, love more dearly and speak so plainly because he genuinely wants people to be safe and secure. If you are in a burning building and you happen to know that only one door is unlocked, there is nothing loving about saying to the people in the building, 'Pick your door.' The loving thing is to push them, if necessary, towards the door that will open. This is what Jesus is doing here. He is lovingly saying that he's the door and we must come to him.

We need to be sensitive and wise in the way we share the gospel with our non-Christian family, friends and colleagues. Sometimes being silent is the best option! However, we can also get into a rut of not sharing our faith at all: essentially saying to those around us, 'Pick your door.' Ask God to help you push people through the right door – through your prayers, kindness, conversations, attitudes and actions. Pray for the opportunity to speak to one person about Jesus today. And when he gives you the opportunity, go for it!

Day 127

Read John 14:1–14
Key verses: John 14:8–11

<hr>

[8] *Philip said, 'Lord, show us the Father and that will be enough for us.'*

[9] *Jesus answered: 'Don't you know me, Philip, even after I have been among you such a long time? Anyone who has seen me has seen the Father. How can you say, "Show us the Father"?* [10] *Don't you believe that I am in the Father, and that the Father is in me? The words I say to you I do not speak on my own authority. Rather, it is the Father, living in me, who is doing his work.* [11] *Believe me when I say that I am in the Father and the Father is in me; or at least believe on the evidence of the works themselves.'*

It would be so much easier if God were to write his will in the sky, speak audibly or even appear in a dream. If God were to speak that clearly, we'd definitely obey him! Just a bit more information, just a little bit more clarity – surely that would make all the difference?

Philip thinks the same. In verse 8, he says, 'Lord, show us the Father and that will be enough for us.' He has seen Jesus turn water into wine, heal the lame man, feed thousands, heal the blind and raise Lazarus from the dead. What Jesus has done and said is extra-ordinary, but still Philip is dissatisfied and says, 'I just wish I had a little more information.'

Jesus replies by telling Philip, 'If you have seen me, you have seen the Father.' And he goes on, 'The words I say to you I do not speak on my own authority. Rather, it is the Father, living in me, who is doing his work.' We expect him to say, 'The words I speak are the words the Father speaks.' But instead, he links the Word of God and the work of God. He is saying, 'My words are the Father's work. When

I speak, God works. So believe that the Father and I are profoundly related and work together.'

Jesus' answer to Philip, and to us if we're dissatisfied, is to go back to his words and his works. Don't wait for God to speak across the sky: that's probably not going to happen. Say to God, 'If you work by your Word and I go back to your Word, would you do a new work in me? Would you renew my trust and my belief? Would you renew my repentance and my obedience? Would you renew my usefulness?'

Be encouraged: we have all the riches of Christ Jesus. We have the Scriptures, and the Holy Spirit is our teacher. We need simply to learn from this anguished conversation with Philip to go back to what we have and to ask God to work with the Word that he has given us.

It is easy to look around at other Christians and become dissatisfied. They seem to be more spiritual than us, to enjoy a deeper communion with God and to receive clearer guidance from him. Our knee-jerk reaction is to look for a quick fix, or to search for the secret spiritual ingredient we must be missing.

Call the search off! The Bible assures us we have everything we need for the life of faith (2 Peter 1:3).

According to Jesus' words here in John, it seems that we determine how spiritual we want to be and we choose how close to God we want to be. Through the Bible and with the help of the Holy Spirit, we can get to know Jesus personally and intimately, and be equipped for holy living. What is holding you back?

Day 128

Read John 14:1–14
Key verses: John 14:12–14

．．

> [12] *Very truly I tell you, whoever believes in me will do the works I have been doing, and they will do even greater things than these, because I am going to the Father.* [13] *And I will do whatever you ask in my name, so that the Father may be glorified in the Son.* [14] *You may ask me for anything in my name, and I will do it.*

Critics often claim, 'You can't take the Bible literally.' And these verses seem to add weight to their argument. Verse 12 certainly looks like an exaggeration, doesn't it?

If you have faith in Jesus, he says, you 'will do even greater things'. And if 'greater' means doing *better* things than Jesus, how can he be serious? Am I really going to turn water into wine? Am I really going to feed more people with a few loaves and fishes? Am I really going to bring more Lazaruses out of their graves? Impossible!

What Jesus means is that you are going to do things of greater quality. Those of you who put your trust in Jesus, you are going to point people to him! You are not going to point people to a loaf of bread, but to the Bread of Life. You are not going to send people to a little lampstand, but to the Light of the World. You are not going to offer people resuscitation on a hospital bed, but the resurrection that outlasts the world. You are going to do greater things, things that all the miracles in John's Gospel have been pointing to – you are going to point people to Jesus.

How will we do these things? By asking Jesus for help: 'And I will do whatever you ask in my name, so that the Father may be glorified.' But be careful not to assume that Jesus is giving carte blanche to our prayer requests. He is speaking here in the context of helping people come to him. He is promising that even though he is going back to the Father, he will help us point people to him. That's what he delights to do.

You have the opportunity of doing greater things than Jesus today! What an incredible thought and an awesome responsibility. Jesus knew that every day he had to be busy with his Father's work – and we must too. Whatever our daily lives look like, whatever our routines or responsibilities, our main role is to point people to Jesus. Think about all the people you will meet today. Will your actions, attitudes and words point them towards Jesus, or away from him? What opportunities could you take to point people to Jesus? Remember, he delights to help you. Will you ask for his help today?

Day 129

Read John 14:12–21

Key verses: John 14:14–15

....

¹⁴You may ask me for anything in my name, and I will do it.
¹⁵If you love me, keep my commands.

Have you been praying for years for the same friends or family members to become Christians? Are unanswered prayers making you feeling discouraged?

We looked at verse 14 briefly yesterday, but it's worth remembering that when you send up your prayers and ask God to act, you are not asking for some small-scale system to work. When we pray, it's not as if we are just calling a plumber and expecting him to come that day. It's not as though we are putting money into a machine and expecting to get a can of Coke back in ten seconds. God may do amazingly speedy things, and we love it when he does so. But we also need to remember that when we pray to our Father, we are putting our requests to someone who is organizing an eternal, cosmic, majestic, huge plan. And if we ask how God is going to be glorified (verse 13), it may be that it is not going to be via a fast answer. It may be that God will be glorified through a long, brilliant process.

God hears every prayer that is uttered – not one of them gets lost. He hears our prayers better than a parent hears the cry of a child, but the whole process of his genius, all the machinery of heaven and the processes of eternity are being worked out by this great heavenly Father, so don't be too impatient.

I'm sure Jacob prayed for his son Joseph to return home that day (Genesis 37), but imagine if God had answered his prayers? What a tragedy! Instead, our great, loving, majestic God replied, 'You have absolutely no idea what I am going to do. I will bring him back, but it's going to be a long and most fruitful path. When he eventually does come back, astronomical things will have been done.'

So don't lose heart when you pray. Jesus says in verse 15, 'If you love me, keep my commands.' I wonder whether this is the command he means. I wonder if Jesus is saying, 'I am commanding you to keep praying because it's a great task I am leaving you to do in the world. I don't want you to forget to ask for help. Totally and brilliantly, I am presenting your case in heaven, and the Holy Spirit is going to help you and wonderfully supply all you need for your ministry in the world.'

Who are you praying for to become a Christian? If you don't pray regularly for a handful of people, start now! We were never meant to be active in pointing people to Jesus without covering all our efforts in prayer. Jesus is your advocate in heaven, bringing every one of your prayers before God's throne. As the Puritans used to say, 'The prayer of the believer is deathless.' If God seems delayed in answering your prayers, don't allow yourself to give up or become discouraged. Keep on praying and keep on trusting. Who knows what marvellous plan God is putting in place?

Day 130

Read John 14:15–21
Key verses: John 14:16–17

....

[16] And I will ask the Father, and he will give you another advocate to help you and be with you for ever – [17] the Spirit of truth. The world cannot accept him, because it neither sees him nor knows him. But you know him, for he lives with you and will be in you.

How well do you know the Holy Spirit? He is probably the least-understood member of the Trinity, and subsequently the subject of many debates.

The word 'advocate' appears five times in the New Testament – four times in these chapters of John's Gospel and once in the first letter of John. The Greek word *parakletos*, 'to be called alongside', has no real English equivalent. We will never find one word to do justice to the majestic, multiple ministry of the Holy Spirit. We know from Scripture that he teaches, convicts, leads, guides and helps; that he can be grieved, resisted and quenched; and that he is a person, not a force or an 'it'. So the translators come up with words like Counsellor, Advocate, Paraclete, Helper, but none of them completely describes the great work of the Holy Spirit.

Wonderfully, verse 16 tells us that the Holy Spirit will be with us, 'for ever'. In the Old Testament, the Holy Spirit left Saul (1 Samuel 16:14), and Psalm 51 records David's desperate plea that the Spirit wouldn't leave him. Here, Jesus promises that the Holy Spirit will never leave us.

He will move in and live with you, and your sin, until you see God face to face, and then you will be sinless. Aren't you grateful that the Holy Spirit stays with us for ever, that when we sin he doesn't leave us, and instead he graciously convicts us?

Whereas the Holy Spirit 'lives with you and will be in you' (verse 17), the world doesn't know, and is hostile to, God's Spirit, for the secular person cannot appreciate the things of the Spirit. This doesn't make Christians any better or smarter than unbelievers; it only means that God's grace has brought us to Jesus and made us alive to the Holy Spirit's work. Interestingly, the word 'you' here is actually in the plural. The Holy Spirit will be in you individually and corporately. That's why when Christians gather together, we have such rich fellowship. That's why being part of the church family is so important.

Read the key verses again, noticing every time the word 'you' is mentioned. Do you see how personal and intimate the Holy Spirit wants to be with you? He is the ever-ready, ever-present 'God with us'.

No matter how much you grieve him, he will never leave you. But he longs for greater access to your heart, for greater obedience from you, and to share greater ministry with you. He wants to work in and through you, to bring transformation and to make you more like Christ. Why resist such an amazing gift? Today, invite the Holy Spirit to have his way in your life. Give him complete access to teach, guide, convict and help you.

Day 131

Read John 14:15–21

Key verses: John 14:18–20

....

> [18] I will not leave you as orphans; I will come to you. [19] Before long, the world will not see me any more, but you will see me. Because I live, you also will live. [20] On that day you will realise that I am in my Father, and you are in me, and I am in you.

Sometimes we struggle to understand Jesus' words. Often, it is only in hindsight that their meaning becomes clear.

For example, what does Jesus mean when he says, 'I will not *leave* you as orphans; I will *come* to you'? Does he mean, 'I'm going to leave you on Friday and come back on Sunday'? Yes. Does he mean, 'I am about to leave you in forty days, fifty days, and I'll come as the Holy Spirit comes and takes residence in your life'? Yes. Does he mean, 'I am about to ascend, but one day I will return'? Yes – he means all of these things. But in verse 19, he says, 'You will see me', and so primarily he means that the disciples will see him quite quickly after the resurrection.

It is only after the resurrection and the coming of the Holy Spirit that the disciples finally understand Jesus' promise: 'Because I live, you also will live' (verse 19). This promise is also for us. He lives so that we who believe might live. As soon as you sent up your prayer to him for salvation, he committed himself to you, Shepherd to sheep: 'I will get you home. Because I live, you will live.'

I love the story of the nineteenth-century Baptist preacher Charles Haddon Spurgeon, who, when visiting his orphanage, got out a basin of water in front of the children and plunged his hands into it. He said to the boys and girls, 'Now, why don't my hands drown?' And one little boy said, 'Because your head's not in the water!' That's it, isn't it? Our head, the Lord Jesus, has risen. He is alive, always alive, so that we, his body, cannot die.

Critics discount it, our peers scoff at it, and even some theologians dismiss it. But Jesus' bodily resurrection is at the core of our faith. It is a doctrine we need to investigate, believe and articulate well. Today, stand on the truth of this marvellous promise: because Jesus lives, we too will live. The reality of Jesus' resurrection means that we will be with the Lord for ever. This is a promise for those who grieve for Christian loved ones, those who are anxious about the future, those who are suffering – it is a promise for all of us. Don't just think about Jesus' resurrection on Easter Sunday. Today, let his resurrection and your hope of eternal life govern your choices, the activities you get involved in, and what your mind dwells on.

Day 132

Read John 14:15–24
Key verses: John 14:21–24

....

> [21] 'Whoever has my commands and keeps them is the one who loves me. The one who loves me will be loved by my Father, and I too will love them and show myself to them.'
>
> [22] Then Judas (not Judas Iscariot) said, 'But, Lord, why do you intend to show yourself to us and not to the world?'
>
> [23] Jesus replied, 'Anyone who loves me will obey my teaching. My Father will love them, and we will come to them and make our home with them. [24] Anyone who does not love me will not obey my teaching. These words you hear are not my own; they belong to the Father who sent me.'

Do you find it unsettling when Jesus says, 'If you love me, you will keep my commandments'?

Most of us would acknowledge that, even in our best moments, our love for Jesus is feeble and cool. Is Jesus actually saying here that obedience is crucial to our security? No, the faithfulness of Jesus is our security. He is faithful to us; his love for us makes us secure. So where does our love for him fit in? The Bible's answer is that our love for him increases the intimacy and enjoyment of that security.

Imagine taking your children on holiday. You help them into the car, put on their seat belts, shut the door and start driving. The security of your children is that you are driving, they are in their seats and the doors are closed. But those of you who have driven small children on long distances will know that their obedience is a big part of the happiness of the journey and a big part of the happiness of the holiday! I think that's what Jesus is saying here: our obedience has the wonderful effect of increasing intimacy, not security.

In verse 22, the other Judas questions why Jesus is going to show himself to so few people. Jesus refuses to discuss his strategy and replies, 'Don't question my plans, but question your heart, Judas. Is it open? Is it humble? We will make our home in such a heart.' This word 'home' in verse 23 is used only here and in John 14:2, where Jesus says, 'My Father's house has many rooms.' So Jesus is simply saying, 'If you are receptive and give a home to the living God, he will be receptive and give you an eternal home.' Welcome him, and he'll welcome you. Refuse him, and he'll refuse you.

Imagine Jesus as a guest in your heart. Are you making him welcome? Think about the books you read, the internet sites you browse, the TV programmes you watch, the relationships you have, the clothes you buy and the language you use. Do they make Jesus feel 'at home'? The security of your relationship with God is not in doubt – that is dependent on Jesus' faithfulness. But your enjoyment of that relationship, your intimacy with God, is dependent on your obedience; it is dependent on how welcoming you are. Today, ask the Holy Spirit to show you what needs to change so that Jesus feels more 'at home' in your heart. Ask for his strength to make those changes.

Day 133

Read John 14:21–31
Key verses: John 14:25–27

....

²⁵All this I have spoken while still with you. ²⁶But the Advocate, the Holy Spirit, whom the Father will send in my name, will teach you all things and will remind you of everything I have said to you. ²⁷Peace I leave with you; my peace I give you. I do not give to you as the world gives. Do not let your hearts be troubled and do not be afraid.

Do you enjoy looking through old photo albums? It's fun looking at ourselves – 'There I am!' 'Look at my hair!' 'What *was* I doing?' But not every photo in the family album is about us, and nor is every verse in the Bible. We need to beware of seeing ourselves in every verse.

Verse 25 is directed primarily at the apostles. The Holy Spirit is going to come, and in the following few weeks, months and years he will teach those apostles and remind them of everything Jesus said. This doesn't mean that the Holy Spirit is going to teach them all the topics of the world, but he's going to teach them all they need in order to be people of faith and faithfulness. How does John remember the very long speeches of Jesus or what he said in chapters 5, 6 or 7? The Holy Spirit enables, teaches and reminds him. And Peter explains that the Holy Spirit drove the apostles on like little sailing boats, enabling them to record the Scriptures (2 Peter 1:21).

Of course, the Holy Spirit is going to teach every generation. But whereas the apostles were taught so that they could record the Scriptures, we are taught in order that we would appreciate the Scriptures. So please remember the things that you hear and are preached to you, and ask for the Holy Spirit's help to drive them home. Remember the words of Bible teacher John Stott who, before preaching, would pray the following prayer:

> Heavenly Father, we bow in your presence.
> May your Word be our rule, your Holy Spirit our teacher,
> And your greater glory our supreme concern,
> Through Jesus Christ our Lord.
> (John R. W. Stott, *Between Two Worlds*, Eerdmans, 1982, p. 340)

And with God's Word in our hearts, it is no accident that peace follows (verse 27). Truth and peace always go together; they are related. Read what Jesus achieved on the cross, read the promises that apply to you, and know peace. Jesus does his atoning work on the cross and he gives his peace to us.

Today, know God's truth; enjoy his peace.

God comes into our frantic and fractured world, offering us his peace, a peace that is so different from the fragile and fleeting cessation of conflict and chaos we aim for. God wants so much more for us. His deep-seated, unshakeable, never-ending peace can't help but spring from a restored relationship with him. Knowing that we are forgiven and loved by our holy heavenly Father, that we have a secure identity, an eternal purpose and a sure hope for the future, guarantees an 'out-of-this-world' peace.

If you feel out of touch with God's peace, then go back to his Word. Think back over the sermons you have heard recently and the Bible passages you have read in the last few days and weeks. What Bible truths have you been reminded of? Which of these truths do you need to cling to today?

Day 134

Read John 14:21–31
Key verses: John 14:28–31

....

²⁸*You heard me say, 'I am going away and I am coming back to you.' If you loved me, you would be glad that I am going to the Father, for the Father is greater than I.* ²⁹*I have told you now before it happens, so that when it does happen you will believe.* ³⁰*I will not say much more to you, for the prince of this world is coming. He has no hold over me,* ³¹*but he comes so that the world may learn that I love the Father and do exactly what my Father has commanded me.*

Come now; let us leave.

Cults and other religions have had a field day with verse 28. Jesus' words, 'The Father is greater than I', at first glance seem to fly in the face of all we know about the Trinity, Jesus' divinity and his oneness with the Father (John 10:30). So what does Jesus mean here?

The clue is in the context. The Father is in heaven, Jesus is on the earth; the Father is in splendour, Jesus is in trouble; the Father is in perfection and Jesus is going to judgment. Where would you rather be? Jesus belongs in heaven. No wonder he is keen to return. He longs to return where he belongs, where the Father is, in a greater position and in a greater place.

Despite wanting to return to heaven, Jesus willingly goes to the cross. He knows the devil is coming to do what God has decided he will do (verse 30). Like a dog on a leash, Satan does not have free rein: his power is limited to what God permits. Nevertheless, Jesus goes to the cross because he loves you (John 3:16), but primarily because he loves the Father. His obedience and his love for the Father are all caught up in this absolutely perfect faithfulness to his Father (verse 31).

Love is not something we can contain; it always finds expression. Love for another person is demonstrated by a hug, a meal, help with the children, a cup of tea and a chat, and in a whole variety of other ways. Jesus' love for his Father is demonstrated on every page of the Gospels. Every act of obedience and every decision to be faithful was Jesus' declaration of love for his Father.

How does your love for God find expression? What act of obedience or faithfulness is God asking of you today? Ask for the Holy Spirit's help and strength as you offer these acts as love gifts to God today.

Day 135

Read John 15:1–8
Key verses: John 15:1, 5

. . . .

¹I am the true vine, and my Father is the gardener . . .
    ⁵I am the vine; you are the branches. If you remain in me and I in you, you will bear much fruit; apart from me you can do nothing.

There is a saying: 'A picture paints a thousand words.' And here the image of the vine and the branches is an incredibly vivid description of the intimacy and fruitfulness God wants us to experience with him.

John 15:1 introduces it along with the seventh of the 'I am' statements in the Gospel of John. But it is not a new image: the Old Testament is full of 'vine' teaching. 'You transplanted a vine from Egypt; you drove out the nations and planted it', but 'Your vine is cut down . . . Restore us, Lord God Almighty' (Psalm 80:8, 16, 19). Isaiah 5:2 says that the Lord had a vineyard and 'planted it with the choicest vines [that is, Israel] . . . Then he looked for a crop of good grapes, but it yielded only bad fruit.'

When the Old Testament disciples have failed to produce fruit, Jesus doesn't say, 'You New Testament disciples will produce good fruit.' He says, 'I am the vine; you are the branches' (verse 5). He'll produce the fruit through us. The Old Testament believers failed, and we New Testament believers will fail, but he will not fail. He will bear the fruit that he is looking for.

Jesus is the vine, the Father is the gardener, believers are the branches, and the purpose is fruit. But what is the fruit? It is not defined in this chapter, but it is referred to. For example, verse 8 says, 'This is to my Father's glory, that you bear much fruit.' And verse 16 gives another clue – it's what God desires: 'I . . . appointed you so that you might go and bear fruit – fruit that will last.' So we can be pretty sure that the fruit is something that brings God glory. It is what he desires – that is, fellowship with Christ, loving one another and being used by God to help other people come to Christ.

We all want to be fruitful. Even unbelievers long to achieve something significant and consequential with their lives. But, according to Jesus, true fruitfulness, fruit that will last, comes only from being a branch on his vine. So stop seeking significance and value from earthly achievements. Don't let a full inbox or recognition from colleagues, tutors and friends cloud your judgment. Instead, meditate on that image of the vine and the branches. You have been grafted 'into Christ'. Draw your life from him, allowing him to sustain you, and ask him to produce in you the type of fruit that will make a difference for eternity and bring him glory.

Day 136

Read John 15:1–8

Key verses: John 15:2, 6

....

> *²He cuts off every branch in me that bears no fruit, while every branch that does bear fruit he prunes so that it will be even more fruitful . . .*
>
> *⁶If you do not remain in me, you are like a branch that is thrown away and withers; such branches are picked up, thrown into the fire and burned.*

Have you ever tried the carrot-and-stick strategy? Perhaps you have used it to encourage good behaviour in your children, to motivate employees at work or to spur yourself on with your diet! A combination of rewards and punishments can be very effective.

Because we are complicated people and this 'remaining' is important, the Lord gives us a good mix of promises and warnings in verses 1–8. The promise is that Jesus desires to bear much fruit through you. The warning is that the fruitless branch goes to the fire. We need both the promises and the warnings in our Christian life – our fears need the promises; our sins need the warnings.

We may like to reduce Christianity to a slogan, but God is too wise for that. We need verses like John 10:28: 'No one will snatch them out of my hand.' And we also need verses like John 15:2: 'He cuts off every branch in me that bears no fruit.' They don't contradict each other. We need them both. God is the perfect Pastor and he knows we are capable of lurching from fear to foolishness. He gives us warnings and promises so that we'll be safe.

If you find yourself in despair, go to John 10:28. But if you are in a casual position where nothing really matters and you don't care, and you think you are getting the best of sin and salvation, it might not be a bad idea to go to John 15:2 and ask yourself whether this is a fruitful time. As long as you don't let verse 2 preoccupy you, it is a good warning.

Even when we find ourselves being pruned – which by definition is hurtful, painful and costly – remember that the person doing this is the Father who loves you. None of it is done with sadistic carelessness, but rather with great affection, love and purpose.

Use the vine illustration to consider and describe the current state of your spiritual life:

- Are you a dead branch, no longer connected to the vine or producing fruit, and needing to be chopped off?
- Are you a branch, grafted on to the main vine and producing fruit, regardless of external conditions?
- Are you being pruned by the gardener so that healthy growth and fruitfulness continue?

Which of God's warnings or promises do you need to take to heart today? Take seriously his warnings so that you don't become a dead branch. Cling to his promises that every bit of painful pruning – in whatever form it comes – is for your good and for his glory. Remember, pruning is the only way a branch keeps on being fruitful. So don't allow suffering or God's discipline to make you bitter, but recognize it for what it is – the loving gardener shaping you into the image of his Son.

Day 137

Read John 15:1–8
Key verses: John 15:4, 7

∙∙

⁴Remain in me, as I also remain in you. No branch can bear fruit by itself; it must remain in the vine. Neither can you bear fruit unless you remain in me . . .

⁷If you remain in me and my words remain in you, ask whatever you wish, and it will be done for you.

How many sermons have you heard that finish with the challenge to 'keep reading your Bible and praying'?

It's a well-worn theme! Shouldn't we have moved on from the basics? Surely there is a danger that our faith will become cold, stale and formulaic because we have heard everything, read everything and sung everything?

Jesus is not interested in this kind of distant, professional relationship with you. He is too jealous a husband for that. He is not satisfied with a cold marriage. Instead, he longs for close, warm, intimate fellowship. The cross has removed the barriers and has made that possible, and the Holy Spirit has brought new life into your heart to make that something you should long for.

The whole emphasis in verses 1–8 is to 'remain in Christ'. In fact, the Greek word that we translate 'remain' occurs ten times in the first eleven verses of this chapter. God's grace has grafted us into him, but we have a responsibility to stick close, to remain, to abide. That is surely why he says in verse 7, 'If you remain in me and my words remain in you, ask whatever you wish, and it will be done for you.' Do you see the combination of Scripture and prayer?

Jesus, the greatest teacher of all time, recognized that reading Scripture and praying provide the key to true fellowship. And every real Christian knows the difference between the dry orthodoxy that just turns the wheels, plays the game and goes to conventions, and the fresh fellowship that Jesus seeks and gives. We need to ask him for it, we need to read the Bible for it, and we need to pray for it. There is no shortcut to good fellowship with Jesus: the only way is by prayer and listening to his Word.

Be honest with yourself. Is your Christian life stale? Are you just going through the motions, or are you enjoying warm, deep fellowship with Jesus? Even if you feel close to him, there is always more intimate fellowship to enjoy. We can't exhaust God!

Jesus' death on the cross has removed the barrier; we can now draw close to him. But how close we get depends on us. The value we place on our fellowship with Jesus is measured by the effort we put into 'remaining in him'. There is no substitute for getting back to the basics – reading your Bible and praying. What are you doing to 'remain in him'? How intentional are you being?

If you don't already have a prayer partner, arrange to meet up regularly with a Christian friend to pray together and discuss what God has been teaching you through the Bible. Encourage each other to keep pressing on in the faith and into deeper fellowship with God.

Day 138

Read John 15:9–17
Key verses: John 15:9–12

....

⁹As the Father has loved me, so have I loved you. Now remain in my love. ¹⁰If you keep my commands, you will remain in my love, just as I have kept my Father's commands and remain in his love. ¹¹I have told you this so that my joy may be in you and that your joy may be complete. ¹²My command is this: love each other as I have loved you.

Many songwriters have told us, 'Love makes the world go round.' The world is certainly in need of true love, and in these verses Jesus teaches us about it.

First, before we can love others, we need to know where we ourselves stand. Although we don't deserve it, Jesus says, 'As the Father has loved me, so have I loved you.' In other words, 'Yes, the Father loved me perfectly and eternally, and I love you perfectly and eternally: that's a fact. You are a greatly loved person.'

Notice that Jesus uses the word 'loved' rather than 'loves'. He doesn't mean, 'I loved you in the past and I don't love you in the present.' He means, 'I loved you in the past and that's how I love you in the present. It's steadfast, fixed, a flag in the ground: I've loved you – it's established; it's decided.'

Second, we need to recognize that obedience blesses the relationship (John 15:10). Jesus is not saying that your security hangs on your obedience; he is saying that your intimacy with him will be affected by your obedience. This means that you can speak to someone today about Jesus because your security does not depend on his or her response. You are loved at the start of the conversation and at the end, regardless of what takes place.

Third, we need to realize what love means. Don't love people as you feel they should be loved or as the world loves; love them as you have been loved (verse 12). We are not going to lay down our lives and die for people, and we are certainly not going to save them, but we can put away self-interest and give freely of ourselves for their good.

Imagine the difference it would make to our church and community if we loved people like this.

You are loved. We don't often spend time thinking about how much God loves us. It seems self-indulgent, somehow. But allow yourself to dwell on this truth for a while:

> We are more than conquerors through him who *loved* us.
> (Romans 8:37, italics added)

> I no longer live, but Christ lives in me. The life I now live . . . I live by faith in the Son of God, who *loved* me.
> (Galatians 2:20, italics added)

> This is love: not that we loved God, but that he *loved* us.
> (1 John 4:10, italics added)

You are loved with a Calvary love. In the past, Jesus demonstrated his love for you on the cross, and that is how he loves you now. Never doubt that God loves you – passionately, completely and eternally. And there is nothing you can do to change that fact. 'Grace means there is nothing I can do to make God love me anymore and nothing I can do to make God love me any less' (Philip Yancey, *What's So Amazing about Grace*, Zondervan, 1997, p. 71).

Today, look for an opportunity to show that Calvary love to someone else.

Day 139

Read John 15:15–25

Key verses: John 15:18–25

···

[18] If the world hates you, keep in mind that it hated me first. [19] If you belonged to the world, it would love you as its own. As it is, you do not belong to the world, but I have chosen you out of the world. That is why the world hates you. [20] Remember what I told you: 'A servant is not greater than his master.' If they persecuted me, they will persecute you also. If they obeyed my teaching, they will obey yours also. [21] They will treat you this way because of my name, for they do not know the one who sent me. [22] If I had not come and spoken to them, they would not be guilty of sin; but now they have no excuse for their sin. [23] Whoever hates me hates my Father as well. [24] If I had not done among them the works no one else did, they would not be guilty of sin. As it is, they have seen, and yet they have hated both me and my Father. [25] But this is to fulfil what is written in their Law: 'They hated me without reason.'

John Piper says that we in the West are not in the fires of persecution, but in the freezer! We probably won't get burnt at the stake, but most of us will have felt cold hostility when we've tried to share the gospel.

But we shouldn't be surprised. 'If the world hates you' (verse 18) basically means, 'When the world hates you'. Jesus is not talking about geography, but the hostile world system that says we are the centre of the universe. If the church agrees that the world rotates around human beings, we'll be left alone – we are saying what the world wants to hear. But if we say that *Jesus* is the centre of the universe, then we will experience hostility.

Jesus wants us to be equipped to deal with this, so he reminds us that we are not the first to experience opposition. Jesus was the lightning rod for three years, attracting criticism; the church is now the lightning rod, but we are actually suffering for him. He is the one who is hated, so don't expect to feel at home. If you belonged to the world, it would love you as its own, but you've been chosen out of the world, so you are something of an alien. Jesus reminds us, 'Remember what I told you: "A servant is not greater than his master." If they persecuted me, they will persecute you also' (verse 20). Jesus lived his life perfectly and he was hated. And if you live your life in a godly way, you will be hated too.

Verse 21 says that the world is blind and ignorant. But individuals are still guilty, because Jesus has come and they have no excuse for their sin. Those lovely people who live near us, and who in some ways are nicer than we are but don't acknowledge Jesus, are heading for hell – they are blind, but they are responsible. Tragically, the world is doing what God said it would do all along; it is just fulfilling the script: 'This is to fulfil what is written in their Law: "They hated me without reason"' (verse 25). God is not taken by surprise, and neither should we be.

We often assume that if only people could see how nice and caring Christians are, they would be won over to the gospel. Of course, believers should be winsome, and our love and kindness for others should be attractive. But if we proclaim with our words and lives that Jesus is the centre of the universe, we will face opposition.

So if you share the gospel with someone or invite them to an Alpha/Christianity Explored course and they respond badly, don't think, 'I should have done that better; someone else could have done that more effectively.' Don't be discouraged by hatred or hostility. Instead, keep telling people about Jesus and keep putting him at the centre of your world and praying that blind eyes would be open to God's truth. Fix your eyes on Christ and leave the results with him.

Day 140

Read John 15:18–27
Key verses: John 15:26–27

· ·

26 When the Advocate comes, whom I will send to you from the Father – the Spirit of truth who goes out from the Father – he will testify about me. 27 And you also must testify, for you have been with me from the beginning.

Have you ever taken part in a race? Do you realize that you are actually part of a relay team right now?

Jesus says, 'The Holy Spirit who is in you for ever and will teach you is going to testify; that is his great delight. And you will testify because you've been with me from the beginning.' Now of course we haven't been with Jesus from the beginning like the apostles had, but we are going to testify as part of the relay team, and he will be with us.

The Holy Spirit is in charge of the case for Christ; he is testifying to the world about Jesus. He orchestrates it and supervises it; he is not surprised by any apparent setbacks and he knows exactly what he is doing. Imagine if it were up to the bishops or the mission organizations to put forward the case for Christ. Thankfully, the Holy Spirit is in charge of the testifying, and, amazingly, he wants to use us.

This doesn't mean we have to get on a soapbox or preach a sermon. We are asked to 'be wise' (Colossians 4:5). Sometimes this will mean initiating a conversation about Christ (Colossians 1:28); at other times it will mean answering somebody's question (Colossians 4:6).

You are part of the Holy Spirit's relay team, and Jesus gives you this promise: 'And surely I am with you always, to the very end of the age' (Matthew 28:20).

Whether you are a first-generation Christian or you come from a family of believers, you have an amazing heritage. You are part of a long line of relay racers that stretches right back to the earliest pages of the Old Testament. Thank God for those men and women who passed the baton of faith to you. Ask God for help to run your section of the race faithfully and to pass the baton on to others.

Today, be alert to the Holy Spirit's promptings to testify for Christ. Ask the Holy Spirit to give you the right words to say, and keep your eyes open for these God-given opportunities. Watch out – they may be simple openings such as someone at work, college or the centre where you volunteer asking you, 'What did you do this weekend?' Be honest and say that you went to church and listened to a message from the Bible. See where the Holy Spirit takes your conversation!

Day 141

Read John 16:1–11
Key verses: John 16:5–7

....

⁵Now I am going to him who sent me. None of you asks me, 'Where are you going?' ⁶Rather, you are filled with grief because I have said these things. ⁷But very truly I tell you, it is for your good that I am going away. Unless I go away, the Advocate will not come to you; but if I go, I will send him to you.

Did Jesus get it wrong?

In John 13:36, Peter asked, 'Lord, where are you going?' In John 14:5, Thomas said, 'Lord, we don't know where you are going.' So why does Jesus say in John 16:5, 'None of you asks me, "Where are you going?"'?

Jesus' point is that his disciples have been concerned that he is leaving, but not about where he is going. Just as you might say to someone who walks out of church during the service, 'Where are you going?', you're not interested in where they are going; you're concerned that they are leaving.

These disciples have been with Jesus for three years, yet they are utterly self-preoccupied. They are not interested in him or his mission. What must it be like for Jesus to have a body of believers like us who are so self-excited and self-preoccupied? It's amazing that he puts up with us. Just imagine having to listen to everybody's prayers – 85 million requests for a parking spot every second!

And the disciples are so distracted that they miss the big issue Jesus wants to tell them about. In verse 7 he says, 'It is for your good that I am going away. Unless I go away, the Advocate will not come to you; but if I go, I will send him to you.' Jesus wants the disciples and us to understand that he needed to die and rise again so that we can enjoy intimate fellowship with God, and the Spirit is the proof, or seal, of that intimacy. The Holy Spirit brings new life, helps us understand the Scriptures and pray, makes us fruitful and gives us access to God's presence.

Take care not to be so preoccupied with 'self' that you no longer hear God speak or see what really matters.

It is easy to be so caught up in the minutiae of daily life, praying about our own needs and concerns, that we forget to look to Christ. We forget about the big picture of salvation history and the eternal plans God has for us. Lift up your eyes: refocus on Christ, the truths of the gospel and what God wants to do in and through you.

> So if you're serious about living this new resurrection life with Christ, *act* like it. Pursue the things over which Christ presides. Don't shuffle along, eyes to the ground, absorbed with the things right in front of you. Look up, and be alert to what is going on around Christ – that's where the action is. See things from *his* perspective.
> (Colossians 3:1–2, MSG)

Use Colossians 3 to help you refocus on some of God's priorities for you.

Day 142

Read John 16:1–11
Key verses: John 16:8–11

....

> [8]*When he comes, he will prove the world to be in the wrong about sin and righteousness and judgment:* [9]*about sin, because people do not believe in me;* [10]*about righteousness, because I am going to the Father, where you can see me no longer;* [11]*and about judgment, because the prince of this world now stands condemned.*

How will the Holy Spirit 'prove the world to be in the wrong'?

Will there be a heavenly court case where the Spirit convinces God that people are guilty and God suddenly admits, 'Oh yes, you're right. They're sinful.'

Of course not! God already knows we are sinful. The Spirit's work is to drive this conviction home in *our* hearts. Jesus explains that the Holy Spirit will bring conviction of:

• *Sin*: 'because people do not believe in me' (verse 9). Not believing in Jesus is a good definition of sin. Sin is not just the random lies we told or the random lust we feel, but that we were fundamentally wrong about Jesus. And so the Spirit clears the fog, and we suddenly say, 'It's all about him.'

• *Righteousness* (verse 10). As people hear the gospel, they will realize that the righteousness of Christ is massive and their own righteousness is pitiful. No longer do we have a low view of Jesus and a high view of self; now we have a high view of Jesus and a low view of self. Everything has been turned the right way up.

• *Judgment* (verse 11). Partly this is recognizing the judging work of Jesus winning victoriously at the cross. But partly it is a healthy fear of judgment, causing us to turn to Christ.

The Spirit convicts unbelievers, enabling them to see that their view of Jesus is hopeless, their view of righteousness is inadequate and their view of judgment is plain wrong. We might say that sin has been shown to be deeper than we ever realized, righteousness higher than we ever realized and judgment closer than we ever realized. And so we call to Christ, and everything about him becomes clear, everything about self becomes clear and we move out of the fog and into the light.

We prefer to dwell on the comforting work of the Holy Spirit: how he illuminates God's Word to us, reassures us that we are children of God and gives us peace. But, today, thank God that the Holy Spirit convicts, for without his conviction no-one could be saved! Pray for your various church ministries where the gospel is shared. Pray that the Holy Spirit would be active in people's hearts, convicting them of sin, righteousness and judgment.

And remember, the Holy Spirit's work doesn't end when we are saved. Today, invite him to convict you of the sins you are still holding on to; to show you the areas where Christ has to become greater and you need to become less; and, in the light of imminent judgment, to give you his power to live a holy life.

Day 143

Read John 16:1–11
Key verses: John 16:8–11

. . . .

[8]*When he comes, he will prove the world to be in the wrong about sin and righteousness and judgment:* [9]*about sin, because people do not believe in me;* [10]*about righteousness, because I am going to the Father, where you can see me no longer;* [11]*and about judgment, because the prince of this world now stands condemned.*

It's easy to get discouraged.

As we look again at verses 8–11, we may wonder why the Holy Spirit doesn't seem to be doing much convicting. In the West, at least, the church does not appear to be growing.

But when the work of evangelism is hard, don't fall into the trap of thinking that things are too difficult for God. Don't imagine God sitting in heaven, wringing his hands and just wishing someone would take him seriously. That's a human-centred view. The Bible's view is that God is utterly sovereign.

Our role is to keep going with the task. We must respond to God ourselves and then tell others about him as best we can – that's our job. Remember when Jesus performs miracles and preaches in the cities, and nobody takes any notice of him, he says, 'I thank you, heavenly Father, because you hide, you reveal, you are totally in charge' (see Matthew 11:25). Then he suddenly turns round and says, 'Come to me, all you who are weary and burdened, and I will give you rest' (verse 28), because the gospel can't be stopped. It goes on like a river; if it hits a rock, it moves round it. It climbs a fence like a vine; if it hits a post, it climbs over it.

Just keep moving with the gospel and don't give up. God knows what he is doing.

Do you have a human-centred or a biblical view of evangelism? Be encouraged that, although we might not see much gospel fruit, God is sovereign, and all over the world people are becoming Christians. Meditate on these Bible verses to remind yourself of the unstoppable power of the gospel. Today, pray for the parts of the world where Christianity is spreading fast. And pray that we would not give up, but would keep sharing our faith and letting the gospel loose in our communities.

> As the rain and the snow
>   come down from heaven,
> and do not return to it
>   without watering the earth
> and making it bud and flourish,
>   so that it yields seed for the sower and bread for the eater,
> so is my word that goes out from my mouth:
>   it will not return to me empty,
> but will accomplish what I desire
> and achieve the purpose for which I sent it.
> (Isaiah 55:10–11)

> For I am not ashamed of the gospel, because it is the power of God that brings salvation to everyone who believes.
> (Romans 1:16)

> All people are like grass,
>   and all their glory is like the flowers of the field;
> the grass withers and the flowers fall,
>   but the word of the Lord endures for ever.
> (1 Peter 1:24–25)

Day 144

Read John 16:1–15
Key verses: John 16:12–15

. . . .

¹²I have much more to say to you, more than you can now bear. ¹³But when he, the Spirit of truth, comes, he will guide you into all the truth. He will not speak on his own; he will speak only what he hears, and he will tell you what is yet to come. ¹⁴He will glorify me because it is from me that he will receive what he will make known to you. ¹⁵All that belongs to the Father is mine. That is why I said the Spirit will receive from me what he will make known to you.

Has anyone ever said to you, 'God has told me . . .' and launched into a viewpoint that is totally at odds with what the Bible teaches?

The problem with this is that the Holy Spirit is not an independent thinker who speaks and acts contrary to how God has spoken and acted in his Word.

As John points out, the Holy Spirit is like the executor of a will. He passes on truth; he doesn't invent or withhold information. His role is to pass on what he has been given. He guides us into all the truth we will need for salvation and service.

Here, in John 16:13, Jesus is launching the New Testament from the upper room. He says, '[The Holy Spirit] will guide you into all the truth . . . and he will tell you what is yet to come.' And Peter corroborates this in his letter when he explains that the apostles were driven by the Holy Spirit to record the Holy Scriptures (2 Peter 1:21). And so the Holy Spirit leads us into the Word because that's where the riches and treasures are found, but also because he is obedient to his task. His whole aim is to glorify Jesus: his work throughout the Old Testament is to get ready for Jesus, and his work throughout the New Testament is looking to Jesus.

A comment by one of the bishops in Sydney struck me deeply. He said, 'I wonder whether the Holy Spirit is interested in what we are doing in proportion to our interest in the glory of Christ?'

How interested are you in the glory of Christ? It's difficult to unravel our motivations, but think through the ministries you are involved in, the voluntary work you do, your studies or employment, the role you have in your family, where you spend your free time and money. How different would it look to do each of these things for the glory of Christ?

> Not to us, LORD, not to us
>> but to your name be the glory,
>> because of your love and faithfulness.
> (Psalm 115:1)

Day 145

Read John 16:16–23
Key verses: John 16:19–22

....

¹⁹Jesus saw that they wanted to ask him about this, so he said to them, 'Are you asking one another what I meant when I said, "In a little while you will see me no more, and then after a little while you will see me"? ²⁰Very truly I tell you, you will weep and mourn while the world rejoices. You will grieve, but your grief will turn to joy. ²¹A woman giving birth to a child has pain because her time has come; but when her baby is born she forgets the anguish because of her joy that a child is born into the world. ²²So with you: now is your time of grief, but I will see you again and you will rejoice, and no one will take away your joy.'

Most of us have a list of questions we would like to ask Jesus when we meet him. I suspect that, when we see him, we will be too busy worshipping him to ask the questions. But having questions is OK.

In verses 16–23, Jesus is keen to answer the question the disciples are grappling with: what does he mean when he says, 'In a little while you will see me no more, and then after a little while you will see me'? Does Jesus mean, 'I'm leaving at Calvary; I'll be back at Easter'? Does he mean, 'I'm leaving at the ascension; I'll be back at Pentecost by the Spirit'? Does he mean, 'I'm leaving at the ascension and I'll be back at the second coming'? Well, all three of them involve grief and joy, don't they? All three of them would fit the gospel.

I think we can be pretty sure, however, that Jesus means he's leaving at Calvary and coming back at the resurrection. That's his primary meaning, because the weeping is appropriate to the weekend more than it is to the fifty days or the 2,000 years, and the childbirth illustration is a relatively short struggle, not one that will be drawn out over weeks or years.

Verse 22 is a treasure of a text, isn't it? 'Now is your time of grief, but I will see you again and you will rejoice, and no one will take away your joy.' That's what Jesus says to the apostles, and the principle is utterly true for us today, especially when we say farewell to someone we love. The Lord says to us, 'Now is your time of grief', but you will see them again, 'and you will rejoice, and no one will take away your joy'. The reunion of 1 Thessalonians 4 is just around the corner.

'Now is your time of grief.' Grief comes in many guises: the loss of a loved one; intense sadness at the end of a marriage; coming to terms with long-term suffering; seeing hopes and dreams for the future come crashing down; acknowledging that your child with additional needs will never experience the life you wished for them. Grief is intertwined with life now; joy and sorrow go hand in hand. But one day in heaven we will see Jesus. There will be no more tears; our joy will be unquenchable. Can you imagine it? Let the impact of verse 22 sink into your heart and give you hope today:

> Then I saw 'a new heaven and a new earth' . . . And I heard a loud voice from the throne saying, 'Look! God's dwelling-place is now among the people, and he will dwell with them. They will be his people, and God himself will be with them and be their God. "He will wipe every tear from their eyes. There will be no more death" or mourning or crying or pain, for the old order of things has passed away.'
>
> He who was seated on the throne said, 'I am making everything new!'
> (Revelation 21:1, 3–5)

Day 146

Read John 16:23–33
Key verses: John 16:23–28

....

²³In that day you will no longer ask me anything. Very truly I tell you, my Father will give you whatever you ask in my name. ²⁴Until now you have not asked for anything in my name. Ask and you will receive, and your joy will be complete.

²⁵Though I have been speaking figuratively, a time is coming when I will no longer use this kind of language but will tell you plainly about my Father. ²⁶In that day you will ask in my name. I am not saying that I will ask the Father on your behalf. ²⁷No, the Father himself loves you because you have loved me and have believed that I came from God. ²⁸I came from the Father and entered the world; now I am leaving the world and going back to the Father.

We get used to ending our prayers, 'in Jesus' name', don't we? It trips off our tongues and means hardly anything to us.

For three years the disciples have been asking Jesus for things, but now their prayer life is going to be radically different because Jesus is going and the Spirit is coming. Their prayers, and ours, will now be 'in Jesus' name'.

For us it may just have become a formula, but God the Father never gets used to hearing 'in Jesus' name'. It never bores him or becomes predictable, and it never grows stale. When the Father hears 'in Jesus' name', everything gets moving. It's as if you were a waiter at some special function and the Prime Minister asked you for some butter. You go to the kitchen and you are a nobody, but when you say, 'The Prime Minister has asked for butter', everything gets moving, doesn't it?

When you say your prayers 'in Jesus' name', that's a loaded phrase. It may not mean much to you, but it means everything to the Father. He has made sure that it carries huge significance; all the strength and wisdom are found in him.

'In Jesus' name' is not a magic formula that ensures we receive everything we ask for; it is the only way we can approach God. Jesus' death opened the way to God for us (1 Timothy 2:5). When you pray today, know that God embraces you warmly, but you are standing on holy ground, and your access to the Almighty was costly. Prayer is a privilege to use often, but never to be taken casually.

'In Jesus' name' is how we approach God, but it also shapes the content of our prayers. It means praying according to Jesus' agenda, purpose and will, and praying for things that will honour and glorify him.

Think about your prayers – how you approach God and the words you say. If you are stuck in a rut or your prayers seem like a shopping list, try something new. For example, write out your prayers so you can be more intentional about what you're saying to God.

Day 147

Read John 17:1–26
Key verses: John 17:1–5

••

¹After Jesus said this, he looked towards heaven and prayed:
'Father, the hour has come. Glorify your Son, that your Son may glorify you. ²For you granted him authority over all people that he might give eternal life to all those you have given him. ³Now this is eternal life: that they know you, the only true God, and Jesus Christ, whom you have sent. ⁴I have brought you glory on earth by finishing the work you gave me to do. ⁵And now, Father, glorify me in your presence with the glory I had with you before the world began.'

After all the waiting, it is finally over.

'The hour has come': literally, the *time* has come.

This hour has been a long time coming. The wedding at Cana (John 2): the hour has not yet come; Jesus talking with his brothers (John 7): the hour has not yet come; the Greeks arrive (John 12): the hour has come. And now in John 17 it has really come! The hour of the cross, the glorification followed by the resurrection and ascension, the hour of the work that Jesus has come for has finally come.

And so Jesus prays. You might ask, 'Why would Jesus pray? It's all organized. God is sovereign, so why pray?' It never occurs to Jesus not to pray. Jesus knows the Father is sovereign, as well as loving and wise, and therefore the Father is the best person to speak to, and so that's what Jesus does.

Do we turn to prayer as readily?

Our prayer life will never be free from doubt, guilt, tiredness, struggle, preoccupation and all sorts of things. There is never going to be a book, a DVD or a conference that will make praying easy. Prayer is part of the spiritual battle (Ephesians 6). Speaking to the invisible God, although we have access, although we are intimate, although the Holy Spirit helps us, is nevertheless difficult.

But keep praying! Prayer is crucial: it is fellowship with God, it puts joy and hope into our Christian walk and it is God's gift to us.

When good things happen, who is the first person you tell? When something goes wrong, who is the first person you call? Even though Jesus is God, although he was involved in orchestrating the plan of salvation, although he trusted God's sovereignty, although he knew his death would result in resurrection and eternal life – knowing all of this – when the hour came, he turned to his Father in prayer. He knew there was no-one better.

Yes, God knows your requests before you make them. Yes, he knows your thoughts even before you have them (Psalm 139:1–4). However, like a father, he delights to hear your voice; he wants to share intimate fellowship with you.

Speak to God throughout the day. When you receive good news, when you face a difficult task or when you are feeling lonely, turn to God first. Before you rush to other people for advice and affirmation, seek God. Let your prayer life prove to God that you know there is no-one better to trust with your joys and sorrows.

Day 148

Read John 17:1–26
Key verses: John 17:1–5

....

*¹After Jesus said this, he looked towards heaven and prayed:
'Father, the hour has come. Glorify your Son, that your Son
may glorify you. ²For you granted him authority over all people
that he might give eternal life to all those you have given him.
³Now this is eternal life: that they know you, the only true God,
and Jesus Christ, whom you have sent. ⁴I have brought you
glory on earth by finishing the work you gave me to do. ⁵And
now, Father, glorify me in your presence with the glory I had
with you before the world began.'*

Is Jesus' passion for his own glory selfish and egotistical?

In this prayer, Jesus' first request is for his own glory. The Old Testament says that God does not share his glory with another (Isaiah 42:8), but Jesus unashamedly asks to be glorified. His two reasons are significant: he wants to be glorified so that the Father will be glorified (verse 1), and to bring people eternal life (verse 2). He wants God to be honoured and people to receive eternal life through his death and resurrection.

Could Jesus really be glorified as he hangs on the cross in excruciating pain and indignity? Yes! What bursts out of the cross is: this God must be loving and just. There's no sweeping of sin under the carpet. It is being graphically dealt with. And this God must be wise, because he is doing what nobody in the world can do: bringing a perfect God and sinful people together. And this God must be powerful: millions and millions of people are going to live for eternity because this event has taken place at Calvary.

The prayer that Jesus would be glorified in his death is wonderfully answered. The cross screams the glory of God: his love, wisdom, power and justice. And when it is explained, the power of the gospel changes the way people think, understand and, God willing, live.

Jesus seeking his own glory isn't egotistical. In fact, it is the exact opposite. It is a demonstration of his love for us. As John Piper explains,

> God's passion for his glory is the essence of his love to us . . . God's love for us is *not* mainly his making much of us, but his giving us the ability to enjoy making much of him forever. In other words, God's love for us keeps God at the center . . . O how we need to help people see that Christ, not comfort, is their all-satisfying and everlasting treasure . . . Magnifying the supremacy of God in all things, and being willing to suffer patiently to help see and savor this supremacy is the essence of love. It's the essence of God's love. And it's the essence of your love. Because the supremacy of God's glory is the source and sum of all full and lasting joy.
> (John Piper, 'How Is God's Passion for His Own Glory Not Selfishness?', <www.desiringgod.org/articles/how-is-gods-passion-for-his-own-glory-not-selfishness>, 24 November 2007)

Turn your eyes to the cross. See the lengths Christ went to so that you could savour the glory of God. And, like Jesus on the cross, Paul's thorn in the flesh, Lazarus' death and countless other examples, God can and will use suffering to glorify his name. So don't long for comfort, security and a pain-free life. Choose to see even your troubles as opportunities to magnify God's name.

Day 149

Read John 17:6–19
Key verses: John 17:11, 15

....

> [11] *I will remain in the world no longer, but they are still in the world, and I am coming to you. Holy Father, protect them by the power of your name, the name you gave me, so that they may be one as we are one . . .*
> [15] *My prayer is not that you take them out of the world but that you protect them from the evil one.*

How do you usually pray for your children, parents, close friends and other family members?

Jesus has two prayer requests for his apostles. The first is that they will be kept or protected.

Jesus is not praying that the disciples will be kept from trouble; he knows most of them will be martyred. Rather, he wants them to be kept from the world (verse 11) and the devil (verse 15). 'Whatever happens to their bodies,' Jesus might be saying, 'guard their souls.'

And in verse 11, Jesus prays specifically that the Father will keep them 'by the power of your name', which, of course, means his character. Jesus is praying that the Father would keep the apostles by his faithful character, and God answers that prayer. All the evidence we have is that the eleven apostles were kept until the end.

I think this is a rebuke to our trivial prayers and the way we pray for our loved ones. When we live in reasonably good circumstances, we can easily absorb all the middle-class, bourgeois trivia of the world around us. And we find ourselves praying that our children would be happy and successful, although we don't put it quite as boldly as that. Our prayers are not much different from what pagans would want for their children. Do you see the sting of this? Do you want your children

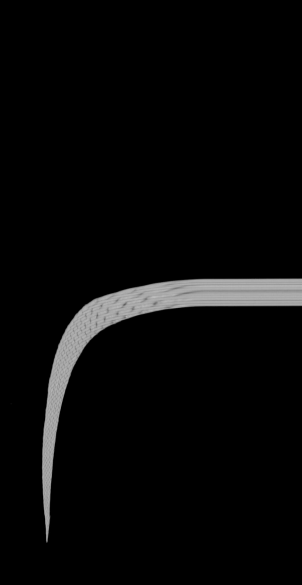

know who they are, why they are there, what they are doing, why they are doing it and where it will all end.

We too need to learn the truth if we are going to do our task in the world.

> Jesus' followers will be 'set apart' from the world, reserved for God's service, insofar as they think and live in conformity with the truth, the 'word' of revelation [John 17:6] supremely mediated through Christ (himself the truth, 14:6, and the Word incarnate, 1:1, 4) – the revelation now embodied in the pages of this book.
> (Don Carson, *The Gospel According to John*, IVP, 1991, p. 566)

So what better prayer could we pray for our loved ones than Jesus' own simple prayer: 'Keep them; sanctify them'?

As our prayer goes up, the Father graciously hears us, and the thousand darts being aimed at that man or woman are diverted. The temptation that is going to face them down the street finds no great interest in them. The sinful impulse that we all look for a way to indulge gets no opportunity. The things of Jesus suddenly appear very wonderful, and the things of this world look very small and temporary, because the Father has heard someone pray, 'Keep them; sanctify them.'

Start a habit today. Each time you pray for your loved ones, ask God to 'keep them and sanctify them'.

Day 151

Read John 17:20–26
Key verses: John 17:20–23

....

20 My prayer is not for them alone. I pray also for those who will believe in me through their message, 21 that all of them may be one, Father, just as you are in me and I am in you. May they also be in us so that the world may believe that you have sent me. 22 I have given them the glory that you gave me, that they may be one as we are one – 23 I in them and you in me – so that they may be brought to complete unity. Then the world will know that you sent me and have loved them even as you have loved me.

Jesus knows us well.

He knows all our flaws – our desire for recognition, our tendency to want our own way, our slowness to say 'sorry'.

Not surprisingly, then, Jesus' prayer for believers down through the centuries, including us, starts with a request for unity – 'that all of them may be one' (verse 21).

Importantly, our unity is to be grounded in the truth (verse 20). We need to belong to the same apostolic message. That's why we need to keep humbly reading our Bibles. God has made us one family by his Spirit. We may disagree on lots of things, but we are still family. The only way to stay united in heart and mind is by sitting under the Bible and reading it humbly together. The Word of God is going to make us not just family, but a mature family. We are not just going to be united in the Spirit; we are going to be united in the truth. Jesus explains that unity is possible because he's given us the truth (verse 22). He says, 'I've given them the revelation of myself: I've shown them what I think, what I say and what I do. I've given them the glory, the revelation.'

But this unity is not just in the truth; it is relational, as Jesus explains in verse 21: 'Father, just as you are in me and I am in you. May they also be in us.' The bonds we have with other believers might be very superficial. But in a thousand years we'll enjoy fellowship which will be so close, so special, so rich, so perfect that we won't believe it. That's what God has begun: relational unity. And this unity is also progressive. In verse 23, Jesus prays 'that they may be brought to complete unity.' This is not just spiritual unity, but being one in heart and mind as the Scriptures are heeded.

If you have been hurt by the comments and behaviour of other believers, it is hard to keep working towards unity. But don't give up! Unity is our witness to the world. It is deeper than differences over worship styles and any number of other secondary issues that cause controversy. As Paul reminds the Galatians, our unity is based on Christ (Galatians 3:28–29).

Meditate on Philippians 2:1–5 and ask God how you can contribute to unity in your church:

> Therefore if you have any encouragement from being united with Christ, if any comfort from his love, if any common sharing in the Spirit, if any tenderness and compassion, then make my joy complete by being like-minded, having the same love, being one in spirit and of one mind. Do nothing out of selfish ambition or vain conceit. Rather, in humility value others above yourselves, not looking to your own interests but each of you to the interests of the others.
>
> In your relationships with one another, have the same mindset as Christ Jesus.

Day 152

Read John 17:20–26

Key verses: John 17:24–26

. . . .

²⁴ Father, I want those you have given me to be with me where I am, and to see my glory, the glory you have given me because you loved me before the creation of the world.

²⁵ Righteous Father, though the world does not know you, I know you, and they know that you have sent me. ²⁶ I have made you known to them, and will continue to make you known in order that the love you have for me may be in them and that I myself may be in them.

When the well-known preacher Martyn Lloyd-Jones was at the end of his life, at the age of eighty-one, his friends and family gathered round him. Many people thought they should be praying for a miracle. But apparently Lloyd-Jones wrote a shaky little note to his wife telling them not to bother because he didn't want to be kept from glory!

That we arrive in glory is Jesus' prayer for each one of us (verse 24). Why are we going to arrive? Because Jesus went through the crucifixion: 'I go and prepare a place' (John 14:3). He did it; he prepared a place. He didn't prepare a place for good people or successful people. He prepared a place for believers.

Do you wonder sometimes whether you will ever be in glory? Do you wonder sometimes whether such a thing as glory exists? Jesus prays for us to be taken to glory, and every single prayer he has prayed has been answered. He prayed for himself to be glorified on the cross: he was. He prayed to be glorified back with the Father: he was. He prayed for the apostles to be kept: they were. He prayed for the apostles to be sanctified: they were.

Look at verse 24. Do you notice the words? Jesus doesn't say, 'Father, I'm asking.' He says, 'Father, I want.' The phrase in the original is, 'I will it.' Jesus says to the Father, 'I'm telling you what my will is. I will that they be with me.'

One day we will arrive in heaven. Until then, run your race well!

Jesus' death on the cross and his prayers for you are your guarantee of glory. One day you will arrive in heaven. That's the end of the story, but what happens in the meantime? Well, Jesus is at the Father's side, interceding for you, and the Holy Spirit is continuing his work of sanctification in you. What is our role? Are we just to wait passively with our eyes on the horizon? No! Because we are bound for heaven, Peter urges us, 'You ought to live holy and godly lives as you look forward to the day of God and speed its coming' (2 Peter 3:11–12). Whatever today holds for you, ask God to help you to keep your final destination in mind.

For further study

If you would like to do further study on John's Gospel, the following may be useful:

- Don Carson, *The Gospel According to John* (IVP, 1991).

- R. Kent Hughes, *John: That You May Believe*, Preaching the Word (Crossway, 2014).

- Colin Kruse, *John*, Tyndale New Testament Commentaries (IVP, 2008).

- Bruce Milne, *The Message of John: Here Is Your King*, The Bible Speaks Today (IVP, 1993).

If God has fed you through your study of the Gospel of John 14 – 17, why not buy the individual Food for the Journey on John 14 – 17 and give it to a friend (available from ivpbooks.com)?

Introduction

Romans 5 – 8

John Stott

Is the gospel good news for Christians?

Too many of us behave as if the gospel were only good news for unbelievers, as if, having become a Christian, we have arrived, we have come to a dead end, and there is no further road to travel. But that is not true! Our conversion is only the start. It is the first step on the journey of a lifetime, where the gospel profoundly affects how we think and live. It shapes how we deal with suffering, how we view our identity, how we pray, how we battle against sin, how we face opposition, where we look for security, what we devote ourselves to, what we hope for, and so much more.

Paul urgently wants the church in Rome to appreciate the gospel message and its implications for their present and future. He begins his letter by setting out the need and way of justification. Justification is a legal declaration of 'not guilty'. God declares us righteous because Jesus paid the penalty that we deserved for sin, when he died on the cross. Paul explains that all of us are sinners under the just judgment of God, and only through the redemption that is in Jesus Christ can we be justified, by grace alone through faith alone. Then chapter 5:1 begins, '*Therefore*, since we have been justified through faith . . .' (italics added), and Paul launches into the immense privileges that believers can enjoy both now and in eternity. Chapters 5 – 8 are a glorious description of what the gospel means for Christ's followers: we have peace with God (chapter 5), union with Christ (chapter 6), freedom from the law (chapter 7) and life in the Spirit (chapter 8).

This devotional is based on the seminal Bible Reading series that John Stott gave at the Keswick Convention in 1965. The text is written by Elizabeth McQuoid but reworked from John Stott's original messages. The content of the Bible Readings was revised and published under the title *Men Made New* in 1966. The material was further revised and published by IVP as *The Message of Romans*, part of the Bible Speaks Today series.

Politically, economically and socially, the world is a very different place from when John Stott first gave these talks. Many of the issues facing Christians today would not have been thought of in 1965. And yet the timeless message of the gospel has never been more relevant or needed. Now, more than ever, believers require a robust understanding of the gospel. It is much more than a ticket to glory; it lights up the way to guide you there.

The gospel is good news for you!

Day 153

Read Romans 5:1–5
Key verses: Romans 5:1–2

• •

[1] Therefore, since we have been justified through faith, we have peace with God through our Lord Jesus Christ, [2] through whom we have gained access by faith into this grace in which we now stand. And we boast in the hope of the glory of God.

What happened when you first trusted Christ?

Paul says you were 'justified through faith'. Justification is a legal declaration of 'not guilty'. God declares us righteous because Jesus paid the penalty for sin that we deserved when he died on the cross. This momentary act leads to a permanent relationship with God, summed up by three words:

- *Peace*. Peace with God is the immediate effect of our justification. We were once enemies of God (Romans 5:10) but now, because of Jesus' death on the cross and God's forgiveness, that old hostility has been dealt with.

- *Grace*. The continuing effect of our justification is that 'we have been allowed to enter the sphere of God's grace' (verse 2, NEB) and we are now standing in it.

- *Glory*. The ultimate effect of justification, for which we hope, is 'the glory of God'. In verse 2, this means heaven, since in heaven God himself is fully revealed ('glory' is God revealed). Our 'hope' is our certain confidence that we shall see and share in God's glory, so much so that we can 'boast' or rejoice in it already.

Do you see how that one-off declaration of 'not guilty' has such an impact? It covers the three phases of our salvation. In the word 'peace', we look back to the enmity which is now over. In the word 'grace', we look up to our reconciled Father in whose favour we now continue to stand. In the word 'glory', we look to our final destiny, seeing and reflecting the glory of God, which is the object of our hope or expectation.

Today, reflect on what being justified means:

- Enjoy peace with God. Don't let past failures steal your joy or hinder your service. Christ's work on the cross has dealt with your sin and guilt, so don't let Satan rehearse it.
- Bask in God's grace. There is nothing you can do or need to do to earn God's approval. Because of Christ's death and your restored relationship with God, you are already enjoying God's favour. In response, live gratefully for an audience of One.
- Look forward to eternity with Christ. One day, you will reflect the Lord's glory perfectly. Until then, ask for his help to reflect him more and more in your priorities, values, actions and attitudes.

> But when the kindness and love of God our Saviour appeared, he saved us, not because of righteous things we had done, but because of his mercy. He saved us through the washing of rebirth and renewal by the Holy Spirit, whom he poured out on us generously through Jesus Christ our Saviour, so that, having been justified by his grace, we might become heirs having the hope of eternal life.
> (Titus 3:4–7)

Day 154

Read Romans 5:1–5
Key verses: Romans 5:3–4

· ·

³Not only so, but we also glory in our sufferings, because we know that suffering produces perseverance; ⁴perseverance, character; and character, hope.

What should we expect from the Christian life? Comfort and ease until we see Jesus?

Paul is clear: we shall suffer (verse 3). These sufferings are not, strictly speaking, sickness or pain, sorrow or bereavement, but the pressures of living in a godless and hostile world. Such suffering always precedes glory (Luke 24:26; Romans 8:17). It is not just that the one is the way to the other. Still less is it that we grin and bear the one in anticipation of the other. No, we 'rejoice' in both (RSV).

How can we rejoice, or glory, in our sufferings? Verses 3–5 explain the paradox. It is not the sufferings themselves we rejoice in as much as their beneficial results. We are not masochists who enjoy being hurt. We are not even stoics, who grit their teeth and endure. We are Christians, who see in our sufferings the working out of a gracious divine purpose. We rejoice because of what suffering 'produces'. Look at the three stages in this process:

- *Stage 1 – suffering produces perseverance*. The very endurance we need in suffering is produced by it. We could not learn perseverance without suffering, because without suffering there would be nothing to persevere in.

- *Stage 2 – perseverance produces character*. Character is the quality of something which, or someone who, has stood the test. It is the quality that David's armour lacked, because he had not 'proved' it (1 Samuel 17:39, KJV). We can usually recognize the ripe character of one who has gone through suffering and come out triumphant.

• *Stage 3 – character produces hope*. The character that has a maturity born of past suffering brings a hope of future glory. Our developing Christian character is evidence that God is at work upon us and within us. And he who is maturing us through suffering will surely and safely bring us to glory.

Do you see that there is an indissoluble link between sufferings and glory? The reason why, if we rejoice in hope of the glory of God, we rejoice in our sufferings also, is that our sufferings produce hope. If the hope of glory is produced by sufferings, then we rejoice in the sufferings as well as the glory; we rejoice not only in the end, but in the means that bring us there.

Are you feeling the pressure of living in a godless society? Are you suffering for being a Christian at home or at work? Will you allow this suffering to do its work in your life, to accomplish God's purpose? Will you rejoice in it?

> Consider it a sheer gift, friends, when tests and challenges come at you from all sides. You know that under pressure, your faith-life is forced into the open and shows its true colors. So don't try to get out of anything prematurely. Let it do its work so you become mature and well-developed, not deficient in any way.
> (James 1:2–4, MSG)

Day 155

Read Romans 5:1–5
Key verse: Romans 5:5

....

⁵And hope does not put us to shame, because God's love has been poured out into our hearts through the Holy Spirit, who has been given to us.

How can we know that our hope of future glory is not wishful thinking?

Paul asserts that this 'hope will not lead to disappointment' (NLT). But how can we be sure? He gives his answer in the rest of verse 5. The solid foundation of our hope rests on the love of God. It is because God has set his love on us that we know he is going to bring us safely to glory.

We believe that we are going to persevere to the end, and we have good grounds for this confidence. As we considered on Day 154, our confidence is partly because of the character that God is forming in us through suffering. Remember that 'suffering produces perseverance; perseverance, character; and character, hope (verses 3–4). The argument is that if he is sanctifying us now, he will surely glorify us later. But our confidence is chiefly because of God's love. We know we are going to see and share in the glory of God because we know God loves us and will never let us down, never let us go.

But how do we know God loves us? Because we have an inner experience of it. Verse 5 tells us that the Holy Spirit has been given to every believer, and one of the works of the Spirit is to pour God's love into our hearts – that is, to make us vividly and inwardly aware that God loves us. Or, as Paul expresses the same truth in chapter 8, to witness with our spirit that we are God's children and that he is our Father who loves us.

Note the tenses of the verbs in verse 5. The Holy Spirit 'has been' given to us (aorist), a past, once-for-all event; God's love 'has been' poured out into our hearts (perfect), a past event with abiding results. The Holy Spirit was given to us when we believed. At the same time, he flooded our hearts with God's love. He still does. The flood remains; it continues. The once-given Spirit caused a permanent flood of divine love in our hearts.

Some people are shocked if we say that we know where we are going after we die. Others roll their eyes at our arrogance. Yet we can be sure that we shall one day see and share in the glory of God – not because of our performance, meaning that we have no cause for self-righteousness, but because of the steadfast love of God.

Listen to the Holy Spirit whisper this truth to your soul as you read God's Word: you are loved by God. There is no experience you will go through that will ever get in the way of God loving you (Romans 8:35, 38–39).

> Let the beloved of the LORD rest secure in him,
>   for he shields him all day long,
>   and the one the LORD loves rests between his shoulders.
> (Deuteronomy 33:12)

Day 156

Read Romans 5:6–11
Key verses: Romans 5:6–8

. . . .

> ⁶*You see, at just the right time, when we were still powerless, Christ died for the ungodly.* ⁷*Very rarely will anyone die for a righteous person, though for a good person someone might possibly dare to die.* ⁸*But God demonstrates his own love for us in this: while we were still sinners, Christ died for us.*

No-one likes to hear someone else speaking badly of them. These verses make for very uncomfortable reading as we are described in the most unflattering terms. We are 'powerless' because we are unable to save ourselves (verse 6), 'ungodly' because we are in revolt against God's authority (verse 6), 'sinners' because we have missed the mark of God's righteousness, however hard we may have tried to aim at it (verse 8), and 'enemies' because of the hostility that exists between us and God (verse 10). What a devastating description of us in our sin. We are failures, rebels and enemies, helpless to save ourselves. Yet it is for people like us that Jesus Christ died.

We would hardly die for a righteous person (one who is coldly upright in his or her conduct), although perhaps some people would even dare to die (verse 7) for a good person (warm and attractive in his or her goodness). But God shows *his* love (the word is emphatic – his own love, his unique love) in giving Christ to die for sinners. Not for the upright, not even for the good, but for unattractive, unworthy sinners.

Do you see how much God loves us? The objective ground for believing that God loves us is historical: it is the death of his Son (verse 8). The subjective ground for believing that God loves us is experiential: it is the gift of the Spirit (verse 5).

So we know that God loves us. We know it rationally as we contemplate the cross. God gave his best for the worst. We know it intuitively as the Holy Spirit floods our hearts with a sense of it. This, then, is our assurance of final salvation.

When prayers seem to go unanswered, when you are dealing with inexplicable and difficult circumstances and God seems distant, when you look at your own sin and failings, is your default mode to doubt God's love? In those times will you turn to the cross and accept it as God's proof of his love for you? Then ask him to flood your heart with the Holy Spirit. Let your doubts and fears be swallowed up in the steadfast love of God.

> But because of his great love for us, God, who is rich in mercy, made us alive with Christ even when we were dead in transgressions – it is by grace you have been saved.
> (Ephesians 2:4–5)

> This is how God showed his love among us: he sent his one and only Son into the world that we might live through him. This is love: not that we loved God, but that he loved us and sent his Son as an atoning sacrifice for our sins.
> (1 John 4:9–10)

Day 157

Read Romans 5:6–11

Key verses: Romans 5:9–11

∙ ∙

⁹ Since we have now been justified by his blood, how much more shall we be saved from God's wrath through him! ¹⁰ For if, while we were God's enemies, we were reconciled to him through the death of his Son, how much more, having been reconciled, shall we be saved through his life! ¹¹ Not only is this so, but we also boast in God through our Lord Jesus Christ, through whom we have now received reconciliation.

Hold fast to this truth: you will not fall by the way; you shall be glorified.

Paul continues to set out his case for our full and final salvation by using an *a fortiori*, a 'much more', argument. This is an argument from the lesser to the greater, which reaches up to a new truth by standing on the shoulders of an old one. Paul contrasts the two main stages of salvation, justification and glorification, and shows how the first is the guarantee of the second. Look how he builds his case:

- *He contrasts present justification and future salvation* (verse 9). If we are already saved from God's condemnation because we are justified, surely we shall be saved from his wrath on the day of judgment?

- *He contrasts how they are achieved* (verse 10). Surely the risen life of Christ in heaven will complete what the death of Christ began on earth (see Romans 8:34)?

- *He contrasts who receives them* (verse 10). It was while we were enemies that we were reconciled to God by the death of Jesus. How much more will we be saved by his life now that we are reconciled to him? If God reconciled his enemies, surely he will save his friends!

Paul's argument is not sentimental optimism; it is grounded in irresistible logic. If God performed the more costly service (involving Jesus' death) for his enemies, he will surely do the easier and less costly service now that his former enemies have become his friends.

But don't only look back to justification or on to glorification. We can't always be preoccupied with the past and the future. You have a Christian life to live now. Verse 11 urges us to 'boast' or 'rejoice in God through our Lord Jesus Christ, through whom we have now received our reconciliation' (RSV). We rejoice in the hope of glory (verse 2). We rejoice in our sufferings (verse 3). But, above all, we rejoice in God himself through Jesus Christ.

Through Christ we have peace with God (verse 1). Through Christ we have obtained access into the grace in which we stand (verse 2). Through the blood of Christ we have been reconciled, and through the life of Christ we are going to be saved (verse 9). As the apostle John said, 'From his abundance we have all received one gracious blessing after another' (John 1:16, NLT).

Today, regardless of your present circumstances or struggles, rejoice in God through Christ for all that he has done, continues to do, and will do for you.

Day 158

Read Romans 5:12–21

Key verses: Romans 5:12–14

• •

> [12] *Therefore, just as sin entered the world through one man, and death through sin, and in this way death came to all people, because all sinned –*
>
> [13] *To be sure, sin was in the world before the law was given, but sin is not charged against anyone's account where there is no law.* [14] *Nevertheless, death reigned from the time of Adam to the time of Moses, even over those who did not sin by breaking a command, as did Adam, who is a pattern of the one to come.*

We know that our actions can have a profound effect on others. But, in the case of Jesus, how can one person's sacrifice bring *so much* blessing to *so many*?

To answer this question, Paul draws an analogy between Adam and Christ. Both Adam and Christ demonstrate the principle that *many* can be affected (for good or ill) by *one* person's deed.

Verses 12–14 concentrate on Adam. Verse 12 sums up in three stages the history of humanity before Christ:

• Sin entered the world through one person.

• Death entered the world through sin, because death is the penalty for sin.

• Death spread to all people, because everyone sinned.

In verses 13–14, Paul explains how this present situation of universal death is a result of the original transgression of one man. All people die, not because all have sinned *like* Adam, but because they have sinned *in* Adam. This is clear, Paul argues, because of what happened during the time between Adam and Moses, between the fall and the giving of the law. During that period, people certainly sinned, but their sin was not reckoned against them because sin is not reckoned when there is no law. Yet they still died. Paul explains that they died not because they deliberately transgressed like Adam, and died for their transgressions, but because they and the whole of humanity were involved and included in Adam, the head of the human race. It is because we sinned in Adam that we die today.

Death is the one great certainty of life. We weep and grieve, feeling the loss of family and friends intensely. In the midst of sadness, for believers, there is hope:

> For my Father's will is that everyone who looks to the Son and believes in him shall have eternal life, and I will raise them up at the last day.
> (John 6:40)

Even as we face the pain of dying or watching our loved ones die, there is comfort:

> Even though I walk
>   through the darkest valley,
> I will fear no evil,
>   for you are with me;
> your rod and your staff,
>   they comfort me.
> (Psalm 23:4)

> Death is not the end of the road; it is only a bend in the road. The road winds only through those paths through which Christ himself has gone . . . Often we say that Christ will meet us on the other side. That is true, of course, but misleading. He walks with us on this side of the curtain and then guides us through the opening. We will meet him there, because we have met him here.
> (Erwin Lutzer, *Heaven and the Afterlife*, Moody Publishers, 2016, p. 238)

Day 159

Read Romans 5:12–21
Key verses: Romans 5:15–17

∙∙∙

[15]But the gift is not like the trespass. For if the many died by the trespass of the one man, how much more did God's grace and the gift that came by the grace of the one man, Jesus Christ, overflow to the many! [16]Nor can the gift of God be compared with the result of one man's sin: the judgment followed one sin and brought condemnation, but the gift followed many trespasses and brought justification. [17]For if, by the trespass of the one man, death reigned through that one man, how much more will those who receive God's abundant provision of grace and of the gift of righteousness reign in life through the one man, Jesus Christ!

A pattern is an example, an indication, of what we can expect from the genuine article. Adam is described as a pattern or prototype of Christ because his actions affected many (verse 14). But there the similarities end. Paul contrasts the difference between:

• *The motive behind their deeds* (verse 15a). Adam's behaviour was self-assertive, going his own way; Christ's deed was one of self-sacrifice, of free, unmerited favour.

• *The effect of their deeds* (verses 15b–17). The sin of Adam brought condemnation; the work of Christ brings justification. The reign of death is a result of Adam's sin; a reign of life is made possible through Christ's work.

• *The nature of their deeds* (verses 18–19). What led to condemnation for all was one man's offence, and what led to justification and life for all (in Christ) was one man's righteousness. Adam disobeyed the will of God and so fell from righteousness; Christ obeyed the will of God and so fulfilled all righteousness (see Matthew 3:15; Philippians 2:8).

Looking back over these verses, we see a striking and significant contrast between Adam and Christ. As to the motive for their deeds, Adam asserted himself; Christ sacrificed himself. As to the nature of their deeds, Adam disobeyed the law; Christ obeyed it. As to the effect of their deeds, Adam's sin brought condemnation and death; Christ's righteousness brought justification and life.

So whether we are condemned or justified, alive or dead, depends on whether we belong to the old humanity initiated by Adam or the new humanity initiated by Christ. All human beings are in Adam, since we are in Adam by *birth*. But not all are in Christ, since we are in Christ by *faith*. In Adam by birth we are condemned and die; but if we are in Christ by faith, we are justified and live. The privileges of the justified – peace, grace and glory (Romans 5:1–2) – belong only to those who are in Christ.

There are only two types of people in the world: those who belong to the old humanity and those who belong to the new. Today, as you praise God for all the wonderful privileges that you enjoy because you belong to Christ, pray too for specific friends, family members or work colleagues who don't yet know him. Pray that God would open their eyes and grant them faith to believe. Be ready for the opportunities that God gives you to share the gospel with them.

Day 160

Read Romans 6:1–7
Key verses: Romans 6:1–3

....

¹*What shall we say, then? Shall we go on sinning, so that grace may increase?* ²*By no means! We are those who have died to sin; how can we live in it any longer?* ³*Or don't you know that all of us who were baptised into Christ Jesus were baptised into his death?*

Why should I stop sinning if sin provides an opportunity for God to show his grace by forgiving me? Wouldn't it be better to go on sinning so that grace may increase? Romans 5:20–21 prompts this question, and Paul is quick to reply, 'By no means!' He asks, 'How can we?' If the Christian life begins with death to sin, it is ridiculous to ask if we are free to keep on sinning. How can we go on living in what we have died to?

The burning question is: in what sense have we died to sin? Paul explains this in Romans 6:1–14, and we shall unpack his argument over the next few days. He begins by explaining that we were baptized 'into Christ'. The fact that people can even think of asking whether Christians are free to sin betrays a complete lack of understanding of what a Christian is, and of what Christian baptism is. The Christian is not just a justified believer; he or she is someone who has entered into a vital, personal union with Christ, and baptism signifies this.

Again and again, the preposition employed with the verb 'to baptize' is *eis*, 'into'. In the Great Commission, the Lord says we are to baptize *into* the name of the Father, the Son and the Holy Spirit (Matthew 28:19). In Acts, believers in Samaria and Ephesus are baptized *into* the name of the Lord Jesus (Acts 8:16; 19:5). In Galatians 3:27, 'all of you who were baptised *into* Christ have clothed yourselves with Christ'. And it is just the same here: 'baptised *into* Christ'.

Baptism in the New Testament is a dramatic sacrament or ordinance. It indicates not just that God washes away our sin, not just that he gives us his Holy Spirit, but that he places us *into* Christ. The essence of the Christian life, as visibly signified in baptism, is that God by his sheer grace puts us, places us, grafts us *into* Christ Jesus.

Reflect on the joys and challenges of being united with Christ. Today, if you are going through deep trials, draw comfort from your union with him.

> What shall support us in that trying hour? . . . Nothing, nothing can do it but close communion with Christ. Christ dwelling in our hearts by faith – Christ putting His right arm under our heads – Christ felt to be sitting by our side – Christ can alone give us the complete victory in the . . . struggle.
> (J. C. Ryle, *Practical Religion, CreateSpace Publishing,* 2012, p. 231)

If you haven't been baptized, will you consider taking this step to signify that you are united with Christ and want to identify with him?

Day 161

Read Romans 6:1–7

Key verses: Romans 6:3–5

· ·

> ³*Or don't you know that all of us who were baptised into Christ Jesus were baptised into his death?* ⁴*We were therefore buried with him through baptism into death in order that, just as Christ was raised from the dead through the glory of the Father, we too may live a new life.*
>
> ⁵*For if we have been united with him in a death like his, we will certainly also be united with him in a resurrection like his.*

You are united with Christ. Don't imagine that this is some vague association or over-spiritualized language. We are not united to Jesus in any general sense; we must be more particular than that. The only Jesus Christ with whom we have been identified and made one is the Christ who died and rose again. So you and I have been united to Christ in his death and resurrection. The picture symbolism of baptism in verses 3–5 describes this union and its implications.

Baptism would take place in the open air, in a stream or river. The individual would go down into the water – whether he or she was partially or totally immersed really does not matter! – where he or she would seem to be buried and then to rise again. Baptism would dramatize the individual's death, burial and resurrection to a new life. Baptism is a sort of funeral and resurrection from the grave as well.

So a Christian, by faith inwardly and by baptism outwardly, has been united to Christ in his death and resurrection. We have actually shared in the death and resurrection of Jesus. In fact, the day we came to know Christ was our funeral, the moment when we said 'goodbye' to our old life and began our new life in Christ.

Christianity doesn't just tinker around the edges of our life, promoting self-improvement. Our union with Christ marks a decisive change from our past. Are you living out the symbolism of your baptism, or are you settling for mediocrity, something less than the gospel of Christ?

> I would like to buy about three quid's worth of gospel, please. Not too much – just enough to make me happy, but not so much that I get addicted. I don't want so much gospel that I learn to really hate covetousness and lust. I certainly don't want so much that I start to love my enemies, cherish self-denial, and contemplate missionary service in some alien culture. I want ecstasy, not repentance; I want transcendence, not transformation. I would like to be cherished by some nice, forgiving, broad-minded people, but I myself don't want to love those from different races – especially if they smell. I would like enough gospel to make my family secure and my children well behaved, but not so much that I find my ambitions redirected or my giving too greatly enlarged. I would like about three quid's worth of gospel, please.
>
> (Don Carson, *Basics for Believers: An Exposition of Philippians*, IVP, 2004, p. 9)

Day 162

Read Romans 6:1–12
Key verse: Romans 6:10

••

10 The death he died, he died to sin once for all; but the life he lives, he lives to God.

Some parts of the Bible are easy to understand (though perhaps harder to obey!). But how do we come to understand what more-difficult passages mean? One fundamental principle of biblical interpretation is that the same phrase bears the same meaning in the same context. The phrase 'died to sin' or 'dead to sin' occurs three times in this section. Twice it refers to Christians (verses 2, 11) and once it refers to Christ (verse 10); therefore we have to find an explanation that is true for Christ and for Christians.

When you die physically, your five senses cease to operate. You can no longer touch, see, smell, etc. Some people assume, therefore, that 'dead to sin' means we become unresponsive to sin. We become like a dead person, so when temptation comes, we neither feel it nor react to it. But 'dead to sin' can't mean that Christ became unresponsive to sin, because he was never alive to sin in the first place. We also know that, as Christians, we are not unresponsive to sin. Our fallen nature is alive and kicking! Why else would the Bible exhort us, 'do not let sin reign' (verse 12)? Chapter 8 urges us not to set our minds on the things of the flesh, and in chapter 13:14, Paul says we are not to gratify the flesh. These would be absurd injunctions if the flesh was dead and had no desires.

In fact, in the Bible, death is spoken of not so much in physical terms, but in moral and legal terms. Whenever sin and death are spoken of together in Scripture, the essential relation to them is that death is sin's penalty. From Genesis 2:17, disobedience is linked with death, right through to Revelation 21 where the destiny of sinners is 'the second death' (verse 8).

Death is to be understood as the just reward for sin (see Romans 1:32; 6:23). So Christ died to sin in the sense that he bore sin's penalty. He died for our sins, bearing them in his own innocent and sacred person. The death that Jesus died was the wages of our sin. He met sin's claim, he paid its penalty, he accepted its reward, and he did it once and for all. So sin had no more claim on him and he was raised from the dead to prove the satisfactoriness of his sin-bearing. He now lives for ever unto God. In the same way, by our union with Christ, we have also died to sin. We have borne its penalty; it has no more claim on us.

Marvel at the scandal of God's grace. Christ took our place: he died the death we should have died.

> He was pierced for our transgressions,
>   he was crushed for our iniquities;
> the punishment that brought us peace was on him,
>   and by his wounds we are healed.
> (Isaiah 53:5)

> Bearing shame and scoffing rude,
> In my place condemned He stood;
> Sealed my pardon with His blood.
> Hallelujah! What a Saviour!
> (Philip P. Bliss, 'Hallelujah! What a Saviour!', 1875)

Day 163

Read Romans 6:5–10
Key verses: Romans 6:6–7

....

⁶For we know that our old self was crucified with him so that the body ruled by sin might be done away with, that we should no longer be slaves to sin – ⁷because anyone who has died has been set free from sin.

We feel the pull of sin every day, so how can it be true that we are 'no longer . . . slaves to sin'?

Verse 6 says that the old self was crucified with Christ (stage 1), in order that the sinful body might be done away with (stage 2), so that we might no longer be slaves to sin (stage 3). To understand how the ultimate stage of being set free from sin happens, we must go back to stage 2. The 'body' does not refer to the human body; our body is not sinful in itself. The word refers to our sinful nature that needs to 'be done away with' so that we no longer serve sin. The verb 'to be done away with' is the same verb used in Hebrews 2:14 of the devil. It conveys the idea of being not extinct, but defeated. Not annihilated, but deprived of power. Our sinful nature is no more extinct than the devil, but God's will is that the dominion of both should be broken – and it has been.

How is our sinful nature going to be deprived of power? Go back to the first stage of Paul's argument. It is only possible because of the crucifixion of the old self. The 'old self' is not our old, unregenerate nature; it is not the same as 'the body'. It is our old, unregenerate life, the man or woman we once were. So what was crucified with Christ was not a part of me called my old nature, but the whole of me as I was before I was converted. My 'old self' is my pre-conversion life.

How is it that, having been crucified with Christ and having 'died to sin', in the sense of bearing its penalty, we are delivered from the bondage of sin? Verse 7 gives the answer. The verb that is translated 'set free' is used twenty-five times in the New Testament, each time conveying the sense of being justified. We are freed from sin in the sense that we are justified from it; the penalty has been paid. We are like a convicted criminal who has served his sentence and leaves the prison free. He has paid the penalty; the law no longer has anything against him, and he is now justified from his sin.

We shall be tempted by sin until the day we die. Satan will cajole us to go back to our old ways, try to convince us we can't resist sin's power, and accuse us of past failures. Don't believe the lies! Sin's penalty has been paid, so its authority over you has been broken. Today, as you face opportunities to sin, ask for God's strength to stand firm and to live out the freedom that Christ has won for us.

If the Son sets you free, you will be free indeed.
(John 8:36)

Day 164

Read Romans 6:1–11

Key verse: Romans 6:11

....

> *¹¹ In the same way, count yourselves dead to sin but alive to God in Christ Jesus.*

We have got to become what we are. Paul has explained how we have died to sin, but now he urges us to 'count yourselves dead to sin'. The RSV says, 'consider yourselves'; the KJV says, 'reckon . . . yourselves' as being what in fact we are: dead to sin and alive to God.

This is not make-believe. 'Reckoning' is not summoning our faith to believe something we do not believe. It is not pretending that our old nature has died when we know it has not. It is to realize that our old self – that is, our former self – did die with Christ. Once we realize that our old life is ended, the score settled, the debt paid, the law satisfied, we shall want to have nothing more to do with it. It is finished.

Think of it in terms of a biography written in two volumes. One volume is the story of me before my conversion. The second volume is the story of me after I was made a new creation in Christ. We are simply called to reckon this – not to pretend it, but to realize it. It is a fact and we need to lay hold of it. We have to let our minds meditate on these truths until we grasp them firmly.

You see, the secret of holy living is in the mind. It is *knowing* that 'our old self was crucified with [Christ]' (verse 6). It is *knowing* that baptism into Christ is baptism into his death and resurrection (verse 3). It is *counting*, intellectually realizing, that in Christ we have died to sin and live for God (verse 11). Know these things, meditate on these things, reckon these things.

Can a Christian live as though he or she were still in his or her sins? I suppose it is not impossible. But it is utterly incongruous. It is like an adult returning to his or her childhood, a freed prisoner to his or her prison cell. By union with Christ, our whole status has changed. Our faith and baptism have cut us off irrevocably from the old life and committed us to the new. Our baptism stands between us and the old life as a door between two rooms. It has closed upon one room and has opened into another. We have died; we have risen. How can we live again in what we have died to?

Why must we count ourselves to be something we already are? Because being 'dead to sin' is like a privilege or legal right. Though it may be true or in force, a person might not realize or utilize the right/privilege. For example, you may have a trust fund put into your name, but unless you draw on it, it won't change your actual financial condition . . . So we must 'count ourselves dead to sin' because unless we act on this great privilege, it will not automatically be realized in our experience. We have to appropriate it, live it, enjoy it.

(Tim Keller, *Romans 1–7 for You*, The Good Book Company, 2014, pp. 143–144)

Day 165

Read Romans 6:8–14

Key verses: Romans 6:12–13

• •

[12] Therefore do not let sin reign in your mortal body so that you obey its evil desires. [13] Do not offer any part of yourself to sin as an instrument of wickedness, but rather offer yourselves to God as those who have been brought from death to life; and offer every part of yourself to him as an instrument of righteousness.

What should be the stand-out features of volume 2 of our biography? What behaviour should characterize our lives?

Paul advocates a two-pronged approach. First he gives us a negative charge: 'do not let sin reign' – do not let sin be your king; do not let it rule over you (verse 12). 'Do not offer' – do not go on yielding yourself, allowing sin to use you to further its unrighteous purposes (verse 13). Then he gives us a positive charge: 'offer yourselves to God' as those who are alive from the dead, which is precisely what you are. You have died to sin, bearing its penalty; you have risen again, alive from the dead; now yield yourselves to God. In other words, do not let sin be your king to rule over you; let God be your king to rule over you. Do not let sin be your lord, to use you in its service; let God be your Lord, to use you in his service.

Why yield ourselves to God and not to sin? Because we are alive from the dead (verse 13), so we are no longer under law, but under grace. God in grace has justified you in Christ; in Christ, sin's penalty is paid, and the law's demands are met. Neither sin nor the law has any further claim on you. You have been rescued from their tyranny. You have changed sides. You are no longer a prisoner of the law but a child of God, under his grace.

To know ourselves under grace and not under law, far from encouraging us to sin in order that grace may increase, actually weans us away from the world, the flesh and the devil (Ephesians 2:1–3). By grace we have opened a new volume in our biography, and there is no going back.

Living as a Christian does not simply mean avoiding sin. As Paul explains, we need a two-pronged approach. We also need to be positively striving for holiness; offering every part of ourselves to God. What disciplines have you put in place to help you in this pursuit? How are you getting on? Are there areas where you need more grace-driven effort?

> If you want to be Christlike, you need to have communion with Christ, and if you want communion with Christ you need to do it on his terms with the channels of grace he's provided [prayer, Bible reading, church fellowship, Lord's table]. And that means the only way to extraordinary holiness is through ordinary means.
> (Kevin DeYoung, *The Hole in Our Holiness*, Crossway Books, 2012, p. 135)

Day 166

Read Romans 6:15–23
Key verses: Romans 6:20–23

••

²⁰ When you were slaves to sin, you were free from the control of righteousness. ²¹ What benefit did you reap at that time from the things you are now ashamed of? Those things result in death! ²² But now that you have been set free from sin and have become slaves of God, the benefit you reap leads to holiness, and the result is eternal life. ²³ For the wages of sin is death, but the gift of God is eternal life in Christ Jesus our Lord.

'Gotta Serve Somebody' is the title of a famous Bob Dylan song. He was right. We like to think we're free, but in reality we all serve somebody. The Bible says we are either slaves to sin or slaves of God. Paul contrasts these two types of slavery. He highlights the differences:

- *Beginning* (verse 17). Our slavery to sin began at birth: 'you used to be slaves to sin'. We are slaves to sin by nature. But our slavery to God began by grace when we obeyed the gospel.

- *Development* (verse 19). The slavery of sin has as its result the grim process of a moral deterioration, but the slavery of God has as its result the glorious process of a moral sanctification. Each slavery develops; neither slavery stands still. In one we get worse and worse, and in the other we get better and better.

- *End* (verses 20–22). When we were slaves to sin, the end was death, but now that we are slaves of God, the end is eternal life. Verse 23 sums it up: sin pays the wages we deserve: death; but God gives us a gift that we do not deserve: life.

Here, then, are two totally different lives, opposed to one another: the life of the old self and the life of the new self. And they are two slaveries: by birth we are slaves to sin; by grace we have become the slaves of God. The slavery of sin yields no return except a moral deterioration and finally death. The slavery of God yields the precious return of sanctification and finally eternal life.

So you see, the argument of verses 15–23 is that our conversion, this act of yielding or surrender to God, leads to a status of slavery, and slavery involves obedience.

In Old Testament times, every seven years, Hebrew slaves were set free from their masters. But just occasionally there was a slave who loved his master so much that he chose to commit himself to that master for life. The slave would go through a special ceremony to mark this commitment, when his ear would be pierced with an awl (Exodus 21:2–6). Today, will you renew your commitment to be a slave of God? Are you willing to say, 'Pierce my ear, Lord. I want to be yours for life. Help me, by your grace, to be obedient to you and devoted to your service'?

Day 167

Read Romans 6:1–23
Key verses: Romans 6:15–17

∙∙∙

[15] What then? Shall we sin because we are not under the law but under grace? By no means! [16] Don't you know that when you offer yourselves to someone as obedient slaves, you are slaves of the one you obey – whether you are slaves to sin, which leads to death, or to obedience, which leads to righteousness? [17] But thanks be to God that, though you used to be slaves to sin, you have come to obey from your heart the pattern of teaching that has now claimed your allegiance.

Sometimes we need to stand back from the details and take a look at the big picture. Today we'll take a bird's-eye view of chapter 6.

Both sections (verses 1–14 and verses 15–23) begin with virtually the same question: 'Shall we continue in sin?' Paul's critics, who intend to discredit the gospel, ask this. And it continues to be asked by enemies of the gospel. Satan often whispers this question in our ear to entice us into sin: 'Why not continue in sin? God will forgive you. You are under grace. Go on. Do it again.'

How should we answer the devil? With the same outraged response as Paul: 'By no means!' (verses 2, 15). But we must go further than that and give a logical, irrefutable reason why the insinuations of the devil must be repudiated. Our answer is based on what we are. It is that we are one with Christ (verses 1–14) and we are slaves of God (verses 15–23). We became united to Christ by baptism, at least outwardly and visibly, and we became enslaved to God by the self-surrender of faith. But whether we emphasize the outward baptism or the inward faith, the point is the same. It is that our Christian conversion has had this result: it has united us to Christ, and it has enslaved us to God.

Now what we are has inescapable implications. If we are one with Christ – and we are – then with Christ we died to sin, and we live to God. If we are enslaved to God – which we are – then by that fact we are committed to obedience. It is inconceivable that we should wilfully persist in sin, presuming on the grace of God. The very thought is intolerable.

> You and I need to be talking to ourselves, and saying, 'But don't you know that you are one with Christ; that you have died to sin, and risen to God? Don't you know that you are a slave to God, and committed therefore to obedience? Don't you know these things?' Go on asking yourself that question until you reply to yourself, 'Yes, I do know. And by the grace of God I shall live accordingly.'

Day 168

Read Romans 7:1–6

Key verse: Romans 7:6

....

⁶But now, by dying to what once bound us, we have been released from the law so that we serve in the new way of the Spirit, and not in the old way of the written code.

As Christians, do we need to obey the law that God gave Moses? Does it even apply to us?

Paul uses the illustration of marriage. A woman is only bound to her husband while he is alive. When he dies, she is free to marry again. His point is that, just as death terminates a marriage, so death has terminated our bondage to the law. Of course, it was Christ who died on the cross, but, by our union with him, it is as if we have died and death has removed us altogether out of that sphere where the law exercises lordship. Using Paul's illustration, we were, so to speak, married to the law. Our obligation to obey the law was as binding as a marriage contract. But now we have been set free to marry Christ. Do you appreciate the intimacy of our union with Jesus Christ? Can you believe it? We are married, joined, to Christ.

But notice that this freedom from the law does not mean we are free to do what we please. We have another kind of bondage. We are free not to sin but to serve. And our new Christian slavery is literally 'in the new way of the Spirit, and not in the old way of the written code'. In the old covenant, the law was written on tablets of stone, but now the Holy Spirit writes the law in our hearts.

So is the law still binding upon the Christian? Yes and no! The law is not binding in the sense that our acceptance before God depends on it. Christ, in his death, has met the demands of the law, so it has no claim on us. But the law is still binding in the sense that our new life is still a bondage; we are still slaves. What has changed is the motive and means of our obedience. The motive: we don't obey the law because it is our master and we have to, but because Christ is our husband and we want to. The law says, 'Do this and you will live.' The gospel says, 'You live, so do this.' This means that we serve not by obeying an external code, but by surrendering to the indwelling Spirit. The Christian life is serving the risen Christ by the power of the indwelling Spirit.

Stop trying to undermine the value of Jesus' death by seeking to win God's approval through your works. Your relationship with God is not dependent on keeping all the rules or obeying the law. Jesus has met the demands of the law and you are justified. You are God's dearly beloved child. Serve him not to get his attention, nor to win his approval, but out of sheer gratitude and joy for all that he has done for you. Try this burden on for size – it is much lighter to carry.

Day 169

Read Romans 7:7–13
Key verse: Romans 7:7

• •

[7]What shall we say, then? Is the law sinful? Certainly not! Nevertheless, I would not have known what sin was had it not been for the law.

Can you remember what you wanted to do the last time you saw a sign saying, 'Keep off the grass'? You may well have immediately wanted to walk on the grass! As soon as we are given a law, we often want to do the opposite; we want to do what is forbidden. In the same way, as soon as we receive God's law, we sin. Does that mean I can blame God's law for my sin?

Paul is quick to respond: 'Certainly not!' He goes on to explain that the law itself is not sinful, but rather it:

• reveals sin (verse 7);

• provokes sin (verse 8) – the verb translated 'seizing the opportunity' is a military term for a springboard for offensive operations; sin found a foothold, an opportunity within us;

• condemns sin (verses 8–13) – when we try to live under the law's obligations, we die under its judgment.

Imagine a man caught red-handed committing a crime. He is arrested, brought to trial, found guilty and sent to prison. As he languishes in his cell, he is tempted to blame the law for his imprisonment. It is true that the law has condemned, convicted and sentenced him, but he has only himself to blame, because he committed the crime. And so Paul exonerates the law because although it reveals, provokes and condemns our sin, it cannot be held responsible for it.

The law itself is actually good (verse 12). The problem is our sin. It is our indwelling sin, our fallen nature, that explains the weakness of the law to save us. The law cannot save us, for the simple reason that we cannot keep it, and we cannot keep it because of indwelling sin.

We don't like to admit our sin. Instead, we often look around and blame everyone and everything else for our moral and spiritual failures. At times we even blame God and his commands for our dearth of holiness. Today, recognize the ugliness of your sin. Gaze on the cross and see your crucified Saviour. This is how much God abhors sin. We can't trifle with it or excuse it any longer. We need to hate sin as much as God does, and deal with it in our lives.

O Lord our God, grant us grace to desire Thee with our whole heart; that, so desiring, we may seek, and seeking, find Thee; and so finding Thee, may love Thee; and in loving Thee, may hate those sins from which Thou hast redeemed us.
(St Anselm, ed. Martin H. Manser, *The Westminster Collection of Christian Quotations*, John Knox Press, 2001, p. 233)

Day 170

Read Romans 7:7–25
Key verses: Romans 7:14–15

· ·

[14] We know that the law is spiritual; but I am unspiritual, sold as a slave to sin. [15] I do not understand what I do. For what I want to do I do not do, but what I hate I do.

Do you struggle daily with sin? Don't be surprised and don't despair! It is part of Christian living. Paul knows about this struggle. Bible-believing Christians have differing opinions, but my view is that verses 7–13 describe Paul's life before his conversion, and verse 14 onward describe his present continuous conflict with sin. The fight is fierce and he refuses to accept defeat.

Some people resist the idea that a believer as mature as Paul would have to struggle with sin to such a degree. They prefer to read verses 14–25 as his pre-conversion experience. But look at the opinion he has of himself. Verse 18: 'I know that good itself does not dwell in me.' Also verse 24: 'What a wretched man I am!' Only a mature believer thinks of himself like that! An unbeliever is characterized by self-righteousness, and an immature believer by self-confidence; he or she doesn't ask, 'Who will rescue me?' Only a mature believer feels such disgust and despair when he or she sees his or her sinfulness. Notice also Paul's opinion of the law. He calls the law good (verse 16) and longs with all his being to obey it (verses 19, 22). That is not the language of an unbeliever.

In verses 7–13, Paul shows that, as an unbeliever, he could not keep the law. From verse 14 onward, he shows that, even as a Christian, by himself he cannot keep God's law. His fallen human nature, which was his undoing before his conversion, leading him to sin and death, is still his undoing after his conversion – unless the power of the Holy Spirit subdues it (which he comes to in chapter 8).

We, too, need honestly and humbly to acknowledge our utter sinfulness. We shall never put our trust in the Holy Spirit until we despair of ourselves. We need to cry out, 'What a wretched person I am!' We need to reach that self-despair Paul experienced, because it is the first step on the road to holiness.

Contrary to popular belief, your struggle with sin is not going to get easier as you mature as a disciple. It is going to get harder, because the more of God's holiness you see, the more aware of your own sin you become. The light exposes the darkness. Thank God that, in his kindness, he reveals your sin and provides the means for obedience. Today, in God's strength, press on in your struggle against sin:

> Flee from all this [false teaching, love of money], and pursue righteousness, godliness, faith, love, endurance and gentleness. Fight the good fight of the faith. Take hold of the eternal life to which you were called when you made your good confession in the presence of many witnesses.
> (1 Timothy 6:11–12)

Day 171

Read Romans 7:14–25

Key verses: Romans 7:21–23

. . . .

²¹ So I find this law at work: although I want to do good, evil is right there with me. ²² For in my inner being I delight in God's law; ²³ but I see another law at work in me, waging war against the law of my mind and making me a prisoner of the law of sin at work within me.

When we want to emphasize a point in our emails or texts, we underline, use capital letters or change the font to bold. Here, Paul emphasizes the importance of his message by reiterating it in parallel sections.

Verses 14–17 and 18–20 both begin with a frank acknowledgment of our sin (verses 14, 18). Paul is aware that on his own he is a slave of sin, albeit a reluctant, resistant slave. Even as a Christian, he is brought into captivity and bondage by sin. Both sections continue with a vivid description of the resulting conflict. Christians who know, love and long to do the will of God, but who are not walking according to the Spirit, cannot do it. Because of their sinful nature, they cannot do what they want to do. So when they sin, it is against their mind and will, and the whole tenor of their life. Both sections conclude that, apart from the Holy Spirit, sin means that obedience to God is impossible.

In verse 21, Paul sums up the general principle at work: 'although I want to do good, evil is right there with me'. There are two opposing forces at work: his mind and his flesh (verse 23). This is a real, bitter, unremitting conflict in every Christian's experience. Our mind is simply delighting in God's law and longing to do it, but our flesh is hostile to it and refuses to submit.

Paul's response? A cry of despair: 'What a wretched man I am! Who will rescue me from this body that is subject to death?' (verse 24). This is followed by a cry of triumph: 'Thanks be to God, who delivers me through Jesus Christ our Lord!' (verse 25). Both of these are the cries of a mature believer. We cry out because of the inner corruption of our sinful nature and we long for deliverance. But then we cry out in triumph because we know that God is the one and only deliverer. He is the one who gives us deliverance now through the Holy Spirit, and he is the one who, on the last day, at the resurrection, will give us a new body, without any sin or corruption.

Praise God! He is our rescuer, our great deliverer:

The LORD is my rock, my fortress and my deliverer;
  my God is my rock, in whom I take refuge,
  my shield and the horn of my salvation, my stronghold.
(Psalm 18:2)

The Lord will rescue me from every evil attack and will bring me safely to his heavenly kingdom. To him be glory for ever and ever. Amen.
(2 Timothy 4:18)

Day 172

Read Romans 7:25 – 8:4
Key verses: Romans 8:1–2

....

[1] Therefore, there is now no condemnation for those who are in Christ Jesus, [2] because through Christ Jesus the law of the Spirit who gives life has set you free from the law of sin and death.

Sin within us is like one of those tricky birthday candles that keeps reigniting when we think we've blown it out.
(Christopher Ash, *Teaching Romans*, Christian Focus, 2009, p. 268)

I don't believe that the Christian ever passes once and for all out of Romans 7 and into Romans 8, out of the cry of despair and into the cry of victory. We are always crying out for deliverance and we are always exulting in our deliverer. Whenever we are made conscious of the power of indwelling sin, it is the same.

In verse 25, Paul sums up with beautiful lucidity this double servitude: 'I myself in my mind [we might say, with all my heart and soul] am a slave to God's law, but in my sinful nature [unless it is subdued by the Holy Spirit] a slave to the law of sin.' Whether we serve the law of God or the law of sin depends on whether our mind or our sinful nature is in control. And the question is, 'How can the mind gain ascendency over the flesh, our sinful nature?' That question brings us to chapter 8:1–4 and the ministry of the Holy Spirit. Although he has never been far away in the background of chapter 7, the Holy Spirit has not yet been named.

Chapter 8:1–4 views the same battle as chapter 7, but from a different perspective and with a different outcome. In chapter 7 the conflict is between my mind and the flesh: between what I want to do and what, in myself, I cannot do. But in chapter 8 the conflict is between the Spirit and the flesh. The Holy Spirit is coming to my rescue, allying himself with my mind, the renewed mind he has given me, and subduing the flesh. Whereas in chapter 7:22–23 the believer delights in the law of God but cannot do it in himself because of indwelling sin, now, according to chapter 8:4, he not only delights in it, but actually also fulfils the law of God, because of the indwelling Spirit.

The battle continues. The Holy Spirit lives within us, but we can never say that we've 'dealt' with sin in a particular area of life because it keeps raising its head, usually when we least expect it. The enemy can attack anyone at any time. Christopher Ash (*Teaching Romans*, Christian Focus, 2009) cautions:

- the respectable and happily married business traveller against sexual temptation;
- the generous donor against becoming complacent in her giving;
- the hard-working person approaching retirement who does not suspect that laziness may be lurking around the corner;
- the prayer warrior who thinks he has his prayer life under control; and
- the melancholy believer prone to self-pity who thinks she has got over this and has it under control.

Be alert and of sober mind. Your enemy the devil prowls around like a roaring lion looking for someone to devour.
(1 Peter 5:8)

Day 173

Read Romans 8:1–4

Key verses: Romans 8:3–4

....

> ³ *For what the law was powerless to do because it was weakened by the flesh, God did by sending his own Son in the likeness of sinful flesh to be a sin offering. And so he condemned sin in the flesh,* ⁴ *in order that the righteous requirement of the law might be fully met in us, who do not live according to the flesh but according to the Spirit.*

Imagine a painter standing back to appreciate how all the details and nuances have come together in his completed work. Paul is doing something similar at the beginning of chapter 8. In verses 1–2, the apostle steps back and surveys the whole Christian landscape, portraying the two great blessings of salvation that we have in Christ. We are delivered from condemnation (verse 1) and delivered from the law of sin and its bondage (verse 2).

Verses 3–4 tell us how this salvation is made available to us. God has done what the law could not do. The law cannot sanctify, the law cannot justify, because we cannot obey it. But God has done it! Praise his name! Through the death of his Son he justifies us (verse 3), and through the power of the indwelling Spirit he sanctifies us (verse 4).

He delivers us from bondage by the Spirit, in order that the 'righteous requirement of the law might be fully met in us'. Notice that verse 4 teaches some major truths about holiness:

• *Holiness is the purpose of the incarnation and the death of Christ.* God sent his Son not only that we might be justified, but also in order that the righteousness of the law might be fulfilled in us – in other words, that we might obey the law.

- *Holiness is the righteousness of the law.* Far from the law being abolished in the Christian life, it is God's purpose that its righteous requirement might be fulfilled in us.

- *Holiness is the work of the Holy Spirit.* The righteousness of the law is only fulfilled in us if we walk according to the Spirit.

So the reason for holiness is the death of Christ; the nature of holiness is the righteousness of the law; and the means of holiness is the power of the Holy Spirit.

> God wants you to be holy. Through faith He already counts you holy in Christ. Now He intends to make you holy with Christ. This is no optional plan, no small potatoes. God saved you to sanctify you. God is in the beautification business, washing away spots and smoothing out wrinkles. He will have a blameless bride. He promised to work in you; He also calls you to work out. 'The beauty of holiness' is first of all the Lord's (Ps. 29:2, KJV). But by His grace it can also be yours.
>
> (Kevin DeYoung, *The Hole in Our Holiness*, Crossway Books, 2012, p. 146)

Day 174

Read Romans 8:5–13
Key verse: Romans 8:5

....

⁵ *Those who live according to the flesh have their minds set on what the flesh desires; but those who live in accordance with the Spirit have their minds set on what the Spirit desires.*

It all starts in the mind. Ultimately our thoughts govern our behaviour. How we live, what the Bible sometimes calls our 'walk', depends on the focus of our mind, as Paul outlines in verse 5. To set our mind either on what the flesh desires or on what the Spirit desires means to occupy ourselves with the things of either the flesh or the Spirit. It is a question of our preoccupations, the ambitions that compel us and the interests that engross us – how we spend our time, money and energies; what we give ourselves to. That is what we set our mind on.

Verse 6 describes the result of these two outlooks. To set the mind on the flesh *is* death. Not it '*will be*'; it *is now* death because it leads to sin, and therefore to separation from God, which is death. To set your mind on the Spirit is life now, because it leads to holiness, and so to continuing fellowship with God, which is life. It also brings peace. Peace with God which is life, and peace within ourselves which is integration and harmony. In contrast, there is no peace for the one whose mind is set on the flesh. That person is hostile to God, and will not submit to his law (verse 7).

So there are two categories of people. If we are in the flesh, we set our minds on the things of the flesh, so we walk according to the flesh, and so we die. But if we are in the Spirit, we set our mind upon the things of the Spirit, and so we walk according to the Spirit, and so we live. What we are governs how we think; how we think governs how we behave; and how we behave governs our relationship to God: death or life.

What is going on in your mind? What do you think most about? What are you feeding your mind with? Will you keep up the process of renewing your mind, focusing on the things of the Spirit, so that you will be transformed more and more into the likeness of Christ (Romans 12:2)?

> [We] must understand that Christianity is not served by mindlessness, but by the knowledge of God through the Word of God. Such knowledge engages our minds, stirs our hearts, and transforms our lives. This knowledge is personal. How is it fostered? By listening to what He says (the priority of preaching), by engaging Him in conversation (the emphasis on prayer), by spending time in His company (the need for a devotional life), and by being with others who know Him too (the need for gathered worship). This knowledge is progressive and dynamic, not static. At the end of our journey, we should still be exclaiming with Paul: 'I want to know Christ' (1 Corinthians 2:2).
>
> (Alistair Begg, *Made for His Pleasure*, Moody Press, 1996, p. 22)

Day 175

Read Romans 8:5–13

Key verses: Romans 8:9–10

∙∙

⁹You, however, are not in the realm of the flesh but are in the realm of the Spirit, if indeed the Spirit of God lives in you . . . ¹⁰But if Christ is in you, then even though your body is subject to death because of sin, the Spirit gives life because of righteousness.

What is the distinguishing mark of a Christian? What sets him or her apart from unbelievers? It is that the Christian is indwelt by the Holy Spirit. In verses 17 and 20 of chapter 7, Paul talks about the sin that dwells in him. Now he focuses on the privilege of the Christian being indwelt with the Spirit, who subdues and controls sin. Notice in verses 9–10 that the Spirit of God and the Spirit of Christ are the same person. Similarly, to have the Spirit dwelling in us and having Christ dwell in us are the same thing.

So what difference does the indwelling Spirit make? Life! Verses 10–11 tell us that the Holy Spirit brings life for our spirits now and life for our bodies at the end. Because the Holy Spirit is the Spirit of life; he is the Lord, the life-giver. Although our bodies are mortal, our spirits are alive; the Holy Spirit has given them life. Because of Adam's sin we die physically, but because of Christ's righteousness we live spiritually. Our spirits are alive because Christ, by his Spirit, dwells in us and has given us life. And although at present it is only our spirits that live, on the last day our bodies are going to live as well, incorruptibly. The same Spirit that quickens our hearts now will quicken our bodies.

Paul concludes that we are debtors (verse 12, KJV). He breaks off before completing the sentence, but the implication is that we are debtors to the Holy Spirit. If the Spirit has given life to our spirits, then we must put to death the misdeeds of the body so that we may continue to live the life that the Spirit has given us. So we have an obligation to holiness. We have an obligation to live up to our Christian status and privilege, and to do nothing that is inconsistent with the life of the Spirit that is in us, but rather to nourish and foster this life.

We are debtors to the Holy Spirit, debtors to God for all the grace he has shown us. Today, pray for God's help to live up to your true status and privilege.

O to grace how great a debtor
Daily I'm constrained to be!
Let Thy goodness, like a fetter,
Bind my wandering heart to Thee.
Prone to wander, Lord, I feel it,
Prone to leave the God I love;
Here's my heart, O take and seal it,
Seal it for Thy courts above.
(Robert Robinson, 'Come Thou Fount of Every Blessing', 1759)

Day 176

Read Romans 8:5–13

Key verse: Romans 8:13

· ·

¹³For if you live according to the flesh, you will die; but if by the Spirit you put to death the misdeeds of the body, you will live.

Most of us like to settle our debts. But how are we going to settle our debt to the Holy Spirit? If we are going to be honourable and discharge our debt, there will be two processes involved: mortification and aspiration.

Mortification, putting to death the deeds of the body, means a ruthless rejection of all practices we know to be wrong. It involves a daily repentance, turning from every known sinful habit, practice, association or thought. It is cutting out the eye, cutting off the hand, cutting off the foot, if temptation comes to us through what we see or do, or where we go. The only attitude we can adopt to the flesh is to kill it.

Aspiration, setting the mind on the things of the Spirit, is a whole-hearted giving of ourselves in thought, energy and ambition to whatever things are true and honest, just and pure, lovely and of good report. In order to give our mind to the things of the Spirit, we will need a disciplined use of the means of grace – prayer, reading and meditation on Scripture, fellowship, worship, the Lord's Supper and so on.

In both cases, the verbs mortification and aspiration are in the present tense, because they are attitudes to be adopted, which are then constantly and unremittingly maintained. We are to keep putting to death the deeds of the body, or, as Jesus said, to 'take up [our] cross daily and follow me' (Luke 9:23–24). We are to keep setting our minds on the things of the Spirit, daily. These are the secrets of life in the fullest sense. There is no true life without the death called mortification, and there is no true life without the discipline called aspiration. To sum up: it is as we mortify the flesh in the power of the Holy Spirit and set our minds on the things of the Spirit that the Spirit himself subdues our flesh.

We talk flippantly of carrying our cross when we refer to dealing with difficult relatives or a minor health issue. When a person carried a cross-beam through the streets in the first century, it meant one thing: they were on their way to their execution. Jesus doesn't pull any punches when he describes discipleship. It is a daily – minute-by-minute, in fact – putting to death of our agenda and programmes, our sinful flesh, and a yielding to him.

Imagine carrying your cross into your work meeting, as you care for your elderly relative, serve in church, study for exams, speak to non-Christian family members or look after young children. Feel the weight of the cross.

Now, at this point in your life, what does it mean to 'take up your cross daily and follow' Christ?

Day 177

Read Romans 8:12–17
Key verses: Romans 8:14, 17

....

> [14] *For those who are led by the Spirit of God are the children of God . . .* [17] *Now if we are children, then we are heirs – heirs of God and co-heirs with Christ, if indeed we share in his sufferings in order that we may also share in his glory.*

Most unbelievers would assume that, if there is a God, surely we are all his children. Paul makes a sobering statement that not all human beings are God's children. Verse 14 definitely and deliberately limits this status to those who are being led by the Spirit, who are being enabled by the Spirit to walk along the narrow road of righteousness. To be led by the Spirit and to be a child of God are synonymous.

When we were converted, we received the Spirit of sonship or adoption. The Holy Spirit given to us when we believe makes us sons and daughters, not slaves. He does not recall us to the old slavery spoiled by fear. He grants us a new relationship in which we can approach God as our Father; more than that, he assures us of the status that he brings us. When we cry out, 'Abba, Father' (the very words that the Lord Jesus used in intimate prayer to God in John 17:1), it is the Holy Spirit bearing witness with our spirits that we are children of God. It is in our access to God in prayer that we sense our filial relationship to God, and we know ourselves to be the children of God. In prayer, the Holy Spirit bears witness to our spirit that we are God's children.

As God's children we are heirs, indeed co-heirs with Christ (verse 17). If we share his sonship, we shall share his inheritance in glory, but notice that if we share his glory, we must first share his sufferings. Suffering is the pathway to glory for Christ and for us. So we share his sufferings, his sonship and his glory. Indeed, the whole of the Christian life is identification with Christ.

> See what great love the Father has lavished on us, that we should be called children of God!
> (1 John 3:1)

We can call the Almighty God 'Our Father'. This sets Christianity apart from all the other religions of the world. Other religions invite their followers to worship and placate their gods, but Jesus came so that we could be adopted into God's family, so that we could relate to God in a personal way. As God's dearly loved child, come to him in prayer often, delight to spend time with him and bring him pleasure by the obedience of your life. Submit to his discipline, knowing that he only wants the best for you; that is Christ's likeness formed in you. In times of suffering rest in him; find your comfort and strength in his Word.

If you struggle with assurance that you are part of God's family, come to him in prayer today and let the Holy Spirit minister this truth to your soul.

(See also John 1:12–13; Galatians 3:26–29; 4:4–7; Hebrews 12:4–11; 1 John 3:2, 10.)

Day 178

Read Romans 8:18–27
Key verses: Romans 8:20–21

....

> ²⁰ *For the creation was subjected to frustration, not by its own choice, but by the will of the one who subjected it, in hope* ²¹ *that the creation itself will be liberated from its bondage to decay and brought into the freedom and glory of the children of God.*

Can you imagine what future glory will be like? Paul does not leave us wondering: 'I consider that our present sufferings are not worth comparing with the glory that will be revealed in us' (verse 18). Paul knows all about suffering (2 Corinthians 11:23–28), he knows that we will suffer as Jesus' disciples (Romans 8:17), and yet his conviction is that our present suffering is a drop in the ocean compared to the future glory that we shall experience.

Paul proves his claim by explaining that the glory we are waiting for is so great that even creation is longing for it. He lifts our heads up from our suffering and gives us a cosmic view. As nature has shared humanity's curse (Genesis 3), so nature now shares humanity's tribulation, and is going to share in humanity's glory. 'For the creation waits in eager expectation [as if standing on tiptoe with eager longing] for the children of God to be revealed' (Romans 8:19). Creation is waiting for this because this is the time when it too will be redeemed.

Creation is mentioned four times in verses 19–22, once in every verse. And notice how its present sufferings are described. It was subject to *frustration* (verse 20), not by its own will but by God's will. It is held in *bondage to decay* (verse 21), and it is *groaning* in pain (verse 22). Frustration is the same word that is translated 'vanity' in the Greek version of the Book of Ecclesiastes. The whole creation has been subjected to vanity. This frustration is explained as a bondage to decay – a continuous process in the universe that appears to be running down. And this process is, whether literally or metaphorically, accompanied by pain.

But the present suffering of creation, of nature, is only temporary. There is hope of future glory – from bondage to freedom, from decay to glory incorruptible. Just as we are going to share Christ's glory, creation is going to share ours. The groans and pains that creation endures now are like the pains of childbirth (verse 22). In other words, they are not meaningless or purposeless pains; they are pains necessarily experienced in the bringing to birth of a new order.

When Paul talks about 'glory', he is not talking about your individual place in heaven. God's vision is far more magnificent and expansive. Creation is craning its neck in eager anticipation of the day when our transformation is complete and we, perfectly like Christ, are ruling a redeemed and restored new creation. That's glory!

Today, lift your head up from your suffering and enjoy Paul's cosmic view. Cling to this certain hope that soon your suffering will give way to glory. Also, accept the challenge: if the groans of creation are not death throes but birth pains, rethink your stewardship of God's world. How could you better look after the resources that God has entrusted to our care?

Day 179

Read Romans 8:18–27
Key verse: Romans 8:23

....

²³ *Not only so, but we ourselves, who have the firstfruits of the Spirit, groan inwardly as we wait eagerly for our adoption to sonship, the redemption of our bodies.*

We groan because of the ravages that sin makes in our lives, and in the lives of those we love . . . We groan in disappointment, in bereavement, in sorrow. We groan physically in our pain and our limitation. Life consists of a great deal of groaning.
(Ray Stedman, *From Guilt to Glory, vol. 1*, Word, 1981, p. 241)

Our bodies are weak, fragile and mortal, subject to tiredness, sickness, pain and death (2 Corinthians 5), and they are indwelt by sin. Physical frailty and our fallen nature cause us to groan and long for future glory. On that last day we are going to be given new, redeemed, resurrection bodies, without sin. But there's more. Future glory is also about our 'adoption'. In one sense we have already received our adoption, but in another sense we are still waiting. We are God's children, but we are not yet conformed, in either body or character, to Christ. Neither has our sonship been publicly recognized or revealed. This will happen on the last day (verse 19).

How can we be sure of this glorious inheritance? We have the firstfruits of the Holy Spirit (verse 23). The Holy Spirit is the guarantee and foretaste of our full inheritance. Sometimes Paul uses a business metaphor and describes the Holy Spirit as the first instalment, the down payment, which certifies that the remainder is going to be paid later (2 Corinthians 1:22). Here he uses a farming metaphor. The firstfruits of the harvest are a pledge of the full crop to come. So the Holy Spirit not only makes us children of God by the Spirit of adoption; he not only witnesses with our spirit that we are children of God; he himself is the pledge of our complete adoption to be the sons of God when our bodies are redeemed. In the meantime, we wait patiently for future glory (verse 25).

Are you groaning today, overwhelmed by circumstances, frustrated by sin? You don't need to groan in despair or doubt, because we have a sure hope. We groan as adopted children longing for our Father to usher in his promised future. Like creation, be on tiptoes eagerly awaiting your deliverance: the day your sinful body will be done away with. You will see Christ and experience the fullness of your salvation.

In the meantime, wait. Wait with endurance, bearing up under all sorts of trials, because you have hope in God. Also wait patiently because you are confident in God's promise that the firstfruits will be followed by the harvest.

> For the grace of God has appeared that offers salvation to all people. It teaches us to say 'No' to ungodliness and worldly passions, and to live self-controlled, upright and godly lives in this present age, while we wait for the blessed hope – the appearing of the glory of our great God and Saviour, Jesus Christ.
> (Titus 2:11–13)

Day 180

Read Romans 8:18–27
Key verses: Romans 8:26–27

∙∙

26 In the same way, the Spirit helps us in our weakness. We do not know what we ought to pray for, but the Spirit himself intercedes for us through wordless groans. 27 And he who searches our hearts knows the mind of the Spirit, because the Spirit intercedes for God's people in accordance with the will of God.

Do you struggle to pray? Often we find it hard to settle down to pray, and then, when we do, we get distracted! At other times we just don't know what words to say.

Helping us in our prayer life is another ministry that the Holy Spirit fulfils. He is mentioned four times in these two verses. We don't often talk about the Holy Spirit's role in prayer, yet we are taught in the Bible that our access to God is not only through the Son, but also by the Spirit. The Holy Spirit's inspiration is as necessary as the Son's mediation in our access to God in prayer. Here Paul is talking specifically about our ignorance in prayer. When we don't know precisely what to pray for as we ought, the Holy Spirit helps us in our weakness.

Sometimes when believers don't know how to pray in words, they groan. Sometimes we groan because of the intensity of our longing. At other times we are so burdened by our own mortality, or by our sin, that we can only groan. But what J. B. Phillips calls 'those agonising longings which never find words' (Romans 8:26) are not to be despised, as if we ought to be able to put them into language. On the contrary, when we sigh with inarticulate desires, it is the Holy Spirit himself interceding on our behalf, prompting these groans. We do not need to be ashamed of these wordless prayers. God the Father understands prayers that are sighed rather than said, because he searches our hearts. He can read our hearts and our thoughts and he knows the mind of the Spirit, because the Holy Spirit always prays in accordance with the will of God. And so the Father in heaven answers the prayers prompted by the Spirit in our hearts.

There are times when we struggle to pray. When we are lying in a hospital bed too ill to speak; when someone we love is suffering so intensely that we are too numb to articulate our thoughts; when we are not sure if we should be asking God to relieve us of our suffering or give us the strength to endure it. But our inability to pray doesn't stop God's will unfolding in our lives. In those times, God the Holy Spirit carries our prayers to God the Father. And he always knows what to pray for because he knows God's will. How amazing that God prays to God on our behalf! And not only that, we have two intercessors: Jesus in heaven (Romans 8:34) and the Holy Spirit in our hearts, both praying to God the Father for us. Surely we are greatly loved.

Day 181

Read Romans 8:28–39
Key verses: Romans 8:28–30

• •

²⁸And we know that in all things God works for the good of those who love him, who have been called according to his purpose. ²⁹For those God foreknew he also predestined to be conformed to the image of his Son, that he might be the firstborn among many brothers and sisters. ³⁰And those he predestined, he also called; those he called, he also justified; those he justified, he also glorified.

What is the best-known verse in the Bible? A few vie for first position, but Romans 8:28 surely must come close. Many Christians have taken comfort from the fact that God works all things together for good – including the pains and the groans we thought about yesterday – for those who love him and are 'called according to his purpose'.

In verses 29–30, Paul sets out five affirmations that explain what is meant by the divine calling, and in what sense God works all things together for good. These affirmations explain God's purpose in saving sinners. First, he foreknew, and second, he predestined. The difference between foreknowledge and predestination is, perhaps, that God's electing choice was formed in his mind before he willed it. His decision preceded his decree. The implication clearly is that everyone who is saved can ascribe each stage of his or her salvation not to his or her merit or obedience, but only to God's favour and action. Notice that the purpose of God's predestination is not favouritism, but holiness, Christlikeness.

The third affirmation is that God called; and the fourth is that he justified. The call of God is the historical outworking of his eternal predestination, and those whom God calls respond in faith to the call. And those who believe, God justifies, accepting them in Christ as his own. Fifth, he glorified, bringing them to resurrection and to heaven, with new bodies in a new world. So certain is this final stage of glorification that it is expressed in the aorist tense as if it were past, like the other four stages which *are* past.

These five affirmations are like a chain with five unbreakable links. God is pictured as moving on steadily from stage to stage, from an eternal foreknowledge and predestination, through a historical call and justification, to a final glorification of his people in heaven.

When we say, 'All things work together for good', we don't mean that life will always turn out as we'd like, that healing will come or a difficult situation will be resolved. Rather, it means we can have great confidence that in God's sovereignty, he will use everything that happens to us in life for our good. The 'good' that Paul is talking about is our ultimate good, that one day we will be conformed to the image of Christ. So whatever is happening in your life right now, whatever struggles you are dealing with, you can be sure that God will finish his work in you. You will be glorified, and your eternal destiny is secure.

Day 182

Read Romans 8:28–39
Key verses: Romans 8:38–39

. . . .

38 For I am convinced that neither death nor life, neither angels nor demons, neither the present nor the future, nor any powers, 39 neither height nor depth, nor anything else in all creation, will be able to separate us from the love of God that is in Christ Jesus our Lord.

In our suffering, when our own faith falters and the world is full of insecurity, can we be sure of God's love?

Paul responds by asking five questions.

- *'If God is for us, who can be against us?'* (verse 31). If he'd simply asked, 'Who can be against us?', we could have come up with a long list! Unbelievers, indwelling sin, death and the devil all oppose us. But Paul's question is, 'If the God who foreknew, predestined, called, justified and glorified us is for us, who can be against us?' Our enemies may set themselves against us, but they can never prevail if God is on our side.

- *'He who did not spare his own Son, but gave him up for us all – how will he not also, along with him, graciously give us all things?'* (verse 32). If Paul had simply asked, 'Will God not give us all things?', we might have wondered. But Paul banishes any lingering doubts. God has already given us his Son: 'with this gift how can he fail to lavish upon us all he has to give?' (NEB). The cross proves the generosity of God.

- *'Who will bring any charge against those whom God has chosen?'* (verse 33). We are in a court of law. If the question had been, 'Who will bring any charge against us?', we might well answer, 'My conscience and the devil' (Revelation 12:10). But the devil's accusations fall to the ground; they do not hurt us. They are like arrows off a shield because we are God's chosen, whom he has justified. And if God has justified us, no accusation can stand against us.

- *'Who then is the one who condemns?'* (verse 34). Our critics, all the demons in hell and even our own hearts seek to condemn us (1 John 3:20–21). But their threats are idle. Jesus died for the sins that should have condemned us. His resurrection proves that the penalty for sin has been paid in full.

- *'Who shall separate us from the love of Christ?'* (verse 35). Verses 35–39 list all the perilous and painful things that could separate us from the love of God. But far from separating us from Christ's love, in the experience and enduring of these sufferings, 'we are more than conquerors' (verse 37). The Greek word conveys the idea of being 'super-conquerors'. These adversities cannot separate us from Christ's love because we conquer in them through him who has proved his love at the cross. Christ has proved his love by his sufferings, so our sufferings cannot separate us from his love.

There is nothing that you will go through today – or in the coming days – that can separate you from God's love: no broken romance, financial hardship, tragedy or even death. Although at times your hold on God may be frail, he has you in his grip and will not let you go. God loves you and is for you. Hold fast to this unshakeable conviction: live in the confidence, comfort and joy of it.

For further study

If you would like to do further study on Romans, the following books may be useful:

- F. F. Bruce, *Romans,* Tyndale New Testament Commentaries (IVP, 2008).

- R. Kent Hughes, *Romans: Righteousness from Heaven,* Preaching the Word (Crossway, 1991).

- Douglas Moo, *Epistle to the Romans,* New International Commentary on the New Testament (Eerdmans, 1996).

- Thomas Schreiner, *Romans,* Baker Exegetical Commentary on the New Testament (Baker, 1998).

- John Stott, *The Message of Romans,* The Bible Speaks Today (IVP, 1994).

If God has fed you through your study of the book of Romans 5 – 8, why not buy the individual Food for the Journey on Romans 5 – 8 and give it to a friend (available from ivpbooks.com)?

Day 183

Read Psalm 13
Key verses Psalm 13:1–2

....

For the director of music. A psalm of David.
¹ *How long, Lord? Will you forget me for ever?*
   How long will you hide your face from me?
² *How long must I wrestle with my thoughts*
   and day after day have sorrow in my heart?
   How long will my enemy triumph over me?

In the last study, we saw in Romans 8 how we can be sure of God's love in our suffering, when our own faith falters and the world is full of insecurity. Our next three sets of studies, on Habakkuk, James and 2 Timothy, all engage in different ways with the question of suffering. Behind it lies the question of how God is acting in the world.

One kind of response too often forgotten by Christians can be found in many of the psalms (sometimes called psalms of lament). These remind us that it is OK to come to God *as we are* and *as we feel* and almost to say the unsayable. Psalm 13 is one such psalm. It is remarkably plain-speaking in addressing God when *shalom* is absent, when things are not as they should be, or, more accurately, when things are not as they one day will be.

Notice how it begins, with an address: 'How long, Lord?' (verse 1). It is an act of trust, that God is there. It is an act of commitment, a recognition of belonging, to address God as the 'Lord', who has acted in history to save.

It continues with the trouble (verses 1–2). As John Calvin says of these psalms, 'Here the Holy Spirit has represented to life all the griefs, sorrows, fears, doubts, hopes, cares, anxieties, in short all the stormy emotions by which human minds are wont to be agitated' (*Works*, ed. 1553, vol. III, p. 356).

Then comes the request (verse 3). While we may often tell God what needs to happen, the psalms tend to ask God to hear and to help, and they trust that he will know best what to do!

Then there is a reason, or motive (verses 3b–4). Here it focuses on the psalmist's need. Elsewhere the reason can be the relationship between the psalmist and God, or the character of God.

Finally, there is an expression of trust or confidence (verses 5–6). While this expression of trust might seem out of kilter with the earlier pleas, in reality the whole psalm stems from trust.

In the garden of Gethsemane, Jesus prays, 'My Father, if it is possible, may this cup be taken from me' (Matthew 26:39). On the cross, he cries out, 'My God, my God, why have you forsaken me?' (Matthew 27:46). We too can pray these prayers for God to act. But, of course, we need to remember his, 'Yet not as I will, but as you will' (Matthew 26:39).

> What a friend we have in Jesus,
> All our sins and griefs to bear!
> What a privilege to carry
> Everything to God in prayer!
> Oh, what peace we often forfeit,
> Oh, what needless pain we bear,
> All because we do not carry
> Everything to God in prayer!
> (Joseph Scriven, 'What a Friend We Have in Jesus', 1855)

Will you bring *everything* to God in prayer? Today, pray this psalm for yourself or for someone you know who is in need.

Introduction
Habakkuk

Jonathan Lamb

Who is in control?

The sustained threat from rogue states, international terrorism, violence perpetrated by religious extremists, and the moral confusion arising from liberal views of all kinds beg the question: what is happening to our world?

We sense that we have entered into an era of bewildering uncertainty where no-one is in control. There is a fault line in our world, a deep vulnerability that many people express. And it is not simply to do with global events. Our own personal world often seems out of control as we reel from suffering, family tragedies and unanswered prayers.

The prophet Habakkuk knows God is in control, but, like us, his personal experience seems to contradict this. His belief does not match his experience, and he wrestles with the tension.

A contemporary of Jeremiah, Habakkuk sees that wickedness and oppression are rife in Judah, and he can't understand why God doesn't act. He is even more perplexed when God tells him he will use the evil Babylonians to bring judgment on Judah.

The book is a dialogue between the prophet and God. Habakkuk confronts God with his confusion and, in doing so, he expresses the voice of the godly in Judah, and he speaks for us. He articulates the questions that believers ask and expresses the certainties we must embrace. His memorable closing doxology is no easy believism or superficial triumphalism. He makes a demanding journey from the bewildered questions of chapter 1 to offering the worship of an individual who has discovered that, when everything is stripped away, God is enough.

Habakkuk invites us to discover the foundations of faith in an uncertain world and to join the journey from 'why?' to 'worship'.

Day 184

Read Habakkuk 1:1–11
Key verses: Habakkuk 1:2–3

· ·

> ²*How long, LORD, must I call for help,*
>   *but you do not listen?*
> *Or cry out to you, 'Violence!'*
>   *but you do not save?*
> ³*Why do you make me look at injustice?*
>   *Why do you tolerate wrongdoing?*
> *Destruction and violence are before me;*
>   *there is strife, and conflict abounds.*

'How long?' 'Why?' – these are two questions we often ask.

The prophet Habakkuk is also overwhelmed by these questions. He is living in Jerusalem in the final days of the seventh century BC. Josiah, the great king who discovered the law, pulled down the pagan altars and restored the temple, but he has been followed by Jehoiakim, who quickly succeeded in reversing all his good work.

King Jehoiakim built his wonderful palaces, exploiting the people in the process, but shows no repentance. And so the priests, politicians and civil servants take their cue from him. They too have become perpetrators of violence and injustice, adding to the moral confusion rather than resolving it (verse 3). No wonder Habakkuk declares, 'The wicked hem in the righteous' (verse 4). The few who do remain faithful to the Word of the Lord are completely surrounded by ungodly behaviour which threatens to snuff out all signs of spiritual life.

Habakkuk watches this terrible moral and spiritual decline set in. God's Word has been frozen out, and the law has been paralysed (verse 4). Justice has been replaced with anarchy. The people are determined to forget what God said and to live life on their own terms.

But it is not just the sinfulness of the people that brings Habakkuk close to despair; it is also the delay in God's action. It is actually Habakkuk's understanding of God that leads him to voice this complaint: 'If what I know about you is true, God, then why aren't you acting? Why the delay?' There is an intensity in verses 2–4, suggesting that the prophet shouts, screams, roars, 'Help, Lord! Why are you allowing people to drift away? Why are you not intervening?'

These questions are not simply academic. Habakkuk is bewildered and is crying out to God with deeply felt pain. As the novelist Peter de Vries puts it, 'The question mark twisted like a fish hook in the human heart' (*The Blood of the Lamb*, University of Chicago Press, 2005, p. 243).

Are there question marks twisting 'like a fish hook' in your heart? Many of us have unresolved 'why' questions in our lives. We won't always find the answers to perplexing questions this side of eternity. When everything seems out of joint, it is okay to admit your bewilderment. But don't believe Satan's lie that God's apparent silence means he is not interested, or not working on your behalf. Like Habakkuk, lay out your complaint honestly before God. Ask him to help you trust his character and learn to live with unanswered questions and mystery.

Day 185

Read Habakkuk 1:1–11
Key verse: Habakkuk 1:5

....

⁵*Look at the nations and watch –*
  and be utterly amazed.
For I am going to do something in your days
  that you would not believe,
  even if you were told.

Sometimes we have particular expectations of how God ought to work in our lives and in our world. We think we know how our prayers should be answered. So it is important to note here what God tells Habakkuk: 'Look carefully.'

God's response in verse 5 begins with the word 'Look', which picks up Habakkuk's complaint in verse 3: 'Why do you make me look at injustice?' Habakkuk *is* looking, but he needs a different perspective. He needs to see God's perspective.

God has heard Habakkuk's prayer and in fact is already at work. He is not standing by, indifferent to the prophet's concerns. No, he says, I am already at work; if only you had eyes to see it. Verses 6–11, which outline God's plan, describe the devastation the Babylonians are about to bring on God's own people. The Babylonians are guilty of international terrorism, ethnic cleansing and the exercise of ruthless power. This great military power will crush everything in its path. And the Lord is behind the series of devastating events that will change the course of history in Habakkuk's day. He has not abandoned his plans. Judah and all of the nations are still under God's watchful eye, if only Habakkuk could see it.

Do you remember Paul's testimony in Philippians 1? He is confined in prison. For an activist like Paul, this could be frustrating in the extreme. But he writes, 'I want you to know, brothers and sisters, that what has happened to me has actually served to advance the gospel' (Philippians 1:12). Paul may be imprisoned, but he knows God is at work. Every day one of Caesar's personal bodyguards is chained to him; there are four teams of four soldiers – a captive audience! We know that members of the imperial household become Christians. The gospel is reaching social circles it never would have reached were it not for Paul's witness, extending right up to Nero himself. Paul also mentions that other Christians are encouraged to speak the Word of God more fearlessly (Philippians 1:14). Paul can see that, however unpromising the situation looks, there is another story: God is at work.

Perhaps you belong to a very small church or are working in a demanding situation. Maybe you live in a country where the church is under enormous pressure, or your personal or family situation exerts what seems like a strongly restrictive influence over all you do. God is not indifferent to your struggles; he does not stand aloof. He is watching over you. Take heart – beneath the surface story of your life there is another more glorious story unfolding; there is the reality of God at work. Ask God to help you take a fresh look at your circumstances and to open your eyes to what he is doing.

Day 186

Read Habakkuk 1:1–11
Key verses: Habakkuk 1:6–7

....

> ⁶*I am raising up the Babylonians,*
> *that ruthless and impetuous people,*
> *who sweep across the whole earth*
> *to seize dwellings not their own.*
> ⁷*They are a feared and dreaded people;*
> *they are a law to themselves*
> *and promote their own honour.*

Some Christians appear to live as if they were in a *Star Wars* adventure, surrounded by equal and opposite forces of good and evil. If something good happens, God has won that battle. If something bad happens, the devil must have triumphed in that round.

But the Bible teaches that God is always in control, always ultimately sovereign.

In fact, what is so troubling for Habakkuk is that, although the Babylonians are in the driving seat of this great war machine, God is the Commander. God is disciplining his people. They have ignored his justice, and so they will be subjected to Babylonian justice. God's people are guilty of perpetuating violence and destruction, so that is what they will receive.

But the Babylonians are not just an instrument under God's sovereign authority; they are also an instrument for God's purposes. These verses underline a very profound truth: God is in control. He even controls the movements of ruthless powers and pagan nations. Calvin commented on these verses: 'It is not by their own instinct, but by the hidden impulse of God . . . God can employ the vices of men in executing his judgments. The wicked are led here and there by the hidden power of God' (*Commentaries on the Twelve Minor*

Prophets, Volume 4: Habakkuk, Zephaniah, Haggai, CreateSpace Publishing, 2015, pp. 23–24). It might seem that the military prowess of the Babylonians will eventually result in their success, but it is God who has raised them up to fulfil his purposes. God really is in control.

The book of Job underlines this point. God grants permission to Satan to test Job, but God sets the boundaries (Job 1:8–12). Exactly the same principle appears in the New Testament. The early Christians are bewildered when Jesus is crucified. In their prayer meeting they state that Herod, Pontius Pilate, the Gentiles and the people of Israel conspired against Jesus. But then they add, 'They did what your power and will had decided beforehand should happen' (Acts 4:28).

The Babylonians might think they are in control; the British or the Americans or ISIS might think they are in control. But the rise and fall of nations and empires, of dictators and terrorists, is in God's hands.

The Bible often urges us to 'remember', because reflecting on God's faithfulness strengthens our resolve to trust and obey him in our present struggles. Remember and reflect on examples from the Bible and your own life when you have witnessed God's control in difficult times. Thank him that even today he is fulfilling his good purposes for your life. Acknowledge his sovereign control and ask for his help to be obedient during dark days.

Day 187

Read Habakkuk 1:12–17
Key verse: Habakkuk 1:12

. . . .

> [12] LORD, are you not from everlasting?
> My God, my Holy One, you will never die.
> You, LORD, have appointed them to execute judgment;
> you, my Rock, have ordained them to punish.

'Never doubt in the dark what God has told you in the light' (Warren Wiersbe, *Be Comforted*, David C. Cook Publishing, 2009, p. 148).

Habakkuk understands that judgment is necessary for Israel, but he can't understand how all the violence and devastation can possibly fulfil God's purposes for righteousness. How will it fulfil God's promise of blessing, and when will it all end?

But, like many of the psalmists and other prophets, Habakkuk sets his questions in the context of his certainties and affirms the foundational truths of the Christian faith. He expresses confidence in:

- *God's commitment*. He speaks to God in direct and personal terms: 'My God, my Holy One'. He is implying, 'You are the faithful, covenant-keeping God; I belong to you.' That is our confidence too. God will not let go of us. Whatever happens, we belong to him. This security is not dependent on our capacity to believe, but on God's faithful commitment to us.

- *God's eternity*. 'LORD, are you not from everlasting?' God is engaged in history, but he is also above all of its turbulent ebb and flow. Whatever our fears and uncertainties, God is eternal, the Rock, the one stable element in an uncertain world. If things are shaking in our lives or in our world, we must hold on to God's changelessness.

- *God's purpose.* Habakkuk realizes that the coming Babylonian invasion is something God has ordained. Other prophets, like Ezekiel, Jeremiah and Isaiah, also realize that international events are not random. They are all part of God's sovereign purpose.

Habakkuk doesn't ignore his troubling questions. He is realistic about the terrible judgment the Babylonians will bring and he cries out honestly to God. But, crucially, in the midst of it all he affirms what he knows to be true about God.

When we are in difficult situations, it is very easy for questions and doubts to overwhelm us. We need to remind ourselves of the certainties of God's Word and repeat to ourselves the confident realities we have examined. If we respond as Habakkuk did, even in the blackest moments, we will discover that God is our refuge and strength.

> Most of your unhappiness in life is due to the fact that you are listening to yourself instead of talking to yourself.
> (D. Martyn Lloyd-Jones, *Spiritual Depression*, STL, 1965, p. 20)
>
> Today, as you struggle with perplexing questions and are concerned with all that is going on in the world, rehearse the great certainties of faith. Choose five rock-solid affirmations of faith, write them down, meditate on them and let these truths fill you with confidence in God's sovereignty. For example:
>
> God has said,
>   'Never will I leave you;
>   never will I forsake you.'
> (Hebrews 13:5)
>
> Jesus Christ is the same yesterday and today and for ever.
> (Hebrews 13:8)

Day 188

Read Habakkuk 1:12–17

Key verse: Habakkuk 1:13

....

¹³Your eyes are too pure to look on evil;
    you cannot tolerate wrongdoing.
Why then do you tolerate the treacherous?
    Why are you silent while the wicked
    swallow up those more righteous than themselves?

No doubt you have heard the phrase, 'The cure is worse than the disease.'

This is exactly how the situation appears to Habakkuk. As a prophet, he understands that judgment is inevitable. His problem is that instead of God's purposes being advanced, they seem to be going in exactly the opposite direction.

God seems to be being inconsistent (verse 13). If he is the God of awesome purity, why is he going to allow the ruthless Babylonians to do their worst? The suspicion is that if he is to use them, he must be like them. The imagery of verses 14–17 underlines their ruthless behaviour. As if fishing with a rod and net, the Babylonians sit beside the stream that God has generously stocked with human fish: 'he gathers them up in his drag-net; and so he rejoices and is glad' (verse 15). Historians tell us that the Babylonians placed hooks into the lower jaw of their captives to lead them along with chains. No wonder Habakkuk is appalled by the brutality.

We, too, are perplexed at what is happening in our world. Like Habakkuk, we are shocked by the violence. We are also bewildered by personal tragedies, which seem to contradict our understanding of God's character. We can't grasp how God can use these present circumstances to fulfil his purposes.

I find my experience of sailing helpful here. Once, when we were in the Sound of Mull in Scotland, the winds rose to almost storm force, but the skipper was determined we would make the journey. We soon learnt how to 'beat against the wind'. This is a manoeuvre whereby you sail in one direction and then tack to travel in another direction, in a sustained zigzag movement. You make very slow progress, but the remarkable thing is this: you are using the winds that are against you to make that progress.

It strikes me that this is also a realistic model of the Christian life. Sometimes we think we must always be riding high on some success-orientated spirituality. But Jesus never promised us that. He did promise that whatever winds and waves are thrown at us, we will still make progress to our destination. God uses even those opposing forces to help us move forward.

Are you in the middle of a storm, figuratively speaking? Don't be content just to tread water in these days of difficulty and testing. Allow the winds and waves that are battering your life right now to be a means of spiritual progress. Practise 'beating against the wind'. Whatever your circumstances, today, look for opportunities to:

- trust God;
- grow in your knowledge and appreciation of his Word;
- deepen your discipleship relationships with other believers;
- pray more fervently;
- serve him wholeheartedly.

Day 189

Read Habakkuk 2:1–3
Key verse: Habakkuk 2:1

....

> ¹*I will stand at my watch*
>   *and station myself on the ramparts;*
> *I will look to see what he will say to me,*
>   *and what answer I am to give to this complaint.*

How should we pray when we are riddled with questions and doubts?

Here, at the start of chapter 2, Habakkuk is quietly, patiently listening. It seems a million miles away from the mood of Habakkuk's praying that we observed in chapter 1. He has poured out his heart to God and now he is waiting on God.

It is helpful to see that both aspects of prayer are expressed by the same man. Habakkuk, after honestly communicating his concerns and questions, turns away from every distraction and waits on God. It must be enormously difficult for him to do that. We should not forget what is happening in Jerusalem – a situation that provokes the sustained refrain of 'violence' and 'injustice'. But it is vital for Habakkuk to step away from the turbulence of the city, and of his own heart and mind, in order to hear God's still, small voice.

Psalm 73 reflects this pattern. The psalmist has similar questions and pours out his complaint: 'Why do the wicked always seem to succeed and the righteous suffer? Why, God, do you allow this to continue?' But then in verses 16–17 we reach the turning point in the psalm:

> When I tried to understand all this,
>   it troubled me deeply
> till I entered the sanctuary of God;
>   then I understood their final destiny.

Like Habakkuk, the psalmist takes time to come into God's presence, and it is there that his perspective changes. Perhaps you can identify with some of the questions Habakkuk asks in chapter 1. What is your response to those challenges? Sometimes we live more by the maxim, 'Why pray, when you can worry?' Committing these perplexities to God is one of the most important disciplines in our lives.

How often have you 'waited' on God? When faced with a difficult situation, we tend to agonize over it, talk it through with friends or rush to solve the problem. It is harder to take ourselves off to a quiet place, to enter God's sanctuary and pray, allowing him, if necessary, to change our perspective. Don't let prayer be a last resort. Get rid of the distractions and join with the psalmist:

Wait for the LORD;
   be strong and take heart
   and wait for the LORD.
(Psalm 27:14)

I wait for your salvation, LORD,
   and I follow your commands.
(Psalm 119:166)

I wait for the LORD, my whole being waits,
and in his word I put my hope.
(Psalm 130:5)

Day 190

Read Habakkuk 2:1–3

Key verse: Habakkuk 2:1

....

> ¹*I will stand at my watch*
> *and station myself on the ramparts;*
> *I will look to see what he will say to me,*
> *and what answer I am to give to this complaint.*

When you pray or read the Bible, are you expectant that God will speak?

Here, Habakkuk describes himself as someone standing on the ramparts, keeping watch above the city of Jerusalem. He is waiting expectantly for God to speak. You may remember the sense of expectancy in Jerusalem some years later, when Ezra stands in the city centre and reads from the Book of the Law. The account is recorded in Nehemiah 8. God's people have returned from exile and have rebuilt the walls of the city. Now, as they prepare for their new life back home, they are desperate to hear and obey the Word of the Lord. Their eagerness and expectancy are expressed in the fact that 'all the people listened attentively' (Nehemiah 8:3), and in the way they stand up when the Book is opened and bow down in worship as they come into God's presence. They are ready to hear and respond (Nehemiah 8:1–12).

There is little to be gained from reading the Bible without that kind of expectancy. Jesus' own ministry is frustrated when there is no expectancy on the part of his hearers. He begins to teach in the synagogue and he is met by cynicism and incredulity. Expectant faith is the soil in which God's Word will bear fruit, and this is an element in our spiritual life that we need to nurture.

It is one of the lessons from Habakkuk chapter 1. Although he feels the weariness of it all (1:2), Habakkuk keeps on praying with perseverance and expectant faith, believing that God will finally speak his Word. Don Carson offers some very useful advice:

> Pray until you pray . . . Christians should pray long enough and honestly enough at a single session to get past the feeling of formalism and unreality that attends a little praying. Many of us in our praying are like nasty little boys who ring front door bells and run away before anyone answers.
> (Don Carson, *A Call to Spiritual Reformation*, IVP, 1992, pp. 36–37)

Will you 'pray until you pray'?

How would you describe your spiritual posture as you read the Bible and pray? God wants us to be like watchmen on a rampart, waiting expectantly for what he will say. The psalmist uses another image:

> As the deer pants for streams of water,
> so my soul pants for you, my God.
> My soul thirsts for God, for the living God.
> (Psalm 42:1–2)

Today, spend unhurried time in God's presence, listening for his voice and cultivating that sense of expectancy. Acknowledge that God's Word alone sustains you. Be willing to 'do whatever he tells you' (John 2:5), and 'pray until you pray'.

Day 191

Read Habakkuk 2:1–3
Key verse: Habakkuk 2:1

....

> ¹I will stand at my watch
>   and station myself on the ramparts;
> I will look to see what he will say to me,
>   and what answer I am to give to this complaint.

Nobody enjoys being rebuked, but sometimes it is necessary.

Habakkuk is aware of how bold he was in God's presence in chapter 1 and knows that a rebuke is in order. He says, 'I will look to see what he will say to me, and what answer I am to give to this complaint' (2:1). But there is an alternative way to translate the phrase, which says, 'what to answer when I am rebuked'. Or it could read, 'I will look to see what he will say to me and the correction that I am going to receive.' It is almost shocking to see the way he addresses God with his complaints and his anxious questions, and so now, as he stands on the city ramparts, he realizes he must be prepared for the Lord's rebuke, 'the correction that I am going to receive'. He has presented all of the arguments, so now he is submissive enough to wait for the Lord's reproof and discipline.

David Prior rightly observes that 'God looks not just for honesty, but he also looks for humility' (*The Message of Joel, Micah & Habakkuk*, IVP, 1988, p. 233). In all prayer we must be submissive as well as honest, ready for what God is going to say to us and open to any reproof or discipline that may be necessary.

Maybe you have heard the story of an announcement in a missionary magazine concerning the former general director of a mission agency who was retiring, but was going to continue to serve the Lord 'in an advisory capacity'! We are not the ones with the answers when it comes to praying. We are not in control. Coming into God's presence, in the way Habakkuk does, requires that we are 'teachable as well as frank', as David Prior puts it. We are to be submissive as well as honest, open to listening to what the Lord has to say to us.

He will change our lives if we come into his presence with this kind of submissive attitude. That is certainly the case for Habakkuk.

Sometimes we have the wrong attitude: we speak unwisely and act impulsively. Will you accept God's rebuke as a gracious display of his love for you? Will you submit to his discipline (Hebrews 12:5–6)?

Today, kneel in God's presence, bending your head and your heart humbly before him. Be like Mary, who sat at her Master's feet, listening and learning from him (Luke 10:38–42). Savour God's pleasure, knowing:

> These are the ones I look on with favour:
>> those who are humble and contrite in spirit,
>> and who tremble at my word.
>
> (Isaiah 66:2)

Day 192

Read Habakkuk 2:1–3
Key verse: Habakkuk 2:2

....

² Then the Lord replied:
'Write down the revelation
and make it plain on tablets
so that a herald may run with it.'

With our multiplicity of Bible versions and translations, we can become quite complacent about what we are actually reading.

Habakkuk 2:2 reminds us that we are holding God's Word in our hands. The key word in this exchange is 'revelation'. It is God's revealed Word that Habakkuk receives, and which he is told to write down so that the herald may run with it. And verse 2 points back to the opening verse of the prophecy, which describes the oracle that Habakkuk saw. It is this vision, or revelation, that God is calling him to record. The words of revelation from God are the vital turning point for Habakkuk, as they are for all of God's people who listen to his voice.

If we are perplexed about what is happening in the church, by the uncertainties of the world or the dilemmas in our own lives, then the starting point is to strengthen our confidence in God's revelation, his authoritative Word to us in all of the Scriptures. Men and women of faith believe that God's Word matters. That Word is authoritative, dynamic and life-giving. It is of lasting importance and must be preserved and passed on to others (2:2). As we come to the pages of Scripture, we look at that Word 'to see what he will say to me' (2:1). Throughout its pages, Scripture urges us to have responsive hearts.

Calvin's commentary on this section of Habakkuk provides us with a lovely illustration:

As long as we judge according to our own perceptions, we walk on the earth, and while we do so, many clouds arise and Satan scatters ashes in our eyes and wholly darkens our judgment and thus it happens that we lie down altogether confounded. It is hence wholly necessary that we should tread our reason underfoot and come nigh to God himself. Let the word of God become our ladder.
(Quoted in Elizabeth Achtemeier, *Nahum – Malachi: Interpretation*, John Knox Press, 1986, p. 41)

This very beautiful expression conveys exactly what Habakkuk does – coming humbly to God to receive his Word. This is our task as well: to let the Word of God become the ladder into God's presence, lifting us above the turmoil of this world so that we listen to God's will and purpose in Scripture and are determined to obey.

If we forget that the newspapers are footnotes to Scripture and not the other way around, we will finally be afraid to get out of bed in the morning. The meaning of the world is most accurately given to us by God's Word.
(Eugene Peterson, *Run with the Horses*, IVP, 1983, p. 54)

Is there a situation in your personal life, church, community or the world where God's Word is challenging your thoughts and feelings? Will you allow Scripture to be your authority, the foundation of your confidence, the lens through which you understand the world?

Day 193

Read Habakkuk 2:1–5
Key verse: Habakkuk 2:3

....

> ³*For the revelation awaits an appointed time;*
>   *it speaks of the end*
>   *and will not prove false.*
> *Though it linger, wait for it;*
>   *it will certainly come*
>   *and will not delay.*

Are you known for keeping your promises?

Sometimes we worry when God doesn't act according to our time-scale. However, verse 3 reminds us that there is an appointed time, a specific moment, when God's promise will be fulfilled. The ESV says, 'it hastens to the end': the verb conveys the sense of 'breathing' or 'panting', with the idea of gasping like a runner heading for the finishing line.

Habakkuk can be absolutely sure that what God now declares about the coming judgment of his people *will* take place. That is the first circle of application, the immediate context in which Habakkuk hears God's promise. And, sure enough, God's people are carried off into exile, just as Jeremiah predicted. But the Babylonians, who are the tool in God's hand to bring about that initial judgment, will also be judged. God's Word has an appointed time for them as well. And we can go out in further concentric circles to the ultimate end, when God will finally act in judgment. Habakkuk is looking outward and forward to what the Old Testament calls the 'day of the LORD' (see Joel 1:15; Amos 5:18), to what the New Testament refers to as the day of Christ (see 1 Corinthians 1:8; Philippians 1:6). There is an 'appointed time'. God speaks and God acts, whether in Habakkuk's day, our day or in that future day when everything will be put to rights through the coming of Christ.

If, like Habakkuk, we are tempted to think that God must have abandoned his people or given up on his promises, then we too must remember that 'the revelation awaits an appointed time'. I realize that this is rather cold comfort if you are going through difficulties. It doesn't always help heartbroken people to be told to hang on, with the assurance that things will get better eventually. But from a pastoral point of view, it is very important to try to retain the longer-term perspective.

Hebrews 11 reminds us that Moses had this eternal perspective. He was 'looking ahead to his reward' (verse 26). The verb conveys the sense of fixing your eyes on something, like an artist intently gazing at the portrait she is painting. Faith that makes a difference is faith that fixes its eyes on the ultimate, not just the immediate. We must learn to take the long view, for God has today and tomorrow under his control.

> A prime mark of the Christian mind is that it cultivates the eternal perspective. It looks beyond this life to another one. It is supernaturally orientated and brings to bear upon earthly considerations the fact of heaven and the fact of hell.
> (Harry Blamires, *The Christian Mind*, SPCK, 1963)
>
> Today, let 'the fact of heaven' guide your priorities, attitudes and behaviour.

Day 194

Read Habakkuk 2:1–5
Key verse: Habakkuk 2:3

....

> ³ *For the revelation awaits an appointed time;*
> *it speaks of the end*
> *and will not prove false.*
> *Though it linger, wait for it;*
> *it will certainly come*
> *and will not delay.*

Political spin, 'post truth' and 'fake news' hit us from every angle. This constant stream of manipulation and deception washes over us daily.

In complete and refreshing contrast, God does not lie. And so it follows that because this revelation in chapter 2 is God speaking, 'it . . . will not prove false.' There is an absolute certainty about that word.

From where Habakkuk stands above Jerusalem, appearances certainly seem to contradict the message of God's ultimate control. In fact, the opposite seems to be the case. Likewise, for Abraham, who was told by God that he would be the father of many nations, appearances suggested the exact opposite, since not even a single child seemed possible. So the message to Habakkuk comes with this assurance: God is not stringing you along. He doesn't lie. 'It . . . will not prove false.'

Peter says exactly the same thing to the cynical people of his day. They doubt that the Lord will ever come back, that God will ever deliver on the promises he has made. And so Peter reminds them that when God spoke in creation, it produced results; when God spoke in judgment in Noah's day, no-one could avoid the resulting flood; and by that same word he will judge in the future (2 Peter 3:2–7). It is a reliable message: 'it . . . will not prove false.'

Isaiah uses the simple picture of the water cycle – the rain falls, achieves its purpose and then returns. He makes the connection: as in the natural world, so in the spiritual world. When God sends his word, it achieves its purpose: 'it . . . will accomplish what I desire and achieve the purpose for which I sent it' (Isaiah 55:11). Little by little, then, Habakkuk is learning that God is in control. It is a reliable message: 'it . . . will not prove false.'

Today, ask God to help you share his Word with others. Be alert for the opportunities he gives you. For example, you may have an opening to talk to a non-Christian friend about the reliability of Scripture. Perhaps you could text a verse of encouragement to a Christian friend who is going through difficult times, or you could read and talk about a Bible story with your children or grand-children. Remember:

The law of the LORD is perfect,
    refreshing the soul.
The statutes of the LORD are trustworthy,
    making wise the simple.
The precepts of the LORD are right,
    giving joy to the heart.
The commands of the LORD are radiant,
    giving light to the eyes.
The fear of the LORD is pure,
    enduring for ever.
The decrees of the LORD are firm,
    and all of them are righteous.

They are more precious than gold,
    than much pure gold;
they are sweeter than honey,
    than honey from the honeycomb.
(Psalm 19:7–10)

Day 195

Read Habakkuk 2:1–5
Key verses: Habakkuk 2:4–5

. . . .

> ⁴*See, the enemy is puffed up;*
> *his desires are not upright –*
> *but the righteous person will live by his faithfulness –*
> ⁵*indeed, wine betrays him;*
> *he is arrogant and never at rest.*
> *Because he is as greedy as the grave*
> *and like death is never satisfied,*
> *he gathers to himself all the nations*
> *and takes captive all the peoples.*

We like having options. In fact, often we put off making decisions or plans, just in case a better option comes along.

But verse 4, the key verse of the whole book, confronts us with the reality that, ultimately, we have only two options: faith or unbelief.

> See, the enemy is puffed up;
> his desires are not upright –
> but the righteous person will live by his faithfulness.

This pithy statement sets the context for the whole book. It marks the contrast between the faithful righteous who trust God, and the proud, bloodthirsty Babylonians. It speaks of the contrasted motives of true and false living, of the godly and the ungodly, the Christian and the pagan perspective.

Habakkuk gives a graphic description of the ungodly. They are inflated with pride and completely self-reliant, and that, of course, is why they are unable to find a righteousness outside of themselves. They live their lives in a completely self-contained way, imagining that they need nothing. It is quite the opposite of Jesus' opening beatitude: 'How blest are those who know their need of God' (see Matthew 5:3).

The ungodly delude themselves in their proud and arrogant independence. They are 'never at rest' – or, as some translations say, 'he does not stay at home' (verse 5, NASB). They are restless with their consuming ambition to get more. Nothing will satisfy. Verse 5 explains that, like death itself, the ungodly person or nation just can't get enough. Here there is an echo of the description of the Babylonians in chapter 1, swallowing up nations to satisfy their greedy appetite (verses 15–17).

Verses 4–5 give a sketch of the self-contained, self-obsessed person who shakes a little fist at God and says, 'I have no need of you.' Such a person is living a lie.

We are not immune from pride, arrogance and self-reliance. As Romans 6:11–14 teaches, we have to be intentional about saying 'no' to self. Helen Roseveare evokes a scene from her missionary days:

> He [the African pastor] drew a straight line in the dirt floor with his heel. 'I,' he said, 'the capital I in our lives, Self, is the great enemy. Helen . . . the trouble with you is that we can see so much Helen that we cannot see Jesus. I notice that you drink much coffee. You stand there holding it, until it is cool enough to drink. May I suggest that as you stand and wait, you should just lift your heart to God and pray . . .' And as he spoke, he moved his heel in the dirt across the I he had previously drawn, 'Please, God, cross out the I.' There in the dirt was his lesson of simplified theology – the Cross – the crossed-out I life. 'I have been crucified with Christ and I no longer live, but Christ lives in me' (Galatians 2:20).
> (Noël Piper, *Faithful Women and Their Extraordinary God*, Crossway, 2005, p. 160)

Day 196

Read Habakkuk 2:1–5
Key verse: Habakkuk 2:4

∙∙

> ⁴*See, the enemy is puffed up;*
>   *his desires are not upright –*
>   *but the righteous person will live by his faithfulness.*

What does it mean to 'live by faith'?

Habakkuk's phrase is actually used in several New Testament passages to express the heart of the Christian gospel. In Romans 1, Paul describes how all have sinned and deserve God's judgment. Justification is based not on what we do, but it is by faith in Jesus Christ alone, for Jew and Gentile alike. 'For in the gospel the righteousness of God is revealed – a righteousness that is by faith from first to last, just as it is written: "The righteous will live by faith"' (Romans 1:17).

Similarly, in Galatians 3, Paul asks how Abraham was made righteous. It was not through careful obedience to the law. No, a person is reckoned by God to be righteous on the basis of faith. We are justified freely by his grace. It is by faith in Christ's work on the cross that we are made right with God, and we can see how this attitude represents the exact opposite of the proud, self-sufficient unbeliever.

Habakkuk comes to see that the attitude of steadfast faith is the only way to live. It is to recognize that the whole of your life is in God's hands. The writer to the Hebrews also quotes from Habakkuk 2:4, demonstrating that such faith is a matter of perseverance, waiting for what God has promised (Hebrews 10:36–39). The writer urges us to trust God that the Coming One will ultimately arrive (quoting Habakkuk 2:3, but changing 'it' to 'he'):

'he who is coming will come
   and will not delay.' . . .
'But my righteous one will live by faith.
   And I take no pleasure
   in the one who shrinks back.'
But we do not belong to those who shrink back and are destroyed, but
to those who have faith and are saved.

Faith involves not only the initial act of believing when we receive the gospel of God's grace, but also the steady perseverance of faithfulness. We depend entirely on him and we are to live day by day under the controlling principle that God is absolutely true to what he has said.

The word of the Lord to Habakkuk, and to all believers, is that the only way to live is by wholehearted trust in the God who rules the entire universe.

William McConnell was Deputy Governor of the Maze prison in Northern Ireland. Shortly before his assassination, he said:

> I have committed my life, talents, work and action to Almighty God, in the sure and certain knowledge that, however slight my hold of him may have been, his promises are sure and his hold on me complete.
> (Quoted by Roger Carswell, *Where Is God in a Messed-Up World?*, IVP, 2009, p. 131)

Do you share his conviction?

Will you live by faith, trusting God with your life, your family, your future and the world?

Day 197

Read Habakkuk 2:6–20

Key verses: Habakkuk 2:6–7

. . . .

> [6]*Will not all of them taunt him with ridicule and scorn, saying,*
>   *'Woe to him who piles up stolen goods*
>   *and makes himself wealthy by extortion!*
>   *How long must this go on?'*
> [7]*Will not your creditors suddenly arise?*
>   *Will they not wake up and make you tremble?*
>   *Then you will become their prey.*

For many people, shopping centres are the new places of worship. The creed of our day is to grab all you can and to look after number one. We are driven to want more and more, without regard for those we might injure in the process.

The Babylonians are also known for their greed and injustice. This taunt song (2:6–19) begins by mocking them for their selfish ambition. They have robbed many nations and accumulate more and more by trampling on others. They feather their own nest at the expense of everybody else and constantly want more (see what Habakkuk says about the ungodly in chapter 2:5).

The outcome is described in verse 7. The proud Babylonians might think they are invincible; they might seem triumphant as they mock God, but they will not get away with it. Throughout this taunt song, we see that the Lord will turn the tables. The plunderer will be plundered (verse 8).

The judgment of Babylon is recorded in Daniel chapter 5. Belshazzar, king of Babylon, is feasting, enjoying the fruit of all his ill-gotten gains, when the finger of God begins to write on the wall: 'That very night Belshazzar, king of the Babylonians, was slain, and Darius the Mede took over the kingdom' (Daniel 5:30–31).

This is an important reminder for all who wonder about the apparent success of evil in our world and who might be tempted to imagine that the fat cats really will succeed. One day, God says, the plunderer will be plundered; the victor will become the victim.

Are you distressed at how evil is prospering in the world, in your community, in your office or college? Meditate on Psalm 73. The psalmist echoes Habakkuk's observation in chapter 2:4 that there are two ways to live: having faith in God or trusting your own rules (see also Matthew 7:13–14). He also reminds us that judgment is coming, when God will right all wrongs. With this in mind, will you pray for increased desire and opportunities to share the gospel, even with those who appear to be prospering? Will you also pray that your resolve to live righteously would be strengthened?

My flesh and my heart may fail,
but God is the strength of my heart
and my portion for ever.

Those who are far from you will perish;
you destroy all who are unfaithful to you.
But as for me, it is good to be near God.
I have made the Sovereign LORD my refuge;
I will tell of all your deeds.
(Psalm 73:26–28)

Day 198

Read Habakkuk 2:6–20
Key verse: Habakkuk 2:9

···

> ⁹*Woe to him who builds his house by unjust gain,*
>   *setting his nest on high*
>   *to escape the clutches of ruin!*

My wife and I recently enjoyed a friend's birthday party, but the conversations there surprised both of us. For Christians and non-Christians alike, the subject of security dominated the conversation. I suppose it was because most of us were fifty-somethings confronting our midlife crises and wondering about the future!

Verse 9 is a graphic description of people or nations who think they are in control. In reality, it is a picture of false security. We know that one military manoeuvre employed by the Babylonians was to capture territories around them and thereby create buffer zones to provide a measure of security. Although the tactics are different, the attitude is common enough today. People do everything they can to protect themselves against disaster. Using whatever means at their disposal, and with scant regard for the needs of others – not least, the poor and defenceless – they build their imagined security with wealth. They think they've made it, they've got away with it . . .

But have they? In verse 11, the Lord again pronounces the outcome: the stones of their buildings will give testimony against them. Those who have built their fortresses on the basis of ill-gotten gains will discover that those very things will return to haunt them. Their schemes will backfire, and their great edifices will cry out for vengeance.

Nebuchadnezzar is enormously proud of his palace complex. In the outer courts the wall is some 136 ft (approximately 41 m) thick, with each brick inscribed with the name 'Nebuchadnezzar'. And there is considerable irony in verse 10: 'You have . . . forfeit[ed] your life.' Nebuchadnezzar of Babylon thinks he has the whole world. But 'What good is it for someone to gain the whole world, yet forfeit their soul?' (Mark 8:36). It is a terrible thing to get to the end of your life and discover you have completely missed the point.

Maybe the graphic image of the stones of the wall crying out is a hint of what will happen when God's finger writes the damning message on the walls of the king's palace. Once again, the message in Habakkuk's day and ours is plain: judgment will come. The writing is on the wall. It is an inescapable certainty.

What 'buffer zones' have you created? What people and things provide you with a sense of security? Having spare cash in the bank, a pension plan, family living close by, a comfortable house? There is nothing intrinsically wrong with these things, but, if we are not careful, they lull us into a false sense of security. We trust them instead of trusting in God. Reflect on what it would mean for you to live with a true dependence on the security of Christ and his Word when we have so many material things that support us:

> Some trust in chariots and some in horses,
>   but we trust in the name of the LORD our God.
> (Psalm 20:7)

Day 199

Read Habakkuk 2:6–20

Key verses: Habakkuk 2:12–13

. . . .

> ¹²Woe to him who builds a city with bloodshed
>   and establishes a town by injustice!
> ¹³Has not the Lord Almighty determined
>   that the people's labour is only fuel for the fire,
>   that the nations exhaust themselves for nothing?

'People look at the outward appearance, but the Lord looks at the heart' (1 Samuel 16:7).

Nebuchadnezzar's palace would undoubtedly impress the tourists. The grand scale and magnificent opulence certainly draw the crowds, but they do not impress God. He sees something else.

> He saw only the blood of untold numbers of people who were slaughtered in ruthless warfare in order to obtain the means which made these buildings possible. He saw only the iniquity, the perversity, the crookedness of the builders.
> (Theo Latsch, quoted in R. D. Patterson, *Nahum, Habakkuk,*
> *Zephaniah: An Exegetical Commentary*, Moody Press, 1991, p. 194)

Despite Nebuchadnezzar's show of ruthless power, the outcome is devastating: it all goes up in smoke (see Jeremiah 51:58). The psalmist is absolutely right: 'Unless the Lord builds the house, the builders labour in vain' (Psalm 127:1). The word the psalmist uses for 'vain' is the same one used in Habakkuk 2:13: they are working for 'nothing'. It is the same message that is recorded by the Teacher in Ecclesiastes. Vanity! Futility! They are working for nothing more substantial than a puff of smoke.

The chapter makes it clear that everything the Babylonians have done will be fuel for the fire of God's judgment. And so it will be for all those who choose not the way of faith but the way of the proud. For the wicked, their world will be reduced to ashes; it will disappear in a cloud of smoke. How can we be certain? 'Has not the LORD Almighty determined' it? (verse 13). If he is the Lord Almighty, his judgment is certain and sure.

Judgment is certain because of the reality of God's holy character. Although sin inevitably produces its own destructive consequences, the book of Habakkuk reminds us that God's active judgment is also at work – if not immediately, then most certainly in the future. It is God's world and it is under his control. His judgment will surely punish sin and set things right.

Despite all the effort and attention to detail, Nebuchadnezzar's palace went up in a puff of smoke. This image takes us to 1 Corinthians 3, where Paul explains that our lives are secure on the one foundation of Jesus Christ, but he asks, what materials are you using as you build on that foundation? How you live your life now matters, because one day it will be tested. Will you look back on your life and see that you have built only with things that are temporary, or will you have used your time, gifts and talents to build something that will last for eternity? Will it disappear in a cloud of smoke because it has all been selfish ambition, or will it be lasting, built for eternity?

Day 200

Read Habakkuk 2:6–20
Key verses: Habakkuk 2:15–16

••

> ¹⁵*Woe to him who gives drink to his neighbours,*
> *pouring it from the wineskin till they are drunk,*
> *so that he can gaze on their naked bodies!*
> ¹⁶*You will be filled with shame instead of glory.*
> *Now it is your turn! Drink and let your nakedness*
> *be exposed!*
> *The cup from the Lord's right hand is coming round to you,*
> *and disgrace will cover your glory.*

What lengths would you go to in order to get what you want?

Habakkuk laments the Babylonians' shameless exploitation. They are damaging the environment and causing cruelty to animals (verse 17). They are also using alcohol to seduce people (verses 15–16). But the point of this woe is broader than that. The ungodly have very little respect for the dignity of other human beings. They will go to any means to achieve their purpose. Other people are simply objects to be manipulated and exploited.

This appalling lack of regard for the dignity of others is the depraved behaviour of those who live their lives without God.

Notice the same pattern in this woe as in all the others. The wicked have brought shame on others, so now the Lord will bring shame on them. We can imagine Belshazzar back at the feast. At the beginning of Daniel 5, they are in festive mood, for the Babylonians are renowned for their drunkenness. Then Belshazzar gives orders to bring in the gold and silver goblets that Nebuchadnezzar took from the temple in Jerusalem. And as they drink their wine and praise their gods, the hand of the Sovereign Lord appears and writes on the wall. Habakkuk 2:16 is fulfilled: 'Now it is your turn! Drink . . . The cup from the LORD's right hand is coming round to you.'

Habakkuk chapter 2 reminds us that God sees what is happening, and he acts. The cup of judgment will come. The image of the cup is used by various Old Testament prophets to express the same awful truth. 'This cup filled with the wine of my wrath,' records Jeremiah 25:15. 'A cup large and deep; it will bring scorn and derision,' predicts Ezekiel 23:32.

In fact, these words take us to Gethsemane. Jesus, who knows all these Old Testament passages, takes from his Father the cup of judgment. It is no wonder that initially he shrinks from taking it, for the cup represents God's judgment, which our sins deserve, but which Jesus is to face at the cross. He drinks that cup to the dregs: he bears our sin and takes our judgment.

Jesus' drinking of that cup of judgment means that we will never hear God's 'woe' to us. For all true believers, Paul's confident assertion should be written across the woes of Habakkuk chapter 2: 'There is now no condemnation for those who are in Christ Jesus' (Romans 8:1). Today, praise God for this gospel truth and determine to live in the light of it.

Day 201

Read Habakkuk 2:6–20
Key verses: Habakkuk 2:18–19

• •

> ¹⁸*Of what value is an idol carved by a craftsman?*
>   *Or an image that teaches lies?*
> *For the one who makes it trusts in his own creation;*
>   *he makes idols that cannot speak.*
> ¹⁹*Woe to him who says to wood, 'Come to life!'*
>   *Or to lifeless stone, 'Wake up!'*
> *Can it give guidance?*
>   *It is covered with gold and silver;*
>   *there is no breath in it.*

It has been well said that when people stop believing in truth, they don't believe in nothing; they believe in anything.

Here the woe is the folly of worshipping dumb idols. The Babylonians often ascribe their success to their gods and look for guidance from idols of their own making. There is a fair amount of satirical mockery in verses 18 and 19, as in descriptions of idolatry elsewhere in the Old Testament, and the purpose is to demonstrate the difference between the powerless nonentities of the pagan nations and Israel's living, all-powerful, all-controlling God:

> For the one who makes it trusts in his own creation;
>   he makes idols that cannot speak . . .
> Can it give guidance?'
> (verses 18–19)

We may think this is merely pagan religion, distant from contemporary Western culture, but it is very typical of our society as well. People long for guidance, hoping to make sense of their lives and gain some control. So they turn to astrology, Ouija boards or New Age superstitions. Contemporary idolatry is all around us. Every generation seeks substitute deities. Perhaps most obviously in our culture, the main idol is the self. The social commentator Bryan Appleyard suggests:

> The only possible sin today is the sin against oneself. The idea is everywhere – self-help, self-esteem, making the best of oneself, looking one's best and self-realisation are the great contemporary virtues. Therefore the one recognised sin is failure to look after *numero uno*.
> (Bryan Appleyard, 'Are You Sinning Comfortably?', *The Times*, 11 April 2004)

We have become the centre of our own little universe. And whatever the substitute god might be – possessions, plans or self-obsession – God pronounces his woe upon all who trust in the things of their own creation. Notice verse 18: 'Of what value is an idol carved by a craftsman? Or an image that teaches lies?' It's an intriguing suggestion – an idol that lies. It is counterfeit. The idols in people's lives are self-deceiving, blinding them to their own helplessness. The supposed worship of an idol blinds them about their guilt and their need of forgiveness. They are ignorant of the fact that they depend on God himself for every breath they take.

Many idols vie to displace God from his rightful place on the throne of our lives. How is your obsession with 'self' diminishing your devotion to God? None of us is immune. Today, pray John the Baptist's words: 'He must become greater; I must become less' (John 3:30)

> Have Thine own way, Lord! Have Thine own way!
> Thou art the Potter, I am the clay.
> Mould me and make me after Thy will,
> While I am waiting, yielded and still.
> Have Thine own way, Lord! Have Thine own way!
> Hold o'er my being absolute sway!
> Fill with Thy Spirit till all shall see
> Christ only, always, living in me.
> (Adelaide Pollard, 'Have Thine Own Way', 1907)

Day 202

Read Habakkuk 2:6–20
Key verse: Habakkuk 2:20

....

²⁰*The LORD is in his holy temple;*
let all the earth be silent before him.

When life does not turn out as we'd anticipated, we have a certainty we can cling to: 'The LORD is in his holy temple; let all the earth be silent before him' (verse 20).

This verse comes in the middle of the sequence of woes where the idols are declared to be dumb – silent. Unlike the idols, God is never unable to hear, speak or act. He is the Lord of heaven and earth. The word 'silent' is onomatopoeic in Hebrew, like our word 'hush': be silent, stop all the arguments, all the arrogant assertions of human power, the efforts of human glory, the petty ambitions. It is a call for reverence, because the one who is speaking is the Lord of the universe. He is the Sovereign Lord, active in history; he calls all men and women, all nations and governments, to bow the knee to him.

In these few words we have the answer to Habakkuk's complaint. Why isn't God acting in the way Habakkuk thinks he should? The answer is stated in a simple assertion.

The Lord is seated on his kingly throne, in the place of ultimate authority, above heaven and earth, high above his creatures. Before him there is no room for asserting our independence. Instead, we are called to humble submission to the Lord of the universe. Unlike the impotent deities of paganism, here is the God who is in control, who can be relied upon. Here is absolute certainty, for this God is the unchanging Ruler of the universe, which he created and sustains, and which ultimately he will wrap up and bring to completion. The people in Habakkuk's day are foolish to turn to the substitute 'godlets', whether idols, magic or black arts, for they are called into relationship with the Sovereign Lord.

The simplicity of verse 20 speaks clearly to the fractured world of our day too. The more we grow in our understanding of the majesty of the God whom we worship – the God who calls us into fellowship with himself and who cares for his children – the more we will learn to entrust the uncertainties of our lives to his good purposes.

Lift the curtain of heaven and glimpse the Lord on his throne. Read Isaiah 6, Ezekiel 1, Daniel 7 or Revelation 4, and imagine the scene those writers saw: 'I saw the Lord, high and exalted, seated on a throne; and the train of his robe filled the temple' (Isaiah 6:1). Whatever problems or issues you are facing today – anxiety about the future, ill health, unanswered prayers, financial struggles or family strife – remember this certainty: 'The LORD is in his holy temple.' Repeat this phrase as you bring your prayer requests to God. Our sovereign God is on the throne. He is in complete control over all the various strands of our lives and he will fulfil his good purposes in and through you.

Day 203

Read Habakkuk 2:6–20
Key verse: Habakkuk 2:14

. . . .

¹⁴For the earth will be filled with the knowledge of the glory
of the Lᴏʀᴅ
as the waters cover the sea.

In a pitch-black room, even the faintest flicker of a candle makes all the difference. And verse 14 is an incredible shaft of light in the darkness of Habakkuk's prophecy.

Here, in the context of the power of empires and the pretensions of human rulers, the Lord speaks of the certainty of what will be left on that final day: the universal knowledge of the glory of God. Similar words are used by Isaiah:

They will neither harm nor destroy
on all my holy mountain,
for the earth will be filled with the knowledge of the Lᴏʀᴅ
as the waters cover the sea.
(Isaiah 11:9)

The earlier part of Isaiah 11 refers to a shoot that will come up from the stump of Jesse. It is a prophecy of great David's Greater Son, pointing towards the ultimate victory of the Lord Jesus, to the completion of his purposes in the destruction of evil and the establishment of a new heaven and earth, the home of righteousness.

Intriguingly, Habakkuk adds to the words of Isaiah: he includes the word 'glory'. 'The earth will be filled with the knowledge of the *glory* of the Lord.' Why is that? Perhaps because the word 'glory' encompasses the ultimate goal of all human history. If we are uncertain about what is happening in our world, we should remember that this is where everything is heading. The ultimate truth, the final word, the enduring reality, will be the glory of the Lord. And all other human glories, such as those described and mocked in the woes of chapter 2, will fade away in the light of that supreme glory, his royal majesty. It is a wonderful description of the ultimate triumph of God.

The last word will not belong to earth's kingdoms. Habakkuk gives us a very different perspective of who is in control. It will be a glorious world filled with the awareness of God's purposes, presence and glory.

What are you passionate about? What puts a smile on your face, gets your heart racing and causes you willingly to make sacrifices?

God's passion is for his own glory. He is jealous for his name to be treasured and magnified above all else, and he wants this to be your chief passion too. What will that look like? It will mean a readiness to 'declare his glory among the nations' – sharing the good news of the gospel with friends, neighbours, work colleagues, calling them to worship him (Psalm 96:3). It will also mean being intentional about your inner life: rooting out idols, those relationships and things that compete for first place in your heart. The goal is to make God your all-consuming treasure.

As John Piper says, 'God is most glorified in us when we are most satisfied in him' (*Desiring God*, IVP, 2004, p. 10).

Day 204

Read Habakkuk 3:1–19
Key verse: Habakkuk 3:2

....

> ² LORD, I have heard of your fame;
>   I stand in awe of your deeds, LORD.
> Repeat them in our day,
>   in our time make them known;
>   in wrath remember mercy.

Do you enjoy singing?

You don't need to have the most melodious voice or be able to read music to sing. In fact, singing about what God has done for you is one of the best ways to help you persevere during difficult days. Just think about Paul and Silas in their prison cell (Acts 16)!

Although it is introduced as a prayer, there are several clues that chapter 3 is actually a song. *Selah* (verses 3, 9, 13) is a term possibly designating a musical break; at the close of the chapter there is a musical instruction (verse 19); and in verse 1 there is a rather unusual word, *shigionoth*, probably an instruction about tempo, implying a strong rhythm. This particular song is no funeral dirge. Given its extraordinarily dramatic descriptions and dynamic pace, it is certainly up-tempo. As we read it, we can almost hear the brass section, the drums, the driving rhythm of the bass!

So, after all we have looked at, all the struggles, challenges and turmoil that Habakkuk faces, what does he do? He starts to sing – and he encourages others to start singing too.

> LORD, I have heard of your fame;
>   I stand in awe of your deeds, LORD.
> (verse 2)

We can sense immediately the change of tone from the anxious prayers and appeals of chapter 1. Here there is a sense of humble commitment. Habakkuk is no longer arguing, for he recognizes that everything that God has said and done is just. Calvin translates the verse, 'I heard Thy voice.' Standing there on the walls above Jerusalem, Habakkuk heard God's word, the report of God's work, both in the past and in the prophecies of what is to come. He stands in awe, probably alarmed, with a sense of submission and godly fear.

We will see this stated even more starkly when we come to verse 16. But by this point in the prophecy, Habakkuk has recognized that God is in control of the situation. He is ready to accept God's just purposes. It is a kind of 'Amen' to what God had been saying to him, a humble response: 'Yes, Lord, now I understand. It is your work.'

Today, will you sing to God? Not because your circumstances are wonderful, but because you acknowledge his control, you accept his purposes and you want him to continue his work.

Because you are my help,
I sing in the shadow of your wings.
(Psalm 63:7)

I will sing of the LORD's great love for ever;
with my mouth I will make your faithfulness known
through all generations.
I will declare that your love stands firm for ever,
that you have established your faithfulness in heaven itself.
(Psalm 89:1–2)

I will sing of your love and justice;
to you, LORD, I will sing praise.
(Psalm 101:1)

Day 205

Read Habakkuk 3:1–2
Key verse: Habakkuk 3:2

....

> [2] LORD, I have heard of your fame;
>   I stand in awe of your deeds, LORD.
> Repeat them in our day,
>   in our time make them known;
>   in wrath remember mercy.

What are you praying for?

Habakkuk prays fervently that God's powerful work in the past will be seen in his own day, so that the people of God will know that God is in control of their lives and of history (verse 2). Chapter 3 has many references to the story of the exodus, celebrated frequently by the psalmists and the prophets as their finest hour. And so he appeals, 'Please, Lord, repeat that kind of redemption. Renew your work now and act just as you did in the past.' It is a call for God's action. He wants to see the work of God in the past renewed now, not in the distant future. And he is clear about what matters: renew *your* work. He wants God's purposes fulfilled, God's work established in his day. It is a prayer with which we are familiar: 'Your kingdom come, your will be done.'

As I read these verses, I can't help thinking about what dominates my praying. Is this the kind of prayer that I pray? Am I longing for God's purposes to be fulfilled, for the church to be renewed? Christians in Europe live in a continent where, by and large, the church is not growing. The majority of God's people today are found in the southern hemisphere, and one reason for this shift in the centre of gravity is undoubtedly the extraordinary gospel passion and committed prayer of Christians in these countries. I have a friend who lives and works in the Majority World, and he wonders whether there is some connection between the suffering, poverty and daily challenge of living in some of these countries and the extraordinary sense of dependence that Christians express – and therefore the blessing of God that they enjoy. There is surely a correlation between those things: dependent prayer and God's blessing.

When Habakkuk appeals, 'in our day, in our time', perhaps he means, 'Even in the midst of judgment, Lord, come in deliverance.' Habakkuk does not want an experience that is just hearsay or second-hand. Rather, he appeals that they would experience God's saving presence now, just as they have in the past.

We want God to act in our day, but for some reason that is not reflected in our prayer life. If we are honest, most of our prayers tend to stay close to home, concerned with the needs of family and friends. Today, will you start to pray like Habakkuk? Will you look up, look out, and plead with God to act in your day and generation?

> Oh, that you would rend the heavens and come down,
>   that the mountains would tremble before you!
> As when fire sets twigs ablaze
>   and causes water to boil,
> come down to make your name known to your enemies
>   and cause the nations to quake before you!
> (Isaiah 64:1–2)

Day 206

Read Habakkuk 3:1–2
Key verse: Habakkuk 3:2

....

> ² LORD, I have heard of your fame;
>   I stand in awe of your deeds, LORD.
> Repeat them in our day,
>   in our time make them known;
>   in wrath remember mercy.

I saw a cartoon not long ago, depicting a husband and wife standing in a queue before the gates of heaven. As they wait for their turn to face judgment, the wife whispers to her husband, 'Now, Harold, whatever you do, please don't demand what's coming to you.'

Despite being aware of what our rebellion deserves, we are still uncomfortable with the idea of God's wrath. Some Christians today hesitate to ascribe such emotions to God. We might be disturbed to discover that in the Old Testament alone, there are more than twenty words for God's wrath and anger, and apparently more than 580 references to him acting in that way.

Indeed, wrath is essential to our understanding of God. How can God be God if he does not reveal his wrath 'against all the godlessness and wickedness of people' (Romans 1:18)? Paradoxically, it is because of God's wrath against wickedness that we have the comfort of knowing that his justice will be fulfilled, that the day of restoration will finally come.

Nevertheless, we can identify with Habakkuk's cry: 'in wrath remember mercy'. He has heard of God's judgment on his own people in Judah, the fearful reality of God's anger against sin, and so he prays that, alongside his wrath, God would remember mercy. Once again, his prayer is a model to us. The essence of prayer is to plead God's character in God's presence. Remember mercy, Lord. Be true to your character.

It is important to hold these two truths of mercy and wrath together, for sometimes Christians tend to emphasize one truth over another. In our desire to make the Christian message acceptable, we might be tempted to emphasize God's love and play down the idea of his wrath. But the Bible frequently describes this duality within God. God's wrath and mercy belong together as two dynamic concepts, which are complementary both in God's nature and in his actions.

In our praying, we must take the words of Habakkuk's prayer and appeal to God's mercy on the grounds of Christ's work. Whatever Habakkuk teaches us about the inevitability of judgment and God's wrath, it also points us to the Lord who shows mercy.

Confess your personal sins and the sins of our nation to God. Cry out to him, 'In wrath remember mercy.'

Pray with King David:

> Have mercy on me, O God,
>   according to your unfailing love;
> according to your great compassion
>   blot out my transgressions.
> Wash away all my iniquity
>   and cleanse me from my sin.
>
> For I know my transgressions,
>   and my sin is always before me.
> Against you, you only, have I sinned
>   and done what is evil in your sight;
> so you are right in your verdict
>   and justified when you judge.
> (Psalm 51:1–4)

Day 207

Read Habakkuk 3:3–15

Key verses: Habakkuk 3:3–4

³*God came from Teman,*
    the Holy One from Mount Paran.
His glory covered the heavens
    and his praise filled the earth.
⁴*His splendour was like the sunrise;*
    rays flashed from his hand,
    where his power was hidden.

What will it be like when the Lord returns?

Eugene Peterson describes it like this:

> Skies are blazing with his splendor,
>   his praises sounding through the earth.
> His cloud-brightness like dawn, exploding, spreading,
>   forked-lightning shooting from his hand –
>   what power hidden in that fist!
> (Habakkuk 3:4, MSG)

This vision, which sweeps Habakkuk off his feet (see 3:2, 16), begins by proclaiming that God is on the move. As he draws nearer, the impact of his glorious presence becomes more and more dramatic. Verse 3 is a reference to the area of Sinai where God first revealed himself to Moses at the burning bush and where, subsequently, in a dramatic revelation of his power and presence, he revealed the law to his people.

Verses 3 and 4 conjure up the images of fire and cloud that characterized that Mount Sinai encounter, reminding Habakkuk and all singers of this song of the glory and power of God whenever he comes to his people. Just as at Sinai, his coming is accompanied by a radiance that is overwhelming and awe-inspiring. Habakkuk sees it here illuminating the entire world.

He remembers those great events of the past, but, as throughout the song, there is also an anticipation of God's future intervention. His coming will always be a source of hope for God's people. As we saw earlier, the writer to the Hebrews quotes from Habakkuk chapter 2:3, making application to the coming of the Lord:

> Do not throw away your confidence; it will be richly rewarded.
> You need to persevere . . . For,
>> 'In just a little while
>>> he who is coming will come
>> and will not delay.'
> (Hebrews 10:35–37)

The glorious manifestation of God's coming described in Habakkuk 3:3–4, witnessed by the entire universe, also anticipates that day when we will see Jesus coming (see also Matthew 24:27, 30).

Habakkuk's vision is pointing us to that ultimate day. In essence, God is saying, 'Watch, I am coming.' It will be a day of judgment and of deliverance, a day of wrath and of mercy, a day when human history will finally be wrapped up. We are to look 'for the blessed hope – the appearing of the glory of our great God and Saviour, Jesus Christ' (Titus 2:13).

Habakkuk does not receive a neat solution to his problems. Instead, he is given an overwhelming vision of the coming of the Lord. Today, meditate on John's vision of Christ's return in Revelation 1:12–18. One day soon he 'will come down from heaven, with a loud command, with the voice of the archangel and with the trumpet call of God' (1 Thessalonians 4:16). Jesus will be 'revealed from heaven in blazing fire with his powerful angels' (2 Thessalonians 1:7); 'every eye will see him' (Revelation 1:7), and 'every knee will bow' (Romans 14:11).

Keep this vision in the forefront of your mind today. It won't change your situation, but it will help you persevere and focus on what really matters.

Day 208

Read Habakkuk 3:3–15
Key verses: Habakkuk 3:6–7

. . . .

> ⁶*He stood, and shook the earth;*
>   *he looked, and made the nations tremble.*
> *The ancient mountains crumbled*
>   *and the age-old hills collapsed –*
>   *but he marches on for ever.*
> ⁷*I saw the tents of Cushan in distress,*
>   *the dwellings of Midian in anguish.*

We like to feel in control. It gives us a sense of comfort, security and, at times, power.

Habakkuk stops us in our tracks and reminds us that God is the one who is all-powerful. He is in control.

Just as there were great convulsions at Sinai when God came to his people, so his power is demonstrated whenever he comes in salvation and deliverance. The poetry of verse 6 demonstrates the almost cosmic implications of his arrival. He is the Creator, and at his coming even the mountains crumble before him. The eternal hills bow before the splendour of this eternal God. The nations of Cushan and Midian bordered Egypt, so they have seen the great deliverance that God has brought about for his people and would be trembling with distress and anguish (verse 7). In Habakkuk's vision, no nation will be exempt from God's power and judgment.

Many of the descriptive images in Habakkuk 3 are picked up in the New Testament. Peter describes the cataclysmic events of the end times:

> The heavens will disappear with a roar; the elements will be destroyed by fire, and the earth and everything done in it will be laid bare . . .

That day will bring about the destruction of the heavens by fire, and the elements will melt in the heat. But in keeping with his promise we are looking forward to a new heaven and a new earth, where righteousness dwells.
(2 Peter 3:10, 12–13)

Peter is making it abundantly clear to the people of his day, just as Habakkuk did, that this *will* happen. God is in control of this world. As Habakkuk says at the end of verse 6, 'His ways are eternal' (AMP). We are reminded once again: he is in control.

In chapter 3, Habakkuk is describing the powerful Lord of the universe, the one who is eternal. He is the Sovereign Lord, in control of creation, history and all of the nations. No wonder they will tremble at his coming! The power of the Lord is the foundation for our security and comfort in hard-pressed situations.

It only takes the result of a blood test, a freak accident or unexpected news for our world to turn upside down. We soon realize that we have very little control over the circumstances of our lives. Thank God that when we are powerless, he is all-powerful. When our lives seem to spin out of control, he remains sovereign. The truth is that when we trust in what Christ achieved for us on the cross, we are eternally secure. So, whatever happens in life, we can be confident of God's eternal control, and that is the basis for our perseverance, joy and hope. Today, praise God that he has set your feet on a rock and given you a firm place to stand (Psalm 40:2).

Day 209

Read Habakkuk 3:8–15
Key verses: Habakkuk 3:12–13

....

> ^{12} In wrath you strode through the earth
> and in anger you threshed the nations.
> ^{13} You came out to deliver your people,
> to save your anointed one.
> You crushed the leader of the land of wickedness,
> you stripped him from head to foot.

Do you remember Habakkuk's first prayer: 'How long . . . must I call for help, but you do not listen?' (1:2). Chapter 3 is the proof that God hears and acts, for this is an account of God's deliverance of his people. It is the very thing that Habakkuk is crying out for, the assurance he needs that God keeps his promises and remembers his covenant.

The poetry is powerful. God tramples the enemy under his feet and crushes the head of the wicked. With allusions to the Red Sea deliverance, God is portrayed as the General leading his forces to victory. And the battle is fought for one clear purpose. Although there are descriptions of judgment, there are also significant references to salvation. Notice in verse 8 that God is riding upon his chariot to victory. The word used for 'victory' is actually 'salvation'. The Greek version of the Old Testament renders it, 'Your chariot which is salvation'.

The purpose of God's coming is the salvation of his people (verse 13). What God did in the exodus deliverance he will do again. He will rescue his people and bring them home. That will be fulfilled for some of God's people after the immediate judgment that Habakkuk and Jeremiah predict, for after the exile some finally return to Jerusalem. But these verses also anticipate the deliverance of God's people in the future. Verse 13 speaks about 'your anointed one'. The anointed one is the Messiah, translated in the Greek as 'Christ'. The word 'anointed' was sometimes used of the kings of Israel, even of a pagan king, Cyrus, who was used by God to deliver his people. But the word also points to the true Messiah: Jesus, the Christ. At the cross, the Lord Jesus is our substitute in bearing God's righteous anger. It is there that wrath and mercy meet. God raises Jesus to life, or – to use the language of verse 13 – saves his anointed. So Jesus wins the decisive battle over human sin, over all the cosmic hosts of wickedness. What Habakkuk describes in his overwhelming vision is finally fulfilled in Christ: the victory of the Lord.

Perhaps Paul has Habakkuk's vision in mind when he describes Christ's work on the cross: 'Having disarmed the powers and authorities, he made a public spectacle of them, triumphing over them by the cross' (Colossians 2:15). Today you will feel the pull of sin and witness the influence of evil, but Christ's death and resurrection mean his victory is certain. So:

• You don't need to fear evil.
• You don't need to give in to sin.
• You don't need to be riddled with guilt because of past sins.
• You are free to serve Christ.

Day 210

Read Habakkuk 3:1–19
Key verse: Habakkuk 3:16

. . . .

> ¹⁶*I heard and my heart pounded,*
>   *my lips quivered at the sound;*
> *decay crept into my bones,*
>   *and my legs trembled.*
> *Yet I will wait patiently for the day of calamity*
>   *to come on the nation invading us.*

Habakkuk has got the message.

Having encountered God's majesty and power, having seen God's judgment, he is shaken to the core of his being. His response is described either side of the vision, in verses 2 and 16, which are both saying similar things. He trembles like a leaf; he shakes from head to toe; he is speechless. Habakkuk records that he feels the impact of this encounter, not simply hearing God's word, but now also experiencing God himself. In the past he has questioned God about his character, his work and his righteousness. He has appealed for evidence of God's power and control in this uncertain world of his. And now that he has heard, now that he has seen the vision, the revelation from the Lord, he can barely stand up. He is profoundly shaken with a sense of awe, a deep respect for the Lord.

Habakkuk's reaction isn't simply fear as he thinks about the judgment to come, though doubtless that contributes to it. His reaction must also be a response to the extraordinary revelation of God's character that he has just experienced in the vision of chapter 3.

There are many examples in the Bible of similar reactions on the part of those who come into God's presence. Job's response to his encounter with the living God is, 'I am unworthy' (Job 40:4). Like Habakkuk, he is speechless in the face of what God says and does.

Is Isaiah proud that he has been enabled to witness the greatness and holiness of God? Quite the reverse. He cries out, 'Woe to me! . . . I am ruined! For I am a man of unclean lips' (Isaiah 6:5).

Every so often in the Gospels there are glimpses of Jesus' own glory and power. Following that incredible fishing expedition, Peter says, 'Go away from me, Lord; I am a sinful man!' (Luke 5:8). And what is John's response when he has a profound vision of the ascended Christ among the lampstands? 'When I saw him, I fell at his feet as though dead' (Revelation 1:17).

Today, enter God's presence with reverence and awe.

> Unaccustomed as we are to mystery, we expect nothing even similar to Abraham's falling on his face, Moses' hiding in terror, Isaiah's crying out 'Woe is me', or Saul being knocked flat . . . Reverence and awe have often been replaced by a yawn of familiarity. The consuming fire has been domesticated into a candle flame, adding a bit of religious atmosphere, perhaps, but no heat, no blinding light, no power for purification . . . We prefer the illusion of a safer deity and so we have pared God down to manageable proportions.
> (Donald McCullough, *The Trivialization of God*, cited in Peter Lewis, *The Message of the Living God*, IVP, 2000, pp. 320–321)

Silence the grumbling and the questions. Get rid of overfamiliarity. Take a step back and gaze at the majestic holiness of Almighty God. Get on your knees and worship him.

Day 211

Read Habakkuk 3:16–19
Key verse: Habakkuk 3:16

. . . .

¹⁶*I heard and my heart pounded,*
my lips quivered at the sound;
decay crept into my bones,
and my legs trembled.
Yet I will wait patiently for the day of calamity
to come on the nation invading us.

Habakkuk declares, 'I will wait patiently.'

The situation hasn't changed. 'Nations still rage . . . the arrogant still rule, the poor still suffer; the enslaved still labour for emptiness and false gods are still worshipped' (Elizabeth Achtemeier, *Nahum – Malachi: Interpretation*, John Knox Press, 1986, p. 58). But Habakkuk knows the one who is working out his purposes, unseen behind the turmoil. Habakkuk knows the end. He knows that God's Word can be trusted and his promises will be fulfilled (2:3).

Habakkuk shows us how to live in the meantime, how to live in the waiting room. Not with anxiety, not with uncertainty, but resting in the sure knowledge that the God who has spoken will bring about his purposes, that the earth will be filled with the knowledge of the glory of God. 'The righteous shall live by his faith' (Habakkuk 2:4, ESV). The Lord told Habakkuk in chapter 2 to take the long-run perspective. And the patient waiting here in 3:16 is part of that same response.

How is he able to rest, to wait patiently? It is his faith in the word of God, that word of revelation. There will be discipline for God's people – he knows that is coming. Both he and Jeremiah prophesied it and, as promised, the people are carted off into exile by the Babylonians (1:6). And now, at the close of his prophecy, Habakkuk points to the inevitable judgment on their enemies too (3:16). Sure enough, Nebuchadnezzar, Belshazzar and all subsequent empires are judged by God.

Habakkuk has to look through the fog as he wonders about God's purposes and whether God really is in control. But, as believers in Jesus Christ, we now know what God's ultimate purposes are. They are expressed in Paul's incredible mission statement in Ephesians. He tells us that God will 'bring unity to all things in heaven and on earth under Christ' (Ephesians 1:10). So the Christian church must also walk by faith. We too must rest in God's promise and trust in his Word as we wait for that final deliverance.

The Victorian pastor and preacher Charles Spurgeon said:

> We have been assured by people who think they know a great deal about the future that awful times are coming. Be it so; it need not alarm us, for the Lord reigneth. Stay yourself on the Lord . . . and you can rejoice in His name. If the worst comes to the worst, our refuge is in God; if the heavens shall fall, the God of heaven will stand; when God cannot take care of His people under heaven, He will take them above the heavens and there they shall dwell with Him. Therefore, as far as you are concerned, rest; for you shall stand . . . at the end of the days.
> (Quoted in Elizabeth Achtemeier, *Nahum – Malachi*, p. 60)

Day 212

Read Habakkuk 3:16–19
Key verses: Habakkuk 3:17–18

....

¹⁷ *Though the fig-tree does not bud*
    and there are no grapes on the vines,
though the olive crop fails
    and the fields produce no food,
though there are no sheep in the sheepfold
    and no cattle in the stalls,
¹⁸*yet I will rejoice in the L*ORD*,*
    I will be joyful in God my Saviour.

Everything has gone.

It is possible that Habakkuk is anticipating the ultimate day of the Lord. But it is also highly likely that he is describing the devastating impact of the predicted invasion of the Babylonians described in chapter 1. Verse 17 begins with the apparent luxuries of figs, grapes and olives, but moves very quickly to show that there is no food at all. It isn't simply a devastated economic and social infrastructure; it is total destruction.

That's what makes this small word 'yet' all the more remarkable. Habakkuk has been stripped of everything and still this man of faith sings, 'Yet I will rejoice in the LORD' (verse 18). It is Job saying, 'Though he slay me, yet will I hope in him' (Job 13:15). It is Paul saying, 'We are hard pressed on every side, but not crushed' (2 Corinthians 4:8).

How can Habakkuk respond as he does? What is there left for him to rejoice in? It is not his possessions; it is certainly not his circumstances. Like Job, he has been stripped of everything else but God. And that is the key to his joy: finding that God the Creator, the Redeemer, the covenant-keeping God is enough. That is how

Habakkuk concludes his prophecy. All those things on which we rely may be stripped away, but God is enough.

All we have seen in the book of Habakkuk points us to this fact: for men and women of faith, evil has lost the initiative. When we become Christians, we are not protected from the hardships of this world. There is no guarantee that we will be immune from suffering or from God's discipline, from the oppression of enemies, or from the pains and dangers of living in this broken world. But we know that the Lord will not let go of his people, that he has not abandoned his world. He is still in control and his purposes will be fulfilled.

People of faith have discovered that Habakkuk's song rings true. When everything is taken away, we can say, 'I will rejoice in God.'

As you face life's uncertainties and turbulence, will you respond like Habakkuk: 'Yet I will rejoice in the Lord, I will be joyful in God my Saviour'? When everything you have come to rely on is stripped away, will you acknowledge that God is enough?

God has *enough* to supply our needs. *Enough* for salvation, *enough* for forgiveness, *enough* to overcome temptations, *enough* to persevere in adversity, *enough* to calm our fears and anxieties. *Enough* grace, *enough* love, *enough* power . . . This is summed up in the promise: 'My grace is sufficient for you' (2 Cor, 12:9) . . . By his grace we have everything we need to live the life he has planned for us, everything we need to live a life that is pleasing to him. (Helen Roseveare, *Enough*, Christian Focus, 2015)

Day 213

Read Habakkuk 3:16–19
Key verse: Habakkuk 3:19

∙∙∙

> ¹⁹*The Sovereign* LORD *is my strength;*
> *he makes my feet like the feet of a deer,*
> *he enables me to tread on the heights.*

Many of us experience 'spiritual vertigo'. We grow queasy at the thought of some of the spiritual challenges, the mountains that lie ahead of us. Our legs begin to buckle when we think about threatening circumstances. So the result is that we live our lives within cautiously safe limits.

Because of his encounter with the living God, Habakkuk knows he can face these spiritual challenges. He declares, 'The . . . LORD is my strength.' The Hebrew word could also mean 'army'. The Lord is my army, the one who sustains my life, the life of the 'righteous who live by faith'. He provides for the person who might have lost everything else and been pushed right to the limits. He is all I need.

This is similar to Paul's testimony in 2 Corinthians 12. Frequently, Paul prays for the removal of his thorn in the flesh. And how does the Lord reply? 'My grace is sufficient for you, for my power is made perfect in weakness' (verse 9). It is an unexpected answer, but it makes a powerful impact on Paul's life. Now God's all-sufficient grace is poured into his life, not in spite of the thorn, but because of that very weakness. The breakthrough for Paul is to see that weakness has the special advantage of making room for God's grace. It is when God can work most effectively, when his power can be seen most clearly.

As with Paul, God is giving Habakkuk a strength that will enable him to accept his weakness and fears and still stand up to the world. He is now sure-footed. He has both stability and energy: 'he enables me to tread on the heights' (verse 19). So, as I put my faith in him, I can live with unstumbling security, rising above all the oppression of the world. God enables his people to keep walking, to keep climbing.

Some writers remind us that 'the heights' could refer to the 'high places', those centres of pagan worship. It was thought that the gods controlled the high ground and were therefore in charge of the whole area. So is it possible that Habakkuk means that God enables us to go even into those spiritual territories, those high places of the enemy? By God's power, by God's Word and by God's Spirit, he enables us to see the gospel advance, whatever the situation, whatever hostile forces may be ranged against Christ and against his people. He enables me to go on to those very heights.

Are you looking up at an impossibly high mountain, wondering how you are going to face this next spiritual challenge? Meditate on Psalm 121. Lean on the Lord's strength. He will enable you and keep your feet from slipping:

> I lift up my eyes to the mountains –
>   where does my help come from?
> My help comes from the LORD,
>   the Maker of heaven and earth.
>
> He will not let your foot slip –
>   he who watches over you will not slumber.
> (Psalm 121:1–3)

For further study

If you would like to do further study on Habakkuk, the following books may be useful:

- David W. Baker, *Nahum, Habakkuk, Zephaniah*, Tyndale Old Testament Commentary (IVP, 2009).

- James Bruckner, *Jonah, Nahum, Habakkuk, Zephaniah*, NIV Application Commentary (Zondervan, 2004).

- John Mackay, *God's Just Demands: Jonah, Micah, Nahum, Habakkuk, Zephaniah* (Christian Focus, 2008).

- O. Palmer Robertson, *The Books of Nahum, Habakkuk and Zephaniah*, New International Commentary on the Old Testament (Eerdmans, 1994).

- David Prior, *The Message of Joel, Micah & Habakkuk*, The Bible Speaks Today (IVP, 1988).

If God has fed you through your study of the book of Habakkuk, why not buy the individual Food for the Journey on Habakkuk and give it to a friend (available from ivpbooks.com)?

Introduction
James

Stuart Briscoe

Faith works

They are fleeing for their lives.

Stephen's martyrdom in Jerusalem signals a mass exodus as believers flee throughout the Roman Empire.

As leader of the Jerusalem church, what words of encouragement will James write to these persecuted Christians?

Perhaps a little surprisingly, his key message is: faith works. Genuine belief inevitably transforms our speech, suffering, compassion for the poor, humility, prayers, priorities and every other aspect of life. In just five chapters, James introduces and briefly touches upon a whole variety of issues that concern these new believers. He doesn't give an exhaustive treatise on suffering or any other topic, but in a simple, forthright style he urges them to live out their faith, knowing that God's grace is sufficient for every trial, and that there is a value and purpose to their suffering.

James's own life illustrates his message. He grew up with Jesus and naturally was sceptical about his brother's messianic claims. But a post-resurrection encounter with Jesus revolutionized his life. He has been transformed from a vocal critic into a key leader of the early church and a prime mover in the Jerusalem Council (Acts 15).

His own experience of transformation and seeing God's grace at work, in tandem with personal obedience, convinced James that true faith is demonstrated by deeds. There is no such thing as faith without works. The dichotomy doesn't exist – it is not either–or, but both–and. Not that any of these works justify us before God, but they are evidence that we have been justified, that the Holy Spirit is changing us, that sanctification is underway.

Today, in our increasingly secular and materialistic world, as we face a growing tide of pressure to privatize our faith, James's message is still on target. The world is not looking for cheerful triumphalism, statements of belief or empty promises. What the world desperately needs to see is genuine faith demonstrated in the suffering, chaos and unpredictability of everyday life. It needs to witness the transformation that the Holy Spirit makes possible when we yield and are obedient to him.

What do people see when they look at your life?

Do they see faith that works?

Day 214

Read James 1:1–4
Key verses: James 1:1–2

· ·

> ¹*James, a servant of God and of the Lord Jesus Christ,*
> *To the twelve tribes scattered among the nations:*
> *Greetings.*
> ²*Consider it pure joy, my brothers and sisters, whenever you*
> *face trials of many kinds.*

Think back to when you became a Christian. What did you expect? How did you anticipate your life unfolding? Did the preacher promise you blue skies, bright sunshine and a wonderful life?

Jesus challenges this type of thinking when he says to his disciples, 'In this world you will have trouble' (John 16:33). And without any preamble or introduction, James picks up this theme at the start of his letter. He wants his readers to know that trials are inevitable. James does not say, 'Consider it pure joy, my brothers and sisters, *if* you face trials.' There is absolutely no question about it: Christians *will* face trials.

James knows that trials are inevitable because:

- *He watched his half-brother, Jesus, suffering intensely.*

- *He knows the twelve tribes are scattered among the nations.* In verse 1, James could be thinking primarily about Jewish history: their captivity under the Assyrians and Babylonians and then dispersion under the Romans. James is well aware that the Jews have been scattered from their homeland all over the world. But it is also possible that he is thinking of the dispersion of the early church. After Stephen was martyred, Christians scattered, fleeing the persecution in Jerusalem. We can't say conclusively to whom he is writing, but the point is that, seeing the scattering of believers and the Jews, James is well aware that trials are inevitable.

- *He himself has suffered.* In verse 1, James calls himself 'a servant of God and of the Lord Jesus Christ'. It is true that he is a pillar of the church in Jerusalem (Galatians 2:9) and he chaired the Council at Jerusalem (Acts 15), but nevertheless he calls himself a 'servant'. Servants give of themselves without any regard for their own well-being and do not have any rights to their own life. As James knows, this is a very testing experience because it militates against everything that is inherently human.

James is a church leader who has gone through times of deep testing. Writing from his own wealth of experience, he encourages the scattered and suffering believers to stand firm.

God never said that we would escape suffering. He never suggested that serving him would guarantee us a smooth passage to heaven. Quite the opposite, in fact! Yes, some trials are of our own making because we made wrong choices and have to live with the consequences. But even if we live for God wholeheartedly, trials are inevitable and unavoidable. Don't let them unsettle you or throw you off course on your journey of faith (1 Thessalonians 3:2–4). And, don't be surprised when it is your time to suffer.

> Dear friends, do not be surprised at the fiery ordeal that has come on you to test you, as though something strange were happening to you. But rejoice inasmuch as you participate in the sufferings of Christ, so that you may be overjoyed when his glory is revealed.
> (1 Peter 4:12–13)

Day 215

Read James 1:1–4
Key verse: James 1:2

● ●

²Consider it pure joy, my brothers and sisters, whenever you face trials of many kinds.

If we knew trials were coming, most of us would do our best to avoid them. But that's the trouble: trials usually come suddenly, without any warning.

On a visit to the Philippines I saw an open manhole, and was told it was extremely dangerous during the rain and floods – sometimes people would forget it was there under the water and fall into it. The word James uses for trials conveys the same kind of image: you encounter them unexpectedly.

The same word is used in the story of the Good Samaritan about a certain man going down from Jerusalem who 'fell among robbers' (Luke 10:30, ESV). You remember also that Paul and his companions were sailing in a storm. The ship was falling apart, and then it 'struck a sand-bar' (Acts 27:41). It's exactly the same word.

You fall into a flooded manhole, you fall into the hands of robbers on the way from Jerusalem or you hit a sandbank. Before you know it, you are in over your head. This is the image that James uses to describe how these testing times will come.

And these testings come in many forms. The word James uses is often best translated 'many-coloured', 'variegated'. Christian psychologist Jay Adams says that our testings can come 'in the fiery reds of affliction, the icy blues of sorrow, the murky browns of failure, the sickly yellows of illness and disease' (*A Thirst for Wholeness: How to Gain Wisdom from the Book of James*, Institute of Nouthetic Studies, 1997, p. 20).

But just as testing times come in various forms, so does God's grace. Peter, writing on a similar subject, points out that the grace of God comes in variegated forms, using that same word (1 Peter 4:10).

It may not feel like this right now, but whatever your situation, the grace of God is adequate for it.

Bring to God your many-coloured afflictions. Imagine him covering over each one with the rainbow colours of his grace. Allow his grace to equip and restore you, and to be reflected through you:

'My grace is sufficient for you, for my power is made perfect in weakness.' Therefore I will boast all the more gladly about my weaknesses, so that Christ's power may rest on me.
(2 Corinthians 12:9)

Be strong in the grace that is in Christ Jesus.
(2 Timothy 2:1)

Let us then approach God's throne of grace with confidence, so that we may receive mercy and find grace to help us in our time of need.
(Hebrews 4:16)

And the God of all grace, who called you to his eternal glory in Christ, after you have suffered a little while, will himself restore you and make you strong, firm and steadfast.
(1 Peter 5:10)

Day 216

Read James 1:1–4
Key verses: James 1:2–4

....

²Consider it pure joy, my brothers and sisters, whenever you face trials of many kinds, ³because you know that the testing of your faith produces perseverance. ⁴Let perseverance finish its work so that you may be mature and complete, not lacking anything.

When you're suffering, there is nothing more annoying than someone casually telling you to 'smile – it could be worse'.

James isn't telling us just to cheer up. He says, 'Consider it joy', because trials are valuable, and they have a purpose.

Trials test the centre of our faith. We all have faith. The big question is: faith in what? You can have tremendous faith in your own physical fitness until you get sick. You can have tremendous faith in your doctor until he tells you he can't diagnose your problem. The whole point is that faith should be centred on God, who is worthy of our faith. And sometimes it takes testings – trials – to prove to us that the centre of our faith is not where it should be.

Trials are also valuable because they produce perseverance. This does not mean a fatalistic resignation to the inevitable. If we respond appropriately, these testings will produce in us a rugged, patient steadfastness.

And when this spiritual perseverance has been produced, it becomes productive in and of itself. As James explains, 'Let perseverance finish its work so that you may be mature and complete, not lacking anything' (verse 4). The word James uses for 'mature' conveys the idea of attaining the goal, reaching the end point. And the word for 'complete' speaks of a sense of wholeness. In other words, God has a goal in mind for you: to be completely like Christ.

And as you trust God and persevere through testing times, the result will be that, slowly but surely, you become more and more like Christ. You will become the person God designed you to be – 'conformed to the image of his Son' (Romans 8:29).

It seems counterintuitive, but trials are valuable and purposeful. They come so that we might not be 'lacking anything'.

Consider the trials you are going through. Why do you think God has permitted them? What lessons does he want to teach you? Are these trials:

• making sure your faith is centred on God?
• purifying your faith?
• developing steadfastness in you?

Don't waste your suffering. Ask God to give you his perspective. Pray that you would be able to see these trials as a gift to make you into the person God designed you to be.

> God is using the difficulties of the here and now to transform you, that is, to rescue you from you. And because he loves you, he will willingly interrupt or compromise your momentary happiness in order to accomplish one more step in the process of rescue and transformation, which he is unshakably committed to.
> (Paul David Tripp, *What Did You Expect?: Redeeming the Realities of Marriage*, Crossway, 2015, p. 22)

Day 217

Read James 1:2–11
Key verses: James 1:5–8

....

⁵If any of you lacks wisdom, you should ask God, who gives generously to all without finding fault, and it will be given to you. ⁶But when you ask, you must believe and not doubt, because the one who doubts is like a wave of the sea, blown and tossed by the wind. ⁷That person should not expect to receive anything from the Lord. ⁸Such a person is double-minded and unstable in all they do.

How are you coping with your present trials and testing?

James gives us pointers for how to manage. He encourages us to:

- *Carefully consider.* Verse 2 begins, 'Consider'. It means to 'count' or 'direct your thinking'. The way you think about a situation will largely determine how you respond to it. And so it is imperative that we get our thinking straight.

- *Continually confess.* We have to confess our lack of wisdom (verse 5). Wisdom is different from knowledge. Knowledge is possessing data, but wisdom is knowing what to do with it. When we talk of lacking wisdom in trials and testing, what we are really saying is, 'What is the right thing to do in response to this situation? And how do I do it?'

As verse 5 reminds us, we have to confess that we need help and ask God for it. We don't just have to roll up our sleeves, grit our teeth and make the best of it; we can ask God for help. We ask in faith, recognizing that we are totally dependent on him for the power to cope with the testing, so that the desired end might be achieved – we don't want to be 'double-minded' or 'unstable'.

- *Cheerfully celebrate*. Verse 2 is not telling us to celebrate the tests, but rather to say, 'Today I have a rainbow of varied, many-coloured tests. But I'm glad that you are a generous and gracious God. I know that you have an end in view, and I'm glad that these tests give me a chance to identify the centre, core and calibre of my faith. I believe there's a high probability that if I respond to the wisdom you give me, I'm going to come out of this trial tested and tried like pure gold.'

How are you managing your trials? Are you burying your head in the sand and pretending they're not happening? Are they making you bitter and disillusioned with God? Are you looking around and wondering why other people's lives seem so trial-free? Are you putting on a smile and false triumphalism, waiting for a rose-tinted, pain-free future?

It might be hard, but today will you:

- face your trials head on and acknowledge them for what they are?

   See, I have refined you, though not as silver;
      I have tested you in the furnace of affliction.
   (Isaiah 48:10)

- confess your need for God's wisdom and strength?

   My God will meet all your needs according to the riches of his glory in Christ Jesus.
   (Philippians 4:19)

- celebrate what God is doing in and through you?

   In all this you greatly rejoice, though now for a little while you may have had to suffer grief in all kinds of trials. These have come so that the proven genuineness of your faith – of greater worth than gold, which perishes even though refined by fire – may result in praise, glory and honour when Jesus Christ is revealed.
   (1 Peter 1:6–7)

Day 218

Read James 1:12–18

Key verses: James 1:13–15, 17–18

· ·

¹³*When tempted, no one should say, 'God is tempting me.' For God cannot be tempted by evil, nor does he tempt anyone;* ¹⁴*but each person is tempted when they are dragged away by their own evil desire and enticed.* ¹⁵*Then, after desire has conceived, it gives birth to sin; and sin, when it is full-grown, gives birth to death . . .*

¹⁷*Every good and perfect gift is from above, coming down from the Father of the heavenly lights, who does not change like shifting shadows.* ¹⁸*He chose to give us birth through the word of truth, that we might be a kind of firstfruits of all he created.*

'God is tempting me;' 'It's God's fault;' 'The devil made me do it.' We use many creative excuses to rationalize our sin!

Each of us has a whole catalogue of 'desires'. Many of these desires are perfectly legitimate, but they can be twisted, warped and abused. If that happens and we are exposed to external testing, it is possible to be dragged into sin (verse 14). The idea is similar to hooking a fish and dragging it out of the water.

So imagine, for example, a situation comes along and it's not my fault. There is a desire within me that at first was legitimate, but now it has become warped and twisted and I've hung around long enough so the hook is set in my mouth. Before I realize what is happening, I'm being dragged away, and the situation that was a testing to prove me has turned into a temptation that has produced sin and death.

That is how temptation works.

In contrast, there is nothing in God that would respond to an external event in such a way that it could produce sin. He does not tempt. He permits, he ordains, he allows, he uses tempting, but never with a view to our sinning, always with a view to our maturing. And just as the sun, moon and stars go on shining, so he goes on graciously, generously giving to us, unchanging, pure and holy in his character, making available to us all we need, in order that we might respond as we ought. Indeed, God took the divine initiative to give us his Holy Spirit and generate within us a response that would result in new birth. The whole point of this new birth is that we might become mature, holy, a kind of firstfruits to God, the beginning of the harvest.

Have you tasted the metal in your mouth? Your desires have been warped; wrong thinking about yourself and God has made you vulnerable to being dragged into sin. All of a sudden, without realizing it, the devil has you hooked like a fish.

• Ask for God's forgiveness today.
• Ask for foresight to recognize when you are being tested.
• Ask for God's strength not to fall into temptation.
• Ask for God's help to use difficult times as a means of maturity and spiritual growth.

Personalize Paul's prayer and make it your own:

We continually ask God to fill you with the knowledge of his will through all the wisdom and understanding that the Spirit gives, so that you may live a life worthy of the Lord and please him in every way: bearing fruit in every good work, growing in the knowledge of God, being strengthened with all power according to his glorious might so that you may have great endurance and patience, and giving joyful thanks to the Father, who has qualified you to share in the inheritance of his holy people in the kingdom of light. For he has rescued us from the dominion of darkness and brought us into the kingdom of the Son he loves, in whom we have redemption, the forgiveness of sins.
(Colossians 1:9–14)

Day 219

Read James 1:19–27
Key verses: James 1:19–20

. . . .

19 My dear brothers and sisters, take note of this: everyone should be quick to listen, slow to speak and slow to become angry, 20 because human anger does not produce the righteousness that God desires.

Some parts of the Bible may be opaque and provoke endless discussion and conjecture. But this last section in James 1 couldn't be any clearer. Here he lists, without much comment, God's requirements of us.

These are the things God wants us to do:

• Deal with our anger.

• Deal with our moral filth.

• Do what God's Word says.

• Keep a tight rein on our tongue.

• Help the needy people around us.

The objective behind all these things is to cultivate within us the righteous life that God desires (verse 20). If we do them in the power of the Spirit, drawing on the generous, gracious, ungrudging provision of our God, then when we go through trials, they will not degenerate into temptations, and we will become increasingly mature: the first-fruits, set apart for God.

Read verses 19–27 again slowly.

Then divide the passage into sections – verses 19–20, 21, 22–25, 26, 27 – and meditate on each topic.

Put these challenges into your own context and situation. Pray through how you can be obedient to God's demands. This isn't about trying harder in your own strength, but rather relying on God's power and wisdom to grow in the midst of trials. God's aim is our spiritual transformation: that we become all that he designed us to be – or, as the Danish philosopher Søren Kierkegaard is said to have prayed, 'And now Lord, with your help, I shall become myself.'

Day 220

Read James 2:1–4

Key verse: James 2:1

• •

¹My brothers and sisters, believers in our glorious Lord Jesus Christ must not show favouritism.

Are you judicious and courteous when you are trying to make your point, or are you direct and forthright? We each have our own individual style!

James's style is usually blunt and straight to the point.

He is eager to remind his readers that their religion is to be characterized by a marked concern for the underprivileged. He introduced this theme in 1:27: 'Religion that God our Father accepts as pure and faultless is this: to look after orphans and widows in their distress.' His concern is that practical spiritual experience should manifest itself in compassion for orphans, widows and the impoverished.

However, there is warmth to his plea. He addresses it to 'my brothers and sisters', those who, because they have been born of the same Spirit, born through the same engrafted Word, are members of the same family. He is speaking to his fellow believers: literally, 'those who hold the faith'.

The reason why we are not to show favouritism is because of 'our glorious Lord Jesus Christ'. He is our standard, the One we look to, our model. And Jesus doesn't show favouritism, because his Father doesn't. Remember that God strictly instructs the Levites, 'Do not pervert justice; do not show partiality to the poor or favouritism to the great, but judge your neighbour fairly' (Leviticus 19:15). Or think back to Peter's vision as he sleeps on the rooftop of Simon the tanner's house. His vision of the unclean foods teaches him that God does not discriminate between Jews and Gentiles, and when he arrives at Cornelius' house, he declares, 'I now realise how true it is that God does not show favouritism' (Acts 10:34). God's lack of favouritism is not an isolated theme; it runs throughout Scripture (see Romans 2:11; Ephesians 6:9; Colossians 3:25; 1 Timothy 5:21).

The very title, 'Lord Jesus Christ', reminds us that he is Lord of all, not just of some; he is Jesus the Saviour, who died for all, not just for some; he is the Christ, the Anointed One, the sent One, who came for all, not just for some.

The glory of the Lord Jesus insists that we model ourselves on him and do not show favouritism.

Who are you modelling your faith on? Sometimes our role models are church leaders. Their public display of Christianity informs how we behave and what we prioritize. Often, without intending to, we make our Christian friends our role models. We let their spirituality set the temperature for ours; their passion for Christ and level of discipleship dictate ours.

James challenges us not to let other believers set the pace for our devotion to God. Our only model must be the 'glorious Lord Jesus Christ'. He longs for us to model Christ in our:

- prayer life;
- faithful service;
- compassion for the sick and marginalized;
- humility;
- obedience to God;
- perseverance and patience during trials;
- passion to share the gospel.

Pray through all the aspects of your day. Ask for the Holy Spirit's help to model Jesus everywhere you go, in everything you do: in all your conversations and decisions, your thoughts and attitudes, at work and in your leisure time.

Day 221

Read James 2:1–4

Key verses: James 2:2–4

· ·

²Suppose a man comes into your meeting wearing a gold ring and fine clothes, and a poor man in filthy old clothes also comes in. ³If you show special attention to the man wearing fine clothes and say, 'Here's a good seat for you,' but say to the poor man, 'You stand there' or 'Sit on the floor by my feet,' ⁴have you not discriminated among yourselves and become judges with evil thoughts?

Have you ever looked at some politician, celebrity or athlete and thought, 'Wouldn't that person make a wonderful Christian?' Why? Because it would be wonderful for *us* if he or she was a Christian! It would help our finances, status and credibility.

That is just one example of favouritism. In these verses, James gives his readers another. He describes the poor people in this impoverished church evaluating a newcomer according to external criteria. They reason that because he is wearing fine clothes and a gold ring, he must be a man of substance, and because he is a man of substance, he must be deserving of special treatment.

At the same time a poor man comes in, in filthy old clothes. The congregation wonder where they can park him! The decision is made: 'Go and stand over there in the corner,' or, 'There's a seat here at my footstool.' If there is one thing that insults a Jew more than anything else, it is telling that person to sit down at somebody's feet. It is like saying, 'Lick my boots!'

James's example probably isn't hypothetical. We know that the church in Jerusalem, where he is a prominent leader, is very poor. Remember that the apostle Paul spends a considerable amount of time raising money to go to the aid of this Jerusalem church. So if a very poor church were to be visited suddenly by an ostentatiously wealthy man, what a temptation it would be to put on a show for him.

James's point is that these Christians are evaluating by externals. They are quick to act in prejudice. And they are opportunistic; doubtless they can see advantages in befriending a wealthy newcomer. James wants them to see that they are discriminating among themselves; they are coming to judgmental positions about people, and this is evil thinking!

Think through your own propensity for favouritism:

- At the end of the church service, do you tend to make a beeline for your friends, or do you look out for those who need encouragement and a listening ear?
- Do you look for ways to ingratiate yourself with the 'influencers' in your church?
- Think about the Christians you invite round for meals or meet up with during the week – are they mainly people in your social bracket, those with children the same age as yours?

To gauge whether favouritism is operating in your church, consider how newcomers feel. Do they receive a warm welcome on a Sunday and at the various midweek groups? Or would they feel that they have to act, dress and worship a certain way in order to be accepted?

Paul reminds us that natural affiliations have no place in how we are to treat one another. We are all children of God and blood-bought brothers and sisters in Christ. Meditate on Galatians 3:26–29. Ask God to show you any favouritism you need to tackle and evil thinking you need to correct.

> So in Christ Jesus you are all children of God through faith, for all of you who were baptised into Christ have clothed yourselves with Christ. There is neither Jew nor Gentile, neither slave nor free, nor is there male and female, for you are all one in Christ Jesus. If you belong to Christ, then you are Abraham's seed, and heirs according to the promise.
> (Galatians 3:26–29)

Day 222

Read James 2:5–10
Key verses: James 2:5–7

. . . .

⁵Listen, my dear brothers and sisters: has not God chosen those who are poor in the eyes of the world to be rich in faith and to inherit the kingdom he promised those who love him? ⁶But you have dishonoured the poor. Is it not the rich who are exploiting you? Are they not the ones who are dragging you into court? ⁷Are they not the ones who are blaspheming the noble name of him to whom you belong?

Have you 'dishonoured the poor'?

This may seem rather an extreme statement. Perhaps you feel you have not 'dishonoured the poor' as much as not thought about them. Except, of course, when you see someone selling *The Big Issue* in the shopping centre.

For many of us, God's care for the poor stands in sharp contrast to our own.

Far from overlooking the poor, God often chooses them to be rich in faith (verse 5). Amazingly, God chooses, enriches and uses the most unlikely people. He has a delightful way of doing things in exactly the opposite way to how we would do them. So if we look at people simply on the basis of their external appearance, we might miss somebody who, under their shabby clothing, is actually rich in faith – a wonderful believer, a member of the kingdom, somebody who really loves the Lord.

You are making a wrong choice if you side with the rich rather than the poor. James says that these people insult those whom God honours, exploit the poor and drag you into court (verse 6). He may have been thinking about how his half-brother Jesus was treated. It wasn't the common people who dragged him into court, but those from the top echelons of society. And in many parts of the world those who hold power are still persecuting the poor. Often those who exploit the poor are the same ones who slander 'the noble name of him to whom you belong' (verse 7).

James wants us to remember that we bear the name of Christ: we are members of his kingdom, we belong to him, we love him. And all that is true of us is true of the believer who is poor.

Care for the poor isn't an isolated issue mentioned only in James's letter. It is a core theme that pulsates throughout Scripture. We are following God the Father and the example of Christ if we love the poor.

Spend time meditating on Isaiah 58:6–8:

Is not this the kind of fasting I have chosen:
to loose the chains of injustice
    and untie the cords of the yoke,
to set the oppressed free
    and break every yoke?
Is it not to share your food with the hungry
    and to provide the poor wanderer with shelter –
when you see the naked, to clothe them,
    and not to turn away from your own flesh and blood?
Then your light will break forth like the dawn,
    and your healing will quickly appear;
then your righteousness will go before you,
    and the glory of the Lord will be your rear guard.

Consider your own situation, opportunities and sphere of influence. How is God asking you to demonstrate love and care for the poor?

Day 223

Read James 2:5–13
Key verses: James 2:8–13

⁸*If you really keep the royal law found in Scripture, 'Love your neighbour as yourself,' you are doing right. ⁹But if you show favouritism, you sin and are convicted by the law as law-breakers. ¹⁰For whoever keeps the whole law and yet stumbles at just one point is guilty of breaking all of it. ¹¹For he who said, 'You shall not commit adultery,' also said, 'You shall not murder.' If you do not commit adultery but do commit murder, you have become a law-breaker.*

¹²*Speak and act as those who are going to be judged by the law that gives freedom, ¹³because judgment without mercy will be shown to anyone who has not been merciful. Mercy triumphs over judgment.*

We are sons and daughters of the King. This means we have privileges, but also responsibilities.

We are subject to the royal law that tells us to love our neighbour as ourselves (verse 8). James reminds us that we are not free to be selective, but must apply this law across the board. Notice, he adds, that this law condemns those who break it, but liberates those who keep it.

So, for example, picture a poor person – someone in need, whom you're tempted to think is a nuisance and isn't going to help you at all. When you obey the law to love that person as yourself, it's remarkably liberating. It liberates you from many of your fears, prejudices and selfishness, and you begin to find yourself free to love and care. But if you don't, you will find that you are constrained by your own selfishness, greed and supercilious attitude, and you're condemned.

Having been trained as a bank manager, I find it the easiest thing in the world to evaluate people quickly, to be critical and to dismiss them with alacrity. But I have discovered that if I am to be a member of the kingdom and see people as God sees them, evaluate them as God evaluates them and operate under the royal law of the King which requires me to love my neighbour as myself, then I will stop being critical, analytical and judgmental, and begin to be merciful, kind and generous towards them. And the remarkable thing is that I find myself wonderfully liberated. But every time I refuse, I find myself in a straitjacket of my own prejudice.

Most of us find it very easy to be critical of others. So the command to 'love your neighbour as yourself' is staggering:

> It seems to demand that I tear the skin off my body and wrap it around another person so that I feel that I am that other person; and all the longings that I have for my own safety and health and success and happiness I now feel for that other person as though he were me.
> (John Piper, 'Love Your Neighbor as Yourself, Part 1', 30 April 1995, <www.desiringgod.org/messages/love-your-neighbor-as-yourself-part-1>)

But notice that the second part of this royal law overflows from the first (Luke 10:27). Loving others is the natural consequence of wholeheartedly loving God. Invite the Holy Spirit to work in your heart today so that your love for God deepens, manifesting itself in loving others. No more criticism, snap judgments or snide comments. Let mercy triumph over judgment!

Day 224

Read James 2:14–19
Key verses: James 2:14–17

....

¹⁴*What good is it, my brothers and sisters, if someone claims to have faith but has no deeds? Can such faith save them?* ¹⁵*Suppose a brother or a sister is without clothes and daily food.* ¹⁶*If one of you says to them, 'Go in peace; keep warm and well fed,' but does nothing about their physical needs, what good is it?* ¹⁷*In the same way, faith by itself, if it is not accompanied by action, is dead.*

These verses have courted a lot of controversy. Martin Luther, in particular, was concerned that James was teaching justification by works, in direct contrast to Paul's doctrine of justification by grace through faith.

But James's question in verse 14, 'Can such faith save them?', indicates that he assumes people can be saved and that they are saved by faith. However, his point is that some faith can be fake, and therefore needs to be carefully evaluated.

It is not just *what* we believe that is important; James wants to underline that *how* we believe is tremendously significant. The object of our faith determines the validity of our faith; you can put minimal faith in thick ice and be safe. Conversely, you can have great faith in thin ice and you will drown. Yes, what you put your faith in is of vital importance. But James is adamant that the calibre and quality of our faith are also desperately important.

The example James uses here is that faith is dead if it is devoid of compassion. Faith is demonstrated by our obedience to the Lord. The Lord has required us to adhere to the royal law. Therefore, if the royal law says I should love my neighbour, and I say, 'I have faith in the Lord of that law,' then the reality of my faith will be shown in the compassion I demonstrate in obedience to that command.

If you were brought into a court of law, would there be enough evidence to convict you as a Christian? Would your neighbours, work colleagues, family members and friends say your faith was something you just talked about, or something that had a significant impact on your life?

Using James's example, when was the last time you showed compassion? Being compassionate can be exhausting and time-consuming. It means our own agenda is put on hold as we get involved in other people's lives. Certainly there is little reward or glamour in dealing with the practical, mundane matters of every-day life. But it is living proof of your faith. Look for heaven-sent opportunities to demonstrate compassion today.

Day 225

Read James 2:14–19
Key verses: James 2:18–19

· ·

¹⁸But someone will say, 'You have faith; I have deeds.'
Show me your faith without deeds, and I will show you my
faith by my deeds. ¹⁹You believe that there is one God. Good!
Even the demons believe that – and shudder.

Should we use creeds in our worship services?

Creeds can be wonderful tools for learning and discovering the faith. But it is also possible to recite them in a way that is totally devoid of meaning.

'You believe that there is one God' (verse 19) probably relates to the great statement in Deuteronomy 6:4, the beginning of the Shema, which orthodox Jews would recite every single day: 'The LORD our God, the LORD is one.'

But there is no point in reciting a creed and thinking that makes us all right. Even the demons believe the creeds! 'The demons believe that – and shudder' (verse 19). The demons believe thoroughly and are shaken by what they believe, but no-one imagines that the demons are saved!

There is no merit in saying, 'Well, I go in for faith; you go in for works. I'm a passive, contemplative sort; you are a doer.' We can't create these divisions. Indeed, James is adamant that this dichotomy doesn't exist – it is not either–or; it is both–and. Faith and deeds are not optional.

If we are a people of faith, we will be a people of action, looking for ways to demonstrate our faith. As James urges us repeatedly, 'Show me your faith.'

Some of us tend towards social action; others are keener to open the Bible with people. But the challenge, the glorious vision, is to hold both these aspects together and minister to the whole person.

• Think about the friendships you have with non-Christians. How can you demonstrate that you truly care? In what ways are you 'showing your faith' as well as talking about it?
• Think about the ways you serve in church – looking after the children in crèche, providing transportation for the elderly and serving meals to international students, for example. What is your motivation, your reason for serving? What drives you to keep on going?

Pray today for opportunities to 'show your faith' in practical, God-honouring ways.

Day 226

Read James 2:14–26
Key verses: James 2:20–26

....

²⁰*You foolish person, do you want evidence that faith without deeds is useless?* ²¹*Was not our father Abraham considered righteous for what he did when he offered his son Isaac on the altar?* ²²*You see that his faith and his actions were working together, and his faith was made complete by what he did.* ²³*And the scripture was fulfilled that says, 'Abraham believed God, and it was credited to him as righteousness,' and he was called God's friend.* ²⁴*You see that a person is considered righteous by what they do and not by faith alone.*

²⁵*In the same way, was not even Rahab the prostitute considered righteous for what she did when she gave lodging to the spies and sent them off in a different direction?* ²⁶*As the body without the spirit is dead, so faith without deeds is dead.*

'Look at the evidence!'

This is James's challenge to us.

Perhaps he is responding to a person who challenged him during his sermon. Or possibly he is engaging in 'diatribe', an old Jewish way of communicating. Either way, we have an argument with someone here. James responds, 'Do you want evidence that faith without deeds is useless? Look at the life of Abraham.'

In verse 23, he quotes Genesis 15:6: 'Abraham believed God, and it was credited to him as righteousness.' How can we be sure that Abraham believed? Because of what he did. When God called him to go to a place and didn't tell him where it was, he went (Genesis 12). When God covenanted with him, he believed (Genesis 15). And the point James focuses on: when God told Abraham to sacrifice his son Isaac, in whom all the covenant blessings were locked up, he was ready to obey (Genesis 22).

In complete contrast to the patriarch Abraham, James's second example is the disreputable Rahab. Hers was the oldest profession in the world. But when the children of Israel came to spy out Jericho, she told them she believed in their God: 'The LORD your God is God in heaven above and on the earth below' (Joshua 2:11). How do we know that she believed? She stuck her neck out! She rescued those men from certain death.

These two simple illustrations point to the fact that faith and actions go hand in hand. Just as the body without the spirit is dead, so faith that doesn't demonstrate itself in compassion, concern, companionship and courage is not real faith at all. James is not saying that we are justified by these things – we are justified by grace through faith – but the evidence for saving faith is that it works. In the same way that a body without the spirit is a corpse, so a faith that doesn't show itself in lively activities is dead.

It doesn't matter whether you come from a wealthy, respectable background like Abraham or have a chequered past like Rahab, you can be a friend of God (verse 23). This relationship is not dependent on your achievements, but solely on Christ's work on the cross. Of course, when you begin to understand all the implications of this new relationship, you experience a sense of gratitude, a desire to serve others and a passion to please God bubbling up inside. Living faith, by its very nature, produces righteous deeds. You may not feel as courageous as Abraham or Rahab, but today look for opportunities to put your faith into action. Is there something specific God is asking you to do? A promise you need to believe, a command you need to obey, a moral stand you need to take, a person you need to share the gospel with?

Day 227

Read James 3:1–5
Key verse: James 3:1

· ·

[1] Not many of you should become teachers, my fellow believers, because you know that we who teach will be judged more strictly.

'Sticks and stones may break my bones, but words will never hurt me' is a playground chant. But it is not true! Words are incredibly powerful and have potential for good or evil.

In this letter, James has been at great pains to remind us that true faith demonstrates itself in behaviour. And here he points out that our behaviour is often demonstrated in how we use our tongues.

He has already introduced the topic of the tongue in 1:26: 'Those who consider themselves religious and yet do not keep a tight rein on their tongues deceive themselves, and their religion is worthless.' And here in chapter 3, James starts by impressing on leaders the need to control their tongues.

In James's day, a teacher would be addressed as 'Rabbi', which literally means 'My great one': perhaps a fitting title for someone who was 'entrusted with the mysteries God has revealed' (1 Corinthians 4:1). Teachers were charged with explaining God's truth to others. And such a responsibility inevitably brought with it a privileged and prestigious role in society.

Today, as in past generations, we are in danger of inviting people to teach in church who perhaps ought not to hold that position. And sometimes, perhaps, with motives that are less than honourable, we want to be teaching when we may not be guarding ourselves as we ought.

Remember, 'From everyone who has been given much, much will be demanded; and from the one who has been entrusted with much, much more will be asked' (Luke 12:48).

James's message is primarily to preachers and church leaders. And while you may not hold this particular role, you still have influence on others. Your children, grandchildren, the young people at church, younger Christians in your home group or Alpha course are listening to how you speak about the Lord and others. They are paying attention to how you respond to personal suffering and division in the church, and they are watching whether the words you say match up with your actions.

Who is listening to your words? Who are you influencing? Recognize the privileged position God has entrusted to you. Pray for those taking note of your life. Determine, in God's strength, that your words will not bring them harm or discouragement, but rather will help them press on in the faith.

Set a guard over my mouth, LORD;
   keep watch over the door of my lips.
(Psalm 141:3)

Day 228

Read James 3:1–6
Key verses: James 3:2–5

....

²We all stumble in many ways. Anyone who is never at fault in what they say is perfect, able to keep their whole body in check.
³When we put bits into the mouths of horses to make them obey us, we can turn the whole animal. ⁴Or take ships as an example. Although they are so large and are driven by strong winds, they are steered by a very small rudder wherever the pilot wants to go. ⁵Likewise, the tongue is a small part of the body, but it makes great boasts. Consider what a great forest is set on fire by a small spark.

How do you measure maturity? Do you look for wrinkles, impressive qualifications and achievements, or someone's practical 'know-how'?

James believes maturity is measured by what comes out of our mouths.

In verses 2–5, James, with characteristic skill, makes use of a variety of illustrations. He thinks of a horse with a bit in its mouth, a rudder controlling a great ship out at sea, and a little spark setting off a raging forest fire. His point is that this little member of our body, which so often we don't regard as particularly significant, is in fact phenomenally important, because unless it is controlled, it leads to all kinds of disaster and damage. Conversely, this little member, if it is properly controlled, will lead to the control of one's whole life.

Consequently, the tongue is a measure of maturity. If someone's tongue is out of control, that person is invariably spiritually, emotionally or intellectually immature. If, on the other hand, someone speaks wisely, judiciously, carefully, positively and helpfully, you have found a mature individual.

And spiritual maturity is God's goal for us (Ephesians 4:13–15). As Paul explains:

> Not that I have already obtained all this, or have already arrived at my goal, but I press on to take hold of that for which Christ Jesus took hold of me . . . forgetting what is behind and straining towards what is ahead, I press on towards the goal to win the prize for which God has called me heavenwards in Christ Jesus.
> (Philippians 3:12–14)

Will you press on to maturity?

What does your language say about you?

What do the jokes you laugh at, the gossip you share, your comments about church leaders or employers reveal about you? How well do you fare on the maturity meter? Could God be asking you to 'grow up'?

It is very easy to say whatever pops into our heads, to speak simply to fill the silence, and to destroy someone with an unkind word. It is much harder and requires more prayerful discipline to control our tongue. Meditate on the following verses as you press on to maturity:

> May these words of my mouth and this meditation of my heart
>   be pleasing in your sight,
>   Lᴏʀᴅ, my Rock and my Redeemer.
> (Psalm 19:14)

> Like apples of gold in settings of silver
>   is a ruling rightly given.
> (Proverbs 25:11)

> Do not let any unwholesome talk come out of your mouths, but only what is helpful for building others up according to their needs, that it may benefit those who listen.
> (Ephesians 4:29)

Day 229

Read James 3:1–12
Key verses: James 3:5–12

· ·

⁵*Likewise, the tongue is a small part of the body, but it makes great boasts. Consider what a great forest is set on fire by a small spark.* ⁶*The tongue also is a fire, a world of evil among the parts of the body. It corrupts the whole body, sets the whole course of one's life on fire, and is itself set on fire by hell.*

⁷*All kinds of animals, birds, reptiles and sea creatures are being tamed and have been tamed by mankind,* ⁸*but no human being can tame the tongue. It is a restless evil, full of deadly poison.*

⁹*With the tongue we praise our Lord and Father, and with it we curse human beings, who have been made in God's likeness.* ¹⁰*Out of the same mouth come praise and cursing. My brothers and sisters, this should not be.* ¹¹*Can both fresh water and salt water flow from the same spring?* ¹²*My brothers and sisters, can a fig-tree bear olives, or a grapevine bear figs? Neither can a salt spring produce fresh water.*

A hastily written email, a sharply worded text message, an outburst of anger when we are tired can all cause immense damage.

Our words are so powerful because they reveal our true thoughts and attitudes. Our words, even careless ones, show what our hearts are like.

Using a series of illustrations, James forces us to dwell on this point. He describes our tongues as:

• *A spark from hell.* That spark of godlessness, rebellion and obscenity in our speech is set on fire in hell. Just like the forest fire, the damage is irreparable; it corrupts our whole body, producing a 'world of evil'.

- *A wild animal*. Although we can train wild animals, it is a strange irony that we can't tame our tongues. When we don't bring them under control, they become a 'restless evil'.

- *A polluted well*. It would be strange to go to a well and sometimes draw fresh water and at other times draw salt water. Similarly, it is inconsistent and unacceptable to use our tongue both to praise God *and* to hurt someone made in his image. How we treat one another is actually a marker of what we think of God.

- *A fruit tree*. You can tie apples onto a pear tree, but it does not make it an apple tree. The fruit of the tree demonstrates its root. Similarly, what comes out of my mouth is an indication of what is going on in my heart.

Your casual conversations, your responses when you are tired or angry, your comments about people when they are not present, all reveal the state of your heart (Matthew 12:34–35). So guarding your tongue begins with guarding your heart (Proverbs 4:23).

What measures are you taking to look after your heart? Are you taking double-pronged action: not only steering away from negative influences, but also pursuing positive ones? Think about the programmes you watch, the websites you browse, the books you read and the music you listen to. Ask the Holy Spirit to help you guard your heart today so that the words you say are wise, honest and helpful.

Day 230

Read James 3:13–16
Key verse: James 3:13

···

13 Who is wise and understanding among you? Let them show it by their good life, by deeds done in the humility that comes from wisdom.

Are you living the good life?

Our society and media portray the good life in terms of acquiring 'goods' or possessions. We are living the good life if we can buy what we want when we want it, if we can indulge our every whim.

However, the word 'good' used by James in verse 13 means 'good' in the sense of 'lovely' – not superficially glamorous, but intrinsically beautiful; not extravagant, but significant.

God's good life is not found in acquiring possessions, but is the result of wisdom that is deeply embedded in the heart and demonstrates itself in our behaviour, and particularly in our speech.

Where can we find this sort of wisdom? Proverbs 9:10 tells us that 'The fear of the LORD is the beginning of wisdom'. In other words, it is only when we begin to understand who the Lord is and what role he plays in our lives that we're even close to the beginning of wisdom.

This wisdom that begins with acknowledging who the Lord is blossoms into 'understanding' (verse 13). The word 'understanding' means 'well informed'. So the fear of the Lord begins to inform a person about all aspects of life. The Lord is integrated into all dimensions of his or her being. Sometimes we try to keep the Lord and spiritual things in a watertight compartment, separate and distinct from the rest of our life. But James insists that this wisdom that begins with the fear of the Lord permeates every dimension of our being and every aspect of our lives.

This is the good life.

To the world, the good life is about acquiring 'things'. The more 'things' we have, the more 'things' we can do, the better our life must be. In complete contrast, Jesus says that the good life is not pursuing *many* things, but only *one*: him.

Perhaps you need to hear his words to Martha: 'You are worried and upset about many things, but few things are needed – or indeed only one' (Luke 10:41–42).

This single pursuit of Christ is liberating. You no longer need to be looking over your shoulder at what others have or what they are doing; you don't have to strive to impress anyone; your worth is not determined by your bank account. Instead, your sole aim, your glorious lifelong ambition, is to pursue Christ. So today, at regular points, perhaps on the hour, pause to worship God; look for every opportunity to obey him and uphold his values. Today, live for an audience of One.

Day 231

Read James 3:13–16

Key verse: James 3:13

....

13 Who is wise and understanding among you? Let them show it by their good life, by deeds done in the humility that comes from wisdom.

We have all met them.

Christians who walk into a room with an 'I've arrived, look at me' attitude; believers who radiate an 'I know it all' aura.

But this is worlds away from James's call to demonstrate our good life 'by deeds done in the humility that comes from wisdom'. Godly wisdom is displayed not by a superior attitude, but by our humility. The word is 'meekness'. It is not the same as weakness. Rather, it is strength that chooses not to exert itself. Humility is not someone simply pretending to be terribly submissive and persuaded. Someone with humility has a genuine, realistic evaluation of self, and is prepared to respond and yield to what is going on.

In 1:21, James uses the word 'meekness' again, concerning our attitude to the Word of God. John Calvin says that it means we have 'a mind disposed to learn' from the Scriptures. We are to have a humble attitude towards God and his Word.

When it comes to our relationship with God, we have an awful lot to be humble about. Therefore, humility and meekness would seem very appropriate indeed. Meekness towards the Word, towards God and towards people – that is heavenly wisdom.

If you've gotten anything at all out of following Christ, if his love has made any difference in your life, if being in a community of the Spirit means anything to you, if you have a heart, if you *care* – then do me a favor: Agree with each other, love each other, be deep-spirited friends. Don't push your way to the front; don't sweet-talk your way to the top. Put yourself aside, and help others get ahead. Don't be obsessed with getting your own advantage. Forget yourselves long enough to lend a helping hand.

Think of yourselves the way Christ Jesus thought of himself. He had equal status with God but didn't think so much of himself that he had to cling to the advantages of that status no matter what . . . Instead, he lived a selfless, obedient life and then died a self-less, obedient death – and the worst kind of death at that – a crucifixion.

(Philippians 2:1–8, MSG)

Don't be afraid to be countercultural. Follow Jesus' example and willingly humble yourself. Be humble in how you approach God, how you respond to his Word and how you treat other people. Then, just as God exalted Christ, one day he will exalt you. Humility now means glory later!

Day 232

Read James 3:14–18
Key verses: James 3:14–16

∙∙∙

¹⁴But if you harbour bitter envy and selfish ambition in your hearts, do not boast about it or deny the truth. ¹⁵Such 'wisdom' does not come down from heaven but is earthly, unspiritual, demonic. ¹⁶For where you have envy and selfish ambition, there you find disorder and every evil practice.

Sometimes our common sense and God's wisdom converge, but not always. Take care not to confuse the two.

James points out that there are two types of wisdom. There is a wisdom that comes from heaven (verse 17), but there is another kind of wisdom – 'earthly, unspiritual, demonic' – which has to be guarded against.

Much of earthly wisdom is sound common sense, but it is devoid of any spiritual understanding. So, for example, the Spirit of God may call you to share the gospel in a dangerous location, but your unbelieving family, being highly practical and very realistic, dissuade you, telling you it is a crazy thing to do. That is earthly wisdom and it is unspiritual. Yes, a good, loving family can pump wisdom into us that is purely secular, has nothing to do with the Spirit and manages to achieve the devil's end.

It happened to Peter. He didn't want the Lord to go to Jerusalem, because he loved him and didn't want him to be in danger. Did Jesus turn to him and say, 'Thank you for that very sensible, solid advice'? No! He said, 'Get behind me, Satan!' (Mark 8:33). Sometimes totally common-sense arguments from well-meaning people will achieve purely secular, humanistic, devilish ends. That is why it is utterly imperative that we keep in step with the Spirit.

In verse 16, James points out that the wrong advice, being estranged from heavenly wisdom and out of touch with the Word of God and the Spirit of God, being out of step with divine purposes, can mean you become inordinately concerned about yourself (that's what 'envy' means here), totally committed to looking out for number one, and pursuing your own dream of the good life.

God's plans often contradict common sense. For example:

- planting a church in your village instead of joining the more established fellowship in the next town;
- turning down a well-paid job in order to work for a Christian charity;
- encouraging your children to train and be involved in full-time Christian ministry rather than secular employment;
- giving generously to kingdom ministry rather than stockpiling for your pension or a rainy day.

Make sure you are not being swept along with the world's distorted view of the good life. Instead, make every effort to 'keep in step with the Spirit' (Galatians 5:22–26; see also Romans 8:9–14).

> Trust in the LORD with all your heart
>   and lean not on your own understanding;
> in all your ways submit to him,
>   and he will make your paths straight.
>
> Do not be wise in your own eyes;
>   fear the LORD and shun evil.
> (Proverbs 3:5–7)

Day 233

Read James 3:13–18
Key verses: James 3:17–18

....

17 But the wisdom that comes from heaven is first of all pure; then peace-loving, considerate, submissive, full of mercy and good fruit, impartial and sincere. 18 Peacemakers who sow in peace reap a harvest of righteousness.

What is the hallmark of this 'wisdom that comes from heaven'? How can you tell if someone is wise, according to God's definition?

Using his favourite word, 'show' (verse 13; see also 2:18), James has already underlined that wisdom needs to be visible and tangible. So what is the evidence?

You can tell the people who are deriving wisdom from above, who are integrating it into their lives so that it is becoming the dominant factor in their thinking about life, because they become increasingly:

• *pure*: related to the word 'holy' and meaning free from blemish;

• *peace-loving and peace-making*: (James himself exemplifies this in Acts 15 and 21);

• *considerate*: accepting, amenable and not inflexible;

• *submissive*: being persuasive in communication and capable of being persuaded;

• *merciful*: having a concern and reaching out practically to those who are hurting;

• *impartial*: not in two minds;

• *sincere:* the word is often translated 'not hypocritical'. The Greek word for hypocrite is a 'play actor'. Actors in those days hid behind a mask, and their own feelings were irrelevant. A hypocrite is someone who lives behind a mask.

How are these virtues demonstrated? There is going to be a 'sowing in peace'. St Augustine actually defined peace as 'the tranquillity of order'. Those who are living out God's wisdom are people of peace, whose lives are in order and who are concerned about bringing order. There is also a great concern for putting things right. Such wisdom results in a 'harvest of righteousness', which means right living, right behaviour, treating people right and living rightly before God.

What a crop! What a harvest!

How wise are you? To what extent have you grown in wisdom this past week, month or year?

Growth in wisdom is measurable – not by increased possessions, university degrees or even the number of candles on your birthday cake, but by the increase in these godly virtues, by your growth in godliness.

Pray that God's wisdom would be integrated more and more into your life and increasingly on display in your:

• marriage;
• family life;
• credit card statement;
• attitude to work/career/unemployment/retirement;
• worship;
• Bible reading;
• contribution to church life.

Imagine what an advertisement we would be for Christ if every day we were pure, peace-loving, considerate, submissive, merciful, impartial and sincere . . .

Imagine how different our conversations and behaviour would be if our driving passion was to live righteously before God . . .

Imagine the impact on our family, workplace or street if God's wisdom dictated every area of our life . . .

Imagine how different our church would be if careless conversations were replaced with a concern to treat people right and to put situations right . . .

Imagine . . .

Day 234

Read James 4:1–3
Key verse: James 4:1

· ·

¹What causes fights and quarrels among you? Don't they come from your desires that battle within you?

Stop burying your head in the sand! Don't ignore the tensions any longer. Ask yourself the hard question James poses here.

Although he has been talking about God's wisdom producing a peace-loving, peace-making lifestyle, as far as this very practical man is concerned, we have to face up to the fact that war, strife, tension, violence, disintegration and disorderliness are everywhere. As well as international and national conflict, we have family breakdown, marital discord and even schisms within our church fellowships.

James himself doesn't shy away from answering his own question: 'What causes fights and quarrels among you? Don't they come from your desires that battle within you?'

He has talked about 'desire' before (1:14–15), and has been careful to point out that the perfectly legitimate desires God has planted within us can become warped and twisted and agents of devilish activity. He not only talks about 'desires', but also in verse 2 he speaks of wants and coveting.

This belief that one owes it to oneself to experience everything that gives pleasure is called hedonism. This is the dominating ethos of our generation, and inevitably leads to the disintegration of society. Of course it does! If I am only interested in myself, I am going to become so utterly dominated by my intrinsic selfism and become so selfish that I will have no time for anyone else. And when others' self-interest collides with mine, there will be squabbles and fights.

At the root of the fights we see internationally, nationally, in families, in marriages and in churches is what Freud called the 'pleasure principle': these desires, wants and covetousness are the evidence of self-centredness. Alec Motyer says, 'It is at root no more than the existence in each of us of a self-centred heart, a controlling spirit of self-interest' (*The Message of James*, IVP, 1998, p. 145).

How sobering to think that the squabbles in my church, marriage and family boil down to this 'pleasure principle'. It may seem that they hang on other issues, such as style of worship or which side of the family to spend Christmas Day with. But James is saying that, in essence, the problem is that I am selfish and want my own way.

If you are involved in any sort of quarrel, ask God to search your heart and to show you where the selfishness lies. Ask him to give you the strength to put 'self' to death and to put the needs of others first.

Meditate on what Jesus' words mean for you in your own particular situation: 'Whoever wants to be my disciple must deny themselves and take up their cross daily and follow me' (Luke 9:23).

Day 235

Read James 4:1–3
Key verses: James 4:2–3

....

²You desire but do not have, so you kill. You covet but you cannot get what you want, so you quarrel and fight. You do not have because you do not ask God. ³When you ask, you do not receive, because you ask with wrong motives, that you may spend what you get on your pleasures.

How would you describe your church prayer meeting? Vibrant? Small? Stagnant? Perhaps you have never attended.

Interestingly, the second reason James gives for the tensions and fights Christians experience is to do with prayer. He raises two issues:

• *Prayerlessness.* 'You do not have because you do not ask God' (verse 2). It is fairly easy for believers to live their church life purely on the basis of self-effort, self-assertion and self-interest. You don't need to pray to operate on any, or all, of these principles. Does your church operate on these principles? Or is there a higher, nobler objective – to begin to discover what the will of God is, to identify with the plan of God, to live in the power of God and to produce a church that is explicable only in terms of divine intervention in human affairs?

• *Inappropriate prayer.* 'When you ask, you do not receive, because you ask with wrong motives, that you may spend what you get on your pleasures' (verse 3). Sometimes our prayers end with that lovely little phrase, 'for Jesus' sake', but they have nothing to do with Jesus' sake; they're for *our* sake. We might try to legitimize our prayers by adding 'for Jesus' sake', but we are not really concerned about the honour of Christ, the extension of his kingdom, the hallowing of his name or doing his will on earth as it is done in heaven. What we are really concerned with is self-interest.

What difference would it make in your church if nobody prayed? Sometimes we get so caught up in our own efforts and agenda that we actually forget to pray. And so we miss out on seeing God at work. Instead of God's power and glory being showcased, arguments and tensions fester.

Prayer is our opportunity to enter God's throne room – to enjoy his presence, experience his peace, recognize our dependence on him, learn his will and join him in his work.

What are you praying for now? How different would your prayer requests be if you really prayed 'for Jesus' sake'?

Day 236

Read James 4:1–5
Key verses: James 4:4–5

. . . .

> [4]*You adulterous people, don't you know that friendship with the world means enmity against God? Therefore, anyone who chooses to be a friend of the world becomes an enemy of God.* [5]*Or do you think Scripture says without reason that he jealously longs for the spirit he has caused to dwell in us?*

James does not pull any punches. He is relentless in his efforts to help us understand how conflicts and tensions arise among us.

The term 'adulterous' here does not necessarily mean that James's readers are engaging in sexual immorality. He is simply using an Old Testament illustration (Hosea 1:2). In effect, he's saying that God's people sometimes claim to be betrothed to Christ, but have actually gone off with other lovers. They've got their priorities wrong. Instead of pursuing a friendship with God, they have chosen a friendship with the world.

What does it mean to have a friendship with the world? Definitions of 'worldliness' vary from place to place and age to age. But the Bible is actually quite explicit with regard to what constitutes worldliness: it is 'the lust of the flesh, the lust of the eyes, and the pride of life' (1 John 2:16).

So when we think in terms of worldliness, we have to decide: is God my friend, or is my desire for position (the pride of life), possessions and passions (the lust of the flesh and the lust of the eyes) the dominating factor? If those are my chief concerns, and if everyone in the fellowship is like that, everything will be wonderful! Until your passions and my passions collide, or your position challenges my position, or your possessions are better than my possessions. Then all kinds of tensions will result (verse 1).

There has to be something grander than this, and there is. It's the love of God.

So what is the priority? Which path will you choose?

There is an antagonism between God and the world; there's a mutually exclusive friendship and enmity. It is either–or. Either we are motivated by the Spirit, or we are motivated by intrinsic selfishness.

When we put it as starkly as this – friendship with God or friendship with the world – it hardly seems much of a choice. But usually the temptations of position, possessions and passions creep upon us stealthily and are altogether more subtle. Pinpoint your weaknesses regarding friendship with the world. Where will the devil most likely pounce: the lust of the flesh, the lust of the eyes or the pride of life? With God's help, keep on your guard. Pray also for members of your family and church – those in your small group, those you serve on a rota with, your prayer partner – that they too would choose friendship with God today.

Finally, be strong in the Lord and in his mighty power. Put on the full armour of God, so that you can take your stand against the devil's schemes. For our struggle is not against flesh and blood, but against the rulers, against the authorities, against the powers of this dark world and against the spiritual forces of evil in the heavenly realms.
(Ephesians 6:10–12)

Day 237

Read James 4:1–6

Key verse: James 4:6

. . . .

> [6]*But he gives us more grace. That is why Scripture says:*
> *'God opposes the proud*
> *but shows favour to the humble.'*

Have you been following James's argument so far?

He's saying, 'If you want to show me your faith, show me your works.' One of the works we can anticipate is that you'll be a peace-loving, peaceable, peace-making person. But we do this in the midst of various tensions and conflicts.

James has given a number of reasons for these struggles: our selfishness, our prayerlessness and wrong motives in prayer, our pursuit of worldliness rather than Christ. The final reason he identifies here is pride.

Quoting Proverbs 3:34, James sets out the two options. On the one hand, if I insist on exalting myself in the fellowship of believers, there are others who will accept it as their God-given responsibility to bring me down. If you have a church with a lot of proud, arrogant people who are becoming increasingly hard and embittered and committed to their own way of doing things, it's only a matter of time until you have all kinds of problems.

On the other hand, if I insist on humbling myself before God and laying myself low before him, I'm in the right position – I am waiting for God's grace and favour; I am waiting for him to raise me up. You see, my worth doesn't depend on the adulation of others; it is only God's exaltation that counts. I can humble myself before others, I can be open and honest with them, and I can trust God with my reputation and all the circumstances of my life, because he has promised to raise me up one day.

Reflect honestly: is there any evidence of pride in your life? Signs could be: always assuming you are right, reluctance to ask for advice, satisfaction in your own achievements, or a determination to protect your reputation.

In the final analysis, we have little to be proud about. All we are and have comes from Christ, and any self-aggrandizement will pale into insignificance compared to the way God will exalt us.

Be willing to humble yourself, and wait for God to exalt you. Join the frequent refrain of Scripture: 'Let the one who boasts boast in the Lord' (1 Corinthians 1:31; see also Psalms 34:2; 44:8; 2 Corinthians 10:17).

> This is what the LORD says:
>> 'Let not the wise boast of their wisdom
>>> or the strong boast of their strength
>>> or the rich boast of their riches,
>> but let the one who boasts boast about this:
>>> that they have the understanding to know me,
>> that I am the LORD, who exercises kindness,
>>> justice and righteousness on earth,
>>> for in these I delight,'
>>>> declares the LORD.
> (Jeremiah 9:23–24)

Consider what it means for you to 'boast in the Lord' and how you can do this today.

Day 238

Read James 4:5–12
Key verses: James 4:7–10

. . . .

> *⁷Submit yourselves, then, to God. Resist the devil, and he will flee from you. ⁸Come near to God and he will come near to you. Wash your hands, you sinners, and purify your hearts, you double-minded. ⁹Grieve, mourn and wail. Change your laughter to mourning and your joy to gloom. ¹⁰Humble yourselves before the Lord, and he will lift you up.*

How do we begin to address the problems in our hearts that so often engender strife in our marriages, families and churches?

By holding on to two spiritual truths.

First, recognize that God supplies grace to equip us to deal with the problem (verse 6). You can surely count on grace to deal with all that is required of you. Second, there are commands God gives that we must obey. In verses 7–10 we encounter some of the fifty-plus commands to be found in the 108 verses of James's letter.

Have you noticed how our temperament largely determines which of these spiritual truths we latch on to?

On the one hand, there are very detailed, organized, goal-setting individuals, who love immediate, measurable goals. These are the kind of people who make lists of the fifty-plus commands in James. They get out their phones and computers, and they say, 'I've got twenty-four hours in a day and there are fifty commands here; fifty into twenty-four . . . Tick, tick, tick.' If you are one of those people, remember there is grace available.

On the other hand, there are those who know that grace is available, and they haven't even bothered to read the commands! They are just trusting God in his grace to do it. If this is your inclination, remember that these commands of God are to be taken seriously.

There is always a balance to be found. The old hymn puts it perfectly: 'Trust and obey.' We don't have to choose between appropriating God's grace and obeying his commands. Whichever comes naturally to you, ignore it, and concentrate on the other one!

If there are problems in your marriage, family or church, humble yourself before God. Analyse the situation before him and, on the basis of this, seek the grace of God to empower you to begin to rectify the problem, and then start being meticulously obedient.

If you do so, you will begin to demonstrate the reality of your faith.

Reread the commands listed in verses 7–10. Is there a particular command God is asking you to obey? In what way do you need to appropriate his grace? Pray through your day – the activities, concerns, people and situations you will have to deal with. Consider all the ways you will be able to demonstrate – to believers and unbelievers – the reality of your faith; all the ways your life can point them to God. Ask God to teach you what it means to both 'trust and obey' him in this season of your life.

Day 239

Read James 4:7–17

Key verses: James 4:13–17

....

¹³Now listen, you who say, 'Today or tomorrow we will go to this or that city, spend a year there, carry on business and make money.' ¹⁴Why, you do not even know what will happen tomorrow. What is your life? You are a mist that appears for a little while and then vanishes. ¹⁵Instead, you ought to say, 'If it is the Lord's will, we will live and do this or that.' ¹⁶As it is, you boast in your arrogant schemes. All such boasting is evil. ¹⁷If anyone, then, knows the good they ought to do and doesn't do it, it is sin for them.

At the end of personal letters, along with the signature, you used to see the initials DV. This was shorthand for *Deo volente* – God willing.

Nowadays, in the church as well as the world, attitudes have changed. We make plans with very little thought of God. In effect, we are saying, 'I've all the time in the world. I can go anywhere I wish. I can do my own thing. I will carry on business, and I'll make money.'

This attitude overlooks the simple fact that we don't even know what will happen tomorrow; we are like 'a mist that appears for a little while and then vanishes'. It is hard to see how anybody could be dominated by self-interest and self-assertion when Scripture says, 'You're like a mist'!

Instead of this arrogant, self-sufficient, self-assertive, self-interested lifestyle, which is the antithesis of a humble dependence on God and obedience to his commands, we ought to be saying, 'If it is the Lord's will, we will live and do this or that' (verse 15).

And if you persist in arrogance and refuse to humble yourself, you're not just creating all kinds of division and tension in your marriage, family and church; to put it bluntly, you're sinning. Because if you know the way to go, and you won't go that way, that's rebellion.

We avoid thinking of ourselves as 'a mist', and we act and plan as if we will be around for ever. We may seek God's will for the big decisions – who to marry and where to live – but we tend not to consult him on the smaller, daily decisions because we feel able to handle these on our own. How foolish!

Recognize that what happens next, even your very breath, is DV – 'God willing'. All the plans you made for today are subject to his sovereignty. Don't let arrogance and self-confidence lead you into sin and rebellion. Humbly submit your plans to him. Pray that instead of holding on tightly to your own agenda, you will be obedient to all that God wants you to do today.

In their hearts humans plan their course,
　　but the Lord establishes their steps.
(Proverbs 16:9)

Day 240

Read James 5:1–20
Key verses: James 5:1–6

· ·

> ¹Now listen, you rich people, weep and wail because of the misery that is coming on you. ²Your wealth has rotted, and moths have eaten your clothes. ³Your gold and silver are corroded. Their corrosion will testify against you and eat your flesh like fire. You have hoarded wealth in the last days. ⁴Look! The wages you failed to pay the workers who mowed your fields are crying out against you. The cries of the harvesters have reached the ears of the Lord Almighty. ⁵You have lived on earth in luxury and self-indulgence. You have fattened yourselves in the day of slaughter. ⁶You have condemned and murdered the innocent one, who was not opposing you.

While major segments of the world are dying because of malnutrition, in the West people are dying because of their extravagant indulgence.

James now turns to address these sins of prosperity. Having talked about humility, speech, silly squabbles in church, messy marriages and bad relationships, James now speaks about money. It shouldn't be surprising that faith is demonstrated not only in our conversations and relationships, but also in our bank statements and direct debits.

Verses 1–6 are James's diatribe against prosperity. It is not sinful to be wealthy. God owns the cattle on a thousand hills; Abraham was very wealthy; Jacob became wealthy; Jesus was buried in the tomb of a wealthy man. So prosperity in and of itself is not sinful.

But there are issues we must consider:

• The means that we use to gain prosperity may be sinful.

• The attitudes that prosperity produces may well be sinful.

• The way we utilize our prosperity may be sinful.

In these verses, James is talking about extravagance, indulgence, selfishness – all the sins that come through prosperity. He's asking us to look at what we have and how we could better reflect our faith in God.

Whether we have a little or a lot, we tend to become attached to our money. Think through James's points: how do you gain your money, what is your attitude to it and how do you spend it? As a practical exercise, look through your bank statement: what are you spending most of your money on? What amount are you giving back to God? Is there evidence of indulgence or greed? Be willing for the Holy Spirit to point out some painful home truths. As you make your next purchase, pay your next bill, receive your next pay cheque, pray that God would fix in your mind a godly view of resources: we are stewards of his money and will one day be called to give an account.

Day 241

Read James 5:1–20
Key verses: James 5:7–9

....

⁷Be patient, then, brothers and sisters, until the Lord's coming. See how the farmer waits for the land to yield its valuable crop, patiently waiting for the autumn and spring rains. ⁸You too, be patient and stand firm, because the Lord's coming is near. ⁹Don't grumble against one another, brothers and sisters, or you will be judged. The Judge is standing at the door!

The Lord is coming again.

Christians have an end in view. We know history is not just repeating itself meaninglessly, nor is it a chance collision of circumstances. It is the unfolding of the divine purpose, and God is working inevitably, relentlessly, inexorably towards the consummation of his eternal will.

Part of God's will is that, at the appropriate time, Christ will return. James reminds us about this future hope (verses 7–9) because it needs to inform how we live now. Knowing that Christ will return and we will live with him for ever is a powerful motivator to holy living: to put our faith into action in our speech, relationships at home and church, our plans, how we use our money, and all the other examples James has given in his letter.

James is echoing the apostle Peter's plea:

Therefore, with minds that are alert and fully sober, set your hope on the grace to be brought to you when Jesus Christ is revealed at his coming. As obedient children, do not conform to the evil desires you had when you lived in ignorance. But just as he who called you is holy, so be holy in all you do; for it is written: 'Be holy, because I am holy.' (1 Peter 1:13–16)

Since everything will be destroyed in this way, what kind of people ought you to be? You ought to live holy and godly lives as you look forward to the day of God and speed its coming. That day will bring about the destruction of the heavens by fire, and the elements will melt in the heat. But in keeping with his promise we are looking forward to a new heaven and a new earth, where righteousness dwells. (2 Peter 3:11–13)

'The Lord is coming again': whisper it to yourself, repeat it aloud, and let the truth and magnitude of these words sink into your soul afresh. He could return this morning or before you get home from work tonight. Keep this glorious thought in the forefront of your mind today. Let it shape how you speak to your children and spouse, apply yourself to your work, use your free time, deal with church conflict and decide what to purchase.

With all that lies ahead and all we have to look forward to, use this waiting time to grow in godliness and prepare yourself for your new home 'where righteousness dwells'.

Day 242

Read James 5:1–20

Key verses: James 5:13–16

. . . .

¹³ *Is anyone among you in trouble? Let them pray. Is anyone happy? Let them sing songs of praise.* ¹⁴ *Is anyone among you ill? Let them call the elders of the church to pray over them and anoint them with oil in the name of the Lord.* ¹⁵ *And the prayer offered in faith will make the sick person well; the Lord will raise them up. If they have sinned, they will be forgiven.* ¹⁶ *Therefore confess your sins to each other and pray for each other so that you may be healed. The prayer of a righteous person is powerful and effective.*

There is nothing special about a well-known preacher's prayers, your pastor's prayers or your parents' prayers. Yes, it is good to have other people pray for you, but remember that you have direct access to God too.

Whom does James exhort to pray? Those who are in trouble, happy or sick. That covers all of us, all the time! Prayer is a powerful, dynamic force that makes a difference (verse 16).

In verse 14, James goes on to talk specifically about prayer for those who are sick. Notice we have the twin truths of obedience and faith mentioned again (see Day 238). There are commands to be obeyed: 'Let them pray . . . Let them sing songs of praise . . . Let them call the elders.' But notice that, when the elders are called to pray over someone who is sick, it is the prayer offered in faith that makes the sick person well. Both obedience and faith are required.

Does praying in faith always work? There have been many occasions when I, along with fellow elders in our church, have gone in faith and prayed over the sick. We have asked God to work, we have sought his face, and God has always raised people up. Always.

That doesn't mean that they have been physically healed every time; they haven't. But everyone has testified to a tremendous spiritual uplift; everyone has testified to an emotional release; and not a few have testified to the fact that God has wonderfully healed them physically.

But remember: everyone who is healed subsequently goes to glory. So keep it in perspective!

Your prayers are precious to God; he listens and remembers each one.

> The four living creatures and the twenty-four elders fell down before the Lamb. Each one had a harp and they were holding golden bowls full of incense, which are the prayers of God's people.
> (Revelation 5:8)

Be obedient to God's commands and keep praying in faith, trusting him to act according to his will and in his time. Also, intercede for the believers whom God brings to your mind today. Ask him to 'raise' them up.

Day 243

Read James 5:1–20

Key verses: James 5:19–20

∙∙∙

[19] My brothers and sisters, if one of you should wander from the truth and someone should bring that person back, [20] remember this: whoever turns a sinner from the error of their way will save them from death and cover over a multitude of sins.

God loves wanderers (Matthew 9:36; Luke 15:4–7).

Indeed, Jesus left heaven when we were wandering to bring us back to God.

And now God invites us to join him in his mission and to show that our faith is working by bringing the wanderers home.

Of course, God is the One who ultimately brings wanderers home, but he does have a habit of using people in the process. So watch out for believers who wander from the truth, who start heaping up a multitude of sins because they are living in error. Don't hesitate to take action, because they are in danger of losing their souls.

If you turn wanderers back to God, you are engaged in the most wonderful work, which glorifies God, brings blessings and shows that your faith is working. You are being used to turn a sinner from error, to save a soul from death and to cover a multitude of sins.

None of us is immune to wanderlust. Each generation faces its own temptations, its own array of idols and attractive false teaching. Are you being intentional about spiritual growth and obedience to Christ? If not, it is easy to drift away from a God-focused life and to be lured by the bright lights of the 'broad road' (Matthew 7:13).

Cling to Christ today. Don't let your heart be distracted by anything less.

> People do not drift toward Holiness. Apart from grace-driven effort, people do not gravitate toward godliness, prayer, obedience to Scripture, faith, and delight in the Lord. We drift toward compromise and call it tolerance; we drift toward disobedience and call it freedom; we drift toward superstition and call it faith. We cherish the indiscipline of lost self-control and call it relaxation; we slouch toward prayerlessness and delude ourselves into thinking we have escaped legalism; we slide toward godlessness and convince ourselves we have been liberated.
>
> (Don Carson, *For the Love of God, Volume 2* (IVP, 2011, January 23)

Also, look out for your Christian friends and the others in your small group. Help them not to deviate from God's path: pray for one another, share deeply, speak out when you see sin, show heartfelt compassion, accept rebuke as from God, and cheer each other on as you see the finish line ahead, so that each of you can say:

> I have fought the good fight, I have finished the race, I have kept the faith. Now there is in store for me the crown of righteousness, which the Lord, the righteous Judge, will award to me on that day – and not only to me, but also to all who have longed for his appearing.
>
> (2 Timothy 4:7–8)

For further study

If you would like to do further study on James's letter, the following books may be useful:

- Sam Allberry, *James for You* (The Good Book Company, 2015).

- R. Kent Hughes, *James: Faith that Works*, Preaching the Word (Crossway, 2015).

- Douglas Moo, *James*, Tyndale New Testament Commentaries (IVP, 2015).

- Alec Motyer, *The Message of James*, The Bible Speaks Today (IVP, 2014).

James mentions suffering a number of times in his short letter. If you would like to explore this subject further, there are many excellent resources available, including:

- Don Carson, *How Long, O Lord? Reflections on Suffering and Evil* (IVP, 2006).

- Sharon Dirckx, *Why? Looking at God, Evil and Personal Suffering* (IVP, 2013).

- Timothy Keller, *Walking with God through Pain and Suffering* (Hodder & Stoughton, 2015).

- Paul Mallard, *Invest Your Suffering: Unexpected Intimacy with a Loving God* (IVP, 2013).

If God has fed you through your study of the book of James, why not buy the individual Food for the Journey on James and give it to a friend (available from ivpbooks.com)?

Introduction

2 Timothy

Michael Baughen

Last words

Last words are important. They are a brief glimpse into another person's soul. A final unveiling of what mattered to them most.

The second letter of Timothy records Paul's last words. He is in prison, near to death, dictating this letter to Luke for his young pastor friend Timothy. As he sits chained to a Roman soldier, Paul's passion for the gospel shines out. He uses his farewell message to urge Timothy to maintain his focus on the fundamentals of the faith. There will be distractions, opposition and even suffering, but Timothy is to keep Christ and the gospel central to his life and ministry. Paul charges Timothy, and the church in every subsequent generation, to share this gospel faithfully and urgently.

This intensely personal letter invites us into Paul's prison cell, allows us to hear his last words and gives us an insight into his devotion to God. It challenges us to think about our own legacy. What are we living for? Or rather, whom are we living for?

Day 244

Read 2 Timothy 1:1–18
Key verses: 2 Timothy 1:1–2

....

¹Paul, an apostle of Christ Jesus by the will of God, in keeping
with the promise of life that is in Christ Jesus,
²To Timothy, my dear son:
Grace, mercy and peace from God the Father and Christ
Jesus our Lord.

All of us are called to serve Christ. That service may be in your home,
your workplace, your university campus or your church. God has put
you there, he has called you there and you serve him there 'by the
will of God'.

Paul knows he is an apostle 'by the will of God'. He is in prison. He
will never again be able to pioneer new churches. There will be no
more missionary journeys. He is about to die for his faith. But Paul is
still convinced that he is what he is and where he is 'by the will of
God'. It's a phrase that should burn into us. When difficulties come,
cling to this truth like a rock in a storm. It may be that, like Paul, you
are no longer able to do many of the things you did in the past; if
that is the case, still see that what you are and where you are is 'by
the will of God'.

As an apostle, Paul's goal is to preach the good news, to share the
'promise of life that is in Christ Jesus'. This letter is Paul's charge to
Timothy, a young pastor in Ephesus, and to us, to pass on to the next
generation all that the apostles witnessed. He wants us to guard,
follow and share the truth about Jesus with others.

Paul's role as an apostle was unique. But each of us, in our own situations, is called to share the life of Christ with others. Wherever you
are, 'by the will of God', whatever your daily circumstances, look for

opportunities to speak and live out the good news of Jesus. And do so confident of God's:

- *grace*: all the wonder of being in Christ, of full and free salvation and of undeserved love;

- *mercy*: the withholding of the punishment our sin deserves;

- *peace*: the wholeness of mind, body, spirit and soul as Christ makes us fully his.

Consider for a moment your job, your family responsibilities, your church ministry – all the different strands that make up your life. It might not be the scenario you'd imagined or hoped for, but God has placed you there. And his greatest delight is to see Christ's life shine out as, with the Holy Spirit's help, you daily choose to live for him. Amazingly, God uses our ordinary, weak and often broken lives to display Christ's life to others (2 Corinthians 4:7). Today, as you meditate on God's grace, mercy and peace, thank him for where he has placed you. Look for ways to share the promise of life that is in Christ.

Day 245

Read 2 Timothy 1:3–18
Key verses: 2 Timothy 1:3–5

....

³I thank God, whom I serve, as my ancestors did, with a clear conscience, as night and day I constantly remember you in my prayers. ⁴Recalling your tears, I long to see you, so that I may be filled with joy. ⁵I am reminded of your sincere faith, which first lived in your grandmother Lois and in your mother Eunice and, I am persuaded, now lives in you also.

Your concern and interest in someone else's life could have a profound impact, without you even realizing it.

Paul is deeply concerned for Timothy. Timothy is not an extrovert or a strong personality. He doesn't find it easy to be a Christian leader, particularly when the going is rough. He has a natural tendency – one that we're all familiar with – to duck out of problems, suffering or controversy. And Paul wants to strengthen him. So, in verses 3 and 4, he reminds Timothy that he is deeply concerned for him.

Each of us needs to demonstrate concern for others. We can show concern for young people going off to college. It only takes a moment to pray, to write, to show you care. How Timothy's heart must be thumping in his throat as he reads Paul's letter: 'I thank God, Timothy, as I remember you.' Paul remembering and thanking God for me! Believing that God is working in me! Paul, this giant in Timothy's eyes, is actually somebody who thanks God for him. He is on Paul's prayer list!

Who is on your prayer list? Whom are you concerned for and showing an interest in? The church is full of people needing our support and prayers – parents with children who have additional needs, those with older children and an 'empty nest', young people facing the pressure to conform in secondary school, older folk feeling the burden of advancing years. The list is endless!

Praying for someone is more than sentimental encouragement. It is more than a reminder of the deep desire that we should run well for Christ, although it includes all of these things; it is a means of the grace of God in answer to prayer. Timothy will be strengthened by the reminder that Paul's heart aches for him in the bonds of deep love, and is expectant of his service for Christ.

Life is busy. It's easy for every day to be filled with our immediate needs and responsibilities, with little or no time left to remember others. But think back to those mature Christians who supported you. What difference did their prayers make? For whom could you be praying? How could you express interest and support for a younger person? Just think – your prayers could be the means of God's grace in someone else's life.

Prayer (this side of heaven) will always be hard and will always take discipline, but when I see it as a means to communion with God, it feels more like a 'get to' than a 'have to'.
(Kevin DeYoung, *The Hole in Our Holiness*, Crossway Books, 2012, p. 131)

Day 246

Read 2 Timothy 1:3–18
Key verses: 2 Timothy 1:6–7

. . . .

⁶For this reason I remind you to fan into flame the gift of God, which is in you through the laying on of my hands. ⁷For the Spirit God gave us does not make us timid, but gives us power, love and self-discipline.

Do you know what your spiritual gift is? Paul tells us that each of us has a gift (1 Corinthians 7:7), but many of us are not sure how to discover it or what to do if we find it!

Paul reminds Timothy that God has called him to ministry and equipped him for it. He encourages Timothy to think back to when his gift was received through the laying-on of hands. This laying-on of hands is normally a sign of prayer to God in response to a person's commitment. So the church responded to Timothy's commitment to the task by the laying-on of hands. Together they asked God to equip Timothy for the task to which God had called him. The important point is that Timothy didn't sit around doing nothing, waiting for God to send him the right gifts. God sends the right gifts when we respond to the right task.

Imagine God's spiritual gifts as being like the flames of a fire. You have to keep fanning the flames and fuelling the fire to keep it fully alive. How do you keep your spiritual gift alive? By reflection, prayer, devotion, using the gift and proving God's grace, and training to be a better user of the gift. Don't try to serve God without using his gifts. It's pointless, careless and fatal for effective ministry.

So Paul urges Timothy that, whatever the opposition – the materialism of society, his own immaturity, ill health or shyness – he is Christ's man. He is called by him and equipped by him, and he must keep that equipment fresh.

Like Timothy, God has equipped us for serving him with spiritual gifts and the indwelling of the Holy Spirit. God's Spirit in us means we can serve, not in fear, but with:

- *power*: power that enables us, gives us boldness, helps us endure, and means we can triumph even in weakness;

- *love*: self-giving love that thinks of others and does not count the cost;

- *self-discipline*: attitudes and behaviour that seek God's glory, not our own.

What task has God given you? There are many jobs in church life, such as putting the chairs out, that just have to be done. But there are other tasks for which you have been uniquely designed and equipped. These tasks often change through the various seasons of life. Ask God to show you what he wants you to do for him now. Pray that he will equip you for the task, whether it's parenting, preaching or catering. Be conscious of serving God today in his power, with love and with self-discipline.

Day 247

Read 2 Timothy 1:3–18
Key verses: 2 Timothy 1:8–12a

⁸*So do not be ashamed of the testimony about our Lord or of me his prisoner. Rather, join with me in suffering for the gospel, by the power of God.* ⁹*He has saved us and called us to a holy life – not because of anything we have done but because of his own purpose and grace. This grace was given us in Christ Jesus before the beginning of time,* ¹⁰*but it has now been revealed through the appearing of our Saviour, Christ Jesus, who has destroyed death and has brought life and immortality to light through the gospel.* ¹¹*And of this gospel I was appointed a herald and an apostle and a teacher.* ¹²*That is why I am suffering as I am.*

Do you believe the gospel? Do you believe it enough to work for it, to share it and to accept the inevitable suffering that comes with it?

Paul wants to encourage Timothy that the gospel is the only answer for humankind. It's worth all the effort, the tiredness, the slog, the mockery, the persecution. He says to Timothy, and to us: don't avoid the gospel to avoid suffering, but share the gospel, whatever the cost.

And there will be a cost. It is inevitable that those who share the ministry of the gospel will suffer (verse 12). But in the midst of our suffering God promises us his grace and power, enabling us to endure.

Whenever we feel ashamed of the suffering or of standing up for the gospel, we need to take ourselves in hand and rehearse the gospel's unique and transforming truth. This is what Paul is doing in verses 9–10: 'He has saved us and called us to a holy life – not because of anything we have done but because of his own purpose and grace.' Our holy calling is by grace, not works, and was part of God's divine plan from the beginning of time. Jesus has 'brought life and immortality to light through the gospel'. With Christ, the floodlights come on and we see what it means to say that death has lost its sting, the grave has lost its power, and all in Christ have eternal life with him. And all this is 'through the appearing of our Saviour, Christ Jesus'. Our salvation is rooted, grounded and assured in Christ, because it's achieved by Christ.

This is the gospel! This is eternal truth. There is nothing to be ashamed of. We stand upon what God himself has done.

Are you suffering for the gospel? Not many of us face physical persecution, but there will be consequences if we let the gospel shape our decisions and values: strained relationships with non-Christian family members; being passed over for promotion because you don't indulge in office gossip; tiredness because you serve in church ministries during the week. If you are struggling in this area, tell yourself the gospel, remind yourself of its truth. Ask God to give you his grace and power as you serve him today.

Day 248

Read 2 Timothy 1:3–18
Key verse: 2 Timothy 1:12

· ·

¹²That is why I am suffering as I am. Yet this is no cause for shame, because I know whom I have believed, and am convinced that he is able to guard what I have entrusted to him until that day.

What do you say to someone who is suffering for being a Christian? What do you say to yourself when you are suffering for the sake of the gospel?

Notice what Paul does. He lifts Timothy's eyes to Jesus. He encourages Timothy to look to Jesus who is the Lord of the gospel, and therefore the guarantor of the gospel.

The text does not say '*in* whom I have believed' but '*whom* I have believed'. '*In whom* I have believed' is an arm's-length relationship, but '*whom* I have believed' speaks of a close, devoted relationship to Christ. How often have you seen people who, after forty or fifty years in the church, by the grace of God come to trust Christ for the first time? That is the movement from '*in whom*' to '*whom*'.

Knowing the Lord in this personal way is how our hearts are convinced of the gospel. We can be sure that, although the world mocks and ignores Christianity, the gospel is for ever. It will be vindicated on the final day as the power of God for salvation. And because we know Jesus, we trust that 'he is able to guard what I have entrusted to him until that day'. Jesus will guard the truth of the gospel throughout the generations, because it is his gospel.

More than that, if we give ourselves to Jesus, we can be sure that he will guard and keep us until the final day. This doesn't mean we'll avoid suffering and hardships, but it does mean that, as we live faithfully for God, we don't need to worry about the results of our ministry or the outcome of our lives; we can leave those with him. We can trust him with all that is precious to us, knowing he is completely trustworthy.

Today, look to Jesus. It may be difficult for you to share the gospel or live out gospel values but, in God's strength, press on! One day you will be vindicated. It's Jesus' responsibility to preserve the gospel, and he will do it! Our role is to live and serve him wholeheartedly. Stop worrying about results or what other people think of you. Don't let your suffering get in the way of living 'all out' for God. Entrust yourself totally to God's care and keeping. Trust him with the outcome of your life and service.

> But you, beloved, build yourselves up on your most holy faith; pray in the Holy Spirit; keep yourselves in the love of God; wait for the mercy of our Lord Jesus Christ unto eternal life.
> (Jude 20–21, RSV)

Day 249

Read 2 Timothy 1:3–18
Key verses: 2 Timothy 1:13–14

....

13 What you heard from me, keep as the pattern of sound teaching, with faith and love in Christ Jesus. 14 Guard the good deposit that was entrusted to you – guard it with the help of the Holy Spirit who lives in us.

What are the fundamentals, the non-negotiables, of our faith?

In verses 13–14, Paul gives us two commands: 'keep' and 'guard'. What we are to keep is 'the pattern of sound teaching'. The 'pattern' is like an architect's sketch, showing the main fabric of a building, not just the finishing touches. Paul is saying to Timothy that the foundations of the building are fixed for ever. They are non-negotiable. They are sometimes called the *kerygma* – that is, the central truths of the faith.

The truths of the gospel are living truths, brought about by Jesus Christ in his incarnation, atonement, resurrection and ascension, and by the Holy Spirit poured out upon the church. You cannot disagree with or compromise on these fundamental facts of the gospel. Other things can be altered or disposed of; the external bricks of the building, such as leadership structures and worship styles, may vary. But the central girders and foundations are for ever!

And we are to 'guard' this gospel. Today, as always, there are attacks on the gospel. All Christians are called to be guardians of the faith. As people seek to subtract from it, add to it or alter it, we must hold on to it because it is the only gospel whereby people can be saved.

So how do we 'keep' and 'guard' the gospel? By reciting a creed or shouting slogans? No. We 'keep' and 'guard' the gospel when:

- we take Christ and his Word seriously, spending time studying and meditating on Scripture;

- we daily live by gospel values with our faith and love in Jesus;

- we rely on the love and power of the Holy Spirit in all we do.

Church is full of a variety of people, from different backgrounds, denominations, races, ages and genders. How can we work together? What binds us together when so much else divides? Christian unity is based on the core elements of the gospel on which we are to build our lives. This week, serve together with other Christian brothers and sisters. Whatever your differences, unite around the core truths of the gospel, and don't fall out over secondary issues. As we live out these gospel truths, we will face opposition. There will be temptation to 'dilute' the gospel or to 'sugar-coat' it. Today, ask the Holy Spirit for help to 'guard' the gospel in your family, workplace and even church, with God's love and grace.

Day 250

Read 2 Timothy 1:3–18
Key verses: 2 Timothy 1:15–18

. . . .

¹⁵ *You know that everyone in the province of Asia has deserted me, including Phygelus and Hermogenes.*
¹⁶ *May the Lord show mercy to the household of Onesiphorus, because he often refreshed me and was not ashamed of my chains.* ¹⁷ *On the contrary, when he was in Rome, he searched hard for me until he found me.* ¹⁸ *May the Lord grant that he will find mercy from the Lord on that day! You know very well in how many ways he helped me in Ephesus.*

Think about the Christians who have made an impact on your life. What did they say? What did they do? What character traits most impressed you?

Paul has served God long enough to experience the disappointment, as well as the joy, of serving with other Christians. He was grieved when the believers in Asia deserted him. He mentions Phygelus and Hermogenes by name. Perhaps they were the ringleaders? We don't know anything about these two characters apart from their unfaithfulness – what a thing to be remembered for! Paul was deeply hurt by their unfaithfulness to him and the gospel.

But he was also greatly cheered by faithful Christians. He mentions Onesiphorus to Timothy. Onesiphorus searched him out on visits to Rome and kept coming back. He and his household helped Paul in 'many ways'. The key verse is verse 16: 'he . . . was not ashamed of my chains.' Onesiphorus was an encouragement to Paul, who wants him to be an encouragement to Timothy too. Paul prays for this fellow worker, and mentions him by name as an encouragement to Timothy not to be ashamed of Paul, of the gospel, or of suffering for it.

When believers watch your life, are they spurred on by your loyalty to God? Do they see gospel values lived out? Do they see you faithfully serving others for the extension of God's kingdom? Are you a breath of fresh air for their soul? Are you like Onesiphorus to them? Meditate on the following verses as you consider how you can encourage other Christ-followers today.

And Saul's son Jonathan went to David at Horesh and helped him to find strength in God.
(1 Samuel 23:16)

News . . . reached the church in Jerusalem, and they sent Barnabas to Antioch. When he arrived and saw what the grace of God had done, he was glad and encouraged them all to remain true to the Lord with all their hearts.
(Acts 11:22–23)

For everything that was written in the past was written to teach us, so that through the endurance taught in the Scriptures and the encouragement they provide we might have hope.
(Romans 15:4)

Do not let any unwholesome talk come out of your mouths, but only what is helpful for building others up according to their needs, that it may benefit those who listen.
(Ephesians 4:29)

Your love has given me great joy and encouragement, because you, brother, have refreshed the hearts of the Lord's people.
(Philemon 1:7)

Day 251

Read 2 Timothy 2:1–13
Key verse: 2 Timothy 2:1

• •

¹You then, my son, be strong in the grace that is in Christ Jesus.

Have you ever read a Christian biography and thought, 'That could never happen to me,' or, 'God could never work in my life like that'? Sometimes we struggle to believe God is able to work through us.

Paul is about to die. The thought of being without him must be overwhelming for Timothy. But Paul's response is unequivocal: 'You then, my son, be strong in the grace that is in Christ Jesus.' In effect, he is saying, 'You are stepping into the breach, and you are to prove the God of Paul to be the same God for Timothy, and for every Christian.'

I had to wrestle with this idea when I was preparing to preach a sermon series on Moses. Do I believe that the God who brought Moses out of Egypt, crossing the Red Sea and taking all those people through the wilderness, is the same God I worship through Christ Jesus? If I do, then I cannot go on acting as though I am cooped up in the wilderness with no way through it. He is my God.

There are lots of people who have been converted but are still living off other people's experiences. They are dependent on a famous preacher or their church minister. They have never moved into that position where they themselves draw on the grace of Christ. God bids Timothy to move into that position and to prove 'the grace that is in Christ Jesus'.

He commands him to 'be strong' and 'be strengthened': the expression can be used both ways. As we hunger for God, he meets us in grace and strength. If we don't abide in him and he in us, we remain weak, like hungry people sitting at a banqueting table, too lazy to reach out for food; like thirsty people lying by a fountain, too lazy to reach out and drink. We have so many resources to help us grow as Christians. The food is all around us, the fountain is beside us; let us eat and drink.

There are great Bible texts on this theme. 'I can do all this through him who gives me strength' (Philippians 4:13), or, 'Be strong in the Lord . . . so that you can take your stand against the devil's schemes' (Ephesians 6:10–11), or, 'My grace is sufficient for you, for my power is made perfect in weakness' (2 Corinthians 12:9). Our weakness is no excuse. God revels in our weakness, as it shows his strength. I believe it's vitally important for Christians to rediscover the pounding theme of the New Testament: it is in Christ that we find our strength.

But being 'strong in the grace that is in Christ Jesus' doesn't mean waiting until you're strong enough to go out; it's about going out into the waters and finding that they recede. It's when you put your foot forward that the power of God enables you. If you wait until you feel strong enough to serve, you'll wait for ever.

God wants to work through you! He is not just the God of Paul or Timothy, of your parents or your minister. He is your God and he wants you to experience his grace. Don't settle for someone else's spiritual leftovers. Feed on God for yourself. Think about the books you read, the music you listen to, the TV you watch. Are they nourishing your soul? When you are connected to God, you will experience his strength in your life. Don't believe the lie that your weakness disqualifies you from service – it is a prerequisite! Our weakness is the backdrop for God to display his strength. So be strong in God's grace and step out in service.

Day 252

Read 2 Timothy 2:1–13
Key verse: 2 Timothy 2:2

....

²And the things you have heard me say in the presence of many witnesses entrust to reliable people who will also be qualified to teach others.

Do you struggle to discern God's will? What university should I attend, what career should I choose, when should I retire, where should I live?

Sometimes it's difficult to work out what God wants us to do. But one thing we can be certain of: wherever we live, work or study, God wants us to teach the gospel to others. The principle is to teach others, who can teach others, who can teach others, ad infinitum. If that strategy had not been followed, you would not be a Christian. The strategy of the Christian church, throughout the New Testament, is to train people who can train others.

Paul explains, 'The things you have heard me say' – the apostle is handing on the apostolic truth – 'in the presence of many witnesses'. We believe that the central truths of the Christian faith are truths that have been hammered out before witnesses. Paul is not handing on some secret tradition, which you have to be in the inner circle to know. Before many witnesses, God broke into the world and showed his glory. He worked out his saving purpose not in a corner, but on the public stage of the world.

And Timothy must entrust the gospel to 'reliable people'. If you entrust this truth to unreliable people, it will be destroyed or twisted. If they hand it on to others, it becomes more twisted and distorted until people are destroyed. Jesus demonstrated this principle of teaching reliable people who could entrust the good news to others. He withdrew from public ministry after the halfway point of his own work in order to teach the Twelve, to concentrate on explaining and deepening their understanding. He could have spent his time preaching and performing miracles for the crowds. Instead, he sat down with the Twelve and trained them. That is why, when he went back to glory, the church went forward in the power of the Spirit.

God is committed to the gospel and he wants all of us to be involved in passing his truth on to the next generation. Whatever else we're involved in, this is God's will for each of us. Unfortunately, most of us are like sheep: only interested in what's in front of our nose! When you have your nose down on the immediate things, you lose sight of the greater purposes in which you are taking part. God says to us today, 'Come on, get your head up. Realize who you are; realize the greater purposes into which I have called you. Head up! Head up!'

Life is full of pressing decisions, and we want to follow God's will at every stage. But look up! You are part of God's story of salvation. He has a great purpose planned for you which doesn't depend on geography or your stage of life. You are called to share the gospel with others, to teach and train them up in God's truth. Whom are you training? Your children, grandchildren, a younger person at church, a work colleague? Ask God to give you opportunities to pass on the baton of faith. Lift your head up and delight in the great purpose God has in mind for you.

Day 253

Read 2 Timothy 2:1–13
Key verses: 2 Timothy 2:3–4

....

³*Join with me in suffering, like a good soldier of Christ Jesus.* ⁴*No one serving as a soldier gets entangled in civilian affairs, but rather tries to please his commanding officer.*

Consider the choices you are making, the priorities you have, the relationships in which you are investing. Do you think Jesus is pleased with them? Is he pleased with how you are living?

Paul sees himself as a soldier whose aim is 'to please his commanding officer' (verse 4). One translation says the soldier's goal is to be 'wholly at his commanding officer's disposal' (NEB). It is a personal aim. Paul echoes this sentiment in 2 Corinthians 5:9: 'We make it our goal to please him.'

Of course, we please Christ by obeying him. Christ wants us to have unquestioning allegiance to his authority. A good soldier is one who says, 'Your will be done.' Saying this to God is the deepest expression of our faith. How else can you explain Gethsemane? In agony, with sweat falling from his face like drops of blood, Jesus was obeying his Father.

Tragically, some Christians treat God like a genie in a bottle. You rub the lamp, and the genie appears and says, 'Yes, Master, what do you want?' But in the New Testament it is the other way around. Of course, God is there to meet us in saving grace and love. That is the glory of being in his family. But commitment means coming to him and saying, 'Yes, Master, what do *you* want?'

Saying, 'Your will be done,' involves a readiness to suffer. So verse 3 says, 'Join with me in suffering, like a good soldier of Christ Jesus.' God is looking for men and women who rule nothing out, who are willing to go wherever and do whatever he asks, regardless of the suffering involved.

If you are going to be committed in this way, you cannot be 'entangled in civilian affairs'. The word in Greek is *empleko*, from which we get our word 'implicated'. It's like when your hair gets so knotty you can't get a comb through it. God is not asking us to avoid family responsibilities or never enjoy hobbies; these are important. He means we must not be so entangled that we cannot go where, and do what, our commanding officer requires.

Is it your goal to please God?

Bring to God all the situations and issues with which you are struggling. Stop wrestling. Stop trying to manipulate the outcome. Stop trying to fix things. Imagine writing over each of these scenarios, 'Your will be done.' Gladly submit your will to God's in each circumstance. As you go through your day, accept from God's hand the suffering that comes with obedience. But also enjoy the freedom that comes from not having to please everyone else. Let your soul delight in having a single focus to pursue. Our sole aim, our single passion, is to please God.

Day 254

Read 2 Timothy 2:1–13
Key verse: 2 Timothy 2:5

....

> [5] *Similarly, anyone who competes as an athlete does not receive the victor's crown except by competing according to the rules.*

If you had to describe your spiritual life, what image would you choose? I imagine that not many of us would describe ourselves as athletes straining towards godliness!

But Paul encourages us that we have a race to run, and it has to be 'according to the rules'. In the ancient Olympic Games, the athletes had to swear on oath that they had undergone constant training for ten months – these were the rules.

Not many Christians show that degree of determination. Many of us find it difficult to snatch a quick quiet time before we go off to work. But athletes are a graphic illustration of the dedication we must devote to our own spiritual training: runners who practise, whatever the weather, to reach the finishing line and obtain the prize; swimmers who get up at five in the morning to swim for two or three hours while the pool is quiet.

If you are serious about your commitment to Christ, you will want to pursue the holiness that is vital to the Christian race. In 1 Corinthians 9:24–27, Paul talks about the strict training of spirit, mind and body he engages in:

> Do you not know that in a race all the runners run, but only one gets the prize? Run in such a way as to get the prize. Everyone who competes in the games goes into strict training. They do it to get a crown that will not last; but we do it to get a crown that will last for ever. Therefore I do not run like someone running aimlessly; I do not

fight like a boxer beating the air. No, I strike a blow to my body and make it my slave so that after I have preached to others, I myself will not be disqualified for the prize.

If we want to receive a crown that will last for ever, then a determined pursuit of holiness is not a luxury, but a necessity. Devote yourself like an athlete to your spiritual training. Daily, set aside time to read the Bible and pray. Ask the Holy Spirit to help you say 'no' to sin and 'yes' to what pleases God. Meet up with other believers to spur one another on. Keep pressing on!

For most of us, the Christian race is not a sprint, but a marathon. At many points along life's course, we lose sight of the prize and get tired or discouraged. We could have avoided this gruelling pursuit of holiness if God had instantly transformed us to be like his Son. God could have done that, but he chose not to. Instead, he wants to partner with us. He wants us to learn to rely on him, to trust him and yield ourselves to him more fully. He wants us to experience the joy of wholehearted devotion and the Holy Spirit's enabling power. Perhaps you have let your spiritual training lapse. Don't give up; get your running shoes back on! Keep your eye on the prize and look forward to God cheering you on to the finishing line, saying, 'Well done, good and faithful servant.'

Day 255

Read 2 Timothy 2:1–13
Key verses: 2 Timothy 2:6–7

••

⁶The hardworking farmer should be the first to receive a share of the crops. ⁷Reflect on what I am saying, for the Lord will give you insight into all this.

Church is often compared to a football match: twenty-two people doing all the work and everyone else sitting watching them! But being a Christian is never a spectator sport.

In verse 6, Paul gives us the picture of a farmer. There's little glamour or excitement in farming. A farmer labours in all weathers. He works relentlessly in the lashing rain, the gale-force winds and even the dark winter mornings.

In the same way, although it's a wonderful privilege to serve Christ, it's also hard work. It's an effort to go out to the prayer meeting after a long day in the office; it's usually a thankless task to be on the rota for the church sound system; it's not thrilling to prepare meals for Alpha or Christianity Explored. Most of the ways in which we serve Christ are not glamorous or exciting – just hard work.

Paul describes his own commitment to the gospel as 'sowing', 'watering', 'reaping', 'pioneering', 'contending' and 'defending'. Like a farmer, he has worked tirelessly in all circumstances.

But though the work is hard, we will be rewarded. 'The hardworking farmer should be the first to receive a share of the crops.' This doesn't mean financial remuneration, but we'll be rewarded with joy as we see the gospel change lives. We'll see the results of our efforts as people are transformed by the good news.

So Paul says to Timothy and to us, 'Reflect on what I am saying.' Reflect on the images of the soldier, the athlete and the farmer.

Acknowledge the dedication required to serve Christ and joyfully persevere, knowing that he and the gospel are worth it.

Are you working hard for God? If your answer is 'no', think about what God requires of you. How does he want you to serve him at church, at work or in your family? If you are already working hard for God, don't waste time seeking praise or thanks; this is the way life is meant to be! Instead, focus on your reward. Think how the gospel is bearing fruit in the lives around you. It's true that we won't always see the difference our service for God is making. But in heaven our reward will be on display for all to see. There will be people there because you shared the gospel with them, you provided a meal at an Alpha course, you prayed for a missionary's work overseas. Hard work now guarantees friends in heaven later!

Day 256

Read 2 Timothy 2:1–13
Key verses: 2 Timothy 2:8–10

....

> [8] *Remember Jesus Christ, raised from the dead, descended from David. This is my gospel,* [9] *for which I am suffering even to the point of being chained like a criminal. But God's word is not chained.* [10] *Therefore I endure everything for the sake of the elect, that they too may obtain the salvation that is in Christ Jesus, with eternal glory.*

Appliances wear out, batteries wear down . . . Not much is built to last these days. What about you? Is endurance a trait you possess?

In these verses and throughout the New Testament, endurance is praised as a key character quality. Peter talks about endurance in the context of persecution (1 Peter 2:20). The apostle James knows the importance of it (James 5:11). While this epistle is being written, John calls for the endurance of the saints, 'those who keep God's commands and hold fast their testimony about Jesus' (Revelation 12:17).

Paul, too, 'chained like a criminal', endures for the sake of Christ. He endures prison, knowing that many of the Praetorian Guard now trust Christ because of his witness (Philippians 1:13). As he reminds the Corinthians, endurance is one of the ways to serve the Lord:

> As servants of God we commend ourselves in every way: in great endurance; in troubles, hardships and distresses; in beatings, imprisonments and riots; in hard work, sleepless nights and hunger.
> (2 Corinthians 6:4–5)

Endurance literally means to stay behind, not to run away when the fight is on. Another word for endurance would be 'stickability'. Jesus himself understood what it meant to endure, and that's why Paul urges us, 'Remember Jesus Christ'. The writer to the Hebrews reminds us, 'For the joy that was set before him [Jesus] endured the cross, scorning its shame, and sat down at the right hand of the throne of God' (Hebrews 12:2).

We are called to endure in the heat and pain of suffering for the gospel. Our endurance is the background against which people will come to faith as the gospel is preached. Paul wouldn't endure the suffering if he didn't believe that the gospel was supremely worth the cost. Nor would he be content to be in prison if that would stop the gospel spreading. But he is convinced that 'God's word is not chained'.

This great truth burns in Paul's heart and helps him to endure. May it burn in ours.

God's Word is not chained. It will do its work in:

- antagonistic offices;
- Islamic countries;
- atheist universities;
- secular societies;
- uninterested friends and family.

So don't despise your chains! You can't begin to imagine how God will use your suffering to spread his love and hope to others. Let God do his work. In the meantime, keep enduring. Live out the gospel with your eyes fixed on Jesus. He endured to save you and he uses your endurance to save others. What a plan!

Day 257

Read 2 Timothy 2:1–13
Key verses: 2 Timothy 2:11–13

....

¹¹ *Here is a trustworthy saying:*
   If we died with him,
      we will also live with him;
   ¹² *if we endure,*
      we will also reign with him.
   If we disown him,
      he will also disown us;
   ¹³ *if we are faithless,*
      he remains faithful,
      for he cannot disown himself.

Life looks better when we have something to look forward to. We can cope with hospital appointments, exams and our daily routine if we know we have a holiday, a meal out with friends or even a favourite TV programme to look forward to.

With these words from an early Christian hymn, Paul encourages us to persevere in our suffering, because we have something to look forward to. Jesus will return soon and take us home to heaven. We can die to self and submit ourselves to God now, because we know heaven is on the horizon. We can endure suffering for the gospel, knowing that one day soon we will reign with God for ever.

Of course, God is faithful to his warnings as well as his promises, because he cannot deny himself. So, 'If we disown him, he will also disown us.' Jesus himself makes this point clear in Matthew 10:32–33: 'Whoever acknowledges me before others, I will also acknowledge before my Father in heaven. But whoever disowns me before others, I will disown before my Father in heaven.' Jesus is talking about those who persistently refuse to acknowledge his sovereignty.

Parables like the foolish virgins and the unfaithful steward in Matthew 25 encourage us to nail our colours to the mast, to live faithfully for God now, ready for Christ's return.

We know there will be times, even as Christians, when we fail God. But thank God that his commitment to us is not based on our fickle character or our performance. God's faithfulness to us is based on his own unchanging and perfect character. Because we can trust his character, we can hold on to his promises and endure through difficult days, waiting confidently for heaven.

Read Revelation 4, 5, 21 and 22. Let your mind wander as you imagine what heaven will be like. Much of the time we are too satisfied with life here to think about heaven. But get into the habit of thinking about it each day. Keep your eyes on the reality that awaits us, the heavenly city we shall one day call 'home'. Let the thoughts of the new heaven and earth give you an eternal perspective on your failure, suffering and heartbreak. Let the reality of the new heaven and earth shape your choices and priorities now. Let the certainty of the new heaven and earth give you strength to endure until the very end.

Day 258

Read 2 Timothy 2:14–19

Key verse: 2 Timothy 2:14

· ·

¹⁴Keep reminding God's people of these things. Warn them before God against quarrelling about words; it is of no value, and only ruins those who listen.

Every now and again, a fad infiltrates the church. Discernment goes out of the window and we are caught up with some overemphasis of an aspect of Christian truth. We are swept along by the crowds and our love of the spectacular. Often, these secondary issues are promoted by brilliant communication, money and publicity. It is easy to start believing that this single issue is all that really matters.

Paul has seen this happen before and he is concerned that we are able to discern between truth and secondary matters. He has seen the damage that these senseless controversies cause, the danger of holding a form of religion but denying its power, and the insidious nature of counterfeit faith. We are not to play games like this when we bring the gospel to the world.

Paul cautions against 'quarrelling about words'. This is when we allow the minutiae to absorb a totally disproportionate amount of time and energy. We judge other Christians by whether or not they give importance to, and a particular interpretation of, this issue. Paul warns that this type of quarrelling 'only ruins those who listen'. The word used here can be translated 'catastrophe'. It is catastrophic for a Christian to pursue some secondary issue as the thing that matters above all else.

The quality that we need is discernment.

Think about the issues that cause controversy in your church. What topics do you and your friends discuss? Are you majoring on the minors? Are you 'quarrelling about words' and letting the minutiae absorb all your time and effort? Ask God for forgiveness. Pray that he will give you discernment so that you can devote yourself to what really matters in his kingdom. Take care how you use your words at home, at work and in your family. Words are more powerful than we realize; we can use them to tear people down or to build them up. Pray that the conversations you have this week with other Christians are edifying and encouraging: 'Let us consider how we may spur one another on towards love and good deeds' (Hebrews 10:24).

Day 259

Read 2 Timothy 2:14–19
Key verse: 2 Timothy 2:15

· ·

¹⁵*Do your best to present yourself to God as one approved, a worker who does not need to be ashamed and who correctly handles the word of truth.*

Do you feel far away from God, indifferent to his commands and distracted by all that's going on around you? Sometimes we wonder why God isn't speaking to us, why we can't hear his voice. Often the answer is simple: we are not spending time in his Word.

God speaks to us in various ways, but primarily through the Bible. If we want to know God's priorities, wisdom, commands and promises, we need to read the Bible. It is not always easy to understand what is written or how to apply it to our context. However, like diligent workers, we must invest time and effort in our study.

For pastors and teachers, the responsibility is immense. The teaching of God's Word must be their central task. They must give it priority in terms of time and energy. The aim of their preaching is not to entertain or please us. God's approval is what counts. But Paul's charge is not just to pastors. This verse applies to all of us. It is vital that we 'correctly [handle] the word of truth', in a way God approves of.

The word that Paul uses for 'handling' literally means 'cutting a straight road'. Remember that this is what John the Baptist had to do to prepare people for Jesus' coming. The prophecy about John was that he would 'Prepare the way for the Lord, make straight paths for him' (Mark 1:3). He was to level the hills and fill the valleys in preparation for Jesus' coming. In other words, his role was to prepare a straight, clear road so that Jesus could have access.

This is what each of us must do. We must 'handle' God's Word in such a way that we prepare a straight road for the Lord to move on. Our job is to dig and dig and compare and ponder and meditate and pray and plumb the amazing depths of the Word. Whenever we read the Bible, either for ourselves or to teach it to others, our task is to cut a straight road: the straight road of truth. The goal is for Christ to have clear and unhindered access to our hearts.

Are you giving God room to move? Are you spending time reading the Bible, making the path straight for the Holy Spirit to speak to you? Are you removing sin and other obstacles, and giving God direct access to your heart?

Think about any Bible teaching that you do. Could God put his stamp of approval on your ministry? Would God approve of the way you handle his Word when you teach others – not manipulating it to say what you want it to say, but allowing it to speak for itself? Are you putting roadblocks in the way of God's truth, or are you cutting a straight road for him to speak to others?

Day 260

Read 2 Timothy 2:14–19
Key verses: 2 Timothy 2:16–19

· ·

¹⁶Avoid godless chatter, because those who indulge in it will become more and more ungodly. ¹⁷Their teaching will spread like gangrene. Among them are Hymenaeus and Philetus, ¹⁸who have departed from the truth. They say that the resurrection has already taken place, and they destroy the faith of some. ¹⁹Nevertheless, God's solid foundation stands firm, sealed with this inscription: 'The Lord knows those who are his,' and, 'Everyone who confesses the name of the Lord must turn away from wickedness.'

'The Lord knows those who are his' – what comforting words! The fact that God has intimate knowledge and a personal relationship with those who belong to him is certainly a truth to cling to in difficult times.

Paul is dealing with false teaching, which he describes as 'godless chatter'. It is godless because it has nothing to do with the truth of God. This chatter leads people into more and more ungodliness, further and further away from God and his holiness.

The issue seems to be that Hymenaeus and Philetus, leading members of the church, are teaching that the 'resurrection has already taken place'. These two have 'departed from the truth', yet, strangely, they still seem to be Christian leaders. Look what the result is: 'they destroy the faith of some' (verse 18). Their false teaching spreads like gangrene.

Paul cautions us to avoid such heresy, to 'turn away from wickedness'. Don't be upset by the godless chatter and false teaching even of leading churchmen. Instead, be strong in your own faith and focus on God's promises: 'God's solid foundation stands firm, sealed with this inscription: "The Lord knows those who are his."'

God assures us that his church, which upholds his truth, is a solid foundation. Paul's quote in verse 19, 'The Lord knows those who are his', is taken from Numbers 16:5 and Korah's revolt against Moses and Aaron. False teachers were challenging their ministry, and these are Moses' words of challenge to the people. Paul uses Moses' quote to remind us that God is the arbiter. It is God's church, and he knows those who are his.

Whatever attacks the church, either from within or from without, Jesus has promised, 'I will build my church, and the gates of Hades will not overcome it' (Matthew 16:18). The church's future and security are protected by God, and he knows each one who is his.

The church is God's best idea. As Paul explains to the Ephesian believers, it is God's way of displaying his wisdom for all to see (Ephesians 3:10). But as the church faces wave after wave of false teaching, it's easy to become disillusioned. It is bewildering to know the wisest way to oppose the godlessness that subtly infiltrates the body of Christ. Don't waste time being disappointed in church leaders or getting sucked into the heresy. Trust God's promise that he has a future for the church. He will protect and sustain it. Pray for your church and its leaders. Pray that you would stay faithful to God's Word and be a source of truth and light in this present darkness.

Day 261

Read 2 Timothy 2:20–26
Key verses: 2 Timothy 2:20–21

· ·

20 In a large house there are articles not only of gold and silver, but also of wood and clay; some are for special purposes and some for common use. 21 Those who cleanse themselves from the latter will be instruments for special purposes, made holy, useful to the Master and prepared to do any good work.

How holy is your life? We may have lots of good qualities and gifts. We may be hard-working, discerning and determined, but if we are not holy, God can't use us.

To help us understand this, Paul describes the image of a house. We are the house and Jesus is the Master. You and I are not our own; we are bought with a price. If we surrender to Christ, he enters our life as Master.

Imagine Fred's fish and chip shop. It has been on the high street for many years. The greasy wallpaper and cracked lino hasn't been changed since the 1990s. Then one day, to everyone's surprise, there is a banner across the window: 'Under new management'. It becomes Fred's fish restaurant. Fred is still there, but he is no longer in charge; he's an employee. The new owner goes round the building pointing out to Fred all the bits that need to be changed. The old tables are thrown out, new wallpaper is put on, more lights set up – which immediately shows up more to be cleaned! It's the same place, but it has undergone a transformation.

It is the same when Christ enters our life. He can only come as owner–manager. Across our life goes the label, 'Under new management', and immediately he has access to every part of our life. Nothing is outside his gaze. He immediately puts his finger on the things that need changing. And as he brings more light, so we see more that needs to be changed.

The cleaning process begins with a major spring clean. To use Jesus' terminology in John 13, we first have a bath and then the constant foot-washing follows. So verse 21 is concerned with purifying. We are made clean by the Word (John 15:3), by confession of sin (1 John 1:9), by asking for washing and renewal (Psalm 51). We must take action about the things that we know to be a major offence to God. This is an ongoing process. The Christian who has a conversion experience but doesn't go in for foot-washing (constant purification) backslides. We have to go on and on, cleaning, purifying, washing and wrestling with the inner nature that disgraces God. Then God can use us.

Have you washed your feet recently? I'm not talking about the big bath of your conversion. Today, have you confessed your sin and asked God to wash you through his Word? Keep short accounts with God; come to him daily for forgiveness. Don't be discouraged: it will be a constant battle to stay clean. The more God shines his light on every part of your life and the more you clean up your heart, the more the dirty stains stand out! Being aware of your sin and the need to repent is actually a good sign. It means that the owner of our house is making progress with the transformation!

Day 262

Read 2 Timothy 2:20–26
Key verse: 2 Timothy 2:22

....

²² Flee the evil desires of youth and pursue righteousness, faith, love and peace, along with those who call on the Lord out of a pure heart.

Are you the only Christian in your office or your family? At times, being a Christian can be an isolating experience. But Paul encourages us to remember that we are never alone in our pursuit of holiness.

There is strength and encouragement to be gathered from belonging to a Christian community. Church provides fellowship; it grounds us; it helps us persevere, knowing we are running the Christian race 'along with those who call on the Lord out of a pure heart'.

There is both a positive and a negative aspect to our pursuit of holiness. On the one hand, we are to 'Flee the evil desires of youth'. Sexual sin is not restricted to young people, but perhaps it is most prevalent among the young. A sexual relationship in the context of committed married love is a beautiful thing and a gift of God. But outside marriage, it is sin. The word 'flee' means to 'run away'. Remember Joseph? He ran from the house when Potiphar's wife tried to trap him. The cost was prison, misunderstanding and accusation, but he did the right thing. We need to flee from youthful passions, to put distance between ourselves and temptation.

This is true for all of us, but it is vital for ministers and church leaders. In 1 Timothy 3:9, Paul says that deacons 'must keep hold of the deep truths of the faith with a clear conscience'. If you are in church leadership, don't get caught out by sexual sin or temptation; make sure you keep your conscience clear.

The other aspect of holiness is to 'pursue righteousness, faith, love and peace'. Thankfully, we don't have to do this in our own strength. The Holy Spirit not only exposes the wrong in our lives, but also develops the fruit of the Spirit in us.

Draw strength from the Holy Spirit and the support of your Christian brothers and sisters as you pursue holiness today.

Imagine yourself running the race of faith. Look around and see the 'great cloud of witnesses' (Hebrews 12:1) cheering you on – heroes from the Bible, perhaps members of your family, church friends, the person who led you to Christ. Notice that this is not a solo race; many others are running alongside you. How can you spur them on? How can you help one another practically to 'flee the evil desires of youth and pursue righteousness'? Start by being authentic: be honest about your struggles, willing to receive godly advice, generous with your encouragement, and determined to seek one another's good. Support one another practically and prayerfully as you see the finish line come into view.

Day 263

Read 2 Timothy 2:20–26
Key verses: 2 Timothy 2:23–26

....

²³*Don't have anything to do with foolish and stupid arguments, because you know they produce quarrels.* ²⁴*And the Lord's servant must not be quarrelsome but must be kind to every-one, able to teach, not resentful.* ²⁵*Opponents must be gently instructed, in the hope that God will grant them repentance leading them to a knowledge of the truth,* ²⁶*and that they will come to their senses and escape from the trap of the devil, who has taken them captive to do his will.*

How do we share the gospel with people? In our generation, when there is so much opposition and apathy, how do we win people for Christ?

As God's servant, we should be 'kind to everyone'. This phrase is only used one other time in the New Testament, in 1 Thessalonians 2:7, where Paul says, 'We were gentle among you, like a nurse taking care of her children' (RSV). The nurse's chief priority is the patient. He or she is not diverted by minor issues. Similarly, in evangelism, we must not be distracted by the many other issues that matter to us. We are not to be 'quarrelsome' (verse 24) and we are to avoid 'foolish and stupid arguments' (verse 23). We must watch our attitudes, behaviour and speech so that there is nothing about us that is a barrier to the gospel.

A nurse is gentle and kind, and goes very carefully. If a bottle of medicine is labelled 'one tablet per day', a nurse doesn't say, 'Well, I'm going to speed up your recovery. Take the whole lot.' And in verse 25 Paul reminds us that 'opponents must be gently instructed'. You don't win people by violent reactions or by mocking them. You win them by patience, love and correcting them with gentleness.

The false teachers of 2 Timothy 2 are won back to the truth by love and care, not by condemnation or confrontation.

Sharing the gospel means that we listen to people. We spend time with them, often over many months, carefully and patiently helping them to understand what is involved in becoming a Christian. Our role is to prepare the way for God by teaching, loving and nursing, so that he in his mercy may perhaps 'grant them repentance'.

Understanding and obeying God's Word is the only way that people can escape 'the trap of the devil'. The picture here is of becoming sober after being drunk or drugged. The world's standards and way of thinking act like a drug, ensnaring us into the devil's net. But it is our privilege to share God's truth with patience, gentleness, skill and love, and to watch friends, family and colleagues find true freedom in Christ.

Think of the non-Christians God has placed in your life: the friend you meet at the gym, the work colleague, the parent at the school gate, your grandchildren. God has given you these people to love and gently share the gospel with. Your life and speech are to be a demonstration of the gospel to them. What a privilege and responsibility! Commit to pray for them daily. Pray for opportunities to speak to them about Christ, to demonstrate his love, and ask the Holy Spirit to work in their hearts to draw them to faith.

Day 264

Read 2 Timothy 3:1–17
Key verses: 2 Timothy 3:10–13

···

[10] You, however, know all about my teaching, my way of life, my purpose, faith, patience, love, endurance, [11] persecutions, sufferings – what kinds of things happened to me in Antioch, Iconium and Lystra, the persecutions I endured. Yet the Lord rescued me from all of them. [12] In fact, everyone who wants to live a godly life in Christ Jesus will be persecuted, [13] while evildoers and impostors will go from bad to worse, deceiving and being deceived.

How do you feel when yet another scandal about the church hits the headlines?

Paul reminds us that there is no point in getting anxious or distressed. From the beginning, there has been worldliness in the church. It is not new for people to be 'lovers of themselves' and 'lovers of money' (2 Timothy 3:2). Consumerism and materialism have always been prevalent. Sadly, it's common for family life to be warped by ingratitude, unholiness, inhumanity, unforgiveness and children's disobedience.

Many are 'lovers of pleasure rather than lovers of God' (2 Timothy 3:4); they fit God in, but not as Lord. The worthlessness of nominal Christianity is revealed as people holding 'a form of godliness but denying its power' (2 Timothy 3:5). In verses 6–7, Paul shares an example of a group of weak women who idolize an influential person in the church, but never accept the truth of the gospel for themselves. In verse 8, he points to false teachers in the church, with corrupt minds and counterfeit faith.

How do we respond to this bleak picture? Paul urges us to meet it with an unswerving commitment to teaching and living truth: 'Do your best to present yourself to God as one approved, a worker who does not need to be ashamed and who correctly handles the word of truth' (2 Timothy 2:15).

Paul calls us to follow his example. He doesn't run after every false trail. Instead, he perseveres with sound teaching, holy conduct and a godly purpose. He practises faith, patience, love and endurance. He accepts persecutions and sufferings as inevitable in the life of a Christian. He ploughs a straight furrow and cuts a clear road. Whatever else is going on in the church, he clings to the truths of the gospel and lives them out.

There has always been worldliness in the church. But don't let worldly leaders or their practices become a role model for you. Don't get sucked into copying what's going on around you. Instead, look for godly examples to follow, people like Paul who preach the gospel and live it out regardless of the suffering. But best of all, keep your eyes on Christ. Let his priorities set the standard for you, his example shape your life and his return help you persevere in this most holy faith.

Day 265

Read 2 Timothy 3:1–17
Key verses: 2 Timothy 3:14–15

∙∙∙

¹⁴But as for you, continue in what you have learned and have become convinced of, because you know those from whom you learned it, ¹⁵and how from infancy you have known the Holy Scriptures, which are able to make you wise for salvation through faith in Christ Jesus.

How often do you read the Bible? It doesn't matter how long you've been a Christian or what ministry you are involved in; we all need to spend time in the Scriptures. It's fundamental to our faith.

After wrestling with all the sidetracks, godless chatter and worldliness in society and the church, Paul urges Timothy to turn back to Scripture. The word translated as 'continue' means settling in permanently. It's the word you use when you arrive at the place where you are going to live, where you're going to unpack. The context suggests that Timothy's faith may have been rocked by the swirling influences around him. Of course, it's easy to be tossed about by theological debates, to be swept along by something new or to allow worldliness to seep into the church. As a countermeasure, Paul urges us to settle in God's Word permanently.

Coming back to Scripture means coming home for Timothy, because that is how he was brought up. From childhood he has 'known' the Scriptures. He was taught about Abraham, Sarah, Moses, Esther and all the many thousands of millions who make up the family of God.

But even if we haven't been brought up in a Christian family, there is still the challenge to 'continue in what you have learned'. The Scriptures make us 'wise for salvation', but their usefulness doesn't stop there. Our goal must be to study the Bible in order to grasp the foundational truths of the Christian faith. This is more than just academic learning. God wants us to live out these truths by the power of the Holy Spirit. It's a lifelong process and an ongoing cycle. As we become more and more 'convinced' of the truth about God, we increasingly learn to trust his Word and rely on his resources to serve and witness. And, not surprisingly, as we live in the good of God's Word, we become more and more convinced that he is trustworthy!

You will never exhaust the Bible and you'll never outgrow it. From the moment you become a Christian until the end of life's race, it is your light, your strength, your manual for living and your ultimate authority. There is no deviation and no graduation, because we never move on from this core element of the faith. Daily time spent with God in his Word is not a luxury, but a necessity. It's what you need to keep yourself centred in God, grounded in his truth and aware of his presence. Take care to set aside time to read the Bible this week. Make it a priority to cultivate this godly habit.

Day 266

Read 2 Timothy 3:1–17
Key verses: 2 Timothy 3:14–15

....

14But as for you, continue in what you have learned and have become convinced of, because you know those from whom you learned it, 15and how from infancy you have known the Holy Scriptures, which are able to make you wise for salvation through faith in Christ Jesus.

When young people look at you, are they attracted to your faith? Do they see you working out your faith with a testimony of commitment, love, worship and joy? Are they inspired by you?

Look again at verses 14–15. Paul encourages Timothy to press on in his faith because 'you know those from whom you learned it'. Timothy's discipleship began in his family with his mother Eunice and grandmother Lois (2 Timothy 1:5). He witnessed their 'sincere faith', not just in Bible reading and church attendance, but also in the way they lived, relaxed, shared and enjoyed life. It seems likely Timothy's father was an unbeliever, but Timothy watched these two women living for God in good times and bad. Their faith had a deep impact on him.

Timothy can also look to Paul, not only as a teacher of the truth, but also as a demonstrator of that truth in his own life. There can be no doubt of Paul's faith. His life is a glowing testimony of his commitment, love, worship and joy.

It's a great tragedy when churches have some cantankerous older people in them who are a disgrace to the gospel. It's damaging when young people can't look to senior Christians in the church and see them on fire for Christ. The greatest contribution that any older Christian can make to the church is to be a glowing example to the young people. Don't allow yourself to be weighed down by bitterness, resentment or disappointment. Instead, determine to trust God with whatever happens in life and press on to Christlikeness. Make your life and faith worth imitating. Choose to leave a legacy of godliness that is an example to those who follow after you.

What spiritual legacy are you leaving? When your children or the young folk in church look at your life, what do they see? For Timothy's mother, life could not have been easy, yet Timothy could see her faith shine. Her trust in God made an indelible impression on his young heart. We can teach young people the truths of the faith, but unless our 'walk' matches up to our 'talk', it won't have any impact. Or rather, it will have a negative impact as our hypocrisy turns them off Christianity. Ask God to help you have integrity: your private thoughts matching your public actions. Pray that you'll be a godly example. This doesn't mean people won't see our flaws and failures, but they will also notice our repentance and our active desire to become more and more like Christ.

Day 267

Read 2 Timothy 3:1–17

Key verses: 2 Timothy 3:16–17

· ·

> [16]*All Scripture is God-breathed and is useful for teaching, rebuking, correcting and training in righteousness,* [17]*so that the servant of God may be thoroughly equipped for every good work.*

Sometimes we treat God's Word like a bag of pick 'n' mix: we choose the verses we like and ignore the rest. Sometimes we try to manipulate Bible verses so that they say what we would like them to say. In essence, many of us are acting as if the Bible is only partly inspired by God, or perhaps not inspired at all!

But Paul explains that 'All Scripture is God-breathed' through the personalities and characters of people: the poets, the historians, the prophets, the psalmists. However, the emphasis here is that God is the initiator. Scripture is from the mind of God, by his Spirit, in his words – or, in a quotation attributed to Gregory the Great, Bishop of Rome in 684, 'The heart of God is in the words of God.'

It is not just the truth that validates Scripture; it is our experience of it. The fact that the Scriptures are constantly an inspiration to me confirms that they are the Word of God. You can turn back again and again to the Word and hear God speak to you through it. Some believers have tried to make a distinction between the Word and the Spirit, and have said, 'The only thing that matters to us is the experience of Christ, not the Bible.' But this is a false dichotomy – we experience Christ through the Scriptures!

J. B. Phillips was not an evangelical when he started translating the New Testament. He worked simply as a translator. But his experience of God in the Bible was profound. He said, 'Translating the New Testament was like rewiring a house with the mains left on.'

It is dangerous to treat the Scriptures as if they are only the words of human beings. We are holding the very Word of God in our hands!

How do you read your Bible? Like a shopper in a supermarket, only picking the verses that suit you? As if it were a newspaper article, only reflecting an individual's opinion? As if you were connected to the main power supply? Reflect on the fact that you are holding the very Word of God in your hands. Do you need to make changes to how you read the Bible? Ask God to show you Christ through the Scriptures. Pray that God would show you how inspired and powerful his Word is. Prepare to be amazed!

Day 268

Read 2 Timothy 3:1–17
Key verses: 2 Timothy 3:16–17

. . . .

> [16]*All Scripture is God-breathed and is useful for teaching, rebuking, correcting and training in righteousness,* [17]*so that the servant of God may be thoroughly equipped for every good work.*

Sometimes, when pressures mount and the constant plate-spinning wears us down, we skip our Bible reading so that we can get on with our 'to-do' list. It seems such a luxury to read the Bible when so much else needs our attention. But, in fact, the opposite is true. It's in studying and meditating on God's Word that we're equipped to handle all that God allows into our lives.

Today, look again at verses 16–17. Paul wants us to grasp this fundamental truth: because the Scriptures are God-breathed, they are the means of completely equipping each Christian.

He explains that the Bible is useful for *teaching*. We need to study the Bible individually and in small groups; we need to hear expository preaching; the Bible must become our authority so that we learn how to please God in all things.

At times, God's Word will be uncomfortable to read because it is useful for *rebuking*. The Scriptures show us what is wrong; they expose the darkness that needs to be brought to light.

The Bible is also useful for *correcting* (*epanorthosis*). This word means 'lifting a person back on his or her feet', restoring them to a true way of living.

Paul goes on to say that the Scriptures are necessary for *training in righteousness*. This means to be made like Christ, conforming to his will and his way in every aspect of life, 'that the servant of God' – the minister, preacher, leader, but also any Christian – 'may be thoroughly equipped'. It is only as we grow in the Scriptures, obeying, learning and responding, that we can truly be complete and thoroughly equipped for the ministry of Christ.

The Bible is God's gift to us. Jesus never took up a pen, but the Holy Spirit was entrusted with bringing the truth to the apostles and, through them, to you and me.

We often fall into the trap of thinking that reading the Bible is a duty rather than a delight. Yes, we will have days when we seem to be going through the motions. But even on those days, God is using his Word to cleanse, refine and equip us. The Bible is God's gift to us to help us navigate our way through life, deal with uncertainties, face hardships, and cope with the demands of ministry and service. Don't cut yourself off from God's voice. Ask him graciously to use his Word to teach, rebuke, correct and train you in righteousness so that you are thoroughly equipped for all that he puts in your path – today and every day.

Day 269

Read 2 Timothy 4:1–22
Key verses: 2 Timothy 4:1–4

· ·

¹In the presence of God and of Christ Jesus, who will judge the living and the dead, and in view of his appearing and his kingdom, I give you this charge: ²preach the word; be prepared in season and out of season; correct, rebuke and encourage – with great patience and careful instruction. ³For the time will come when people will not put up with sound doctrine. Instead, to suit their own desires, they will gather round them a great number of teachers to say what their itching ears want to hear. ⁴They will turn their ears away from the truth and turn aside to myths.

An individual's last words are significant because they tell us what that person's priorities and passions were. Chapter 4 is Paul's last will and testament to Timothy. And, not surprisingly, his major concern is the gospel.

He charges Timothy to 'preach the word'. Timothy has been commanded to follow it, guard it, learn it, teach it to others, and now to preach it. To the world, preaching is folly. Many won't endure sound teaching. They want something new to tickle their ears and are easily led away from the truth and into myths. But, despite this opposition, all who love Christ and believe his Word need to teach and preach it.

'Be prepared in season and out of season.' Be willing to speak God's truth both when it is welcomed and when it's not. Don't desert your post even if the going gets tough.

However, readiness to speak is not an invitation to be arrogant or rude. Paul's charge to Timothy is to 'correct, rebuke and encourage – with great patience and careful instruction'. We need to be able to explain the gospel without being argumentative and loud, allowing God's Word to bring its own comfort and discomfort to people. We need to appeal for conversion and consecration, and steadily to expound God's Word with patience.

Why persevere? Why keep patiently explaining the gospel amid such opposition? Well, Paul gives his charge to Timothy in 'the presence of God and of Christ Jesus'. Ultimately we are all answerable, not to human beings, but to Christ, 'who will judge the living and the dead'. One day we will face Jesus as our Judge, Lord and King. On that day we shall hand back to him our ministries and all that he has entrusted to us.

What are your main priorities in life? Not all of us are preachers, but sharing the gospel should still be a high priority for us. Think about the ministry that God has given you. What opportunities are there to share the gospel? As you serve God today, remember that you are doing it in 'the presence of God and of Christ Jesus'. Imagine the day when you will hand back to God all the fruits of your service. Keep that in your mind as you serve him joyfully, patiently and with great endurance.

Day 270

Read 2 Timothy 4:1–22
Key verse: 2 Timothy 4:5

....

[5] But you, keep your head in all situations, endure hardship, do the work of an evangelist, discharge all the duties of your ministry.

It's common for businesses, charities and even churches to draw up a mission statement. This is a document outlining their core purposes and objectives, which remain unchanged throughout the years. Verse 5 is the mission statement that Paul wants us and his young friend Timothy to live by.

Paul is in his prison cell, in chains, about to be martyred for the gospel, and he has poured out his soul in this letter to Timothy. Now he sums up his message to Timothy and to the whole church of God – past, present and future – in this four-point charter:

- *Keep your head in all situations.* Don't lose your nerve. Don't be blown away by every new fad. Rather, hold on to the core truths of the faith. Keep Christ at the centre of your life and ministry.

- *Endure hardship.* The great theme of 2 Timothy 1 – 2 is that suffering is inevitable for the servant of God. Like Timothy, when we are afraid, we need to remember that God has given us a spirit of love, power and self-discipline. Are you prepared to endure suffering?

- *Do the work of an evangelist.* We aren't all given the spiritual gift of evangelism, but each one of us is charged to do the work of an evangelist. We need to be prepared, ready to take every opportunity to share our faith. This is the main task of every Christian and every church. The gospel is our primary focus.

- *Discharge all the duties of your ministry*. Whatever task God has given you, see it through to the end. God has entrusted this task to you and he has equipped you for it. Please him by remaining faithful to your calling until the very end. Don't lose your steam in later years!

Often at New Year we set ourselves targets for the coming months – frequently to lose weight! But we don't often spend time thinking about our goals for life. However, we all have them, and, consciously or unconsciously, they shape our values, behaviour and priorities. Be honest with yourself and ask: what are your core objectives, the goals you think are important and want to achieve? How does your mission statement compare to Paul's? What about adopting Paul's mission statement as your own? Memorize his key principles, repeat them often, and pray for God's help in applying them to every situation.

Day 271

Read 2 Timothy 4:1–22
Key verses: 2 Timothy 4:6–8

....

> [6] *For I am already being poured out like a drink offering, and the time for my departure is near.* [7] *I have fought the good fight, I have finished the race, I have kept the faith.* [8] *Now there is in store for me the crown of righteousness, which the Lord, the righteous Judge, will award to me on that day – and not only to me, but also to all who have longed for his appearing.*

We don't often spend time thinking about our own mortality, and yet it is the one certainty of life. Paul's farewell to Timothy is a challenge to us, regardless of the inevitable distractions, temptations and disappointments, to press on and to finish life's race well.

Paul sees himself as a sacrifice, a drink offering to his Lord. 'The time for my departure is near' – the word used is *analusis*, 'setting free'. It's the word used when a boat leaves harbour. For Paul, this is not a reluctant, but rather a purposeful departure. He's packed, ready to go, looking forward to all that lies ahead.

The three pictures in verse 7 are from chapter 2. The retiring soldier – 'I have fought the good fight.' The retiring athlete – 'I have finished the race.' The retiring farmer – 'I have kept the faith', which literally means 'gone on', like a farmer fulfilling a farming task.

All that Paul has encouraged Timothy to do is demonstrated in his own life. Like Christ, Paul has run the race set before him. He has endured suffering and despised the shame. His legs are in chains as this letter is being written. Now the joy is set before him, and Paul is looking forward to hearing the righteous Judge say 'Well done' to his righteous servant.

So often, we resist pouring ourselves out to God as an offering; we'd rather live for our own goals and dreams. We're not ready to depart for heaven; it seems too much of a wrench to leave our loved ones and earthly treasures. We so easily lose sight of the fact that death is the greatest liberation, the start of a more real and precious life. We get caught up in preserving our lives when sacrifice is the only true way to live. Keep your eyes focused on eternity, on Christ's return and on your heavenly reward. And pray that as you wait, you would persevere, so that you will be able to say, 'I have fought the good fight, I have finished the race, I have kept the faith.'

Day 272

Read 2 Timothy 4:1–22
Key verses: 2 Timothy 4:9–21

· ·

⁹*Do your best to come to me quickly,* ¹⁰*for Demas, because he loved this world, has deserted me and has gone to Thessalonica. Crescens has gone to Galatia, and Titus to Dalmatia.* ¹¹*Only Luke is with me. Get Mark and bring him with you, because he is helpful to me in my ministry.* ¹²*I sent Tychicus to Ephesus.* ¹³*When you come, bring the cloak that I left with Carpus at Troas, and my scrolls, especially the parchments.*

¹⁴*Alexander the metalworker did me a great deal of harm. The Lord will repay him for what he has done.* ¹⁵*You too should be on your guard against him, because he strongly opposed our message.*

¹⁶*At my first defence, no one came to my support, but everyone deserted me. May it not be held against them.* ¹⁷*But the Lord stood at my side and gave me strength, so that through me the message might be fully proclaimed and all the Gentiles might hear it. And I was delivered from the lion's mouth.* ¹⁸*The Lord will rescue me from every evil attack and will bring me safely to his heavenly kingdom. To him be glory for ever and ever. Amen.*

¹⁹*Greet Priscilla and Aquila and the household of Onesiphorus.* ²⁰*Erastus stayed in Corinth, and I left Trophimus ill in Miletus.* ²¹*Do your best to get here before winter. Eubulus greets you, and so do Pudens, Linus, Claudia and all the brothers and sisters.*

Church life is full of highs and lows. There are times of joy and celebration when ministries are flourishing, people come to Christ and others are being strengthened in their faith. There are also times of sadness when the church family suffers a bereavement or there is a harsh disagreement between believers.

Paul has experienced a full range of circumstances throughout his ministry. He was deserted by Demas who 'loved this world' and opposed by Alexander the metalworker. He's known the joy of friends such as faithful Luke and practical Mark. He's had practical needs for clothing and books. He has endured difficulties and times of living simply. He's received love and encouragement from various Christian families. But he's also experienced the sadness of watching a friend face illness. And at the end of his life, in a lonely prison cell, he is eager to see the young pastor Timothy again.

The constant in these turbulent times has been that 'the Lord stood at my side and gave me strength'. Like Paul, each of us can draw on the strength of Christ as we serve him. People will come and people will go, but God's resources are unlimited, inexhaustible and incomparable.

Pray through all the circumstances you will face today. Remember, the Lord is at your side, giving you strength. Entrust your loved ones to God's care and keeping. Often there is nothing we can do to alleviate the difficulties they face, but remember that the Lord is at their side. His resources are more than adequate for their deepest needs. Pray that they would be aware of God's strength today.

Day 273

Read 2 Timothy 4:1–22
Key verse: 2 Timothy 4:22

· ·

²² *The Lord be with your spirit. Grace be with you all.*

How does Paul close his letter? With a formulaic 'God bless'? No. To Timothy specifically, he writes in the singular, 'The Lord be with your spirit', and to the whole church reading this letter he adds, 'Grace be with you all.'

This is Paul's final encouragement to Timothy. This whole letter is to urge him and us to live the one life that we have been given totally committed to the Lord, prioritizing the core truths of the faith and the centrality of the gospel. This is Paul's own aim. Indeed, he sees himself not only chained in prison, but, more importantly, also chained to Christ, chained to the core truths of the faith and chained to the gospel. His main focus in this letter is to urge us to share his priorities and become better equipped, cleansed and trained for service. In this way, by God's mercy, at the end of our lives we might be able to say, 'I have fought the good fight, I have finished the race, I have kept the faith.'

In the light of this, to the church, Paul writes, 'Grace be with you all.' Of course, the cross is the greatest demonstration of God's grace to us. He sent his Son to die in our place, to bring us salvation and forgiveness of sins. But daily we see evidence of God's grace overflowing in our lives. We can't earn this grace; it is totally unmerited. Our only response can be to give ourselves wholeheartedly to God's service.

As we do that, each of us can go into our day knowing that the Lord is with our spirit. We are not alone. We are not expected to serve God in our own strength. Our devotion to God is not a matter of simply trying harder. Whatever challenges, temptations and doubts we face, the ever-present, all-powerful God the Holy Spirit is with us, enabling and energizing our spirit. Yield yourself to his control, rely on his strength, submit to his authority and live daily for his pleasure.

What has God been saying to you through Paul's letter to Timothy? Pray through the truths that God wants you to cling to, the priorities he wants you to invest your life in, the commands he wants you to follow and the promises he wants you to believe in.

God did not just show his grace to us at Calvary. Every day our lives are flooded with his grace and mercy. He's sent his Spirit to be with us, even now, strengthening, comforting, guiding, equipping and keeping us. We are truly blessed! Use Psalm 103 as a response as you worship God for who he is and all that he has done for you.

> Praise the LORD, my soul;
>   all my inmost being, praise his holy name.
> Praise the LORD, my soul,
>   and forget not all his benefits.
> (Psalm 103:1–2)

For further study

If you would like to do further study on 2 Timothy, the commentaries listed here may be useful:

- R. Kent Hughes and Bryan Chapell, *1–2 Timothy and Titus: To Guard the Deposit*, Preaching the Word (Crossway, 2012).

- Walter L. Liefeld, *1 & 2 Timothy, Titus*, NIV Application Commentary (Zondervan, 1999).

- John Stott, *The Message of 2 Timothy: Guard the Gospel*, The Bible Speaks Today (IVP, 1999).

- Charles R. Swindoll, *Insights on 1 & 2 Timothy, Titus*, Swindoll's Living Insights New Testament Commentary (Tyndale, 2014).

If God has fed you through your study of the book of 2 Timothy, why not buy the individual Food for the Journey on 2 Timothy and give it to a friend (available from ivpbooks.com)?

Day 274

Read Psalm 2
Key verses Psalm 2:7–9

....

> ⁷I will proclaim the LORD's decree:
>   He said to me, 'You are my son;
>   today I have become your father.
> ⁸Ask me,
>   and I will make the nations your inheritance,
>   the ends of the earth your possession.
> ⁹You will break them with a rod of iron;
>   you will dash them to pieces like pottery.'

Our final group of three sets of devotions, from Ruth, Colossians and Revelation, has as a connecting theme the person of Jesus Christ: born from David's line (Ruth; see Matthew 1:5), supreme in creation and redemption (Colossians 1:15–23), the one to whom the church must listen, the ruling Lamb who was slain (Revelation 22:1). As Paul says in 2 Timothy 2:8, 'Remember Jesus Christ, raised from the dead, descended from David. This is my gospel . . .'

If we were to trace this messianic hope to its source, the spring comes bubbling out of the ground in 2 Samuel 7 and cascades in Psalm 2. The psalm splits neatly into four sections:

• *Verses 1–3*. The scene is in some ways familiar to today – the world of international conflict, the scheming of political and military leaders, anger, posturing, alliances. But in other ways it is very different. For the scheming is 'against the LORD and against his anointed [king]' (verse 2), the king we now know as Jesus Christ.

• *Verses 4–6*. As Christians we may feel isolated, beleaguered, losers. We hear of opposition to God and persecution of his people all over the world. This psalm assures us that this is far from the ultimate reality or our destiny, regardless of what may be happening at the moment. The nations' scheming and plotting is futile (verse 1). The Lord 'laughs'. This is not the mockery of a cruel tyrant, for the Lord loves the world, but it does highlight the stupidity of opposition to the one true God. The nations should be justly fearful because he has 'installed' his 'king' on Zion (verses 5–6).

- *Verses 7–9*. We hear the voice of the king, supremely the voice of King Jesus, the one who has always been God's Son (Matthew 3:17) but who, in one sense, is fully declared God's Son by the resurrection, so that hidden glory becomes publicly known (Acts 13:33; Romans 1:4). Ultimately, every nation will belong to him, every nation will be subject to his rule, though that has started now (Matthew 28:18–20; Revelation 12:10).

- *Verses 10–12*. Everyone needs to respond aright to this king. The blessing of delighting in God's law (Psalm 1:1; see Day 1) mirrors the blessing of taking refuge in God's Son (Psalm 2:12); the destruction of the way of the wicked (Psalm 1:4–6) mirrors the destruction of the way of those who reject God's Son and King (Psalm 2:12).

If you're despairing as you look out on a world that rejects the Lord and his anointed, remember the reality. Jesus is indeed the King who reigns. Remember that there's no refuge *from* him, only *in* him; that it's impossible to run *from* him, so we should urge all to run *to* him before it's too late.

> Every eye shall now behold him,
> Robed in dreadful majesty;
> Those who set at naught and sold him,
> Pierced and nailed him to the tree,
> Deeply wailing, deeply wailing, deeply wailing,
> Shall the true Messiah see.
> (Charles Wesley, 'Lo! He Comes with Clouds Descending', 1758)

Bring those in authority and those who reject the King before our gracious God.

Introduction

Ruth

Alistair Begg

Ordinary people in the hands of an extraordinary God

Bad news.

Newspapers, social media and TV bombard us with it constantly.

Is there any hope, any ray of light, in the midst of this chaos?

We are not the first believers to have asked this question.

The story of Ruth takes place when the Israelites are living in the Promised Land after the death of Joshua. Instead of heeding the warnings God gave through Moses and Joshua, the people rebelled against God's rule. They served foreign gods and were taken over by their enemies, and each time, in response to their cries for deliverance, God sent them a judge. 'But when the judge died, the people returned to ways even more corrupt than those of their ancestors, following other gods and serving and worshipping them. They refused to give up their evil practices and stubborn ways' (Judges 2:19). A vicious cycle ensued, and by the end of the book of Judges, brutality and immorality were commonplace: 'In those days Israel had no king; everyone did as they saw fit' (Judges 21:25).

It was in the midst of this whirl of social, religious and moral chaos that the book of Ruth was written, reminding the children of God that there was hope, that a remnant of true faith remained, that God was continuing to work in the lives of ordinary people as they went about their daily chores.

The book takes our gaze off the heroes. There are no judges here: no Samson, no Gideon, no Jephthah, no amazing story of Rahab. Instead, God is preoccupied with a woman called Naomi. We are given an intimate glimpse into her family life, and we witness, firsthand, God's providence.

The book ends with a genealogy pointing forward to King David who was a 'man after God's heart' (see 1 Samuel 13:14), who would lead the people wisely. But it ultimately points us to Jesus, the great 'son of David' (Matthew 1:1) – the Hope of the Nations, the Light of the World, the Prince of Peace.

Today, we see glimmers of hope and chinks of light breaking through the darkness. But chaos will prevail until Jesus returns to reign. In the meantime, don't lose heart. Be encouraged, for God is still pre-occupied with people like Naomi. In the midst of everything that unfolds in life, in the mystery of his purpose, God sets his love and affection on unlikely people, in unlikely contexts, doing routine things. Quite surprisingly, he chooses to work his eternal purposes out in the ordinariness of the lives of ordinary people.

That includes you.

Day 275

Read Ruth 1:1–5
Key verse: Ruth 1:1

....

> ¹ *In the days when the judges ruled, there was a famine in the land. So a man from Bethlehem in Judah, together with his wife and two sons, went to live for a while in the country of Moab.*

The result of a blood test, the loss of a loved one, a rash decision, and life can unravel very quickly.

Here we find life falling apart in the space of five verses. The catalyst was a famine. God warned his people that famine would be one of the consequences if they failed to obey his commands (Deuteronomy 32:24). The writer doesn't tell us how the famine came about. It could have been caused by the invasion of enemy forces or by a drought. Whatever the cause, the famine is certainly the result of the providential dealings of God. It provides the backdrop for the story, introducing us to this little family of four.

When people heard the word 'famine', they knew that it had often proved to be a moment of great historical significance. 'There was a famine in the land', remember, and Abraham went down to Egypt to live there (Genesis 12:10). 'There was a famine in the land' and Isaac went to Abimelek, the king of the Philistines (Genesis 26:1). It was on account of famine in the land that Jacob and his sons ended up in Egypt (Genesis 42 – 46). In each case, the famine proved to be pivotal, a turning point in the lives of the people of God, as it was in the life of the young man in the story Jesus told in Luke 15:11–32.

Outsiders might have just thought, 'We're down on our crops,' or, 'It's exceptionally rainy', but God's children need to recognize that he is working things out in the very details of history according to the eternal counsel of his will. And in each case of famine, not least of all in this story, his servants are protected and provided for.

Is your life unravelling? It doesn't take much in the way of extra pressure, bad news, family strife or financial woes to feel as if life is fraying at the seams. Most of us are well acquainted with hardship. Suffering, in various guises, is part of our human experience. However, have you considered that this particular time of challenge in your life might be pivotal? A God-appointed time of spiritual growth, a crucial opportunity to exercise faith or develop deeper bonds of fellowship with other Christians? Don't waste your poor health, your unemployment, your financial struggles or your grief. However bleak the backdrop of your life, however difficult your present situation, seek God. Be open and ready to learn the lessons he wants to teach you in this season of your life.

Day 276

Read Ruth 1:1–5
Key verses: Ruth 1:1–2

....

¹*In the days when the judges ruled, there was a famine in the land. So a man from Bethlehem in Judah, together with his wife and two sons, went to live for a while in the country of Moab.* ²*The man's name was Elimelek, his wife's name was Naomi, and the names of his two sons were Mahlon and Kilion. They were Ephrathites from Bethlehem, Judah. And they went to Moab and lived there.*

Are you a decisive person? Many of us struggle with decision-making. When you don't know the outcome, when the future is uncertain, how can you be sure you are making the right decision?

Try to imagine Elimelek and his wife lying in bed, chatting to each other before they fall asleep. He asks, 'What do you think we should do?'

Naomi replies, 'What do you think God wants us to do?'

Elimelek says, 'God wants us to use our brains. He wants us to be discriminating. He wants us to lean on our understanding.'

Naomi says, 'Don't you think it might be good if we trusted in the Lord with all our hearts and trusted him with this famine? Shouldn't we trust him to direct our paths?'

Elimelek sighs and rolls over. 'I'm going to sleep.'

The next morning, he announces to his family that they are leaving to go to Moab.

The author doesn't criticize Elimelek's decision. In one sense it is understandable – he's supposed to provide for his family and he has the means to move to a better place. But from another perspective, it is astonishing. The family are living in Bethlehem, which means 'the house of bread'. Elimelek's own name means 'My God is king'; he knows that God's people are to be in God's place if they are going to live under God's rule and blessing. He also knows that the people of Moab are on the list of those with whom the people of God should not associate. Yet he still goes.

All of us, if we are honest, have made decisions and then thought, 'Maybe, if I had the chance again, I would do that differently.' But the wonderful thing is that, through it all and over it all, God remains in control.

You may be living with the consequences of bad decisions; most of us are. But don't bow to Satan's pressure to keep raking over them. Jesus' death on the cross has paid for your sins and wiped the slate clean. You are forgiven, and God looks at you clothed with the righteousness of Christ. Whatever poor choices you have made in the past, God is still in control. He does not waste any of your tears or suffering, but uses them for your good and his glory.

Moving forward, resist the urge to do just whatever seems right to you. If you have decisions to make, bring them before God. Pray, ask for wisdom, listen to God speaking through his Word and, if it is appropriate, ask the advice of mature believers whom know you well.

Day 277

Read Ruth 1:1–5
Key verse: Ruth 1:2

....

²*The man's name was Elimelek, his wife's name was Naomi, and the names of his two sons were Mahlon and Kilion. They were Ephrathites from Bethlehem, Judah. And they went to Moab and lived there.*

When they were younger, my children used to love hearing what their names meant and why we had chosen them.

The fact that these verses are full of names indicates the importance of what is going on here. As the story unfolds, we'll see that each name carries special significance in the purposes of God.

Elimelek's name means 'My God is king'. That's interesting! If he knows the Lord really is king – and therefore faithful and trust-worthy – then why is he leaving Bethlehem? It causes quite a stir when Naomi returns to Bethlehem with Ruth (Ruth 1:19), so we can assume that it causes a stir when the family leave. They are Ephrathites, an important clan, probably one of the more wealthy families. So everyone notices what they do and that Elimelek fails to live up to his name.

Naomi's name means 'lovely', 'pleasant', 'delightful'. This is significant because of all the bitterness she will experience through losing her husband and two sons.

The boys' names, Mahlon and Kilion, come from two Hebrew words. We might call them 'sickly' and 'pining'. A clue as to what will happen to them!

Names are significant, and throughout this story we shall see God living up to his name and remaining true to his covenant promises.

Many of us are named after someone – perhaps a family member or a celebrity whom our parents admired. Often a name has special connotations for the person who chooses it.

God's name also has special significance; it represents the sum total of his character and power. The Bible often talks about the significance of the name of God:

> The name of the LORD is a fortified tower;
>   the righteous run to it and are safe.
> (Proverbs 18:10)

> Some trust in chariots and some in horses,
>   but we trust in the name of the LORD our God.
> (Psalm 20:7)

> Do not worship any other god, for the LORD, whose name is Jealous,
> is a jealous God.
> (Exodus 34:14)

> No one is like you, LORD;
>   you are great,
>   and your name is mighty in power.
> (Jeremiah 10:6)

> Salvation is found in no one else, for there is no other name under
> heaven given to mankind by which we must be saved.
> (Acts 4:12)

Today, meditate on the name of God and all that it means. Surely, our only valid response is to say with King David:

> I will exalt you, my God the King;
>   I will praise your name for ever and ever.
> (Psalm 145:1)

Day 278

Read Ruth 1:1–5
Key verses: Ruth 1:3–5

••

> ³ Now Elimelek, Naomi's husband, died, and she was left with her two sons. ⁴ They married Moabite women, one named Orpah and the other Ruth. After they had lived there about ten years, ⁵ both Mahlon and Kilion also died, and Naomi was left without her two sons and her husband.

Do you enjoy being the centre of attention? Some of us like the limelight, while others prefer to blend into the background.

If this story were a film, Naomi would certainly take centre stage. Notice that the camera is on her a lot. Usually in the Bible, the women are introduced in the light of the men. Here the man is introduced in the light of his wife; he is described as the husband of Naomi. This is interesting and purposeful.

Naomi is first left without her husband, and then without her two sons. Of course, they have married, and their marriages held the prospect of children coming along; however, not only have no children been born, but now the potential fathers are dead as well. As a result, the family name and the family's future are over. And the importance of the name for posterity's sake is at the heart of the culture of the people of God and at the very heart of this story. Naomi finds herself absolutely hopeless and bereft – the family name has found itself in a cul-de-sac, and she is a lonely widow living as an alien in a male-dominated foreign place minus the protection and provision of a husband or sons.

So much is going on at this point in Israel's history, yet the focus of God is on a sad and lonely lady. This is the only book in the Bible entirely devoted to the domestic story of a woman. It shows the amazing compassion and empathy of God for the backstreets and side alleys and the people who feel themselves to be last, lost and left out. God says, 'The whole world is going on, but I am with you. I hem you in behind and before. I have set my hand upon you.' That is the kind of God we worship.

God has got the whole world in his hands. That's true. But he also has you in the palm of his hands. God is sovereign over the affairs of state, international politics and the weather systems, yet he cares intimately and always for you. You may feel bereft like Naomi, with no silver lining to your circumstances, no way out, nothing to look forward to, but God's hand is upon you. As you bring your circumstances before God today, meditate and rest in the truth of David's words in Psalm 139:1–6.

> You have searched me, Lord,
>   and you know me.
> You know when I sit and when I rise;
>   you perceive my thoughts from afar.
> You discern my going out and my lying down;
>   you are familiar with all my ways.
> Before a word is on my tongue
>   you, Lord, know it completely.
> You hem me in behind and before,
>   and you lay your hand upon me.
> Such knowledge is too wonderful for me,
>   too lofty for me to attain.

Day 279

Read Ruth 1:1–5
Key verses: Ruth 1:3–5

. . . .

> ³ Now Elimelek, Naomi's husband, died, and she was left with her two sons. ⁴ They married Moabite women, one named Orpah and the other Ruth. After they had lived there about ten years, ⁵ both Mahlon and Kilion also died, and Naomi was left without her two sons and her husband.

What did you expect when you first became a Christian? Did you imagine that life would be easier somehow? These opening verses of the book of Ruth serve as an antidote to the notion that the path of faith is strewn with rose petals. Neither the Bible nor human experience encourages us to think in this way.

In the course of verses 1–5, the family find the food that they so desperately need, but they also face circumstances that are dreadfully painful. No details are given, just the bald facts.

With the loss of her husband and two sons, Naomi has to grapple with God's providence in an intensely personal way. And as the drama unfolds, her view of the world remains firmly fixed on the God of Abraham, Isaac and Jacob. She doesn't regard herself as being held in the grip of some kind of blind, impersonal force. Nor does she view her life as if she were a cork bobbing around on the ocean of chance.

Naomi would be a Westminster Confession girl, describing God's providence as 'his most holy, wise and powerful preserving and governing of all his creatures and all their actions' (Westminster Shorter Catechism, 1674). Or, along with the theologian Berkhof, she might say, 'God's providence is the continued exercise of the divine energy whereby the Creator preserves all his creatures, is operative in all that comes to pass in the world and directs all things to their appointed end' (*Systematic Theology*, Banner of Truth Trust, 1971).

Naomi is going to discover, and has now discovered from the vantage point of eternity, that God is doing something far bigger than anything she could ever see. The story before us is a wonderful exposition of Romans 8:28: 'And we know that in all things God works for the good of those who love him, who have been called according to his purpose.'

What is the good that God is working towards? It is the separating out of a people and the transforming of a people into the likeness of his Son. He does use famine. He does use failure. He does use the silly, obviously bad things we do, in order to accomplish his final strategy for us.

Don't be surprised or knocked off course when you face difficulties. Trust in God's providence. In your struggles, unanswered questions and grief, know that 'every detail in our lives of love for God is worked into something good' (Romans 8:28, MSG). Or as William Cowper the hymn writer said,

> Judge not the Lord by feeble sense,
> But trust Him for His grace;
> Behind a frowning providence
> He hides a smiling face.
> His purposes will ripen fast,
> Unfolding every hour;
> The bud may have a bitter taste,
> But sweet will be the flower.
> (William Cowper, 'God Moves in a Mysterious Way', 1774)

Day 280

Read Ruth 1:6–9
Key verses: Ruth 1:6–7

• •

⁶When Naomi heard in Moab that the LORD had come to the aid of his people by providing food for them, she and her daughters-in-law prepared to return home from there. ⁷With her two daughters-in-law she left the place where she had been living and set out on the road that would take them back to the land of Judah.

When you are away from home, do you like to keep in touch?

Naomi, an alien living in a foreign place, obviously keeps in touch with her homeland. She is a bit like Nehemiah, who was constantly hearing news about the state of Jerusalem when he was in Susa. One day, news reaches Naomi in Moab that the Lord has come to the aid of his people. Or, as one translation puts it, 'the LORD had visited his people' (ESV).

On this occasion, he has come to their aid by providing food. We shouldn't miss the simplicity of this statement. When you live in the world of Asda or Tesco, it is possible to forget that God is the provider of everything we have. He makes the rain fall and the sun shine and so on. That is why it is imperative for us to make sure we don't get to the point in our Christian lives where saying grace is perfunctory. We need to guard against taking things, even ordinary things, for granted. Instead, we should recognize God's provision and care each day.

Through the poor, painful tears of Naomi's disappointment, the sun shines in, the news comes and she can testify to Calvin's wise words: 'It is an absurd folly that miserable men take upon themselves to act without God when they cannot even speak except he wills' (*Institutes of the Christian Religion*, Hendrickson Publishers Inc., 2007).

Today open your eyes, pause and take stock of all the instances of God's grace and favour on your life.

Practise being thankful for his care and provision in the big as well as the small things – the clothes you wear, the smile on your child's face, or the words of encouragement someone gives you.

Start to see God's fingerprints all over your life – you arrived at work today not because the train was on time, but because God protected you on your journey; there is food on your table not because you did an online shop, but because God provided the rain and sun to grow the crops; you got a job not because you passed exams, but because God gave you skills and enabled you to use them; you were able to care for a sick loved one today not because you are kind and patient, but because God gave you his strength and compassion.

Worship *Jehovah Jireh* – the God who provides.

Day 281

Read Ruth 1:6–10
Key verses: Ruth 1:8–9

• •

> ⁸ *Then Naomi said to her two daughters-in-law, 'Go back, each of you, to your mother's home. May the* Lord *show you kindness, as you have shown kindness to your dead husbands and to me.* ⁹ *May the* Lord *grant that each of you will find rest in the home of another husband.'*
>
> *Then she kissed them goodbye and they wept aloud.*

We learn a lot if we listen.

Of the eighty-five verses in this book, fifty of them are dialogue. These conversations reveal a jumble of expectations, emotions, affirmations and misgivings.

The provision of food means that Naomi and her two daughters-in-law prepare to head to Judah (verse 6). And at some point along the road, this dialogue takes place. Naomi says goodbye to Ruth and Orpah, and tries to persuade them to return to Moab.

We can picture the raw emotion of the scene: the three women wrapped in each other's arms, weeping together, Naomi pleading with the younger women to leave and them clinging to her.

Some commentators are convinced that Naomi is wrong to urge the girls to return to Moab. They suggest that she is concerned about how it will look if she turns up in Bethlehem with these two foreigners. It will certainly highlight the fact that not only have her family lived among the people of Moab, but they have also gone one step beyond and married their inhabitants. These commentators portray Naomi as a selfish, cantankerous, bitter old lady.

However, the language of verses 8–9 suggests that Naomi's concern is prayerful and God-centred. She is not concerned about her own well-being, but with their well-being and security – a security that is ultimately found in Yahweh but is, in the immediate term, expressed in their mothers' homes and in a husband's embrace.

There is a selflessness here about Naomi as she kisses her daughters-in-law and asks the Lord to show them kindness. The word is *hesed*, God's covenant love. She is commending them ultimately into the care of God. What else can we do for our children and those near and dear to us? The covenant love of God, says Alec Motyer, 'is that wonderful love that combines the warmth of God's fellowship with the security of God's faithfulness'.

Life is full of tearful goodbyes – a boyfriend or girlfriend moving to a different city for work or study; children growing up and leaving home; loved ones dying. Goodbyes of the temporary and more permanent kind are part and parcel of real life. When we are apart from friends and family, there is often little we can do to help them with their daily lives and struggles. One thing – the best thing – we can do is to commend them to the covenant love of God. Though we cannot be with them, we can be sure that God's faithfulness will sustain and keep them. Today, affirm with the psalmist:

> The Lord is good and his love endures for ever;
>   his faithfulness continues through all generations.
> (Psalm 100:5)

Day 282

Read Ruth 1:8–13
Key verses: Ruth 1:11–13

....

> [11] But Naomi said, 'Return home, my daughters. Why would you come with me? Am I going to have any more sons, who could become your husbands? [12] Return home, my daughters; I am too old to have another husband. Even if I thought there was still hope for me – even if I had a husband tonight and then gave birth to sons – [13] would you wait until they grew up? Would you remain unmarried for them? No, my daughters. It is more bitter for me than for you, because the Lord's hand has turned against me!'

Perhaps Naomi thinks she has persuaded her daughters-in-law to return home. She hears them saying, 'We will go back . . .'. But then they add, '. . . with you to your people' (verse 10). And so Naomi launches into a little speech in verse 11, urging them to be sensible.

Her comments may seem strange, but she is referring to the custom of levirate marriage where, if a man dies childless, his brother is supposed to marry the widow to produce heirs to continue the family line. Naomi is saying this can't happen – even if she were to conceive that night, Orpah and Ruth would be too old by the time the boys became men.

Apparently, Naomi is perfectly prepared to believe that God is king over the affairs of her daughters-in-law, even if they are to go back into enemy territory. But when she thinks about her own circumstances, she can only see old age and loneliness beckoning. She recognizes that Ruth and Orpah have lost their husbands and are therefore not free from grief, but adds, 'It is more bitter for me than for you, because the Lord's hand has turned against me!'

Notice her theology. She is not saying, 'God turned his back and everything went wrong,' or, 'God is as surprised by this as I am.' She is not suggesting that the affairs of life are out of control. She affirms God's sovereign control, in that he brings to pass all that he wills. Hubbard says of her statement, 'Here we have bitter complaint cloaked in firm faith' (Robert Hubbard, *The Book of Ruth*, Eerdmans, 1995, p. 113). She recognizes that famine, exile, bereavement and childlessness have all proved to be in God's will for her.

Naomi is a good reminder to us that God is too wise to make mistakes; he is too kind to be cruel.

The commentator Atkinson describes faith not as a still light, but like a nursery mobile above a baby's cot. Imagine the image. When you hang a mobile in a child's room, at times one of the characters or pieces will be in the shadows, and then, as it moves around, it will come out into the sunshine. This is the life of faith for a believer.

Is your life in the light or the shadows? If you are crying out in bitter complaint, know that you are not alone. Believers like Naomi, the prophets Isaiah and Jeremiah, David in the Psalms, and even Jesus in Gethsemane, cried out to God. Like them, will you hold firmly on to faith, trusting that our God is too wise to make mistakes, too kind to be cruel?

Day 283

Read Ruth 1:11–18
Key verses: Ruth 1:14–15

. . . .

¹⁴*At this they wept aloud again. Then Orpah kissed her mother-in-law goodbye, but Ruth clung to her.*
   ¹⁵*'Look,' said Naomi, 'your sister-in-law is going back to her people and her gods. Go back with her.'*

Do you wear your heart on your sleeve? Do you appreciate talking about your feelings? Or are the emotions of this story already exhausting you?

No-one needs to guess how these women are feeling. Their weeping, kissing and clinging make it blatantly obvious. When Naomi finishes her little speech, once again there are tears. Verse 14: 'At this they wept aloud again.' We have this whole scene acted out by the side of the road as, back and forth, these women cry, kiss and say goodbye.

Then the great divide comes. 'Then Orpah kissed her mother-in-law goodbye.' This is the final exchange of kisses and goodbyes. It is a defining moment. Orpah decides to be obedient to Naomi, to make the sensible choice.

What are we to make of this? Can we fault her for doing what Naomi urged? Is she walking away from the Living God? Is this an illustration of a borrowed faith that she decides not to make her own in the moment of opportunity? Or is it possibly an illustration of someone who decides to return to alien territory to live under the shadow of Yahweh's protection? I don't know, and neither do you.

One day, in heaven, we will be able to say, 'Excuse me, has anyone seen Orpah? I'm looking for her because I don't know what happened on that roadway. I don't know if she was saved.' Wouldn't it be tremendous if Orpah's reasoning was, 'Naomi, you have convinced me so much that Yahweh is my protector and my provider that I will go back into that alien environment, and under the shadow of his wings I will rest secure'?

One day, after a lifetime of kisses and tears, it will be our final goodbye. We don't know which goodbye will be our last, so we should make each conversation, each opportunity for the gospel count.

You may never know the impact your life has had on the people in the Alpha/Christianity Explored course, the prodigal who wandered from the faith, the mum at the school gate or the colleague in the office. Imagine if there will be people in heaven because you spoke to them about Jesus? In the raw emotion of everyday life – the hellos and goodbyes, the tears and the laughter, the joys and the sadness – live out your faith. Let people see you trusting God in good times and bad. Pray that your life would be like a signpost, pointing other people to God.

Day 284

Read Ruth 1:11–18

Key verses: Ruth 1:16–18

· ·

¹⁶ But Ruth replied, 'Don't urge me to leave you or to turn back from you. Where you go I will go, and where you stay I will stay. Your people will be my people and your God my God. ¹⁷ Where you die I will die, and there I will be buried. May the LORD deal with me, be it ever so severely, if even death separates you and me.' ¹⁸ When Naomi realised that Ruth was determined to go with her, she stopped urging her.

These verses are often quoted at weddings. But we shouldn't miss their deeper, more profound significance.

The cast is dwindling – there are only two left. Elimelek, Kilion and Mahlon didn't have speaking parts. So far, Naomi has been doing all the talking. Orpah's brief response provides the velvet from the jeweller's store on which the diamond, this remarkable opening statement of Ruth's, shines.

Orpah is still in the distance; she isn't quite round the bend. Naomi urges Ruth to catch up with her, to go while she still has a chance. Ruth's eyes are following Orpah, but her hands are clinging to Naomi. Her heart is pulling her all over the place, her mind is formulating this little speech, and the radical decision she makes reverberates throughout redemption history.

It is fascinating that the same fact that causes Orpah to return causes Ruth to stay. Orpah processes Naomi's childlessness and decides that she will leave, desiring to become a wife. Ruth processes the information and decides that she will stay, committed to being a daughter. The same circumstances, the same information, a momentous decision: 'Wherever you go, I'm there.'

Ruth isn't just agreeing to go on a short-term mission project. Her statement means goodbye to Orpah, goodbye to familiarity, goodbye to everything that has meant security to her, and hello to the great unknown. She is choosing an uncertain future as a widow in a land where she knows no-one. She is agreeing to stay with Naomi 'till death do us part'. Even in death she promises to be buried with Naomi's people; that's a huge commitment. And her deep conviction comes not only because of Naomi herself, but also on account of Naomi's God.

God is still looking for people of deep conviction, those who will nurture a 'till death do us part' kind of commitment.

Can you say these words to Christ?

'I'm committed to you through thick and thin. Where you go, I'll go. What you do, I'll do. Whom you love, I will love. I'm with you not only to death but through death.'

Perhaps, like Ruth, you need to leave something or someone behind to follow Christ. There will be sacrifices; the journey of faith is costly. Even today, your commitment to God will be challenged and tested. But hold on to God, persevere in your faith and don't be afraid to love him wholeheartedly. Because, like Ruth, you know what kind of God he is.

Day 285

Read Ruth 1:15–22
Key verses: Ruth 1:19–21

••

¹⁹*So the two women went on until they came to Bethlehem. When they arrived in Bethlehem, the whole town was stirred because of them, and the women exclaimed, 'Can this be Naomi?'*

²⁰*'Don't call me Naomi,' she told them. 'Call me Mara, because the Almighty has made my life very bitter. ²¹I went away full, but the LORD has brought me back empty. Why call me Naomi? The LORD has afflicted me; the Almighty has brought misfortune upon me.'*

Village life doesn't lend itself to anonymity. If you have a baby, pass exams or even just change your bathroom suite, people tend to know about it!

Ruth and Naomi were never going to be able to slip into Bethlehem quietly. But perhaps even they are surprised at their reception. Women are nudging each other and saying, 'Is that Naomi? She's looking old, isn't she? Do you think she's lost weight? What happened to the boys? Who's the girl she's with?'

'They say she's a daughter-in-law.'

'Really? I'm going to ask her.'

So they go up to her and say, 'Is this really you, Naomi?'

And Naomi replies, 'That's my name, but not my experience. *El-Shaddai* has taken me down a bitter path. Full I went away; empty he has brought me back.'

Again, in this dialogue, Naomi's honesty is striking. No hiding her feelings, no pretending about her life, no attempt to sweep it all aside or maintain a stiff upper lip. Presumably walking into the town and seeing the old familiar places brings back all kinds of memories. Maybe the quick sighting of a friend who's grown old, the glimpse of young men who were contemporaries of her boys, and the paths she walked on in the early days with Elimelek all combine to overwhelm her emotionally. But she deals with her pain theologically. She says, 'Oh, God. You are the Almighty One. Famine, bereavement, sadness and loneliness, yes. But you are the Almighty One, you are *El-Shaddai*. I can leave the explanations and the responsibilities with you.'

Take a deep breath and step back from your current situation. Stop searching for explanations, stop grappling with doubt, stop being sidetracked by other people's questions and opinions. Instead, focus on God. Write down all you know and have experienced of his character: he is all-powerful, all-present, all-knowing and all-sufficient.

Today, choose to rest in his love and faithfulness and say with Naomi, 'But you are the Almighty One; you are *El-Shaddai*. I can leave the explanations and the responsibilities with you.'

Day 286

Read Ruth 1:15–22

Key verse: Ruth 1:22

....

22 So Naomi returned from Moab accompanied by Ruth the Moabite, her daughter-in-law, arriving in Bethlehem as the barley harvest was beginning.

Have you ever watched a TV series, desperate to know the outcome, only for the finale to end on a cliffhanger?

After all the sadness and grief, chapter 1 ends with similar intrigue. Ruth and Naomi arrive in Bethlehem 'as the barley harvest was beginning'. Signs of life and hope are appearing, and Bethlehem is finally living up to its name.

If this story were a film, the background music for the first five verses would be a lament, perhaps a lone piper. But now the sun is forcing its way through the clouds; it is shining through the fields of barley; there's the inkling of a new day. The music changes; the lament ends, the melody line picks up and more strings fill the background. When God is at work, even hopelessness may prove the passageway to fresh starts and new opportunities.

What chapter 1 eventually says to us is that he who is King of the nations has the affairs of the world under his control. The Lord God omnipotent reigns. It may not always seem so, but it is so, and he who is King of the nations is also Lord of the ordinary. So don't overlook the simple stuff – food on your table, companionship, tears, honest questions – and in it all, the awareness that God is sustaining and guiding his children until, at last, the darkness is dispelled. Because, ultimately, the goodbyes of this chapter prepare us for the goodbye of death, and we are waiting for the dawning of the bright and blessed of days, when we shall see Christ in all his fullness.

Can you imagine that day? When the darkness fades, the clouds split open and Christ returns in all his glory; when your grief pales into insignificance in the beauty of his presence; when hope gives place to sight and your tears are wiped away once and for all. You know the final scene, the grand finale, of God's redemption story, so don't be discouraged. You feel the loss of your health, job or loved one keenly, but have you ever considered it was meant to be that way, that the pain has purpose? Perhaps pain and grief are means God uses to train our eyes on the horizon, to keep us looking forward to that eternal hope, and to speed its coming.

> Praise be to the God and Father of our Lord Jesus Christ! In his great mercy he has given us new birth into a living hope through the resurrection of Jesus Christ from the dead, and into an inheritance that can never perish, spoil or fade. This inheritance is kept in heaven for you, who through faith are shielded by God's power until the coming of the salvation that is ready to be revealed in the last time.
> (1 Peter 1:3–5)

Day 287

Read Ruth 2:1–3
Key verse: Ruth 2:2

....

²And Ruth the Moabite said to Naomi, 'Let me go to the fields and pick up the leftover grain behind anyone in whose eyes I find favour.'

When we see someone huddled asleep in a shop doorway or begging on the streets, we are often quick to make assumptions. Usually, we are wide of the mark.

The same applies to Ruth and Naomi. These two women are not poverty stricken as a result of indolence. They are not back in Bethlehem because they have made poor choices and bad decisions or been lazy. They are commendable, particularly this girl Ruth.

We don't know when she formed the plan that now unfolds. We don't know whether she and Naomi talked about their poverty and Yahweh's care for the poor as they walked along the road to Bethlehem.

If they had that conversation, it obviously wasn't a theoretical one. What Ruth is to discover is that God's law, in keeping with his concern for the helpless, the poor and the sojourner, has long made provision for the needy. God stipulated that the poor are not to be exploited (Deuteronomy 24:14), but to be paid daily (Deuteronomy 24:15) and shown justice (Exodus 23:6). A Year of Jubilee was also instituted so that, every seven years, the land would be left un-ploughed and the poor could help themselves to food from it (Exodus 23:11).

We read about another of God's plans to help the poor in Leviticus 23:22:

> When you reap the harvest of your land, do not reap to the very edges of your field or gather the gleanings of your harvest. Leave them for the poor and for the foreigner residing among you. I am the Lord your God.

Picking up the leftover grain from the fields was how those on the margins of society survived. And perhaps it was the sights and sounds of the barley harvest that stirred Ruth into action.

Because God is concerned for the poor, he expects his people to be equally concerned. No matter how prosperous they are, they are to treat individuals like Ruth and Naomi with a compassion that is representative of the compassion of God.

What poverty looks like and how we alleviate it may have changed, but God's expectations of his people haven't.

We talk about 'compassion fatigue' as if the relentless media images of human suffering somehow make us immune to people's needs. Yes, the need is great and sometimes we wonder what difference our small contribution makes. But don't give up on compassion! Again and again, the Bible tells us that God is compassionate (Psalm 86:15), and we his people are to mirror his character and priorities. Compassion is faith in action; it sets us apart as Christ's followers and commends the gospel powerfully (John 13:35). 'Therefore, as God's chosen people, holy and dearly loved, clothe yourselves with compassion' (Colossians 3:12). Put on compassion today – don't leave home without it!

Day 288

Read Ruth 2:1–3
Key verse: Ruth 2:2

• •

²And Ruth the Moabite said to Naomi, 'Let me go to the fields and pick up the leftover grain behind anyone in whose eyes I find favour.'

Can you imagine Ruth's thoughts as she wakes up that first morning in Bethlehem?

No doubt her heart and mind are flooded with all kinds of cares and concerns. But instead of lying in bed, wallowing in self-pity, Ruth gets up and says to Naomi, 'Let me go to the fields and pick up the leftover grain behind anyone in whose eyes I find favour.'

Let's look again at the importance of this verse. Ruth doesn't look at her mother-in-law and say, 'What am I supposed to do now?', or, worse still, 'So what have you got planned for me, Naomi? This is where you live; I am not from here.' Nor does she suggest that it is time for Naomi to get up and start working. No, she goes out on a limb. She risks being ostracized as a foreigner, perhaps even being harmed in the company of the workers. In this she provides a wonderful illustration of a principle that is increasingly absent in our culture: care for the elderly. We need to care for those who have invested their lives in us, who nurtured us and who, in many cases, now find themselves living in poverty or isolation. Any of us who are tempted to give short shrift to the notion of honouring our fathers and mothers, and our extended responsibilities to aunts and uncles, can certainly derive no support from the example of Ruth.

The initiative of Ruth is not only attractive, but definitely also instructive. Up in the morning, she's out to do what she can do. She knows that God will provide, but she knows that he does not routinely provide in a vacuum. She knows that God is sovereign, but she is coming to understand that his sovereignty takes into account her decisions and endeavours.

She walks out in the morning, aware of the fact that what she needs more than anything is grace and favour.

No doubt you have heard the story about the man who, when out walking, fell down the side of a cliff. He cried out to God to save him. When the lifeboat came, he refused to jump in; when the rescue helicopter came and lowered a rope, he didn't grab it; instead he believed that God would save him. The point is, of course, that God rarely works in a vacuum. He expects us to use the means at our disposal, to exercise initiative and to work hard, all the time trusting in his sovereignty and seeking his grace and favour. Consider your own situation. What resources and support has God provided? In what ways could you be taking initiative and working hard? Take action today, and at each step seek God's grace and favour.

Day 289

Read Ruth 2:1–3
Key verses: Ruth 2:1, 3

. . . .

> ¹*Now Naomi had a relative on her husband's side, a man of standing from the clan of Elimelek, whose name was Boaz . . .*
> ³*So [Ruth] went out, entered a field and began to glean behind the harvesters. As it turned out, she was working in a field belonging to Boaz, who was from the clan of Elimelek.*

'It just happened!' That's a cry we often hear from our children when they have had an accident or got into some kind of trouble.

And it just happens that Ruth ends up working in Boaz's field.

With a very light touch, the author has introduced us to Boaz in verse 1. He is a relation in Elimelek's clan and 'a man of standing'. He is a man whose influence isn't tied only to his financial resources (which are to become apparent), but also to his moral integrity.

And, amazingly, Ruth finds herself in Boaz's field. What are the chances of that? There isn't a big sign that says, 'Boaz's field'. In fact, the vast acreage would be divided up into allotments and everybody would have their little bits and pieces. The owners know where they are, but a stranger wouldn't know whose field is whose. Ruth just launches into the first field she can. The King James Version of verse 3 says: 'Her hap was to light on a part of the field belonging unto Boaz.' It just happens that way. She could have gone somewhere else, but she goes there.

One of the things it is important for us to hold on to is the fact that God can overrule the freedom of our choices. Remember Joseph? His brothers were jealous, not because God made them jealous, but because they were bad rascals. They sold Joseph to Ishmaelite traders who transported him into captivity to sell him for a profit. The brothers were acting of their own volition. The Ishmaelites were acting of their own volition. And what was God doing? All of this, in the freedom of their choice, he was using according to the eternal counsel of his will to ensure that Joseph would be in Egypt to be able to provide for the very brothers who had disdained him with jealous hatred.

It is truly beyond our ability to comprehend. So what we should do is put our hands over our mouths and bow before God.

How the sovereignty of God and the freedom of human choice interface is a mystery. But we must hold these truths in tension and remember:

> What is before us? We know not whether we shall live or die, but this we know, that all things are ordered and sure. Everything is ordered with an unerring wisdom and unbounded love, by Thee O God, who art love.
> (Charles Simeon, 1759–1836)

Don't say, 'It just happened.' Today, look out for God's guidance and the means he uses to order your path. Recognize and rejoice in divine coincidences.

Day 290

Read Ruth 2:1–7
Key verses: Ruth 2:4–5

....

> ⁴*Just then Boaz arrived from Bethlehem and greeted the harvesters, 'The Lᴏʀᴅ be with you!'*
>
> *'The Lᴏʀᴅ bless you!' they answered.*
>
> ⁵*Boaz asked the overseer of his harvesters, 'Who does that young woman belong to?'*

If you work in an office, factory or lab, does the atmosphere change when the boss arrives? If you are the boss, do you notice your employees shuffling uncomfortably or shutting down conversations when you appear?

Notice what happens when Boaz arrives on the scene. He greets his workers with a blessing, 'The Lᴏʀᴅ be with you', and they call back, 'The Lᴏʀᴅ bless you!' These are not formulaic greetings, but they express Boaz's godly character, his kindness to his employees and their appreciation of him. What a wonderful place to work!

Boaz clearly knows his workers well. He immediately spots the new girl working in his field and asks his foreman about her. Interestingly, the man responds by giving him a detailed and honest report, under-lining their effective working relationship.

This story has something to say about the importance of employer–employee relationships. If you are a boss, you have a huge respon-sibility for the way you behave among your people. Likewise, how employees respond is of great significance.

How does your work life – whatever that looks like for you – reflect your love for God?

If you go to work, you have a ready-made mission field. Many of us rub shoulders with the same people for more than eight hours every day – what an opportunity to be salt and light, pointing people to Jesus (Matthew 5:13–16). How we work, how we treat people, the values we promote – all of it – can be used by God to commend the gospel.

Whether you are the boss, the lowest employee in the organization or a volunteer for a charity, remember that you are ultimately serving your heavenly master, so 'whatever you do, whether in word or deed, do it all in the name of the Lord Jesus, giving thanks to God the Father through him' (Colossians 3:17).

Consider how Paul's words apply to you:

> Servants, do what you're told by your earthly masters. And don't just do the minimum that will get you by. Do your best. Work from the heart for your real Master, for God, confident that you'll get paid in full when you come into your inheritance. Keep in mind always that the ultimate Master you're serving is Christ. The sullen servant who does shoddy work will be held responsible. Being a follower of Jesus doesn't cover up bad work.
>
> And masters, treat your servants considerately. Be fair with them. Don't forget for a minute that you, too, serve a Master – God in heaven.
> (Colossians 3:22 – 4:1, MSG)

Day 291

Read Ruth 2:4–10
Key verses: Ruth 2:8–10

....

[8]*So Boaz said to Ruth, 'My daughter, listen to me. Don't go and glean in another field and don't go away from here. Stay here with the women who work for me.* [9]*Watch the field where the men are harvesting, and follow along after the women. I have told the men not to lay a hand on you. And whenever you are thirsty, go and get a drink from the water jars the men have filled.'*

[10]*At this, she bowed down with her face to the ground. She asked him, 'Why have I found such favour in your eyes that you notice me – a foreigner?'*

Sometimes we are actually quite surprised when God answers our prayer requests.

It has been a matter of hours since Ruth left Naomi. Her last words to her mother-in-law were, 'Let me go and find favour.' And now, in verse 10, she bows before Boaz and asks, 'Why have I found such favour?'

Boaz has noticed her in the field; he has heard about her background, humility and hard work, and introduces himself. He says, 'I don't want you to go anywhere else. Stay in my fields. Follow along with the girls. You'll be safe here.' Ruth's response in verse 10 indicates the tenderness that must have marked his directives, because she bows her face to the ground in humility. The hopes of the morning have been more than fulfilled. The circumstances are way beyond what she could have asked or even imagined.

We don't find Ruth congratulating herself on her endeavours or for picking out the right field in which to work. She knows she just 'happened' to be there. Furthermore, she is a foreigner. She has worshipped other gods, and would still be doing so if it were not for the intervention of the God of Abraham, Isaac and Jacob in her life when she met Naomi's family. As Ruth reflects on this light that has shone into her darkness, it is thankfulness and humility that are expressed in her very posture. Thankful people are humble, and humble people are thankful; these traits sleep in the same double bed!

Ruth's question ought to be on the lips of every believer, when we come before the One who has made provision for us and under whose protective custody we live: 'Why have I found such favour?'

When you stop to think about it, the examples of God's favour on your life are endless. But today, spend time thanking him for his great gift of salvation:

Remember that at that time you were separate from Christ, excluded from citizenship in Israel and foreigners to the covenants of the promise, without hope and without God in the world. But now in Christ Jesus you who once were far away have been brought near by the blood of Christ.
(Ephesians 2:12–13)

Day 292

Read Ruth 2:11–16
Key verses: Ruth 2:13–16

. . . .

13 'May I continue to find favour in your eyes, my lord,' she said. 'You have put me at ease by speaking kindly to your servant – though I do not have the standing of one of your servants.'

14 At mealtime Boaz said to her, 'Come over here. Have some bread and dip it in the wine vinegar.'

When she sat down with the harvesters, he offered her some roasted grain. She ate all she wanted and had some left over. 15 As she got up to glean, Boaz gave orders to his men, 'Let her gather among the sheaves and don't reprimand her. 16 Even pull out some stalks for her from the bundles and leave them for her to pick up, and don't rebuke her.'

Who or what are you taking refuge in?

We don't like to admit it, but all of us take refuge in something; we seek security and protection in our job, family, reputation, even money.

The distinguishing feature of Ruth's life is that her refuge is in Yahweh.

Boaz has noticed Ruth's kindness to Naomi, so he prays for her, in verse 12: 'May the Lord repay you for what you have done. May you be richly rewarded by the Lord, the God of Israel, under whose wings you have come to take refuge.'

In a sense, Boaz answers his own prayer by welcoming Ruth at the meal, offering her roasted grain and making sure she has enough to take home. Boaz points us forward to Jesus, the great provider, the one who intervenes in the lives of those who are poor, needy and alone.

Ruth's circumstances are uncomfortable, and yet Boaz speaks kindly to her (verse 13). She faces the possibility of antagonism, but he brings her under the jurisdiction of his protection, and so under the Lord's protection. And she is amazed by this – such comfort, such kindness. Especially as she doesn't even have the standing of one of his servant girls. She is not thinking of entitlement. She regards the intervention of Boaz as an act of unmerited favour. She has no standing, but is brought into the protection and provision of a man of standing, who is prepared to give her all she needs and more.

Jesus is our man of standing, able to give us all we need and more.

Whatever your concerns or struggles, take refuge in Jesus today. He is your protector and provider; nestle in the shadow of his wings. He is the only one able to give you all you need – and so much more! Join the psalmist in praise:

How priceless is your unfailing love, O God!
    People take refuge in the shadow of your wings.
(Psalm 36:7)

Whoever dwells in the shelter of the Most High
    will rest in the shadow of the Almighty.
I will say of the Lord, 'He is my refuge and my fortress,
    my God, in whom I trust.'
(Psalm 91:1–2)

Day 293

Read Ruth 2:17–23
Key verses: Ruth 2:19, 22–23

• •

[19] *Her mother-in-law asked her, 'Where did you glean today? Where did you work? Blessed be the man who took notice of you!'*

Then Ruth told her mother-in-law about the one at whose place she had been working. 'The name of the man I worked with today is Boaz,' she said . . .

[22] *Naomi said to Ruth her daughter-in-law, 'It will be good for you, my daughter, to go with the women who work for him, because in someone else's field you might be harmed.'*

[23] *So Ruth stayed close to the women of Boaz to glean until the barley and wheat harvests were finished. And she lived with her mother-in-law.*

I wish I could have been there to see Naomi's eyes when Ruth comes along the road.

She sends her off in the morning with the general idea that she will glean in the fields. And when Ruth comes back, she can barely stand up with all the grain she's carrying. Then it is just as you'd imagine; all those questions. 'Where did you glean?' 'Where did you work?' Eventually, Ruth calms Naomi down and tells her all about her day.

These two women are committed to one another; their lives are woven together. Notice Ruth relaying all Boaz has said to her, and Naomi's motherly instinct in urging Ruth to stay in Boaz's field where she will be protected. Ruth doesn't reply, 'I'll do what I want; I don't need you.' No, she does what her mother-in-law says, gleaning until the barley and wheat harvests are finished.

And look how the chapter finishes: 'And she lived with her mother-in-law.' The author is not telling us about their living arrangements, but wanting us to notice how good it is that they love each other. How good that they live together in peace. How good that they discover together the provision of God. How wonderful that, when their lives are so marked by poverty, they should be introduced to plenty. How fantastic that Naomi, Mrs Pleasant, who has been on such a bitter path, is being warmed up again by the sunshine of God's love.

Have you got a Ruth–Naomi relationship with anyone? Have you got someone you share life with, who celebrates God's grace with you and prays for you regularly? Most of us have good Christian friends, but will you take your friendship to a deeper level? Find ways to share your spiritual journey – pray together, share Bible verses or talk about the opportunities God is giving you at work or at home to live for him – and spur each other on to godliness.

As iron sharpens iron,
  so one person sharpens another.
(Proverbs 27:17)

Let us consider how we may spur one another on towards love and good deeds, not giving up meeting together, as some are in the habit of doing, but encouraging one another – and all the more as you see the Day approaching.
(Hebrews 10:24–25)

Day 294

Read Ruth 3:1–8
Key verses: Ruth 3:1–4

....

[1] *One day Ruth's mother-in-law Naomi said to her, 'My daughter, I must find a home for you, where you will be well provided for.* [2] *Now Boaz, with whose women you have worked, is a relative of ours. Tonight he will be winnowing barley on the threshing-floor.* [3] *Wash, put on perfume, and get dressed in your best clothes. Then go down to the threshing-floor, but don't let him know you are there until he has finished eating and drinking.* [4] *When he lies down, note the place where he is lying. Then go and uncover his feet and lie down. He will tell you what to do.'*

This scene should come with a warning: 'Don't try this at home'!

No mother today would suggest this as a plan of action for her daughter going off to college. But our social and cultural context is very different. Expectations, requirements and obligations within marriage, courtship and interpersonal relationships were different on almost every level in twelfth-century-BC Palestine.

Nevertheless, even in its time, this is an audacious plan. Naomi is trusting God and believing in the character of Boaz as she tries to arrange Ruth's marriage. Boaz is a man of standing, true, but he is still just a man, and the best of men are men at best. We could spend a long time reflecting on whether this is a good idea or not. You can perhaps imagine Ruth's eyes widening as Naomi explains the sheer bravado needed to implement this risky plan.

Having said that, while we may not be as ingenious as Naomi, we shouldn't overlook the privilege and responsibility of helping our young people find life partners. Today, many thousands of people sign up to internet dating sites to find someone compatible with whom to spend their lives. This represents a crying need in our culture. So, if you are able, host meals and social events where, in the company of many others, singles can meet. Many of us can be thankful to friends who helped us in this way.

If only a marriage could be arranged by lying down at someone's feet! Relationships are complex. Even if, like Naomi, God prompts you to take action to pursue a relationship, prayer needs to be the bedrock.

- If you are divorced, bereaved or have never married, pray that your primary focus would be on God – now and in any prospective relationship.
- If you are a parent, pray for your children's salvation. Pray that they would be faithful to God whether they are called to singleness or marriage. Pray also for their prospective marriage partners – that God would keep them pure and devoted to him.
- If you are married, pray that your marriage would be God-centred and God-glorifying.

Day 295

Read Ruth 3:1–8
Key verses: Ruth 3:3–5

....

> ³ *Wash, put on perfume, and get dressed in your best clothes. Then go down to the threshing-floor, but don't let him know you are there until he has finished eating and drinking.* ⁴*When he lies down, note the place where he is lying. Then go and uncover his feet and lie down. He will tell you what to do.'*
> ⁵*'I will do whatever you say,' Ruth answered.*

'I will do whatever you say.' Most parents would be thrilled to hear those words!

In chapter 1, Ruth showed her devotion to Naomi by not doing what she said, by not returning home to Moab. Here in chapter 3, she shows her devotion to Naomi by doing *exactly* what she says.

Naomi is following the law of Moses. The law made provision for those who had become destitute as a result of the death of a spouse. When property was sold in order to ease the poverty, God's law stipulated that a kinsman redeemer would purchase it to secure the property for the impoverished family. This also ensured that the land of Israel would remain within the families of Israel. In the same way, the brother or another close relative would marry the widow in order to produce a child, so as to continue the family name. This is referred to as levirate marriage. As Boaz has been identified as a kinsman redeemer, it seems wise to Naomi to approach him.

Ruth understands exactly what this plan is about; it is not a fool's errand. She has her whole future ahead of her, but she is not thinking about herself or the type of man she would like to marry. She is thinking about what is best for Naomi. 'So she went down to the threshing-floor and did everything her mother-in-law told her to do' (verse 6). But let's not romanticize this scene. There is nothing sexual or sensual about lying on the floor by a pile of grain. This is not an attractive proposition! It is obedience that takes Ruth there.

'I will do whatever you say.' If earthly parents are thrilled to hear those words, imagine how God, our heavenly Father, feels when we set aside our preferences and concerns and determine to obey him wholeheartedly. Perhaps there is a command he is asking you to obey, a promise he wants you to cling to or a place he's sending you to. Will you obey him today, not because it suits you or benefits you in some way, but simply because it delights God's heart?

Day 296

Read Ruth 3:6–14
Key verses: Ruth 3:9–13

....

⁹'Who are you?' he asked.

'I am your servant Ruth,' she said. 'Spread the corner of your garment over me, since you are a guardian-redeemer of our family.'

¹⁰'The LORD bless you, my daughter,' he replied. 'This kindness is greater than that which you showed earlier: you have not run after the younger men, whether rich or poor. ¹¹And now, my daughter, don't be afraid. I will do for you all you ask. All the people of my town know that you are a woman of noble character. ¹²Although it is true that I am a guardian-redeemer of our family, there is another who is more closely related than I. ¹³Stay here for the night, and in the morning if he wants to do his duty as your guardian-redeemer, good; let him redeem you. But if he is not willing, as surely as the LORD lives I will do it. Lie here until morning.'

What do you think Ruth and Boaz looked like?

We may imagine Ruth to be very pretty and Boaz to be a distinguished older gentleman, but, actually, we are never told. It is their characters, not their appearances, that are recorded.

'The mouth speaks what the heart is full of' (Matthew 12:34). Notice how quickly Boaz speaks about the Lord: 'The LORD bless you,' he says. He also expresses kindness to Ruth, calling her 'my daughter', a wonderful tenderness that acknowledges the significance of their age difference. He then commends her kindness to Naomi in leaving Moab. But he recognizes that this marriage proposal is taking kindness to a whole new level. Ruth could marry for love or for money, but the fact that she is on the threshing-floor in the middle of the night, making this proposal on the strength of family loyalty, is an expression of *hesed* love. Ever since her arrival in Bethlehem, people have remarked on her noble character.

The pace of the story now slows right down, and into the drama comes the possibility that the marriage we have been holding our breath for might not happen. Boaz explains that he would gladly marry Ruth, but there is a legal technicality: a kinsman redeemer closer than him. His honesty and integrity could put a stop to Naomi's plan. Boaz's number-one concern is, 'What is the right thing to do?' Even if the situation does not end up as they hope, Boaz is determined to do the right thing.

How would people describe you? Do your godly speech and choices get you noticed? Are you known for doing the right thing even if it costs you? Today:

- Be still and ask God to reveal the areas of your inner life you need to work on.
- Ask the Holy Spirit for help and opportunities to develop a godly character.
- Say 'no' to self and 'yes' to Christ's will.

Set this as a pattern each day, and your character will increasingly display the fruit of the Spirit (see Galatians 5:22–23).

Day 297

Read Ruth 3:9–18
Key verses: Ruth 3:15–17

••

¹⁵*[Boaz] also said, 'Bring me the shawl you are wearing and hold
it out.' When she did so, he poured into it six measures of barley
and placed the bundle on her. Then he went back to town.*

*¹⁶When Ruth came to her mother-in-law, Naomi asked, 'How
did it go, my daughter?'*

*Then she told her everything Boaz had done for her ¹⁷and
added, 'He gave me these six measures of barley, saying, "Don't
go back to your mother-in-law empty-handed." '*

Why does Boaz give Ruth the barley?

Ruth's early-morning adventures could raise questions of inappropriate behaviour. But by carrying the barley, she looks as though she
is just finishing the night shift.

Yet the gift of the barley is more than just a cover-up. Boaz's comment,
'Don't go back to your mother-in-law empty-handed', should remind
us of Naomi's great statement in 1:21: 'I went away full, but the LORD
has brought me back empty.'

There are two kinds of emptiness represented in the life of Naomi:
the emptiness of childlessness and the emptiness of hunger as a
result of famine. With the provision of this grain in amazing abundance, Boaz is saying to Naomi through Ruth, 'You can stop worrying
about what you are going to eat; all that emptiness is dealt with.'

But the Hebrew text in 1:21 can also connote childlessness. If it can
imply that in chapter 1, it can do so here as well. The grain is a suitable
symbol of offspring to come. The commentator Hubbard says that
'the seed to fill the stomach was promise of the seed to fill the
womb' (Robert Hubbard, *The Book of Ruth*, Eerdmans, 1995, p. 226).

Ruth has arrived home with a bundle for her and Naomi to enjoy, and there is the prospect of the arrival of another little bundle in the near future!

This big bundle represents God's answer to the dilemma to which Naomi could see no answer when she left Moab. She urged Orpah and Ruth to leave her because she had no future; she was empty, with no possibility of that emptiness being filled.

But as she listens to Ruth, she realizes that God is able to do exceedingly and abundantly beyond all she can ask or imagine.

God is the same yesterday, today and for ever (Hebrews 13:8). He is always caring and working on behalf of those who love him. If he could satisfy an empty, barren widow like Naomi, surely he can intervene in your situation. Stop letting worry dictate how you feel; instead, determine to trust God with your circumstances. Look to him alone to fill and satisfy you. Put your hope in God, for he 'is able to do immeasurably more than all we ask or imagine' (Ephesians 3:20).

> Blessed are those whose help is the God of Jacob,
> whose hope is in the Lord their God . . .
> (Psalm 146:5)

Day 298

Read Ruth 3:7–18

Key verses: Ruth 3:13–14, 16–18

....

¹³ 'Stay here for the night, and in the morning if he wants to do his duty as your guardian-redeemer, good; let him redeem you. But if he is not willing, as surely as the LORD lives I will do it. Lie here until morning.'

¹⁴ So she lay at his feet until morning, but got up before anyone could be recognised . . .

¹⁶ When Ruth came to her mother-in-law, Naomi asked, 'How did it go, my daughter?'

Then she told her everything Boaz had done for her ¹⁷ and added, 'He gave me these six measures of barley, saying, "Don't go back to your mother-in-law empty-handed." '

¹⁸ Then Naomi said, 'Wait, my daughter, until you find out what happens. For the man will not rest until the matter is settled today.'

Are you a 'big-picture' person or do you enjoy dealing with detail?

For a moment, look up from the details of this story and the everyday lives of these two women, and consider the bigger picture it is pointing to.

Naomi's ingenious plan has been carried out to perfection by Ruth. What Naomi prayed would be part and parcel of Ruth's and Orpah's lives is about to be answered in a far more wonderful way than she could have conceived. In the freedom of the actions of these individuals, God's providence has been at work, using even wrong or strange choices to conform everything to the eternal counsels of his will.

As we await the final instalment of the story, we see how Boaz points forward to the Lord Jesus. For Jesus Christ is our kinsman redeemer, becoming like us, identifying with us in every way and yet without sin. And when we, like Ruth, cast ourselves at the feet of Jesus, depending on his mercy, aware of the fact that we are outsiders, he grants forgiveness, he welcomes us with a steadfast love, and he loads us down with his benefits. In the Lord Jesus we are granted one benefit after another. Boaz takes Ruth to himself, sharing his life and abundance with her. By redeeming us, Jesus makes us his bride; we have a Saviour to whom we may go and for whom we may live.

You are loaded down with benefits. It doesn't always feel like it, because sorrow and worry often cloud our focus. But today, remind yourself of this truth, rehearse God's blessings on your life, say them out loud, write them down. Physically and spiritually, bow at Jesus' feet, signalling your complete dependence on him for all things. And as the psalmist encourages us:

> Praise the LORD, my soul;
>   all my inmost being, praise his holy name.
> Praise the LORD, my soul,
>   and forget not all his benefits –
> who forgives all your sins
>   and heals all your diseases,
> who redeems your life from the pit
>   and crowns you with love and compassion,
> who satisfies your desires with good things
>   so that your youth is renewed like the eagle's.
> (Psalm 103:1–5)

Day 299

Read Ruth 3:18 – 4:4
Key verses: Ruth 3:18 – 4:1

....

¹⁸ Then Naomi said, 'Wait, my daughter, until you find out what happens. For the man will not rest until the matter is settled today.'

^{4:1} Meanwhile Boaz went up to the town gate and sat down there just as the guardian-redeemer he had mentioned came along. Boaz said, 'Come over here, my friend, and sit down.' So he went over and sat down.

Standing in the queue at the supermarket checkout; biding your time until the doctor rings with your test results; being put on hold during a phone conversation. Waiting is part of life – we do a lot of it, but we don't like it.

At the end of chapter 3, Naomi issues the instruction to Ruth to 'Wait . . . until you find out what happens.' Like Naomi and Ruth, the readers are on the edge of their seats. The resolution of this story apparently hinges on the response of an unknown character to this most important question.

Chapter 4 begins, 'Meanwhile Boaz went up to the town gate and sat down there.' There is a lot of sitting around at the end of chapter 3 and here at the beginning of chapter 4. But notice that Boaz is waiting with purpose. He is sitting in the public square, in the place where business is transacted and legal matters are settled, so that he can resolve this situation with the nearer kinsman redeemer. He puts himself in a position to meet this man if he happens to come along.

No doubt people travelling in the early morning to their places of work and to places of opportunity would speak to him on the way. Clearly, Boaz knows it is a big day. It is a big day for him and for Ruth, but he has no idea of the part he is playing in redemptive history.

Waiting is part of life – our physical and spiritual life. We wait for God to intervene in our situation, to answer prayers, to fulfil his purposes and for Jesus to return. But waiting does not mean inactivity. The Bible urges us to wait expectantly (Psalm 5:3), patiently (Psalm 37:7) and with hope (Psalm 33:20). Wait purposefully: pray, grow as a disciple, be active serving God, be available for him to use. Don't begrudge the waiting – like Boaz and Ruth, you have no idea what God is doing behind the scenes and what part your waiting will play in God's plan of salvation.

> I say to myself, 'The Lord is my portion;
>   therefore I will wait for him.'
> (Lamentations 3:24)

Day 300

Read Ruth 4:1–8

Key verses: Ruth 4:1–6

....

¹ Meanwhile Boaz went up to the town gate and sat down there just as the guardian-redeemer he had mentioned came along. Boaz said, 'Come over here, my friend, and sit down.' So he went over and sat down.

² Boaz took ten of the elders of the town and said, 'Sit here,' and they did so. ³ Then he said to the guardian-redeemer, 'Naomi, who has come back from Moab, is selling the piece of land that belonged to our relative Elimelek. ⁴ I thought I should bring the matter to your attention and suggest that you buy it in the presence of these seated here and in the presence of the elders of my people. If you will redeem it, do so. But if you will not, tell me, so I will know. For no one has the right to do it except you, and I am next in line.'

'I will redeem it,' he said.

⁵ Then Boaz said, 'On the day you buy the land from Naomi, you also acquire Ruth the Moabite, the dead man's widow, in order to maintain the name of the dead with his property.'

⁶ At this, the guardian-redeemer said, 'Then I cannot redeem it because I might endanger my own estate. You redeem it yourself. I cannot do it.'

The man with no name.

In a story where names are significant, we are, interestingly, never told the kinsman redeemer's name. Boaz simply calls him over and invites him and the ten elders to sit down. He explains that there is a property to buy, which belonged to Elimelek, and the man readily agrees to the purchase.

The audience gasps. This is not supposed to happen!

But Boaz adds, 'Before you take your sandal off to seal the deal, you should know that, along with the land, you get a wife.' This is a different proposition altogether. If the kinsman redeemer were only required to buy the land, then, although he would pay the purchase price, he would still have an accruing asset. But if he were to take on a wife with the land and they had a child, the child would inherit the land. Therefore, it would be of no economic benefit to him. The heirs of the marriage might become part of the disbursement of his resources, and he doesn't want to jeopardize his retirement strategy. So he declines to redeem the land.

Do you see the paradox? The one who is concerned about securing the rights to his family name is not remembered, and the one who is selflessly concerned for the needs of others is, of course, remembered for his kindness.

Beware of trying to make a name for yourself. Like the builders of the tower of Babel, ultimately you will be frustrated (Genesis 11:1–9). Clinging to your resources, to your reputation, to your 'name' is like trying to hold on to sand. But spend your energy promoting God's name, like the woman who anointed Jesus' feet (Matthew 26:6–13) or the Israelite midwives, Shiphrah and Puah (Exodus 1:15–21), and you will be remembered for ever. What a paradox! Our names are only remembered when our sole aim is to make God's name great. Today, share John the Baptist's prayer: 'He must become greater; I must become less' (John 3:30).

Day 301

Read Ruth 4:9–12
Key verses: Ruth 4:11–12

• •

> [11] *Then the elders and all the people at the gate said, 'We are witnesses. May the LORD make the woman who is coming into your home like Rachel and Leah, who together built up the family of Israel. May you have standing in Ephrathah and be famous in Bethlehem.* [12] *Through the offspring the LORD gives you by this young woman, may your family be like that of Perez, whom Tamar bore to Judah.'*

How do you celebrate good news? Perhaps you phone a friend, post on Facebook or go out for a special meal?

Look at how these well-wishers respond to this wedding announcement. As the details of the transaction are formalized, the crowd cheers in the grandstand. But it is not simply cheering; it is really a praying crowd.

The book has been full of prayers on the lips of all these different characters: 'May the Lord show kindness to you', 'May the Lord be with you', 'May the Lord repay you', 'May the Lord bless you', 'May the Lord grant you favour', and so on.

Now, in verse 11, the elders, who have witnessed Boaz's acquisition of the land and a wife, begin to pray. They have seen Ruth's kindness to Naomi and also Boaz's commitment to this family. Notice Boaz's detailed and solemn statement in verse 10. He is well aware that he is marrying Ruth for the greater purpose of maintaining the name of the dead man's property.

As witnesses of such devotion, the elders pray, first for Ruth. They pray that she will be like Rachel and Leah, the founding mothers of Israel. Then they pray for Boaz, 'May you have standing in Ephrathah and be famous in Bethlehem.' Finally, they pray that this couple would have a family like Perez, who was also born of an outsider, and who became a clan chief in the nation.

These weren't pygmy prayers!

How would you describe your prayer life? Do you use prayer like an Aladdin's lamp, only speaking to God when you need something? Or are you like Daniel in the Old Testament, believing that prayer is worth risking your life for? Most of us are somewhere in the middle of this spectrum, but you shouldn't settle for mediocrity. Determine to pray more, to pray more ambitiously and more biblically. Use one of Paul's prayers as you pray for friends and family today (see Ephesians 3:14–21; Philippians 1:9–11; Colossians 1:9–14).

Devote yourselves to prayer, being watchful and thankful.
(Colossians 4:2)

Day 302

Read Ruth 4:9–13
Key verses: Ruth 4:13

···

> ¹³*So Boaz took Ruth and she became his wife. When he made love to her, the LORD enabled her to conceive, and she gave birth to a son.*

In verse 13, the story shifts from the boardroom to the bedroom.

As marriages crumble, as legal institutions seek to redefine it, as Christians lose their voice to address it because of premarital sex, extramarital sex and total confusion in their minds, society hastens down a track on a fast train with apparently no driver. Therefore, when the Bible expresses God's concerns about marriage, we need to pay very careful attention.

'For this reason a man will leave his father and mother and be united to his wife, and the two will become one flesh' (Ephesians 5:31). Marriage is not some arbitrary arrangement which has been conceived in a moment of time. It is not a contrivance of human beings. Marriage is a creation ordinance (Genesis 2:24). God has designed and established it, and the order of things is vital: leaving, cleaving, being interwoven and conceiving. To alter the structure is to bring chaos into our lives and into the life of society.

When the car drives away with the bride and groom, the people are supposed to watch them and say, 'When they come back, they will be different.' The couple are supposed to go away on their honeymoon as virgins and come back having been physically united. Do you know how seldom that takes place, even within the Christian community? Why? Because people are disobedient. But if Jesus is Lord, then I am not at liberty to disbelieve what he teaches or demands of my behaviour.

Bonhoeffer said:

> Marriage is more than your love for each other. It has a higher dignity and power, for it is God's holy ordinance . . . In your love you only see the heaven of your happiness but in marriage you are placed at a post of responsibility towards the world and mankind.
> (Dietrich Bonhoeffer, *Letters and Papers from Prison, volume 8*, Fortress Press, 2010, p. 83)

Your love is your own private possession, but marriage is something more than personal. It is a status; it is an office that joins you together in the sight of God and man. If the Christian church will not stand up for the nature of marriage, then no-one will. We must clean up our act and pray, 'Oh, that you would rend the heavens and come down' (Isaiah 64:1); judgment needs to start with the family of God (1 Peter 4:17).

- Unlike Ruth and Boaz, not all of us have obeyed God's divine order for love and marriage. Repent for past sin. Receive God's forgiveness and grace. From today onward, serve God joyfully, knowing you are pure and holy in his sight, clothed in the righteousness of Christ.
- If you are married, pray for God's strength to maintain your marriage vows.
- Pray for the marriages of family and friends, that they would be God-honouring and a beacon of hope in our confused culture.

Day 303

Read Ruth 4:13–22
Key verses: Ruth 4:14–17

. . . .

14 The women said to Naomi: 'Praise be to the LORD, who this day has not left you without a guardian-redeemer. May he become famous throughout Israel! 15 He will renew your life and sustain you in your old age. For your daughter-in-law, who loves you and who is better to you than seven sons, has given him birth.'

16 Then Naomi took the child in her arms and cared for him. 17 The women living there said, 'Naomi has a son!' And they named him Obed. He was the father of Jesse, the father of David.

What a wonderful ending.

What a lovely picture: 'Then Naomi took the child in her arms and cared for him' (verse 16).

The film that began in black and white is now in glorious technicolour. The soundtrack that was a lament now swells to a triumphant crescendo, and Ruth, who hasn't had a speaking part since chapter 3:17, is now fading completely from view, and the camera is back on Naomi.

All her concerns of chapter 1 have been more than answered in the providence of God. The women of the community gather together to remind Naomi how much her daughter-in-law loves her and that she is better to her than seven sons. They are delighted that this new baby will renew Naomi's life and sustain her in her old age.

Let this be an encouragement to every Naomi. Through experiences of bitterness and disappointment, God is at work, and Naomi, who changed her name to Mara, is now very happy to be called Naomi again. Wonder of all wonders, miracle of miracles, the God of the nations, who is vitally involved in the personal life of this widow and her daughter-in-law, provides this little bundle that is now on her lap.

God is passionately preoccupied with Naomi – and all those ordinary people like her on the humdrum track of life.

When we face difficulties or go through suffering, it can be tempting to doubt God's love. No matter how long we've been a Christian or how often we have experienced God's faithfulness, we may question whether God hears our prayers and why he doesn't intervene. Today, refuse to believe the devil's lies. Acknowledge that God is passionately preoccupied with you. Let this truth sink deep into your heart.

God cares about all the issues you are facing, and he is providing for you in ways you cannot see. One day soon, in the new creation, the loose ends of life will be tied up and all of God's work behind the scenes will be on display. Until then, commit all the mundane elements of your life to God, trust his care for you and rest secure in the knowledge of his love.

Day 304

Read Ruth 4:13–22
Key verses: Ruth 4:18–22

. . . .

¹⁸ *This, then, is the family line of Perez:*
Perez was the father of Hezron,
¹⁹ *Hezron the father of Ram,*
Ram the father of Amminadab,
²⁰ *Amminadab the father of Nahshon,*
Nahshon the father of Salmon,
²¹ *Salmon the father of Boaz,*
Boaz the father of Obed,
²² *Obed the father of Jesse,*
and Jesse the father of David.

The whole story of the Bible is about getting from Genesis 12 to Revelation 7.

In Genesis 12, God calls Abraham to leave his people and his father's household and go to a land he does not know. God promises to make him into a great nation and to bless all the peoples of the earth through him. In Revelation 7, we see the promise of God fulfilled when John sees a great multitude that no-one could count, from every nation, tribe, people and language.

If you realize that we get to Revelation 7 as a result of the promise of God in Genesis 12, then you will begin to put the big picture together. Remember at the end of the book of Judges it says, 'In those days Israel had no king; everyone did as they saw fit' (Judges 21:25). The implication is that if Israel had a king, life would be so much better. Then you have this story of Ruth, which ends with the genealogy – and who is at the end? David, the shepherd boy who became king. David is a man after God's own heart, but he isn't perfect, and when we watch his reign, we realize he doesn't totally fit the picture. He is clearly not the serpent-crusher who was promised in Genesis 3. He is obviously not the great ruler from the tribe of Judah mentioned in Genesis 49. There is still one greater than David to come, which is made clear to him by Nathan the prophet. In 2 Samuel 7:12–16 are these amazing words that are partially fulfilled in Solomon and are ultimately fulfilled only in Jesus, who puts Solomon in the shadows (Luke 11:31).

This is how redemption history unfolds. Just when we think we have the fulfilment of God's promises, we realize they are only partially fulfilled. The story of Ruth points us forward to King David, but eventually we have to acknowledge that he is not the one we are waiting for. And so the story points us further forward, to a descendant of David: Jesus, our great kinsman redeemer. Ultimately, we discover that these relatively unknown, apparently insignificant lives of Ruth and Boaz are central to all that God is doing in the world.

Jesus is coming back! That scene from Revelation 7 will soon take place. Be encouraged that the eternal significance of your relatively unknown, apparently insignificant life will soon be revealed. Until then, keep your focus on Christ – your kinsman redeemer and King. Determine how you should spend your day, and what your priorities should be, in the light of his imminent return.

For further study

If you would like to do further study on the book of Ruth, the following may be useful:

- David Atkinson, *The Message of Ruth*, The Bible Speaks Today (IVP, 1974).

- Sinclair Ferguson, *Faithful God: An Exposition of the Book of Ruth* (Bryntirion Press, 2005).

- Robert Hubbard, *The Book of Ruth*, New International Commentary on the Old Testament (Eerdmans, 1995).

- John Piper, *A Sweet and Bitter Providence* (IVP, 2010).

- K. Lawson Younger, *Judges, Ruth*, NIV Application Commentary (Zondervan, 2002).

If God has fed you through your study of the book of Ruth, why not buy the individual Food for the Journey on Ruth and give it to a friend (available from ivpbooks.com)?

Introduction
Colossians

Steve Brady

Putting Jesus in his place

The church at Colossae is wrestling with what status to give Jesus. There is a plethora of other gods and spiritual beings to worship. The city is rife with syncretism, the belief that you can worship Jesus but need to supplement your faith by turning to other powers and authorities. If you get sick or want your business to flourish, surely it is expedient to pay allegiance to these other powers and not just to Jesus? In Colossae, Jesus is eminent. The fundamental question is, 'Is he pre-eminent?' Jesus is important, just not all-important; he is adequate, but not totally sufficient for every need. He is better, not the best.

Writing from a prison cell in Rome, Paul warns these new believers of the danger of turning to another Jesus who is less than the Jesus of the Bible, the Son of the living God. If they fail to heed his warning, their faith and everything associated with it will eventually unravel. Their trade-in of the real Jesus will give them a domesticated Jesus, a Jesus who might be Lord of some things, but not Lord of all.

Colossae was a church that had to find its way in the world of its day, without the advantage of all the background knowledge Christians have today, after centuries of Christian civilization. Yet, by God's grace, it was part of a first-century missionary church that outlived, out-thought and out-died its contemporary world, and passed on the baton of faith.

That is why the letter to the Colossians is so important for the church today. We still live in a world full of pluralistic ideologies, philosophies and religions, all competing for our attention and devotion. Every day, in many practical ways, we face the question of whether Jesus is pre-eminent in our lives. Putting Jesus in his place is still something we wrestle with. Be encouraged as you study this epistle to the Colossians. This letter, if we listen to it, will provide challenge, inspiration and a renewed focus to keep on living for Christ in our generation.

Day 305

Read Colossians 1:1–6
Key verse: Colossians 1:1

••

¹*Paul, an apostle of Christ Jesus by the will of God, and Timothy our brother . . .*

How do you introduce yourself?

We often describe ourselves in terms of our significant relationships or what we do for a living – 'I'm John's wife', 'I'm David's son', 'I'm a teacher', 'I'm a nurse', 'I'm a student'.

Writing to the believers in Colossae, Paul introduces himself simply as 'an apostle' (verse 1). The word 'apostle' in Scripture actually means 'sent one'. The equivalent word in Latin means 'missionary'. At one level, every Christian is a sent one: we have been sent by the risen Christ into the world. But there is an exclusive sense to this word too. When Paul says he is an apostle, he means he is someone who has seen the risen Lord and has been personally commissioned by him as a bearer of the apostolic gospel (see 1 Corinthians 9:1–2; 15:1–8). So verse 5 mentions the 'word of the truth', and verse 6 speaks of knowing 'the grace of God in truth' (NKJV). Paul is not an apostle as a result of deciding to get a new job because he thinks Judaism has had its day. Rather, it is the will of God (verse 1). He was converted on the Damascus Road; he saw the risen Lord and was commissioned by him.

If it is the will of God for Paul to be an apostle, it is also God's will for him to write this letter. Colossians is one of Paul's prison epistles, written around the same time as Ephesians, Philippians and Philemon. Paul finds a writing ministry when he is in prison for the gospel. I don't suppose he would have willingly signed up for that, but he realizes it is the will of God that he should be in prison at this time. In prison by the will of God? That is a jarring note for many Christians today. To be a success, to be a winner, to be always on the up: surely that is the will of God? Isn't it God's will for me always to be healthy, wealthy and wise? But here we find Paul in prison by the will of God.

Perhaps we need to rethink what God's will is?

Are you in circumstances you would not choose for yourself? What is your prison? Is it illness, heartbreak, redundancy, bereavement, the onset of old age? Whatever your prison is, God can use it for his purposes, just as he did for Paul. From prison, Paul was able to write this letter that has blessed countless generations of believers. God can use your prison for his glory too.

And we know that in all things God works for the good of those who love him, who have been called according to his purpose. (Romans 8:28)

Day 306

Read Colossians 1:1–2
Key verse: Colossians 1:2

....

2 To God's holy people in Colossae, the faithful brothers and sisters in Christ:
    Grace and peace to you from God our Father.

What gives you your identity – your genes, family background, community, education or job? In verse 2, Paul explains our Christian identity.

He is writing to the 'holy' and 'faithful brothers and sisters in Christ'. Originally these were terms reserved for the Jewish nation. But in this church at Colossae, both Jews and Gentiles are accepted as the people of God.

Paul addresses them as 'in Colossae . . . in Christ'. The Christian has a dual address. We live both in Christ and in our own Colossae, wherever that may be. When we forget either of those addresses, we are in big trouble. Paul is writing to the church in Colossae, a fairly insignificant place at the time, situated in the Lycus Valley, now part of modern Turkey. This church faces both similar and different circumstances and challenges from the churches at Hierapolis and Laodicea (Colossians 4:13), just a few miles up the road.

Do you know where you live? I don't simply mean your address. Do you know the kind of place you come from, the kinds of people your church is seeking to serve? There is a great danger, when we don't know where we live, that we become a Christian ghetto. We are not part of the community we serve; we haven't incarnated. Instead, we simply drive to church, bolt ourselves in and then drive off after the service. We need to learn to live where God has placed us, because where God has placed us has a bearing on how we maintain our witness to the gospel in that community.

However, where we come from isn't the all-important thing. It is being 'in Christ' that makes the difference. That is why Paul can later say, despite the diversity of our backgrounds, that 'there is no Gentile or Jew, circumcised or uncircumcised, barbarian, Scythian, slave or free, but Christ is all, and is in all' (Colossians 3:11). Being a Christian is being in Christ. This is one of Paul's often-repeated phrases.

So, what gives me my identity isn't just where I live or where I come from; rather it is whose I am and to whom I belong. I am in Christ while in my Colossae. It isn't either–or. If I am just in my Colossae, I will capitulate to my culture. If I am just in Christ, I may not be able to relate to my culture.

Believers are in Christ and in their Colossae. That's how Christian identity is formed – through eternity and history coinciding.

Pray for the things that are happening in your Colossae this week. Pray also for increased opportunities to reach the people in your community with the gospel. But don't forget your dual identity. You are 'in Christ', united to him. God gives you his grace and peace (verse 2). So rely on his resources to live the life he designed you for.

Day 307

Read Colossians 1:3–8

Key verses: Colossians 1:3–6

. . . .

> [3]*We always thank God, the Father of our Lord Jesus Christ,
> when we pray for you,* [4]*because we have heard of your faith in
> Christ Jesus and of the love you have for all God's people –* [5]*the
> faith and love that spring from the hope stored up for you in
> heaven and about which you have already heard in the true
> message of the gospel* [6]*that has come to you.*

Do you know anyone who died of too much encouragement? I don't!

Paul has much to say to these believers, some of which will be painful.
But he knows they need encouragement, so he begins by telling
them why he is grateful to God for them. He thanks God for their
faith in Christ, and for their personal trust and commitment to him as
Lord and Saviour. What makes their church a church is that they
believe the gospel.

Next, he mentions their love for all God's people (verse 4). How do we
know somebody is a Christian? Faith in Jesus Christ produces a love
for the people of God that comes from the Holy Spirit (see verse 8).
Notice that this is love for all the saints, not just for people whom
we personally like. Churches are not supposed to be monochrome,
designer churches, full of like-minded people. It is easy to love
people who are just like ourselves. But what real faith produces is a
love for all the saints. God's purpose through the gospel is to produce
a new community from a damaged humanity, and a loving society
out of a hateful world.

Such faith and love spring from hope (verse 5). How can we keep
going on with Christ, year in and year out, beset with problems and
perhaps a less-than-perfect church? What keeps us fired up? Paul
says it is hope stored up in heaven. Whatever benefits we receive

from the gospel now – and they are considerable – are only foretastes. The big deal, the big payload of the gospel, will not come until we see Jesus – it is stored up for us in heaven. The best is yet to come! Don't fall for the lie that we can have it all now. We shall have it all then. One of the secrets of living the Christian life in a God-honouring way is to work out what is for the here and now, and what is for the then and there.

What do people thank God for when they think of you? Your sunny disposition, organizational skills or caring nature, perhaps? Pray that, above all, faith, hope and love would be the hallmarks of your life, worked out in practical ways every day. Paul sees these traits in action in the lives of the Thessalonian believers:

> We remember . . . your work produced by faith, your labour prompted by love, and your endurance inspired by hope in our Lord Jesus Christ.
> (1 Thessalonians 1:3)

Today, look for ways to demonstrate faith, hope and love. See these as opportunities to glorify God and to be an encouragement to your Christian friends.

Day 308

Read Colossians 1:3–8

Key verses: Colossians 1:6–8

....

> [6] *In the same way, the gospel is bearing fruit and growing through-out the whole world – just as it has been doing among you since the day you heard it and truly understood God's grace. [7] You learned it from Epaphras, our dear fellow servant, who is a faithful minister of Christ on our behalf, [8] and who also told us of your love in the Spirit.*

In our small corner of the world, it doesn't always feel as though Christianity is flourishing. But we only need to look to other countries and continents to see that Paul is right: 'the gospel is bearing fruit and growing'.

In verse 6 there is an echo of the 'Be fruitful and multiply' theme that harks back to the book of Genesis. Back then, humankind disobeyed and brought both a curse and chaos into God's world. Now, through the gospel, God is reversing that curse and will one day usher in a new heaven and a new earth. Paul is confident that the gospel of Christ is growing and increasing. How? First, it is via hearing the 'word of truth' (verse 5, NASB). Evangelism entails verbal proclamation: words. We live in an image-conscious age, with brand names and jealously guarded logos. If Christians, however, only use symbols – a cross or a fish, for instance – and don't explain them, the gospel isn't heard. And then it isn't 'understood' (verse 6). The gospel is something we need to hear.

Verse 7 adds that the gospel is something we also learn. The Colossians learned it from Epaphras. In our post-Christian culture, where people are no longer brought up with or surrounded by Christian truth, we need to give people the opportunity to learn the gospel, perhaps through courses such as Alpha and Christianity

Explored. We need to teach the gospel in one-to-one settings, in small groups and from the pulpit. Praise God for men and women like Epaphras who faithfully teach the Word of God.

Thank God for the people in your life who have been like Epaphras and taught you the gospel – a friend, work colleague, Sunday school teacher, parent or pastor. Thank God for the investment they made in your life and their willingness to witness to you. Will you be an Epaphras to someone else? Think about the people God has placed in your life to whom you could teach the gospel. Today, pray for opportunities and boldness to begin this type of gospel partnership with someone.

> [Apollos] had been instructed in the way of the Lord, and he spoke with great fervour . . . He began to speak boldly in the synagogue. When Priscilla and Aquila heard him, they invited him to their home and explained to him the way of God more adequately.
> (Acts 18:25–26)

Day 309

Read Colossians 1:9–14

Key verses: Colossians 1:9–11

....

⁹We continually ask God to fill you with the knowledge of his will through all the wisdom and understanding that the Spirit gives, ¹⁰so that you may live a life worthy of the Lord and please him in every way: bearing fruit in every good work, growing in the knowledge of God, ¹¹being strengthened with all power according to his glorious might so that you may have great endurance and patience.

Becoming a Christian is just the start of a journey.

Paul wants these Colossians to press on towards maturity. He prays for God 'to fill you with the knowledge of his will through all the wisdom and understanding that the Spirit gives' (verse 9). The purpose? To live a life worthy of the Lord and bring him pleasure (verse 10). Is the goal for us to be happy, peaceful and contented? Not in the first instance. Rather, it is that we may have 'great endurance and patience' (verse 11). Are we then stoical, tight-lipped, determined and miserable? Hardly. Note the addition of 'joyful' in verse 12.

Paul prays that these Christians will go the distance of faith. To do that, they need to see the big picture. Without such spiritual insight, they will lose their way. They will live merely for the here and now. Paul prays that they will remember that, from eternity to eternity, God's rescue plan is in Christ. He prays that they might have 20/20 spiritual vision to grasp and hold on to the purposes of God in Christ.

Like these Colossians, we too need spiritual insight, stickability and endurance to tough it out with joy. This is joy inspired by the Holy Spirit, the kind that gives us strength to live the life described in verses 10–11.

You may know the film *Saving Private Ryan*. (Spoiler alert, if you don't want to know the plot!) The film recounts a story from the Second World War when an incredible amount of American resources are used to rescue one soldier, Private Ryan, as all his brothers have already been killed in action. Many men lose their lives to save this one man. Towards the end of the film, the dying captain of the rescue platoon says to Ryan, 'Earn this! Earn what has been done for you.' In the final scene of the film, we see Private Ryan as an old man. He is visiting the graves of those who gave their lives for him and he is asking himself, 'Was I good enough for all that has been done for me?'

The cross of Jesus Christ says Christ has earned it. We were never good enough. He did it for us. But out of sheer gratitude, we are called to lay our lives down for him, daily and consistently. That is what is entailed in pleasing him 'in every way . . . in every good work'.

How well are you doing in living a life worthy of the Lord? Are there specific attitudes and actions that you know are grieving God? Is there an area of life you are resisting laying down for him? As you go through the routines of your day, pray for the Holy Spirit's power to please God 'in every way . . . in every good work'.

If God doesn't rule your mundane, he doesn't rule you, because that's where you live.
(Paul David Tripp, *The Power of Words and the Wonder of God*, Crossway, 2009, p. 24)

Day 310

Read Colossians 1:9–14
Key verses: Colossians 1:12–14

∙ ∙

[12] . . . giving joyful thanks to the Father, who has qualified you to share in the inheritance of his holy people in the kingdom of light. [13] For he has rescued us from the dominion of darkness and brought us into the kingdom of the Son he loves, [14] in whom we have redemption, the forgiveness of sins.

'I did it my way' is the great anthem of our generation.

But, however hard we try, we cannot save ourselves. Our danger is so great, our plight so terrible, that only God Almighty can mount the rescue mission. The gospel is God coming personally in Christ to rescue us from the dominion of sin. That rescue, effected through the cross, brings us redemption. It buys us out of slavery. It sets us free. It brings us forgiveness.

In verses 12–14, Paul, who has echoed the book of Genesis in verse 6, now piles on terms associated with the motley Israelite crew that came out of Egypt at the exodus. Paul reminds the Colossians that they have been rescued from the 'dominion of darkness' (verse 13) – darkness being one of the great plagues of Egypt – and brought into 'the kingdom of the Son'. These Old Testament phrases are now being used to describe what happens when someone becomes a Christian. A great transfer, or rescue, has taken place. We are no longer under the authority of the power of darkness. We are now under the rule and management of a new authority: the kingdom of Jesus.

How does this transfer from the kingdom of darkness into the kingdom of light come about? Because God has qualified us (verse 12). I remember when I was one of the guinea pigs on a new degree course, many years ago. I had to sit a Hebrew exam that nobody had tried before. I sat there for three hours. It might as well have been Sanskrit. I came out, my head whizzing – I was sure I had failed. But everyone else had had the same problem. The exam had been set at a standard that only Regius professors of Hebrew at Oxford and Cambridge could cope with. So the examiners got together, and they must have decided that my name on the paper alone was worth at least 30%! They qualified the whole lot of us. We all passed. It was sheer grace. It bore no relationship to my performance. Likewise, God qualifies us by his grace. To put it another way, Christ has taken the exam for us, but inserts our name, not his – and we therefore pass because of his efforts, not ours.

The Puritan preacher Jonathan Edwards explained, 'You contribute nothing to your salvation except the sin that made it necessary.' As the hymn says:

> Nothing in my hand I bring,
> Simply to Thy cross I cling;
> Naked, come to Thee for dress;
> Helpless look to Thee for grace;
> Foul, I to the fountain fly;
> Wash me, Saviour, or I die.
> (Augustus Toplady, 'Rock of Ages', 1763)

Today, praise God for his extravagant grace.

Day 311

Read Colossians 1:15–20
Key verse: Colossians 1:15

• •

¹⁵ *The Son is the image of the invisible God, the firstborn over all creation.*

We live in an image-conscious age. Image is everything. What is apparently important is what you project, not who you really are.

Confucianism teaches that there are three important elements to a person: there is the person you think you are, the person others think you are, and the person you really are. Image and reality are not the same. The further what we are is from what we project, the more likely we are to have psychological problems, since so much energy is spent on projecting and protecting an image which is a façade. We are then like an actor playing a role, portraying a character, hiding behind a mask. Is that what Paul means when he says in verse 15 of this early Christian song that Jesus is 'the image of the invisible God'? Is he a projection of God, but not the reality? Does he give us an idea of what God is like but is not the real thing?

That's not what Paul intends to convey at all. Rather, the idea of image here is one of exactness, of representation, of revelation, of manifestation. In the ancient world, if you made an image of yourself, it was viewed as part of you, as almost you. Paul is saying that Jesus is the image of the invisible God. He isn't different from God. He is the exact representation of God; he is the exact image. Hebrews chapter 1 talks about the Son as the perfect image of God, the exact representation of his being. We sometimes say, 'Like father, like son.' But Scripture wants us to see: like Son, like Father. That is the picture. What the Son is, so is the Father.

Therefore, in Jesus I don't meet someone who can introduce me to the ultimate God; in Jesus I meet God with a human face. I meet

God in our shape and size. John 1:18 puts it like this: 'No one has ever seen God, but the one and only Son, who is himself God and is in the closest relationship with the Father, has made him known.'

Jesus is 'Immanuel' – God with us. He is the proof that God is not aloof and distant. Jesus experienced life on earth and our frailty. His death on the cross demonstrates that God understands our suffering. But, more than that, it demonstrates the full extent of his love.

> I have turned . . . to that lonely twisted tortured figure on the cross, nails through hands and feet, back lacerated, limbs wrenched, brow bleeding from thorn pricks, mouth dry and intolerably thirsty, plunged in God-forsaken darkness. That is the God for me! He laid aside his immunity to pain. He entered our world of flesh and blood, tears and death. He suffered for us. Our sufferings become more manageable in the light of his. There is still a question mark against human suffering, but over it we boldly stamp another mark, the cross which symbolizes divine suffering.
>
> (John Stott, *The Cross of Christ* (reprint), IVP, 2006, p. 387)

Day 312

Read Colossians 1:15–20
Key verses: Colossians 1:15–17

....

¹⁵[He is] the firstborn over all creation. ¹⁶For in him all things were created: things in heaven and on earth, visible and invisible, whether thrones or powers or rulers or authorities; all things have been created through him and for him. ¹⁷He is before all things, and in him all things hold together.

Who created God? It's a question many children and some adults often ask.

Taken out of context, 'the firstborn over all creation' (verse 15) has led some to deduce that Jesus is a created being. But the Bible does not say 'first created over all creation'. The word is 'firstborn', and it is loaded with Old Testament history. In Exodus 4:22 Israel was called God's firstborn, though it certainly was not the first created nation. The Davidic king, the one who was going to come, is called the firstborn (Psalm 89:27). Firstborn is to do with rank, status and priority. It had little to do with birth at all, but suggested instead the idea of being an heir. Just as the uncreated Father stands before, above and beyond all his creation, so the uncreated Son stands in that same position. He is the eternal Son of God.

In verse 16, Paul tells us that Jesus is the Creator. And note how comprehensive that creation is. Christ is at once the starting point and the goal of all creation. Why is the created universe here? Astonishingly, it is here for Christ. This is a sharp reminder for the church at Colossae. This ancient church is being threatened by principalities, powers, superstition and occult practices, and it is riddled with fear. Paul says that when you belong to Christ, you are safe – this is your Father's world, your Saviour's creation.

His point is that whatever powers there may be, visible or invisible, Christ is ultimately the Lord of them all. In our day these powers are manifested in multinational companies, global conglomerates, economic forces, international politics, the whole structure and fabric of the world. There is nothing outside the majestic reign and sway of Christ. The devil may appear to be in the detail, but Christ is Lord of every detail!

What holds the whole universe together? Christ (verse 17)! He is the sustainer of the whole of creation; he prevents the cosmos from collapsing into chaos. How dare we think that Jesus is just for Christians? No, he is the Lord, the magnificent ruler of the whole universe, everything we can see, however far our telescopes can penetrate, and everything we cannot see, however profound and mysterious. Jesus Christ is Lord of all.

'There is nothing outside the majestic reign and sway of Christ.' Take comfort and strength as you rest in this truth. Whether in political wrangling, international terrorism, family struggles, personal finances, your daily routines or the unexpected situations you will face today, remember that Jesus Christ is Lord of all.

> Is there anyone around who can explain God?
> Anyone smart enough to tell him what to do?
> Anyone who has done him such a huge favor
>   that God has to ask his advice?
> Everything comes from him;
> Everything happens through him;
> Everything ends up in him.
> Always glory! Always praise!
> Yes. Yes. Yes.
> (Romans 11:34–36, MSG)

Day 313

Read Colossians 1:15–20
Key verse: Colossians 1:18

· ·

18And he is the head of the body, the church; he is the beginning and the firstborn from among the dead, so that in everything he might have the supremacy.

From its earliest days, Christianity has faced opposition.

Here, in Colossae, a small town in the Lycus Valley, the Christians are under threat. They are fearful that the surrounding culture is going to overwhelm and sink the church. Paul's encouragement, to them and to us, when our backs are against the wall, is to focus on Christ. He reminds us:

- *Christ is the head of the church.* That is a challenge for those of us who think we are in charge of the churches we serve. God, of course, raises up leaders. But we are not indispensable. Paul tells us that Christ is the cause and the source of the church's life. It is as the church, as Christ's body, stays connected to him, the head, that it draws from him all that is needed to tough it out in difficult situations. The church has one foundation, Jesus Christ her Lord, and one head and supreme governor, the One who runs the universe.

- *Christ is also the firstborn from the dead.* Paul is speaking about the resurrection. Christians don't believe that Jesus just came back as a ghost, or reappeared for a while, resuscitated like Lazarus in John 11. True enough, Lazarus died and was raised again. But he, like the widow of Nain's son, or Jairus' daughter, had to die all over again. The difference is that, having died and risen, Christ will never die again (Romans 6:9). Although he was the first to rise from the dead to endless life, thank God he isn't the last. He is the forerunner of many others. We are going to be raised in power also. Jesus promised, 'Because I live, you also will live' (John 14:19).

Is your church small and struggling? Perhaps you are experiencing opposition from your local community? Take on board Paul's teaching. First, Christ is the head of the church. That means that whether the doors of your local church stay open does not depend on you. Don't let the devil crush you under the weight of false responsibility or fool you into thinking you are indispensable. Don't measure your faithfulness by the fruitfulness of your ministry. Your concern must be to stay connected to Christ, like a body to the head. Draw strength and wisdom from him.

Second, Christ is the firstborn from the dead. His resurrection guarantees yours. You don't need to fear the future. However wonderful or tough life is now, this is not all there is. So make sure your priorities and your values are focused on eternity. Let the prospect of future glory flood you with deep-seated hope and joy.

> When Christ, who is your life, appears, then you also will appear with him in glory.
> (Colossians 3:4)

Day 314

Read Colossians 1:15–20
Key verses: Colossians 1:19–20

....

[19] For God was pleased to have all his fullness dwell in him, [20] and through him to reconcile to himself all things, whether things on earth or things in heaven, by making peace through his blood, shed on the cross.

Often people reject the claims of Christ, not because they aren't true, but because, if they are, they demand a radical response. Here Paul tells us:

• *Christ is the Reconciler.* '. . . and through him to reconcile to himself all things' (verse 20). Note that it isn't 'all men' or 'all people' here. The Greek is neuter. It is 'all things'. One of the Early Church Fathers, Origen, believed in universalism – that there would come a time when Christ would turn back the clock on sin in such a way that not only would everybody be saved, but even the devil himself would be redeemed. But the Bible does not teach that, regardless of repentance and faith in Christ, at the end of time, everybody from St Francis of Assisi through to Adolf Hitler, whether they want to be or not, will be saved.

What does it mean for Christ to reconcile all things to himself? Well, it certainly teaches that the death of Christ atones for the sins of people, and puts us right with God.

In addition, in the death and resurrection of Christ, God is reversing the curse that is on the world, and through Christ he is going to bring in a whole new cosmos, 'a new heaven and a new earth, where righteousness dwells' (2 Peter 3:13; see also Isaiah 11:6–9; Romans 8:19–21). Does that mean everybody becomes a Christian? No. But everybody in the universe and whatever is beyond it, everywhere in the whole cosmos, will acknowledge that Jesus

Christ is Lord. A Christian is someone who believes and acts on that truth now. At the end of time, everybody will believe and confess it. Willingly or unwillingly, every knee will bow to Jesus as Saviour or Judge (Philippians 2:10–11).

- *Christ is pre-eminent*. He is pre-eminent and peerless in every realm (Colossians 1:18). What Jesus Christ was eternally as the Son of God, the Lord, he became in actuality in space and time as he became one of us for our redemption. Similarly, Philippians 2:5–11 reminds us that the One who from all eternity was God and Lord, through his death and rising again, is proclaimed Lord before all the universe. He who was before all things has the pre-eminence in all things. In every part of our lives, as well as in our homes, churches and communities, we are to give Jesus pre-eminence.

If God's Word is true and these titles apply to Christ, what difference does that make to us? First, we have the ministry of reconciliation. As soon as we become Christians, we become Christ's ambassadors – God makes his appeal to the world through us. This is a lifelong commitment to living out and sharing the gospel with others (2 Corinthians 5:11–21). Second, he wants to be pre-eminent in every area of our lives. That means making him central to our career and financial decisions, our choice of spouse and retirement plans, how we raise our children and what we watch on TV. How are you doing in these areas?

Day 315

Read Colossians 1:21–29
Key verses: Colossians 1:21–22

. . . .

²¹ Once you were alienated from God and were enemies in your minds because of your evil behaviour. ²² But now he has reconciled you by Christ's physical body through death to present you holy in his sight, without blemish and free from accusation.

Jesus didn't die only to forgive our sins.

Christ reconciled us to God so that he might 'present you holy in his sight, without blemish and free from accusation' (verse 22). Christ has died so we can be free from that gnawing accusation, that conscience that is always twisting us this way and that. In addition, there is the 'accuser of our brothers and sisters', as Revelation 12:10 describes the devil. But Christ has died for us, and, as we surrender to him, we are presented free from accusation. As the final verse of Wesley's hymn, 'And Can It Be', puts it:

> No condemnation now I dread;
> Jesus, and all in Him, is mine;
> Alive in Him, my living Head,
> And clothed in righteousness divine,
> Bold I approach the eternal throne,
> And claim the crown, through Christ my own.
> (Charles Wesley, 1738)

Consider what is really happening when the devil reminds us of past sins. Alistair Begg explains:

> Satan comes in our imaginations, into the courtroom, and he says to the Father, 'Look at that sinner; how can you declare him justified?' 'Well, yes,' says the Father; 'he is a sinner. The charges you bring are valid, but will you look at my Son's hands? And look at my Son's feet?

And will you look at the wounds in my Son's side? Who are you to condemn? It is Christ who justifies.'
(Jeremy and Elizabeth McQuoid, *The Amazing Cross*, IVP, 2012, p. 75)

This is the good news. You are no longer alienated; you are reconciled. You are no longer guilty; you are free from accusation.

Are you still beating yourself up over past sin? Does it weigh you down and make you feel unworthy to serve God? Stop dredging up what God has cast into the deepest sea (Micah 7:19; see also Psalm 103:12). Look to the cross and see Jesus' blood shed to cleanse your darkest sin. His death satisfied God's wrath, paid the punishment for your sin and frees you for ever from condemnation. Thank God for such a great Saviour and such a great salvation.

> As we come to Christ, then, empty-handed, claiming no merit of our own, but clinging by faith to His blood and righteousness, we are justified. We pass immediately from a state of condemnation and spiritual death to a state of pardon, acceptance, and the sure hope of eternal life. Our sins are blotted out, and we are 'clothed' with the righteousness of Jesus Christ. In our standing before God, we will never be more righteous, even in heaven, than we were the day we trusted Christ, or we are now. Obviously in our daily experience we fall far short of the perfect righteousness God requires. But because He has imputed to us the perfect righteousness of His Son, He now sees us as being just as righteous as Christ Himself.
> (Jerry Bridges, *The Gospel for Real Life*, NavPress, 2002, p. 107)

Day 316

Read Colossians 1:21–29
Key verses: Colossians 1:24–27

• •

²⁴ *Now I rejoice in what I am suffering for you, and I fill up in my flesh what is still lacking in regard to Christ's afflictions, for the sake of his body, which is the church.* ²⁵ *I have become its servant by the commission God gave me to present to you the word of God in its fullness –* ²⁶ *the mystery that has been kept hidden for ages and generations, but is now disclosed to the Lord's people.* ²⁷ *To them God has chosen to make known among the Gentiles the glorious riches of this mystery, which is Christ in you, the hope of glory.*

When Christ calls a man, he bids him come and die.
(Dietrich Bonhoeffer, *The Cost of Discipleship,* SCM Press, 2015, p. 11)

Strong words from Bonhoeffer, a German pastor and theologian who was executed for his opposition to the Nazi regime.

God only ever had one Son without sin, but he has no sons or daughters without suffering. Verse 24 calls us to suffer for Christ. At first reading, it sounds as if Paul is a co-redeemer. But no, it means that Paul is prepared to suffer for the gospel so that others may come to know Christ. Some pay the ultimate price, but all Christians are called to pay something to follow Christ, so that others may hear the gospel.

We suffer now, knowing that one day we shall reign with Christ. In the meantime, we are called to serve him (verses 25–27). Paul says he has found his niche; he knows what he is built for and called to. He's become a servant of the gospel. We are called to be servants of the gospel wherever God has placed us, whether in an old folks' home or in a high-tech company. For some of us, this becomes a calling to full-time service at home or overseas. Whatever and wherever, we are called to share the gospel, as verses 28–29 say:

> He is the one we proclaim, admonishing and teaching everyone with all wisdom, so that we may present everyone fully mature in Christ. To this end, I strenuously contend with all the energy Christ so powerfully works in me.

Paul, how do you do it? How do you keep on suffering; how do you keep on serving? How do you keep on investing in kingdom work without quitting? The key for Paul, and us, is 'Christ in you' (verse 27). The Supreme Governor of the church, the Lord of the universe, Christ the Lord of glory, by his Spirit, is in you. When we are connected to him, we have abilities and resources that we did not have before. His sovereignty is our sufficiency.

No wound? no scar?
Yet, as the Master shall the servant be,
And piercèd are the feet that follow Me;
But thine are whole: can he have followed far
Who has nor wound nor scar?
(Amy Carmichael, *Toward Jerusalem*, CLC, 1989)

Don't leave where you're serving or shy away from sharing the gospel to avoid suffering. This is our calling as a Christ-follower. As you represent him today, remember Jesus is *for* you, *with* you and *in* you.

Day 317

Read Colossians 2:1–7
Key verses: Colossians 2:2–3

. . . .

²My goal is that they may be encouraged in heart and united in love, so that they may have the full riches of complete understanding, in order that they may know the mystery of God, namely, Christ, ³in whom are hidden all the treasures of wisdom and knowledge.

Today, people use tarot cards, look up their horoscopes and talk in vague terms about 'spirituality'. Our syncretistic, pluralistic culture is not unlike Colossae.

In Colossians 2, Paul confronts a world full of elemental spirits that many believe control their lives and need to be respected and placated. But he offers hope by explaining why Christians don't need to be controlled by these powers: in Christ there is freedom from such bondage, and fullness of life.

How do we reach that point of freedom and sufficiency in Christ? First of all, we are to be 'encouraged in heart' (verse 2). We need more than just friendly churches. In friendly churches you may get a nice warm welcome, but then find that that's it. Nobody ever invites you home, takes you out for a coffee, offers to babysit or helps with the ironing. Instead of friendly churches, we need encouraging communities of people who are becoming like Jesus.

Second, we are to be 'united in love', so that we may have the 'full riches of complete understanding'. Paul wants Christians who are full of love, but also those who grow in their faith intellectually so they appreciate all they have in Jesus. If only we could put these two things together: 'full of grace and truth', like Jesus (John 1:14).

Paul wants us to have this understanding so that we may know the 'mystery of God'. We think of a mystery as a puzzle. But in the New Testament, a mystery is something God has previously hinted at in one way or another and now has clearly revealed. The mystery is that, right from the very beginning, God did not intend to make only the Jewish race his chosen people. His Plan A was to bring salvation to the whole world. The Jews' election and special status was for a purpose. Through them, salvation would come through Christ to bless the world.

Why is it important to know about the mystery? Because that mystery is Christ. The whole Old Testament was, and still is, pointing forward to him. He is the key to unlocking its treasures and to understanding what its big picture is all about. Indeed, he is the key to life itself, the one in whom are 'hidden all the treasures of wisdom and knowledge' (verse 3). Christ is what everything, the very structure of reality, is ultimately all about.

How would you rate yourself in terms of demonstrating encouragement, love and understanding? Are you an encourager who puts faith into action? Are you loving, striving to unite with others on the fundamentals of the gospel rather than dividing over minor issues? Are you growing in understanding – taking steps to deepen your knowledge of God's Word? Desire to excel in these three areas – encouragement, love and understanding – so that you may know Christ better.

Love the Lord your God with all your heart and with all your soul and with all your mind and with all your strength.
(Mark 12:30)

Day 318

Read Colossians 2:1–7
Key verses: Colossians 2:4–7

∙∙∙

> *⁴I tell you this so that no one may deceive you by fine-sounding arguments . . . ⁵[I] delight to see how disciplined you are and how firm your faith in Christ is.*
>
> *⁶So then, just as you received Christ Jesus as Lord, continue to live your lives in him, ⁷rooted and built up in him, strengthened in the faith as you were taught, and overflowing with thankfulness.*

Grow up!

That is Paul's charge to these Colossian believers. He commends them for their strong, robust faith, assured of its resources in Christ (verse 5). But he urges them to press on.

The curse of syncretism is afflicting the church in Colossae. The popular argument is that you can turn to other spirits to help you. Yes, by all means, have Jesus – but we also need help from this spirit, that demi-god and some other idol.

Paul's point is that if we are bound up with Jesus as Lord, we discover all we ever need in him. So, in verse 6 he says, 'just as you received Christ Jesus as Lord, continue to live your lives in him'. The word 'live' can be translated 'walk': 'I want you to walk in Christ.' Walk in his footsteps. Then Paul mixes his metaphors a little. He says, 'I want you to be like a tree, well-rooted, or like a house, built up.' In other words, these are pictures of stability, growth and development. Paul says to these Christians, 'It is great to be in Christ, but don't stop developing. Don't remain in spiritual kindergarten, a spiritual Peter Pan in a Neverland of spiritual adolescence. We need to grow in our faith, in our salvation!'

And that's not all: we need to be 'rooted . . . in the faith as [we] were taught, *and* overflowing with thankfulness' (italics added). Thankfulness, an attitude of gratitude, is to mark us out.

Are you growing as a Christian? This growth can be measured not in years or ministry responsibilities, but by how like Christ we are. It is cultivated over a lifetime by daily choosing to obey God and putting him first. Amy Carmichael, the well-known missionary to India quoted earlier, explained:

> Sometimes when we read the words of those who have been more than conquerors, we feel almost despondent. I feel that I shall never be like that. But they won through step by step, by little bits of wills, little denials of self, little inward victories, by faithfulness in very little things. They became what they are. No one sees these little hidden steps. They only see the accomplishment, but even so, those small steps were taken. There is no sudden triumph, no spiritual maturity. That is the work of the moment.
> (Quoted in Tim Hansel, *Holy Sweat*, Word Books Publisher, 1987, p. 130)

Imagine today simply as a series of moments. Each one is an opportunity to submit to God and to walk in his path.

Day 319

Read Colossians 2:8–15
Key verses: Colossians 2:8–10

. . . .

⁸*See to it that no one takes you captive through hollow and deceptive philosophy, which depends on human tradition and the elemental spiritual forces of this world rather than on Christ.*
⁹*For in Christ all the fullness of the Deity lives in bodily form,* ¹⁰*and in Christ you have been brought to fullness. He is the head over every power and authority.*

Have you ever visited a film studio? You can wander past fine-fronted mansions and other impressive buildings, but, if you look behind them, you discover that they are just frontage. There's no substance.

Lack of substance is what Paul is talking about in verse 8. He warns, 'See to it that no one takes you captive through hollow and deceptive philosophy.' Please note that there is nothing wrong with philosophy per se – a genuine love of wisdom, which is what the word means. Paul is warning us of imitations. There are sham philosophies that capture people's minds and the way they think; they are hollow and deceptive because they are based either on human tradition – ancient wisdom passed down from who knows where – or on the basic principles of this world. These principles might refer to wind, earth, fire and water, which the ancients believed to be the four elements of which everything else was made up. But, in this context, Paul is probably talking about the magical powers that are prevalent everywhere in the ancient world. These spiritual realities do not depend on Christ. They exclude him, ignore him or domesticate him by adding him to their pantheon.

In contrast to all these counterfeits, 'in Christ all the fullness of the Deity lives in bodily form' (verse 9). Notice the phrase, 'all . . . the Deity': in Jesus I do not encounter a false deity or an approximation to deity. I meet God himself. And Paul says that this Deity 'lives in bodily form'. Here again is the astonishing story of Christmas and the gospel. The eternal God has joined the human race: he has become one of us, to seek and to save us (John 1:14). What's more, Paul says, all the fullness '*lives* in bodily form', not '*lived*'. Christians believe that the Son of God who became one of us is still one of us. He has joined a human nature to his divine nature. He is one person, God and man, for ever. Think of that: there is a man at God's right hand today! There is someone who has taken our human nature to the very throne of God (1 Timothy 2:5).

Some people, thinking about the size of the universe, ask, 'Do we and our planet really matter?' The gospel tells us we matter infinitely, because God in Christ has personally come to this earth to seek and to save people like us. The Son of God became a son of man so that the sons and daughters of men may become sons and daughters of God (2 Peter 1:4).

If you are ever tempted to wonder whether God loves you, just look at the lengths he went to in order to save you. As Charles Wesley's carol says, 'Our God contracted to a span, Incomprehensibly made man' ('Let Earth and Heaven Combine', 1745). Christ took on flesh, died in our place and now lives to intercede for us before God the Father.

> Let us then approach God's throne of grace with confidence, so that we may receive mercy and find grace to help us in our time of need.
> (Hebrews 4:16)

Day 320

Read Colossians 2:8–15
Key verses: Colossians 2:11–13

. . . .

> ¹¹*In him you were also circumcised with a circumcision not performed by human hands. Your whole self ruled by the flesh was put off when you were circumcised by Christ,* ¹²*having been buried with him in baptism, in which you were also raised with him through your faith in the working of God, who raised him from the dead.*
>
> ¹³*When you were dead in your sins and in the uncircumcision of your flesh, God made you alive with Christ. He forgave us all our sins.*

Why did Jesus come to earth?

Because 'you were dead in your sins' (verse 13). We are made in the image of God, designed for a love relationship with him. But our sinfulness and moral failures have alienated us from God. We are spiritually dead, out of relationship with him. Now, however, we have been 'buried with [Christ] in baptism' (verse 12). What the apostle is speaking about here is not so much the methods or moments of baptism, though they are not excluded; rather it is the spiritual transformation whereby, through the death of Christ, his death counts for me, and my sins are dealt with and buried with him.

Then notice 'raised with him through your faith' (verse 12), or similarly, 'God made you alive with Christ' (verse 13). What does Christ bring us? New, spiritual, eternal life. He brings the life of God into our dead souls. Through faith in Christ, we are born again, changed and being transformed. Eternal life becomes ours by the saving grace of Christ.

When I sit on a plane, I often look at its tons of metal and cargo and ponder the law of gravity. Everything in me tells me that this thing cannot fly. But, as that plane zips along the runway and the aerofoils are tilted, suddenly it leaves the ground and takes to the skies. What has happened to the law of gravity? If it had been suspended, we would be floating around the roof of the plane cabin. No, gravity is still in operation. It has not been suspended so much as superseded as we take to the skies. At some point we come under another law, a higher law, the law of aerodynamics – I am flying!

What does Christ do for me that no-one else can do? He comes and he takes me beyond my law of gravity, the law of sin and death, and by his grace he enables me to fly by his 'law of aerodynamics' – the Spirit of God.

Being a Christian does not mean simply clinging to promises of future glory. Eternal life starts now. Today we are already eternally alive to God through Christ. His resurrection power is at work in us, transforming us into his image.

> Now this is eternal life: that they know you, the only true God, and
> Jesus Christ, whom you have sent.
> (John 17:3)

Day 321

Read Colossians 2:8–15

Key verses: Colossians 2:13–15

. . . .

¹³*When you were dead in your sins and in the uncircumcision of your flesh, God made you alive with Christ. He forgave us all our sins,* ¹⁴*having cancelled the charge of our legal indebtedness, which stood against us and condemned us; he has taken it away, nailing it to the cross.* ¹⁵*And having disarmed the powers and authorities, he made a public spectacle of them, triumphing over them by the cross.*

Have you ever owed someone money and written them an IOU?

The 'charge of our legal indebtedness' in verse 14 is like an IOU. In this case, it isn't money, but a death warrant. My name is on it; I am condemned to death because of my sin (Romans 6:23). And then, wonder of wonders, Christ takes that death warrant and nails it to a cross. He dies in my place and pays my debt.

But the picture isn't of an angry God on one side and poor sinners on the other, and this nice Jesus who says, 'I will sort it for them.' No, it was 'God [who] so loved the world that he gave his one and only Son' for us (John 3:16). The gospel tells me that the cross of Christ is not something extrinsic to God. God, out of love, to forgive us sinners all our sins, 'was in Christ reconciling the world to Himself' (2 Corinthians 5:19, NASB).

The powers and authorities did not know that, in crucifying the Lord of glory, they were fulfilling the plan, purpose and mystery of God. In the very death that Jesus died, he defeated them and robbed death of its power (verse 15).

Paul reminds us that, if Jesus has defeated these principalities and powers, there is no point looking to them for help. Instead, we must look to the cross where God in Christ meets us in grace and mercy.

A friend of mine, a postman, delivered mail to a large house with a huge dog. Every time he opened the gate, this dog would romp towards him, growling and snarling. He was terrified – until he noticed that the dog was on a big chain. The chain allowed the dog a certain amount of freedom. However, it was limited. My friend discovered that as long as he kept to the path, he was safe. Actually, the chain did not keep the dog from the postman. It was what held the chain – a huge concrete post in the ground. So, each morning when the postman entered the garden, he did not look at the dog, nor even its chain. He used to check just one thing: was that post still properly staked into the ground? If it was, he was safe.

Every morning, as you go out into this dangerous world, look and see the stake of the cross holding firmly in the ground. Keep to the path of Christ, look to his cross and walk in liberty, free from bondage, however ugly or terrifying the evil one seems to be. In Christ we are free.

Day 322

Read Colossians 2:16–23
Key verses: Colossians 2:20–23

•••

²⁰ Since you died with Christ to the elemental spiritual forces of this world, why, as though you still belonged to the world, do you submit to its rules: ²¹ 'Do not handle! Do not taste! Do not touch!'? ²² These rules, which have to do with things that are all destined to perish with use, are based on merely human commands and teachings. ²³ Such regulations indeed have an appearance of wisdom, with their self-imposed worship, their false humility and their harsh treatment of the body, but they lack any value in restraining sensual indulgence.

To whom or to what do you turn if you face illness or disappointment in love, or if you find yourself in financial difficulty?

In the ancient world, Gentiles, and even Jews, would call on a whole concoction of angels and powers to help. Paul is reminding the believers that our only mediator is Christ. No matter what we face, we do not need to go anywhere else, since 'all the treasures of wisdom and knowledge' are in Jesus (Colossians 2:3). Therefore we don't need to worry whether we have doffed our cap to this particular power, paid our penance to that particular principality or strayed into some evil spirit's territory. We are set free from all such bondage.

Accordingly, we need to avoid getting caught up in chasing spiritual experiences (verse 18). Such experience isn't self-authenticating. And we always need to beware of people who impose their own rules and regulations on us. They say, 'If you want to be really spiritual you need to do this, that and the other' (verse 21). But this becomes just another form of legalism and bondage. All these little petty rules have an appearance of wisdom, but they cannot make us genuinely good or Christlike (verse 23).

Paul's plea is to avoid such bondage by staying connected to Christ (verse 19). How do we do that? Not by petty rule keeping, that's for sure! If we want to stay spiritually afloat, we must hold on to Christ. Spend time in the Word and in prayer so you can walk with Christ day by day.

If faith connects me to Christ, then I must not lose contact with him. Otherwise, instead of skimming over the waves of life by the grace that connects me to his power, I will be taking in mouthfuls of salty water and feeling pretty grim and miserable. Faith in Christ, heartily trusting Jesus, is the key to freedom from bondage and to fullness of life.

Are you free? Sometimes secular philosophies, traditions and legalistic practices can become ingrained in us without our even realizing it. Instead of trusting wholly in Christ, we rely on our resources, rituals, spiritual experiences and even Christian service. True freedom and the abundant life that Christ promised depend on staying connected to him (John 10:10; 15:1–8). Colossians 2:19 says, 'He is the Head and we are the body. We can grow up healthy in God only as he nourishes us' (MSG). God wants to nourish us; he wants to strengthen, cherish and sustain us. Have you turned to him for nourishment today?

Day 323

Read Colossians 3:1–4

Key verses: Colossians 3:1–2

∙∙

¹Since, then, you have been raised with Christ, set your hearts on things above, where Christ is, seated at the right hand of God. ²Set your minds on things above, not on earthly things.

Focusing on the finishing line is crucial if we want to win a race.

Paul reminds the Colossian believers that if they want to win the race of Christian faith, they need to keep remembering the goal, the finishing line. The challenge is, 'Set your minds on things above' (verse 2). For how long? This is a marathon, not a 100-metre sprint. Christians do not finish the race until either they die or Jesus returns. So this is a daily – indeed, hourly – race.

That said, it is important to understand what such a mindset does *not* mean. Some set their minds on things above as if that were the only reality. Paul isn't saying that. Indeed, the rest of the chapter earths our Christianity into the hurly-burly of life in the home and the family. Nor is he saying that because this world is so evil, we should withdraw from it.

Of course, we must not go to the other extreme. Some Christians react to what is called 'pie-in-the-sky-when-you-die' Christianity. They don't want to wait for the perfection of the new heaven and the new earth; they want to change everything in the world now. They remove all the 'otherness' of the Christian faith, collapsing heaven and the eternal elements of faith into the here and now. So we turn up on a Sunday morning and we hear a riveting sermon on the deforestation of the Amazon or holes in the ozone layer. Christianity does, of course, have something to say about such things. But when we focus exclusively on them, Christianity loses its transcendence. Sometimes people can come to church looking for a spirituality to plug the vacuum in their souls, and leave disappointed, finding no spiritual bread to feed their spirits.

As Christians, we need to hold on to the reality of these two worlds. If I am going to be a wise Christian and make it to the finishing tape with honour, I actually only need two dates in my diary. I need to look to the day when I will appear with Christ in glory. That is my finishing line. The other date is today. And for today I need Jesus. These are the most important dates, the two polarities, between which I must operate.

It is tempting to start crossing bridges that I have not reached, and which may not even exist. I need to learn to set my mind, my affections, my heart, on the finishing line. Today, I need to remember my tomorrow. I am going to be with Christ; I will stand before him and give an account of my time on earth. Imagine hearing Christ saying to you, 'Well done, good and faithful servant!' (Matthew 25:21). Let the vision of that future day give you strength and hope as you live for Christ wholeheartedly today.

Day 324

Read Colossians 3:5–11
Key verses: Colossians 3:5–6

· ·

⁵Put to death, therefore, whatever belongs to your earthly nature: sexual immorality, impurity, lust, evil desires and greed, which is idolatry. ⁶Because of these, the wrath of God is coming.

Are you the type of person who likes having rules to follow? Or are you more of a nonconformist, preferring to test the boundaries?

The rabbis certainly liked rules. They computed that in the Old Testament there are 613 commandments: 248 positive ones and 365 negative ones. But Paul isn't laying out a whole new pile of laws that Christians have to keep scrupulously. These verses are illustrative of what the life of Christ in me is meant to look like. They are moral teachings that do not go out of date. They are principles for Christian living, earthed in the real world.

An imperative starts us off: 'Put to death, therefore, whatever belongs to your earthly nature' (verse 5) – that means whatever belongs to your sinful heart. Then he gives us a list: 'sexual immorality, impurity, lust, evil desires'. We can lump all these together, for the first words, 'sexual immorality', really give the game away. These come from the Greek word *porneia*, from which we derive the English word 'pornography'. It is often a catch-all phrase, covering a multitude of sins. Christian teaching on sexuality is simple to learn, though hard to practise. For instance, the Christian faith does not teach love, sex and marriage. It teaches love, marriage and sex – in that order! Scripture condemns any form of sexual activity outside the bonds of marriage.

Paul adds, 'Because of these, the wrath of God is coming' (verse 6). God will hold me to account one day. In this area of sexuality, here is what the Christ-life looks like: it is walking with God, seeking for a pure heart. The way we view and treat other people, whether of the same or opposite sex, and of whatever age, is to be with absolute purity. It is at this point, of course, that some Christians want to start putting all sorts of rules and regulations in place. But the heart of the principle isn't how long a woman's skirt or a man's hair should be. The issue is being godly, sexually pure and faithful.

In today's society, it is a constant battle to stay sexually pure. Perhaps you need to repent of past sin. You may need to take evasive action so that you make the right decisions before temptation gets too strong. But do not despair; don't be tethered to guilt any longer or believe the lie that your cycle of sin cannot be broken (1 John 1:9). Jesus' blood was shed on the cross for you. Come to him for cleansing and power to live a holy life.

Offer yourselves to God as those who have been brought from death to life; and offer every part of yourself to him as an instrument of righteousness.
(Romans 6:13)

Day 325

Read Colossians 3:5–11
Key verses: Colossians 3:7–8

. . . .

⁷You used to walk in these ways, in the life you once lived. ⁸But now you must also rid yourselves of all such things as these: anger, rage, malice, slander, and filthy language from your lips.

We are often blind to our own sin and adept at excusing wrong behaviour. Certain sins take on a veneer of respectability and are often accepted as part of a middle-class lifestyle. But Paul won't stand for such skewed thinking. He doesn't sugar-coat the seriousness of sin as he continues with his list. Verse 5 refers to covetousness, greed, and unchecked desires for pleasure and money, 'which is idolatry'. For example, the Bible says, 'Six days you shall labour and do all your work' (Exodus 20:9). I understand all the difficulties of the marketplace and demands on employees. But some of us choose to work long hours, excluding time with God and others, not because it is necessary, but so we can accumulate more money and acquire more prestige and possessions. Are we sure it is God-honouring? Isn't the challenge to rearrange our lives and our lifestyles to reflect God's priorities, rather than simply having more money in the bank, a bigger house or a newer car?

Then follow what many might see as the more decent sins: 'You used to walk in these ways . . . now you must also rid yourselves of all such things as these: anger, rage, malice, slander, and filthy language from your lips' (verses 7–8). Many people think that words don't matter. However, Jesus said that by our words we shall be acquitted or condemned (Matthew 12:37). Words can help or heal, hurt or hinder, bless or destroy. They have an incredible power. Some of us have gone through life carrying all sorts of painful baggage because somebody said something unkind to or about us.

God has given us the gift of language. However, before speaking, we need to **THINK** about what we are about to say: is it **T**rue, is it **H**elpful, is it **I**mportant, is it **N**ecessary, is it **K**ind? If it isn't, then don't say it!

Be conscious of the words you use today. Resist off-the-cuff comments, sarcastic banter with family members or crude jokes. Instead, honour God in your speech. Speak kindly, graciously and truthfully to everyone you meet today.

But I tell you that everyone will have to give account on the day of judgment for every empty word they have spoken. For by your words you will be acquitted, and by your words you will be condemned.
(Matthew 12:36–37)

With the tongue we praise our Lord and Father, and with it we curse human beings, who have been made in God's likeness. Out of the same mouth come praise and cursing. My brothers and sisters, this should not be.
(James 3:9–10)

Gracious words are a honeycomb,
  sweet to the soul and healing to the bones.
(Proverbs 16:24)

Day 326

Read Colossians 3:5–11

Key verses: Colossians 3:9–11

∙∙∙

> *⁹Do not lie to each other, since you have taken off your old self with its practices ¹⁰and have put on the new self, which is being renewed in knowledge in the image of its Creator. ¹¹Here there is no Gentile or Jew, circumcised or uncircumcised, barbarian, Scythian, slave or free, but Christ is all, and is in all.*

The world is made up of an endlessly fascinating variety of people with different personalities, skills, interests and outlooks. But we should remember that, fundamentally, there are only two kinds of people.

Paul has in mind two 'bookends' when it comes to people. These bookends are the first Adam and the last Adam: Christ. So, in 1 Corinthians 15 and Romans 5, he talks about being 'in Adam' or being 'in Christ'. A Christian is someone who is no longer just 'in Adam', the old self, who is sinful and wayward and in rebellion towards God. By the grace of God, that person is now 'in Christ'. Paul isn't just giving us a text for self-improvement here. He is saying, 'God has done something radical for us in Christ – Christ died so he might take us out of the old humanity and put us into the new.' In Adam, all humanity dies. In Christ, all who believe live.

We can think of it this way: to be like Jesus is to be truly human; in him, humanity flourishes. The only perfect human being ever seen on planet earth since the fall of Adam is Christ. He is the prototype for a new kind of people. Not the 'old Adam', who was sinful, selfish and wayward. Rather, he is the new Adam type: God-centred, obedient and good. Therefore, to be in Christ is to become authentically and increasingly human. Accordingly, when we are in Christ, we must not forget who we are. Verse 11 reminds us, 'Here there is no Gentile or Jew, circumcised or uncircumcised, barbarian, Scythian, slave or free, but Christ is all, and is in all.' Therefore, we no longer judge people by their background, intelligence, social class or the colour of their skin.

Paul's message is clear. There are only two kinds of people: those in the old Adam and those in the new, or those 'in Christ' and those without him. That is what makes all the difference, in this world and the next.

> We email, Facebook, tweet and text with people who are going to spend eternity in either heaven or hell.
> Our lives are too short to waste on mere temporal conversations when massive eternal realities hang in the balance. Just as you and I have no guarantee that we will live through the day, the people around us are not guaranteed tomorrow either. So let's be intentional about sewing the threads of the gospel into the fabric of our conversations every day, knowing that it will not always be easy, yet believing that eternity will always be worth it.
> (David Platt, *Follow Me*, Tyndale, 2013, p. 187)

Day 327

Read Colossians 3:12–17
Key verses: Colossians 3:12–14

• •

¹²Therefore, as God's chosen people, holy and dearly loved, clothe yourselves with compassion, kindness, humility, gentleness and patience. ¹³Bear with each other . . . Forgive as the Lord forgave you. ¹⁴And over all these virtues put on love, which binds them all together in perfect unity.

Avoiding sin is not enough. If we want to become more like Jesus, we need proactively to pursue holiness. Whereas sin brings fragmentation and disintegration, Paul explains that 'these virtues' bring wholeness to our personalities.

• *Compassion.* This is a word used of Jesus when he saw the crowds in Matthew 9:36. It conveys the idea of being moved to the very core of our being with concern. The early church was noted for its kindness to all sorts of people on the edges of society. This inspirational care for those on the margins has been a constant trait of the church throughout the generations.

• *Gentleness.* This word could be translated as 'meekness' (Matthew 5:5). Meekness is not weakness. It is strength and power under control.

• *Patience.* We are to be known for having a long fuse, not a short temper. We may say that some people 'do not suffer fools gladly'. But here is the quality of suffering fools and everyone else gladly for Jesus' sake. After all, he suffers us! His patience and long-suffering are the reason why we are still here. Likewise, we are mandated to exercise restraint even in the face of extreme provocation – including traffic jams!

- *Forgiveness*. 'Forgive' in verse 13 can be translated as 'grace' – as God has graced you, grace others. This theme of forgiveness is central to the Christian faith, of course. In Christ's death, God has gone to the ultimate length to forgive us so we can go free. But I know, from many years as a pastor, about the troubled lives of people who will not forgive. They damage the people around them as well as themselves. Some of us need to forgive our children or our parents, or that person who broke our heart and wrecked our life all those years ago. We may object, 'But you don't know what she did to me!' No, I don't. But I know what your sins and mine did to Christ, so we could go free (Ephesians 4:32). While we hold on to bitterness, we shrivel our own souls, forfeiting the grace that comes from walking with God and trusting Jesus.

'And over all these virtues put on love' (verse 14). Put on the love that is patient and kind, not jealous or boastful, not arrogant or rude, the love that is the love of Christ.

The Message version of the Bible describes us putting on these virtues like clothes:

> So, chosen by God for this new life of love, dress in the wardrobe God picked out for you: compassion, kindness, humility, quiet strength, discipline. Be even-tempered, content with second place, quick to forgive an offense. Forgive as quickly and completely as the Master forgave you. And regardless of what else you put on, wear love. It's your basic, all-purpose garment. Never be without it. (Colossians 3:12–14, MSG)

What will you wear today?

Day 328

Read Colossians 3:12–17
Key verses: Colossians 3:15–17

....

¹⁵ Let the peace of Christ rule in your hearts, since as members of one body you were called to peace. And be thankful. ¹⁶ Let the message of Christ dwell among you richly as you teach and admonish one another with all wisdom through psalms, hymns, and songs from the Spirit, singing to God with gratitude in your hearts. ¹⁷ And whatever you do, whether in word or deed, do it all in the name of the Lord Jesus, giving thanks to God the Father through him.

Growing in holiness is not a solitary pursuit, but a community endeavour.

Paul is speaking specifically to all the assembled church in verses 15–17, as the 'you' and 'your' in these verses are plural. So, 'Let the peace of Christ rule in your hearts.' Of course, we can individually know the peace of God, but here is a church community full of peace. We live in a warring, hurting, dysfunctional world. The local church is meant to be an oasis of peace, healing and hope for damaged people and communities. When Jesus is central, the church isn't merely happy but healthy, functioning as it should – as salt and light in the community (Matthew 5:13–16). The alternative is tragic: a church fellowship no different from the world outside, with people fighting, gossiping, cold-shouldering each other, playing power games and having turf wars about who does what. Peace and unity in the local church are to be highly prized and carefully guarded.

A peaceful, thankful church can only be God-pleasing because it is a biblical community. Sadly, in too many churches today, Scripture is marginalized and Bible teaching neglected. But the Word of God is crucial for the well-being of the church (Colossians 3:16). Moreover, this is a worshipping church, singing psalms, hymns and spiritual songs. There are other ways of understanding these three categories and how they apply to public worship. But it seems to me to be the path of wisdom, in our specific worship services, to have a blend of psalms, hymns and spiritual songs. Let us be wisely eclectic and flexible, yet testing everything by Scripture. Indeed, over all of life, inside and outside the local church, whatever we do, 'whether in word or deed, do it all in the name of the Lord Jesus, giving thanks to God the Father through him' (verse 17).

Today, pray that the church you attend would be a place of peace where the Bible is central and the worship style is God-honouring. Pray for your minister and leaders, and that your contribution to your local church would bless others (Romans 12:4–8; Hebrews 10:24–25).

> The church gives a visual presentation of the gospel when we forgive one another as Christ has forgiven us, when we commit to one another as Christ has committed to us, and when we lay down our lives for one another as Christ laid down his life for us. Together we can display the gospel of Jesus Christ in a way we just can't by ourselves.
> (Mark Dever, *What Is a Healthy Church?*, Crossway, 2007, p. 29)

Day 329

Read Colossians 3:1 – 4:1
Key verses: Colossians 3:23–24

. . . .

23 Whatever you do, work at it with all your heart, as working for the Lord, not for human masters, 24 since you know that you will receive an inheritance from the Lord as a reward. It is the Lord Christ you are serving.

How do biblical principles work out in practice? Paul gives us some everyday examples:

• *Marriage.* 'Submit' in verse 18 is in the reflexive or middle voice, indicating that it is something the woman does herself, willingly and deliberately. Scripture makes it clear that both by creation (Genesis 1:27–28) and new creation in Christ (Galatians 3:28), men and women are equal in the sight of God. Here the issue is how things operate in the home. In the first century, women had very few, if any, legal rights, and the husband's word was law. Yet remarkably Paul says that the wife actually has something she can do, she has a choice about this: she can learn to submit to her husband willingly, as is fitting in the Lord and appropriate in her culture. Indeed, one of the root meanings of submit has the idea of order. In submitting to her husband, not just any man anywhere, a woman finds God's order for her own life, domestically and otherwise.

Husbands are told to 'love your wives and do not be harsh with them' (verse 19). They are not to be physically or verbally violent in any way. Never become embittered with your wife; rather love her as Christ loved the church (see Ephesians 5:25).

Husbands and wives, let the gospel reorder your marriage relationship.

- *Parents and children.* Like verses 18–19, verses 20–21 are reciprocal. Fathers are not to embitter their children by having family favourites and so on. And children are to be taught to obey, because, in this way, they learn to please the Lord.

- *Workplace.* Nothing is too small, humble or insignificant if it is done for Christ (verse 23). If I am a Christian in employment, whether in bond markets or fixing boilers, I need to do it for Jesus. The Christ-life must show itself in the workplace. That does not mean ramming religion down people's throats, but instead talking the talk. But that will only count if we walk the walk.

Is there a master key to this whole new way of life? Yes, and it is mentioned three times. In the past we were 'raised with Christ' (verse 1); in the present our life is 'hidden with Christ in God' (verse 3); and in the future we 'will appear with him in glory' (verse 4). The secret is *with* – 'with Christ'. Having a relationship with Christ means that in our workplaces, marriages, families and churches, the life of Jesus by the Holy Spirit should be coursing through our veins so that, in all things, Jesus has the pre-eminence in that daily event, made of many little bits, that we call life.

Peter and John were ordinary, uneducated fishermen whose lives had been transformed. The religious leaders' only explanation was that 'these men had been with Jesus' (Acts 4:13). Spend time with Christ. You are already united with him; now cultivate that relationship. Pray that your personal relationship with Jesus would not only transform you, but also have an increasing impact on your closest relationships and daily interactions.

Day 330

Read Colossians 4:2–6
Key verses: Colossians 4:2–3

....

²*Devote yourselves to prayer, being watchful and thankful.* ³*And pray for us, too, that God may open a door for our message, so that we may proclaim the mystery of Christ, for which I am in chains.*

Have you felt like giving up lately? Paul reminds us that one of the ways we press on in our Christian life is through prayer. He urges these Colossian believers to pray, and he outlines how. Be:

• *Faithful*. 'Devote yourselves to prayer' (verse 2). 'Pray continually,' says 1 Thessalonians 5:17. In other words, stay constantly in touch with God throughout the day. Be like Nehemiah when he came before Artaxerxes: 'I prayed to the God of heaven, and I answered the king' (Nehemiah 2:4–5). This was an arrow prayer – a brief, spontaneous prayer asking for God's help without interrupting his conversation with the king. Send quick prayers up to God as you go about your day; keep in touch with him moment by moment.

• *Alert*. Be 'watchful' for answers to prayer, for the Lord's coming, and so that we shall not fall into temptation (Matthew 26:41).

• *Thankful*. Cultivate an attitude of gratitude. Learn to count your blessings! We grieve the Holy Spirit when we are critical. There is nothing like gratitude to God to develop a Christlike spirit within us. As Paul says in 1 Thessalonians 5:18, 'give thanks in all circumstances'.

• *Purposeful*. In verse 3, Paul asks for prayer – in particular for opportunities to preach the gospel. It isn't wrong to pray generally (1 Timothy 2:1–2). But we can only be watchful for answered prayer if we pray specifically.

- *Together*. Notice that all the verbs that Paul uses are in the plural. He is urging the Colossians to pray with one another. Isn't it often so much easier to pray with one or two others alongside (Matthew 18:19–20)? We need to pray personally, but there are times and occasions when praying with friends, family or a partner is likewise vital.

> Prayer is the only entry way into genuine self-knowledge. It is also the main way we experience deep change – the reordering of our loves. Prayer is how God gives us so many of the unimaginable things he has for us. Indeed, prayer makes it safe for God to give us many of the things we desire most. It is the way we know God, the way we finally treat God *as* God. Prayer is simply the key to everything we need to do and be in life.
>
> We must learn to pray. We have to.
>
> (Tim Keller, *Prayer: Experiencing Awe and Intimacy with God*, Hodder and Stoughton, 2016, p. 18)

Day 331

Read Colossians 4:2–6
Key verses: Colossians 4:5–6

••

> ⁵*Be wise in the way you act towards outsiders; make the most of every opportunity.* ⁶*Let your conversation be always full of grace, seasoned with salt, so that you may know how to answer everyone.*

God has placed you where you are. And he wants you to share the good news with the people around you.

Paul is in prison as he writes this letter. But even there he shares the gospel with his captive audience – the guards on duty (Philippians 1:12–14; 4:22). We don't all have Paul's gift of evangelism, but each one of us is called to share the good news. Here, Paul sets out the non-negotiables we need to be an effective witness for Jesus.

• *Live with integrity.* 'Be wise in the way you act towards outsiders' (verse 5). Literally, 'walk in wisdom'. That word 'walk' picks up all the teaching Paul has already given in chapter 3. How are Christians to live? By putting some things off – immorality, misbehaviour – and putting some things on – compassion, mercy and becoming like Christ. If we are going to be good witnesses for Jesus, it isn't only what we say, but also the integrity of our lives that counts. We are to walk the Christian life, to live it out, being a good advert to outsiders, pointing them to an altogether different world and value system.

• *Make the most of every opportunity.* Verse 5 reminds us to snap up the opportunities we have. There are natural opportunities that come up in national life, headlines and stories that grab people's attention. There are personal circumstances that arise for us to bring God's focus, the gospel: a new baby, a birthday, a wedding, a funeral.

• *Speak appropriately.* Let's learn how to be sensitive and gracious as we share the gospel. But we also need to season our words with salt (verse 6). In the ancient world, this phrase could mean using some wit as well as wisdom. The New Jerusalem Bible translates it, 'Always talk pleasantly and with a flavour of wit but be sensitive to the kind of answer each one requires.' Often we need to work out where a person is coming from, and what their problems about faith may or may not be.

The Lord Jesus challenges us to 'open your eyes and look at the fields! They are ripe for harvest' (John 4:35). Let's fix our eyes on the harvest fields of our communities, our countries and the nations of the world.

Where has God placed you – at home, at work, in education, at the school gate or in a retirement home? God has put you there and he has tasks that only you can accomplish. In every situation you encounter and every conversation you have today, you are representing Christ. Pray that you will represent him well by living with integrity and speaking wisely.

> Live such good lives among the pagans that, though they accuse you of doing wrong, they may see your good deeds and glorify God on the day he visits us.
> (1 Peter 2:12)

Day 332

Read Colossians 4:7–18
Key verses: Colossians 4:7, 9

....

> [7] *Tychicus will tell you all the news about me. He is a dear brother, a faithful minister and fellow servant in the Lord . . .* [9]*He is coming with Onesimus, our faithful and dear brother, who is one of you. They will tell you everything that is happening here.*

Some people think of the apostle Paul as a lone ranger who bends the rules and cannot work with anybody. But his letters and the book of Acts mention more than a hundred different Christians with whom he has contact. He is a team player!

Paul introduces us to Tychicus. We don't know much about him other than that he is regularly on the move with and for Paul. He is Paul's equivalent of email, his mobile phone, a key messenger reporting to the Colossian believers the impact that the gospel is having on Caesar's household (Philippians 1:12–14; 4:22).

Tychicus' travelling companion is Onesimus, a new Christian. In reading Paul's epistle to Philemon, we learn about Onesimus, a runaway slave. He ran away from Philemon his master, met Paul, a friend of his master, and was converted. Here is a brilliant little cameo of 'God-incidences' that lead to faith in Christ.

The mention of Aristarchus in verse 10 raises the question – why is he a fellow prisoner? He might have been imprisoned with Paul for his faith. But a prisoner of standing like Paul would be allowed two slaves. It is possible that Aristarchus and possibly Epaphras volunteered to be Paul's slaves. Why? So that they could be with their brother in prison. Now that type of fellowship goes a little beyond tea and biscuits after the service, doesn't it? Don't we all wish for friends like that!

There is also an introduction to 'Jesus, who is called Justus' (verse 11). Jesus was a common name in the first century. This Justus is one of God's unsung heroes. He is only mentioned in passing, but his inclusion is notable. Perhaps, like so many of us, he simply aims to flourish in the inconspicuous, in the daily round and common task.

In contrast to an unsung hero, we are reminded of the famous missionary doctor Luke (verse 14). He wrote both a Gospel and the book of Acts, and was one of Paul's travelling companions. There is also Mark (verse 10). He failed at his first attempt at missionary service, managing to cause a major rift between Paul and Barnabas (Acts 13:13 (where he is referred to as John); 15:36–40). Mark is now with Paul again, a reminder that since failure need never be final with God, it need not be with others.

Paul had the writers of two of the Gospels and the book of Acts in prison with him. Between the three of them, they produced more than half the books in the New Testament. Never underestimate God's power to take ordinary people and make them effective, and sometimes world-changers, for him. You never know who you could be sitting next to in church or on the bus!

You may feel an unlikely candidate for God's service. But he uses all sorts of people, and, by grace, that includes you. Today, thank God that you are part of the body of Christ and joyfully invest your time and talents in serving him.

Day 333

Read Colossians 4:7–18
Key verses: Colossians 4:12–13

. . . .

12 Epaphras, who is one of you and a servant of Christ Jesus, sends greetings. He is always wrestling in prayer for you, that you may stand firm in all the will of God, mature and fully assured. 13 I vouch for him that he is working hard for you and for those at Laodicea and Hierapolis.

Prayer and passion are a dynamic combination.

Paul describes Epaphras as 'always wrestling in prayer for you' (verse 12). Every Christian is called to pray. Clearly, however, this man has a ministry of intercessory prayer. He wrestles in prayer for the spiritual maturity of these believers at Colossae. However, Epaphras is not just prayerful. He is busy for Christ as well: 'I vouch for him that he is working hard for you and for those at Laodicea and Hierapolis' (verse 13). He is a man of prayer and action. That can be a rare combination. Some pray and don't act. Others act and don't pray. For an example of both–and, read Nehemiah chapters 1–6.

Another passionate servant of the gospel is 'Nympha and the church in her house' (verse 15). As you may know, there are different manuscript copies of the New Testament, known as textual variants. Don't worry about that – the New Testament is the best-preserved book by far from the whole of the ancient world. At this point, however, some manuscripts read, 'Nymphas and the church in his house'. Another manuscript confuses us even further, for it says 'their' house. The probability is that it was Nympha – a woman's house. It was unusual for a woman to be the head of a home, but not unique (note Lydia in Acts 16:13–15, 40). Nympha may be single, divorced or widowed. But here is part of the genius of the ancient church: they are so concerned to grow in Christ, to get the gospel out, that they do not bother too much about church buildings. All are called, men and women alike, to be fervent in God's service, eagerly sharing the good news.

Many churches today are consumed by building-related issues and trivial matters. Prayer is no longer a priority; evangelism a lost art. We desperately need modern-day people like Epaphras and Nympha, who exemplify a single-minded passion for God.

Are you too easily pleased with mediocre devotion? Are your prayers and your witnessing half-hearted at best? Repent and ask God for an 'undivided heart' (Psalm 86:11). Pray that God would renew your passion for his glory.

If we consider the unblushing promises of reward and the staggering nature of the rewards promised in the Gospels, it would seem that Our Lord finds our desires not too strong, but too weak. We are half-hearted creatures, fooling about with drink and sex and ambition when infinite joy is offered us, like an ignorant child who wants to go on making mud pies in a slum because he cannot imagine what is meant by the offer of a holiday at the sea. We are far too easily pleased.
(C. S. Lewis, *The Weight of Glory*, William Collins, 2013, p. 26)

Day 334

Read Colossians 4:7–18
Key verses: Colossians 4:17

· ·

17 Tell Archippus: 'See to it that you complete the ministry you have received in the Lord.'

Finish well. That is Paul's final charge to us.

Demas, mentioned here (verse 14), is probably the one to whom Paul refers in his final letter, and who, 'because he loved this world, has deserted me' (2 Timothy 4:10). Demas is the man who does not press on and does not finish well. What a contrast to Archippus, whom Paul encourages to keep going until he finishes what God has given him to do.

Have you received a work from the Lord? Have you completed it? Most people can start a marathon, but the truly difficult part is to complete it. The marathon of faith requires not only starters but 'stickers'.

Clearly, there are times to lay down what God has given us to do. Some of us, getting on in years, may presume that we are to continue what we have always done. God may say, 'I want you to stop doing that now. You have done your bit. Leave it for somebody else to complete.' Conversely, others of us need to keep going where we are, in that little church that sometimes breaks our hearts. God's word to us is, 'Complete the ministry you have received in the Lord' (verse 17).

Fulfil the job given, even if the going is tough. Christ is at the end of the storm and, amazingly, he is with us in the storm: 'When you pass through the waters, I will be with you; and when you pass through the rivers, they will not sweep over you' (Isaiah 43:2). David Livingstone, the great nineteenth-century Scottish missionary and explorer, declared just a few weeks before his death, 'Nothing earthly shall make me give up my work in despair. I encourage myself in the Lord my God and go forward' (plaque in the David Livingstone Centre, Blantyre).

It's often too soon to quit. Jesus completed the work of salvation that his Father had given him to do (John 17:4). As part of his church, don't quit what he has called you to do, till he tells you it's quitting time. Do not lose your reward. Trust God and finish well. Christ is worth it! He is King of heaven, Lord of earth.

Are you determined to finish well the tasks the Lord has given you – raising a family, completing an assignment, leading a ministry? The end may seem a long way off, but how we finish is determined by our daily choices. Finishing well depends on living well. It is a lifelong pursuit, composed of a myriad of moments loving, serving, trusting and obeying the Lord. Finishing well is the culmination of a life devoted to God.

> Be strong and courageous, and do the work. Do not be afraid or discouraged, for the LORD God, my God, is with you. He will not fail you or forsake you until all the work . . . of the LORD is finished.
> (1 Chronicles 28:20)

For further study

If you would like to do further study on Colossians, the following books may be useful:

- David Garland, *Colossians, Philemon*, NIV Application Commentary (Zondervan, 1998).

- R. Kent Hughes, *Philippians, Colossians, and Philemon*, Preaching the Word (Crossway, 2013).

- Dick Lucas, *The Message of Colossians & Philemon*, The Bible Speaks Today (IVP, 2000).

- Douglas Moo, *The Letter to the Colossians and to Philemon* (Pillar New Testament Commentary) (IVP, 2008).

- Sam Storms, *The Hope of Glory* (Crossway, 2008).

- N. T. Wright, *Colossians and Philemon*, Tyndale New Testament Commentaries (IVP, 2009).

If God has fed you through your study of the book of Colossians, why not buy the individual Food for the Journey on Colossians and give it to a friend (available from ivpbooks.com)?

Introduction

Revelation 1 – 3

Paul Mallard

Does the church have a future?

Across the generations, troubled Christians have often asked this question.

Even as early as the end of the first century, the future of the church hung in the balance. False teaching, internal division and persecution were rife. Emperor Domitian had exiled the apostle John, who was probably in his nineties, to the island of Patmos. You can imagine John, Jesus' beloved disciple, pacing up and down the island at night, looking across the sea to the cities on the shore, wondering, 'Does the church have a future?'

Into this situation the Lord comes and makes these glorious revelations. He gives John this vision and tells him to write to the seven churches of Asia Minor, in the eastern part of the Roman Empire, in what is now Turkey. The first letter is to Ephesus, the first place the postman would come to when travelling from Patmos. Then the letters move round in a horseshoe, up from Patmos to Smyrna, to Pergamum and through Thyatira, Sardis, Philadelphia, and finally to Laodicea.

To each of these churches Jesus says, 'I know . . . I know your hopes and dreams, your faults and failings, your joys and sorrows, your temptations and frustrations.' Jesus knows each of these churches, and so he can speak wisely and truthfully into each circumstance. He says some hard things to shake believers out of their apathy. He also speaks words of comfort: 'I am with you. I am going to bring a new world where there will be no pain or sorrow.' Every letter ends by pointing the believers to heaven, a reminder that, despite their present struggles, ultimately, they are on the victory side.

Like those first-century believers, we have so many spiritual blessings in Christ, but at the same time we still struggle with sin, failure, doubt and bereavement. Theologians describe this tension as living between 'the already and the not yet'. But John's glorious vision reminds us that we are on the victory side. When we trusted in Christ, when we were placed in Christ, we were put in a position of ultimate strength.

Today the church still faces internal division. Opposition from media and government is increasing. In various parts of the world the persecution of Christians is rife. In such testing times it is understandable that some believers question, 'Does the church have a future?'

The answer is the same as it has always been.

Absolutely.

Day 335

Read Revelation 1:1–20

Key verses: Revelation 1:13–16

. . . .

> ¹³*Among the lampstands was someone like a son of man, dressed in a robe reaching down to his feet and with a golden sash round his chest.* ¹⁴*The hair on his head was white like wool, as white as snow, and his eyes were like blazing fire.* ¹⁵*His feet were like bronze glowing in a furnace, and his voice was like the sound of rushing waters.* ¹⁶*In his right hand he held seven stars, and coming out of his mouth was a sharp, double-edged sword. His face was like the sun shining in all its brilliance.*

'When I get to heaven, I'm going to ask Jesus about . . .' We often speculate about the questions to which we will finally receive answers when we meet Jesus.

However, the apostle John's experience suggests that talking will be the last thing on our minds.

Revelation begins with this vision of the awesome majesty of Christ. John can barely describe it and he uses the word 'like' or 'as' seven times. He says, 'When I saw him, I fell at his feet as though dead' (verse 17). Jesus is not now the baby of Bethlehem, the pale Galilean, or the man of Calvary bathed in blood. He is King of kings and Lord of lords, the strong Son of God. He is magnificent, glorious and majestic.

John was the beloved disciple, yet, as he looks at Jesus, he acknowledges that there is an awesomeness about him, a terrifying otherness. When we look at Jesus, we also see a terrible beauty about him. He is our friend, but he is not our mate. He is the Holy One of God.

We live in a culture that has lost the fear of God, because the church has lost the fear of God. We no longer think of God as awesome, glorious and majestic. The Hebrew word for 'glory' can be translated as the 'heaviness' of God. God is substantial, significant. We need to regain that sense of the awesome glory of Jesus. If the church is to endure suffering, trials and difficulties, we need to recapture this vision of Christ. The magnificent warrior, who will conquer his enemies and come for his people, is reigning now.

When was the last time you felt the awesomeness of God, his terrifying otherness? So often we domesticate and tame God, reducing him to manageable proportions. In doing so, we strip away his glory, his majesty and the 'blazing fire' of his holiness. Our overfamiliarity gives us a god we can handle, predict and control – a powerless, pygmy god.

Today, come into God's presence with reverence. Meditate on John's vision. Whatever your day holds, this is the God who is with you and for you. He is no longer the helpless baby in the Christmas-card manger scene or the tortured figure on a cross. He is the King of kings and Lord of lords, the mighty warrior who is reigning now and will one day bring in the new heaven and the new earth, where you will take your place. Amen!

Day 336

Read Revelation 1:1–20
Key verses: Revelation 1:17–18

....

17When I saw him, I fell at his feet as though dead. Then he placed his right hand on me and said: 'Do not be afraid. I am the First and the Last. 18I am the Living One; I was dead, and now look, I am alive for ever and ever! And I hold the keys of death and Hades.'

Imagine the book of Revelation as a film.

This scene would be the first of many dramatic cliffhangers. The tension would be palpable. The Lord of glory appears in all his majestic brilliance, and John falls at his feet, lying face down in the dirt. What happens next? What does Jesus do?

He stoops down from his throne and he lifts up his servant. He is the glorious, merciful Saviour who stoops from the glory of heaven to lift sinners out of the dirt and put their feet on a rock. In Psalm 3:3 David refers to God as 'my glory, and the lifter of my head' (ESV). It is a picture of the ancient court, where someone who had offended the king would be thrown on his face. If the king decided there would be no mercy, he would click his fingers and the man would be taken out for execution. If the king decided to have mercy, he might point to one of his officers, who would come and lift up the man's head so that he could see the king. But if the king wanted to demonstrate his forgiveness to the one who had offended him, he would leave his throne and come to where the man was in the dirt and would lift up his head. The first face the man would see would be that of the king.

You can look into the face of your King.

Jesus left his throne and all the splendour of heaven to come to earth. Our glorious King died on a cross to pay the penalty for our sins (Philippians 2:6–8). His death brings forgiveness and a restored relationship with God. It guarantees that you are welcome in his presence. He wants to hear your prayers, praises, concerns and adoration. So don't be afraid to draw near – come and stand on holy ground; gaze into the face of your King.

Live for him today in thankful adoration.

> My heart says of you, 'Seek his face!'
>   Your face, Lord, I will seek.
> (Psalm 27:8)

> I have sought your face with all my heart;
>   be gracious to me according to your promise.
> (Psalm 119:58)

> The Lord bless you
>   and keep you;
> the Lord make his face shine on you
>   and be gracious to you;
> the Lord turn his face towards you
> and give you peace.
> (Numbers 6:24–26)

Day 337

Read Revelation 2:1–7

Key verses: Revelation 2:1, 7

••

¹*To the angel of the church in Ephesus write:*
    These are the words of him who holds the seven stars in his right hand and walks among the seven golden lampstands . . .
        ⁷*Whoever has ears, let them hear what the Spirit says to the churches.*

Christians are often called 'People of the Book'. An apt description for past generations, but is it still applicable today?

Notice that each of the letters starts in the same way: verse 1, 'To the angel of the church in . . . write: These are the *words* . . .' And every one of the seven letters ends on the same note: verse 7, 'Whoever has ears, let them *hear what the Spirit says* to the churches' (italics added). These phrases frame each letter.

What are the marks of being godly? One of the marks, and one of the needs of our spiritual renewal, is to be people who love the Word of God. What we have in our hands is the most precious physical object in the universe. This is the Word of the living God. What the Scriptures say, God says. But the purpose of God in speaking to us is not simply to entertain, enthral or even inform us. The purpose of the Word of God is to transform us.

God the Father is the author of renewal. His plan and purpose for our lives is that we might be holy: 'He chose us in him before the creation of the world to be holy and blameless in his sight' (Ephesians 1:4). Jesus Christ is the model of renewal: to become like Jesus is the goal of our lives, and the Holy Spirit is the agent of renewal. As we go through these letters, every one of them speaks of the ministry of the Spirit: 'Hear what the Spirit says to the churches.' But the Word of God is the instrument of renewal. If we are to be renewed in the power of God to be the kind of people he wants us to be, then we have to listen to what God says to us through his Word.

Do you struggle to spend time in God's Word? When our to-do list is long, sometimes it feels self-indulgent to take time to read the Bible. We forget that this is not a luxury, but a fundamental necessity for our spiritual life and growth. Make every effort to drown out distracting voices and soak in God's Word – study it, memorize it, meditate on it and share it with others.

Let God's Word become your source of strength, joy, comfort and direction, as Psalm 119 describes:

> How can a young person stay on the path of purity?
>   By living according to your word.
> (verse 9)

> My soul is weary with sorrow;
>   strengthen me according to your word.
> (verse 28)

> I run in the path of your commands,
>   for you have broadened my understanding.
> (verse 32)

> Your word is a lamp for my feet,
>   a light on my path.
> (verse 105)

> You are my refuge and my shield;
>   I have put my hope in your word.
> (verse 114)

Day 338

Read Revelation 2:1–7
Key verses: Revelation 2:2–3

••

²I know your deeds, your hard work and your perseverance. I know that you cannot tolerate wicked people, that you have tested those who claim to be apostles but are not, and have found them false. ³You have persevered and have endured hardships for my name, and have not grown weary.

It is nicknamed the Light of Asia.

The city of Ephesus is the most important of the seven cities, famous for its banks, boulevards and harbour. It is a melting pot of people from all over the Roman Empire. People come specifically to worship at the Temple of Artemis (or Diana), one of the wonders of the world (Acts 19).

In this demon-infested, immoral city, the church shines as a bright light. It was founded by the apostle Paul in around AD 52 as part of his third missionary journey, and he spent two years there. Ten years later he writes the letter to the Ephesians, the crown of his theology. Timothy pastors the Ephesian church, and Paul writes 1 and 2 Timothy to him while he is there. According to tradition, John the apostle, who wrote Revelation, also pastored the church at Ephesus.

Perhaps, then, it is not surprising that Christ commends the church. It is:

• *A busy church.* Verse 2: 'I know your deeds, your hard work.' The Greek word conveys the idea of labouring to the point of exhaustion. It is good to be a busy church. If you are saved, you are set aside for service. Indeed, the role of the pastor/teacher is not just to do the ministry, but to prepare God's people for works of service (Ephesians 4:12). Every Christian has a gift that is given by Christ for the glory of God and for the building up of the church. Whoever you are, whatever gift you have, it is for the good of the church, and you are needed.

• *A discerning church.* They vehemently oppose false teachers (verse 2). In verse 6 the sentiment is even stronger: 'But you have this in your favour: you hate the practices of the Nicolaitans, which I also hate.' This church knows that truth is important.

• *A steadfast church.* The Christians have endured hardships and persecution (verse 3). They have seen their pastor, John, thrown into prison, but have not given up.

Are you busy in God's service? Church is not supposed to be like a football match where the majority of us sit in the stands cheering on the active few. God has placed you, with your particular gifts, in your local church (Romans 12:6–8; 1 Corinthians 12; 1 Peter 4:10–11). Of course, church isn't the only place where we serve God, but it is certainly a starting point. Will you find out how you can use your gift in the life of the church? If you are already serving, will you persevere? You may not be recognized or thanked by others, but the Lord knows all your work on his behalf. Determine to wait patiently for his reward (Matthew 16:27; 1 Corinthians 3:10–15).

Day 339

Read Revelation 2:1–7
Key verse: Revelation 2:4

···

⁴Yet I hold this against you: you have forsaken the love you had at first.

It must be one of the most devastating statements in the whole of Scripture: 'You have left your first love' (NKJV).

One person translates it, 'You do not love me as much as you used to. You have given up loving me.' When the church was planted in AD 52, it was on fire for God. When Paul wrote the letter to the Ephesians in AD 62, about thirty years before the book of Revelation was penned, it was a church that had a reputation for love (Ephesians 1:15; 6:24). But now that love has grown cold. You can imagine the Christians there saying, 'We are tired out. Have you seen all our church ministries? Haven't you seen our programme? We are fighting for truth. We have suffered for your name.'

'Yes,' says the Lord, 'but you do not love me like you used to. You can have all those things, but if your love has grown cold, then it is fatal.'

Sometimes we are so busy about the Lord's service that we do not have time for the Lord we serve. The issue is worship. Of course, worship is everything we do: it is 24/7, presenting our bodies as living sacrifices to God. We worship God in the office, in the factory, when we are looking after the kids, struggling with pain and dealing with elderly relatives. The New Testament talks about worship in this broad sense, but it also speaks about those moments we spend gazing on God. We are to come, as individuals or as the body of Christ, and spend time gazing on the beauty of the Lord, declaring his worth, delighting in his character, loving him, adoring him, praising his name, surrendering our will to him.

In verse 4 we are assuming that the love spoken of is a love for Christ, but it could equally be a love for God's people. When we fall out of love with the Lord, we find God's people very hard to love. The only thing that sustains a ministry of loving difficult people is the love of Christ. We cannot love the church unless we love Christ.

Are you bitter as you look around at those in the church who don't work as hard as you do? Do you find yourself criticizing others or feeling overprotective of your ministry? Do you feel exhausted and joyless in serving? Perhaps, like the Ephesians, you have become so busy in the Lord's service that you have forgotten the Lord you serve. God is jealous for your love. It doesn't matter how much you serve, how well you know your Bible, or how many spiritual victories you have experienced in the past, if you don't love the Lord wholeheartedly. Do you love God more now than you did six months, a year or even ten years ago? Are you grieving the Lord? If so, acknowledge his rebuke, repent and ask for forgiveness:

> Today, if you hear his voice,
>   do not harden your hearts.
> (Hebrews 4:7)

Day 340

Read Revelation 2:1–7
Key verses: Revelation 2:5, 7

....

⁵*Consider how far you have fallen! Repent and do the things you did at first. If you do not repent, I will come to you and remove your lampstand from its place . . .*

⁷*Whoever has ears, let them hear what the Spirit says to the churches. To the one who is victorious, I will give the right to eat from the tree of life, which is in the paradise of God.*

Is it possible to recapture the passionate, zealous love for God you had when you were a new Christian?

Absolutely! The living Christ urges these Ephesian Christians, 'Consider how far you have fallen.' Bring it to mind and hold it there. Remember when you first became a Christian. Remember how you fell in love with Jesus. Remember it; keep dwelling on it. Then, 'Repent.' This is a sudden, urgent turning to Christ. And he says, 'Do the things you did at first.' In other words, go back to living as you did when you first became a Christian; go back to doing the same things. Can you remember when you first fell in love with Jesus, when you first went to the cross? Go back to that point – to the primitive, unsophisticated simplicity of that first love.

He gives them two encouragements to go back to that simplicity. One is negative; one positive. The negative one is in verse 5: if you do not do something about it, you will have no future. The positive one in verse 7 is a promise of paradise. The word 'paradise' appears three times in the New Testament. It is used when Jesus is speaking to the thief on the cross (Luke 23:43), and Paul uses it in 2 Corinthians 12. This Persian word refers to a garden of delight.

How do I get this first love back? You can't manufacture it; you can only look at his love for you. When was the last time you looked at that Calvary love and it broke your heart and showed you how much you love your Saviour?

Do you ever wonder how much God loves you? God the Father devised the plan of salvation whereby he sent his only Son to the cross for us. Surely we must agree with John: 'See what great love the Father has lavished on us' (1 John 3:1). And Christ willingly died on the cross to rescue us from our sin and adopt us as sons and daughters of God. Today, gaze on that breathtaking Calvary love.

> Man of sorrows, what a name
> For the Son of God, who came
> Ruined sinners to reclaim:
> Hallelujah, what a Saviour!
>
> Bearing shame and scoffing rude,
> In my place condemned he stood,
> Sealed my pardon with his blood:
> Hallelujah, what a Saviour!
>
> Guilty, helpless, lost were we;
> Blameless Lamb of God was he,
> Sacrificed to set us free:
> Hallelujah, what a Saviour!
>
> He was lifted up to die;
> 'It is finished' was his cry;
> Now in heaven exalted high:
> Hallelujah, what a Saviour!
> (Philip P. Bliss, 'Man of Sorrows', 1875)

Day 341

Read Revelation 2:8–11
Key verses: Revelation 2:9–10

. . . .

> [9] *I know your afflictions and your poverty – yet you are rich! I know about the slander of those who say they are Jews and are not, but are a synagogue of Satan.* [10] *Do not be afraid of what you are about to suffer. I tell you, the devil will put some of you in prison to test you, and you will suffer persecution for ten days. Be faithful, even to the point of death, and I will give you life as your victor's crown.*

The devil hates you, your Christian faith, your marriage, your kids, your church, your pastor.

The believers in Smyrna know they have to take the devil seriously. They live in a beautiful city. It was, according to legend, founded by the Greeks and was the birthplace of Homer, the father of Western literature. It is wealthy owing to an exclusive right to import myrrh – an anaesthetic in great demand in the ancient world. And it is nicknamed the resurrection city because twice in its history it was destroyed and, metaphorically, rose out of the ashes. Interestingly, when Jesus introduces himself to this city, he describes himself as the One who has risen from the dead.

But Smyrna is a dangerous city for Christians. The Roman Empire is huge and covers most of the known world. Loyalty is cultivated by emperor worship. At least once a year every Roman citizen has to go into the temple and burn incense, confessing that the emperor is Lord and God. But the Christians refuse. Their backs are against the wall, and the people who are informing on them are from the synagogue. Jews are exempt from emperor worship, but they claim that the Christians are an upstart sect and encourage Emperor Domitian to take severe measures against them.

Christ tells these Christians in Smyrna that Satan is going to throw some of them into prison; they're going to be persecuted by the Roman Empire. But behind the Roman Empire is Satan. We often think that the devil is a tame little beast whom we can pat on the head. But he is highly intelligent, immensely powerful, remarkably persistent, fiendishly cunning, violently malicious and utterly unscrupulous. He can attack your mind and body. He can bring persecution and false teaching. He will do everything he can to destroy your Christian faith.

Right now, the devil is prowling around you. He is looking for your weak spots, areas where you are prone to temptation, any way he can get a foothold on your life (Ephesians 4:27; 1 Peter 5:8). Stand firm and resist the devil's schemes by putting on each element of the armour of God (Ephesians 6:10–18). Most importantly, remember to whom you belong:

> I'm not afraid of the devil. The devil can handle me – he's got judo I never heard of. But he can't handle the One to whom I'm joined; he can't handle the One to whom I'm united; he can't handle the One whose nature dwells in my nature.
> (A. W. Tozer, *Gems from Tozer*, Moody Press, 1980)

Day 342

Read Revelation 2:8–11
Key verse: Revelation 2:9

. . . .

⁹I know your afflictions and your poverty – yet you are rich! I know about the slander of those who say they are Jews and are not, but are a synagogue of Satan.

Does God want Christians to be happy, healthy and prosperous?

If he does, you might imagine you would find them in the wealthy, influential city of Smyrna. But the church is a small, struggling, frail bunch of people. The Christians at Smyrna are insignificant, down-trodden, despised and threadbare.

Notice the words that Jesus uses to describe them in verse 9:

• *Affliction.* The Greek word *thlipsis* is used, frequently translated as 'persecution' or 'torture'. These believers in Smyrna are facing the weight, the relentless pressure, of persecution.

• *Poverty.* There are different Greek words to describe poverty. The one used here conveys the sense of having nothing at all. This is a destitute church in an affluent community. Probably many of them are slaves or have been ostracized for their faith. There are those who say that if you're a Christian, you should never be sick or have any problems. You should be wealthy and prosperous. But sometimes, in the mystery of God's providence, the choicest Christians go through affliction and suffering.

• *Slander.* Slander comes from those who are the 'synagogue of Satan'. Much of the persecution, certainly in the Acts of the Apostles, comes from the Jewish direction. Not all those who are Israel are real Israel. True Jews are not those descended from Abraham, but those who have faith in Christ.

Given the church's circumstances, you might think these Christians are being punished for some grievous sin. But this is the shortest and warmest of all the letters. No faults or criticisms are mentioned. I'm sure Smyrna isn't a perfect church, and yet this is a letter of unconditional commendation. Christ's message to these struggling believers is that he knows and loves them.

Don't let difficult circumstances cause you to doubt God's love. You are infinitely precious to him. He delights in you. Seek his purpose and plans even in dark days (Ephesians 3:14–19).

> Do you think anyone is going to be able to drive a wedge between us and Christ's love for us? There is no way! Not trouble, not hard times, not hatred, not hunger, not homelessness, not bullying threats, not back-stabbing, not even the worst sins listed in Scripture . . . None of this fazes us because Jesus loves us. I'm absolutely convinced that nothing – nothing living or dead, angelic or demonic, today or tomorrow, high or low, thinkable or unthinkable – absolutely *nothing* can get between us and God's love because of the way that Jesus our Master has embraced us.
> (Romans 8:35–39, MSG)

Day 343

Read Revelation 2:8–11
Key verse: Revelation 2:9

• •

⁹I know your afflictions and your poverty – yet you are rich! I know about the slander of those who say they are Jews and are not, but are a synagogue of Satan.

What makes a person rich?

Surprisingly, Christ says that the church in Smyrna is rich. They are being persecuted, but, in God's eyes, these poor, pitiful Christians are rich.

Can I remind you of the spiritual riches you have in Christ? You have been justified. God has declared you righteous in his sight. You are as righteous as a redeemed sinner ever can be. You will always be righteous and justified in his sight. You are being sanctified; no matter how stubborn you are, the Holy Spirit won't give up on you. He is sanctifying you, and you will be glorified. God, the Creator and Sustainer of the universe, is your Father, King, Master, shield and hiding place. He provides, guides and protects you.

Jesus, the Son of God, lives in you, loves you and prays for you. He is your Brother, Saviour, Lord and Friend. He will never let you go. The Holy Spirit seals you: he is the life of God in the soul of man. He gives assurance, comfort, encouragement and joy. You have an inheritance that will never perish, fade or disappoint, and it's reserved in heaven for you. You are the child of a king, a soldier in his army, a stone in his temple and a sheep in his flock. You have brothers and sisters who love, encourage, support and pray for you. You have the Word of God in your hand and in your heart. It feeds, guides and brings you light in the darkness. It gives you purpose, direction and a goal for your life.

You look up and there's no judgment. You look down and there's no hell. You look in and the peace of God that passes all understanding guards your heart and mind. You look back and your sins are covered. You look forward and the glory dawns in the future because Jesus is coming back for you. You are saved, sealed, satisfied, secured and destined for glory!

You might not have a big bank balance or great career prospects, but you are rich. God has blessed you with 'every spiritual blessing in Christ' (Ephesians 1:3). He has lavished his love upon you, given you a peace that cannot be bought, joy that does not depend on mood or circumstance, and an inheritance that can never run out. The riches you have are unsurpassable, incomparable and inexhaustible. Are you living like a person who is rich in Christ?

Today, be generous with your time and finances, find your confidence and security in Christ, don't fear for the future, trust God for your needs, share the good news of the gospel with someone, and be thankful: 'My God will meet all your needs according to the riches of his glory in Christ Jesus' (Philippians 4:19).

Day 344

Read Revelation 2:8–11
Key verse: Revelation 2:8

. . . .

> [8] *To the angel of the church in Smyrna write:*
> *These are the words of him who is the First and the Last, who died and came to life again.*

When you are suffering, what do you need to know? What truths, what hope do you need to cling to?

The first thing Christ says to the church in Smyrna facing persecution is, 'I am alive.'

Here are the two great facts of Christian history: Christ died once and for all on the cross, and he rose again from the dead. The resurrection is an indisputable historical fact. It is not a symbol, myth or parable; it is a physical, literal and datable event. Of course, it's interesting that John, who wrote this book, was one of the very first to believe the resurrection. In John's account, in chapter 20 of his Gospel, the disciples hear the news from Mary, and John and Peter run to the tomb. John gets there first. That simple fact authenticates the historical relevance and reliability of the story. He arrives at the empty tomb first because he is there on the spot. He doesn't even see the risen Christ. He sees the folded grave clothes and is utterly convinced of the resurrection.

The resurrection is not only an indisputable fact of history, but it also has massive significance for our lives. Just look back at Revelation 1:17–18:

> When I saw him, I fell at his feet as though dead. Then he placed his right hand on me and said: 'Do not be afraid. I am the First and the Last. I am the Living One; I was dead, and now look, I am alive for ever and ever! And I hold the keys of death and Hades.'

What a comfort to know that death is not the end. If you have to go through the veil of death, Jesus is on the other side. Jesus, the Lord of glory, has conquered death and has risen. He now holds the keys of the grave and can unlock it for all his people. When we have to face death, and even when we have to face death for the sake of the gospel, it's wonderful to proclaim that Jesus is alive.

Raising Jesus from the dead was not an arbitrary stunt by God the Father. No, the resurrection has meaning. The resurrection is the outworking and proof of our salvation, because death is the out-working and proof of our sin. Jesus's new life shows us the cycle of sin and death has finally been broken. There is new life to be had. Sin has been conquered.

It is therefore the resurrection of Jesus – and *can* only be the resurrection of Jesus – that assures us of salvation. Only the resurrection proves that our sins have been fully dealt with, that death is no longer our destination, but a gateway to perfect, endless life.

The cross is not a starter pack. God doesn't drum up most of what we need, only to leave us fishing around in our pockets to provide the rest.

By dying and rising for us, the Son has closed the deal. In raising him from the dead, the Father has signed for it.

(Sam Allberry, 'Death Is Dead, Christ Has Conquered', 16 April 2017 <www.thegospelcoalition.org/article/death-is-dead-christ-has-conquered/>)

Day 345

Read Revelation 2:8–11
Key verses: Revelation 2:9–10

. . . .

⁹I know your afflictions and your poverty – yet you are rich! I know about the slander of those who say they are Jews and are not, but are a synagogue of Satan. ¹⁰Do not be afraid of what you are about to suffer. I tell you, the devil will put some of you in prison to test you, and you will suffer persecution for ten days. Be faithful, even to the point of death, and I will give you life as your victor's crown.

When we look at our world, and even at our own lives, we may wonder who is in control.

Jesus wants the church in Smyrna to know that, although the devil is going to put some believers in prison, God is the one calling the shots. Their imprisonment is not an accident. God is not on the sidelines, wringing his hands, saying, 'I'd love to help you but I can't.' No, he is saying, 'I'm in control. The devil will attack you, but it's only part of my purpose and plan.'

The doctrine of the sovereignty of a loving God is the single most comforting doctrine we can possibly have as Christians. We may think of it as a harsh and difficult doctrine, but that is not the case at all. Christ reigns, and I'm in his hands. Whatever I have to go through – even if I suffer death, even if I am persecuted – I'm not in the hands of human beings; I'm in the hands of Jesus. My suffering may be for ten days, which is a limited period, but he will call the shots. He'll start it and he'll finish it.

Whatever you are going through today, God has a purpose in it. The devil might be testing you to destroy you. But God tests you in order to make you strong. Imagine I'm walking along the road and I pick up a lump of rock. There is a seam in it that appears to be gold. What do I do? I crush it and put it in the furnace to extract the pure gold. Why? Not because it's worthless, but because it has value. God looks at our lives and sees the gold of holiness. He crushes us and puts us in the furnace. He produces something that lasts. Whatever trials you are going through today, remember that God is in control and he knows what he's doing.

There is nothing – no circumstance, no trouble, no testing – that can ever touch me until, first of all, it has gone past God and past Christ right through to me. If it has come that far, it has come with a great purpose, which I may not understand at the moment. But as I refuse to become panicky, as I lift up my eyes to Him and accept it as coming from the throne of God for some great purpose of blessing to my own heart, no sorrow will ever disturb me, no trial will ever disarm me, no circumstance will cause me to fret – for I shall rest in the joy of what my Lord is! That is the rest of victory!
(Alan Redpath, quoted in Elizabeth George, *Loving God with All Your Mind*, Harvest House Publishers, 2005, p. 204)

Day 346

Read Revelation 2:8–11
Key verse: Revelation 2:11

....

¹¹*Whoever has ears, let them hear what the Spirit says to the churches. The one who is victorious will not be hurt at all by the second death.*

If we send a text message or an email to someone who is dealing with a difficult situation, we usually try to end on a positive, hopeful note.

Strangely, perhaps, Jesus does not end his letter to the church in Smyrna with warm words of blessing. Instead, his parting comment to the believers is a reminder that they are not going to hell. They will not be hurt by the second death, the death after death.

We struggle with this doctrine of eternal, conscious separation from God. It's intellectually demanding, emotionally draining and morally disturbing. We say, 'Well, that's the God of the Old Testament, the God of wrath, not the God of the New Testament.' But Jesus talked more about hell than anyone else. He spoke about darkness, weeping and gnashing of teeth. He spoke about the two gates, two roads, two crowds and two destinies. It was Jesus who said it is better to pluck out your eye or cut off your hand than fall into hell.

The truth here is a simple reminder of the awesome seriousness of sin. The gravity of sin is seen most clearly and demonstrated most vividly when Christ, the holy Son of God, receives the just punishment for our sins at Calvary. If you have any doubts about hell, look at the cross. Jesus says to these believers facing persecution – and it's a strange thing to say – in the end, just rejoice in the fact that you are saved from hell, at measureless cost.

Every single person you meet today is going to live for ever. Every single face you look into today will live for ever, either in heaven or in hell. What makes the difference? The gospel. Whatever we go through in this world, if we're Christians, we're going to glory – and that's wonderful.

At first it seems strange that Jesus would encourage persecuted believers by saying they will be spared hell. But, on reflection, how wise of Jesus to place their suffering in the context of eternity. How kind of him to remind them that, in the end, the only thing that matters is that their eternal destiny is secure.

> Therefore we do not lose heart. Though outwardly we are wasting away, yet inwardly we are being renewed day by day. For our light and momentary troubles are achieving for us an eternal glory that far outweighs them all. So we fix our eyes not on what is seen, but on what is unseen, since what is seen is temporary, but what is unseen is eternal.
> (2 Corinthians 4:16–18)

Today, give thanks to God that, because of Jesus' sacrifice, you are headed for glory. Pray that God would use your life, witness and words to help point others heavenward. Look for an opportunity to share the gospel with someone you meet today.

Day 347

Read Revelation 2:12–17
Key verses: Revelation 2:12–13

. . . .

¹² *To the angel of the church in Pergamum write:*
These are the words of him who has the sharp, double-edged sword. ¹³ *I know where you live – where Satan has his throne. Yet you remain true to my name. You did not renounce your faith in me, not even in the days of Antipas, my faithful witness, who was put to death in your city – where Satan lives.*

Would you die for your faith? That's the question facing the believers in Pergamum.

Historically, Pergamum is the capital city. The proconsul, or governor of the Roman province, lives there. When he goes down the street, a man walks in front of him carrying a sword as a symbol of his authority. Interestingly, when Jesus writes to this church, he reminds them that he holds the double-edged sword. He is the one with ultimate authority.

Paganism is thriving in Pergamum. On the hillside, overshadowing the whole city, is a massive altar to the Greek god Zeus. The patron god of the city is Asclepius, the god of healing. The symbol of Asclepius is a snake on a stick. Wherever you go in the city, there are images of serpents, and emperor worship is ubiquitous. The devil seems to be rampant in this city, and the forces of evil overwhelming.

Paganism and persecution are a stage further on compared to what is happening in Smyrna. Believers aren't just being thrown into prison; Antipas, who was probably the pastor of the church, has been killed (verse 13). According to the church historian Eusebius, he was arrested for his faith, put inside a bronze bull and roasted alive.

What is the reason for this persecution? Verse 13 says, 'You remain true to my name.' But why are we hated as Christians? Not because we are religious in a general sense – the world can put up with that. It's because we believe that Jesus Christ is the only way to God; the only name under heaven by which we can be saved; the one revelation of God that is full, final and climactic. We are faithful to his name.

To the world, this is scandalous. And if, like the Christians in Pergamum, you stand up for this truth and are faithful to God's name, you'll face opposition too.

We shouldn't be surprised if we suffer for being Christians – missing out on promotion, being ostracized by family or being mocked by the media (John 15:18–25). The signs indicate that, in our generation, persecution will become increasingly overt in the West. We may not have to die for our faith, but we will experience the cost of discipleship.

Today, pray for wisdom to represent Christ well and to be faithful to his name in your particular circumstances. Pray, too, for believers around the world who are being persecuted. Pray that even as they suffer they would know God's love and peace, be encouraged in their faith and continue to witness boldly.

Day 348

Read Revelation 2:12–17
Key verse: Revelation 2:14

···

14 Nevertheless, I have a few things against you: there are some among you who hold to the teaching of Balaam, who taught Balak to entice the Israelites to sin so that they ate food sacrificed to idols and committed sexual immorality.

'The long, dull, monotonous years of middle-aged prosperity or middle-aged adversity are excellent campaigning weather for the devil' (C. S. Lewis, *The Screwtape Letters*, William Collins, 2016, p. 155).

The devil doesn't always attack us with persecution. In fact, a more subtle method of seduction is usually more effective, whatever age we are!

It is certainly working in the church at Pergamum. 'Balaam' is a code word that takes us back to Numbers 22 – 25. The Israelites have come out of the Promised Land and have conquered all their enemies. They come to the plains of Moab, and the king, Balak, realizes that his time is up. So he sends for the prophet Balaam to curse the Israelites so that he could defeat them in battle.

The plan backfires and, instead of cursing Israel, he blesses them. Balaam explains to the king that attacking the Israelites won't work; he needs another plan. So, when the Israelites come to a place called Shittim, the beautiful women of Moab seduce them. They begin to worship idols and commit fornication, and God's wrath falls upon them.

Do you see, seduction is far more dangerous to the church than persecution? When the church is persecuted, very often it grows and flourishes. The second-century Church Father Tertullian said, 'The blood of the martyrs is the seed of the church.' But when the devil joins the church and seduces it with false teaching, it is in real danger.

Remember King David? When the devil attacked him, he just grew stronger and wrote some wonderful psalms. It is in middle age, when he is relaxing at home instead of going to war, that the devil is able to seduce him with the beautiful Bathsheba. He takes her, and his reign is ruined. God forgives him, but the implications go on and on.

The Lord says to this church, 'If you don't stand against this seduction and deal with false teaching and immorality, I'm going to come against you with the sword of my mouth.' Jesus, the divine Warrior, will fight for the purity of his church.

> We are too apt to forget that temptation to sin will rarely present itself to us in its true colours saying, 'I am your deadly enemy, and I want to ruin you forever in hell.' Oh no! Sin comes to us like Judas, with a kiss; like Joab, with an outstretched hand and flattering words. The forbidden fruit seemed good and desirable to Eve; yet it cast her out of Eden. Walking idly on his palace roof seemed harmless enough to David; yet it ended in adultery and murder. Sin rarely seems [like] sin at first beginnings. Let us watch and pray, lest we fall into temptation.
> (J. C. Ryle, *Holiness*, 1877, Ichthus Publications, 2017, p. 7)

> Where are your weak points, those areas where you're particularly susceptible to the devil's schemes? Will you pray for strength to resist and actively root out sin?

Day 349

Read Revelation 2:8–17
Key verse: Revelation 2:13

. . . .

¹³I know where you live – where Satan has his throne. Yet you remain true to my name. You did not renounce your faith in me, not even in the days of Antipas, my faithful witness, who was put to death in your city – where Satan lives.

Do you know that Christians sometimes lie?

They tell more lies on a Sunday morning at the end of a service than at any other time. The pastor shakes your hand and asks, 'How are you doing?' And you say, 'Fine.' Your life is falling apart. Nobody knows the problems you are having at work. Nobody knows that although you have been widowed many years, you still miss your husband every day. Nobody knows the problems in your marriage, no other Christian couples seem to be struggling. Nobody knows about the problems you are having with your children. Everybody else's kids seem to be perfect Christians.

But Jesus knows.

In verse 13, he says to the church, 'I *know* where you live.' Back in verse 9, he said, 'I *know* your afflictions and your poverty . . . I *know* about the slander' (italics added). This isn't the knowledge of observation; it is the knowledge of experience. To put it in a simple way, when we look at those words in verse 9 – affliction, poverty, slander – we could be talking about the earthly ministry of Jesus. He was afflicted on the cross more than any other person. He knew poverty: 'Foxes have dens . . . but the Son of Man has nowhere to lay his head' (Matthew 8:20). He was slandered. People said he was mad and demon-possessed. When Jesus says, 'I *know*', this isn't the knowledge of a distant, removed God. This is the knowledge of a high priest who's been where you are, who looks and sees and knows your sorrows, who is tenderly moved by the concerns and sufferings of his people.

Perhaps nobody else knows your pain. What a comfort that Jesus knows. He's been bruised and broken. He is the man of sorrows, acquainted with grief (Isaiah 53:3).

Whatever your heartache, Jesus knows. The cross of Christ stands as a reminder that God is not aloof or immune from suffering. He entered our world and he understands your pain.

> The real sting of suffering is not misfortune itself, nor even the pain of it or the injustice of it, but the apparent God-forsakenness of it. Pain is endurable, but the seeming indifference of God is not . . . We think of Him as an armchair spectator, almost gloating over the world's suffering, and enjoying His own insulation from it. It is this terrible caricature of God that the cross smashes to smithereens. (John Stott, *The Cross of Christ*, IVP, 1986, p. 329)

Day 350

Read Revelation 2:18–29
Key verse: Revelation 2:18

．．

¹⁸*To the angel of the church in Thyatira write:*
    These are the words of the Son of God, whose eyes are like
blazing fire and whose feet are like burnished bronze.

What happens when our Christian principles clash with society's expectations?

For the believers in Thyatira, this is a daily struggle.

The city is a military colony founded by Alexander the Great. The soldiers worship the Greek god Apollo, who has been given the title, 'The son of god'. It is also a commercial centre. In Acts 16, Paul speaks about Lydia, the first European convert, a dealer in purple cloth, who comes from Thyatira. The city is famous for its trade guilds, and the only way you can get a job is by joining a guild. Each trade guild dedicates a banquet once a month to its patron god. The health of the god is toasted, and burnt offerings are dedicated to the image of the god. Usually these sessions end with an orgy. Of course, Christians are forbidden from eating food offered to idols, or indulging in immorality or fornication, so how can they live and work in a city where they are constantly being asked to go against their moral scruples?

Christ's response is to give these distraught believers a magnificent insight into who he is (verse 18). Apollo, the son of Zeus, is not the son of god; he's just a passing image. Jesus is Lord and King. Truly, he is the Son of God, glorious in majesty. His eyes are like blazing fire, signifying his absolute justice, inflexible integrity and supernatural knowledge. When you look into the face of Jesus, you lay yourself bare before him. His eyes see everything in your soul. We can't hide anything from him. His feet are like burnished bronze.

That's a picture of his strength, power and majesty. It is echoed in Ezekiel's vision of the glory of God. When he stands firm, nothing is going to move him. From head to toe, he is the glorious Son of God.

When we read all the books John wrote – his Gospel, the book of Revelation and his three letters – the theme of the absolute deity of Jesus is underlined again and again. Christ's message to these first believers, and to us, is that he is the co-equal, co-eternal Son of God. He is fully divine.

Today, as you face temptations to compromise your faith and opportunities to stand up for your beliefs, reflect on John's vision of Christ. His searching eyes are the only ones you should fear. His assessment of you is the only one that really counts. As you stand firm, remember you are resting your whole weight on the Son of God. The one with burnished bronze feet is strong enough to carry you, and stable enough to hold you fast:

Listen to me . . .
you whom I have upheld since your birth,
 and have carried since you were born.
Even to your old age and grey hairs
 I am he, I am he who will sustain you.
I have made you and I will carry you;
 I will sustain you and I will rescue you.
(Isaiah 46:3–4)

Day 351

Read Revelation 2:18–29
Key verse: Revelation 2:19

. . . .

¹⁹I know your deeds, your love and faith, your service and per-
severance, and that you are now doing more than you did at
first.

How would people describe your church? What are the standout characteristics?

If you were to go to the church at Thyatira, the first thing you would notice is that it is a wonderfully loving church. The Christians love one another and they love to talk about the Lord.

The foundations of this church are love and faith, which result in service and perseverance (verse 19). In other words, the believers have a love that leads to service, and a faith that leads to perseverance.

Love is crucial in a church. There is not one of the twenty-one letters or epistles of the New Testament written to the early church that doesn't speak about relationships between Christians. The sublime book of Romans deals with relationships between Christians of strong and weak faith. The book of Philemon is written to a slave owner, reminding him that Christianity affects his relationship with his slave now. Whichever book it is, each one speaks about relationships, because the biggest destructive force in churches is disunity amongst brothers and sisters.

Jesus commends this church because they have a wonderful love which leads to wonderful service. The word for 'service' is *diakonia*, conveying the idea of humble service – washing one another's feet or cleaning tables. Real love means getting your hands dirty.

Christ also commends this church for their faith. Saving faith is passive. We receive salvation as a free gift of grace from God. As the hymn writer says, 'Nothing in my hand I bring; simply to thy cross I cling' (Augustus Toplady, 'Rock of Ages', 1885). But living faith is always seen. In Hebrews 11, the proof or evidence that these great men and women had faith was seen by what they did. Faith works. Vision leads to venture. In Thyatira, faith leads to wonderful perseverance. The believers don't give up.

What a commendation!

What is your church known for? Is it like Thyatira, known for love and active faith? Or is it like Ephesus, strict on doctrine but lacking in love? The right theology is important, but it is worth little if it is not accompanied by love. The New Testament is full of reminders about how we should treat one another: bear with one another, forgive one another, be patient and gentle . . .' And over all these virtues put on love, which binds them all together in perfect unity' (Colossians 3:12–14).

Love is our hallmark:

A new command I give you: love one another. As I have loved you, so you must love one another. By this everyone will know that you are my disciples, if you love one another.
(John 13:34–35)

How will you show love to another Christian today?

Day 352

Read Revelation 2:18–29
Key verses: Revelation 2:20–23

....

> [20] *Nevertheless, I have this against you: you tolerate that woman Jezebel, who calls herself a prophet. By her teaching she misleads my servants into sexual immorality and the eating of food sacrificed to idols. [21] I have given her time to repent of her immorality, but she is unwilling. [22] So I will cast her on a bed of suffering, and I will make those who commit adultery with her suffer intensely, unless they repent of her ways. [23] I will strike her children dead. Then all the churches will know that I am he who searches hearts and minds, and I will repay each of you according to your deeds.*

In my years of ministry, I have learned that almost anyone is capable of almost anything, especially in relation to sin. And sin is rampant in the church at Thyatira.

Jezebel is another code word, taking us back to 1 Kings 16. She was the wife of the wicked King Ahab and encouraged his idolatry. They set up an altar to Baal in the city of Samaria and sacrificed their children on it. They promoted immorality and cultic prostitution.

Christ's point in referencing Jezebel is twofold:

- *Truth is important.* As Christians, there can never be spiritual renewal in our lives, or in the church of Jesus, unless we are convicted and convinced about the truth of the great doctrines of the Christian faith. I don't mean that we become pernickety about secondary issues. But there are some things that are non-negotiable: the doctrine of the Trinity, the incarnation, penal substitutionary atonement, the resurrection and the return of Christ. Indeed, the fundamental truth – the material principle of the Reformation – is *sola scriptura*, the authority of the Word of God.

These believers are in trouble because they don't confront false teaching. A mark of a church's truth and discipline is how it deals with falsehood.

- *Lax teaching leads to lax living.* Jezebel teaches that sin isn't serious. This thinking affects the believers and leads to immorality and idolatry. We need to be clear in our thinking and recognize that all sin is vile. Lying is vile. Being unkind to your wife is vile. Internet pornography is vile. But God can forgive the vilest sin. The blood of Jesus is sufficient to cover your worst sin. Failure is not final. God can pour his grace into your life and give you deliverance.

John Bunyan described sin as taking your fist and smashing it into the face of Christ. When Jesus was arrested, the soldiers took him and put a blindfold over his eyes. Then, one after another, they came and smashed him in the face. When we sin, even as Christians, it's like that fist in the face of Jesus Christ.

Today, will you put a marker in the sand and deal with a particular sin you have been indulging in? Repent. Draw on God's strength to resist temptation. If it is helpful, pray specifically with a more mature Christian about this issue.

Day 353

Read Revelation 2:18–29
Key verses: Revelation 2:24–25

....

²⁴ *Now I say to the rest of you in Thyatira, to you who do not hold to her teaching and have not learned Satan's so-called deep secrets, 'I will not impose any other burden on you,* ²⁵ *except to hold on to what you have until I come.'*

Just keep on doing what you're doing. That was the message to the faithful believers in Thyatira.

In essence, what Christ is saying in verses 24–25 is this: 'I'm not going to give you any man-made rules or regulations. Just stick to the apostolic declaration. No immorality, no food offered to idols – just continue to strive to be holy.' Holiness is something we can never hope to achieve in our own strength. It is a work of God. It is also 100% our work. It isn't one or the other, but both at the same time. As Paul explains, 'Therefore, my dear friends . . . continue to work out your salvation with fear and trembling, for it is God who works in you to will and to act in order to fulfil his good purpose' (Philippians 2:12–13).

As the believers stay faithful and press on towards holiness, Christ holds out this great hope for the future: he's going to return (verse 25). He's going to rule 'with an iron sceptre' (verse 27), and 'I will also give that one the morning star' (verse 28). The morning star comes at the end of a dark night. If you are tossing and turning and can't sleep, when the star comes up, you know that the morning is near. Christ reminds these struggling believers that the morning is near, and one of the great joys of heaven will be utter deliverance from sin.

Do you know why I'm looking forward to heaven? I will never, ever sin again. Isn't that wonderful? Not only will I never sin again; I will never be able to sin again and I won't want to sin. I will be like Christ in all his holiness. As I struggle with sin every day, I look to Jesus, and I'm looking forward to that great day when the morning star rises, when I am with Christ and everything is well.

Don't be disheartened – the finishing line is in sight, the morning star is about to rise and your struggle with sin is almost over. In the short time remaining, pursue holiness as your primary ambition:

> You need to persevere so that when you have done the will of God, you will receive what he has promised. For,
>> 'In just a little while,
>>> he who is coming will come
>>> and will not delay.'
> (Hebrews 10:36–37)

> There's far more to life for us. We're citizens of high heaven! We're waiting the arrival of the Savior, the Master, Jesus Christ, who will transform our earthy bodies into glorious bodies like his own. He'll make us beautiful and whole with the same powerful skill by which he is putting everything as it should be, under and around him.
> (Philippians 3:20–21, MSG)

Day 354

Read Revelation 3:1–6
Key verse: Revelation 3:1

....

> ¹*To the angel of the church in Sardis write:*
> *These are the words of him who holds the seven spirits of*
> *God and the seven stars. I know your deeds; you have a reputa-*
> *tion of being alive, but you are dead.*

Most of us would like to be a member of the church at Sardis. It is large, has a tremendous reputation, and everyone flocks to it: it is *the* place to be.

But despite this glorious history, the future is doubtful. The believers have a form of godliness but no power: they are dead. Similarly, the city's glory has faded. The old days of Sardis being a rich commercial centre are long gone. It has been conquered by enemies, suffered an earthquake in AD 17, and now many of the buildings have crumbled and the shops are boarded up. There was an attempt to build a temple to Diana to rival the one in Ephesus, but it was never completed. The city, like the church, had a great beginning, but is not finishing well.

How does that happen? Why do churches with such great histories die? The introduction to the church in verse 1 helps to explain. It talks about the 'seven spirits'. Just as physical death is when the human spirit leaves the body, so death in a church is the absence of the Holy Spirit.

Incidentally, 'seven spirits' does not mean that there are seven Holy Spirits. Revelation is a book of symbols, and seven is a symbol of perfection. The perfection of the living Spirit of God is in the hand of Jesus. Jesus, in his ascension, pours the Spirit upon the church, and so the church has been consumed and changed by the fire of God.

The problem at Sardis is that they have forgotten that we can do nothing without the power of the Holy Spirit.

Remember how God gave the Israelites manna in the desert? Apart from on the Sabbath, they were instructed to gather enough for each day (Exodus 16). The previous day's manna rotted, so they had to trust God for a fresh supply each day. Just like the manna, there is a fresh supply of God's grace, mercy and love each day. Don't rely on past experiences of the Holy Spirit, past answers to prayer, past study of God's Word to fuel your relationship with God. Don't be fooled that your family's history in the church or your reputation are any substitute for genuine discipleship. Today, come to God with a fresh hunger to hear his Word, a new passion to seek his face in prayer, and a renewed desire for his Spirit to reign in every area of your life.

> I am the vine; you are the branches. If you remain in me and I in you, you will bear much fruit; apart from me you can do nothing. If you do not remain in me, you are like a branch that is thrown away and withers; such branches are picked up, thrown into the fire and burned . . . This is to my Father's glory, that you bear much fruit, showing yourselves to be my disciples.
> (John 15:5–6, 8)

Day 355

Read Revelation 3:1–6
Key verses: Revelation 3:2–3

....

²Wake up! Strengthen what remains and is about to die, for I have found your deeds unfinished in the sight of my God. ³Remember, therefore, what you have received and heard; hold it fast, and repent. But if you do not wake up, I will come like a thief, and you will not know at what time I will come to you.

Do you sleepwalk?

Perhaps you did as a child. Today, many of us sleepwalk our way through life, unconscious of all that is going on around us, giving little thought to our purpose or where we are heading.

The church at Sardis is sleepwalking. It is wedded to its tradition and nostalgia, and has no vision for the future. It is great to learn from the past, but we cannot dwell on it. The past is supposed to inspire us, not paralyse us, and if we do not change, we will die. Change can be tough in church life. Of course, we never change the gospel. We cannot change it; it is not ours to change. But a lot of other things have to change.

Jesus says to the church in Sardis, 'You are sleepwalking into death! If you don't wake up and shape up, if you don't repent and deal with the issues in the church, if you don't strengthen the good things that remain, I will come like a thief and take the Holy Spirit from you. Then you will have no future at all.'

As the church of Jesus Christ, and as individual Christians, we need to be filled with the Holy Spirit every day. Being filled by the Spirit is an ongoing, daily thing. 'Keep being filled,' says the apostle Paul (Ephesians 5:18). It is not as if we come to a little fountain with the cup of our life and we fill this little cup. Rather, we come with the cup of our life to a thousand Niagara Falls. We say, 'Lord, fill me today, because I need you. My work is difficult, my marriage is struggling, I don't know how to witness and I don't know how to cope – fill me.' And guess what happens? The great ocean of the fullness of the Spirit comes into our lives and overflows. Every moment of every day we need to be crying, 'Oh God, send your Spirit.'

Bring the cup of your life to God – your work, health, marriage, family, ministry, church – and pray that you would live in the power of the Holy Spirit today.

If you then, though you are evil, know how to give good gifts to your children, how much more will your Father in heaven give the Holy Spirit to those who ask him!
(Luke 11:13)

We continually ask God to fill you with the knowledge of his will through all the wisdom and understanding that the Spirit gives, so that you may live a life worthy of the Lord and please him in every way.
(Colossians 1:9–10)

The Spirit God gave us does not make us timid, but gives us power, love and self-discipline.
(2 Timothy 1:7)

Day 356

Read Revelation 3:1–6
Key verses: Revelation 3:4–5

....

⁴Yet you have a few people in Sardis who have not soiled their clothes. They will walk with me, dressed in white, for they are worthy. ⁵The one who is victorious will, like them, be dressed in white. I will never blot out the name of that person from the book of life, but will acknowledge that name before my Father and his angels.

It is not easy to stay faithful to God when those around you, especially those in the church, are compromising.

But be encouraged. God knows about you, just as he knew about the faithful few in Sardis. Notice that these people are dressed in white robes. In those days white robes were a symbol of festivity: when you were going to a celebration, you would put on white robes. They were robes of victory and purity, and most of all they were robes you would wear to a wedding. When a Roman attended a wedding, he would dress in a white toga, just as today a bride puts on a white dress. But it is more than that.

White robes are a symbol, in John's thinking, of the righteousness of Christ. He is talking about the glorious doctrine of justification by faith. Justification is the work of God for us; it is a declaration that God sees us as righteous in his sight because we are clothed in the pure and perfect righteousness of Christ. God justifies the ungodly. He blots out sin, and does not want you to remember what he has chosen to forget.

But that description of justification does not go far enough. Justification is a positive thing. God takes the righteousness of Christ and covers us with it. Remember when Jesus came out of the waters of baptism? His Father looked at him and said, 'This is my beloved

Son, with whom I am well pleased' (Matthew 3:17, ESV). God was pleased with his perfect righteousness and utter obedience. Those robes of righteousness are laid on your shoulders today, and when God looks at you, he sees the glorious righteousness of Jesus. You are as right with God as you ever can be. It is instantaneous, it is legal, it is declarative and it is glorious. It is the gospel.

You are justified. How does, and should, this truth impact on your thought patterns and behaviour? This is John Bunyan's experience:

> But one day, as I was passing into a field . . . suddenly this sentence fell upon my soul, 'Thy righteousness is in heaven' . . . I saw with the eyes of my soul, Jesus Christ, at God's right hand; there, I say, is my righteousness; so that wherever I was, or whatever I was doing, God could not say 'He wants my righteousness,' for that was just before him. I also saw that it was not my good frame of heart that made my righteousness better; or my bad frame of heart that made it worse; for my righteousness was Jesus Christ himself, 'the same yesterday, and today, and forever'.
> (Hugh T. Kerr and John M. Mulder, *Famous Conversions*, Eerdmans, 1994, p. 79)

Give thanks for this glorious gospel of grace.

Day 357

Read Revelation 3:7–13
Key verses: Revelation 3:8, 11

. . . .

> [8]*I know your deeds. See, I have placed before you an open door that no one can shut. I know that you have little strength, yet you have kept my word and have not denied my name . . .*
> [11]*I am coming soon. Hold on to what you have, so that no one will take your crown.*

What does God demand of us? Successful ministries? Effective evangelism? Expanding churches? No. God demands faithfulness.

Christ's key message to the church in Philadelphia was, 'Don't quit.'

Philadelphia is the youngest of the seven cities. It was set up by Alexander the Great as a means of spreading the Greek culture and way of life to the barbarians. It is a small city and has never really recovered its population following the earthquake in AD 17.

Although it is only thirty miles down the road from Sardis, this church is very different. It is small and struggling. But Christ warmly commends them: 'You are wonderfully faithful. You may be small and lacking strength, but you have kept my word to endure; you haven't denied me.'

Sometimes we think faithful means never changing. It does not. Being faithful to God and to the church sometimes does require change. It also means being obedient, carrying on and not giving up. This is what God loves and commends. That is why he has no criticism for this church, just as he has no criticism for the church in Smyrna.

If you are struggling to stay faithful and feel like giving up, you are in good company. Moses felt like giving up. He was the pastor of 2 million people. Elijah and Jeremiah felt like giving up. Even Paul felt like giving up, in 2 Corinthians. When you feel like giving up and you find yourself just hanging on to God, he can bless you. Because when you are weak, you are strong. This is what Jesus is saying to the church in Philadelphia, and to us: 'You are faithful. I will keep you.'

In Psalm 119:30, David says, 'I have chosen the way of faithfulness; I have set your rules before me.' The life of faithfulness is one in which we daily choose to place our hope in God, with every ounce of certainty that he will not fail us. We choose the way of faithfulness, though we know it will be marked by trials and temptations. We choose it in matters large and small . . . God's will for your life is that you be faithful as he is faithful. Faithful to him. Faithful to others. Faithful in this moment. Faithful to the end. That which he wills, he also enables.

'Now may the God of peace himself sanctify you completely, and may your whole spirit and soul and body be kept blameless at the coming of our Lord Jesus Christ. He who calls you is faithful; he will surely do it' (1 Thess.5:23–24 [ESV]).

(Jen Wilkin, *In His Image*, Crossway, 2018, pp. 106–107)

Day 358

Read Revelation 3:7–13

Key verses: Revelation 3:7, 9, 11

....

⁷These are the words of him who is holy and true, who holds the key of David. What he opens no one can shut, and what he shuts no one can open . . .⁹I will make those who are of the synagogue of Satan, who claim to be Jews though they are not, but are liars – I will make them come and fall down at your feet and acknowledge that I have loved you . . .

¹¹I am coming soon. Hold on to what you have, so that no one will take your crown.

Words of encouragement can have a powerful impact, and when they come from Christ, they are priceless.

Here, Christ speaks words of encouragement to this battle-weary church in Philadelphia and to all present-day believers. He urges them not to give up, not to quit, because he is giving them three blessings:

• *A present opportunity* (verse 7). In the hands of Jesus is the key of David. He lays before the church a wonderful opportunity. Wherever you are spiritually, wherever you are physically, whatever your trials, troubles or heartbreak, Jesus can offer you a door of opportunity. Even in the midst of your suffering, Jesus can bring you to a place where he can bless and use you. I have found that the experiences my wife and I have wept over together, and the breaking and bruising that the Lord has done in our lives, have provided tremendous opportunities for ministry. I would not be without them. (For more on the subject of suffering and my own experience, read my book, *Invest Your Suffering*, IVP, 2013.)

- *A public vindication* (verse 9). Some people assume that the scene in verse 9 refers to the end of time. I suspect that is right, but it may also mean that those who are their worst enemies will become their dearest friends. God will convert these people. He is in the business of converting his enemies and making them his friends. He did it with me and you.

- *A permanent reward* (verse 11). This small church is struggling, but it has a glorious future. Jesus will return and they will receive their crown.

Let Christ's words of encouragement nourish your soul.

As you press on in difficult days, keep in mind the public vindication and the permanent reward you will one day receive. Imagine Christ placing the crown on your head and saying, 'Well done, good and faithful servant!' (Matthew 25:21).

Today, in the midst of your hardships, look out for the door of opportunity God is holding open for you. It could be the opportunity to witness to a non-Christian friend, to grieve with someone who is suffering, or to share with other parents who are dealing with similar issues to you.

> Pray for us . . . that God may open a door for our message, so that we may proclaim the mystery of Christ.
> (Colossians 4:3)

Day 359

Read Revelation 3:14–22
Key verse: Revelation 3:14

....

> ¹⁴ *To the angel of the church in Laodicea write:*
> *These are the words of the Amen, the faithful and true witness,*
> *the ruler of God's creation.*

Why do we end our prayers with 'Amen'?

'Amen' simply means 'let it be so', 'this is the truth', 'this is reliable'. So it is hardly surprising that Jesus calls himself 'the Amen'. He is 'the faithful and true witness'. He is completely honest, true and trustworthy. In the Old Testament, God is described as *Elohey Amen*, meaning the true, reliable God (Isaiah 65:16). Psalm 100 encourages us to praise the Lord and come before him with thanksgiving. Why?

> For the LORD is good and his love endures for ever;
>   his faithfulness continues through all generations.
> (verse 5)

The Hebrew word translated 'faithfulness' could be rendered the 'Amen-ness of God'. The psalmist is reminding us that God is reliable. He is the rock and fortress on which we build our lives, the rock on which we stand. He doesn't move or 'change like shifting shadows' (James 1:17).

Christ also introduces himself as 'the ruler of God's creation'. I don't think it is an accident that he introduces himself in such a powerful way to these believers. They have lost sight of whom they are supposed to serve. The Greek word used here for 'ruler' has a wide range of meanings. It can mean origin, beginning, source, author, ruler, governor or master. This verse tells us that Christ existed before the world. Indeed, he is the one who caused the whole world to come into existence (John 1:3). The Bible begins with those great words: 'In the beginning God created'. Evangelicals have many questions about this topic, but they all agree that God created all things out of nothing, by the power of his Word, for the purpose of his glory.

Jesus made and rules over all things. He holds the universe in place. And yet he came to earth for us. He was nailed to a cross. Such love! Think how much our hearts should beat with love for him.

Are you facing problems today? Come to the solid Rock, which is Christ, and cling to him for strength. He will not let you down. He will not let you go.

> My hope is built on nothing less
> Than Jesus' blood and righteousness;
> I dare not trust the sweetest frame,
> But wholly lean on Jesus' name.
>
> On Christ, the solid Rock, I stand;
> All other ground is sinking sand,
> All other ground is sinking sand.
>
> When darkness veils His lovely face,
> I rest on His unchanging grace;
> In every high and stormy gale,
> My anchor holds within the veil.
>
> His oath, His covenant, His blood
> Support me in the whelming flood;
> When all around my soul gives way,
> He then is all my hope and stay.
> (Edward Mote, 'My Hope Is Built on Nothing Less', 1834)

Don't imagine your concerns are too big or complicated for Christ to deal with. He is the God of the universe! He has pinned the stars in the galaxies and he brings the sun up each morning. Nothing is too big for him.

Day 360

Read Revelation 3:14–22
Key verses: Revelation 3:15–16

....

> ¹⁵*I know your deeds, that you are neither cold nor hot. I wish you were either one or the other!* ¹⁶ *So, because you are lukewarm – neither hot nor cold – I am about to spit you out of my mouth.*

Imagine the government offering your city money for renovations, and city officials replying, 'No thanks. We're so rich, we don't need your help.' It's unthinkable!

But Laodicea is such an immensely rich and prosperous city that it declined help to rebuild after the earthquake in AD 17. This vibrant commercial centre has it all, except one thing: good water. Situated in the Lycos Valley, it is near to Hierapolis, where there are medicinal hot springs, and Colossae, where there is wonderful, cold, gushing water. But Laodicea's water comes from five miles down the road. It contains lime, travels along a lead pipe and is warmed in the sun, so it tastes of lime and lead and is tepid. No wonder you take a drink and instantly spit it out. Jesus says, 'Actually, that's what your church makes me feel like doing.'

The believers are not refreshing like the icy water from Colossae, or hot like the water in Hierapolis. They are just tepid. This brash, proud church makes Jesus sick. It has no power, suffering, sacrifice, emotion or enthusiasm. It is a respectable, nominal, flabby, anaemic, irresolute church. There is no passion for Jesus, for purity, for lost souls or for justice.

It makes Jesus sick. Why? Because he never held back anything for us. He went all the way to Calvary. He died there for us. Jesus said to us, 'Whoever wants to be my disciple must deny themselves and take up their cross and follow me' (Matthew 16:24). When he said that, he was going to Calvary. Death is not just something that happens at the end of the Christian life when you go through terrible suffering. As a disciple, you have to die daily to self. Christianity is not about self-affirmation; it's about self-denial, about putting Jesus first.

It is easy to say we love Jesus. Talk is cheap. But my prayer is, 'Lord, can I love you more each day? Can I respond to Calvary love more fully? Please, God, give me that love in my heart.'

Are you loving God as you should today?

How does God know that you love him? In what ways are you demonstrating your love for God through self-denial and sacrifice? Pray that today you would respond more fully to Christ's Calvary love.

O Love that will not let me go,
I rest my weary soul in thee;
I give thee back the life I owe,
That in thine ocean depths its flow
May richer, fuller be.

O Cross that liftest up my head,
I dare not ask to fly from thee;
I lay in dust life's glory dead,
And from the ground there blossoms red
Life that shall endless be.
(George Matheson, 'O Love that Will Not Let Me Go', 1882)

Day 361

Read Revelation 3:14–22
Key verses: Revelation 3:17–18

....

> [17]*You say, 'I am rich; I have acquired wealth and do not need a thing.' But you do not realise that you are wretched, pitiful, poor, blind and naked.* [18]*I counsel you to buy from me gold refined in the fire, so that you can become rich; and white clothes to wear, so that you can cover your shameful nakedness; and salve to put on your eyes, so that you can see.*

Sometimes, instead of being a light, the church mirrors the world.

The citizens of Laodicea boast of their material prosperity. They are proud of their banks and their clothing industry, and their medical school, which is renowned for its Phrygian powder: a paste applied to your eyes to help you see more clearly. These people think they have it all.

The church mirrors this sickening complacency. Jesus says, 'You're like a wretched beggar and you're not even aware of it. You've got all these wonderful programmes in your church, but, spiritually, you're a million miles away from me.' They are sinning and are not even aware of it. They have seared their consciences and are no longer able to see what is wrong or how serious their sin is.

In verse 18, Christ refers to the three items that the Laodiceans are particularly proud of. In a warm and compelling way, he says, 'Come to me as you are, and I will give you everything you need. I will give you real treasure. There's nothing wrong with having money in the bank, but I will give you a treasure that lasts for ever – myself. I will give you clean clothes. No more black woollen robes that you manufacture as a status symbol, but white robes! My blood will cleanse you of all sin, and you will be clothed in righteousness. I will give you eye salve to help you see clearly for the very first time.'

People without Christ can have all the things of the world, yet they're blind. They don't know where they have come from or where they are going, and they have no purpose. God promises to open our eyes and show us the truth – that we were made in his image, to know, love and experience him. When we leave this world, is it death? No, it's real life. It's out of the prison and into the palace.

There is no heresy or persecution in this wealthy church. From the outside, it looks comfortable, prosperous and successful. But, in truth, this complacent church is bankrupt. It has lost sight of what real treasure is.

We are so easily duped into believing that having plenty of money, clothes with the right labels, and good health make us rich. Don't become like the believers in Laodicea – complacent in their own good fortune, ignorant of how greatly they have sinned against God and how far from him they have fallen. Christ's arms are outstretched, inviting you into a deeper, growing relationship with him. The question is, will you leave the trinkets of this life and pursue real treasure?

Day 362

Read Revelation 3:14–22
Key verses: Revelation 3:19–20

••

19 Those whom I love I rebuke and discipline. So be earnest and repent. 20 Here I am! I stand at the door and knock. If anyone hears my voice and opens the door, I will come in and eat with that person, and they with me.

Why do we discipline our children? Because we love them and we want them to be the best they can be.

The Lord says some very harsh things to this church. He says some very painful things to these Christians. Why? Is it because God is mean? No, it is because he loves them. Sometimes God allows pain in our lives not because he is mean, but because he loves us. He loves us enough to chasten us. God's Word can be incredibly uncomfortable, because he loves us and he wants us to be the best we can be.

And he won't settle. Look at verse 20: 'Here I am! I stand at the door and knock.' This is not an evangelistic text. Jesus is not talking to a non-Christian and saying, 'Let me into your life.' You can apply it that way, I'm sure. But this is primarily a word to the church and to individual Christians. Jesus is saying, 'You have pushed me to the periphery. I want you to put me back in the centre of your life where I used to be.' The results will be radical. When Jesus knocks on the door of your life, he wants to come in and take over. He says, 'This has got to change, this has got to change, and this has got to change as well.' We don't like change. That's why we keep the door shut. Jesus is saying to you today, 'Will you let me in? I want to deal with these issues in your life.'

Some Christians want enough of Christ to be identified with him, but not enough to be seriously inconvenienced; they genuinely cling to basic Christian orthodoxy but do not want to engage in serious Bible study; they value moral probity, especially of the public sort, but do not engage in war against inner corruptions; they fret over the quality of the preacher's sermon, but do not worry much over the quality of their own prayer life. Such Christians are content with mediocrity.

(D. A. Carson, *A Call to Spiritual Reformation*, IVP, 1992, p. 121)

Don't settle for mediocrity! Is Jesus knocking on the door of your life? Is there some area that you have kept compartmentalized, some part you don't want him to touch or change? Swing the door open wide, grant him unlimited access, repent of the sins he points out and, with the Holy Spirit's help, embrace the changes he wants you to make.

Day 363

Read Revelation 3:14–22
Key verses: Revelation 3:21–22

....

> ^{21} *To the one who is victorious, I will give the right to sit with me on my throne, just as I was victorious and sat down with my Father on his throne. ^{22}Whoever has ears, let them hear what the Spirit says to the churches.*

Did you notice that in all these letters there is a little phrase at the end: 'the one who is victorious'. It could be translated as 'the one who conquers' (ESV) or 'the one who overcomes' (NKJV).

Who are these 'overcomers'? We might imagine them to be spiritual giants, such as missionaries, pastors and church leaders – those inspirational Christians whom we typically put on a pedestal. But 'overcomers' are not an elite category of Christians who live triumphant lives and don't seem to have any problems. No! Being an 'overcomer' means that you persevere. You keep going and don't give up. Guess what? I have a million problems and so have you. You struggle in your home, in your marriage, with your kids, with work and with witnessing for Christ. Sometimes you feel terrible and you let Christ down. But if you persevere – and Christ gives you the grace to persevere – you're an 'overcomer'.

This perseverance isn't a passive stance. Over and over again, in every one of the letters we are urged to 'hear what the Spirit says to the churches' (verse 22). If we are going to be 'overcomers', we need to listen to God's Word and obey it, letting it do its work of transformation in our lives. As James taught,

> Do not merely listen to the word, and so deceive yourselves. Do what it says. Anyone who listens to the word but does not do what it says is like someone who looks at his face in a mirror and, after looking at himself, goes away and immediately forgets what he looks like. But

whoever looks intently into the perfect law that gives freedom and continues in it – not forgetting what they have heard but doing it – they will be blessed in what they do.
(James 1:22–25)

There is no elite category of Christian who has a hotline to God and enjoys extra spiritual insights and favour. You can be victorious. You can be an overcomer. There is no deep secret or quick fix to achieving this enduring spiritual life. It is a lifetime commitment consisting of daily decisions to follow God – putting him first, spending time in his Word, obeying him through the power of his Holy Spirit. You may have been on this journey of faith many years, you may be just starting out, or you may have recently come back to God. Christ's word to you is the same: keep persevering.

Blessed is the one who perseveres under trial because, having stood the test, that person will receive the crown of life that the Lord has promised to those who love him.
(James 1:12)

May the Lord direct your hearts into God's love and Christ's perseverance.
(2 Thessalonians 3:5)

768 | REVELATION 1 – 3

Day 364

Read Revelation 3:14–22
Key verse: Revelation 3:21

....

²¹ To the one who is victorious, I will give the right to sit with me on my throne, just as I was victorious and sat down with my Father on his throne.

A seven-year-old boy was asked, 'What is home?'

He thought for a minute and then replied, 'Home is a place that, when you get to it, they've got to let you in.'

Because of what Christ achieved for us on the cross, heaven is our home. Did you notice that at the end of every one of the letters there is a promise of heaven? To the believers in Laodicea the promise is, you will 'sit with me on my throne'. Christ's last word to each of these struggling Christians is, 'You'll be home soon.'

Our great hope of heaven is that we will see Jesus.

He's the apostle of our faith. He's the anointed one, the atoning sacrifice. He's the author of our salvation. He is the altogether lovely one. He is the beautiful Saviour, the bread of heaven, the bridegroom of our souls. He's the bright morning star. He is the chief shepherd and the capstone. He's the captain of the armies of the Lord. He is the conqueror of death.

He is the Christ. He is fully God and fully man, full of grace and truth. He is the fairest of ten thousand. He is the faithful one. He is the friend of sinners. He is the glorious Redeemer, the gate for the sheep, the good shepherd. He is great David's greatest Son. He is the Holy One. He is the head of the church, the high priest, after the order of Melchizedek.

He is the image of the invisible God. He is Immanuel, God is with us. He is the joy of his people and the justifier of the ungodly. He is the King of Israel, the King of the Jews and the King of kings. He is my kinsman redeemer, the light of the world, the lion of Judah, the lamb of Calvary. He is the meek and majestic one. He is the mighty God, the everlasting Father, the Prince of peace. He is the man of sorrows, acquainted with grief.

He is the Passover Lamb. He is the root of David, the rock of ages, the risen and ascended Lord. He is my Redeemer. He is the sinless one. He is the true vine and the tender shoot. He is the true light of true light. He is the wisdom of God. He is the Word of God. He is the way, the truth and the life. He is my Saviour. He is mine.

Heaven is about Jesus. The greatest joy of our hearts is that we'll be able to see him for ever. Prepare for heaven now – serve him with all your heart and live for his glory.

Today, meditate on Revelation 22:1–5. Ultimately, our home will be the new heaven and the new earth. Live your life with this destination in mind, daily investing in eternity.

For further study

If you would like to do further study on Revelation, the following books may be useful:

- Craig Keener, *Revelation*, NIV Application Commentary (Zondervan, 2000).

- Leon Morris, *Revelation*, Tyndale New Testament Commentary (IVP, 2009).

- John Stott, *What Christ Thinks of the Church* (Monarch, 2003).

- Michael Wilcock, *The Message of Revelation*, The Bible Speaks Today (IVP, 1991).

- Tom Wright, *Revelation for Everyone* (SPCK, 2014).

If God has fed you through your study of Revelation 1 – 3, why not buy the individual Food for the Journey on Revelation 1 – 3 and give it to a friend (available from ivpbooks.com)?

Day 365

Read Psalm 98
Key verses Psalm 98:1–3

· ·

> ¹*Sing to the* L ORD *a new song,*
>   *for he has done marvellous things;*
> *his right hand and his holy arm*
>   *have worked salvation for him.*
> ²*The* L ORD *has made his salvation known*
>   *and revealed his righteousness to the nations.*
> ³*He has remembered his love*
>   *and his faithfulness to Israel;*
> *all the ends of the earth have seen*
>   *the salvation of our God.*

We've journeyed through life, nourished by the Word of God, as we've fed on Christ through this book. We've seen his patience, his grace, his deliverance. How should we respond?

If we take the psalms seriously, we'll *sing*.

Psalm 98, like others sometimes classed as 'hymns' (see Psalms 33, 100, 117), has a call to praise God, followed by the reasons. In this psalm, the call comes twice: verse 1 – 'Sing to the L ORD a new song'; verses 4–9a – 'Shout for joy . . .', 'burst into jubilant song', 'make music', 'shout for joy', 'let the sea resound', 'let the rivers clap their hands', 'let the mountains sing together', 'let them sing'. The reasons follow the calls: 'for he has done marvellous things' (verse 1b); these marvellous things are then unpacked in verses 2–3. Then again in verse 9, 'for he comes to judge the earth'; this judgment is then unpacked in the second half of verse 9.

The song is a *new* song because God has done *new* things – he has acted in history, in wonderful ways: 'his right hand and his holy arm have worked salvation for him'; 'The L ORD has made his salvation known and revealed his righteousness to the nations'; 'He has remembered his love and his faithfulness to Israel; all the ends of the earth have seen the salvation of our God.'

God has done something wonderful, marvellous, spectacular. God has done a new thing, so sing a new song. The Lord is centre stage. There's no mention of enemies, no mention of other gods, no hint of anyone to help. It is he who has acted, and he alone. He's acted because of his faithfulness to his promise, not because his people deserved it. They can't take the credit. For us, as Christians, these verses celebrate Christ's great work of deliverance – the *wonderful* things he has done – and what *wonderful* things they are:

• he was born by a *wonderful* birth;
• he lived a *wonderful* life;
• he died a *wonderful* death;
• he rose by a *wonderful* resurrection;
• he ascended *wonderful*ly into heaven;
• he poured out the life-giving Holy Spirit in *wonderful* fashion;
• through this *wonderful*ly poured-out Spirit, his people have done *wonderful* things;
• throughout the world today, God is doing *wonderful* things.

In short – Jesus has won a stunning victory . . . He is the Saviour, the Deliverer, the Victor over sin, death and the evil one. And all the ends of the earth have seen it (verse 3), and all creation can and should join in celebration (verses 4–9).

Will you put Jesus centre stage? Let's join with all creation in letting him fill our horizons. How can we *not* celebrate? As Charles Simeon asks, 'Shall we then be contented to offer to our Lord a few cold and languid acknowledgements?' (*Charles Simeon's Discourses vol. VI* (Ps 73–150), Holdsworth & Ball, 1832, p. 177).

Hallelujah!
    For our Lord God Almighty reigns.
Let us rejoice and be glad
    and give him glory!
(Revelation 19:6–7)

Bible acknowledgments

KESWICK MINISTRIES

Our purpose

Keswick Ministries is committed to the spiritual renewal of God's people for his mission in the world.

God's purpose is to bring his blessing to all the nations of the world. That promise of blessing, which touches every aspect of human life, is ultimately fulfilled through the life, death, resurrection, ascension and future return of Christ. All of the people of God are called to participate in his missionary purposes, wherever he may place them. The central vision of Keswick Ministries is to see the people of God equipped, encouraged and refreshed to fulfil that calling, directed and guided by God's Word in the power of his Spirit, for the glory of his Son.

Our priorities

Keswick Ministries seeks to serve the local church through:

- *Hearing God's Word.* The Scriptures are the foundation for the church's life, growth and mission, and Keswick Ministries is committed to preaching and teaching God's Word in a way that is faithful to Scripture and relevant to Christians of all ages and backgrounds.

- *Becoming like God's Son.* From its earliest days the Keswick movement has encouraged Christians to live godly lives in the power of the Spirit, to grow in Christlikeness and to live under his lordship in every area of life. This is God's will for his people in every culture and generation.

- *Serving God's mission.* The authentic response to God's Word is obedience to his mission, and the inevitable result of Christlikeness is sacrificial service. Keswick Ministries seeks to encourage committed discipleship in family life, work and society, and energetic engagement in the cause of world mission.

Our ministry

- *Keswick: the event.* Every summer the town of Keswick hosts a three-week convention, which attracts some 15,000 Christians from the UK and around the world. The event provides Bible teaching for all ages, vibrant worship, a sense of unity across generations and denominations, and an inspirational call to serve Christ in the world. It caters for children of all ages and has a strong youth and young adult programme. And it all takes place in the beautiful Lake District – a perfect setting for rest, recreation and refreshment.

- *Keswick: the movement.* For 140 years the work of Keswick has had an impact on churches worldwide, and today the movement is underway throughout the UK, as well as in many parts of Europe, Asia, North America, Australia, Africa and the Caribbean. Keswick Ministries is committed to strengthening the network in the UK and beyond, through prayer, news, pioneering and cooperative activity.

- *Keswick resources.* Keswick Ministries produces a range of books and booklets based on the core foundations of Christian life and mission. It makes Bible teaching available through free access to mp3 downloads, and the sale of DVDs and CDs. It broadcasts online through Clayton TV and annual BBC Radio 4 services.

- *Keswick teaching and training.* In addition to the summer convention, Keswick Ministries is developing teaching and training events that will happen at other times of the year and in other places.

Our unity

The Keswick movement worldwide has adopted a key Pauline statement to describe its gospel inclusivity: 'for you are all one in Christ Jesus' (Galatians 3:28). Keswick Ministries works with evangelicals from a wide variety of church backgrounds, on the understanding that they share a commitment to the essential truths of the Christian faith as set out in its statement of belief.

Our contact details

T: 01768 780075
E: info@keswickministries.org
W: <www.keswickministries.org>
Mail: Keswick Ministries, Rawnsley Centre, Main Street, Keswick,
Cumbria CA12 5NP, England

Food for the Journey

If God has fed you through these studies, why not buy the individual Food for the Journey volumes for when you're on the go, or to give to a friend?

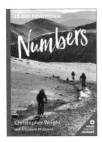

Numbers

978 1 78359 720 8

Ruth

978 1 78359 525 9

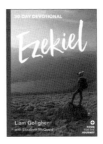

Ezekiel

978 1 78359 603 4

Habakkuk

978 1 78359 652 2

John 14 – 17

978 1 78359 495 5

Romans 5 – 8

978 1 78359 718 5

Colossians

978 1 78359 722 2

1 Thessalonians

978 1 78359 439 9

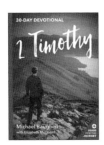

2 Timothy

978 1 78359 438 2

Hebrews

978 1 78359 611 9

James

978 1 78359 523 5

Revelation 1 – 3

978 1 78359 712 3

Available from your local Christian bookshop or **www.ivpbooks.com**

Related titles from IVP

KESWICK FOUNDATIONS

Bible Matters

Meeting God in His Word

Tim Chester

ISBN: 978 1 78359 579 2
176 pages, paperback

Of course the Bible matters. It is God's Word to us. But how do we engage with its message?

Tim Chester creates a sense of expectation, causing our reading of the Bible to become a living experience in which we encounter God. Amazingly, this God of the universe speaks to us each day!

Here is a personal, clear, intentional and sufficient message for our lives. The Bible is truly unique; it speaks into a myriad of situations and brings us back to the deep joy of the gospel.

Praise:

'Will enrich your encounter with God as you engage with his Word.' Elaine Duncan

'This is more than useful; it's inspiring.' Julian Hardyman

'Tim Chester is one of the clearest, most useful and reliable Christian writers in the UK today . . . He comes alongside the reader to instruct and to apply his teaching to life in the modern world.' Peter Lewis

Available from your local Christian bookshop or **www.ivpbooks.com**

Related titles from IVP

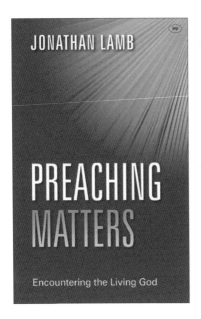

KESWICK FOUNDATIONS

Preaching Matters
Encountering the Living God
Jonathan Lamb

ISBN: 978 1 78359 149 7
192 pages, paperback

Preaching matters. It is a God-ordained means of encountering Christ. This is happening all around the world. The author knows this only too well. He recalls:

- the student who, on hearing a sermon about new life in Christ, found faith which changed his life and future forever

- the couple facing the trauma of the wife's terminal illness who discovered that Christ was all they needed, following a sermon on Habakkuk

When the Bible is faithfully and relevantly explained, it transforms hearts, understandings and attitudes, and, most of all, draws us into a living relationship with God through Christ.

This is a book to ignite our passion for preaching, whether we preach every week or have no idea how to put a sermon together. It will encourage every listener to participate in the dynamic event of God's Word speaking to his people through his Holy Spirit.

Praise:

'Refreshing, clear, helpful and accessible.' **Christopher Ash**

'Buy, read, mark and learn from this superb guide.' **Steve Brady**

Available from your local Christian bookshop or **www.ivpbooks.com**

Related titles from IVP

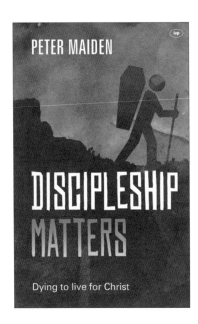

KESWICK FOUNDATIONS

Discipleship Matters
Dying to Live for Christ
Peter Maiden

ISBN: 978 1 78359 355 2
160 pages, paperback

Discipleship involves a gentle journey with our Saviour. Its demands will dovetail happily with our carefully crafted plans.

Wrong. Peter Maiden pulls no punches as he focuses on what a disciple should look like today. Are we prepared to follow Jesus' example? Lose our lives for his sake? Live counter-culturally in a world that values power, prestige and money, and constantly puts self at the centre?

Of all people, Jesus, the Son of God, has the authority to require this of us. And he's calling us to a relationship, not to a set of rules or a miserable, spartan existence. In fact, it is through losing our lives that we find them, and thereby discover the source of pure joy.

What a pity we set the bar too low.

Praise:

'With wisdom, biblical accuracy, maturity and a pastoral heart, Peter unpacks what it means to be a follower of Christ . . . A must-read.' **Andrew Chard**

'Engagingly personal and resolutely biblical. A delight to read. But beware, it is also an exciting challenge.' **Tim Chester**

Available from your local Christian bookshop or **www.ivpbooks.com**